TO WHAT END EXEGESIS?

To What End Exegesis?

Essays Textual, Exegetical, and Theological

GORDON D. FEE

WILLIAM B. EERDMANS PUBLISHING COMPANY
GRAND RAPIDS, MICHIGAN / CAMBRIDGE, U.K.

REGENT COLLEGE PUBLISHING
VANCOUVER, BRITISH COLUMBIA

Published jointly 2001 by
Wm. B. Eerdmans Publishing Co.
255 Jefferson Ave. S.E., Grand Rapids, Michigan 49503 /
P.O. Box 163, Cambridge CB3 9PU U.K.
www.eerdmans.com
and by
Regent College Publishing
an imprint of Regent College Bookstore
5800 University Boulevard, Vancouver, B.C. V6T 2E4

Printed in the United States of America

06 05 04 03 02 01   7 6 5 4 3 2 1

Library of Congress Cataloging-in-Publication Data

Fee, Gordon D.
To what end exegesis? essays textual, exegetical, and theological /
Gordon D. Fee.
p.   cm.
Includes bibliographical references.
Eerdmans ISBN 0-8028-4925-3 (pbk.: alk. paper)
1. Bible — Criticism, interpretation, etc.   I. Title.

BS511.2.F44   2001
225.6 — dc21

2001040361

Regent College Publishing ISBN 1-57383-218-9

The author and publisher gratefully acknowledge permission
to reprint material granted by the sources listed on pp. ix-x.

Contents

THEOLOGICAL STUDIES

Preface

I welcome this opportunity to gather this collection of academic papers that have appeared in a variety of publications over a twenty-five-year period and make them available in this single volume. Hopefully this will offer convenient access to some studies that are otherwise more difficult to find, since in many cases they first appeared in *Festschriften* in honor of scholar friends or in the *SBL Seminar Papers* for a given year, which in both cases by their very nature had a very limited publication. On the other hand, those who come to this volume from two earlier collections of papers (*Listening to the Spirit in the Text* [Eerdmans, 2000] and *Gospel and Spirit: Issues in New Testament Hermeneutics* [Hendrickson, 1991]) may be mildly disappointed that there is less "application" and more pure hermeneutics.

In many ways this collection reflects my varied interests as a New Testament scholar, including textual criticism. But in the end all of them, even the textual studies, focus on my primary, lifelong concern for understanding the biblical text and for coming to terms with the theology inherent in these texts. And all of this for the sake of the believing Christian community. The studies themselves appear in mostly canonical order, except for the final section of theological studies, which combines a canonical order with a more chronological one. The interested reader may wish to begin with chapter 17, from which the title has been drawn, since it is a published lecture which begins with a kind of autobiographical note that may help to make sense of the rest.

On the other hand, I have no illusions that many will actually read this book through, since that is seldom the case with these kinds of collected studies. But since I did read it through (as a proofreader), I wish to make a few further observations about the collection as a whole.

First, even though the first of these studies goes back to 1976 (ch. 10), I have resisted the temptation to update them. I have not made such changes because a primary reason for this publication is to make these studies conveniently available in a single place, and most people who will consult them are interested not in my interaction with later response to them, but with their original expression. Therefore, apart from an occasional bracketed cross reference to chapters in the present volume and several corrections of typographical errors, we have chosen to leave them basically as they originally appeared (although since this volume was produced by scanning the originals and resetting them to the publisher's house style, we may in fact have introduced further typos!)

Second, the order of the essays in part reflects my own journey as a biblical scholar, beginning with work in textual criticism, before turning to more strictly exegetical work and then finally to studies more theological in overall intent.

Third, in the final section of essays one may find a few repetitions. In some ways these are inevitable, since my interests in these various matters have tended over the past decade to focus on christology and pneumatology, and especially on the issue of whether or not it is proper to use trinitarian language with regard to Paul's theology. But repetition also occurs once in the earlier studies, for which I need to offer a word of explanation.

The earliest piece in this collection is the study of the troublesome passage in 2 Corinthians 6:14–7:1. This study arose while I was teaching a Greek course at Wheaton College based on 2 Corinthians, while at the same time I was doing some work on 1 Corinthians for another class. By then I had already taught 1 Corinthians often enough to have come to the conclusion that 1 Corinthians 8–10 was not about marketplace idol food, but about eating that food in temple precincts. What struck me were the verbal ties between the 2 Corinthians passage and some language in 1 Corinthians 10:14-22. So I spent several months researching this issue and published those findings (ch. 10 of this book). Sometime later, when asked to give a lecture at Southwest Baptist Theological Seminary, I reworked the 1 Corinthians part of that paper into what became the substance of the essay that appears as chapter 9. My reason for eventually publishing this separately was that I had come to realize that my greater concern for the suggestion about "food offered to idols" in 1 Corinthians had simply gone unnoticed because it was embedded in the study of a well-known crux in 2 Corinthians.

Finally, I should note that studies like these often precede the writing of major books or commentaries. Indeed, in an earlier day (before electronic publishing changed so much for both authors and publishers), I used to tell students to watch for a rash of articles by one scholar on a given topic because that may give hints about forthcoming books (e.g., C. E. B. Cranfield's score of studies on Romans, which were the harbinger of his major commentary). The reason for this is that it gave a scholar opportunity to explore some matters in more depth than the constrictions of a book or commentary would allow. This is also true of several studies in this volume (chs. 5, 7, 9, 11, 12, and 21).

But this present collection also reflects some interests that go in reverse of this. In some of the exegetical work that went into the publication of *God's Empowering Presence: The Holy Spirit in the Letters of Paul* (Hendrickson, 1994, a manuscript that was actually finished in late 1992), I thought I might be plowing new ground at several places. In the meantime I had received several requests to contribute to *Festschriften* in honor of some friends and colleagues in the academy. So I took the opportunity of those requests to reconfigure some of this exegesis and publish it in new and expanded form so as to reach a wider audience. Studies of this kind appear as chapters 13–16 and 18.

I here record my thanks to Michael Thomson, former student and teaching assistant at Regent College and now Sales Director at Eerdmans, for his interest in this project, which caused it all to happen. Thanks also to Eerdmans for their willingness to take it on. And finally I need to acknowledge the original place of publication of these various items, and thereby thank the publishers for permission to reprint them in their present form.

1. *New Testament Textual Criticism, Its Significance for Exegesis: Essays in Honour of Bruce M. Metzger* (ed. E. J. Epp and G. D. Fee; Oxford: Oxford University Press, 1981), pp. 61-75. © Oxford University Press 1981. Reprinted by permission of Oxford University Press.

2. *The Evangelical Quarterly* 54 (1982): 207-18. Used by permission of Paternoster Publishing.

3. *The Four Gospels 1992: Festschrift Frans Neirynck* (ed. F. Van Segbroeck, C. M. Tuckett, B. Van Belle, and J. Verheyden; Leuven: Leuven University Press, 1992), III.2193-2205. Used by permission of Leuven University Press.

4. *Scribes and Scripture: New Testament Essays in Honor of J. Harold Greenlee* (ed. David Alan Black; Winona Lake, IN: Eisenbrauns, 1992), pp. 1-15. Used by permission of Eisenbrauns, Inc.

5. *Society of Biblical Literature 1992 Seminar Papers* (ed. Eugene H. Lovering Jr.; Atlanta: Scholars Press, 1992), pp. 165-83. Used by permission of the Society of Biblical Literature.

6. *The Expository Times* 89 (1977/78): 116-18. Used by permission of T&T Clark.

7. *Journal of the Evangelical Theological Society* 23 (1980): 307-14. Used by permission.

8. *New Testament Studies* 24 (1977/78): 533-38. Reprinted with the permission of Cambridge University Press.

9. *Biblica* 61 (1980): 172-97. © 1980 Editrice Pontificio Istituto Biblico, Rome.

10. *New Testament Studies* 23 (1976/77): 140-61. Reprinted with the permission of Cambridge University Press.

11. *Review and Expositor* 91/2 (1994): 201-17. Used by permission.

12. *Bulletin for Biblical Research* 2 (1992): 29-46. Used by permission of Eisenbrauns, Inc.

13. *Pauline Theology, Volume II: 1 and 2 Corinthians* (ed. D. M. Hay; Minneapolis: Fortress, 1993), pp. 37-58. Used by permission of the Society of Biblical Literature.

14. *Jesus of Nazareth: Lord and Christ, Essays on the Historical Jesus and New Testament Christology* (I. H. Marshall *Festschrift;* ed. J. B. Green and M. Turner; Grand Rapids: Eerdmans, 1994), pp. 312-44.

15. *Gospel in Paul: Studies on Corinthians, Galatians and Romans for Richard Longenecker* (ed. L. Ann Jervis and Peter Richardson; JSNTSS 108; Sheffield: Academic Press, 1994), pp. 111-33. Used by permission of Sheffield Academic Press.

16. *Spirit and Renewal: Essays in Honor of J. Rodman Williams* (JPTSS 5; Sheffield: Academic Press, 1994), pp. 129-44. Used by permission of Sheffield Academic Press.

17. *Bulletin for Biblical Research* 9 (1998): 75-88. Used by permission of Eisenbrauns, Inc.

18. *To Tell the Mystery: Essays on New Testament Eschatology in Honor of Robert H. Gundry* (ed. T. E. Schmidt and M. Silva; JSNTSS 100; Sheffield: JSOT Press, 1994), pp. 196-215. Used by permission of Sheffield Academic Press.

19. *Society of Biblical Literature 1997 Seminar Papers* (Atlanta: Scholars Press, 1997), pp. 732-49. Used by permission of the Society of Biblical Literature.

20. *The Trinity: An Interdisciplinary Symposium on the Trinity* (ed. Stephen Davis, Daniel Kendall, and Gerald O'Collins; Oxford: Oxford University Press, 1999), pp. 49-72. © Oxford University Press 1999. Reprinted by permission of Oxford University Press.

21. *The Way of Wisdom: Essays in Honor of Bruce K. Waltke* (ed. J. I. Packer and Sven Soderlund; Grand Rapids: Zondervan, 2000), pp. 251-79. Used by permission of Zondervan.

TEXTUAL STUDIES

CHAPTER 1

"One Thing Is Needful"? (Luke 10:42)
(1981)

In my review of Professor Metzger's *Textual Commentary*, I concluded by noting that "even where . . . the individual scholar feels the committee to have erred, [the *Commentary*] will serve as a useful point of departure for further discussion."[1] I take the occasion of this *Festschrift* in honor of Professor Metzger to follow up that suggestion by discussing one such text: Luke 10:41-42.

I

This passage is a well-known exegetical crux, the final resolution of which is inextricably bound to textual criticism. The exegetical question is: Did Jesus intend no comparison between the two sisters at all, but merely say, "Martha, Martha, Mary has chosen the good portion," or did he rebuke Martha for her anxiety over many things, while commending Mary for her choice of the good portion? And if the latter, did he say to Martha: (1) few things are needed, (2) one thing is needed, or (3) few things are needed, indeed only one?

These differences are a reflection of the textual evidence, which comes down to us in four basic forms, with some minor variations within each:[2]

---

1. *Bib* 55 (1974): 455.

2. The supporting data are given in this order: line 1, the Greek evidence, with a notation of minor variation in brackets (θορυβάζῃ/τυρβάζῃ and Μαριάμ/Μαρία are omitted); line 2, the versional evidence: line 3 (and following), the patristic evidence, which is given in full when it has some bearing on the discussion in this paper.

(1) Μάρθα Μάρθα· ⁴²Μαρία . . .

D [+ θορυβάζῃ]

a b e ff² i l r¹ (c) [c + *conturbaris erga plurima*]

Ambrose, *exp. Lc.* 1.9 (CChL 14.11) [cites vv. 40-42]

Possidius, *vit. Aug.* (MPL 32.34)

[Clement (*Q.d.s.* 10.6 [GCS 3.166]) is sometimes cited as supporting the OL Codex Colbertinus *(c)*. His text reads: σὺ περὶ πολλὰ ταράσσῃ· Μαρία τὴν ἀγαθὴν μερίδα ἐξελέξατο. But the loose nature of this adaptation, plus the context, clearly shows that Clement is not intending to cite all of vv. 41-42.]

(2) Μάρθα Μάρθα, μεριμνᾷς καὶ τυρβάζῃ περὶ πολλά, ⁴²ὀλίγων δέ ἐστιν χρεία· Μαρία δέ . .

38

syrᵖᵃˡ arm geo bo (2 MSS)

[Origen, *fr. 78 in Jo.* (GCS 4.545) is often cited in support of this variant. But as we shall note later, this is extremely dubious. His text reads: καὶ οὐκ ἀπιθάνως διὰ τὴν ἐν τῷ Μωϋσέως νόμῳ πολιτείαν φησὶν εἰρῆσθαι τῇ Μάρθᾳ· "Μάρθα Μάρθα, περὶ πολλὰ θορυβῇ καὶ περισπᾶσαι, ὀλίγων δὲ ἐστιν χρεία." εἰς σωτηρίαν γὰρ οὐ τῶν πολλῶν κατὰ τὸ γράμμα τοῦ νόμου ἐντολῶν χρεία, ἀλλ' ὀλίγων, ἐν οἷς κρέμαται ὅλος ὁ νόμος καὶ οἱ προφῆται, τῶν περὶ ἀγάπης νενομοθετημένων.]

(3) Μάρθα Μάρθα, μεριμνᾷς καὶ (θορυβάζῃ) περὶ πολλά, ⁴²ἑνὸς δέ ἐστιν χρεία· Μαριὰ(μ) δέ . . .

𝔓⁴⁵ 𝔓⁷⁵ A C* W Θ Ξ Ψ unc^*rell* 22 118-209 892 1241 f¹³ *pler*

[𝔓⁷⁵ A Ψ 69 892 1241 *pc* γάρ *l.* δέ (2°)]

itᵃᵘʳ ᶠ ۹ vg sa syrᶜ, ᵖ, ʰ

[aur vg   *porro unum est necessarium*

f   *unum est autem opus*

q   *unius autem est opus*]

Chrysostom, *hom. 44 in Jo.* (MPG 59.249a)

Evagrius, *rer. mon.* (MPG 40.1253c)

Nilus, *de mon. praest.* (MPG 79.1079b)

Ps-Basil, *const. asc.* 1.1 (MPG 31.1325c)

[This is incorrectly cited as by Basil both by F. H. A. Scrivener, *A Plain Introduction to the Criticism of the New Testament* (1894), 2.350, and the UBSGNT. That the tract is not by Basil is almost certain; it appears to have been written under Messalian influence. See J. Quasten, *Patrology*, 3.213.]

Ps-Macarius, *ep. mag.* 32 (W. Jaeger, *Two Rediscovered Works of Ancient Christian Literature* [1954], 288)

John-Damascus, *de fid. orth.* 2.11 (MPG 94.916a) [γάρ *l.* δέ]

Augustine, *serm.* 103.2 (MPL 38.614) *unum autem opus est*
        serm. 104.1 (MPL 38.616) *quando unum est necessarium*
        serm. 104.2 (MPL 38.617) *quando unum est necessarium*
        serm. 170.14 (MPL 38.925) *porro unum est necessarium*
        serm. 179.3 (MPL 38.967) *porro unum est necessarium*
        serm. 256.6 (MPL 38.1189) *porro unum est necessarium*

[Later Latin Fathers (except Cassian, noted below under reading 4), e.g., Gregory the Great, Bede, Antiochus (St. Saba), all cite the Vulgate.]

(4) Μάρθα Μάρθα, μεριμνᾷς καὶ θορυβάζῃ περὶ πολλά, [42]ὀλίγων δέ ἐστιν χρεία ἢ ἑνός· Μαριὰ(μ) γὰρ . . .

$\mathfrak{P}^3$ ℵ B C² L 1 33 579 2193

[B ~χρεία ἐστίν; ℵ* *om.* χρεία; 579 δέ *l.* γάρ]

syr^hmg bo^rell eth it^μ

[OL Codex Mulling reads: *paucis vero opus est vel etiam uno*]

Origen, *fr. 39 in Lc.* (GCS 9.298): δύναται δὲ Μάρθα μὲν εἶναι καὶ ἡ ἐκ περιτομῆς συναγωγὴ εἰς τὰ ἴδια ὅρια δεξαμένη τὸν Ἰησοῦν, περισπωμένη περὶ τὴν ἐκ τοῦ γράμματος τοῦ νόμου πολλὴν λατρείαν, Μαρία δὲ ἡ ἐξ ἐθνῶν ἐκκλησία τὴν ἀγαθὴν τοῦ πνευματικοῦ νόμου μερίδα ἐκλεξαμένη ἀναφαίρετον καὶ μὴ καταργουμένην ὡς ἡ ἐπὶ τοῦ προσώπου Μωϋσέως δόξα, ὀλίγα τὰ χρήσιμα ἐκ τοῦ νόμου ἐπιλέξασα ἢ πάντα ἀναφέρουσα εἰς ἓν τὸ ἀγαπήσεις. καὶ εἰς μὲν τό· "ἑνός ἐστι χρεία" χρήσῃ τό· "ἀγαπήσεις τὸν πλησίον σου ὡς σεαυτόν", εἰς δὲ τό "ὀλίγων ἐστὶν" "τὰς ἐντολὰς οἶδας· οὐ μοιχεύσεις· οὐ φονεύσεις" καὶ τὰ ἑξῆς.

Basil, *moral.* 38.1 (MPG 31.760) [in a citation of vv. 38-42]
    reg. fus. 20.3 (MPG 31.973) [with an exegesis of the two parts]

Cyril-Alexandria, *Lc.* 7.33 (MPG 72.621) [Greek fragments of the commentary]; also in Syriac, *serm.* 39 (CSCO 70.77); *serm.* 69 (CSCO 70.188)

Olympiodorus, *comm. Ezek.* 1.14 (MPG 93.489)

Jerome, *ep. 22 (ad Eustoch.)*.24 (Labourt [1949], 1.136) *pauca autem necessaria sunt aut unum* [written at Rome, AD 384]

Cassian, *conlatio* 1.8 (CSEL 13.15) *paucis vero opus est aut etiam uno*

Each of these text-forms has had its recent advocates. In his commentary in the Pelican series G. B. Caird has argued for reading 1.[3] In this he was following a tradition that goes back to F. Blass,[4] who in turn was followed *inter al.* by J. Wellhausen,[5] J. Moffatt,[6] W. Bousset,[7] E. Klostermann,[8] and W. Manson.[9] Here, not only is the shorter reading preferred, but the other three are to be "regarded as variants of an early gloss."[10]

Reading 2 has recently been defended by Monika Augsten.[11] As far as I can tell, von Soden has been its only other advocate.[12] Nonetheless this variant has played a crucial role in the discussions, for it is repeatedly argued that reading 4 is a conflation of readings 2 and 3.[13] Most of those who so argue favor reading 3 as the original. Augsten prefers reading 2 — as the *lectio difficilior.*

Reading 3 is the traditional reading, both in Christian antiquity East

---

3. G. B. Caird, *Saint Luke* (Baltimore: Penguin, 1963), pp. 149-50; repr. Westminster (SCM) Pelican Commentaries series (Philadelphia: Westminster, 1977).

4. F. Blass, *Evangelium secundum Lucam* (Leipzig: Teubner, 1897). In his *Philology of the Gospels* (London: Macmillan, 1898), pp. 148-49, he considered the textual evidence of this passage as one of the strong arguments in favor of two editions of Luke.

5. J. Wellhausen, *Das Evangelium Lucae* (Berlin: Reimer, 1904), p. 54.

6. J. Moffatt, *The New Testament: A New Translation* (New York: Hodder and Stoughton, 1913).

7. *Die Schriften des Neuen Testaments neu übersetzt* (Göttingen, 1917).

8. E. Klostermann, *Das Lukasevangelium* (HNT 5; Tübingen: Mohr, 1919), p. 485.

9. W. Manson, *The Gospel of Luke* (MNTC; New York: Harper, 1930), pp. 132-33.

10. J. M. Creed, *The Gospel According to St. Luke* (London: Macmillan, 1930), p. 154; cf. Caird, *Saint Luke,* p. 150.

11. M. Augsten, "Lukanische Miszelle," NTS 14 (1967-68): 581-83.

12. Augsten also claims Scrivener to be in support, but she has apparently misread him. Scrivener is a strong advocate of reading 3; and he is so opposed to reading 4 that he says: "We confess that we had rather see this grand passage expunged altogether from the pages of the Gospel than diluted after the wretched fashion adopted by ℵ and B." He finds reading 2 to be "less incredible than that of ℵ B L" (*A Plain Introduction to the Criticism of the New Testament* [4th edn.; 2 vols.; London: Bell, 1894], 2.350). It may be that the adoption of this reading is also the intent of the notes in A. Pallis, *Notes on St Luke and the Acts* (Oxford: Oxford University Press, 1928), p. 22, and W. R. F. Browning in the Torch commentary (London: SCM, 1960), p. 112.

13. It is difficult to trace the origin of this idea. It appears as early as H. Alford, *The Greek Testament* (3rd edn.; 4 vols.; London: Rivingtons, 1861), p. 542. It has been repeated frequently since, both in articles (e.g., G. D. Kilpatrick, "The Greek New Testament Text of Today and the *Textus Receptus*," in *The New Testament in Historical and Contemporary Perspective,* ed. H. Anderson and W. Barclay [Oxford: Blackwell, 1965], p. 192; A. Baker, "One Thing Necessary," CBQ 27 [1965]: 136; Augsten, "Lukanische Miszelle," p. 581) and in commentaries (e.g., Ragg [1922], Creed [1930], Gilmour [1952], Ellis [1966], Stuhlmueller [1968]).

and West and in the majority of commentaries[14] and English translations.[15] It has enjoyed the support of the critical editions of Tischendorf, Vogels, Bover, Nestle,[16] and now the UBSGNT. It was recently defended in an extensive discussion by A. Baker as the reading that best explains the others and is most in keeping with Lucan style.[17] The presentation of the arguments in favor of this reading has been succinctly set forth by Professor Metzger in the *Textual Commentary*. Since I will have occasion to debate some of these conclusions, his comments are here given in full:

> [The] variations seem to have arisen from understanding ἑνός to refer merely to the provisions which Martha was then preparing for the meal; the absoluteness of ἑνός was softened by replacing it with ὀλίγων . . . ; and finally in some witness . . . the two were combined though with disastrous results as to sense. The omission of both clauses (as well as γάρ after Μαριάμ) from it[a,b,e,ff²,i,l,r¹] syr[a] (D retains only θορυβάζῃ) probably represents a deliberate excision of an incomprehensible passage, if it is not a sheer accident, perhaps occasioned by homoeoarcton (Μάρθα . . . Μαριάμ).[18]

Reading 4 has enjoyed the support of the critical editions of Westcott-Hort, B. Weiss, Lagrange, and Merk, as well as of many commentaries[19] and a few English translations.[20] However, it has never had a full-scale defense.

14. *Inter al.*, Alford (1863), Godet (1875), Farrar (1889), Sadler (1889), Zahn (4th edn., 1920), Ragg (1922), Boles (1941), Lenski (1946), Geldenhuys (1951), Gilmour (1952), Thompson (1972).

15. *Inter al.*, *KJV* (1611), *RV* (1881), *ASV* (1901), Weymouth (1903), Montgomery (1924), Knox (1944), Verkuyl (1945), *RSV* (1946), Rieu (1952), C. K. Williams (1952), Confraternity (1953), Kleist (1954), *NEB* (1961), Beck (1963), *TEV* (1966), Barclay (1968), *NAB* (1970), *NIV* (1973), Translators (1973), Estes (1973).

16. The longer reading is printed in the text; from the 20th edition (1950) the siglum (!) has indicated preference for reading 3.

17. "One Thing," pp. 127-37.

18. *A Textual Commentary on the Greek New Testament* (London: UBS, 1971), pp. 153-54. This appears to be dependent upon Alford, *Greek Testament*, 1.543: "The variations have arisen from understanding ενος to refer merely to the provisions then being prepared, — then softening it by ολιγων, and finally combining both readings."

19. *Inter al.*, Plumptre (1881), B. Weiss (9th edn., 1901), Plummer (1902), A. B. Bruce (n.d.), Lagrange (1919), Easton (1926), Rengstorf (1936), Grundmann (1939), Leaney (1958), Ellis (1966), Danker (1972), Karris (1977).

20. *Inter al.*, Twentieth Century (1898), Ballantine (1923), Greber (1937), C. B. Williams (1937), Phillips (1947), New World (1950), Wuest (1956), *NASB* (1963), *JB* (1966), Klingensmith (1972).

The purpose of this present essay is to fill that lacuna, by showing the weaknesses in the argument presented in the *Textual Commentary* and by arguing that reading 4 is the only variant that adequately explains all the data.

II

Despite the frequency with which it has been asserted, the suggestion that ὀλίγων δέ ἐστιν χρεία ἢ ἑνός is a conflation must be laid to rest. The possibility of conflation here has several strikes against it, all having to do with the weak support for reading 2, ὀλίγων δέ ἐστιν χρεία.

In order for conflation to have occurred one would have to establish the very early existence (especially in Egypt) of reading 2. Indeed, one would think from the word order of the longer reading, ὀλίγων . . . ἑνός, that for simple conflation to have occurred (the mere *adding* of ἢ ἑνός) the reading ὀλίγων δέ ἐστιν χρεία should have been predominant in Egypt. But the evidence for an early existence of this variant is so slight as to be nearly worthless.

To be sure, it has been recently argued by Augsten that the fragment from Origen's commentary on John is the evidence we were needing — and now have.[21] A. Baker, on the basis of the fragment from Origen's commentary on Luke, had already suggested that Origen was "probably the source of the conflate."[22] However, both of these suggestions seem to be an inadequate handling of Origen's evidence.

First, the comment in the Luke fragment can scarcely be the source of the conflation — for two reasons: (1) There are many instances in Origen's commentaries and homilies of precisely the kind of "exegesis" found in the Luke fragment, and in no other instance is he conflating texts. Origen's comment here is standard for him and indicates, as we should expect, that he was working with the same text as one finds in ℵ B *et al.* For him, Martha represented Judaism, who, though they had received Jesus into their borders, were nonetheless still distracted with much (πολλήν) service based on the letter of the law. Mary, on the other hand, is like the Gentile church, which has chosen the "good portion" of the "spiritual law." Thus, Origen says, just a few things (ὀλίγα) set forth in the law are beneficial (χρήσιμα); indeed (ἤ), all things in the law are brought forward into the one (ἕν) commandment, "you shall love." He then illustrates from two sayings of Jesus how this is so. The "one

21. "Lukanische Miszelle," p. 582.
22. "One Thing," p. 136.

thing necessary" refers to the saying "you shall love your neighbor as your-self"; the "few things necessary" to the saying "you know the command-ments; you shall not commit adultery, nor murder, etc." The ease with which Origen moves from πολλά to ὀλίγα to ἕν makes it clear that he *presupposes* this text and is therefore not the creator of it.

(2) Furthermore, there is ample evidence available in Origen of places where he *does* know of two or more variants.[23] In such cases, he always gives a clear statement of the existence of the various readings, and frequently he comments on them. Therefore, we may conclude quite positively that in writ-ing the commentary on Luke, Origen knew only a text with the longer read-ing, and that he is in no way responsible for creating it.

Second, it is equally clear that it is basically *this same comment* that Origen had previously made in the commentary on John 11:2.[24] There he had already seen Mary as a σύμβολον τῶν ἀπὸ ἐθνῶν, and Martha as τῶν ἐκ περιτομῆς. In this case, however, he is commenting on John 11, *not* Luke 10; and his interest now is solely in "Martha," who, as the Jews, was distracted about πολλά when only ὀλίγα were necessary for salvation. Thus he "cites" the text somewhat loosely — and only partially. But his final comment in which he ties the "few things" to the law of love in Matthew 22:40 makes it clear that he presupposes the same kind of comment he will make in full on the Luke passage; and therefore even here he presupposes the longer text, even though he cites it partially.

Furthermore, even if we did not have such clear contextual evidence as Origen affords in these two fragments, this kind of "short text" in a patristic ci-tation is of dubious value. As I have shown elsewhere, one can scarcely make any case at all of a Father's citation when the debated words are missing at the beginning or end of his citation.[25] This is especially true when in other cita-tions the same Father cites the text in full and *includes* the debated words! For example, I have noted this about Origen's alleged support of 𝔓[45] *et al.* in the "omission" of καὶ ἡ ζωή in John 11:25.[26] The full evidence from Origen makes it plain in that instance that he knew only the longer text. The same is true here.

---

23. See B. M. Metzger, "Explicit References in the Works of Origen to Variant Readings in New Testament Manuscripts," *Biblical and Patristic Studies in Memory of Robert Pierce Casey,* ed. J. N. Birdsall and R. W. Thomson (Freiburg: Herder, 1963), pp. 78-95.

24. This section of the commentary on John would have been written at Caesarea, *c.* 232. The homilies on Luke were probably among those taken down in shorthand during his later years. See Eusebius, *H.E.* 6.36.

25. G. D. Fee, "The Text of John in *The Jerusalem Bible:* A Critique of the Use of Patristic Evidence in New Testament Textual Criticism," *JBL* 90 (1971): 163-73.

26. In my review of Metzger, *Bib* 55 (1974): 454.

This catena fragment, therefore, simply will not bear the weight that many would give it as evidence of Origen's knowledge of a text without ἢ ἑνός.[27]

Thus the *only* evidence for the variant ὀλίγων δέ ἐστιν χρεία is from codex 38 (thirteenth century); from three versions: the Palestinian Syriac (trans. after AD 400),[28] the Armenian (*c.* 410), and the Georgian (*c.* 450); and from two MSS of the Bohairic (‎א [ninth century], J1 [13th c.]). But to argue from these diverse witnesses for a common denominator that goes back to the second century is to lose historical perspective, or at least is to fail to grapple with the *a priori* logic of genealogy.

First of all it should be noted that these witnesses represent three quite unrelated traditions. Codex 38 is a Byzantine MS, which von Soden listed as I^k; the Armenian and Georgian have well-known textual affinities, while there is a recognized, but unclear, relationship between the Armenian and Syriac; the Bohairic version is a witness to the Egyptian text. One might propose that three such strands of evidence, all independent of each other, argue well for a common archetype that must go back as early as the second century. But that is precisely what is difficult to believe in this case. Given the nature of these particular witnesses, it is much more likely that this is simply a "subsingular" reading, i.e., "a non-genetic, *accidental agreement in variation* between two MSS which are not otherwise closely related."[29]

Let us begin with the two Bohairic MSS. According to Horner, both of these MSS are subject to omissions of various kinds.[30] This means that what we have here are not two related Bohairic MSS that somehow represent an independent expression of this version, and therefore represent a *Greek* text that read ὀλίγων δέ ἐστιν χρεία. Rather, these two MSS are independent corruptions (omitting ἢ ἑνός) of the *only* text of Luke 10:42 known in Bohairic, namely the longer text.

The same is probably also true for the other versions. That is, since there is no early Greek evidence of any kind for ὀλίγων δέ ἐστιν χρεία, it is far more

---

27. All of this only confirms the point made by R. M. Grant many years ago that "patristic citations are not citations unless they have been adequately analyzed." See "The Citation of Patristic Evidence in an Apparatus Criticus," *New Testament Manuscript Studies,* ed. M. M. Parvis and A. Wikgren (Chicago: University of Chicago, 1950), p. 124.

28. For the dating of the various versions, see B. M. Metzger, *The Early Versions of the New Testament* (Oxford: Clarendon, 1977).

29. This definition was offered in an unpublished paper read before the Textual Criticism Seminar of the SBL, 5 October 1974, entitled "Toward the Clarification of Textual Variation: Colwell and Tune Revisited," p. 10.

30. G. W. Horner, *The Coptic Version of the New Testament in the Northern Dialect, otherwise called Memphitic and Bohairic* (4 vols.; Oxford: Clarendon, 1898), 1.xxxviii, cv.

likely that they represent mistranslations, or simple corruptions of the *longer* reading, than that they represent the softening of ἑνός δέ ἐστιν χρεία.

The text of codex 38 is equally suspect. Surely no one will seriously argue that this thirteenth-century MS alone among all its close and distant relatives preserved this reading from the second century. On the contrary, ὀλίγων δέ ἐστιν χρεία is simply a singular reading in codex 38. One cannot tell whether it is a corruption of ἑνὸς δέ ἐστιν χρεία or of ὀλίγων δέ ἐστιν χρεία ἢ ἑνός (probably the former). In either case, the only available Greek evidence for ὀλίγων δέ ἐστιν χρεία belongs to the thirteenth century, and cannot easily be traced back to the second.

Altogether, the evidence for ὀλίγων δέ ἐστιν χρεία is so weak that neither can it be the original text itself nor can it serve as an early source for the alleged "conflation" in reading 4.

III

A similar judgment must be made about reading 1. Although it is sometimes true that *lectio brevior potior,* this is most highly improbable in Luke 10:41-2. To be sure, the omission is difficult to explain. If it is accidental, then the suggestion first made by G. D. Kilpatrick[31] and repeated in a slightly different form in the *Textual Commentary* may well be right — homoeoteleuton or homoeoarcton.

A deliberate omission would be more difficult to explain. If, as Metzger suggests, it is a "deliberate excision of an incomprehensible passage," it must be admitted that the resultant text is even more incomprehensible (Moffatt's translation notwithstanding). One might have expected what happened in Codex Colbertinus *(c)*, but not this. But if in fact it is deliberate, then this Western text is further evidence of the early widespread existence of ὀλίγων δέ ἐστιν χρεία ἢ ἑνός. For by everyone's admission, this is the only reading of the remaining two (3 and 4) that might have been thought to be incomprehensible.

But as difficult as the omission is to explain, it is even more difficult to explain all the data if the short text were original. It falls among several such omissions in the Western text (Hort's "Western non-interpolations"), few of which have commended themselves to recent scholars as the original text.[32]

31. G. D. Kilpatrick, "Western Text and Original Text in the Gospels and Acts," *JTS* 44 (1943): 27.

32. For a recent survey and evaluation see K. Snodgrass, "Western Noninterpolations," *JBL* 91 (1972): 369-79.

Besides its poor external attestation, the short reading here faces two other difficulties.

(1) The doubling of the vocative Μάρθα, followed immediately by a word about Mary, is difficult under any circumstances. But in this case it also runs counter to a clear feature of Lucan style. The doubling of personal name vocatives is a Lucan peculiarity in the NT (Luke 10:42; 22:31; Acts 9:4; 22:7; 26:14). In the other instances, the vocative is followed, as one would expect, by a word spoken in the second person to the one addressed. The words μεριμνᾷς καὶ θορυβάζῃ περὶ πολλά fit this stylistic feature exactly, and therefore surely belong to Luke, not to some glossator.

(2) The saying, μεριμνᾷς καὶ θορυβάζῃ περὶ πολλά· ὀλίγων δέ ἐστιν χρεία ἢ ἑνός, with the following γάρ, is very difficult to explain as a gloss. In the first place, "glosses" usually have the nature of explanatory comment (John 5:4), or catechetical/theological comment (Acts 8:37; 1 John 5:7b). But what does this "gloss" explain? And why does it take the form of a Jesus word (unless it came from an existing tradition of the story)? Furthermore, it is obvious from the textual variation that the "glossed" explanation created as many difficulties as it hoped to solve. And why did the one who finally introduced it into the text insert a γάρ rather than a δέ following Μαριάμ? To suggest that this saying is a gloss is simply to put too much confidence in a reading (the omission) that is already suspect by the company it keeps.

IV

What all of this means, therefore, is that the textual variation in Luke 10:42 boils down to a choice between *two* readings, *not* four. Either Luke wrote ἑνὸς δέ ἐστιν χρεία or ὀλίγων δέ ἐστιν χρεία ἢ ἑνός. Both existed as far back as the second century; and in either case, there is no accident involved. One is clearly the deliberate revision of the other. The real question then is, which variant came second? That is, which one can best be explained as the revision of the other?

Those who have opted for the traditional reading have usually taken one of three stances toward reading 4: (1) ignore it altogether,[33] (2) dismiss it with contempt,[34] or (3) dismiss it as a conflation that yields an intolerable

33. As, for example, does N. Geldenhuys, *Commentary on Luke* (Grand Rapids: Eerdmans, 1951), pp. 315-17.

34. See, for example, M. F. Sadler, *The Gospel According to St. Luke, with Notes Critical and Practical* (3rd edn.; London: Bell, 1889), p. 288: "In this case the so-called neutral text substitutes an unintelligible sentence for one of the Lord's most important words. And this against the authority of all Christendom."

sense.[35] We have already seen the improbability of conflation. If, however, it is the *revision* of reading 3, then one must be prepared to argue also that it did yield a tolerable sense to the reviser. F. Godet saw this many years ago. He himself argued for the originality of ἑνός, which he believed had a purposeful double reference for Jesus himself: one kind of nourishment is sufficient for the body, as only one is necessary for the soul. Of the longer reading Godet goes on to say: "This is probably the meaning of the Alex. reading: '*There needs but little* (for the body), *or even but one thing* (for the soul).'" He adds: "There is subtilty in this reading; too much perhaps."[36]

Godet is surely right on two counts: this is the probable meaning of reading 4; and it is subtle. But it is *not* an intolerable sense. The only question is whether it is *too* subtle. There is a long and worthy tradition that thinks otherwise, which argues both that this is the original text and that this meaning is more than tolerable — it makes good sense! As to its being too subtle, this would, however, be very likely true as the work of a second-century scribe — especially so, if the original text were ἑνὸς δέ ἐστιν χρεία. For this text never seems to have given anyone trouble in antiquity, at least not among those who comment on the text. Since *both* variants lead eventually to the same result, it is difficult to imagine why an early scribe would have felt impelled to this kind of subtlety in order to achieve that result.

On the other hand, if ὀλίγων δέ ἐστιν χρεία ἢ ἑνός were original, one can well imagine an early scribe being perplexed by the text (as apparently many later commentaries have been). Thus, taking his clue from the ἑνός, plus the following comment about Mary's choice of τὴν ἀγαθὴν μερίδα, he rewrote what was for him a perplexing text into something much more manageable. Reading 4, therefore, surely is a case of *lectio difficilior potior*.

Although it has never been included in the discussion, there is one further piece of evidence that seems to confirm this choice, and that is the interchange of γάρ and δέ following Μαριάμ. Several things are significant in this regard: (1) No matter which textual choice is made between readings 3 and 4, all critical texts have Μαριὰ(μ) γάρ. (2) This is surely correct, for it is inconceivable that a scribe under any circumstances would have expunged a δέ for a γάρ here. (3) However, elsewhere Luke's use of γάρ in direct discourse very clearly expresses cause or reason. For example, there are thirty-five such instances in the Gospel up to 10:42, and the *RSV* translates every one of them "for." (4) On the

---

35. See, for example, Creed, *Gospel of Luke,* p. 154; Baker, "One Thing," p. 135; Metzger, *Textual Commentary,* pp. 153-54.

36. F. Godet, *A Commentary on the Gospel of St. Luke* (trans. E. W. Shalders and M. D. Cush; 3rd edn.; 2 vols.; New York: Funk & Wagnalls, 1890), 2.45.

other hand, in this passage the English translations (including the *RSV*) that are made from a text reading ἑνὸς δέ . . . Μαριὰμ γάρ invariably treat γάρ as an untranslatable particle, rather than as a conjunction. (5) Rightly so, because γάρ scarcely follows ἑνὸς δέ ἐστιν χρεία meaningfully. Later scribes, who had only ἑνὸς δέ ἐστιν χρεία in their texts, were quite right to substitute for γάρ a consecutive δέ: "One thing is needful, *and* Mary has chosen. . . ."

How then does one account for the original γάρ, especially, in light of Luke's rather careful usage elsewhere? The answer of course is that it goes with an original text that read ὀλίγων δέ ἐστιν χρεία ἢ ἑνός. It functions as an explanation of ἢ ἑνός, thus suggesting that the ἤ has normal disjunctive force here. Thus the original text reads: "Martha, Martha, you are worried and upset about *many* things. However (δέ) few things are really needed, or, if you will (ἤ), only *one*; for that is indeed what Mary has chosen, the good portion. . . ."

It may be of interest finally to note that the other Egyptian witnesses (𝔓⁷⁵ Ψ 892 1241) all reflect their true origins in this regard by reading γάρ, even though they have picked up the secondary ἑνὸς δέ ἐστιν χρεία.

V

One final argument against the longer reading must be noted. It is sometimes suggested that this reading is "very much confined to Alexandria" and is therefore a local, transient revision.[37] Indeed, the evidence of 𝔓⁴⁵ and especially 𝔓⁷⁵ seemed to make this all the more true. So much was this so, in fact, that one can trace the pendulum of scholarship oscillating from Westcott-Hort back to the traditional text with the discovery of these two papyri. Since the influences behind the UBSGNT text are very clear, it is most probable that 𝔓⁷⁵ as much as anything else led to the choice of ἑνὸς δέ ἐστιν χρεία with a (C) rating.[38]

This is one of those rare places, however, where the text of 𝔓⁷⁵ is probably secondary both to the original text and to its own textual tradition. I have shown elsewhere[39] that the relationship between 𝔓⁷⁵ and B is such that they must have common ancestry anterior to 𝔓⁷⁵. Occasionally, one finds a bifurcation in this text-type, where two clearly early readings exist among the wit-

37. Baker, "One Thing," p. 131.

38. On the influence of 𝔓⁷⁵ on the UBSGNT text, see the reviews by I. A. Sparks, *Int* 22 (1968): 92-96, and I. Moir, *NTS* 14 (1967-68): 136-43. Sparks notes that 𝔓⁷⁵ "has clearly usurped the place of honor previously given to the great uncials" (p. 95).

39. G. D. Fee, "𝔓⁷⁵, 𝔓⁶⁶, and Origen: The Myth of Early Textual Recension in Alexandria," in *New Dimensions in New Testament Studies*, ed. R. N. Longenecker and M. C. Tenney (Grand Rapids: Zondervan, 1974), pp. 31-44.

nesses, one of which is often destined to become the Byzantine reading. On rare occasions 𝔓⁷⁵ and B also reflect this bifurcation, where now one and then the other picks up the variant that is secondary both to the mainstream of the text-type and to the original text. Ἑνὸς δέ ἐστιν χρεία appears to be one of those readings.⁴⁰

Thus, even though 𝔓⁷⁵ shows that both readings existed very early in Egypt, the reading ὀλίγων δέ ἐστιν χρεία ἢ ἑνός seems to have predominated there. This is evidenced not only by the Greek MS tradition, but also by the facts that both the Bohairic (although not the Sahidic) and the Ethiopic versions translate this text and that this is the only text cited in any extant evidence from the Egyptian Fathers (Origen, Cyril, Olympiodorus, plus John Cassian).

But is this text which predominated in Egypt to be found only in Egypt as a local aberration? The evidence from West and East (outside of Egypt) suggests otherwise.

(1) There is no evidence from extant sources that either reading 3 or 4 had early existence in the West. As noted above, the early OL omits the clause altogether. Ambrose and Possidius, the biographer of Augustine, reflect the continuing predominance of the omission into the fifth century. Earlier Latin Fathers unfortunately are silent.

The earliest appearance of either of the other readings in the West is in Jerome's letter to Eustochium, written at Rome in 384, at about the same time he was creating the Vulgate of the gospels. However, one cannot tell whether this reading already existed in Rome, or whether Jerome brought it from the East. In either case, it is clearly a text that he knew well and one that existed outside Egypt.⁴¹

Interestingly enough, the earliest evidence for ἑνὸς δέ ἐστιν χρεία in the West is also from Jerome. Again, it is not possible to know whether it already existed or whether he introduced it. The earliest appearance of this text-form is in Augustine, and his citations clearly reflect the Vulgate's *porro unum est necessarium*.⁴² The only evidence for a non-vulgatized rendering of this vari-

40. For the graphs that present all these data see "𝔓⁷⁵, 𝔓⁶⁶, and Origen," pp. 34-39.

41. The later existence in Latin of the longer reading, *paucis vero opus est vel etiam uno*, in John Cassian and the Irish Book of Mulling is attributable first of all to the lengthy stay of Cassian in Egypt, and then to his residency at Lérins, which in turn influenced Irish monasticism (and the text of Mulling). See G. G. Willis, "Some Interesting Readings of the Book of Mulling," *Studia Evangelica* 1, ed. K. Aland *et al.* (TU 73; Berlin: Akademie-Verlag, 1959), pp. 811-13.

42. F. C. Burkitt believed that this reading, among others, is evidence that Augustine accepted Jerome's version, even though he also continued to use the OL throughout his life. See "Saint Augustine's Bible and the Itala," *JTS* 11 (1910): 263.

ant is to be found in the "revised" OL codices *f* and *q* and in one citation from Augustine. This latter evidence may indicate that the variant had some existence in the West independently of the Vulgate. However, the likelihood is that this reading appeared in the West only after Jerome introduced it.

(2) The evidence from other parts of the East, on the other hand, suggests a situation much like that in Egypt, where both variants existed side by side from early on. However, in this case, the shorter reading came to predominate. The longer reading is known in the Syriac traditions (in the marginalia of the Harclean, and in the corrupted, shortened form [omit ἢ ἑνός] in the Palestinian). It is also cited and commented on by Basil of Caesarea and is clearly the only text he knew. This reading probably also lies behind the Armenian (and thus the Georgian) version.

This is not abundant evidence, but it is substantial. When joined with the evidence from Jerome, it seems clear that this reading had a widespread history in the East. However, ἑνὸς δέ ἐστιν χρεία eventually came to predominate. It was known early in Syriac. By the end of the fourth century and thereafter it is the only text known outside of Egypt.

What must be concluded from all of this, therefore, is that the external evidence is simply indecisive. Both variants existed early in Egypt; both existed frequently outside of Egypt in the fourth and fifth centuries. The question finally is whether the Egyptian text-type, as in so many other cases, also preserves the Lucan original. In this case transcriptional probability argues strongly in the affirmative.

VI

All of this evidence converges to suggest that Luke 10:42 should read: ὀλίγων δέ ἐστιν χρεία ἢ ἑνός. If so, then the text is not so much a "put down" of Martha as it is a gentle rebuke for her anxiety. For a meal, Jesus says, there is no cause to fret over πολλά, when only ὀλίγα are necessary. Then, having spoken of "necessity," he moves on to affirm Mary's "outrageous" action. "Indeed," he says, "in another sense only one thing is necessary. For this is indeed what Mary has chosen."

CHAPTER 2

On the Inauthenticity of John 5:3b-4
(1982)

New Testament scholarship by and large has regarded the reference to the angel's stirring of the waters of Bethesda (John 5:3b-4) to be a gloss and therefore no part of the original text of the Fourth Gospel. The well-known and off-repeated reasons for this conclusion are briefly summarized by Metzger:[1] (1) its absence from the earliest and best witnesses, (2) the presence of non-Johannine words or expressions, and (3) the rather wide diversity of variant forms in which v. 4 was transmitted. Indeed, so certain for most scholars is this an "assured result" that one looks in vain to the scholarly literature for a full-scale presentation of the data; it simply seemed too certain to be necessary.

Nonetheless there have been a few exceptions to this consensus, especially among Roman Catholic scholars.[2] Most notable of these was the willingness of D. Mollat to include the disputed verses in the French original of the *Jerusalem Bible*. After acknowledging the majority opinion, he notes: "Cependant il est attesté par l'assemble des Mss de VetLat et nous paraît authentique."[3] He further suggests that the verses might have been suppressed because of the rather unorthodox character of this "sanctuary of healing."

More recently, Z. Hodges, whose text-critical methodology had already

---

1. B. M. Metzger, *A Textual Commentary on the Greek New Testament* (London: United Bible Societies, 1971), p. 209.

2. See, e.g., J. M. Bover, "Autenticidad de Jn. 5,3b-4," *Est Bib* 11 (1952): 69-72; T. Antolín, "La autenticidad de Jn. 5,3b-4 y la exégesis dels vs. 7," *Verdad y Vida* 19 (1961): 327-41. It also appears in the translation by Ronald Knox (1944).

3. *L'Évangile et les Épîtres de Saint Jean* (2nd edn.; Paris: Cerf, 1960), p. 105. In the 3rd edition (1973) the final sentence has been softened to "et pourrait être authentique."

given him a prior commitment in favor of inclusion,[4] has offered an extensive defense of their authenticity.[5] In response to the traditional arguments against them, Hodges argues that the "omission" is a basically Alexandrian phenomenon, and that the presence of non-Johannine words and expressions is a matter that counts for little. On the contrary, he argues that v. 7 demands the presence of 3b-4 and that their suppression can be explained as an early theological aversion to what would have been considered a "vestige of paganism" in some parts of the church.

It is Hodges' article in particular that has prompted this present paper, which is an attempt to fill a lacuna by offering a full-scale discussion of the reasons for rejecting the passage as spurious. The discussion will proceed under the traditional rubrics of transcriptional probability, intrinsic probability, and external evidence.

Transcriptional Probability

It is especially important at the outset to set forth the textual data in full, because the discussion of transcriptional probabilities must embrace all the phenomena. The data:

(1) Include both 3b-4 $\quad$ A[2] C[3] K X[comm] Δ Θ Ψ Ω 063 078 f[1] f[13] 28 565 700 892 1241 Byz it[a, aur, b, c, e, ff2, j, r1] syr[p,pal] cop[bomss] arm eth Diatessaron[a] (Tertullian) Ambrose Augustine Chrysostom

(2) Include with asterisks $\quad$ S Λ Π 047 1079 2174 pc sy[h]

(3) Include only v. 4 $\quad$ A* L Diatessaron[l, i, n]

(4) Include only v. 3b $\quad$ D W[supp] 0141 38 it[d, f, l] vg[ww]geo

(5) Omit both 3b-4 $\quad$ P[66] P[75] ℵ B C* 0125 it[q] syr[c] cop Cyril-Jerusalem (Amphilochius) Pseudo-Amphilochius (Didymus) Nonnus (Cyril Alexandria)

There is, of course, no possible way this material could have been added or omitted by accident; it was either intentionally expunged or intentionally inserted. Furthermore, we are not dealing with a *single* addition or deletion. The data demand a process — of independent additions or deletions of more than one kind.

4. See, e.g., "The Greek Text of the King James Version," *Bibliotheca Sacra* 125 (1968): 334-45.

5. "The Angel at Bethesda — John 5:4," *Bibliotheca Sacra* 136 (1979): 25-39.

Traditionally, it has been believed that variant 5 is original and that all of 5:3b-4 (variant 1) was added as a gloss to explain the otherwise puzzling statement in v. 7: "I have no one to help me into the pool when the water is stirred. While I am trying to get in, someone else goes down ahead of me" (NIV). That, of course, would explain how one gets from variant 5 to variant 1. However, it seems far more likely that we are here dealing with *two* independent glosses (variants 3 and 4), which had already been joined at an early stage in the West, but which also had a period of independent existence. In any case, a variety of *additions* of two separate, and then joined, glosses is a historically probable explanation of all the textual phenomena.

On the other hand, neither variant 5 nor 3 or 4 is easily explained if 5:3b-4 had been original to John's Gospel. The question, of course, is why one would have expunged such a pertinent datum. The only possible answer is a theological one. For some reason, someone had a theological uneasiness about an angel's giving salubrious qualities to a pool of water, and therefore omitted the offending sentence when copying his text. But the problem with this answer is twofold: (a) It fails to reckon with all the textual phenomena, especially variants 3 and 5, and (b) it fails to take seriously the theological proclivities of second-century Christianity.

First, this answer fails because it works as a transcriptional explanation *only* for variant 4 (the "omission" of v. 4 only). What cannot be explained with any degree of historical probability is why, given v. 7, anyone would also have expunged the words ἐκδεχομένων τὴν τοῦ ὕδατος κίνησιν from v. 3. Furthermore, what is even more unlikely is variant 3 itself. If variant 1 were original, then one is faced with the improbability that someone deleted *only* these words from v. 3. This in turn means that someone else deleted only v. 4, and still someone else deleted them both. If it is argued that variant 5 was the original corruption and that variants 3 and 4 are partial restorations of the original, that might well explain the reading of A and L (variant 3), but it presses the imagination as an explanation of variant 4 — why should one have restored only the "moving of the water" and have left out the explanation itself? If variant 1 were original, there seems no viable alternative to the necessity of postulating at least *two independent* deletions, one of vv. 3b-4 and another of v. 4. While this is historically possible, it is most highly improbable.

Second, there seems to be no historical basis whatever for someone in second-century Alexandria, not to mention elsewhere in the early church, to have had a theological aversion to such activity on the part of angels. On the contrary, the writers of the second century who speak of angels at all do so with great favor. In Hermas's *Shepherd* (*Vis.* 4.2.4) an angel shuts the mouth of a wild beast for Hermas's sake (cf. Dan. 6:22); in Clement of Alexandria angels watch over nations, cities, and individuals (*Strom.* 6.157.5); and later, in Origen, the whole created order (air and water) is kept pure through the agency of angels (*Cels.* 8:31). Angels play a major role in apocryphal and heretical literature as well. There is simply no known aversion to angelic activity in second-century Christianity.

To be sure, Professor Hodges attempts to find the theological milieu necessary for such a deletion in a passage from Tertullian's *De Baptismo* (ch. 5), where Tertullian is arguing that pagan ritual cleansings, though demonic, in their own way bear witness to Christian baptism. In ch. 4 Tertullian argued that the Spirit through an angel sanctified the waters of Christian baptism. In ch. 5 he contrasts this work of the Spirit and his angel with the demonic spirits present at pagan cleansings. In the midst of this argument he asks: "Why have I referred to such matters? So that no one should think it over-difficult for God's holy angel to be present to set waters in motion for man's salvation, when an unholy angel of the evil one often does business with that same element with a view to man's perdition. If it is thought strange that an angel should do things to waters, there has already occurred a precedent of that which is to be."[6] And with that Tertullian argues that the angel of Bethesda is the precursor of his baptismal angel. Hodges italicizes the protasis of this final sentence and argues that Alexandria provided just such an intellectual atmosphere for a textual deletion "motivated by a falsely perceived 'pagan tinge.'"[7] That is, he perceives someone actually to have had the hypothetical difficulty Tertullian suggests and thereby to have deleted 5:4 from the text of John.

This argument, however, seems totally *non sequitur.* The problem with which Tertullian is wrestling at this point is not with angels *per se,* nor with the activity of angels in waters *per se,* but with his own non-biblical view of angels at the waters of baptism. Thus it is not a falsely perceived vestige of paganism that Tertullian is anticipating, but a response to his own view of Christian baptism. Hodges is correct that Tertullian argues *from* John 5:4 as though that were the only known text. But it is precisely for such a reason that he thinks he can argue with impunity. No one would deny the sacred text. Thus there is not a hint in any of this that Christians as early as, or in this case (because of P[66] and P[75]) earlier than, Tertullian had an aversion to angelic activity in first-century Jerusalem.

In the matter of transcriptional probability, therefore, the dictum *lectio difficilior potior* prevails, and the more difficult task is to explain the deletion(s). The addition(s) are fully explicable on the basis of v. 7.

6. Translation by E. Evans (London: SPCK, 1964), pp. 13-15.
7. "The Angel," p. 39.

Intrinsic Probability

This aspect of textual criticism, having to do with whether or not a given author wrote the words in question, is admittedly the most subjective dimension of our science. But it is not thereby to be discounted — or disregarded — as some today are wont to do. Professor Hodges' study again offers an interesting case in point. In the first place, apart from his confidence in the Majority Text, his argument rests on the supposition that the response of the invalid in v. 7 "demands the presence of verse 4 in order to make John's text genuinely comprehensible."[8] This seems to be a case of subjectivity of the highest order; in any case it affirms the author of the Fourth Gospel to have been a much tidier writer than the evidence allows.[9]

Indeed, the problem of intrinsic probability lies elsewhere, in this case with the unusually high incidence of non-Johannine words or expressions in such a short passage. Hodges has countered that "this argument has no real force," because "special subject matter often elicits special vocabulary." As an example he points to seven Johannine *hapax legomena* (including three New Testament *hapaxes*) that appear in John 2:14-16.[10]

Hodges, however, seems to have missed the nature of the problem here. It is true that in the 60 words in 2:14-16 John uses 11 words he does not use elsewhere; and it is further true that in this case the special subject matter has elicited the special vocabulary (after all, 8 of the 11 words are nouns). But it is further true that everything else in 2:14-16, except for 8 special nouns and 8 special verbs, is very Johannine; the adverbs, the conjunctions, the word order, the paraphrastic style — all accord with ordinary Johannine usage. It should be further noted that even these kinds of passages are extremely rare in John (cf. 4:52 and 12:3).

The problem in 5:3b-4, however, is significantly different from the sudden increase of special nouns found in 2:14-16. The problem here has to do with Johannine and New Testament *hapax legomena,* plus non-Johannine stylistic features, where a new or special vocabulary is in fact not required by the subject matter. Let us comment on each of the linguistic and stylistic *hapaxes* in their order of appearance:

1. ἐκδεχομένων — This word occurs only here in John, and six times

---

8. "The Angel," p. 39.

9. Besides the well-known aporias, there are similar local matters left unexplained, which would have been equally puzzling to ordinary readers (e.g., 4:20: "Our fathers worshipped on this mountain").

10. *Art. cit.,* p. 37. Actually Hodges has sold himself a little short. There are eleven Johannine *hapaxes*. Hodges has missed ἐκχέω, τράπεζα, ἀνατρέπω, and ἐμπόριον.

elsewhere in the New Testament. It presents no special problems to authenticity, since the concept of "waiting" does not occur elsewhere in John. In all likelihood this would be normal usage.

2. κίνησιν — This word presents special problems for Johannine authenticity. In this case the special subject matter has not called for this word. In v. 7 John refers to the water as having been "troubled" (ταράσσω). Whoever wrote v. 4 was sensitive enough to this usage to repeat it, both in its verbal and nominal forms. Since such repetition is one of the outstanding Johannine characteristics,[11] it is difficult to understand his having used κίνησις in v. 3b and ταραχή in v. 4.

3. τὴν τοῦ ὕδατος κίνησιν — This use of an enclosed genitive presents extraordinarily difficult problems for Johannine authenticity. The difficulties have to do with two realities about Johannine style. On the one hand, one of the marked characteristics of John's style is his frequent repetition, in close sequence, of identical words or phrases, but frequently with the second or following items appearing in word order variation. Thus, for example, he regularly varies the position of possessive or demonstrative pronouns or of subject-verb-object. On the other hand, there are some word-order invariables (e.g., ἀμὴν ἀμὴν λέγω ὑμῖν; never ὑμῖν λέγω). Another of these invariables is with genitive constructions where both nouns are definite (e.g., *the* eyes of *the* blind). There are 97 such occurrences in the Gospel (*not* including those places where both nouns are genitives, as in 12:3 τῆς ὀσμῆς τοῦ μύρου), plus 27 others in 1 and 2 John. In every case the word order invariably is *the* moving of *the* water.

It is as improbable for John to have written τὴν τοῦ ὕδατος κίνησιν as it would be for a proper Bostonian to say, "I'm fixin' to go up town; y'all come with me, ya hear?" One may count on it: had John written 5:3b he would have said τὴν ταραχὴν τοῦ ὕδατος.

4. ἄγγελος κυρίου — almost all of the early uncials have κυρίου, which is lacking in the later majority. This use of κυρίου without the τοῦ is a septuagintalism, which occurs frequently in Matthew, but elsewhere in John only in citations of the LXX (1:23; 12:13; 12:38). In 1:51 he speaks of τοὺς ἀγγέλους τοῦ θεοῦ. In no other instance in fact does John refer to God as κύριος.

5. κατὰ καιρόν — This idiom, with the meaning "from time to time," is a New Testament *hapax legomenon*. The phrase occurs elsewhere only in Romans 5:6, where it has the sense of an appointed time. John does not use κατά in a distributive sense elsewhere; on the other hand, there is nothing unusual about the usage.

---

11. See Edwin A. Abbott, *Johannine Grammar* (London: A. and C. Black, 1906), pp. 437-65.

22

6. κατέβαινεν ἐν τῇ κολυμβήθρᾳ — Although M. Zerwick allows that this use of ἐν with καταβαίνω could be accounted for as a "pregnant construction" (i.e., with the connotation of *preceding* motion, now at rest),[12] the usage of ἐν with any of the βαίνω compounds (ἀναβαίνω, καταβαίνω, ἐμβαίνω) is totally out of keeping with *Johannine* style, which always reads εἰς. Again, it is not a case of John's *not* being able to say καταβαίνω ἐν; it is a matter of a proper Britisher saying "ain't."

7. ἐμβάς — Elsewhere in the New Testament, including John 5:7(!), people καταβαίνουσι into water and ἀναβαίνουσι out of it — unless they are cast, or cast themselves, into the water, in which case βάλλω is used. Ἐμβαίνω is reserved for getting into boats. The usage is unusual on every count. In this case the special subject matter has not only *not* called for the usage, but on this matter John elsewhere is in total conformity to the rest of the New Testament.

8. οἴῳ δήποτ' — This construction is also a New Testament *hapax legomenon*. And again, it is *not* called forth by the special subject matter. This idiom poses nearly insurmountable problems for Johannine authorship. First, because John nowhere else uses unique constructions as subordinating conjunctions; second, because John does subordinate elsewhere with the concept of "whatever" and uses a variety of standard forms: ὅσα ἄν, ὅτι ἄν, ποταπός.

9. κατέχω — This is a Johannine *hapax legomenon*. As a verb to express being "held" by sickness or disease, it is a New Testament *hapax* (cf. the variant in D at Luke 4:38). Again, the usage is *not* dictated by the special subject matter. In the immediate context (5:5), John has ἔχω, which is the standard New Testament usage.

10. νοσήματι — Here again we have a New Testament *hapax legomenon*, which again is not elicited by the special subject matter. Indeed, this word is unusual in two ways. First, the word ordinarily refers to disease proper (cf. Josephus, *Contra Apion* 1.282, where it refers to leprosy), a category that does not seem to be included in John's three words in v. 3, which describe the kinds of ἀσθενούντων of those who were lying at the pool (blind, lame, withered). Second, John elsewhere always uses a form of ἀσθενεία to describe sickness.

In sum: No one of these perhaps is sufficient in itself to cause one to question the authenticity of 5:3b and 5:4. But the effect is cumulative — and it is devastating. In the space of 34 words there are 10 unusual words or non-Johannine features of style, only two of which (ἐκδεχόμενοι and κατὰ καιρόν) might have been called for by the special subject matter. The others are not only non-Johannine in the sense that he does not use them elsewhere, but

---

12. Maximilian Zerwick, *Biblical Greek* (Rome: Pontifical Biblical Institute, 1963), pp. 33-34.

more significantly in the sense that John uses different words or phrases when he expresses identical ideas elsewhere.

Contrary to Hodges, this argument has real force. Since John is not noted for unique expressions, but for constant repetition, it is particularly difficult to account for so many non-Johannine expressions in such a short span. Coupled with the difficulty of transcriptional probabilities, it seems unlikely in the highest degree that John could have written either 5:3b or 5:4.

The External Evidence

The final (or first!) argument that favors variant 5 as the original is the external evidence itself. The three criteria of early, best, and geographically widespread all favor this variant, and alternatively indicate the secondary character of the others. To be sure, Professor Hodges, with something of a *tour de force*, argues the opposite in favor of variant 1, but to do so he seems to push historical data beyond recognizable limits.

There is no question that the evidence *for* both 5:3b and 5:4 is early, but it is certainly questionable whether that evidence is diverse and widespread. On the other hand, the evidence against both glosses is equally ancient, and in this case can be shown to be *independently* widespread. (In what follows we will limit our discussion only to the variant of v. 4.)

First, it must be noted that the early evidence for the gloss is *strictly Western*. Indeed, it appears to be the predominant text in the West and is found as early as Tertullian (ca. 200) in North Africa and in Codex Vercellensis (*a;* 4th c.) in Italy. The only other "early" evidence is from the Diatessaron, which has clear affinities with the Western text.

The earliest Greek evidence for the addition is to be found in the homilies on John by Chrysostom, which were delivered around 391. It is often asserted that Didymus (d. 398) also knew the reading, but this is not quite accurate. It is clear from *De Trinitate* 2.14 that Didymus knew the *tradition* about the angel. But it seems equally clear that he was not acquainted with the actual text of the tradition, for there is not a single verbal correspondence to John 5:4 in his sentence. Furthermore, he says the water was stirred by the angel *once a year*! That is a far cry from the κατὰ καιρόν of the text.

Similarly, it is likely that Amphilochius of Iconium (d. post 394) also knew the tradition, since he refers to an *angel* who ἐσάλευσεν the water.[13] But

---

13. See *homilia in John 5:19* (C. Datema, editor, *Amphilochii Iconiensis Opera*, in *Corpus Christianorum Graecorum* 3 [Leuven: University Press, 1978], p. 176).

again such language gives little confidence that he had this verse in his text of John. The lack of precise verbal correspondence is especially relevant in his case, because his homily is on John 5:19, and he picks up the narrative at 5:1. Although he does not cite every verse along the way, the *language* of his references and allusions is in every other case very close to the Johannine text.

The earliest Greek *manuscript* to have 5:4 is Codex Alexandrinus (although it has failed to pick up 5:3b). From the ninth century on it is found in almost all the Greek evidence, which by then of course was limited to the Byzantine Church. Early evidence for this verse in the Eastern Church, therefore, simply does not exist.[14]

On the other hand, the evidence against it is not only early, but far more diverse and widespread than Hodges allows. It is the only reading known in Egypt, with the possible exception of Cyril of Alexandria, where the verse is found in the *lemma* of his commentary, but is not cited in the commentary itself.[15]

This text is also known very early in Syria in the form of the Old Syriac version. Although Hodges doubts the antiquity of this version he does so against the conclusions of most Syriac scholars.[16] In any case, the Old Syriac is early evidence from Syria for a text without John 5:4 in a manuscript that has *no* significant textual relatedness to Egypt, except in those several instances where it agrees with the Egyptian tradition simply because both are early representatives of the original text over against the later Byzantine.

This reading also has substantial Western support in the form of Codex D and the Old Latin *q*. Codex D, despite its being a fifth/sixth-century manuscript, is the major *Greek* witness to the text that circulated very early in the East. Where it does *not* reflect the early Western text, it has generally been influenced by a later textual tradition. Here we have evidence quite unrelated to Egypt *in a direct way* for the early circulation of a text of John without 5:4 in the same area where early texts that have it are also circulating.

14. The Diatessaron, which influenced later Syriac traditions, is basically "Western," even though it found its greatest response in the East.

15. *Jo.* 2.5 (Pusey 3, p. 304). Following v. 7 (p. 307) Cyril does allude to the tradition, but he mentions "angels" in the plural and seems to reflect the "once a year" tradition known to Didymus, specifying the angels to come to the pool on the Day of Pentecost. Again, there is nothing in his language that gives one confidence that he actually knew a text of *John* with this verse.

The few and late Coptic Mss. that have 5:4 have all clearly been influenced by later texts. The original Coptic versions themselves know nothing of this reading.

16. *Art. cit.*, 31, n. 18. See B. M. Metzger, *The Early Versions of the New Testament* (Oxford: Clarendon, 1977), pp. 47-48.

The other two Old Latin manuscripts (*f* and *l*) without v. 4 were heavily influenced by the Vulgate and therefore add their substantial weight to the fact that the original Vulgate did not have v. 4.[17] In fact it is nearly impossible to account for the Vulgate evidence if v. 4 were in Jerome's original. The *addition* of this verse to any number of Vulgate manuscripts is totally explicable, given its widespread presence in the Old Latin tradition, plus the initial difficulty the Vulgate had in gaining acceptance. The fact that it was *added* to the Vulgate is confirmed by the fact that *three different recensions* can be found in the Vulgate manuscripts, each of which follows differing expressions of the Old Latin! On the other hand, if v. 4 *were* original to the Vulgate, several *independent omissions* are required (in the Irish Codex Dublinensis, the Italian Codex Harleianus, and some earlier manuscripts that influenced *f* and *l*). Such widespread omissions in the early medieval period, allegedly influenced by Egyptian texts, are nearly impossible to account for.

But the evidence from the Vulgate against v. 4 is probably not Western itself. Since the Vulgate is a *revision* of the Old Latin on the basis of Greek manuscripts available to Jerome in the environs of Bethlehem, and since the Old Latin tradition generally contained this verse, Jerome becomes strong evidence *outside of Egypt* for Greek manuscripts that lacked the verse. Jerome seems scarcely ever to have adopted a reading only from the Old Latin without support from his Greek manuscripts. We may deduce, therefore, that John 5:4 was in *none* of the Greek witnesses to which Jerome had access.

Such a deduction is strongly supported from Jerome's older contemporary, Cyril of Jerusalem (d. 386), who has an extant homily on the story of the healing of the invalid in John 5. It is certain from Cyril's homily that he knew nothing of a text with the gloss in it.[18] Although Jerusalem is close to Egypt, Cyril's New Testament text shows affinities not with Egypt, but with other evidence from Palestine during the fourth century.[19] It is clear from Origen's evidence that a text similar to Cyril's existed in Caesarea *before* he got there (ca. 232) and that he was influenced by this kind of text in his later writings,[20] whereas Origen's own Egyptian text, which has been proven to have accom-

17. Hodges (28, n. 10) wishes to leave doubts on this matter as well; but again he does so without evidence and over against the clear force of the data.

18. See J. Rupp, *Cyrilli Opera* (Munich, 1860), II, 408.

19. See J. Harold Greenlee, *The Gospel Text of Cyril of Jerusalem,* Studies and Documents 17 (Copenhagen: Ejnar Munksgaard, 1955).

20. This is especially true of his text of Mark and Matthew. See K. Lake, R. P. Blake, and Silva New, "The Caesarean Text of the Gospel of Mark," *Harvard Theological Review* 21 (1928): 259-77; K. W. Kim, "The Matthean Text of Origen in his *Commentary on Matthew,*" *Journal of Biblical Literature* 68 (1949): 125-39.

panied him to Caesarea,[21] does *not* appear to have had further influence in that area.

There is one further piece of significant Eastern, but non-Egyptian evidence for the text that lacks v. 4. An early homily on the feast of Mid-Pentecost, which was attributed both to Chrysostom and Amphilochius, is almost certainly the work of neither. This has been demonstrated recently by C. Datema in his critical edition of the works of Amphilochius.[22] A check of the New Testament text in this homily against the text in the genuine works of Amphilochius has further corroborated Datema's conclusion. Datema dates this homily at the end of the sixth century. The author seems to have come from Asia Minor, and his New Testament text is early Byzantine, very much like that of the Cappadocian Fathers. However, in a long citation of John 5:1-6 he was using a Greek text with neither 3b nor 4, and there is no hint in his comments that he even knew of the tradition about the angel. Such a text, therefore, continued to exist in Asia Minor alongside that known by Chrysostom.

All of this evidence together indicates that not only was the text without John 5:4 very early in the East, but it also is the only text found in all the extant evidence from disparate parts of the East *before* Chrysostom — except for the Diatessaron, which came from the West, and in turn influenced the later Syriac versions.

Conclusions

We may rightly conclude that the confidence with which New Testament scholarship has almost unanimously rejected both 5:3b and 5:4 is well founded. Hodges' explanation as to how a deletion of this kind may have taken place does not appear to be an adequate reading of the evidence from Tertullian nor from all the other extant second-century Christian literature. Given the love of angels found everywhere in early Christian piety, it is easy to account for the addition of the prevailing superstition about the pool to texts of the Gospel of John, but it still remains a singular mystery as to why anyone in the second century would have rejected it. In any case there are no *known* historical reasons for such a thing.

Furthermore, the fact that there is such early and widespread evidence for a text of John without 5:4, among witnesses with no *direct* textual related-

---

21. See my study of "The Text of John and Mark in the Writings of Chrysostom," *New Testament Studies* 26 (1971-80): 525-47.

22. Datema, *Amphilochii Iconiencis Opera,* pp. xx-xxi.

ness, suggests that the "omission" would have to have been made more than once, a possibility that seems most highly improbable. Since the passage is so thoroughly non-Johannine in style and language, we may confidently regard both additions as having had no place in the Johannine original.

A Theological Postscript

Although this is not a part of the investigation *per se,* one might add that this is a passage one gladly gives up for theological reasons. And it is not antipathy towards angels nor doubts about the miraculous that is involved. Rather, on the one hand, the idea of an angel giving healing properties to water has all the earmarks of ancient superstition, rather than a New Testament view of the miraculous; on the other hand, the view of God presented in this particular superstition seems to stand over against a biblical view of God.

There is a kind of capriciousness to "grace" that allows only one person to be healed, and only the first one into the pool at that. It is no surprise that the invalid whom Jesus cured had lain there 38 years. His condition was such that he could never have been the first one into the pool. One wonders how this can be grace that loads all the advantages toward the one who is least sick, and thus most able to jump into the pool, while month after month, year after year, those who need it most must lose hope of ever being made whole. One can gladly affirm that such an account is no part of the inspired original.

CHAPTER 3

On the Text and Meaning of John 20:30-31
(1992)

It is of more than passing interest that the one Gospel which has an explicit statement of purpose should also be the Gospel for which there has been such little agreement within scholarship as to its purpose. Part of the reason for this lies with the richness of content in the Gospel itself, with its wide variety of internal hints as to possible life settings; and part of it lies with the statement of purpose in 20:30-31, which has both textual and denotative ambiguity. So much is this so, that the current attitude toward the text and grammar of v. 31 is that it does not really matter too much one way or the other.[1] This paper is written in response to this deferential attitude toward the text and grammar of this passage.[2] I do not hereby propose to solve the mystery of

1. Lindars, Schnackenburg, and Beasley-Murray are representative: B. Lindars, *The Gospel of John* (NCB) (London: Oliphants, 1972); R. Schnackenburg, *Das Johannesevangelium: III. Teil* (Freiburg: B. Herder, 1975); ET: *The Gospel According to St John*, vol. 3, trans. D. Smith and G. A. Kon (New York: Crossroad, 1987); G. R. Beasley-Murray, *John* (WBC 36) (Waco, Tex.: Word, 1987). Each of them notes the uncertainty of the text, although Lindars notes that the majority lean toward the present subjunctive, and makes common disclaimers as to the grammar. Thus, Schnackenburg: "The tense used is no worthwhile argument in this matter" (p. 338); and Beasley-Murray: "A decision like this can hardly rest on a fine point of Greek grammar, not least in view of the fact that the Evangelist does not always keep the rules in his use of tenses" (p. 387). So also the most recent article on this passage by D. A. Carson, "The Purpose of the Fourth Gospel: John 20:31 Reconsidered," *JBL* 106 (1987): 639-51, who says of the textual and grammatical question: "In short, the text-critical evidence is not determinative, not only because it is evenly balanced but also because both the present subjunctive and the aorist subjunctive can occur both in the context of coming to faith and in the context of continuing in faith" (p. 640).

2. Cf. K. Wengst, *Bedrängte Gemeinde and verherrlichter Christus. Der historische Ort des Johannesevangeliums als Schlüssel zu seiner Interpretation*, Biblisch-theologische Studien 5 (Neu-

purpose, nor even to suggest that the resolution of its text and grammar is the key to such a solution. My purpose rather is twofold: (1) to suggest that the textual question of 20:31 can be resolved with a much greater degree of certainty than is often allowed; and (2) to propose grounds for believing that the original text (πιστεύητε, present subjunctive) is grammatically meaningful for John.[3] I am delighted to offer the study, modest as it is in comparison with his own work on John's Gospel, to Professor Neirynck with appreciation for friendship and collegiality in the common enterprise of Gospel study.

I. The Textual Question

D. Carson represents the majority opinion with regard to the text of 20:31: "The external evidence is very finely balanced, but probably a majority of recent commentators prefer the present subjunctive."[4] What degree of doubt remains (as, for example, Schnackenburg), is related to Carson's suggestion that "the external evidence is very finely balanced," which in turn reflects the ambiguity set in motion by the UBS Greek New Testament[5] and its companion *Textual Commentary*.[6] In one of its less scintillating moments textually, the UBS committee decided to make no choice at all on the variation in John 20:31. Thus, despite the "C" rating, they present the text with brackets, ἵνα πιστεύ[σ]ητε. The comment in the *Textual Commentary* is especially puzzling. An opening sentence spells out one dimension of the difficulty: "Both πιστεύητε and πιστεύσητε have notable early support." But thereafter the comment has little to do with textual criticism per se, and notes instead the possibilities of these two readings in terms of meaning for the Gospel. Without mention of transcriptional or intrinsic probabilities or the relative value of the external evidence, the comment concludes: "In view of the difficulty of *choosing between the readings by assessing the supposed purpose of the Evangelist (assuming that he used the tenses of the subjunctive strictly)*, the Committee

---

kirchen, 1981), pp. 32-35, who takes a much more vigorous stance on this matter than I am ready to do.

3. So that I will not need repeatedly to use such circumlocutions as "the author of the Fourth Gospel," I will call the author "John" with no intent of speaking to the question of authorship or the source of the traditions in the Gospel.

4. *Purpose* (n. 1), p. 640; cf. Beasley-Murray (n. 1): "the evidence is evenly balanced" (p. 387).

5. Published jointly by the United Bible Societies, third edition, 1975.

6. B. M. Metzger, *A Textual Commentary on the Greek New Testament* (London–New York: United Bible Societies, 1971), p. 256.

considered it preferable to represent both readings by enclosing σ within square brackets" (italics mine). Thus we are not only left with no textual reasons for what appears in the text, but we are not even given the Committee's choice in this case.[7]

I submit that we can do better than that. The two readings are well known, and have the following support:

πιστεύητε   P⁶⁶vid ℵ* B Θ 0250 892
πιστεύσητε   A C D K L rell

Related to this is the reading in 19:35, one of two other places where the author of the Gospel speaks directly to his readers, in this case in language very much like that of 20:31:

πιστεύητε   P⁶⁶vid ℵ* B Ψ Origen
πιστεύσητε   rell

Before looking at this evidence in detail, some words are needed about the readings of P⁶⁶, because along with Origen on 19:35, this MS places this reading firmly in Egypt at the end of the second century. In the case of 20:31 the *videtur* is in deference to textual conventions, which insist that only totally visible readings be listed as such in an apparatus. But there can be no question of the reading of P⁶⁶ in this case.[8] Even though πιστεύηται[9] is partly lacunose, the letters that remain and are plainly visible make this reading certain. Both the τ (partly rubbed out) and the η are plain. The partial lacuna between them is capable of sustaining only two letters in this scribe's ordinary hand; and the visible remains of those two letters are clearly the left side of an ε and the tip end of the right "arm" of an υ.[10] The reading at 19:35 can only re-

---

7. One wonders further how such complete indecision merits a "C" rating.

8. The unfortunate use of *videtur* in this instance can be seen by the reluctance of some to include P⁶⁶ in their list of supporting evidence (e.g., Lindars [n. 1]).

9. This is one of many *e/ai* interchanges in the MS; see Appendix D in G. D. Fee, *Papyrus Bodmer II (P⁶⁶) — Its Textual Relationships and Scribal Characteristics,* Studies and Documents 34 (Salt Lake City: University of Utah Press, 1968), pp. 131-36.

10. If one has access to the superior photographs in the editio princeps (V. Martin and J. W. B. Barns, *Papyrus Bodmer II, Supplement, Évangile de Jean chap. 14–21,* Cologny-Genève, Bibliotheca Bodmeriana, 1962, plate no. 145), one might note (1) the same combination of τε in the line immediately above, where the scribe (regularly) elevates the ε following a τ or π (he apparently concluded the τ or π with the top stroke, and then followed the same plane and made the median of his ε before finishing with the half circle); and (2) that the only visible υ on this page (line 1) also (typically) ends mid-letter to the α that follows.

main *videtur,* since the beginning πιστ and concluding ι are on two different scraps of the MS. Thus the crucial portion remains lacunose; nonetheless, when one lines up these two pieces *both verso and recto* (they are much too far apart in the photograph), the amount of available space cannot possibly exceed five letters (thus ευητα, not ευσητα). Thus, it is certain that P[66] supports the present subjunctive in 20:31, and relatively certain that it does so in 19:35.

What this means, of course, is that, contrary to what is implied in the *Textual Commentary* (that "both [readings] have notable early support"), in fact the only "notable early support" is for the present subjunctive. Here the primary Egyptians (P[66] ℵ B, the earliest and best of the MSS for this Gospel [P[75] is lacunose]),[11] plus some secondary witnesses from this tradition (0250 892) and the non-Egyptian Θ, form a considerable combination of evidence in favor of πιστεύητε. As a general rule in the textual criticism of the Fourth Gospel, one chooses against this combination of evidence only on fairly strong intrinsic or transcriptional grounds. But in this case, as we shall note momentarily, these criteria also favor the present, not the aorist, subjunctive. On the other hand, the earliest evidence for the aorist is a group of witnesses from several textual traditions from the fifth century (A C D W), which have in common that they are frequently the earliest witnesses to readings, usually patently secondary readings, that form the basis of the Byzantine textual tradition. All of this to say, then, that the external evidence is not even; rather, it weighs significantly in favor of the present subjunctive.

So also with the questions of intrinsic and transcriptional probability. Since the matter of intrinsic probability can be especially treacherous waters — particularly in a case like this one where one's exegetical proclivities toward the whole Gospel can play such a significant role — I will hold that dis-

---

11. For this judgment, based on stylistic, grammatical, and transcriptional considerations, see G. D. Fee, "P[75], P[66] and Origen: The Myth of Early Textual Recession in Alexandria," in *New Dimensions in New Testament Study,* ed. R. Longenecker and M. C. Tenney (Grand Rapids: Zondervan, 1974), pp. 19-45, repr. E. J. Epp and G. D. Fee, *Studies in the Theory and Method of New Testament Textual Criticism* (Grand Rapids: Eerdmans, 1993). The significance of P[66] in this case must not be overlooked. Although this MS is the earliest representative of the Egyptian text-type, it is less pure in this regard than either P[75] or B; and when it deviates from its basic tradition, it does so in the vast majority of instances toward a smoother, more readable variant. In fact, in the matter of present/aorist interchanges in moods outside the indicative, it picks up the secondary reading (always the aorist) in nine instances, but never does so the other way about (see Fee, *Papyrus Bodmer II* [n. 9, 46-47]). That it reflects its basic tradition in these two readings, therefore, is the certain evidence that this is not the creation of the scribe of P[66], and is in fact the only way these passages were known early on in Egypt, in a tradition that has been demonstrated not to be "recensional" in any meaningful sense of that term, but rather that has preserved a relatively pure line of very ancient text (Fee, "Myth," p. 44).

cussion until the next section on "significance and meaning." But one can make some general observations about scribal proclivities that lean heavily in favor of the present subjunctive as the original.

Two matters are significant here. First, since final ἵνα-clauses are one of the certain stylistic features of this Gospel,[12] one can measure the author's own proclivities regarding *Aktionsart* in such clauses, and have a broad enough sampling so as to insure relatively reliable conclusions.[13] Second, one can check the manuscript tradition against the subjunctives in these clauses to see if there are clear tendencies in one direction or the other when scribal errors are made with these subjunctives.

First, then, the data from the author of the Gospel (on the basis of the textual tradition where it is firm). According to Hendriksen's tabulation, there are 101 final ἵνα-clauses (with 110 subjunctives) in the Fourth Gospel, plus 40 non-final (with 49 subjunctives). The number of aorists in final clauses is 77 (26 presents), giving a ratio of 3:1, which increases to 4:1 in the non-final clauses (37/9).[14] Two general observations about these data can be made: (a) The predominance of aorists in the subjunctive mood is quite in keeping with ordinary Greek prose; in contrast to the way the language is learned by us, the aorist would be the normal tense in the non-finite moods, and either fixed usage or a good reason prevails when the present occurs. (b) But that very fact suggests also that there is a much higher incidence of the present tense in the Gospel of John (35 in all) than one would expect in normal prose. We will note the possible significance of these data momentarily.

Second, as to what the copyist(s) may have done, there are basically three options: (a) we are dealing with a simple inadvertent error (the adding or dropping of a σ); (b) the copyist(s) made a deliberate change, because he (they) considered tense to be meaningful, i.e., to have significance as to the purpose of the Gospel; or (c) he (they) made a deliberate change, but did not

12. Cf. C. F. Burney, *The Aramaic Origin of the Fourth Gospel* (Oxford: Oxford University Press, 1922), p. 69: "[This is] one of the most remarkable phenomena in this Gospel."

13. The most useful tabulation of these clauses, in terms of statistical data, can be found in W. Hendriksen, *Exposition of the Gospel According to John* (Grand Rapids: Baker, 1953), pp. 45-53. For the grammar itself, see E. A. Abbott, *Johannine Grammar* (London, 1906), pp. 369-89, whose analysis of the aorist and present subjunctives is still the absolutely basic starting point for this discussion; it is of some wonder that so many are willing to speak to grammatical points in this Gospel as if Abbott had never written a thing. See also cf. H. Riesenfeld, "Zu den johanneischen ἵνα-Satzen," *Studia Theologica* 19 (1965): 213-20, who, however, must finally resort to usage in 1 John to make his point stick. Carson, *Purpose* (n. 1), p. 641 n. 6, also has a convenient tabulation, which differs slightly from the one used here; but these are minor matters.

14. The ten occurrences of εἰμι have been excluded from the count of present subjunctives, since the verb has no aorist.

33

consider it meaningful, i.e., he (they) made it on other grounds, such as uniformity or common usage or grammar. Although reason (b) can be shown as the probable cause in some cases of present/aorist interchange in this Gospel,[15] reason (c) can be shown to be far more likely. In which case, one can further show that the direction of change would almost certainly have been from the present to the aorist. Several data support this conclusion:

(1) While one must always be open to the possibility of an inadvertent error (in the sense of a slip of eye or ear), an analysis of the copying tradition in the ἵνα-clauses in the Gospel suggests that such did not happen very often.[16] Of the 159 verbs in ἵνα-clauses, there are variants in only 16. Seven of these involve variations other than tense.[17] The remaining nine (4:34; 5:20; 6:29, 38, 50; 13:19; 17:21; 19:35; 20:31) involve variants between aorist and present subjunctives, three of which require changes in the stem (4:34; 6:38, 50) and therefore cannot be accidental in the sense we are now using the term. The other six, five of which involve the verb πιστεύειν (6:29; 13:19; 17:21; 19:35; 20:31), allow for the slip of an eye involving a σ. Several factors suggest that this is not the cause of the five instances of variation with πιστεύειν. (a) This is in fact the best explanation for the θαυμάσητε of P[75] and 1241 in 5:10; and the slip, it should be noted, is toward the aorist; (b) the three interchanges that require stem changes, where there is significant support for both readings, indicate that scribes tended to be thoughtful about this matter; (c) there are several other places where such a slip might easily have occurred, but did not (e.g., 1:17 [λύσω]; 9:39 [βλέπωσιν], a most logical place for such an "error"!). All of this to say that it seems highly unlikely that the aorist/present interchange in five of eleven appearances of πιστεύειν should have been accidental; moreover, even if one or two of them were, the evidence is heavily weighted toward the addition, not the omission, of a σ.

(2) That the variation is most likely deliberate and in the direction of the aorist from the present is supported by another significant piece of textual datum. In all five instances involving πιστεύειν, D and the Byzantine tradition

---

15. E.g., in 13:19, if the πιστεύητε of B C is original, the change to πιστεύσητε would most likely have been a "sense" variant, based on the implications of the following "when it happens." To "believe when it happens" seems to beg for the aorist, which not only makes the reading of B C the *lectio difficilior*, but leaves one little confidence that a σ was accidentally omitted from their exemplar. Cf. the discussion below.

16. Some may object to looking only at ἵνα-clauses, but a random checking of other kinds of interchanges, plus the large number in this sampling, indicated that some general conclusions may be based on this evidence.

17. 1:19; 4:15; 6:28; 8:56; 10:38; 15:8; 17:2. Several of these are changes from subjunctive to indicative; two involve substitutions of other words.

always read the aorist, while B and supporting Egyptians always read the present. This is quite in keeping with a singular textual phenomenon in John's Gospel. As is well known, there are several kinds of grammatical and stylistic features of this Gospel, which are Johannine peculiarities and which also run at crosscurrents with more standard Hellenistic Greek (e.g., anarthrous personal names; the abundance of asyndeton; the redundant nominative personal pronoun; the idiom ἀπεκρίθη Ἰησοῦς καὶ εἶπεν αὐτ[ῷ]; the vernacular possessive). In all of these cases, the Johannine idiom is certain; it is also the case that the Egyptian tradition is generally faithful to John's idioms while D and the Byzantines regularly conform John's Greek to more standard usage.[18] The present interchange seems to be a case in point.

(3) The evidence is overwhelming in the textual tradition that changes such as these generally move in the direction of more common, less idiosyncratic Greek. That makes the present subjunctive the *lectio difficilior* in this case.

All of this together, therefore, suggests most strongly that in John 20:31 the author wrote ἵνα πιστεύητε, and that later scribes changed it to ἵνα πιστεύσητε, either because they thought such a sentence leaned toward the notion of "coming to faith" or because the aorist subjunctive would have been a more common idiom for them. This suggests further that the indecision on the part of the UBS editors should be put to rest. The reading πιστεύητε may be confidently placed in the text, and I would think with a "B" rating.

II. Is the Present Subjunctive "Meaningful"?

This question in effect is two-pronged. The first is whether one can demonstrate that John used *Aktionsart* in a meaningful way. Assuming a positive answer to that question, the second is whether the present subjunctive in 20:31 has "meaning," and if so, what, or how much? It is probably illusory to think that the present tense in itself demonstrates that the Gospel was intended for the believing community; on the other hand, the question is open as to whether it might lend support to such a notion if other evidence were also present. In any case, an analysis of the 159 subjunctives in ἵνα-clauses in John suggests that John tended to be sensitive to this Greek idiom, so much so that it is worth one's while always to ask if the use of the present subjunctive was purposeful.

---

18. For a demonstration of these matters see Fee, *Papyrus Bodmer II* (n. 9), pp. 36-56; for a full demonstration of the use of the article with personal names, see G. D. Fee, "The Use of the Definite Article with Personal Names in the Gospel of John," *NTS* 17 (1970-71): 168-83.

First, as to the *aorist subjunctive*, it should be noted that by the very nature of the language one is hard pressed to find "significance" in most instances of this tense. That is, the aorist is what an author would be expected to use if he had no specific "kind of action" in mind. Thus, it occurs in ἵνα-clauses in this Gospel on a regular basis and very often has no further significance at all. Many of these are fixed phrases (e.g., 23 are passives, which are always aorist, including eight instances of ἵνα πληρωθῇ); most of them are strictly punctiliar, and would make no sense in any other tense. Some of them are undoubtedly constative, as in 1:8, for example, where the Evangelist seems interested only in the concept of the Baptist's bearing witness to Jesus; it would be pushing the use of tense all out of proportion to suggest that he had a specific moment in mind. Here he could well have used the present tense to suggest "over a period of time," but there is no reason why the aorist could not also bear that sense — that is, John bore witness to Jesus in a variety of ways, all of which are summed up in this aorist. Moreover, there are certain verbs that one can expect always to appear in the aorist in the subjunctive, simply because the sense of the verb is aoristic (e.g., λαβ[ῃ], 6:7; 10:17; βαλ[ῃ], 5:7; δ[ῳ], 1:22; 13:29; 17:2; or "eat," "die," "raise up").

This feature of the language in itself should cause one due caution as to whether an aorist in 20:31 would be "meaningful" in some way. If it were original, it could be ingressive, of course, but it could also refer to the simple act of believing, without making a point of when.

But it is otherwise with the *present subjunctive*. To be sure, some are fixed expressions, where the verb itself carries a durative sense (e.g., ἔχειν is always present [8×]. Others could perhaps fall into this category, such as "love" and "bear [fruit]," but in this case these would also fit with what appears to be a strong sensitivity to the significance of this tense.

The certain evidence that for John the use of the present tense could have meaning, of course, is the oft-noted clause in 10:38, ἵνα γνῶτε καὶ γινώσκητε, which can only mean something like, "that you may come to know and keep on knowing."[19] Similarly, and now outside the subjunctive, the imperative combination ἄρατε . . . μὴ ποιεῖτε seems to show sensitivity to *Aktionsart* (cf. the imperatives in 5:8). What this demonstrates, of course, is that John knew the significance of tense; what it does not demonstrate is that he therefore always used the present tense with this kind of significance.

19. This has been changed to read ἵνα γνῶτε καὶ πιστεύσητε in ℵ (πιστεύητε) A K Byz pler. This is secondary on all counts (it is impossible to imagine the circumstances in which a scribe would have changed this reading to the compound of γινώσκω); this is another "C" rating in Metzger's *Textual Commentary* (n. 6) that defies explanation.

A close look at several of the present subjunctives in ἵνα-clauses, however, suggests that John shows a general sensitivity to *Aktionsart*, when choosing to use this tense. This phenomenon first occurs in the narrative of the Samaritan woman. John's narration of her reply to Jesus' offer of living water is: "Give (aorist) me this water, ἵνα μὴ διψῶ μηδὲ διέρχωμαι ἐνθάδε ἀντλεῖν." The present subjunctives suggest the iterative sense of not continuing to go thirsty, nor needing to come out to this well on a daily basis. Similarly, the present ἐρωτᾷ in 16:30 implies that Jesus needs no one to "keep on asking." In 5:20, on the other hand, it is unlikely that the present θαυμάζητε carries this sense; i.e., it is probably pedantic to suggest "in order that they may continue to marvel." Even so, the present in this case suggests sensitivity to the sense of the sentence. Jesus' word that he will do greater works than these implies ongoing mighty deeds, and in each case they will marvel, hence ἵνα ὑμεῖς θαυμάζητε. So also with the concept of "honoring the Son" in 5:23.

Of still greater significance to this study is the group of present subjunctives appearing in the Last Supper Discourse (chs. 13–17), which are best explained in terms of long-term discipleship, a concern which the discourse itself seems intended to address. Thus in 13:15, the disciples are expected to keep on doing (ἵνα ποιῆτε) what Jesus has done (aorist); above all they are to keep on loving one another (13:34; 15:12, 17); likewise they are to continue bearing fruit (15:8, 16); and Jesus prays that they might continue to know and behold his glory (17:3, 24).

In light of this usage, therefore, there are two sets of interchanges that hold special interest, because they apparently stem from the author himself. Very likely there is significance here as well. One of these is found in similar clauses about Jesus' doing the will of his Father. Thus:

4:34 (UBS)	ἐμὸν βρῶμά ἐστιν ἵνα ποιήσω τὸν θέλημα τοῦ πέμψαντός με καὶ τελειώσω αὐτοῦ τὸ ἔργον
ποιήσω	P⁶⁶ P⁷⁵ B C D K L N W Θ Ψ 083 1 33 al
ποιῶ	ℵ A f¹³ Byz
6:38 (UBS)	ὅτι καταβέβηκα ἀπὸ τοῦ οὐρανοῦ οὐχ ἵνα ποιῶ τὸ θέλημα τὸ ἐμὸν ἀλλὰ τὸ θέλημα τοῦ πέμψαντός με
ποιῶ	P⁶⁶ P⁷⁵ B rell
ποιήσω	ℵ D L 1010 pc

At first blush this may appear to lend support to the demurrers, that John "does not use tenses with . . . precision."[20] But on closer look, this usage

---

20. Lindars, *Gospel*, p. 617 (n. 1). I have purposely left out Lindars's word "absolute," since

may be more precise than first meets the eye. The present tense in 6:38 makes perfectly good sense: while it is true that a (constative) aorist could have given the same meaning,[21] the present suggests that the sentence has to do with Jesus' earthly ministry as a whole. All of his words and works constitute a continual "doing" of the Father's will. This likewise explains the change to the present tense in the Byzantine tradition at 4:34. Indeed, the (almost certainly original) aorist[22] in this case can also be explained as "meaningful." On the one hand, it could be constative; more likely, in keeping with the τελειώσω that follows, this whole clause looks forward to the one specific moment, hinted at often in the Gospel, when Jesus "finishes" the will of the One who sent him — namely, on the cross.[23] In this case, the aorist not only makes sense, but very likely gives insight into John's intent. While this exegesis falls short of "proof" as to the point at hand, when one begins — on the basis of such usage as in 10:38 — with the *assumption* that *Aktionsart* is probably meaningful, it will not only affect the exegesis of such texts as these, but can also provide possibly helpful insight into John's intent.

Much the same can be said of the similar interchange of the present and aorist of πιστεύειν in 13:19 (UBS): ἀπ' ἄρτι λέγω ὑμῖν πρὸ τοῦ γενέσθαι, ἵνα πιστεύσητε ὅταν γένηται ὅτι ἐγώ εἰμι

> πιστευσητε   P[66] rell
> πιστευητε   B C [P[75] lac]

in light of 14:29 (UBS): καὶ νῦν εἴρηκα ὑμῖν πρὶν γενέσθαι, ἵνα ὅταν γένηται πιστεύσητε (no variation).

If the UBS is correct on 13:19, then there is little to be said; the aorist subjunctive is what one might well expect in conjunction with the clause ὅταν γένηται. But in this case the UBS is almost certainly wrong, for several

---

this may very well be true; but the demurrer seems clearly intended to suggest that the problem is more widespread than simply at 20:31. Cf. Beasley-Murray, *John*, p. 387.

21. Which, along with scribal proclivities toward the aorist in this mood, explains the reading of ℵ D L 1010 pc.

22. Although C. K. Barrett, without explanation, prefers the present (*The Gospel According to St. John* [Philadelphia: Westminster, ²1978], p. 240); cf. the *puzzling* comment by Schnackenburg, *St. John I* (n. 1), p. 447 n. 81, who first says, "the present seems to bring out better the present nature of the action," but concludes, "Hence ποιῶ should be preferred, as the *lectio difficilior*." These two sentences are textually *non sequitur*. The first sentence offers the reason for the change on the part of scribes, which makes the aorist in the case the *lectio difficilior*.

23. Cf. Beasley-Murray, *John* (n. 1), p. 63: "The entire ministry of Jesus is represented by the Evangelist as obedience in action, which leads him finally to the surrender of himself in death."

reasons, not especially different from those in 20:31: (1) the reading of the present subjunctive is altogether unlikely as an inadvertent error, since such errors in this direction (dropping a letter) are rare in the textual tradition in comparison to additions; in any case (2) scribal proclivities would go the other direction, thus arguing for the present tense as original, which (3) is made the more certain both because of the textual character of the readings of B and because the ὅταν γένηται makes the reading of the present tense the undoubted *lectio difficilior*.[24]

If, then, the Egyptian tradition once again preserves the Johannine original, these two very similar sentences suggest subtleties of usage with this idiom that are quite in keeping with that of 10:38. The present tense in 13:19 is to be accounted for in light of the object clause, ὅτι ἐγώ εἰμι. It is not the moment of believing "when it happens" (which alone accounts for the textual variation) that here concerns John, but that the disciples will thereafter continue to believe that "I am," after what Jesus has said beforehand is fulfilled.[25] However, even though similar in language and structure, the opposite prevails in 14:29, where the concern is simply with "believing" at the time that "it happens." This may seem like overly subtle exegesis to some; but John himself is the one who sets us up for such subtleties. It is not that he is trying to "make a statement" by the use of the present in these texts, but that he shows considerable sensitivity to the subtleties of *Aktionsart* inherent in the language itself.

These various texts seem to suggest a clear sense of nuanced usage in the Gospel whenever John uses the present tense with ἵνα; to test this suggestion further, a brief look at all of the ἵνα-clauses with πιστεύειν may prove instructive, again not in the sense that one can squeeze a great deal of "meaning" out of his choice of the present subjunctive, but in the sense that such usage is almost certainly deliberate and sensitive to *Aktionsart*.

There are 11 such clauses in the Gospel (1:7; 6:29, 30; 9:36; 11:15, 42; 13:19; 14:29; 17:21; 19:35; 20:31); six are aorist subjunctive; there is textual variation in the other five (6:29; 13:19; 17:21; 19:35; 20:31), although the present is almost certainly original in each case. The six instances in the aorist all refer to general or specific instances of "belief" within the "historical" situation of the narrative. Thus in 1:7 (ἵνα πάντες πιστεύσωσιν δι' αὐτοῦ) the context is clearly that of people coming to believe through the witness of John. The aorist is to be expected. So also in the several specific instances of belief, as for example

---

24. Contra R. Brown, *The Gospel According to John (xiii–xxi)* (AB 29A) (Garden City, N.Y.: Doubleday, 1970), pp. 554-55.

25. Cf. Hendriksen, *Exposition* (n. 13), pp. 239-40, who is one of the rare commentators to note the significance of this present subjunctive and the textual variation.

in the reply to Jesus of the man born blind ("Who is he, in order that I might believe [πιστεύσω] in him?"). Our interest lies with the five instances of present tense:

6:29-30. Here is another case of apparently subtle awareness of tense that should be taken into account in the exegesis of this dialogue. When Jesus is asked "what should we be doing (ποιῶμεν) so that we might be performing (ἐργαζώμεθα) the works of God?" his answer is in keeping with the question, except for the significant change from "works" to "work": "This is the work of God, that you believe (πιστεύητε) in him whom (εἰς ὅν) that one sent." The implication of their question is not that they are asking about what single thing they might do to please God, but what kind of "works" over the long run they should be doing so as to be living in keeping with God's will. Jesus' answer, therefore, quite in keeping with the perspective of the Gospel, also does not have to do with a call to faith in Christ, but with that single "work" that all should be doing over the long run, namely (a lifelong) believing in Jesus, the one whom the Father sent. All of this is nicely captured in Barrett's comment: "The present (continuous) tense of πιστεύητε is perhaps significant: not an *act* of faith, but a *life* of faith."[26] It is the failure to catch John's own nuances and the influence of the next question (in v. 30) that caused the later textual tradition (D K W Γ Δ 0145 f¹³ 28 700 892 1241 Byz) to change this present to an aorist. But precisely the opposite prevails in v. 30. Here, in light of the implications of his answer to their question in v. 29, they want to know what sign he does so that "we might see (ἴδωμεν) and believe you (πιστεύσωμέν σοι)." The clear implication, both of the aorist subjunctives and the context, is that they are asking about coming to believe; and since such people never become true disciples in John's view, the usage is "believe him," not "believe in him."[27]

13:19. We have noted this usage above.

17:21. On the surface this passage seems a bit more difficult for the position being argued here. But again, that is only at first blush; if one begins with the presupposition that John used the present tense meaningfully, then this one too can be shown not only to make good sense, but also to caution interpreters of John that they should at least begin their exegesis by assuming that John knew what he was about. Here Jesus prays that his followers and those who follow them might be one, so that "the world might believe (πιστεύῃ) that you sent me." It is no wonder that the later textual tradition changed this

26. *Gospel* (n. 22), p. 287.
27. Cf. Barrett, *Gospel* (n. 22), p. 288: "πιστεύειν is no longer constructed with εἰς; but with the dative; that is, the Jews contemplate no more than putting credence in the words of Jesus."

present to an aorist (the present is read by P⁶⁶ ℵ* B C*). But here all of John's linguistic subtleties and grammatical sensitivities are at work. In this prayer there are three clearly distinct groups: the disciples, their disciples, and the world. The world is no longer the arena of salvation (as in 3:16-17), but refers to those who do not — and never will — believe in him (in the sense of having faith in Christ).[28] Hence the issue here is not in their coming to faith; just as in v. 23 which follows (ἵνα γινώσκῃ ὁ κόσμος ὅτι . . .), conversion is not in view. The world will continue to be the world, but on the strength of Christian unity, it will have to take seriously that the Father sent Jesus into the world. Again, as in some earlier instances, it would be pedantic to translate, "keep on believing." But the tense is the proper one for what John here intends; this is what the world will come to believe and know about Jesus (over the long haul), not in the sense of coming to faith, but in the sense of their knowing it as long as the world endures.

19:35 and 20:31. In light of all of these passages, it seems altogether likely that the Evangelist also had such a nuance in mind in these two instances where he directs his words to the readers of his Gospel. Since the present tense is clearly to be preferred in both cases, and since, if one assumes that what is clear in some instances (e.g., 10:38) is also likely in others, one can make good sense of Johannine usage throughout the Gospel, then there is no good reason to think otherwise in these two instances.

But how much "meaning" one should thereby give to the present tense is another matter. It is possible, of course, that John intends something maximal, that he has written his Gospel for the believing community in order that, in light of defections or external pressures, they "may continue to believe" — as though the Gospel were intended to keep people from drifting away from faith in Christ. Although I think this case could be made on other grounds, I for one would be reluctant to press for that much intent in the use of tense alone. But I would argue that the use of the present subjunctive is both original and "meaningful" in the sense that it presupposes a document intended for those who are already members of the believing community.[29] In this

---

28. Although not so earlier, κόσμος is used exclusively in a hostile sense in the *Abschiedsreden* (chs. 14-17). This has been set up by the clear line of demarcation in the double conclusion to the Book of Signs in 12:37-50.

29. This conclusion stands over against that of Carson, *Purpose* (n. 1), who tends to dismiss the significance of this clause and argues on other grounds that the primary purpose of the Gospel is evangelistic. The major flaw in his argument, and one that he himself notes that others have argued (p. 648), is his reliance on L. C. McGaughy's *Toward a Descriptive Analysis of EINAI as a Linking Verb in New Testament Greek* (SBLDS 6) (Missoula, Mont.: SBL, 1972), in which McGaughy's observations are made on the basis of the verb εἶναι, without adequate attention to

more minimalistic view, the present tense simply fits the pattern of this usage throughout — that John does not so much "mean" anything by it, but that he is sensitive to this usage; and for a Gospel written for believers, this is the usage that fits (just as with the world in 17:21). After all, those who "confess" Jesus in this Gospel in the language of this sentence (that Jesus is the Christ, the Son of God) are not coming to faith, but represent those from within a context of faith who must be encouraged to a deeper measure of that faith, in the sense of deepened understanding (e.g., Nathanael, Peter, Martha, Thomas).

In sum: There can be little question that the present subjunctive is the original text in both 19:35 and 20:31. Although not all will be convinced by the evidence adduced in this paper, it also seems clear that John had a good sense of the distinctions between the aorist and present tenses and that he regularly used the present tense in ἵνα-clauses in the Gospel with awareness of its implications and sometimes in quite "meaningful" ways. It therefore seems altogether likely that in 20:31 John used the present tense in this sense.

Such a conclusion does not mean that one has thereby solved the issue of purpose for this Gospel; but it does add its own weight to those several studies in recent years that see the Gospel as making most sense as having been produced within, and for the sake of, a believing community that stands over against various forces from within and without, with the meaning and significance of Jesus as the central point at issue.

John's own usage of the article with proper names. On this matter, see Fee, "Use" (n. 18), where it has been demonstrated that Johannine usage in particular and NT usage in general favor an anarthrous personal name in ὅτι-clauses when the name precedes the verb (p. 179). This especially Johannine feature would seem to be of more significance than "syntactical links to ἐστίν." Thus, while it is possible that Ἰησοῦς is the predicate noun in this sentence, this cannot be demonstrated on the basis of its being anarthrous. Johannine usage on the whole suggests that Ἰησοῦς functions as the subject in this clause.

CHAPTER 4

Textual-Exegetical Observations
on 1 Corinthians 1:2, 2:1, and 2:10
(1992)

I take this opportunity to honor Dr. Greenlee by elaborating on three textual questions in 1 Corinthians, beyond what I was able merely to outline in my commentary (Fee 1987). In each case the textual issue has bearing on the exegesis of the particular passage — and therefore on its proper translation — as well as on some larger questions of meaning in 1 Corinthians as a whole.[1] In pursuing such questions I hope to illustrate by example a major concern of Dr. Greenlee's: that textual criticism is not an end in itself, but must ultimately be brought to bear on the meaning and message of the New Testament.

1 Corinthians 1:2

The textual variant in question is a matter of word order. Did Paul write "to the church of God which is in Corinth, sanctified in Christ Jesus" (variant 1: supported by $\mathfrak{P}^{61}$ ℵ A D^c Maj lat sy$^{(p)}$ co), or "to the church of God, sanctified in Christ Jesus, which is in Corinth" (variant 2: supported by $\mathfrak{P}^{46}$ B D* F G b m Ambrosiaster)? In relating the divided opinion of the UBS committee, Metzger (1971: 543) says that variant 2,

> though supported by a notable combination of witnesses . . . , appeared to the majority of the Committee to be intrinsically too difficult, as well as

1. The variants have further in common that they are three of nineteen instances where I have opted for a text different from that found in the modern "standard text" (UBS^3 — NA^{26}). They also represent the (only) two instances where I differ with both UBS^3 — NA^{26} and Zuntz 1953.

quite un-Pauline in comparison with the style of the salutations in other Pauline letters. The reading apparently arose through the accidental omission of one or more phrases and their subsequent reintroduction at the wrong position.

On this point the majority of the committee were influenced by Zuntz (1933: 91-92), who had previously argued:

> This is really more than a mere variation of order. As arranged in $\mathfrak{P}^{46}$ &c., the clauses make a jumble which defies interpretation. This jumble cannot have come about, at this place, by mere scribal slips in these outstanding witnesses.... Variants of this kind arise through the insertion of additional or the reintroduction of omitted words. At some very early stage, or even originally, one of the two clauses must have been absent from the text.... [The] impossible reading [of $\mathfrak{P}^{46}$] is most easily accounted for if the "sanctified"-clause is supposed to have been absent from some ancestor manuscript; it could penetrate into the text at this unsuitable point if in some less distant ancestor it had been added above the text or in the margin.

Zuntz goes on to argue that the "sanctified" clause is probably not original with Paul, since "οἱ ἡγιασμένοι is not a Pauline term to describe believers." Three observations, however, are in order:

1. The external evidence strongly favors variant 2, which is also, as Zuntz himself recognized, decidedly the *lectio difficilior*. Indeed, this combination of earliest and best manuscripts both east and west supporting the harder reading would ordinarily be decisive. Again, as Zuntz has rightly seen, the combination of $\mathfrak{P}^{46}$ and the western evidence puts this reading back very early and must be accounted for. On the other side, the evidence for variant 1 is basically Egyptian and Byzantine.[2] In any case, it is arguable that one would need considerable and good reasons to overturn the ordinary canons of NT textual criticism for this variant. The question is whether the proffered arguments are that weighty.

2. The primary reason for rejecting the *lectio difficilior* comes under the rubric of intrinsic probability — it seems too difficult. By this is meant that one can scarcely imagine Paul to have written variant 2. To this

2. It is doubtful whether the "lat" of NA[26] is a useful siglum, since it represents the Vulgate and two Old Latin manuscripts (a [9th cent.] and r [6th/7th cent.]). This may reflect later influences or may be of little value at all, since it could easily be a "translational" variant, such as one would tend to find in any modern English translation of variant 1.

Zuntz adds the alleged evidence of Paul's not referring to believers as "the sanctified," thus casting suspicion on the phrase altogether.

3. Zuntz has the integrity to admit that variant 2 is equally difficult to account for under the ordinary canons of transcriptional probability. No scribe would intentionally have created variant 2 from variant 1. Therefore, it must have been accidental, but not by any one of the scribes responsible for our present witnesses, since any mere scribal slip "in these outstanding witnesses . . . would have been quickly mended" (Zuntz 1953: 91). Thus Zuntz resorts to a three- or four-stage process:

   a. Either variant 1 or the next stage (b) is original.
   b. Very early on one or the other of the phrases, or both, was dropped accidentally.
   c. Another scribe, having the text of step *b* in hand, but also aware of the text of step *a,* reinserted the missing clause, but carelessly put it in the wrong place.
   d. The text of step *c* had a very early and very wide circulation but was finally overcome by the original itself.

But there are considerable difficulties with this view of things. First, as to transcriptional probabilities: It is nearly impossible to account for any direct corruption moving in the direction of variant 1 to variant 2. That is, variant 2 simply cannot be explained on the basis of variant 1 alone. On the other hand, the opposite is perfectly explicable. Any number of scribes could have — indeed would have — "corrected" variant 2 if it had been original. It is inevitable that variant 1 should finally triumph.

Therefore, in order to get from variant 1 to variant 2, Zuntz must theorize the unlikely possibility of a double error of rare kinds,[3] and then argue that the text based on the double error had such widespread early circulation that it took years for the original to overtake it — although it had to have existed side by side — and that the intermediate stage (the text with the omission, which makes perfectly good sense) had no further known existence. No wonder Zuntz himself ultimately preferred the intermediate-stage text as the Pauline original.

3. That is, omission of a considerable piece of text, followed by its reintroduction at the wrong place. On the one hand, there is no easy way to account for either phrase's having been dropped out accidentally; and why would anyone have done so on purpose? On the other hand, reintroduction from an interlinear correction or marginal note is explicable; but in its position in variant 2? Why should something "impossible" for Paul be somehow easier for a scribe — especially since Paul arguably would have been dictating, and thus open to such disjunction, whereas a scribe might be expected to show more care?

Finally, since someone had to create the text of variant 2, either Paul or a subsequent scribe, why is it inherently more probable for a scribe to have done it than Paul himself? In the final analysis, one will either believe that a scribe "corrected" in this bizarre fashion or else that Paul himself did the "bizarre" thing in the first place. The rest of this analysis will try to give a plausible reason for Paul's being responsible for it.

Is the *lectio difficilior* impossible for Paul to have written? The answer is no, on two counts. First, one must always be careful about asserting too quickly what an author may or may not have done, especially in matters of style in ad hoc documents. There are just enough instances of unusual word order in this letter to give one reason to pause before announcing that variant 2 is impossible.

Second, and more importantly, both the phrase itself and the word order may significantly reflect the urgency of this letter. Paul's basic problem with this church was their emphasis on being πνευματικοί "spiritual" and possessing higher σοφία "wisdom" and γνῶσις "knowledge," which at the same time had been rather largely divorced from Christian behavior. Part of his own response to this is to describe Christian conversion, as well as community life, with ἅγιος "holy" words. There are three significant texts in this regard: 1:30; 3:17; 6:11.

In 1:30, in contrast to their enchantment with σοφία and on the basis of what he had earlier said in v. 23, that Christ crucified is God's only wisdom, Paul says again that God has made Christ to become wisdom for us. Ulrich Wilckens and others to the contrary, σοφία is not a christological word,[4] but a soteriological word, as is evidenced by the appositives, δικαιοσύνη "righteousness/justification," ἁγιασμός "sanctification" and ἀπολύτρωσις "redemption."[5] All of these are soteriological metaphors, and, in the case of the first two, Paul is using metaphors that seem clearly to be moving over into the ethical sphere as well. Thus God made Christ himself to become "sanctification" for them; that is, through him they were saved ("set apart") for God's purposes, to be his holy people in the world.

Likewise in 6:11, when describing how the wicked will not inherit the kingdom, and thereby warning them of the same, he describes their conversion in these terms: "But you were washed, you were sanctified, you were justified," etc. Again, each verb can be shown to be a soteriological metaphor,

4. Wilckens (1959: 68-76) sees it in terms of an alleged Gnostic redeemer myth; compare Windisch (1914), who sees it in terms of Jewish speculative wisdom.

5. Thus Paul has moved σοφία from the sphere of philosophy and rhetoric to that of the history of salvation. "Wisdom" is what God has done to effect salvation for his people through the work of Christ.

each appropriate to describe the ethical dimension of the new life that is expected in Christ. You were "washed" from your former wickedness (described in vv. 9-10); you were "set apart" for a life different from before; you were made "right" with God so that you could be "righteous" (δίκαιος) rather than "wicked" (ἄδικοι).

So also 3:17. By their pursuit of wisdom, with its consequent strife over their teachers, they were destroying the church, God's temple in Corinth. In a prophetic word of judgment, Paul announces that God will destroy those who so destroy the church, because his temple is to be ἅγιος "holy," set apart to be his eschatological people, living out the life of the future in stark contrast to all that was Corinth.

Given this kind of emphasis and usage within the letter, it is not quite precise for Zuntz to suggest that the language of οἱ ἡγιασμένοι "who have been sanctified" is not used by Paul to describe believers. This is in fact thoroughly Pauline language; and in this letter — especially in significant theological texts — it is crucial language used to describe the believers' new existence in Christ. Thus it should not come as a surprise that this is the first note struck in the salutation. "To the church of God," Paul writes; but before he goes on to locate them geographically, he first describes them in terms of who they are in Christ. Thus, "to the church of God, sanctified in Christ Jesus, which is in Corinth — called to be saints," etc.

Variant 2, therefore, is explicable as a Pauline phenomenon, whereas it is nearly impossible to account for, had Paul actually written variant 1. But if this be the case, then it also presents a special problem for translators. On the one hand, if we follow the ordinary principles of dynamic equivalence and translate as though variant 2 were original after all, we may thereby also eliminate a Pauline emphasis; on the other hand, if we follow Paul's original word order, we end up with a kind of awkwardness that, if left unexplained, leaves the modern reader wondering. I for one would be willing to argue a case for the latter.

1 Corinthians 2:1

The choice here is between μυστήριον "mystery" (supported by 𝔓[46] ℵ* A C 88 436 pc a r sy[p] bo Epiph Ambst) and μαρτύριον "testimony" (supported by B D F G P Ψ 33 81 614 1739 Maj b vg sy[b] sa arm). On this variant Metzger (1971: 545) has written:

> From an exegetical point of view the reading μαρτύριον τοῦ θεοῦ, though well supported . . . , is inferior to μυστήριον, which has more limited but

early support. . . . The reading μαρτύριον seems to be a recollection of 1.6, whereas μυστήριον here prepares for its usage in ver. 7.

But that will hardly do, since scholarship has been largely divided on this question, and one may read elsewhere (Zuntz 1953: 101):

> The latter assumption [that μαρτύριον is original] can alone account for all the data of the problem. The variant μυστήριον in ii.1 is explicable as being due to assimilation to ii.7.

The questions are two: (1) Did Paul write μυστήριον in anticipation of the argument in vv. 6-16, or did he write μαρτύριον, referring to his preaching as bearing witness to what God had done in Christ crucified? (2) Did a scribe change μυστήριον to μαρτύριον under the influence of 1:6, or μαρτύριον to μυστήριον under the influence of v. 7? Despite the swing of contemporary opinion to the contrary,[6] the evidence seems overwhelmingly in favor of μαρτύριον in answer to these two questions.

On the matter of transcriptional probability, two things need to be noted. First, the two words are so similar that this is less likely a deliberate change than it is a simple case of a scribe's seeing one word and having the other called to mind. The question then is which would be the more common term for a scribe in the early church; that is, which one would he tend automatically to see, no matter which one was before him? A simple glance through Lampe's *Patristic Lexicon* will reveal that the former had become common stock for talking about the gospel, as well as the sacraments, whereas μαρτύριον is seldom so used. It does no good in this regard to appeal to the commonness of the word μάρτυς "witness" for martyrdom during the second century, since to be a μάρτυς is one thing, but to call the gospel itself μαρτύριον "testimony" is quite another; and the latter simply does not happen in the early church.

Second, both the distance and the relative obscurity of 1:6 make it extremely unlikely that a scribe would recall that text, having μυστήριον before him here, since the scribe himself well knows what is coming in v. 7. But that is what could easily have happened if μαρτύριον were before him. He saw μαρτύριον, but thought μυστήριον, in light of what was about to be said.[7]

6. Interestingly enough, this is less so in commentaries (Orr and Walther 1976, Mare 1976, and Senft 1979 are exceptions) and translations (GNB and Williams are exceptions), as in a variety of other studies, many of whom, it should be pointed out, have a vested interest in Paul's use of "mystery" language. See, inter alia, Bornkamm 1967: 819; Brown 1968: 48-49; Wilckens 1959: 45; Funk 1966: 295; Schütz 1975: 91; Trites 1977: 203; Kim 1981: 75.

7. Zuntz argued that the interchange of Χριστοῦ "Christ" and θεοῦ "God" in 1:6 is a re-

The issue of intrinsic probability is more highly subjective in this case, since no one questions whether or not either variant is Pauline. The real question then is the appropriateness of either word at this point in the argument.[8] Metzger and others have argued that μυστήριον here "prepares for its usage in ver. 7." If original, it would surely do so, but the question is whether Paul himself would have done so at this point. The actual flow of Paul's argument suggests otherwise.

Up to this point, and through 2:5, Paul has had a singular concern: to set out in stark contrast his own gospel of Christ crucified over against the self-styled σοφία "wisdom" of the Corinthians. They are prating wisdom; he is reminding them that the gospel of a crucified Messiah is the divine contradiction to wisdom humanly conceived. Thus in three paragraphs (1:18-25; 1:26-31; 2:1-5) he reminds them of three realities from their original experience of the gospel as Paul preached it that give the lie to their present stance. First, the message itself, with its central focus on Christ crucified (which, he argues, is in fact the true wisdom of God), stands in contradiction to that σοφία (1:18-25); as does, second, the fact that God chose them, not Corinth's beautiful people, to become his people in that city (1:26-31). In this third paragraph Paul now reminds them that when he came among them, his preaching was both materially and formally consonant with such a gospel. The emphasis in this paragraph, therefore, is still on the contradictory nature of the gospel of a crucified Messiah, not on the heretofore secret nature of that gospel. Just as in 1:6, he is recalling here his original preaching, in which he did not engage in rhetoric and philosophy, but rather bore "witness" to God's saving activity in Christ. In such an argument μαρτύριον is a most appropriate — and natural — expression, while "mystery" would be much less so, since Paul's first preaching was not in terms of revealing God's secret, but of bearing witness to what God had done in Christ.

At v. 6, however, there is a decided turn to the argument. In 1:18–2:5 Paul

---

lated matter, which it probably is. That is, the change from the unquestionably original Χριστοῦ to θεοῦ was probably influenced by the reading μαρτύριον τοῦ θεοῦ in 2:1. But that admittedly says little as to whether the latter is original here, only that such a text was predominant and influenced the scribe(s) who made this interchange.

8. It is of some interest that scholars on both sides have argued for the appropriateness of either word with καταγγέλλω "I proclaim." Findlay (1900: 774), for example, says, "[μαρτύριον] suits better καταγγέλλω," while Bornkamm (1967: 819, n. 141) says, "Since . . . the linking of μαρτύριον with καταγγέλλειν . . . is unusual in the NT, μυστήριον is to be preferred." Bornkamm's is less than impressive argumentation, since μαρτύριον itself as a word for the gospel is rare in the NT (only at 1:6, here, and in 2 Thess. 1:10), and καταγγέλλω is nowhere used with μυστήριον!

has twice pointed out that the message of Christ crucified is God's wisdom (1:24, 30), because it was God's power at work doing what worldly σοφία could not, namely bringing salvation to the perishing. In 2:6-16 Paul has two concerns: (1) to point out that the gospel of Christ crucified is recognized as God's wisdom because it has been so revealed by the Spirit, whom we have received; and (2) to nudge them gently to recognize their own inherent contradiction: they think of themselves as πνευματικοί "spiritual"; Paul's point is that if they truly were so, then they would have recognized that what the Spirit has revealed, namely salvation through the divine contradiction of Christ crucified, is God's wisdom indeed. It is in this context, then, that in v. 7 he now speaks of this wisdom as "hidden," "in mystery," unknown to the important people of the present age, whom God used to carry out his foreordained plan. God's wisdom can only be known as such by revelation of the Spirit; hence until that revelation it was "in mystery." Thus "mystery" is as appropriate to the argument here as it would have been inappropriate in vv. 1-5.

Finally, it should be noted that the absolute use of μυστήριον as a synonym for the gospel is otherwise unknown in the earlier Paul. The first clear usage is found in Colossians 1:26-27. This does not mean, of course, that he could not have done so earlier; the question is, given the variety of early uses of this word, whether he did in fact do so. Most likely it is this usage in Colossians that had become so popular in the early church, which, along with the usage in v. 7, caused some early scribes to alter Paul's original μαρτύριον in favor of the more familiar (to them) μυστήριον.

1 Corinthians 2:10

The variants in this case are δέ "but" (‭א‬ A C D F G P Ψ 33 81 Maj latt sy Epiphanius) and γάρ "for" (𝔓46 B 6 365 1175 1739 al Clement Spec). Although the interchange of one conjunctive signal for another may not seem terribly significant for exegesis or translation, here is a case where quite the opposite prevails. One's understanding of both the meaning of v. 9 and its relationship to the rest of the paragraph hinges on this exegetical choice. In fact, a prior commitment to an understanding of that relationship is the only plausible explanation as to how the UBS committee in this instance abandoned its better text-critical judgment for the secondary reading.

Of this interchange Metzger (1971: 546) says: "The loose use of the connective δέ . . . is entirely in Paul's manner, whereas γάρ, though strongly supported . . . , has the appearance of being an improvement introduced by copyists." Zuntz (1953: 205) concurs, adding that "the opposite change, from γάρ to δέ, is rare." But in this case these arguments lack force. Indeed, I hope to show that the situation is exactly the opposite of what Metzger has argued.

First, even though the external evidence is basically limited to Egypt, it has the advantage of being the earliest (Clement 𝔓⁴⁶) and best (𝔓⁴⁶ B 1739) of this evidence. Here this external evidence is supported by both transcriptional and intrinsic probabilities, and in this case the questions of Paul's style and intent offer a way through some of the difficulties in understanding this notorious crux.

Despite Metzger and Zuntz to the contrary, transcriptional probabilities are all in favor of γάρ. Except for sheer carelessness, which is not easy to account for (and in any case would favor γάρ over δέ as original),[9] it is difficult to imagine any circumstance under which a scribe, faced with δέ in this text, would have substituted γάρ. This is especially so, since, as the history of translation and interpretation makes plain, an adversative force to this sentence in contrast to "what eye has not seen," etc. in v. 9 seems to make such good sense. On the other hand, for that very reason one can understand how any number of scribes, who failed to make sense of Paul's γάρ, might have expunged it for what seemed to them to be the more natural adversative sense; all the more so, given the fact that the next two sentences also are joined by an explanatory γάρ. Is one to argue that a scribe deliberately created three consecutive uses of γάρ, especially when the first one made such little sense?

Given, then, that γάρ is easily the *lectio difficilior* and is supported by the best of the Egyptian tradition, can one make sense of it in Paul's argument? An affirmative answer to that question, I hope to show, not only resolves the textual question but also offers help for understanding v. 9, which reads literally:

> *But* [ἀλλά] even as it stands written:
> (1) What things [ἅ] eye has not seen,
> (2)   and   ear has not heard,
> (3)   and has not entered into the heart of man
> (4) What things [ἅ] God has prepared for those who love him
>   *for* [γὰρ] or *but* [δὲ]
>   to us God has revealed through the Spirit.

Besides the question of the source of the quotation, which does not concern us here, there are two basic problems with this verse. (1) The sentence itself is

---

9. For the very reason noted in Metzger: that the use of δέ here would be "entirely in Paul's manner," which is why a scribe could have carelessly so conformed it, whereas no amount of carelessness could account for an interchange in the other direction.

an anacolouthon: the problem has to do with the double ἅ "what things" and how one is going to understand what Paul intended to be the subject and object of the sentence. (2) How does the quotation function in the argument itself? Is it the conclusion of vv. 6-8, or does it begin a new direction to the argument? On these matters interpreters and English translations differ considerably.

With regard to the first item there are basically three options. (a) Omit the first ἅ and translate the second as "what," so that line 4 functions as the object of the three verbs in lines 1-3 (NIV: "No eye has seen, no ear has heard, no mind has conceived what God has prepared for those who love him"; compare NAB and Montgomery). (b) The opposite of that: Omit ἅ in line 4, so that lines 1-3 function as the object of the verb "has prepared" in line 4 (GNB: "What no one ever saw or heard, what no one ever thought could happen, is the very thing God prepared for those who love him"). (c) Make both occurrences of a coordinate and the whole of the quotation function as the object of the verb ἀπεκάλυψεν "has revealed" in v. 10 (RSV: "What no eye has seen, nor ear heard, nor the heart of man conceived, what God has prepared for those who love him, God has revealed to us through the Spirit"; compare NEB).[10] These latter assume a text with δέ, but then proceed to run roughshod over it, as if conjunctive signals were irrelevant.

The second question gets equally diverse treatment. (a) Some avoid the question by simply translating all of vv. 6-16 as a single paragraph — which it is, but one cannot thereby tell how v. 9 functions in the argument. (b) NIV and NEB see the first subparagraph to be vv. 6-10a. In the scheme of NIV, v. 9 is adversative to vv. 6-8 ("however"), although it is not at all clear how so: in the scheme of NEB, v. 9 is also adversative to vv. 6-8, but because they treat it as part of v. 10a, the whole of vv. 9-10a expresses the revelatory character of what the "rulers" did not understand. (c) By adding a comma after the strong adversative (ἀλλά) that begins v. 9, RSV and GNB take this verse to begin a new subparagraph (RSV: "But, as it is written," etc.). This comes out at the same place as NEB, even though the paragraphing is different. That is, in all such cases, even though the quotation in v. 9 touches on the subject matter of vv. 6-8, its real role is to set up the contrast that begins the new subject matter of vv. 10-13.

I would like to suggest another alternative, which sees γάρ in v. 10 as in-

---

10. JB has taken the opposite stance of this one, by reworking the introductory formula so that the quotation becomes the object of γέγραπται "it is written" ("We teach what scripture calls: the things that no eye has seen and no ear has heard, things beyond the mind of man, all that God has prepared for those who love him").

tentional on Paul's part and therefore as an integral part of his argumentation.[11]

First, although it will not be argued for here, the linguistic and contextual evidence overwhelmingly favors "the rulers of this age" as referring to the human rulers responsible for the death of Jesus,[12] who thereby also represent for Paul the "leaders" in terms of σοφία that is merely of this age. Thus he sets them up as those who represent the σοφοί ("wise") whom the Corinthians would now emulate in their feverish pursuit of σοφία.

Second, the stylistic clue to this passage lies with the introductory formula, ἀλλὰ καθὼς γέγραπται "but even as it stands written." Most translations take this to be an independent clause, the whole of which is adversative-supportive of vv. 6-8. This exact formula, however, appears two other times in Paul, in Romans 15:3-4 and 15:20-21, and in both cases ἀλλά "but" functions with the preceding sentence, as part of an οὐ/ἀλλά "not/but" contrast. Thus:

> Romans 15:3-4: For Christ did *not . . . But* as it is written . . .
>
> 15:20-21: . . . so that I would *not . . . but* just as it is written . . .

It should also be noted that in the case of 15:3, the succeeding sentence is connected with γάρ and is clearly explanatory of the citation. This stylistic feature suggests (a) that v. 9 is intended to provide support for vv. 6-8, as the adversative to the negatives in v. 8 ("The rulers did *not* understand, for if they had, they would *not* have crucified the Lord of glory, *but . . .*"); (b) that v. 9 thus belongs with vv. 6-8, which together form the first subparagraph of the argument; and (c) v. 10 therefore begins a new subparagraph by means of an explanation of v. 9.

11. Frid (1985) offers a slightly different solution, which has a similar net result. He sees the sentence in v. 9 as elliptical and would add the verb "we know" from v. 8. Thus: "None of them knew, but, as it is written, what things . . . , these things we do know."

12. The oft-repeated assertion that this term refers to demonic powers, either on their own or behind the earthly rulers, needs to be laid to rest. The linguistic evidence is decisive: (1) the term ἄρχοντες "rulers" is never equated with the ἀρχαί "principalities" of Col. 1:16 and Eph. 6:12; (2) when ἄρχων "leader" appears in the singular it sometimes refers to Satan; but (3) there is no evidence of any kind, either in Jewish or Christian writings until the second century, that the term was used of demons; furthermore, (4) in the NT in the plural it invariably refers to earthly rulers and unambiguously does so in Paul in Rom. 13:3; and (5) it is used regularly by Luke to refer to those responsible for the death of Jesus. It has been argued that the case for demonic powers rests on the addition "of this age," as in the singular "ruler of this world" in Eph. 2:2 (cf. John 12:31). But that still will not work in this case, since the phrase *of this age* comes directly from 1:20-21, where the Jewish expert in the law and the Greek philosopher are further styled "the disputer of this age."

Third, the argument of vv. 6-9, therefore, goes something like this. In v. 6 Paul has argued that, despite his pejorative treatment of wisdom in 1:17–2:5, there is nonetheless true σοφία for the believer (God's σοφία), which is not available to the leaders of the present age — because they pursue wisdom that is merely human (of this world, of this age). The divine σοφία, he goes on to explain in vv. 7-8, which was held "in mystery" and "once hidden" in God, was destined by God for our glory. Such wisdom, Paul repeats in v. 8, was not known by those who thought they had wisdom. That he intends nothing new or esoteric here is demonstrated by the next clause: *had* they known this hidden wisdom, they would *not* have crucified the Lord of glory. That is, divine wisdom is once more joined to Jesus Christ and him crucified, as in 1:23, 1:30, and 2:2. Right at this point, he adds a contrast: "But even as it stands written." Thus: "Had they known, they would *not* have crucified him, *but* as it is written, what things eye has not seen," etc.

Fourth, this leads, then, to some clues about the structure of the quotation. First, the two parts of the quotation, lines 1-3 and 4, support the two emphases in vv. 6-8. Lines 1-3 correspond to the rulers who did not understand, for if they had, they would not have crucified Christ (note especially line 3, "the heart of ἀνθρώπου [man] has not conceived"); line 4 corresponds to "what God has determined from before the ages for our glory." Second, since the quotation functions as a contrast to the rulers of this age, its whole point aims at line 4: what God has prepared for those who love him. Third, since the aim of the quotation is line 4, this suggests that both occurrences of ἅ be understood in a way similar to Moffatt's translation, where the second ἅ functions something like ταῦτα "these things." This means that the second ἅ is best understood as in apposition to the first and that both function as the object of the verb "has prepared." Thus: "What eye has not seen, and ear has not heard, and the heart of man has not conceived, these things God has prepared for those who love him." Therefore, even though it gives scriptural support for the lack of understanding by the rulers of this age, the quotation also picks up the motif of those who do understand. What Paul will now go on to explain in v. 10 is how we understand, the key to which of course is the Spirit.

How then does v. 10 function? Given the stylistic feature of Romans 15:3-4, v. 10a begins the new subparagraph that gets to the point of the whole section — our being able to understand what the rulers could not, because we have the Spirit while they do not. The first three sentences begin with an explanatory γάρ, each of which explains the former sentence.[13]

---

13. This compounding of explanatory γάρ is a unique feature of 1 Corinthians (see, e.g., 1:18-21; 3:2-4; 4:15; and 9:15-16).

> *For* to us God has revealed by his Spirit;
>> *for* the Spirit searches all things, even the depths of God;
>>> *for* [by way of analogy] who knows the mind of man, etc.

The first γάρ functions as the explanatory conjunction to the quotation in v. 9, especially as it climaxes with line 4. Thus Paul says, "What things were not formerly known are the things that God has prepared for those of us who love him; *for* to us God has revealed them by his Spirit." In this view, not only is sense made of the *lectio difficilior* of v. 10, but also v. 9 is placed in its proper role in the argument, to bring support and closure to vv. 6-8 as well as to lead into vv. 10-13.

I trust that these brief exercises in textual criticism, as it impacts exegesis and translation, will not only be an honor to Dr. Greenlee, but will also help us better to understand God's Word, to which task all of Dr. Greenlee's academic labors have been devoted.

References

Bornkamm, G.

1967   "μυστήριον." Vol. 4: pp. 802-27 in *Theological Dictionary of the New Testament*. Edited by Gerhard Kittel and Gerhard Friedrich. Grand Rapids: Eerdmans.

Brown, Raymond E.

1968   *The Semitic Background of the Term "Mystery" in the New Testament*. Philadelphia: Fortress.

Fee, Gordon D.

1987   *The First Epistle to the Corinthians*. New International Commentary on the New Testament. Grand Rapids: Eerdmans.

Findlay, G. G.

1900   "St. Paul's First Epistle to the Corinthians." Vol. 2: pp. 727-953 in *The Expositor's Greek Testament*. Edited by W. Robertson Nicoll. London: Hodder & Stoughton.

Frid, Bo

1985   "The Enigmatic ΑΛΛΑ in I Corinthians 2.9." *New Testament Studies* 31:603-11.

Funk, Robert W.

1966   "Word and Word in 1 Corinthians 2:6-16." Pp. 275-305 in *Language, Hermeneutic, and Word of God*. New York: Harper & Row.

Kim, Seyoon
1981   *The Origin of Paul's Gospel.* Tübingen: Mohr.

Mare, W. Harold
1976   "1 Corinthians." Vol. 10: pp. 173-297 in *The Expositor's Bible Commentary.* Edited by Frank E. Gaebelein. Grand Rapids: Zondervan.

Metzger, Bruce M.
1971   *A Textual Commentary on the Greek New Testament.* London: United Bible Societies.

Orr, William F., and James Arthur Walther
1976   *1 Corinthians.* Anchor Bible. Garden City: Doubleday.

Schütz, John H.
1975   *Paul and the Anatomy of Apostolic Authority.* Cambridge: Cambridge University Press.

Senft, Christophe
1979   *La Première Épître de Saint-Paul aux Corinthiens.* Neuchâtel: Delachaux & Nestlé.

Trites, Allison A.
1977   *The New Testament Concept of Witness.* Cambridge: Cambridge University Press.

Wilckens, Ulrich
1959   *Weisheit und Torheit.* Tübingen: Mohr.

Windisch, Hans
1914   "Die göttliche Weisheit der Juden and die paulinische Christologie." Pp. 220-34 in *Neutestamentliche Studien: Georg Heinrici zu seinem 70. Geburtstag.* Edited by Hans Windisch. Leipzig: Hinrichs.

Zuntz, Günther
1953   *The Text of the Epistles.* Schweich Lectures 1946. London: Oxford University Press for the British Academy.

CHAPTER 5

On Text and Commentary
on 1 and 2 Thessalonians
(1992)

For the purposes of this seminar, I have set for myself two tasks: (1) some observations on the role of textual criticism in the writing of a commentary, based on an analysis of recent English-language commentaries on 1 and 2 Thessalonians; and (2) a practical discussion of the issues by illustrations of various kinds from the text of 1 and 2 Thessalonians.

My urgencies are twofold. First, I carry the concerns of a text critic who happens also to write commentaries: that contemporary English-language commentaries evidence general impoverishment regarding textual questions — except for the most notable issues — thus leaving their users with an inadequate awareness of this dimension of the exegetical task. On this matter, the giants of an earlier time dwarf us considerably.[1] Thus the first section of this paper, as well as the set of illustrations in section II, takes up the issue of commentaries and textual questions of apparently lesser significance; i.e., when are "trivia" just that, and when do they make a difference in our understanding of texts, and therefore are no longer trivia? Second, in several papers before this section in the past several years I have shown interest in textual matters where I differed with some decisions made by the editors of the UBS³/NA²⁶. But in two key textual questions in 1 and 2 Thessalonians, taken up in section III of this paper, I wish to plead

---

1. Their failure lay on the other side of things; they tended to be experts in every kind of imaginable detail, but were less concerned with a readable exposition of the text, in which they offered contextual reasons for things. Their concentration on detail, of course, assumed a more narrowly defined readership, whose training made them capable of following terse textual or grammatical notes.

the cause of the editors of these editions[2] over against the majority of English commentaries.[3]

I. Commentaries and Textual Criticism

My concerns here stem from my own history, first as one who has been working in textual criticism over many years — but always with the greater urgency as to how these matters impact our understanding of the biblical text[4] — and second as one who has long made use of commentaries and who more recently has assayed to write such volumes, and even more recently to edit them.

The primary point of tension between textual criticism and commentary writing has to do with the twin issues of *what* to include — and *how*. Some of the difficulties here, of course, stem from the nature and format of the various series. In series such as Black's/Harper's and the New Century Bible, which aim at a readable exposition of the text itself with minimal exposition of the exegetical process by which the commentator arrived at his or her conclusions, one can hardly fault the commentator either for the lack of more textually related comments or for the brevity of those that do appear. Indeed, in this regard Ernest Best (Black's) is a model of excellence, given the limitations imposed by the series. But in other series, such as the Word Biblical Commentary (F. F. Bruce), the New International Commentary (Leon Morris), and the New International Greek Testament Commentary (C. A. Wanamaker),[5] one is allowed the option of significant and sub-

---

2. In one case (1 Thess. 2:7) I am pleading the cause of the majority over against the minority report.

3. It should be noted that the choice of texts in this case is not the result of writing a commentary on these letters per se, but comes from the Thessalonians chapter in my forthcoming monograph on the Spirit in the Pauline letters. All but one of the illustrations, therefore, come from "Spirit texts" in these two letters.

4. This explains in part my own role as one of the editors of the Metzger Festschrift (with E. J. Epp, *New Testament Textual Criticism: Its Significance for Exegesis: Essays in Honour of Bruce M. Metzger* [Oxford University Press, 1981]). Although we were only partly successful — and finally yielded to other kinds of papers — the goal of that volume was to invite scholars who were working in the field of textual criticism to bring their expertise to bear on specific textual issues that affected the exegesis of the biblical text.

5. Unfortunately, the commentaries on Thessalonians in Hermeneia (H. Koester) and the Anchor Bible (A. Malherbe) are not yet available. In other commentaries in both of these series textual notes and commentary are a mixed bag. In some cases the notes are considerable and the comment substantial (in Hermeneia, Galatians by Betz, or in AB, 2 Corinthians by Furnish).

stantial textual commentary. Here the results are mixed at best. There are two matters for concern: (1) The question of choice, as to what is noted and what is not, often seems to be a matter of whim; and in any case, the lesser items, even though they could make a difference in understanding the text, tend to get little or no attention at all. My plea here is in the cause of textual variation, both in terms of the reader's need to be informed and in the interest of the history of interpretation — which textual variation very often puts one in touch with. (2) The second matter is that of how textual questions are actually treated, which in some cases is even more perplexing. One wonders at times for whom some textual notes might be intended. My plea here is in the cause of the reader, for whom a great many textual notes must seem worthless.

a. The Question of Choice

Ideally, questions of textual criticism should be treated in the same way as questions of grammar: all such matters should be noted which actually impact the meaning of the text; however, since not all such questions impact meaning in the same way, the commentator must also be sensitive as to which variations should merely be noted briefly — but informatively — and which should be discussed at length. Moreover, even though questions of textual variation are based on the hard data of actual differences in the transmission of the text, not all of the hard data are of equal weight, so one still must exercise considerable judgment, e.g., as to when to note singular or sub-singular readings and when to pass them by altogether. On this last matter one should expect commentators to make differing judgments. If indeed one chooses to include a textual note, then the reader should be given the benefit of at least the minimal form of "comment," including the commentator's best judgment as to the original text and at least some comment on the probable cause of variation and what meaning of the text is thereby implied.

My plea, therefore, is ultimately for both more and better notations about textual matters than is often the case presently, especially in cases (a) where there is substantial and divided support for two or more textual options, and (b) where the textual options make some degree of difference in the understanding of what Paul has written. Thus one should obviously include the major items, such as the νήπιοι/ἤπιοι interchange in 1 Thess. 2:7, the συνεργόν/διάκονον etc. interchange in 3:2, the add/omit δέ in 5:21, the ἀνομίας/ἁμαρτίας interchange in 2 Thess. 2:3, the add/omit ὡς θεόν in 2:4, and the ἀπαρχήν/ἀπ' ἀρχῆς interchange in 2:13, all of which need discussion in the body of the commentary. But I would urge that a commentary in series which make provision for such should also minimally include all the variants discussed in Metzger's *Textual Commentary*[6] — even if ever so slightly, and even if such "discussion" is limited to notes.[7]

I would argue further that one's exegesis, and thus the writing of the commentary, should be based either on NA[26] or on one's own reconstructed text based on NA[26] (and Tischendorf), so that the broader textual picture can also be included. Thus in 1 Thessalonians 1, for example, one should probably include notes to the add/omit ὑμῶν in v. 2, the add/omit ἐν (2x) in v. 5, the add/omit καί in v. 8, and the ἡμῶν/ὑμῶν interchange in v. 9. I would also include the addition of καί by B and some Vulgate MSS in v. 6 (both because of the significance of B and, in the interest of the history of interpretation, the slight difference between "full of the joy *of* the Holy Spirit" and "full of joy *and* the Holy Spirit"). Similarly, I would include the add/omit ἐν τῇ with Ἀχαΐᾳ in v. 8, on the grounds that it does make a difference in meaning as to whether Paul now intended to group the previously mentioned — but separated — Macedonia and Achaia together[8] or to continue to view them as separate entities when he adds his further geographical note. Whether one would include the add/omit article with θεοῦ in v. 4 would depend on how much technical data the series can bear and whether one has special interest in the arthrous/anarthrous use of θεός in this earliest of the Pauline letters. It is in this regard that I would press, e.g., for the inclusion of the two items noted in section 2 below.

6. B. M. Metzger, *A Textual Commentary on the Greek New Testament* (London/New York: United Bible Societies, 1971). This would mean that at least all the variants in the apparatus of the UBS[3] are discussed, as well as several others included in the Commentary but not in the apparatus of the edition itself.

7. For the sake of the discussion in the next section, the 14 variants in 1 Thessalonians discussed in Metzger's *Commentary* appear in Appendix I.

8. Surely in this case the text without the ἐν τῇ (following B K 6 33 365 614 630 1739 it[r] vg[mss]) is to be preferred to that of the majority. It is arguable, of course, that a scribe might have omitted these two words as unnecessary in light of v. 7; but rhetorically, one might ask, why should he? Scribes are not notorious for wanting to "save space" in such matters. But one can easily understand a scribe, having missed Paul's nuance, thereby adding these words from v. 7. Paul's point seems to be that, having mentioned the notoriety of the Thessalonians' conversion in the two provinces of immediate and direct concern (Macedonia and Achaia), travelers through Corinth (apparently) have also informed him of how widely this news has spread. Hence he now notes that it is well known not only in Macedonia and Achaia (now thought of together as one unit) but in "every place." Cf. H. Koester, "The Text of 1 Thessalonians," in *The Living Text: Essays in Honor of Ernest W. Saunders*, ed. D. E. Groh and R. Jewett (Lanham, Md.: University Press of America, 1985), pp. 220-21, who also argues for removing this bracketed error from NA[26].

A survey of how these matters are treated in six of the more recent commentaries in English (Best [1972]; Thomas [EBC, 1978]; Bruce [1982]; Marshall [1983]; Wanamaker [1990]; Morris [²1991]) in comparison with three earlier ones (Milligan [1908]; Moffatt [EGT, 1910]; Frame [1912]) can be found in Appendix II. A few observations are in order: First, only three variants (2:7; 3:2; and 5:4) are either noted or discussed in all nine commentaries. Second, only Bruce has a textual notation on all the items on the list;[9] the disappointing nature of these notations is discussed in the next section. Third, of the two commentaries in the style of "readable exposition," Best makes maximum use of textual data, while Marshall makes minimal notations. Fourth, for a commentary on the Greek text, Wanamaker's is especially disappointing in the area of textual discussions; not only does he fail to include any discussion at all of seven of the items in Metzger's *Commentary* (which should at least serve as a secondary source to be reckoned with on these matters), but what discussions are included are not always thorough or sensitive to matters that are especially text-critical (e.g., the weight of external evidence and transcriptional probabilities). Finally, Morris's commentary, even in its revised form, gets mixed reviews. On the one hand, one is puzzled by several omissions of textual discussions, especially since the format allows for such discussion in the notes and since in some notes he makes a point of what is found in the preferred text without so much as acknowledging textual variation. On the other hand, of the six contemporary commentaries surveyed, his textual discussions are easily the most complete and textually the best informed.

But on the whole, one will have to rate these commentaries as less than satisfactory on textual questions in general, and even more so on the so-called lesser items in particular.

b. The Question of Presentation

Two matters concern us here: (1) All too often commentators include notations about textual data without adequate discussion so as to make those data user-friendly; thus (2) some suggestions are offered as to how this material might be presented in a more useful way.

The problem of inadequate discussion. I would urge that two kinds of

---

9. With the exception of the add/omit ἐν with πληροφορίᾳ in 1:5. But this was surely an oversight of some kind (perhaps at the editorial level), since in the comment itself he brackets the ἐν, thus acknowledging the variation and since he has notes on all such textual variation.

nearly useless "commentary" should be forever eliminated from this genre: (a) textual notation pure and simple, in which variants and supporting witnesses are given but with no discussion one way or the other; (b) textual discussion that offers conclusions either without supporting evidence or argumentation or without explanation as to what difference it makes in understanding the text.

The first of these faults finds its ultimate expression in the Word Biblical Commentary (F. F. Bruce), where almost every variant listed in the apparatus of NA²⁶ is noted in the commentary, but with little information or help beyond what one can find for oneself in that apparatus. Of what value, one wonders, are the footnotes to the author's translation that read: "ἀπὸ θεοῦ πατρὸς ἡμῶν καὶ κυρίου Ἰησοῦ Χριστοῦ added by ℵ A I byz lat^vgcodd syr^hcl** (from 2 Thess. 1:2)" or "τύπους ('examples') is read for τύπον by ℵ A C F G Ψ byz syr^hcl," to cite only the first two variants listed in Appendix I? Unfortunately, such textual notation is the only "discussion" one gets in this commentary, except for the more significant items such as at 2:7 or 3:2. And since Bruce seldom made textual choices contrary to the text of NA²⁶, one is here simply getting a replay of the Nestle-Aland apparatus.[10]

Equally unhelpful to the reader are notations (which are hardly discussions) such as this comment by Thomas on the double add/omit ἐν in 1:5: "In v. 5 two appearances of ἐν . . . — before πληροφορίᾳ . . . and before ὑμῖν — have weak MS support. The sense is not greatly affected by their absence" (p. 245). If that is the case, and especially so in a series that has such severe space limitations, then why the comment at all? Who will be helped to know this? Unfortunately, neither are the assertions in this case strictly accurate. On the one hand, the "weak MS support" for the first addition happens to include the entire textual tradition except for ℵ B 33.[11] On the other hand, if the sense is "not greatly affected," it is arguable (as I will argue below) that it is affected enough to deserve meaningful comment, and not simply to be cavalierly brushed aside. This picks on Thomas a bit, whose textual notes for the most part are better than average, especially so in light of his space limitations. The problem is that such "comments" can be illustrated scores of times over in most of these commentaries. I would argue that in all inclusions of textual data in a commentary, the reader should be given the benefit of some discussion, as to the reasons for and

10. F. F. Bruce did opt for the "minority report" on 2:7 (ἤπιοι), but on all other variants selected for this study, he simply reflects NA²⁶.

11. Also lat, but its Greek text cannot be assumed in this case. The support for the second ἐν is equally strong, including B D F G Ψ Maj it. One wonders whether Thomas did not misspeak himself here, intending actually to say the opposite.

against the chosen variant and its rejected alternatives[12] as well as to its significance for understanding.

Some suggestions about presentation. On this matter commentaries are of two kinds: those which allow footnotes of various kinds and those which do not. The latter are especially strapped when it comes to textual matters, where, as in the case of Wanamaker, one either must offer notations in parentheses or offer discussion that seems to intrude on the comment/exposition itself.[13]

For those commentaries where one can make copious use of notes, there are basically two ways of handling textual matters. Either textual notes should occur in conjunction with the English translation itself (the *lemma*), or else the notes should appear in the commentary *ad loc.* The advantage of the former is that it allows for discussion at the point of translation itself, where the reader has immediate access both to the options involved and to their translational significance. The disadvantage is that many readers do not consult the translation at all, but move directly to the comment *ad loc.* The solution to this, of course, is some further comment about textual matters in the exposition itself, either by way of referral footnote or by way of direct comment.

In any case, I would urge two matters on the writers of all such commentaries. First, the textual discussion in the footnotes should be as complete as possible, so that, on the one hand, it can stand by itself as a form of "textual commentary" for all those interested in such matters for their own sake, and that, on the other hand, one can for the most part comment on the resultant text itself in the exposition, without cluttering the exposition with reasons for and against.

Second, for all of the more significant variants, as well as for many of the lesser ones, some form of further comment is needed in the exposition itself, so that the reader can see the exegetical significance of the textual choices made in the footnotes. Only for major — and difficult — choices like the two chosen in section 3 below should there be considerable discussion in the ex-

12. Cf., e.g., Wanamaker's comment on the κλέπτης/κλέπτας interchange in 1 Thess. 5:4 (pp. 181-82), which offers a good explanation of the differences in meaning, but chooses κλέπτης without offering any textual argumentation (the alternative simply represents "a secondary reading"). On this variant, one might add, Metzger's *Commentary* (p. 689) fares little better, by noting that the accusative plural results "in near nonsense." That may be a bit cavalier, given that this is the choice of WH, and is the accepted reading — and argued for — by Moffatt and Frame (cf. Milligan).

13. It should be noted that this fault was remedied in the NIGTC commentary by P. T. O'Brien, *Philippians* (Grand Rapids: Eerdmans, 1991).

position itself, precisely because the textual choice affects one's understanding of Paul's sentence in a rather thoroughgoing way.

In the discussions that follow, I hope both to illustrate such a way of approaching textual discussion in a commentary and to argue the case for my own textual choices.

II. Commentaries and Textual Variation of Lesser Significance

In order to illustrate my concerns here, I have chosen textual questions from two of the Spirit texts in 1 Thessalonians: the add/omit ἐν with πληροφορίᾳ in 1:5; and the three variants in 4:8 found in the NA²⁶ apparatus (add/omit καί; διδόντα/δόντα; ὑμᾶς/ἡμᾶς).

a. 1 Thessalonians 1:5

My translation (with various translational and textual notes) reads:

> . . . how that¹⁴ our gospel came to you not in word alone, but also with power, namely,ᵃ with the Holy Spirit and full conviction, just as you know what manner of men we were towardᵇ you for your sakes;

Textual notes a and b read as follows:

ᵃ This translation is based on the textual choice which lacks the ἐν before πληροφορίᾳ with ℵ B 33 lat. This is almost certainly the original text, since one can offer no reasonable explanation for its omission by scribes (esp. in light of its certain presence before the two preceding nouns, ἐν δυνάμει καὶ ἐν πνεύματι ἁγίῳ), whereas that very fact easily explains why subsequent scribes would have added an ἐν before πληροφορίᾳ as well — to make all three nouns coordinate (so also Rigaux, 374; Koester, "Text," 220). What this means, therefore, is that we are not here dealing with a "triad" (Collins, Studies, 192, n. 95), but (most likely) with epexegesis, where the second (compound) phrase further qualifies the first (cf. Moffatt, 24).

ᵇ The textual choice between ὑμῖν (ℵ A C P 048 33 81 104 326* 945 1739 1881 pc) and ἐν ὑμῖν (B D F G Maj it sy) is not an easy one. The change could have been purely accidental: an additional ἐν or its omission resulting from dittography or

14. Rather than "causal," as in most translations and commentaries (cf. O'Brien, *Thanksgivings*, p. 151, n. 49; Wanamaker, 78; Morris, 45), the ὅτι that begins this clause is probably epexegetic, and offers an elaboration-explanation as to how the Thessalonians can be sure that God's love for them has resulted in their election. For this usage in Paul (οἶδα, followed by an object, followed by an epexegetic ὅτι), see esp. 2:1; cf. 1 Cor. 16:15; Rom. 13:11.

haplography (from the preceding ἐγενήθημεν). From the perspective of intrinsic probability (in this case, author's style), one could argue for its presence in the Pauline original, since the use of two prepositional phrases in this manner (ἐν ὑμῖν δι' ὑμᾶς) is quite in keeping with Paul's style (cf. 3:7; 4:14). On the other hand, on the grounds of transcriptional probability — assuming the change were not accidental — ὑμῖν is most likely the original, since scribes would tend to add prepositions, unless a good reason could be found for their having omitted it, which is not forthcoming in this case. Since this reading also has the better external support (it is clear that B abandons its relatives in this case), it should probably be preferred as the original. Although the overall sense of the sentence comes out at about the same place, the text without ἐν emphasizes Paul's (and Timothy's/Silas's) relationship *toward,* or *before* (so Frame), the Thessalonians; whereas ἐν ὑμῖν emphasizes their conduct while *among* them. The argument of 2:1-12, which emphasizes Paul's *relationship with the Thessalonians* while present among them, also favors the former reading.

The comment itself (some two pages later) proceeds as follows (I have included extended comment in this case so as to illustrate how the earlier textual note can be fitted into the discussion as well as to make my own case for this reading and its meaning):

Paul's concern seems clear. He grounds their experienced faith in God's prior love and election (v. 4); but since he is appealing to their own conversion as a means of encouragement in the midst of present suffering,[15] the reminder is twofold: of the nature of *Paul's proclamation* of the gospel, that it was accompanied by the Holy Spirit's power (v. 5); and of their own *experience* of receiving the gospel ("the word"), that it was accompanied by an untrammeled joy produced by the Holy Spirit — despite the sufferings they also came to experience (v. 6).[16]

All of that seems plain enough in context. But what is less plain in the present verse is to determine the precise referent in the twin phrases "in/with power" and "in/with the Holy Spirit and deep conviction."[17] Does this refer to Paul's actual preaching of the gospel,[18] to "signs and wonders" that accompanied that preaching (as in the similar passage in Rom. 15:19),[19] or, as is almost certainly true of the similar passage in 1 Cor. 2:4-5,

15. This seems to be the ultimate reason for this recall, even though it is expressed in terms of his (and Silas's and Timothy's) being reminded of their conversion when giving thanks in prayer.

16. This appeal to the *experience* of conversion, evidenced by the work of the Spirit, is not dissimilar to that found in Gal. 3:1-5.

17. On these as "twin phrases" and not a "triad," see n. a above.

18. As most commentaries.

19. As, e.g., C. H. Giblin, *The Threat to Faith* (AnBib 31: Rome: Pontifical Biblical Insti-

to the Thessalonians' actual conversion?[20] Or perhaps do two or all three of these somehow coalesce in this sentence?

Most likely the answer lies with this last suggestion, so that at least the two realities of Paul's Spirit-empowered preaching and their Spirit-experienced conversion are both in view, the latter being the consequence of the former (or in this case, they represent the two sides of one reality). Nonetheless even though in context (especially vv. 2-4 and 6-10) the overall emphasis is on their becoming and being Christian believers, the *primary* emphasis in v. 5 seems to be on Paul's Spirit-empowered preaching of the gospel that brought about their conversion. This seems certain from the contrasting phrase, "not only in word," as well as the concluding clause, "even as you know what manner of men we were toward you for your own sakes." The latter in particular focuses on Paul's and his co-workers' preaching and behavior — and surely anticipates 2:1-12.

The phrase "not only in word," it should be noted, is not an attempt to play the Spirit off against the Word.[21] Paul seems to be doing two things with this contrast: First, he is setting up the argument in 2:1-12, that his preaching and their response are quite unrelated to the kind of "word" one finds among the religious and philosophical charlatans. As they well know, and as he will argue in 2:1-12, his manner of life among them as proclaimer of the gospel was quite in contrast to such purveyors of empty words, who used "flattery as a mask for greed" (2:5). Paul's "word" was accompanied by the power of the Holy Spirit and carried deep conviction.

Second, Paul wants to remind them, as he will the Corinthians in yet another context (1 Cor. 2:1-5), that the message of the gospel is truth accompanied by experienced reality. It did indeed come "in word," meaning in the form of proclaimed truth, as a message from God himself (see 2:4 and 13). But for this appeal the proof is in the eating. Thus it was not "in word *alone*." God verified its truthfulness by a display of his power through the ministry of the Holy Spirit.

What this means, then, is that the twin phrases, "but in power" and "with the Holy Spirit and deep conviction," refer primarily to Paul's

---

tute, 1967), p. 45: "Paul's teaching was given in the power of the Spirit in that it was attended with miracles (1 Thess. 1,5. . .)." Cf. Marshall, 53-54; Grundmann, *TDNT* 2.311; Wanamaker, 79.

20. As, e.g., Whitely, p. 36: "The *power* associated with the gospel was . . . the power to work the 'miracle' of causing the heathen to believe."

21. On this point Kemmler's critique of much of the exegesis of this text is well taken. But his own solution, which sees the "but with" phrases as "additional testimonies" to the effectiveness of Paul's "word," seems to miss Paul's concern and argument by too much (see D. W. Kemmler, *Faith and Human Reason: A Study of Paul's Method of Preaching as Illustrated by 1–2 Thessalonians and Acts 17,2-4* [NovTSup 40; Leiden: Brill, 1995], pp. 149-68).

preaching, but not so much to the *manner*[22] (or style) of the preaching, as to its Spirit-empowered *effectiveness*. This seems to be the best way to make sense of what might at first blush look like a mere compounding of words. Contrary to some,[23] the appeal can scarcely be to Paul's *own sense* that his ministry was accompanied by power. The sentence insists that his gospel "came to *you*"[24] in a certain manner. Thus the initial phrase on the positive side is not "with the Holy Spirit and power,"[25] but simply "in power," precisely because that is for Paul the proper contrast to coming merely "with speech" (cf. 1 Cor. 2:1-5; 4:19). But lest "power" not be properly understood, Paul immediately qualifies by adding, "that is, with the Holy Spirit and deep/full conviction." Thus, the Holy Spirit is being designated as the source of the power in his preaching the gospel, the evidence of which was the full conviction that accompanied his preaching and resulted in their conversion.

b) 1 Thessalonians 4:8

Translation:

For that very reason the person who rejects [this instruction][26] does not reject a man but rejects the God who also[a] gives[b] his Holy Spirit unto you.[c]

Here the textual notes read as follows:

[a] The presence (with ℵ D* F G Maj lat Clement) or absence (with A B I 33 1739* b pc) of this καί is not easy to resolve; but in the final analysis, it seems more likely that scribes omitted it as unnecessary, than that it was added (precisely because it is difficult to imagine *why* they would have done so); cf. the similar expression in 2:12, where no such "addition" exists in the textual evidence. The presence of this καί would seem to be especially telling against those various

22. Contra Frame, 81, among others.
23. For example, O'Brien, *Thanksgivings*, p. 132, who argues that "ἐν δυνάμει does not so much refer to the outward signs of the presence of the Holy Spirit, as to the sense the preachers had that their message was striking home." That seems to miss Paul's own emphasis, which throughout is on the Thessalonians' own recall of their conversion including their remembering Paul's preaching as Spirit-empowered — and thus effectual *in their behalf*.
24. ἐγενήθη εἰς ὑμᾶς. The idiom basically means "to come to someone."
25. As, e.g., in 1 Cor. 2:4 ("with the demonstration of the Spirit and power") and Rom. 15:19 ("with the power of the Spirit").
26. There is no object to the verb "rejects," but the context seems to demand something like this, rather than a rejection of Paul himself.

commentators who think the emphasis here is on the substantival idea of "God the giver," rather than on the verbal, "the one who gives." See the discussion below.

b Gk. διδόντα (א* B D F G I 365 2464 pc); later witnesses (A Ψ Byz sy co) changed it to the aorist δόντα, on the pattern of Paul's usage elsewhere (Rom. 5:5; 2 Cor. 1:22; 5:5; cf. Gal. 3:2; 4:6; Rom. 8:15). Rigaux, 514, adopts it on the pattern of the preceding ἐκάλεσεν (so also now Koester, "Text," 223); however, this is but another reason for later scribes to make the change (as Frame, 156, pointed out many years earlier). Indeed, *pace* Koester, everything favors the reading of the present tense (external evidence, transcriptional probability [a deliberate change from the aorist to the present is nearly impossible to account for; and the accident of copying Koester argues for, following B. Weiss, is improbable in the highest degree — especially crossing the two earliest textual traditions], Paul's own point in context). As to whether the present tense is significant, see the discussion below.

c The ἡμᾶς ("us") found in A 6 365 1739 1881 a f m t pc is probably a secondary conformation to the ἡμᾶς found in v. 7. An earlier generation of Catholic scholars adopted this reading and used it as support for the apostolic succession, i.e., to reject Paul's teaching is the same as to reject God, who gave his Spirit to Paul in order to teach authoritatively. But even if ἡμᾶς were the original reading, which it almost certainly is not, it would mean "us Christians collectively" (Frame), as elsewhere in Paul where in semi-creedal formulations he changes from the second plural to the all-inclusive first plural (e.g., Gal. 4:6).

The paragraphs that discuss this matter *ad loc.* proceed as follows:

In this first mention in the Pauline corpus of the actual "gift of the Spirit," Paul designates the Spirit as being given εἰς ἡμᾶς ("into you"). This somewhat unusual usage is reminiscent of LXX Ezek. 37:6 and 14 (καὶ δώσω τὸ πνεῦμα μου εἰς ὑμᾶς, "I will give my Spirit into you"), which probably means something like, "I will *put* my Spirit in you."[27] In any case, such a usage reflects a Pauline understanding of the gift of the Spirit as the fulfillment of OT promises that God's own Spirit will come to indwell his people, "and you shall live" (Ezek. 37:14; cf. 11:19). In later letters Paul will make this same point by referring to the Spirit as "given (or sent) into your hearts" (2 Cor. 1:22; Gal. 4:6; cf. the emphatic language in 1 Cor. 6:19, "the temple of the in you Holy Spirit").

Despite some debate here, the use of the present participle, "who also gives" (see notes *a* and *b* above), almost certainly stresses the ongoing work of the Spirit in their lives. Although their previous conversion by the Spirit is the obvious presupposition of this usage, had Paul in fact intended to refer to their conversion as such (as in 1:5-6),[28] he would have

27. Cf. Frame, p. 156, "the εἰς is for the dative or for ἐν; 'give to be in,' 'put in.'"
28. As Hiebert (p. 176), e.g., explicitly says.

used the simple aorist, as in v. 7 and as he does elsewhere with regard to the Spirit.[29] This is very similar to the use of the present tense with "calls" in 2:12 and 5:24; and especially to the use of the present tense with the "supplying" of the Spirit in Gal. 3:5 (cf. Phil. 1:19). All of this is to say that Paul's concern here is not with their conversion, but with their present experience of God's *Holy* Spirit, given to them by God precisely so that they might walk in holiness. Thus the Spirit is understood as the constant divine companion, by whose power one lives out holiness, i.e., a truly Christian ethic.

Such discussions as these, it may be argued, not only help readers get in touch with the issues of Paul's text, but also help them to recognize the significance of text-critical questions — even apparently lesser ones — in the exegetical process.

III. Commentaries and Major Textual Decisions

The two textual matters taken up in this section — 1 Thess. 2:7 and 2 Thess. 2:13 — were chosen not only because they are well-known textual questions in which the editors of the NA[26] seem to have the better of it over the commentaries, but also because they reveal the worst side of textual criticism in commentaries: the tendency to make textual decisions ultimately on the weakest — at least most subjective — of all the textual criteria, namely intrinsic evidence, based on our prior commitments to what is most in keeping with Pauline usage/theology. The problem from a text-critical point of view is that mere lip-service is paid to truly text-critical questions, so as to dismiss them, in order to comment on the text one believes is most in keeping with Pauline style or theology.

In both cases, as in the former section, I will illustrate by offering my translation with textual footnotes; however, in the interest of space the "commentary" is basically limited to the textual arguments.

---

29. Apparently to avoid the implication of the present participle, some suggest that the emphasis is substantival, "God the Giver of the Holy Spirit" (e.g., Moffatt, 35; Findlay, 90; Hiebert, 176; Dunn, *Baptism,* 106, at least as referring to conversion). The expressed concern here is to avoid the concept of "continuous or successive impartation" (Moffatt). But that is to avoid "second blessing theology" by an unnecessary expedient. Paul's concern is not on "successive gifts" of the Spirit, but on the present, ongoing work of the Spirit in their lives.

a. 1 Thessalonians 2:7

Translation:

> [6]. . . nor seeking glory from people, neither from you nor from others — [7]although as apostles of Christ we could have made our weight felt — but[30] we became babes[a] among you. Even as a nurse cares for her own children, [8]so we, deeply yearning after you, were willing to impart to you . . .

The textual note reads as follows:

[a]Gk. νήπιοι (supported by P[65] ℵ* B C* D* F G I Ψ* 104* 326[c] 2495 pc it vg[ww] sa[mss] bo Clement); ἤπιοι ("gentle") is read by A MajT, as well as the correctors of ℵ C D Ψ and some MSS of the Sahidic. Historically, this has proven to be a very difficult textual choice. The external evidence, it should be noted, is *overwhelmingly* in support of νήπιοι, being read by all the significant early evidence both East and West. Transcriptionally, the issue is, first, whether the variant is the result of a copying accident or whether it was intentional, and second, which variant *best* explains how the other came about. For the full argument in favor of νήπιοι as the original reading, see the commentary.

The commentary reads as follows:

> Paul's concern up through v. 6 has been easy to follow, both in terms of the argument itself and in light of its Hellenistic (Cynic) background. But with vv. 7-8, everything in Paul's sentence begins to break down, both structurally and metaphorically. The problem is twofold: the structure of the sentence itself, and the textual choice in v. 7 between "babes" and "gentle,"[31] which rests upon the presence or absence of a single Greek letter *(nu)*. These two issues in fact are interrelated, since if one understands Paul to have written "babes," one will structure the clauses in one way; if one thinks he wrote "gentle," the structures will be seen in another way (see n. 30 above). Since the structural question is largely determined by

---

30. Depending in large measure on how one resolves the textual matter in note a, the punctuation of this especially complex sentence is not at all easy. Most translations and commentaries put a full stop after the first clause in v. 7 (here bracketed with dashes) and begin a new clause with 7b. Thus they read this ἀλλά as beginning a new clause, as they also do the οὕτως that begins v. 8. That also means that the ὡς ἐάν that begins the third clause in v. 7 (here seen as the beginning of a new sentence) is understood as dependent on 7b (= "But . . . even as . . ."). Read this way, there is indeed a "violent transition in the same sentence" (B. M. Metzger, *The Text of the New Testament* [2nd edn.; New York: Oxford University Press, 1968], p. 231); but as argued below, this is a most unnatural way to handle Paul's Greek.

31. See n. a above.

the textual one, some words are first of all necessary about the text itself, as to what Paul is most likely to have written.

While it is true that a very good contextual case can be made for "gentle," there are in fact no purely textual arguments that *favor* this reading. On the other hand, the following textual considerations strongly favor "babes" as the Pauline original.[32]

1. The most common text-critical "reason" for choosing "gentle" suggests that νήπιοι is the result of common dittography, wherein a scribe (or scribes) repeated the final *nu* of the immediately preceding verb. In fact, however, this is no textual argument at all, but is rather an explanation as to how νήπιοι might have arisen *if one makes the prior assumption* that ἤπιοι is the original reading. But in such a case the textual choice is made on the prior grounds of what Paul is most likely to have written in context, not on textual grounds, since if one begins with the opposite prior assumption, that νήπιοι is original, then one can just as easily argue that ἤπιοι came about as the result of haplography — which happens just as frequently, since there is no scribal predilection toward one or the other. The point is that the possibility of dittography or haplography is open-ended. Either may have happened; but neither is an argument for one reading or the other as original.[33]

The textual question, therefore, must be answered on other grounds. At this point the issues are two — whether the interchange was accidental or intentional — both of which favor "babes." That is, (a) if the add/omit *nu* were *accidental,* then one should surely opt for νήπιοι on the basis of its superior attestation (see next paragraph); (b) likewise if the add/omit were *intentional,* then one should also opt for νήπιοι on the twin grounds that the "more difficult" reading is to be preferred as the original and that that reading which best explains the origin of the other is most likely the original. A few more words about each of these matters.

2. The external evidence is decisively in favor of νήπιοι, being supported by the earliest evidence in the West (all the Old Latin) and in the East (Clement, P[65]), as well as by the predominance of what is most often considered the best evidence (in this case, all but Codex A of the Egyptian

---

32. Contra Metzger, *Text,* pp. 280-83; cf. his minority report in the *Textual Commentary,* p. 630; so also Best, Bruce, Ellicott, Hendriksen, Marshall, Moffatt, Thomas, Wanamaker. Cf. Koester, "Text," p. 225, who is characteristically bold: "There cannot be the slightest doubt that νήπιοι is wrong." In fact, of course, there is every kind of doubt, since all the purely textual arguments are quite in its favor. It is also favored, inter alia, by Westcott-Hort, Frame, Lightfoot, Milligan, and Morris.

33. In fairness it must be pointed out that Metzger, *Text,* p. 231, acknowledges this reality — although not all commentators do so.

witnesses). One would seem to need especially strong transcriptional arguments to overrule this combination of evidence. In fact, the evidence for ἥπιοι is so much weaker than for νήπιοι that under ordinary circumstances no one would accept the former reading as original.

What is seldom noted, however, is a further significant historical factor: Since all the known early evidence — empire-wide — attests νήπιοι, anyone who favors ἥπιοι needs to offer good *historical* reasons as to how the (accidental) corruption happened so early (and so often) that it came to be the only text known for several centuries, while the "original" reading escaped all the known early evidence only to emerge much later in the monolithic, but patently secondary, evidence of the Byzantine tradition. This is not thereby to deny that such could have happened; but one wonders why only the "accident" is universally known in the first four Christian centuries.[34] On this matter, I want to "plead the cause of history, and in the name of history to plead the cause of the documents."[35]

3. The same holds true with regard to the issues of transcriptional probabilities (having to do with scribal proclivities). It turns out, in fact, that the *only* thing that favors ἥπιοι is internal evidence, predicated on what scholars deem Paul most likely to have written. But the arguments raised in favor of ἥπιοι and against νήπιοι on transcriptional grounds actually favor νήπιοι only. That is, it was to alleviate the very difficulty that present-day scholars have with νήπιοι, as malapropos to the argument, that best explains why some (not very early) scribes changed it to read ἥπιοι. This is further corroborated by the fact that several manuscripts have been "corrected" in this case, and that the direction of correction in every case but one is away from νήπιοι in favor of ἥπιοι. Such "corrections" are obviously intentional, suggesting that most of the later corruptions to this text also moved intentionally in this direction (thus it is unlikely the result of pure accident).

What this means, then, is that all the evidence that is purely textual favors the reading "babes." The task of the interpreter, it must be pointed out, is not to choose the more weakly attested reading for theological or stylistic reasons, but to make sense contextually of the reading which alone best accounts for the other, which is almost certainly the Pauline original.

But what about the questions of Pauline usage? Here again the evi-

34. It must be noted that the split evidence of Clement and Origen noted in the UBS apparatus offers no substantial evidence at all, since the reading ἥπιοι is almost certainly due to corruptions in the transmission of these patristic texts.

35. The language is Jean Duplacy's.

dence favors "babes." If "usage" = the meaning of words, it must be pointed out that ἤπιος is found elsewhere in the NT only in 2 Tim. 2:24,[36] whereas νήπιος occurs as a frequent metaphor. This latter fact has sometimes been used to condemn "babes" here, on the grounds that this metaphor is always pejorative in Paul. But such a comment is at best prejudicial, and fails to come to terms with Paul's own fluid use of metaphors. After all, in 1 Corinthians alone he uses it pejoratively in 3:1-2, in a neutral sense in 13:11, and positively in 14:20.[37]

Furthermore, when "usage" is expanded to include syntax and sentence structures, the evidence again favors "babes." If "gentle" were the original text, then one seems compelled to structure Paul's sentence in the following way (cf. NRSV, NIV, NASB):

> Nor did we seek praise from mortals,
> > neither from you nor from others,
> > > even though as apostles of Christ we might have made our weight felt.
> > *But* (ἀλλά) we were gentle among you,
> > > like (NRSV for ὡς ἐάν) a nurse tenderly caring for her own children.
> > So (NRSV for οὕτως) deeply do we care for you . . .

But there are several problems with this structural arrangement, having to do with Pauline usage elsewhere. First, under all normal circumstances an ἀλλά following a negative (in this case the intensified threefold repetition of οὔτε) would be understood as the second part of a "not/but" contrast. The same holds true, secondly, for the combination of ὡς . . . οὕτως, which would seem to require overwhelming evidence of an unusual kind for the one (ὡς) to be the concluding member of a former clause, and the latter (οὕτως) the beginning member of the following clause.[38] The solution of such translations as the NRSV and NASB, which treat the normally correlative οὕτως as an adverb denoting degree, found-

---

36. It has sometimes been argued that this makes ἤπιοι the "more difficult" reading in this case. But that implies, quite incorrectly in a case like this one, that a scribe was more conscious of how many times Paul used each word than he was of the sense of the immediate context. Scribes, after all, did not carry concordances with them, and ἤπιοι is a common enough word, even if found only once in the NT.

37. See G. D. Fee, *The First Epistle to the Corinthians* (Grand Rapids: Eerdmans, 1987), p. 679, n. 15. This point has also been made recently by Beverly Roberts Gaventa, "Apostles as Babes and Nurses in 1 Thessalonians 2:7," in *Faith and History: Essays in Honor of Paul W. Meyer,* ed. J. T. Carroll, C. H. Cosgrove, and E. E. Johnson (Atlanta: Scholars Press, 1991), p. 196.

38. And with asyndeton at that, which makes for triple jeopardy in terms of Pauline usage.

ers on Pauline usage elsewhere, not to mention ordinary Greek usage. There are simply no parallels in Paul where this adverb functions as the first member of its clause and intensifies a verb form. All other examples are correlative (either stated or implied).

On the other hand, the preferred textual choice, "babes," yields to a structural and syntactical arrangement that is quite in keeping with ordinary Pauline usage:

> Nor did we seek glory from people,
>> neither from you nor from others,
>>> although as apostles of Christ we could have made our weight
>>>> felt,
>> but we became babes among you.
> Even as a nurse cares for her own children,
>> so we, deeply yearning after you, were willing to impart to you. . . .

If this seems like an abrupt change of metaphors, it is so only if one thinks the "nurse" clause is syntactically related to the "babes" clause. But seen as separate sentences, they can be easily explained as in keeping with similar sudden shifts of metaphor elsewhere in Paul, where one metaphor triggers another in the apostle's mind, and thus are related primarily by "catchword" and not by consistency in application.

At this point, of course, the commentary needs to explain both the *sense* of the two metaphors and how they most likely function in the argument. Given that one can in fact make perfectly good sense of these metaphors in context — as concluding one and beginning another sentence[39] — one should all the more opt for the reading that best explains the existence of the other. It should be noted finally that although this discussion is somewhat longer than most textual discussion in a commentary, such can be justified here on two grounds: that the choice so thoroughly affects the meaning of the whole passage, and that several significant exegetical points are being made in the course of this discussion (especially as to the structures of Paul's argument).

---

39. As, e.g., does Gaventa, "Apostles" (n. 87). Even if one were disinclined toward her specific interpretations of the metaphors, she has demonstrated both the tenuousness of Malherbe's contention as to the Cynic background of "gentle as a nurse" and the possibility of making perfectly good sense of the two metaphors "babes" and "nurse" as one following the other.

b. 2 Thessalonians 2:13

Translation:

> *But we, on the other hand, are bound always to give thanks to God for you, brothers and sisters beloved by the Lord,*[40] *that God chose you to be firstfruits*[a] *for salvation by means of the sanctifying work of the Spirit and your own belief in the truth.*

The textual note reads as follows:

[a] On the surface, this is one of the more difficult textual choices in 2 Thessalonians (between ἀπαρχήν, "firstfruits" [B F G P 33 81 326 1739 it[c,dem,div,f,x,z] vg syr[h] cop[bo]] and ἀπ' ἀρχῆς "from the beginning" [ℵ D K L Ψ 104 181 pler it[ar,e,mon] syp[p] cop[sa]]). The external evidence is nearly evenly divided, both East and West. Nor is the change likely to have happened by pure accident (except in the sense noted below that a scribe looked at one thing but "saw" another). The commentaries and translations tend to favor ἀπ' ἀρχῆς (Best, Ellicott, Frame, Hendriksen, Hiebert, Marshall, Morris, Plummer, Thomas, Wanamaker; otherwise Weirs, Moffatt, Bruce), while the English translations are more divided ("from the beginning," KJV RSV NASB JB NEB; "firstfruits," NIV GNB NAB Moffatt Knox). Nonetheless, the weightier arguments both transcriptional and intrinsic point to ἀπαρχήν as the original text. Given its lack of theological grist in comparison with "from the beginning," it is easily the *lectio difficilior*. That this same interchange (from ἀπαρχή to ἀπ' ἀρχῆς) happens twice elsewhere in the NT (Rom. 16:5 [P[46] D* g m]; Rev. 14:4 [ℵ 336 1918]) illustrates the ease with which scribes, who were actually looking at one thing, in fact "saw" another (in each case ἀπαρχή lay before them; they "saw," or anticipated Paul to have said, ἀπ' ἀρχῆς). The primary argument usually raised against ἀπαρχήν is that the Thessalonians were not in fact the "firstfruits" of Macedonia; but this makes the rather unwarranted assumption that Paul would indeed have intended "of Macedonia" had he used this word (it is common to note that although Paul uses ἀπαρχή elsewhere [Rom. 8:23; 11:16; 16:5; 1 Cor. 15:20, 23; 16:15], only in Rom. 11:16 does he use it without a qualifying genitive [most recently Wanamaker, 266]). To the contrary, Paul almost certainly intended "the firstfruits of Thessalonica," wanting them to see themselves as the "firstfruits" of many more in Thessalonica who would come to know the Savior — despite (or as the result of?) the persecution that they are presently enduring. Added to this is the fact that when Paul elsewhere wishes to place something "in eternity," he never uses the phrase ἀπ' ἀρχῆς nor anything close to it (cf. 1 Cor. 2:7; Col. 1:26; Eph. 1:4).

The commentary reads as follows:

40. As argued for in the preceding section of this paper, in a commentary I would also note the reading of θεοῦ here by D* b m vg, as conforming to Pauline usage in 1 Thess. 1:4, but as thereby missing the trinitarian implications of Paul's inclusion of Christ in this sentence by this shift from "God" to "Lord."

As noted above (in note *a*), it is not absolutely certain as to how Paul in this case modifies the verb "God chose," whether he said "God chose you from the beginning for salvation," or whether he said, "God chose you as firstfruits for salvation." Although the textual evidence finally seems to be against it, what favors the former is Paul's strong emphasis in this passage on God's prior activity (where he is contrasting their "salvation" — and its security — with the "judgment" of the deceived in vv. 10-12). Thus he would be assuring them that God's choice of them is "from the beginning [of time, can be the only possible intent, if original]." Great confidence can indeed be gained from such theological reassurance.

Nonetheless, the textual arguments seem rather fully on the side of "firstfruits," which is likewise intended to be an encouraging word, but in a slightly different way. Since Paul does not qualify "firstfruits,"[41] he almost certainly intends them to see themselves as God's "firstfruits" in Thessalonica. Thus the imagery would function in two directions. First, it is intended to encourage them that right in the midst of those who are responsible for their present grief, who are described in vv. 10-12 as to their wickedness and eventual ruin, God has chosen a people for his own name — his firstfruits, if you will, of the great eschatological harvest alluded to in v. 14, a theme that recurs throughout this letter. At the same time, therefore, it would also function to encourage them that God has chosen still others from among their Thessalonian compatriots, who also shall escape the deception and resultant judgment and be "sanctified by the Spirit, as they believe the truth." If the believing community is relatively small and currently heavily persecuted, they need to hear that from the divine perspective, from the perspective of "God's having chosen them for salvation," there are many more — even from among their own townspeople — who will join them "for the obtaining of the glory of our Lord Jesus Christ."

These solutions and comments are not expected to satisfy all. But they are presented to this seminar both as plea and illustration for those who are involved in the writing of commentaries, that they take the textual task much more seriously than most currently tend to do.

---

41. As noted in n. a, this is often seen as condemning the choice of ἀπαρχήν in this passage, but that is hardly so. In fact, Paul qualifies this word geographically only in Rom. 16:5 and 1 Cor. 16:15, in both cases referring to individuals, with no particular emphasis on the "ingathering" of others. The qualifier "of the Spirit" in Rom. 8:23 is most likely appositional (the Spirit himself is the firstfruits, guaranteeing the future reality). In the other three cases, whether qualified or not, the metaphor images the "firstfruits" of a much greater "ingathering." That would seem to be precisely the point being made here, so that the lack of a genitive (geographical) qualifier is altogether irrelevant.

Appendix 1
Lists of Textual Variants in 1 Thessalonians
for the Survey in Appendix II

A. The 14 textual variants in 1 Thessalonians listed in Metzger's *Textual Commentary* (those with * are discussed in the *Commentary* but are not in the UBS[3] apparatus)

1.	1TH 1:1	omit	B F G Ψ 629 1739 1881 pc lat sy[p] sa
		ἀπὸ θεοῦ πατρὸς ἡμῶν καὶ κυρίου Ἰησοῦ Χριστοῦ	ℵ A (D) I Maj sy[h]
*2.	1TH 1:7	τύπον	B D 6 33 81 104 1739 1881 pc lat sy[p]
		τύπους	ℵ A C F G Ψ Maj sy[h]
3.	1TH 2:7	νήπιοι	p[65] ℵ B C* D* F G I Ψ* 104* 325[c] 2495 pc it vg[ww] bo Clem
		ἤπιοι	A 33 1739 Maj vg[st] sa[mss]
4.	1TH 2:12	καλοῦντος	B C D F G Ψ 33 1739 pler
		καλέσαντος	ℵ A 104 326 945 2464 pc a f vg sy co
5.	1TH 2:15	προφήτας	ℵ A B D* F G I P 0208 6 33 81 629 1739 1881 pc latt
		ἰδίων προφήτας	Ψ D[l] Maj sy
6.	1TH 3:2	συνέργον τοῦ θεοῦ	D* 33 b m* Ambrosiaster
		συνεργοῦ	B pc vg[mss]
		διάκονον τοῦ θεοῦ	ℵ A P Ψ 6 81 629 1241 1739
		διάκονον καὶ συνέργον τοῦ θεοῦ	Maj
7.	1TH 3:13	omit	B F G Ψ Maj it sy sa
		ἀμήν	ℵ A D 81 629 pc a m vg bo
*8.	1TH 4:1	καθὼς καὶ περιπατεῖτε	Rell
		omit	B* 33 629 630 1175 1739* vg[mss] sy[p] bo
*9.	1TH 4:9	ἔχετε	ℵ* A H Maj sy[p] co
		ἔχομεν	D* F G Ψ 6 104 365 1739 1881 2464 pc lat sy[h]
		εἴχομεν	B I t vg[mss]
*10.	1TH 4:15	κοιμωμένων	ℵ A B 33 81 326 1175 1739 pc Origen
		κεκοιμημένων	D (F G) Ψ Maj
11.	1TH 5:4	κλέπτης	Rell
		κλέπτας	A B bo[pt]
12.	1TH 5:21	δέ	B D G K P Ψ 181 326 436 1241 1739 Byz[pt] it sy[h] sa
		omit	ℵ* A 33 81 104 614 629 630 945 Byz[pt]
13.	1TH 5:25	καί	p[30] B D* 33 81 104 326 330 436 451 1739 1877 1881 2492
		omit	ℵ A G K P Ψ 88 Maj

14. 1TH 5:27 τοῖς ἀδελφοῖς   ℵ B D F G 431 436 1311 1907 2004 pc
             τοῖς ἁγίους ἀδελφοῖς   A K P Ψ 33 1739 Maj

B. An additional list of variants in 1 Thessalonians 1, culled from NA²⁶

15.	1:1	omit	Rell
		ἡμῶν	A 81 (629) pc a r vg^mss
16.	1:2	omit	ℵ* A B I 6 33 81 323 630 1739 1881
		ἡμῶν	C D F G Ψ Maj it sy
17.	1:5	ἐν³	ℵ B 33
		omit	Rell
18.	1:5	ἐν⁴	B D F G Ψ Maj
		omit	ℵ A C P 048 33 81 104 326 945 1739 1881 pc
19.	1:6	omit	B vg^mss
		καί	Rell
20.	1:8	ἐν τῇ	ℵ C D F G Ψ Maj lat
		omit	B K 6 33 365 614 629 630 1739 1881 al r vg^mss
21.	1:8	ἀλλ'	(ℵ*) A B C D* F G P Ψ 33 81 1739 1881 al
		ἀλλὰ καί	Maj m
22.	1:9	ἡμῶν	Rell
		ὑμῶν	B 81 323 614 629 630 945 al a d vg^mss
23.	4:8	διδόντα	ℵ B D F G I 365 2464 pc
		δόντα	A Ψ Maj sy co

Appendix 2

Nine English commentaries in relationship to the textual choices noted in Appendix 1 ["yes" means that there is at least a text-critical note, however inadequate; "no" means that the textual question is not mentioned at all]

	Milligan	Moffatt	Frame	Best	Thomas	Bruce	Marshall	Wanamaker	Morris
1.	yes	no	yes	no	yes	yes	no	no	no
2.	yes	yes	yes	no	yes	yes	no	no	no
3.	yes	yes	yes	yes	yes	yes	yes	yes	yes
4.	yes	no	yes	yes	no	yes	no	no	no
5.	yes	yes	yes	yes	no	yes	no	no	no
6.	yes	yes	yes	yes	yes	yes	yes	yes	yes
7.	yes	no	yes	yes	no	yes	no	yes	no
8.	yes	no	no	no	no	yes	yes	no	no
9.	no	yes	yes	no	no	yes	no	no	no
10.	no	no	yes	no	no	yes	no	no	yes
11.	yes	yes	yes	yes	yes	yes	yes	yes	yes
12.	yes	yes	yes	yes	yes	yes	no	yes	yes
13.	yes	no	yes	yes	yes	yes	yes	yes	yes
14.	yes	yes	yes	no	yes	yes	no	yes	yes
15.	no	no	no	no	no	yes	no	no	no
16.	no	no	yes	no	no	yes	no	yes	no
17.	no	no	yes	yes	yes	no	no	no	yes
18.	yes	no	yes	yes	yes	yes	no	no	yes
19.	no	no	no	no	no	yes	no	no	no
20.	no	yes	yes	no	yes	yes	no	no	yes
21.	no	no	yes	no	no	yes	no	no	no
22.	no	no	yes	yes	no	yes	yes	no	no
23.	yes	no	yes	yes	yes	yes	no	yes	yes

EXEGETICAL STUDIES

CHAPTER 6

Once More — John 7:37-39
(1978)

John 7:37-39 has long been a notorious crux. The basic problems, as formulated by R. E. Brown,[1] are: (1) Who is the source of the rivers of living water, Jesus or the believer? That is, to whom does the αὐτοῦ refer in v. 38? and (2) What passage of Scripture is cited in v. 38? These two questions are interrelated; for since there is *no* Old Testament passage that looks very much like v. 38, a series of passages can be mustered to support the two answers to question (1).

Ordinarily the solutions have been related to how one punctuates the whole of vv. 37-38.[2] On the one hand, the solution which is traditional in English translations (first found in Origen and supported by P[66]) is to make αὐτοῦ refer to the believer, whose antecedent, ὁ πιστεύων εἰς ἐμέ, functions grammatically as a *nominativus pendens*. Thus it is translated (RSV):

> "If anyone thirst, let him come to me and drink.
> He who believes in me, as the scripture has said,
> 'Out of his heart shall flow rivers of living water.'"

On the other hand, there is increasing support among scholars (though, interestingly, not among translations) for the "christological" interpretation, which can be traced as far back as Hippolytus. This solution puts a full stop,

---

1. *The Gospel According to John (i-xii)*, Anchor Bible 29 (Garden City, N.Y., 1966), pp. 320-21.

2. This note does not intend to list all the scholars or translations that support one view or the other. Brown, who supports the "christological" interpretation, has fairly complete listings. His presentation of that case is comprehensive. Since Brown, the commentaries by L. Morris (Grand Rapids, 1971) and B. Lindars (London, 1972) both favor the English tradition. The most recent and comprehensive presentation of this position may be found in J. B. Cortes, "Yet Another Look at Jn 7[37-38]," *Catholic Biblical Quarterly* 29 (1967): 75-86.

with quotation marks, after ὁ πιστεύων εἰς ἐμέ, which is thus understood to be the subject of the preceding πινέτω. Verse 38 then becomes a Johannine comment, and the αὐτοῦ is seen to refer to Jesus. Thus it is translated (NEB):[3]

"If anyone is thirsty let him come to me;
    whoever believes in me, let him drink.
As Scripture says, 'Streams of living water
    shall flow from within him.'"

As long as the questions are posed the way Brown poses them, the solutions appear to be stalemated — for obvious reasons: equal arguments can be mustered on either side. Stylistically it can be shown that the *nominativus pendens* is a recurring feature of Johannine style (see, e.g., 1:12; 6:39; 15:2; 17:2); but it is also true that the chiastic parallelism of the second solution fits Johannine style (cf. 6:35) and that the καθὼς εἶπεν ἡ γραφή formula is ordinarily the first member of its clause in the Fourth Gospel.[4] Likewise, either solution can gather a group of Old Testament texts which imply that the water of the new age more appropriately belongs either to the Messiah or to the believer.[5] Finally, either solution is fully in accord with Johannine theology, where Jesus is the one who pre-eminently has and gives the Spirit (1:33; 4:10; 7:39; 20:22), but also where the believer has (or will have) the Spirit "within him" (4:14; 14:17).

The purpose of this note is to suggest that the solution to these problems lies in framing the exegetical question in quite a different way. Barnabas Lindars has recently suggested: "In order to make a decision, John's own comment in v. 39 must be given due weight."[6] Exactly right. However, Lindars limits his comments to the *meaning* of v. 39 vis-à-vis vv. 37-38; I would suggest that the solution lies as well in the thoroughly Johannine stylistic feature at the beginning of v. 39: τοῦτο δὲ εἶπεν. The real question is, What did the au-

---

3. It should be noted in passing that although these are the two basic — and historic — interpretations, there have been others. Both C. F. Burney (*The Aramaic Origin of the Fourth Gospel;* Oxford, 1922) and C. C. Torrey ("The Aramaic Origin of the Gospel of John," *Harvard Theological Review* 16 [1923]: 305-34) found the solution in mistranslations of a hypothetical Aramaic original, where v. 38 referred to the Temple Mount (Burney) or Jerusalem (Torrey). J. Blenkinsopp has more recently argued that ὁ πιστεύων εἰς ἐμέ is a gloss, a mere parenthetical insertion to explain in the logion itself who are the believers in v. 39. See "John vii. 37-39: Another Note on a Notorious Crux," *NTS* 6 (1959): 95-98.

4. Cf. G. D. Kilpatrick, "The Punctuation of John vii. 37-38," *JTS*, n.s. 11 (1960): 340-42.

5. See E. D. Freed, *Old Testament Quotations in the Gospel of John* (Leiden, 1965), pp. 21-38.

6. Barnabas Lindars, *The Gospel of John* (London, 1972), p. 301.

thor intend by that editorial remark? To what did he intend τοῦτο to refer? Or to put it in another way, to whom did the author intend to attribute v. 38 (from καθώς on)? Are these the words of the Johannine Jesus, or are they the author's own comments?[7]

Once the question is posed in this way, the most viable exegesis of the passage is the traditional one. For the author of v. 39 almost certainly intended the content of v. 38 *to belong to the words of Jesus;* therefore, the most natural meaning of the third person pronoun αὐτοῦ is the believer, rather than the Messiah.

First, it should be noted that the stylistic feature τοῦτο δὲ εἶπεν is typically Johannine. Although the formula is not always the same, there are seven other instances in the gospel where the author (or redactor) similarly comments on or interprets what has been said:[8]

of Jesus' words

    2:21 ἐκεῖνος δὲ ἔλεγεν περὶ. . .

    6:6 τοῦτο δὲ ἔλεγεν πειράζων. . .

    6:71 ἔλεγεν δὲ τὸν ᾽Ιούδαν. . .

    12:33 τοῦτο δὲ ἔλεγεν σημαίνων. . .

    21:19 τοῦτο δὲ εἶπεν σημαίνων. . .

of Caiaphas's words

    11:51 τοῦτο δὲ ἀφ᾽ ἑαυτοῦ οὐκ εἶπεν. . .

of Judas's words

    12:6 εἶπεν δὲ τοῦτο οὐχ ὅτι. . .

In each instance the formula refers specifically to a saying that immediately precedes it. Therefore, τοῦτο δὲ εἶπεν περὶ τοῦ πνεύματος ὃ ἔμελλον λαμβάνειν οἱ πιστεύσαντες εἰς αὐτόν is a comment that includes the content of v. 38. Since the emphasis in the comment of v. 39 is clearly on the believer's reception of the Spirit, rather than the Messiah's *giving* the Spirit, this further supports αὐτοῦ as referring to the believer.[9]

7. This problem remains even if one assumes a variety of editors/redactors for the gospel. The exegete finally must interpret the text in its last form, not only hypothetical prior stages. For after all, the final form is the one we actually have; and the final redactor is himself interpreting the text, so that our interpretation must take this final view into account.

8. This does not include 11:13, which, because it lacks τοῦτο and has the perfect εἰρήκει, is a special case (see below). Nor does it include two other instances (13:11, 28) where the formula is a part of the Evangelist's "knowing/not knowing" editorial comments (cf. 2:22; 4:53; 8:27; 10:6; 11:13; 12:16; 16:19).

9. J. R. Michaels has recently offered a unique interpretation of τοῦτο δὲ εἶπεν. He sug-

One must insist, therefore, that the translation of the NEB creates something of an absurdity. By putting quotation marks around vv. 37-38a, the translators clearly intend "As Scripture says . . ." to be the comment of the evangelist. He then makes a further comment, which in this case must exclude the "rivers of living water" and refer back to vv. 37-38a. But in such a case one would expect him to have written εἰρήκει, precisely as he did in 11:13 where there is a break between Jesus' words and the evangelist's further comment.

Bultmann recognized the inherent difficulty of this kind of translation and argued (correctly) that it made "an inadmissible break between Jesus' words in vv. 37, 38a and v. 39." But his own solution is surely not correct — to argue that v. 38b is "a gloss, inserted by the ecclesiastical editor."[10] No one has followed Bultmann at this point, for good reasons: (1) Such a redactor would be expected to cite Scripture with enough accuracy as to make it identifiable. That is, if a later redactor is going to break into the text like this, one would expect him to do so because he had a precise text in mind, which this logion could be seen as fulfilling. (2) The content and style of v. 38 are thoroughly Johannine. (3) Most importantly, the τοῦτο δὲ εἶπεν demands the content of v. 38 in order to make sense. To make it refer to vv. 37-38a as do the NEB and Bultmann means that Jesus' invitation to the thirsty to come to him and the believer to drink of him somehow refers to the Spirit whom the believers were to receive. This makes *both* vv. 37 and 39 altogether too cryptic. Being cryptic, of course, would not in itself rule it out in the Gospel of John, but it would certainly be out of keeping with the other explanatory comments in the gospel.

Bultmann is correct that the τοῦτο δὲ εἶπεν must refer to what immediately precedes; the NEB is correct in leaving v. 38 there, because even by mistake (or careless writing) the author intended τοῦτο δὲ εἶπεν to refer to what he himself had said in that verse.

R. E. Brown offers yet another option, although there seems to be ambiguity in his commentary. On the one hand, his translation includes all of vv. 37-38 within quotation marks. This means that in the gospel's final form Jesus spoke the words of v. 38, and thereby referred to himself in the third person.

---

gests that "the δὲ which introduced v. 39 should thus be taken in at least a mildly adversative sense. The close proximity of εἶπεν in v. 39 to the same form in v. 38 suggests that what is being *directly* qualified is the Scripture quotation." Thus he translates v. 39: "But it [i.e., the Scripture] said this about the Spirit." See "The Temple Discourse in John," in *New Dimensions in New Testament Study,* ed. R. N. Longenecker and M. C. Tenney (Grand Rapids, 1974), pp. 208-9. The difficulty with this would seem to be its uniqueness. Elsewhere the τοῦτο δὲ εἶπεν formula always refers to a spoken word, and the implied subject of εἶπεν is the speaker. There seems to be no good reason to abandon that pattern here.

10. *The Gospel of John: A Commentary* (Eng. trans. Oxford, 1971), p. 303, n. 5.

But that seems to make the author far more careless than one ordinarily finds him to be. Since the Old Testament "text" is as loosely constructed as it is, why did he not simply say, "From the Messiah shall flow rivers of living water"?

Brown himself, however, recognizes the problem this creates and attributes v. 39 to the final redactor,[11] suggesting that it "has a parenthetical character which makes us wonder if it represents the primary meaning of 37-38."[12] But this seems to solve the problem in reverse order: to predetermine (for good reasons, to be sure) that the αὐτοῦ of v. 38 must refer to Jesus, and then to find v. 39 somewhat out of step with that interpretation. Furthermore, every stylistic feature in v. 39 is thoroughly Johannine: τοῦτο δὲ εἶπεν; the use of μέλλω for things that *have already happened* from the author's perspective (cf., e.g., 6:71; 11:51; 12:4, 33; 18:32); εἰς αὐτόν with πιστεύω; the anarthrous Ἰησοῦς following ὅτι;[13] the entire vocabulary is distinctively Johannine.

Therefore, since all other arguments are stalemated, and are usually resolved by what one thinks is more in accord with Johannine theology, Lindars is surely right. The solution lies in v. 39, where both the τοῦτο δὲ εἶπεν and the emphasis there on the believer's reception of the Spirit break the deadlock and decide in favor of the tradition of the English-language translations.[14]

---

11. *The Gospel of John: A Commentary,* p. 324.

12. *The Gospel of John: A Commentary,* p. 328.

13. See G. D. Fee, "The Use of the Definite Article with Personal Names in the Gospel of John," *NTS* 17 (1971): 179.

14. The question of what scripture is being cited in v. 38 is beyond the concern of this note. In any case, since no OT passage fits precisely, the answer to that question cannot have priority as to whom αὐτοῦ refers. Probably Freed is correct here (*Old Testament Quotations in the Gospel of John,* p. 37): "It appears more likely that John was motivated by a combination of several passages and then from memory wrote down a quotation to support his theology."

CHAPTER 7

1 Corinthians 7:1 in the NIV
(1980)

In a public response to an open question, I was once quoted (correctly) by *Christianity Today* as commending the *NIV* for being "gutsy" in its translation methodology.[1] I meant by that that they were willing to make tough choices about the meaning of texts and that they translated according to those choices rather than trying to escape through the safe route of ambiguity.

I still stand by my former applause. Being courageous in translation also has its obvious pitfalls, however, especially when the wrong choice misleads the reader as to the meaning of the text. There is one such text in the *NIV* that has regularly given me concern, especially so now that the whole Bible is available and the revision of the NT has neither corrected what seems to many of us to be a mistranslation nor offered even a marginal note to the (more surely correct) alternative.[2]

The text is 1 Cor. 7:1, translated in the *NIV*: "Now for the matters you wrote about: It is good for a man not to marry."[3] My problem with this trans-

1. See *Christianity Today* 21 (January 21, 1977): 42 [462]. It should be noted that I was not one of the *NIV* translators. Cf. my letter to the editor (March 4, 1977): 8 [616].

2. My urgency to write this paper was finally prompted by a recent evaluation of "The Literary Merit of the New International Version" by L. Ryken (*Christianity Today* 23 [October 20, 1978]: 16-17 [76-77]). He says: "And I hope it will dispel some follies to read that 'it is good for a man not to marry' instead of 'not to touch a woman.'" I fear that this translation creates even greater follies.

3. The *NIV* is not the first so to translate. I checked over thirty of the nearly eighty English translations since 1900. Those that translate "to marry" are *Twentieth Century* (1898), *Weymouth* (1903), *Goodspeed* (1923), *Williams* (1937), *Amplified* (1968), *Living Bible* (1962), *TEV* (1966). My reason for "picking on" the *NIV* is precisely because I think it is such a good translation and, contrary to Ryken (see n. 2), I wish to see it have long usefulness as a pew Bible. While it is true that no translation will please all the people all the time — and I have several other

lation is twofold: philological (the meaning of *gynaikos haptesthai* = literally "to touch a woman") and exegetical (the meaning of the whole chapter, and especially of vv. 1-7). The purpose of this paper is (1) to present all of the available philological evidence, which seems so incontrovertible as to render the translation "to marry" to be without foundation; (2) to offer an exegesis of 7:1 in light of the whole of 1 Corinthians 7, which argues that the ordinary meaning of the idiom makes the most sense here; and (3) to suggest that such an interpretation fits well with current thinking as to the nature of the Corinthian false theology. If the reconstruction of the Corinthian position is somewhat speculative, it is not so with the philological evidence or the exegesis.

I. The Meaning of the Idiom

The idiom *haptesthai gynaikos* or its equivalent occurs at least seven times (excepting our passage) in extant literature from antiquity from the fourth century B.C. to the second century A.D. In all of these occurrences it is a euphemism for sexual intercourse, and in not one of them is there the slightest hint that the idiom extends to something very close to "take a wife" or "marry." The evidence (in roughly chronological order):

(1) Plato *Leges* 8.840a: "During all the period of his training (as the story goes) he never touched a woman *(gynaikos hēpsato),* nor yet a boy." (LCL 11.162-163)

(2) Aristotle *Politica* 7.14.12: "As to intercourse with another woman or man, in general it must be dishonourable *(mē kalon)* to be known to take any part in it *(haptomenon)* in any circumstances whatsoever as long as one is a husband." (LCL 21.624-625)

(3) Gen. 20:6 LXX (of Abimelech with Sarah): "That is why I did not let you touch her *(hapsasthai autēs)." (NIV)* Cf. Ruth 2:9 LXX: "I have told the men not to touch you *(hapsasthai sou)." (NIV)*

(4) Prov. 6:29 LXX: "So is he who sleeps with another man's wife; no one who touches her *(ho haptomenos autēs)* will go unpunished." *(NIV)*

(5) Plutarch *Alex. M.* 21.4: "But Alexander . . . neither laid hands upon these women, nor did he know any other before marriage, except Barsine. This woman . . . was taken prisoner at Damascus. And since she had a Greek education, . . . Alexander determined . . . to attach himself to a

---

places where I think the *NIV* could be improved — for many of us who teach NT, and especially 1 Corinthians, its handling of this text seems to be a glaring error.

woman *(hapsasthai gynaikos)* of such high birth and beauty." (LCL 7.284-285)

(6) Josephus *Ant.* 1.163: "The King of the Egyptians . . . was fired with a desire to see her and on the point of laying hands on her *(hapsasthai tēs Sarras)*. But God thwarted his criminal passion." (LCL 4.80-81)

(7) Marcus Aurelius *Ant.* 1.17.6: "That I did not touch Benedicta or Theodotus *(mēte Benediktēs hapsasthai mēte Theodotou)*, but that even afterwards, when I did give way to amatory passions, I was cured of them." (LCL, pp. 22-23) Cf. Josephus *Ant.* 4.257: "Should a man have taken prisoner . . . a woman . . . and wish to live with her, let him not be permitted to approach her couch *(eunēs hapsasthai)* and consort with her until. . . ." (LCL 4.598-599)

Given this overwhelming philological evidence, one might wonder how the translators of the *NIV* and their predecessors ever translated the text "to marry." The answer of course lies in their understanding of the context,[4] which sees the whole chapter as addressing the question of "to marry or not to marry" and vv. 1-7 as an introduction to the whole. Thus it is suggested that on this question Paul prefers celibacy (v. 1) but that because of sexual passions (v. 2 interpreted in light of vv. 9, 36) he concedes marriage (vv. 2, 6). If there is a marriage, then there should be full sexual relations (vv. 3-4) except for occasional periods of abstinence for prayer (v. 5). In v. 7, however, Paul reverts to his initial preferences expressed in v. 1. Since Paul so clearly affirms sexual relations in vv. 3-5 it is hard for these interpreters to believe that he would deny them in v. 1, and hence the idiom — with no philological support — is expanded into "to marry."[5]

As common as that interpretation has been, it seems to be faced with several insuperable difficulties. Not only is the meaning of the idiom *haptesthai gynaikos* against it, but this interpretation leads to two further

4. See, e.g., the arguments in F. W. Grosheide, *Commentary on the First Epistle to the Corinthians* (NICNT; Grand Rapids: Eerdmans, 1963), pp. 154-56; L. Morris, *The First Epistle of Paul to the Corinthians* (Tyndale NT Commentary; London: Tyndale, 1958), pp. 105-6.

For the translators of the *NIV* the context apparently included an understanding of 6:12-20 as well. One of the anomalies of the translation is that quotation marks indicating the Corinthian point of view are found only at 6:12-13 and 10:23 (at 8:1 — but not 8:4! — there is a marginal note). Apparently, since they considered 6:12-13 to reflect the Corinthian point of view they cannot imagine that 7:1b could also come from Corinth.

5. Morris, *First Epistle,* p. 105, simply asserts: "In this context *touch* refers to marriage." Grosheide acknowledges that the idiom is "a euphemism for sexual intercourse" but then goes on to say that it is a "question whether or not one should marry" (*Commentary,* p. 155).

anomalies. First, it promotes an understanding of the whole chapter that seems to avoid, or abuse, the clear structural signal *peri de* ("now concerning") in 7:25. Thus Paul's argument is seen to move to and fro from celibacy and marriage (vv. 1-7), to marriage once again (vv. 8-9), to divorce (vv. 10-16), and back to marriage twice again (virgins in vv. 25-38 and widows in vv. 39-40). Second, this interpretation fails to do justice to vv. 1-7, since it sees the main concern (vv. 3-5) as a digression and the surrounding matter as the main point.

II. The Structure of the Chapter

Any valid interpretation of 1 Corinthians 7 must take seriously the probability that the *peri de* in 7:25 functions as do all the other occurrences of *peri de* in 1 Corinthians (8:1; 12:1; 16:1, 12; cf. 15:1) — to take up a new topic from the Corinthian letter to Paul. That seems clearly to be the case here. There are two recurring terms in vv. 25-38 that control the discussion throughout: *parthenos* = "virgin" (vv. 25, 28, 34, 36, 37, 38) and *gameō/gamizō* = "to marry" (vv. 28 [2], 33, 34, 36, 38 [2]). The term *parthenos* does not occur in vv. 1-24; the verb *gameō*, in the sense of "get married," occurs in vv. 1-24 only in v. 9 in connection with the widowed, a theme to which Paul returns in vv. 39-40.

There is of course a long debate as to the meaning of *parthenos* in this section. But at the very least it refers to a young woman who has not yet been married. Verses 36-38, which are to be seen as the conclusion of the whole section and not some additional special case (as by Conzelmann),[6] make it abundantly clear that the *parthenos* refers to one who has not yet been married. Furthermore, the apparent distinction in v. 34 between "virgin" and *hē gynē hē agamos* (= "unmarried woman") suggests that the "virgin" is a special class of unmarried woman distinguishable from others. The best solution to all the data is that which understands the "virgin" to be a young woman engaged to be married.[7]

But the significant point here is that in 7:25 Paul begins a new topic, whether or not the never-before-married should get married. It follows,

---

6. H. Conzelmann, *A Commentary on the First Epistle to the Corinthians* (Hermeneia; trans. J. W. Leitch; Philadelphia: Fortress, 1975), pp. 134-36.

7. There is a considerable tradition that sees this section as referring to celibate marriage (as in the *NEB*). For the most recent argument of this point of view see J. C. Hurd, *The Origin of I Corinthians* (London: SPCK, 1965), pp. 169-82. For the point of view adopted here see J. K. Elliott, "Paul's Teaching on Marriage in I Corinthians: Some Problems Considered," *NTS* 19 (1973): 219-25.

therefore, that 7:1-24 is most likely not dealing with marriage at all in the sense of getting married (except of course vv. 8-9). What then?

The clue to 7:1-24 lies in the clear structural arrangement of vv. 8-16, where Paul in successive paragraphs speaks *tois agamois kai tais chērais* (v. 8; *NIV:* "to the unmarried and the widows"), *tois de gegamēkosin* (v. 10; *NIV:* "to the married"), and *tois de loipois* (v. 12; *NIV:* "to the rest"). Of the four classes mentioned, three (the widows, the married, the rest) are clearly groups of people who are now or at one time were married. W. F. Orr pointed out several years ago[8] that the *agamois* of v. 8 are masculine and the *chērais* feminine, thus continuing the balanced pairs from vv. 2-4. He further points out, from LSJ, that *agamos is* the ordinary word in Greek for "widower." And since widows would already be included among the "unmarried" in the term *agamos,* why should they be singled out unless they are the female counterpart to the *agamoi?* This evidence, plus the fact that Paul takes up the question of the not-yet-married in v. 25, makes a strong case for "widower and widow" as the proper meaning of vv. 8-9. This suggests therefore that all of vv. 8-16 is addressed to people who are or who have been married. If that is the case, then how do vv. 1-7 function? Surely not as an introduction to vv. 8-9 and then to the new topic of vv. 25-40, but rather as the first step in an argument with the Corinthians about behavior within marriage.

III. The Meaning of 7:1-7

The heart of this paragraph takes up a very singular concern: mutual sexual responsibility within marriage. Indeed, as we shall see, the imperatives in vv. 2-5 are directed toward married couples living in full marital cohabitation, and the single prohibition (*mē apostereite,* v. 5) is for the Corinthians to "stop depriving one another." One wonders therefore why Paul would take such a forceful stance on this matter, if he were merely taking up the question of "getting married" or, better, not "getting married." The clue to all of this of course lies in v. 1. But since our understanding of that verse is the controversial point, let us begin with v. 2.

V. 2. In many ways this is the crucial text. At least it is the context for those who think v. 1 has to do with not getting married. All interpreters are agreed that the *de* ("but") in v. 2 has strong adversative force. The question is

8. W. F. Orr, "Paul's Treatment of Marriage in 1 Corinthians 7," *Pittsburgh Perspective* 8 (1967): 5-22, esp. 12-14.

whether Paul is qualifying his preference for celibacy by conceding marriage, or whether he is rejecting the Corinthians' advocacy of marital celibacy. All of the language of v. 2 argues for the latter.

If v. 1 means "not to marry," then the imperative "let each man/woman have his/her own wife/husband" must mean that men and women should seek marriage. The problem with this interpretation — besides the difficulties in the words "each one" and "his own" — is that the idiom "to have a wife/husband (or woman/man)" occurs frequently in antiquity but in no known instance does it mean to acquire a mate.

For example, the idiom occurs eight times in the LXX[9] and nine times in the NT.[10] In some cases it has the minimal meaning of "have" in the sense that one has anything (with scarcely any emphasis on possession). Thus Absalom "had eighteen wives and thirty [v.l., sixty] concubines" (2 Chron. 11:21; cf. 1 Esdr. 9:12, 18). Sometimes in the LXX it means "to have sexually" (Exod. 2:1; Deut. 28:30; Isa. 13:16). More often it means to be married or to be in continuing sexual relations with a man or woman. Thus Herod has his brother's wife (Mark 6:18); the seven brothers have the same woman as a wife (Luke 20:33); the Samaritan woman has had five men, and the one she now has is not her husband (John 4:18). Similarly Josephus (*Ant.* 4.259) rewrites Deuteronomy 21:14 to speak of the man as disdaining to have the woman as his spouse. More significantly, this usage with strong sexual overtones is found elsewhere in 1 Corinthians (5:1, a man is having his father's wife; cf. 7:29).

If this normal usage is also what Paul intends in 7:2, then the imperative "let each man/woman have his/her own wife/husband" assumes marriage and is encouraging married partners to continue marriage. This will involve both continuing in full sexual relationships (vv. 3-5) and not dissolving marriages through divorce (vv. 10-16).

This meaning of the imperatives in v. 2 also makes sense of the other troublesome words in this sentence: "because of the fornications," "each man/woman," and "his/her own."

The term "each man/woman" along with "his/her own" has always created trouble for the traditional interpretation. The text should mean literally that everyone is to get married but only to his or her own spouse. Since that makes little sense, we are variously told that the terms "imply monogamy"[11]

---

9. Exod. 2:1; Deut. 28:30; 2 Chron. 11:21; 1 Esdr. 9:12, 18; Tob. 3:8 (BA); Isa. 13:16; 54:1.

10. Mark 6:18; 12:33 (= Matt. 22:28; Luke 20:33); Luke 20:28; John 4:18 *(bis);* 1 Cor. 5:1; 7:29.

11. See, e.g., Grosheide, *Commentary,* 155; cf. A. Robertson and A. Plummer, *A Critical and Exegetical Commentary on the First Epistle of St. Paul to the Corinthians* (ICC; Edinburgh: T. & T. Clark, 1911), p. 133.

or mean "as a general rule."[12] There is no difficulty with the terms at all, however, given the ordinary meaning of the idiom "to have a wife." Paul simply means: "Let each man who is already married continue in relations with his own wife, and each wife likewise."

This interpretation also makes sense of *dia tas porneias* ("because of the fornications"). The traditional view must make this mean "to avoid fornication"[13] in the sense of premarital promiscuity. But much more likely this phrase is to be understood in light of the similar phrase in v. 5: *dia tēn akrasian hymōn* ("because of your lack of self-control"). This latter phrase can refer only to extramarital sexual intercourse, since it is in the context of Paul's conceding temporary abstinence for married couples. Most likely, therefore, "because of the fornications" in v. 1 has direct reference to 6:12-20, where men (probably married men) were going to the *pornai* (probably the temple prostitutes).

Vv. 3-4. Given this meaning of v. 2, then vv. 3-4 further elaborate by emphasizing two things: (1) that sexual relations are a "due" within marriage (v. 3), and (2) that there must be full mutuality in this matter (v. 4). It should be noted in passing how totally unlike anything else one finds in antiquity (and even in many moderns as well) is the emphasis in v. 4. Sex is not something the husband does to his wife. The wife "possesses" her husband's body in the same way he does hers.

Vv. 5-6. Again, this emphasis on conjugal rights and mutuality makes little sense for the traditional view. But it makes full sense in light of the prohibition in v. 5. It is true that the present tense of a prohibition like *mē apostereite* in Paul may mean nothing stronger than "while we are on the subject, do not forbid sex to one another either, except by mutual consent and for prayer." But it is much more likely, given the urgencies of this whole paragraph, that what Paul intends is the full force of the present *Aktionsart*: "Stop depriving one another." For it is precisely such deprivation that they are probably arguing for and that Paul is here contesting. The point of v. 5 is clear: Sexual abstinence within marriage is not the norm. It may be allowed, but it is only to be temporary, by mutual consent and for prayer.

In v. 6, however, Paul makes it clear that such abstinence is not necessar-

12. See C. Hodge, *An Exposition of the First Epistle to the Corinthians* (New York: Carter, 1860), p. 109.

13. See, e.g., Hodge (*An Exposition*), who actually translates: "Nevertheless, to avoid fornication. . . ." Cf. also the comments by Robertson-Plummer, Grosheide, and Morris.

ily to be desired. It is only a concession — and most likely in this case a concession to the Corinthians' own position. To take the *touto* ("this") to refer back to v. 2 is perhaps the most difficult feature of the traditional view, since it forces one to disregard Paul's emphases in vv. 3-5 as almost irrelevant.

V. 7. This is the sentence, of course, that has seemed to give the strongest support to the traditional interpretation. This is especially so since Paul seems to repeat the *hōs kai emauton* ("as I am") in the context of not getting married in v. 8 *(hōs kagō).* But these two sentences do not necessarily refer to the same thing. There is little question that Paul is both single and celibate and that he demands celibacy of all singles. But celibacy and singleness are not identical ideas, especially in a context where some are arguing for celibacy (abstinence from sexual relations) within marriage. What then does v. 7 mean?

Paul at this point seems to be affirming their position in v. 1. But true celibacy as a *charisma* does not mean simply singleness. Rather, as Barrett following Bachmann argues,[14] it means to be completely free from any need of sexual fulfillment. Celibacy of this kind, however, is a gift. It is equally clear to Paul that not all are so gifted. Thus in principle he can agree that it is "good for a man not to have relations with a woman." But this is true only for the single, not the married.

V. 1. All of this leads us to argue, therefore, that v. 1 not only means that "a man is better off having no relations with a woman" *(NAB)*[15] but also, as many have suggested,[16] that this is a position being argued by the Corinthians themselves in their letter. The basic reason for seeing it as their position is the fact that Paul so sharply contradicts it in vv. 2-5. But who among the Corinthians was saying this — and why?

IV. The Corinthian Position

The current debate over the nature of the problem in Corinth to which 1 and 2 Corinthians is directed revolves around two foci: (1) The relationship of the party strife in 1:10-12 to the other issues addressed in 1 Corinthians, and

14. C. K. Barrett, *The First Epistle to the Corinthians* (HNTC: New York: Harper, 1968), p. 158.

15. This translation is excellent in two respects: (1) It keeps the euphemistic nature of the original idiom; (2) at the same time it preserves the meaning of the original.

16. See the table in Hurd, *Origin*, p. 68, for a partial list, which should also include Hurd himself.

(2) the nature of the Corinthian false theology. It is not my purpose here to try even to survey the give-and-take of these debates.[17] Rather I shall simply state the positions that I find most convincing and then show how these might be reflected in Paul's answer in 1 Corinthians 7.

It seems most likely, as Hurd has argued,[18] that the Corinthian letter to Paul is not from one of the parties in the Church but from the community as a whole. Furthermore, Hurd seems quite correct also in seeing their letter as over against Paul (= "why can't we?" or "why shouldn't we?"), not as a friendly seeking of advice (= "Paul, what do you think about . . . ?"). With regard to the Corinthian false theology I am persuaded by the view that sees their problem as basically an over-realized eschatology informed by an improper understanding of spiritual enthusiasm. While I agree with Thiselton that it is quite "unnecessary to resort to theories about gnostic influences there,"[19] it seems to me most probable that some form of Hellenistic dualism entered into their understanding of being "spiritual."

If this is a correct view of things, then the problem in ch. 7 is probably a direct reflection of their over-realized eschatology combined with their Hellenistic dualism. On the one hand they were arguing that they should be living out their new eschatological existence both by abstaining from sex within marriage[20] (or by divorce, if marital celibacy will not work) and by denying marriage to the "virgins." This argument is reinforced by their low view of the body, reflected elsewhere in 6:12-20 and 15:1-58. This would be very similar to the position that Paul is attacking in ch. 15, where they are denying both a future resurrection and the bodily nature of such a resurrection (from their point of view, "who needs it?").

Thus they have taken as a basic premise: In light of our new existence it is "good for a man not to have relations with a woman" — even within marriage. Nor should the widowed (or unmarried) seek marriage, since they are already freed from it. And since abstinence might be too difficult for some,[21]

---

17. On the first issue see Hurd, *Origin*, pp. 117-25, 155-58, 164-65. For a good recent overview of the second issue see A. C. Thiselton, "Realized Eschatology at Corinth," *NTS* 24 (1978): 510-26.

18. Hurd, *Origin*, passim.

19. Thiselton, "Realized Eschatology," p. 525.

20. Hurd (*Origin*, pp. 276-77) suggests that there might be a tie with Mark 12:24-25 and parallels — that is, the Corinthians were trying to be "like the angels" in the present age.

21. Hurd, who divorces this section from the concern in vv. 1-7 (*Origin*, p. 167), seems to miss the force of this argument. He says: "If Christian couples were willing to practice intramarital asceticism, then divorce would seem to serve no useful function." But it is precisely because some may have been unwilling to do so that their spouses would be seeking divorce.

then surely divorce is a viable alternative — most certainly so when the marriage partner whom "one touches" is an unbeliever. This same view would also be the reason for their arguing that the "virgins" should never get married.

Paul's answer is consistent throughout. In principle he agrees with their premise: It is good, from his own point of view, for a man not to have relations with a woman. But he altogether rejects their applying it to the marriage relationship. Furthermore, divorce is not permissible except under the circumstance that the pagan partner seeks it — never the Christian.

In 7:25-40 Paul is caught in something of a dilemma. He agrees with their premise but disagrees with their reasons for holding it. Thus he cannot appear to agree overmuch, lest it reinforce their own false theology. As a result Paul makes some strong affirmations of marriage and gives some different grounds for celibacy.

Admittedly there is a real problem with this reconstruction. How does one explain 6:12-20, where just a few sentences earlier the Corinthians seem to have taken quite the opposite position?[22] The usual response to this problem is that the Corinthian false theology, especially the denigration of the body, can logically move in two directions: asceticism (the body is evil, so deny it) or libertinism (the body is irrelevant, so indulge it).[23] While this is altogether possible — indeed, given their arguments in 6:12-13 and 7:1, most probable — one nonetheless wonders whether they might not have had a different view toward sexual relations within and without the community of faith.

It is of interest to note that in 6:12-20 every word reflecting the believer is masculine, while the *pornē* is clearly a female prostitute.[24] On the other hand everything in 7:1-16 is set out in balanced pairs so as always to include the female believer. And in 7:10 Paul's answer implies that the wife is the one seeking divorce — a known but rare occurrence in antiquity. It seems alto-

22. It should be noted that the juxtaposition of 6:12-20 and 7:1-40 is a problem for any interpretation of the letter — except for those who deny the unity of 1 Corinthians.

23. See, e.g., W. Barclay, *The Letters to the Corinthians* (2nd edn.; Philadelphia: Westminster, 1956), pp. 65-66.

24. I suggested earlier that this is probably temple prostitution. There are two reasons for this: (1) Paul's ordinary use of the temple imagery refers to the local church as a whole (1 Cor. 3:16-17; 2 Cor. 6:16; cf. Eph. 2:21). Why then does he take the same image and here apply it to individual believers? Most likely because the temples were where the problem literally lay. (2) The phrase *pheugete tēn porneian* has its exact counterpart in Paul only at the other place where the Corinthians are arguing for going to the temples (*pheugete apo tēs eidōlolatreias*, 1 Cor. 10:14). See G. D. Fee, "II Corinthians vi.14–vii.1 and Food Offered to Idols," *NTS* 23 (1977): 140-61, esp. 148-54.

gether possible that the wives are responsible for 7:1b[25] while at the same time they are urging their husbands to go to the temple prostitutes if they need sexual fulfillment. That is, they were arguing for "no sex" within Christian marriage (7:1, 5) as a reflection of life in the new age but for "free sex" down at the temples for those who had not yet attained new-age maturity with regard to bodily appetites. For those whose husbands still wanted sexual relations within marriage they would argue for the right to divorce.

V. Conclusion

It should be noted in conclusion that the exegesis of 7:1-7 is in no way dependent on the reconstruction of the Corinthian position argued for in this paper. Such a reconstruction is contended for only as making good sense of the data. The exegesis of 7:1-7 here presented, however, is contended for as the only interpretation that adequately deals with all the data of that paragraph. The idiom *haptesthai gynaikos* simply cannot be extended to mean "to marry." The ambiguous "not to touch a woman" of the *KJV* is better than that. Preferable is a true dynamic equivalent, such as "to have relations with," that keeps the euphemistic nature of the original and at the same time has the same meaning as the original.

25. J. Moffatt (*The First Epistle to the Corinthians* [MNTC; New York/London: Harper, 1938], p. 78) had earlier argued that 7:10 reflects the position of the "feminist party in the local church." I have not found this suggestion taken up elsewhere.

The problem with this possibility of course is that in the slogan, "It is good for a man not to have sexual relations with a woman," the "woman" has been narrowed to mean only his wife, while apparently it would not be true of prostitutes — hence the tentative nature of this suggestion.

CHAPTER 8

ΧΑΡΙΣ in 2 Corinthians 1:15: Apostolic Parousia and Paul-Corinth Chronology (1978)

The clause ἵνα δευτέραν χάριν σχῆτε in 2 Cor. 1:15 has long been an exegetical crux. The clause interrupts, by way of explanation, an otherwise clear presentation of Paul's previous plans about visits to Corinth. With four infinitive phrases joined by καί, Paul says he planned (a) to come to Corinth first,[1] (b) to go through Corinth to Macedonia, (c) to return to Corinth from Macedonia, and (d) to be sent by the Corinthians to Judea. The ἵνα-clause is inserted after the first infinitive and explains why he had intended to make two visits. The explanation was apparently necessary because, on the one hand, this plan reflected a clear change from 1 Cor. 16:5-7, and because, on the other hand, the second part (phrases c and d above) of this new plan had not been carried out. The question is, what did Paul mean by δευτέραν χάριν? How would his saying this help to alleviate the problem of his twofold change of plans in coming to Corinth?

Although a variety of nuances have been offered as to how this is to be taken, interpreters have been almost unanimous in suggesting that the χάριν is active from Paul's perspective and passive from the Corinthians'. That is, χάριν is something to be received by the Corinthians as a result of Paul's being present with them twice on this proposed journey rather than once. Thus χάριν is variously translated as "benefit,"[2] "kindness,"[3] "blessing,"[4] "opportu-

---

1. This follows the majority of interpreters and translations in taking πρότερον to go with ἐλθεῖν rather than ἐβουλόμην. See the argument in Hans Windisch, *Der zweite Korintherbrief* (Göttingen, 1970), pp. 61-62.

2. AV, RV, NEB, JerusBib, NIV; J. Calvin, J. J. Lias, J. Denney, P. E. Hughes.

3. C. K. Barrett, *Commentary* (London, 1973), p. 69.

4. NASB, Berkeley, TEV.

nity of spiritual profit,"[5] "mark of esteem,"[6] or "proof of goodwill."[7] The text of this interpretation may be displayed thus:

(a) ἐβουλόμην <u>πρότερον πρὸς ὑμᾶς ἐλθεῖν</u>,
     (ἵνα δευτέραν χάριν σχῆτε)
(b)   καὶ δι' ὑμῶν διελθεῖν εἰς Μακεδονίαν,
(c) καὶ <u>πάλιν</u> ἀπὸ Μακεδονίας <u>ἐλθεῖν πρὸς ὑμᾶς</u>,
(d)   καὶ ὑφ' ὑμῶν προπεμφθῆναι εἰς τὴν Ἰουδαίαν.

The emphasis here is on phrases (a) and (c) with their corresponding equivalents: πρότερον πρὸς ὑμᾶς ἐλθεῖν and πάλιν ἐλθεῖν πρὸς ὑμᾶς.

The purpose of this note is to offer an alternative to this traditional interpretation. I suggest that Paul's emphasis is on phrases (b) and (d) and that χάρις here is active from the perspective of the Corinthians. What Paul is saying is not that they will receive χάρις twice because of his presence, but that they will experience it twice *as they help him along the way*. In such a case the emphasis is not on πρὸς ὑμᾶς ἐλθεῖν but δι' ὑμῶν διελθεῖν (with δι' ὑμῶν here denoting agency)[8] and ὑφ' ὑμῶν προπεμφθῆναι. The whole sentence would thus be translated: "I planned to visit you first, so that you might have a double opportunity for kindness. I planned by means of you to go to Macedonia, and then to come back to you from Macedonia and have you send me on my way to Judea."

I

Χάρις, of course, has been the troublesome word. It is not that it cannot bear the traditional meaning of "benefit" or "favor" — it obviously can — but that such a usage is altogether unusual for Paul. Χάρις as "favor" is generally limited to Luke in the New Testament (Acts 2:47; 7:10; cf. Luke 1:30; Acts 4:33; 7:46). In Paul the word is always filled with theological content, even in the "collection" passages noted in this paper.[9] Furthermore, it seems highly un-

5. Ronald Knox.
6. E. B. Allo (Barrett's translation).
7. Bauer-Arndt-Gingrich.
8. While it is granted that διά with διέρχομαι would ordinarily mean nothing more than "through," the argument of this paper is that Rom. 16:22-29 is the clue to much of what is said here, both conceptually and linguistically. In the Romans passage, where it is abundantly clear that his basic reason for coming to Rome was to be sent on his way by them, he concludes by saying: ἀπελεύσομαι δι' ὑμῶν εἰς Σπανίαν.
9. The only other place in Paul where χάρις could bear the meaning it is traditionally

likely in this context. One must grant that Paul had a rather large view of the "apostolic parousia."[10] Indeed, anyone who could tell a church that he would come to them ἐν πληρώματι εὐλογίας Χριστοῦ (Rom. 15:29) could also see his parousia as χάρις for the church. Nonetheless, it is difficult to escape the latent egotism and condescension that the traditional translations imply.

Interpreters have long felt these difficulties and in various ways have hedged on χάρις. The earliest attempt to overcome the problem was to change χάριν to χαράν (read by B L P bo pc Theodoret), thus softening the idea from "grace received" to "joy experienced." This is so attractive that some have argued for χαράν as original. Thus B. B. Warfield affirms that "assuredly this is the right reading" and interprets the clause to mean: "He was confident, at that time, that his coming would bring joy."[11] But χαράν is surely secondary for the very reason that it alleviates the difficulty in finding a proper meaning for χάριν. Others have followed Chrysostom, who apparently did not know the variant reading, but stated that χάριν here means χαράν.[12] But this interpretation seems forced, or at least wishful, since such a usage is found nowhere else in Paul for this word which is ordinarily loaded with theological overtones.

Other interpreters, therefore, suggest that such theological overtones are precisely what Paul intended. Thus Wendland suggests: "Ein ungeheures Vollmachtsbewusstsein kommt in diesen Worten zutage . . . : der Apostel ist Träger der göttlichen Gnade, and seine Anwesenheit in der Gemeinde bedeutet daher eine Zeit den Gnadenwirksamkeit in Korinth."[13] This is surely possible, and it is usually supported by reference to Rom. 1:2: "I long to see you so that I may impart to you some χάρισμα πνευματικόν." However, in this case, he sharply qualifies what might sound like impertinence — even for an apostle — by indicating that he really intended his coming to have mutual benefit. Furthermore, such an interpretation sounds almost too theological.

given here is as a variant for καύχημα in 1 Cor. 9:16 (א* D E F G pc). But χάρις is so suspect here that even Tischendorf refused to follow the combined evidence of א and D.

10. For an analysis of this feature in the Pauline letters see Robert W. Funk, "The Apostolic *Parousia:* Form and Significance," in *Christian History and Interpretation: Studies Presented to John Knox,* ed. W. R. Farmer, C. F. D. Moule, and R. R. Niebuhr (Cambridge, 1967), pp. 249-68.

11. "Some difficult passages in the first chapter of II Corinthians," *JBL* 6 (1896): 38, 36.

It is difficult to know whether translators are translating χάριν as "joy" or simply reading the variant itself. See the RSV, Twentieth Century NT, Weymouth, Moffatt, Goodspeed, Rotherham. Some of these at least use the Westcott-Hort text, which reads χαράν. χαράν is also favored by A. Plummer and J. Hering.

12. *Hom. 3 in 2 Cor.*

13. *Die Briefe an die Korinther,* Das Neue Testament Deutsch 7 (Göttingen, 1968), pp. 170-71. Cf. J. A. Beet, *A Commentary on St Paul's Epistles to the Corinthians* (London, 1885), p. 326.

That is, it seems to argue for more than Paul would have intended for a mere passing visit.

On the other hand, the meaning suggested in this paper is quite in keeping with (1) Paul's usage elsewhere in 1 and 2 Corinthians (with regard to the collection) and with (2) his emphasis in a similar passage on his reason for visiting a church (Rom. 15:22-24).

(1) Although Paul's basic word for the collection is the technical term λογεία, he uses it only twice (1 Cor. 16:1-2). Elsewhere he uses words that at the same time are filled with theological content. Thus the collection is called κοινωνία (Rom. 15:26; 2 Cor. 8:4; 9:13), λειτουργία (Rom. 15:27; 2 Cor. 9:12), διακονία (2 Cor. 8:4; 9:1, 12, 13; cf. Rom. 15:25), and χάρις (1 Cor. 16:3; 2 Cor. 8:4, 6, 7, 19). The usage in 2 Cor. 8:7 is especially significant. In the same way that they excel in other dimensions of Christian life, including certain χαρίσματα (faith, word, knowledge), as well as love for Paul,[14] he urges them to excel ἐν ταύτῃ τῇ χάριτι. The meaning here obviously moves beyond a mere equation with λογεία (= gift) to the act of giving itself (thus the RSV: "gracious work"; cf. NIV: "grace of giving").

This is precisely the kind of χάρις Paul probably had in mind in 1:15. This would also explain the use of σχῆτε rather than λάβητε (Rom. 1:5; 5:17) or δέξησθε (2 Cor. 6:1). Although such χάρις is, as Barrett rightly observes about 2 Cor. 8:7, "as much a divine gift as *gnosis* or tongues,"[15] the emphasis here is not on the Corinthian reception of such grace per se, but on their experiencing it by service toward others (in this case Paul and his companions).

This interpretation also fits the context of at least one of Paul's difficulties with this church, namely his failure to have allowed them to assist in his ministry. He had already found it necessary to speak on that question (1 Cor. 9:3-18), and it may well be that this is the cause of his change of plans from 1 Cor. 16:5-7. Even though it would only be a passing visit — precisely what he had wanted to avoid in 1 Cor. 16:7 — he determined on such a visit so that they might have a double opportunity to assist him, where they had had none in the past.

(2) In the John Knox *Festschrift*, R. W. Funk offered an extremely helpful analysis of the form and significance of the "apostolic parousia."[16] How-

14. Barrett, *Commentary*, p. 216 and B. M. Metzger, ed., *A Textual Commentary on the Greek New Testament* (London and New York, 1971), p. 581. Both consider ἡμῶν ἐν ὑμῖν to be the more difficult reading. I demur. Most of the other things wherein the Corinthians are here said to abound are benefits received (faith, speech, knowledge). Love from Paul to them fits nicely in that context. What is "difficult," and a sensitive scribe would have sensed it, is any suggestion in 2 Corinthians that their love abounded toward Paul. Surely this is the *lectio difficilior*.

15. Barrett, *Commentary*, p. 222.

16. Funk, *The Apostolic Parousia*.

ever, in attempting to be as complete as possible so as to discover "the form" of such passages, he has tended to blur distinctions between *two kinds of visits:* (a) where the specific reason for Paul's coming was to minister in some way to the church, and (b) where he was visiting "on his way through," as it were; as always Paul would indeed be ministering to the church, but the main purpose lay beyond the immediate visit.

Most of the Pauline *parousia* passages are of the former kind (1 Cor. 4:14-21; 1 Thess. 2:17–3:13; Phil. 2:19-24; and probably Philem. 22). However, the collection visit of 1 Corinthians 16:1-12 clearly is of the second kind. His emphasis on staying with them for a time (vv. 6-7), combined with 4:14-21, makes it certain that he felt a need to minister to the church. But in v. 6 he also ties their service to him to his long stay (ἵνα ὑμεῖς με προπέμψητε οὗ ἐὰν πορεύωμαι). This is also true of the passage in Rom. 15:14-33, which serves as the basic model for Funk's analysis. Although Paul expects his coming to be of benefit to the church (15:32; cf. 1:11), the emphasis throughout is on their "benefit" to him.

The similarities of these passages with 2 Cor. 1:15-16 are so striking that the latter, too, must belong to this second kind of visit. One should especially note the correspondence with Romans 15:23-24:

ἐπιποθίαν δὲ ἔχων τοῦ ἐλθεῖν πρὸς ὑμᾶς . . . , ὡς ἂν πορεύωμαι εἰς τὴν Σπανίαν· ἐλπίζω γὰρ διαπορευόμενος θεάσασθαι ὑμᾶς καὶ ὑφ' ὑμῶν προπεμφθῆναι ἐκεῖ . . .

This is the same pattern one finds in 2 Cor. 1:15-16, with the exception of the twofold visit. Thus in 2 Corinthians Paul uses χάρις to describe the visits, not because of what they are to receive by his presence, but because of how God's grace is going to be working through them.

II

If this is the correct interpretation of 2 Cor. 1:15, then the following reconstruction of Paul's visits to Corinth seems to bring some order out of much of the chaos.[17]

(1) Paul's original plan (1 Cor. 16:1-12) was to visit Macedonia first on his way to Corinth. The purpose of this visit was almost certainly to pick up the collection. The given reason for this plan was so that he might be able to spend time in Corinth, intimating a passing visit through Macedonia.

---

17. This reconstruction supports that suggested by Barrett, *Commentary*, pp. 5-10.

(2) For reasons not precisely known, Paul changed those plans and decided to pay a passing visit to Corinth, "in order that they might have a double opportunity for kindness." The first part of this double visit was surely not to pick up the collection, but perhaps to pick up some of the brothers to accompany him (cf. 1 Cor. 16:3-4). In any case, it was an added opportunity for the church to do something they had not yet had a hand in — ministering to Paul's needs.

(3) However, on his arrival he found that things had deteriorated. Instead of χάρις in any direction, Paul was abused by someone in the church (2 Cor. 2:5 and 7:12; perhaps because of his change of plans, but more likely because of the infiltration of the "super-apostles"), and the church failed to support Paul. Paul's departure was as sudden as his arrival; the visit was a "painful" one (2 Cor. 1:23–2:4), so Paul determined to forgo the plan of 1:15. It is this new change of plans that he is trying to explain in 2 Cor. 1:12–2:4.

(4) Probably he went on to Macedonia, but he did not at that time pick up the collection. Rather, he returned to Ephesus, which was never in his plans, and he now had two problems: to straighten out the church in Corinth and still to follow through with the collection and subsequent trip to Jerusalem. To accomplish the former, he sent Titus, along with a very strong letter; to accomplish the latter, he reverted to the first plan (1 Cor. 16:5-7), to make Corinth the last stop on the way to Judea. How, or even whether, that visit would come off would depend in large measure on Titus's report when he was to meet him at Troas (2 Cor. 2:13-14).

(5) Meanwhile Paul suffered a great θλίψις in Ephesus (2 Cor. 1:8-11), which probably delayed his getting to Troas and thereby increased his anxiety in not finding Titus. Thus he set off for Macedonia, where he picked up their collection along with the accompanying brethren (2 Cor. 8:1-7; 9:1-4). Meanwhile Titus arrived with basically cheering news. The first problem was essentially resolved, but there was still the matter of the collection.

(6) Thus he sent Titus and two others on ahead to make sure the collection would be ready on Paul's arrival with the Macedonians. With Titus he sent a letter (our 2 Corinthians, at least chs. 1–9) explaining all of this, including the reasons for his earlier failure to return after going on to Macedonia. His plans had been made so that they might have χάρις twice (2 Cor. 1:15). But the first χάρις did not work out, so now they were to see to it that they excelled in the second (2 Cor. 8:7).

CHAPTER 9

Εἰδωλόθυτα Once Again:
An Interpretation of 1 Corinthians 8–10
(1980)

Paul's answer to the Corinthians' stance on εἰδωλόθυτα, food sacrificed to idols, has long posed difficulties for modern interpreters. The problems basically have to do with (1) the relationship of the various parts of Paul's answer to one another, and (2) the nature of the problem in Corinth and its relationship to the Corinthians' letter to Paul.

First, it is almost universally recognized that 1 Cor. 8:1–11:1 takes up three clearly different, yet somehow related, issues. In 10:14-22 Paul prohibits the eating of sacrificial food at the pagan temples in the presence of the idol-demons. In 10:23–11:1 he deals with the same food, but now as it is related to its purchase in the marketplace, and says that such food may be freely eaten without any questions. In 9:1-27 he offers a strong defense of his apostolic authority, with special emphasis on his apostolic freedom. The problem here is twofold: (1) How are these three items related to one another, or are they? (2) How are the large sections 8:1-13 and 10:1-13 related to any, or all, of these three issues?

The section 8:1-13 is where most of the difficulties lie. First of all, vv. 1-6 seem to be a *non sequitur*. What do a contrast between knowledge and love and a discussion of Christian theology and idolatry in nearly henotheistic terms have to do with "food sacrificed to idols"? Moreover, vv. 7-13 seem to be related in some ways to both 10:14-22 and 10:23–11:1, yet scholars at various times have also found these verses to be in conflict with one or the other of these later two sections. The problem has to do with εἰδωλόθυτα in this section. Is it referring to participation at the temple meals or to idol food sold in the marketplace?

Second, the issue of food sacrificed to idols has been raised by the Corinthians themselves in their letter to Paul. But how was it raised? There is nothing in Paul's answer that suggests they were merely asking for his advice. To the contrary, the combative nature of Paul's answer indicates that he was taking issue with them on this matter. Moreover, unless the "weak" of 8:7-12 are merely hypothetical, as Hurd argues,[1] the church does not appear to be unanimous on this matter. What, then, was going on in Corinth, and how did the Corinthians express themselves to Paul in their letter?

I. The Traditional Answer and Some Alternatives

The traditional interpretation views the problem in terms of "weak" and "strong" factions within the church, often related to the divisions in 1 Cor. 1:12, and does in fact see their letter to Paul as asking his advice. Typical of this stance is the recent comment by R. Kugelman:[2] "The Corinthians had inquired in their letter whether it was permitted to eat the flesh of animals that had been sacrificed to idols." After noting the variety of ways this could have been a problem — marketplace food, social occasions at the temples, invitations to private homes — he continues: "With reference to their attitude toward this problem Paul distinguishes two groups among the Christians: those who have an enlightened conscience about Christian liberty because they have knowledge and those with 'a weak conscience,' who attributed a tangible impurity to sacrificial meats."

According to this view, the problem primarily had to do with marketplace idol food, which is what Paul is seen to be speaking to in 8:1-13, 10:23–11:1, and (usually) 10:1-13. This tradition generally allows that some of the "strong" were so bold as even to advocate going to the temples, so that Paul feels constrained to speak to that question as well, but it is strictly a side issue.

As to Paul's answer, it is usually argued that 8:8 reflects Paul's real position (idol food *per se* is a matter of indifference), but that for the sake of the "weak" the "strong" should forbear. Since the problem in Corinth apparently was not the food in itself, but rather the ἐξουσία and ἐλευθερία of the "strong," Paul digresses slightly in ch. 9, by way of a defense of his own conduct, to illustrate the proper use of "freedom." Then, on the way back to εἰδωλόθυτα (10:1-13), he takes yet another digression to remind them that such food eaten at the temples is strictly forbidden (10:14-22). This "digres-

---

1. J. C. Hurd, *The Origin of 1 Corinthians* (London, 1965), pp. 117-25.

2. R. Kugelman, "The First Letter to the Corinthians," in *The Jerome Biblical Commentary* (Englewood Cliffs, N.J., 1968), p. 266.

sion" is often viewed as a concession to the "weak," in which Paul is seen to be affirming the correctness of their view of idolatry. But when he finally returns to their question about εἰδωλόθυτα (10:23–11:1), Paul once again emphasizes that such food really is a matter of indifference, but at the same time repeats his concern about not offending the weaker person's conscience.

Thus the traditional answer tends to see no conflict at all between chs. 8 and 10. Paul's answer is not necessarily tidy, but neither is it contradictory. By means of digressions he simply touches several bases, and in so doing he speaks both to the "strong" and the "weak."

Not all scholarship is pleased with this state of affairs, however, and several alternatives have been offered. Most commonly the problem has been to reconcile what seem to be differing points of view expressed in 8:7-13 and 10:14-22. As Conzelmann[3] has put it:

> Paul's argument appears to vacillate. In chs. 8 and 10:23–11:1 he adopts in principle the standpoint of the "strong": sacrificial meat is not dangerous and can accordingly be eaten. The restriction on freedom is imposed not by the meat, but by the conscience, by the bond with the "weak" brother. The *strong* are *admonished*. In 10:1-22, on the other hand, Paul appears to vote in favor of the weak. Eating is dangerous. *All* are *warned*. . . .
>
> Now both forms of argumentation are Pauline in content. The question is, however, whether Paul can argue both ways in the same breath.

One solution to this problem is that proposed by J. Weiss, W. Schmithals, *et al.* — to see 1 Corinthians as a compilation of two or more letters.[4] But in most cases this is simply to give the traditional answer (digression) a new dress. Schmithals, for example, makes considerable point of trying to differentiate between εἰδωλολατρία (= the actual worship of idols) and εἰδωλόθυτα (= the substance of the meat itself, now sold in the market). He argues that 10:1-22, dealing with εἰδωλολατρία, belongs to Epistle A, whereas 8:1–9:23 + 10:23–11:1, which shifts to the theme of εἰδωλόθυτα, belongs to Epistle B. And in this latter case, the Corinthians are merely "asking Paul for information on this point."[5]

3. H. Conzelmann, *1 Corinthians* (Hermeneia; Philadelphia, 1975), p. 137.

4. J. Weiss, *Der erste Korintherbrief* (KEK, [10]1925), pp. xl-xliii; W. Schmithals, *Gnosticism in Corinth* (Nashville, 1971), pp. 87-96, 224-29. For a discussion of these and others who propose this solution, see Hurd, *Origin*, pp. 43-47, 131-42.

5. Schmithals, *Gnosticism*, p. 227.

A different tack altogether was taken by H. F. von Soden,[6] whose concern in the exposition of this passage was the resolution of "sacrament and ethics" in Paul. He saw the tension as between the "strong," who, as "unrestrained enthusiasts," had a magical view of the sacrament (as long as they participated in Christ's body, no evil could harm them) and the weak, who (probably) were filled with "legalistic anxiety" and were "terrified of every defilement." Paul moves beyond the position of both with a dynamic view of sacrament (Christ as present in Spirit, but also as bringing man under obligation to God) that involves an ethic of proper intention.

Thus for von Soden the tension between eating εἰδωλόθυτα at home or in the temple is a false one. Paul really forbids neither as such — only those temple meals that had as their clear intent the worship of idol-demons. He argues that almost all meals to which one would have been invited would have been in the temple precincts. What Paul does, then, is to try to move both the strong and weak beyond their present positions: by reforming their wrong view of the sacrament, but at the same time rejecting any legal regulation. The sacrament, which binds them to Christ, should lead them to "mutual heed and concern."

Although von Soden offers a number of helpful insights in understanding the passage, his basic concern to resolve what he calls the antinomies in Paul leads to some questionable assertions. He has a legitimate concern to keep Paul's gospel from becoming law. But that concern becomes misguided when it leads him to negate the clearly prohibitive force of 10:14-22.

More recently J. C. Hurd has moved in still another direction.[7] On the one hand, he has affirmed the traditional view that the conflict between 8:7-13 and 10:14-22 is more apparent than real. He argues, *inter alia,* (1) that there were no actual "weak" and "strong" *as parties* in the church, (2) that the church as a whole is responsible for the letter to Paul in which they have taken a somewhat anti-Pauline stance, and (3) that Paul's answer is basically a single argument with them in which he actually agrees with them (eating idol food sold in the marketplace is a matter of indifference), but does not want to appear to agree overmuch because his *reasons* differ from theirs. As a result, he offers the *hypothetical* qualifications of the "weaker" brother and attendance at the temples.

6. H. F. von Soden, "Sakrament und Ethik bei Paulus: Zur Frage der literarischen und theologischen Einheitlichkeit von I Kor. 8–10," in *Marburger Theologische Studien,* Rudolf Otto Festgruss, ed. M. Frick (Gotha, 1931), pp. 1, 1-40. An excerpted English translation appeared as "Sacrament and Ethics in Paul," in *The Writings of St. Paul,* ed. W. A. Meeks (New York, 1972), pp. 257-68. The references in this paper are to the English translation.

7. Hurd, *Origin,* pp. 115-49.

I find Hurd's points (1) and (2) persuasively argued. Furthermore, I quite agree that the alleged tension between 8:7-13 and 10:14-22 has been considerably overdrawn. Nonetheless, his conclusion as to the hypothetical nature of attendance at the temple feasts is equally unsatisfying. There is simply too much urgency in all of this for temple attendance to be purely hypothetical.

The burden of this paper is that the real conflict between chs. 8 and 10 is not between 8:7-13 and 10:14-22 at all, but rather is between 8:7-13 and 10:23–11:1. However, it has been so often assumed that these sections speak to the same issue that any tension between them either is not noted at all or is lightly brushed aside.[8]

The common interpretation is that 8:7-13 and 10:23–11:1 both speak to the question of idol food sold in the marketplace. But there are several problems with this view: (1) The nature of the answer in 8:1-13 is argumentative and combative: "Knowledge puffs up . . . ; if anyone thinks he knows anything . . . ; not everyone has knowledge . . . ; take care lest this authority of yours . . . ; if anyone sees you, the one who has knowledge . . . ; the weak brother, for whom Christ died, is destroyed by your knowledge . . . ; when you sin against your brothers in this way. . . ." In this regard 8:7-12 is one with all of 8:1–10:22, where Paul is clearly on the attack, parrying and arguing with all his usual resourcefulness. Sometimes it is direct encounter, other times it is appeal, but always it is an attempt to convince the Corinthians that he is right and they are wrong. On the other hand, this is scarcely so with 10:23–11:1. Although set in the context of edification and loving concern for "the other person," here Paul simply gives advice. There is no attack, and very little of the urgency one feels throughout 8:1–10:22. This section is almost totally devoid of argument, except for vv. 29b-30, which, however, seem far more to reflect Paul's own defense in 9:19-23 than the concern for the "weak" in 8:7-13.

(2) The so-called "stumbling-block principle" seems to receive different treatment in the two sections. In 8:7-13 the concern is for a brother with a "weak conscience," who will be tempted to emulate the "gnostic" brother's action. Thus he is not merely offended by what he sees the "gnostic" doing (as in, "How can a Christian possibly eat such food?"); rather, he is himself "encouraged" to buy and eat marketplace idol food (according to the traditional view) — to his own destruction. For this reason, Paul's answer has the practi-

---

8. One is hard pressed to find anywhere in the commentaries that these two sections are in conflict. Those who seem to sense that the answer in 10:23–11:1 is not really the same as in 8:7-13 treat 10:23–11:1 as a generalizing conclusion. Others (e.g., R. C. H. Lenski, *The Interpretation of St. Paul's First and Second Epistle to the Corinthians* [Columbus, Ohio, 1946], pp. 419-21) see 10:25-27 as addressing "the weak," whereas 8:7-13 and 10:28-30 address "the strong." This admits to the conflict without articulating it.

cal effect of prohibition. After all, if my eating such food causes the fall of a brother who would be destroyed were he to follow my example, then love surely prohibits such eating. Such an outcome is the practical effect of the appeal in v. 13.

In 10:23–11:1, however, there is not the slightest hint that someone will fall by imitating another's action. The only problem suggested seems to be a matter of "offense" pure and simple; that is, the informant apparently would be distressed, or "offended," by the other person's action. And Paul's response in this section does *not* prohibit eating marketplace food. Indeed, he says quite the opposite: buy and eat; accept invitations and eat; and never so much as inquire as to whether the food had been sacrificed to an idol. For the buying and eating of such food *there are no restrictions whatsoever.* In fact, vv. 29b-30 suggest that not even the scruples of someone else should affect one's action in this matter! For the accepting of invitations there is one proviso: Forbear if someone else calls attention to the temple origins of the food. But the objector here is not called a "weaker" brother; in fact the use of ἱερόθυτον to describe the food in v. 28 makes it altogether unclear whether he is a brother.

(3) The only specific mention of eating in 8:7-13 refers not to marketplace food at all but to attendance at the temple (v. 10), which in fact a little later Paul will outright prohibit. In contrast, 10:23–11:1 does not so much as allude to the temple, but specifically refers to food sold at the *macellum,* which is then eaten at home or at a neighbor's home.

On close examination it does not seem possible to reconcile these differences, if in fact both passages speak to the same issue. If they do, then Paul in 10:23–11:1 surely undercuts his own argument in 8:7-13. If the "gnostic's" eating of marketplace idol food endangers a brother's life in 8:7-13, then how possibly can Paul be so relaxed about their eating the same food in 10:23-28, even to the point of making it an imperative in 10:25? And any suggestion that Paul is addressing two different groups, the "weak" and the "strong," is ruled out by the content of 10:23-30. Paul is unquestionably addressing the "strong" in 8:7-13. One might argue, as Lenski, e.g., does,[9] that in 10:25-27 he addresses the "weak," that they should not have such scruples. But the problem with this solution is that in vv. 28-29 we are back to *another person's conscience,* not the eater's. If it is the "weak" who are here being addressed, who then are the new "weak" whose conscience causes one to forbear? Yet it is this second person's conscience that has caused exegetes to see a relationship between these two passages in the first place.

The answer, therefore, must lie elsewhere. In this paper I wish to defend

9. Ibid.

yet another alternative,[10] namely that εἰδωλόθυτα in 8:1-13 does not at all refer to the sacrificial food sold in the marketplace. That indeed is the issue in 10:23–11:1. In 8:1-13, I suggest, Paul is dealing primarily with the eating of sacrificial food at the temple itself in the presence of the idol-demon. Furthermore, Paul's answer best makes sense if this practice is something that the Corinthians, in their letter to Paul, are arguing for as a "right."

This means, further, that the prohibition in 10:14-22, rather than a digression, is in fact the main point, to which the whole argument of 8:1–10:13 has been leading. The question of marketplace food is then taken up after the fact as another issue altogether — although it has close ties to Paul's defense in 9:19-23 — and to this issue Paul gives a considerably different answer.

This interpretation can be shown to offer a reasonable reconstruction of the Corinthian situation, including their letter to Paul, as well as a consistent and coherent exegesis of the whole of Paul's answer in chs. 8–10.

II. The Problem in Corinth

It is generally recognized that any viable interpretation of 1 Corinthians 8–10 must try to reconstruct the situation in Corinth to which Paul is responding. What have they asked, or in my view *asserted*, in their letter that calls forth this combination of arguments from Paul? This is precisely where the traditional interpretation comes up short: The effect (Paul's argument and defense) does not seem adequate to the cause (a letter asking his opinion on issues where they are divided). On the other hand, the great strength of Hurd's book lies in his ability to give an adequate, and consistent, answer to this question for all of 1 Corinthians.

a. The Corinthian Position

In the first place, Hurd is surely correct in seeing the Corinthian letter as being over against Paul, not simply as a series of questions calling for his advice.

10. I first suggested this alternative in a paper on 2 Cor. 6:14–7:1 ("II Corinthians vi.14–vii.1 and Food Offered to Idols," *NTS* 23 [1976/77]: 140-61, esp. 148-54). Since then I have discovered that this alternative is the basic point of view in the small commentary by R. St. John Parry, *The First Epistle of Paul the Apostle to the Corinthians* (Cambridge Greek Testament for Schools and Colleges; Cambridge, ²1926), pp. 125-55, although he presents no argument for it. It is also hinted at, but not thoroughly argued, in H. Lietzmann, *An die Korinther I/II* (HNT 9; Tübingen, ⁴1949), pp. 37-52.

The combative nature of 8:1–10:22 noted above argues for this; and Paul's inclusion of his defense (9:1-22) in this section seems to clinch it.

Second, given that Paul had previously addressed at least one of the issues taken up again in our 1 Corinthians (πορνεία; see 5:9), Hurd's argument is also well taken that whatever it is the Corinthians were arguing *for* in their letter, it is something Paul had already forbidden in his previous letter. This again makes sense both of the argumentative nature of his reply and of the need for his defense. Furthermore, it is also altogether probable that the letter comes from the church as a whole, not from one of the factions in the church. After all, Paul implies that he has received the whole community in the persons of Stephanas, Fortunatus, and Achaicus (16:17). This does not mean that all the church is necessarily agreed on the issues in their letter, but it does mean that Paul is giving a singular, unified response to their argument with him.

My point of disagreement with Hurd is in the *content* of their letter. Rather than arguing in their letter for the right to buy and eat idol food, a point Paul has no argument with, they are much more likely arguing for the right to continue to join pagan friends in the feasts at the temples. In so doing they make four points:

(1) They all have γνῶσις about idols, namely that Jewish-Christian monotheism by its very nature rules out any genuine reality to an idol. On this point they can expect Paul's agreement. But the point is almost too trivial if their concern were marketplace food; it has its bite only if, thinking they "have Paul on this one," they want it to apply to their actual attendance at the temples, where the "nonentities" stood.

(2) They also have γνῶσις about food itself, namely that it is a matter of indifference to God. It has been a moot point whether 8:8 reflects their position or Paul's;[11] but again, it is highly likely that at least 8:8a is something on which they are both agreed. The Corinthians' point in this case, however, would have been not simply *what* we eat, but *where* we eat it. Here again they would think they have Paul: "Since idols are nonentities and since food per se is a matter of indifference, how can you forbid our eating at the temples?"

(3) They have an "enthusiast's" or a "magical" view of the sacraments, namely that those who partook of the Christian sacraments were thus out of danger from falling. As von Soden put it: "They put their trust . . . in the belief that those initiated by Christ's sacraments are charmed against all powers and therefore possess a limitless *exousia*."[12] This alone makes sense of 10:1-13,

---

11. For a recent discussion of the options, see R. A. Horsley, "Consciousness and Freedom among the Corinthians: 1 Corinthians 8–10," *CBQ* 40 (1978): 577-79.

12. "Sacrament and Ethics," p. 259.

where Paul uses the analogy of Israel's "sacraments" and yet their "overthrow in the desert" to warn the Corinthians that the one who thinks he stands is indeed in danger of falling (10:12).

(4) They also use this occasion to question Paul's apostolic credentials, which in turn led them to question his authority to forbid them on this matter at all. From the content of ch. 9 it may be assumed that they questioned his authority because he himself seemed ambiguous about it at two points: his failure to accept their financial support and his own compromising stance toward marketplace food, which he ate on some occasions but refused to eat on others. Such vacillation does not seem worthy of an apostle.

Add these all together and you have them *asserting,* not asking, something like this: "Since we all know that there is only one God and therefore that an idol has no reality, and since food is a matter of indifference to God, it not only does not matter what we eat, but where we eat it. Besides, we are saved and protected by the sacraments. Why can't we then continue to join our friends at their feasts, even at the temples? Besides, Paul, you seem to be unable to use your authority as an apostle. Indeed, are you really an apostle? You have repeatedly refused our offer of financial support, and you also have been known to eat idol meat in Gentile homes, but refuse it when Jews are present. If you cannot settle on your own authority, why should you restrict ours to act in Christian freedom?"

This view of things is further supported by the background to the term εἰδωλόθυτα as well as its usage throughout 1 Corinthians 8–10.

b. The Meaning of εἰδωλόθυτα

The term εἰδωλόθυτον occurs four times in ch. 8 (vv. 1, 4, 7, 10) and one further time in 10:19. It seems reasonably clear that in 10:19 it refers to sacrificial food that is partaken in the idol temple. Not only does the context argue for such a meaning, but so also does the balanced nature of the two rhetorical questions in v. 19. In a context of eating food in the presence of a deity, Paul asks whether either the idol or the food has reality in itself, questions clearly intended to recall 8:4-6. The expected response of course is negative. The "reality" involved is to be found in the demonic nature of idolatry; and eating the sacrificed food in the context of the idol-demon constitutes becoming κοινωνοὺς τῶν δαιμονίων. Since eating the food in the temple is surely the meaning here, the question is whether εἰδωλόθυτα should carry another meaning in ch. 8. Yet it is either stated or assumed by almost all who have written on the subject that εἰδωλόθυτα throughout the NT refers to idol food sold in the market. There are in fact several converging data that lend support to this view.

(1) It is well known that Jews forbade the eating of idol food, and in their case εἰδωλόθυτα could have referred only to marketplace food, since there was no danger of the Jews' going to the idol temples. Thus *m. Abod. Zar.* 2:3 says: "Flesh that is entering in unto an idol is permitted, but what comes forth is forbidden" (Danby); and the Babylonian Talmud comments that the idolatrous sacrifice caused defilement in the same way a dead body defiled what it touched (*b. Hul.* 13b; cf. 4 Macc. 5:2).

(2) The apostolic decree in Acts 15:29 also forbids εἰδωλόθυτα, along with blood, things strangled, and πορνεία. Since these prohibitions were written to Gentile converts, the most common view is that they place some minimum "Jewish" requirements on Gentile believers; so that they may have social intercourse with Jewish Christians. In this case εἰδωλόθυτα would again refer to idol food sold in the market.[13]

(3) In some later Christian writers εἰδωλόθυτα also has the Jewish sense of marketplace food. This is especially true of Justin, since the Jew Trypho is made to say that he knows some Christians who eat idol food (*Dial.* 34), and of Irenaeus, who says that the heretics both eat εἰδωλόθυτα and attend pagan festivals in honor of the idols (*Haer.* 1.6.3), which seems to imply a distinction between the two.

But despite this strong linguistic evidence from both Jewish and Christian sources, there are real problems with making εἰδωλόθυτα equal marketplace idol food in 1 Corinthians 8, besides the fact that it surely does not mean that in 10:19.

(1) It is extremely doubtful whether sacrificial food sold in the marketplace would have been a problem to a Gentile convert, apart from contact with Jewish Christians. Such scruples could only have stemmed from the Jewish abhorrence of idolatry. While it is true that Gentile converts are characterized by Paul as having "turned to God from idols" (1 Thess. 1:9), there is no reason to believe that they would also have adopted Jewish thinking about marketplace food, especially so when Paul himself had no scruples about such things. This is why several scholars have suggested that the problem in

---

13. There has been considerable speculation as to the possible relationship of the Apostolic Decree to 1 Corinthians 8–10. Usually it is suggested that the question had been raised in Corinth by Peter, or at least in his name. See, e.g., A. Ehrhardt, "Social Problems in the Early Church," in *The Framework of the New Testament Stories* (Manchester, 1964), pp. 276-78; and T. W. Manson, "The Corinthian Correspondence (1)," in *Studies in the Gospels and Epistles* (Philadelphia, 1962), p. 200. Cf. the discussion in C. K. Barrett, "Things Sacrificed to Idols," *NTS* 11 (1964/65): 142-43.

Corinth is in fact to be linked to outside attempts to introduce the apostolic decree into the Corinthian church.[14] The problem with this as a solution to 1 Cor. 8:1-13, however, is the non-Jewish character of everything in the text. The offended person, whose conscience is weak, is not a Jewish Christian, but a Gentile convert (8:7).[15] Moreover, there is not a hint in the text that his anxiety over idolatry has an outside source or that it is related to contaminated food; rather it is inherent to his former *pagan* understanding of idolatry in light of his Christian conversion. And finally his "fall" in 8:10-12 does not rest on his being "offended" by a brother's eating of marketplace food nor in that person's "idolatry"; rather, it rests in his *seeing,* and thereby being encouraged to *imitate,* a brother's going to the temple meals (8:10).

It is appropriate, therefore, for us to seek the meaning of εἰδωλόθυτα in 1 Corinthians not in the Jewish abhorrence of idolatry but in the nature of idol-worship in pagan antiquity.[16]

(2) It is a well-known phenomenon that worship in both Jewish and pagan antiquity very often involved eating a meal in the presence of the deity. At the regular seasonal feasts or at irregular but important times, like marriages, good fortune, and especially at death,[17] worshipers would invite family or friends to join them at the temples or shrines. There they would sacrifice food to the deity, some of which became the burnt offering for the deity, some of which became the priests' portion, but most of which was prepared for the eating of a festive meal before the god. Especially in pagan antiquity such feasting usually meant drunkenness and sexual play.[18]

Such sacrificial meals before Yahweh are specifically enjoined in Deut. 14:22-26 and are referred to elsewhere in the OT (Exod. 24:11; 1 Sam. 9:13; 1 Kings 1:25; Hos. 8:13). Special chambers for these meals are found in the first temple (Jer. 35:2) and probably in the second (Neh. 13:7-8; cf. Ezek. 42:13).

Besides the evidence from other sources, such sacred feasting among the nations that surrounded Israel is also noted in the OT. It is found among

14. See the preceding note.

15. For the opinion that Jewish Christians are involved, see J. Dupont, *Gnosis: La connaissance religieuse dans les épîtres de Saint Paul* (Louvain, 1949), pp. 265-377.

16. It should also be noted that one must not be so quick to read this passage in light of Romans 14. Although Paul's answer in both cases has some analogies, the subject matter is completely different. In Romans 14 there is no mention of idolatry; it seems rather to be a question of ritualistic asceticism. In our passage there is no mention of "weak" and "strong" — only ὁ ἔχων γνῶσιν and another having a "weak conscience." Nor is food *per se* the issue in 1 Corinthians 8–10 as in Romans 14. Thus the clearly Jewish background in Romans is of no help here.

17. See especially the evidence accumulated by M. H. Pope, *Song of Songs* (AB; Garden City, N.Y., 1977), pp. 210-29.

18. Pope, *Song of Songs,* pp. 210-29.

the Canaanites (Judg. 9:27) and the Babylonians (Dan. 5:1-4); Egyptian practices, including their sexual overtones, are reflected in Exod. 32:6. Indeed, it was the combination of feasting and sexual intercourse that apparently was one of the great attractions on the part of Israel to the idolatry that surrounded them (Num. 25:1-2; Hos. 4:10-14; 7:4-5, 14; cf. Isa. 28:7-8).

By the first century C.E., however, the phenomenon of eating before Yahweh had disappeared from Judaism — almost certainly because of its close ties to πορνεία among the Gentiles. Instead God was worshiped by sacrifices and prayer in the temple, but more commonly by prayer, singing, and Scripture in the synagogue. The meal apparently persisted only as an eschatological hope, in the form of the messianic banquet.[19]

In contrast to contemporary Judaism, there is considerable evidence that the meal in the presence of the deity continued to be a commonplace in the Hellenistic world in the first century C.E.[20] The chance discovery among the papyri of the two invitations to meals at the Serapeum[21] is mute evidence of what must have been the regular practice of most non-Jews in the Hellenistic world, whether they believed in the gods or not. For those who believed, the cultic meal probably also had participatory significance.

Indeed, it is the *commonness* of such meals in a city like Corinth, with its abundance of shrines to the "gods many and lords many,"[22] over against the lack of "Jewishness" in the text of 1 Corinthians 8–10, that argues strongly for temple attendance as the real concern in this passage. As A. Ehrhardt has said:

> Even today we are surprised to read from the pen of St. Paul, 'but if somebody seeth thee, who hast gnosis, lying at table in the temple of an idol', as

19. One of Jesus' table partners gave expression to what was probably a common hope: "Blessed is the one who will eat at the feast in the Kingdom of God" (Luke 14:15; cf. Matt 8:11; 22:1-14; 26:29; Rev. 19:9). The phenomenon of worship in the form of a meal reappearing among the earliest Christians is probably best explained as a form of realized eschatology, stemming both from Jesus' table fellowship with "the poor" and from his instituting the Lord's Supper in a context of eschatology.

20. See the excursus in Lietzmann, *Korinther I/II*, pp. 49-51.

21. P. Oxy. 1.100[2] (2nd c. C.E.) ἐρωτᾷ σε Χαιρήμων δειπνῆσαι εἰς κλείνην τοῦ κυρίου Σαράπιδος ἐν τῷ Σαραπείῳ αὔριον, ἥτις ἐστὶν ιε, ἀπὸ ὥρας θ' ("Chaeremon requests your company at the table of the lord Serapis at the Serapeum tomorrow, the 15th at 9 o'clock"); P. Oxy. 111.523 (2nd c. C.E.) ἐρωτᾷ σε Ἀντώνιο(ς) Προλεμ(αίου) διπνῆσ(αι) παρ' αὐτῷ εἰς κλείνην τοῦ κυρίου Σαράπιδος ἐν τοῖς Κλαυδ(ίου) Σαραπίω(νος) τῇ ιϛ ἀπὸ ὥρας θ' ("Antonius, son of Ptolemy, requests your company at the table of the lord Serapis in the house of Claudius Serapion on the 16th at 9 o'clock").

22. In Pausanias's description of Corinth a century later one can count at least 26 temples or shrines to the "lords" and "gods" (Loeb, 1.255-72).

if that were the most obvious thing in the world. Let us state plainly that such was indeed the case: For it has to be realised that it was the temples of the ancient world which had to supply the need for restaurants, particularly in the Greek cities.[23]

(3) One further thing needs to be noted in this regard, namely the combination of idolatry as eating along with πορνεία in 1 Cor. 10:7-8.

The whole of 10:1-13 is controlled by a single concern. Paul is using the history of Israel to give a severe warning to the Corinthians, who are in a similar danger as Israel. In vv. 1-5 he first establishes that Israel, as Corinth, had its own form of baptism and the Lord's Supper. Yet this did not provide them with security. In vv. 6-10 Paul goes on to give reasons for the fall of "most of them." In so doing, he selects four examples from Israel's time in the desert, where they had been overthrown. The exegetical question is whether these examples were chosen because of Israel or because of Corinth, i.e., were they simply chosen at random to illustrate Israel's fall, and as such become for the Corinthians simply another Pauline sin list, or were they chosen because in a very precise way they reflect the situation in Corinth. Surely it is the latter, and vv. 7-8 are the keys.

In v. 7 Paul says, "Do not be like them in εἰδωλολατρία." In citing the passage from Exodus 32, however, he makes no mention whatever of the idolatry of making the golden calf or of Israel's acclaiming it as the god who delivered them (vv. 2-4). Rather, he quotes v. 6: "The people *sat down to eat and drink* and *rose up to play*." This is exactly the εἰδωλολατρία that is forbidden in 10:14-22.

Verse 8 is the interesting text. For the illustration of πορνεία is from one of the OT texts (Num. 25:1-2) where sexual intercourse took place in conjunction with the meals in the presence of pagan idols! There are two things to note here that are of significance for our argument.

(a) Every mention of εἰδωλόθυτα in the NT is also accompanied by πορνεία (Acts 15:29; Rev. 2:14, 20; and here). Moreover, in Rev. 2:14 there is the same allusion to Num. 25:1-2.[24] It is highly probable, therefore, that in each case these two sins really belong *together*, as they did in the OT and pagan precedents. And εἰδωλόθυτα and πορνεία go together *at the temples*. There is evi-

---

23. A. Ehrhardt, "Social Problems," p. 279 (see above, n. 13).

24. The mention of Balaam in the Revelation passage intrigues one about Jude v. 11. For here, in the context of false teachers as blemishes on Christian love feasts (v. 12!), they are said to walk in the way of Cain (= unworthy sacrifice?), to rush into Balaam's error for profit, and to be destroyed in Korah's rebellion. Is it perhaps possible that here, too, we have an allusion to εἰδωλόθυτα and πορνεία?

dence, in fact, that sacred meals and sexual immorality were still a part of the temple cults of the first century c.e.[25] Thus in all of these texts the sins are probably *not* the eating of sacrificial food sold in the marketplace and sexual promiscuity in general, but sacred meals and sexual immorality at the temples.

(b) It is instructive that Paul has a very similar kind of combative argument with the Corinthians in 6:12-20 over πορνεία, as he does in chs. 8–10 about εἰδωλόθυτα. One should note the following: (1) In 6:12-20 the Corinthians also seem to be arguing for the "right" of πορνεία, based on "freedom" and on some partly true assertions about the nature of the body. (2) Paul's argument involves a contrast to being "joined" to the Lord or to a πόρνη, very much like the contrast between "becoming partners" with the Lord or demons in 10:14-22. (3) Paul takes the "temple" imagery that he uses elsewhere of the church and applies it to the human body. One wonders whether all of this does not suggest — and in any case it is surely an open option — that temple, rather than brothel, fornication is in view in 6:12-20.

This is *not* to argue that the sacred meals to which the Corinthians are inclined to go also involved temple prostitution. But it is to argue that any Corinthian who argued for the "right" both to eat at the temple and to engage in πορνεία would from time to time have occasion for both activities at the same place. Thus both are here warned against.

This is probably how we are also to understand 1 Cor. 10:9. The Corinthians, by insisting on their "rights" to the temple meals and fornication, were *testing* the Lord. In v. 22 Paul asks rhetorically: "Are we trying to arouse the Lord's jealousy? Are we stronger than he?" (NIV).

According to this exegesis, v. 10 also fits the scheme. They are arguing for their "rights" because Paul has previously forbidden both εἰδωλόθυτα and πορνεία. In the case of πορνεία we know that Paul had previously forbidden it; the nature of the argument in 6:12-20 implies that they have taken exception to such a prohibition. The same appears to be true in chs. 8–10. But they are not "to grumble," for in the past such grumblers were also overthrown by God.

Thus the evidence from contemporary Hellenistic culture and from Paul's specific statements in 8:10 and 10:1-22 combines to make a strong case for temple meals as the real problem Paul is addressing in all of 8:1–10:22. It

---

25. See, e.g., the story in Josephus (*Ant.* 18.65-80) where the lady Paulina "after supper" had night-long sex with Mundus, thinking him to be the god Anubis. Conzelmann has shown that sacred prostitution probably did not exist in the Corinth of Paul's day ("Korinth und die Mädchen der Aphrodite," *NAG* 8 [1967-68]: 247-61). Nonetheless, sexual immorality of the kind described by Josephus certainly could have been a part of "worship" in some of the Corinthian temples.

remains to be shown by a brief exegesis of the whole passage that this also makes good sense of Paul's answer.

III. Paul's Response

The most noticeable feature about the beginning of Paul's response (8:1-13) is that although he *says* περὶ δὲ τῶν εἰδωλοθύτων, in fact he scarcely speaks to that question at all. What controls the whole of 8:1-13 is not idol food at all; rather, it is γνῶσις. In fact the words γνῶσις and γινώσκω occur nine times in ch. 8 and not at all in chs. 9–10. That should clue us in that although εἰδωλόθυτα is indeed the issue even here (8:1, 4, 7, 10), the greater problem to be wrestled with in this connection is the Corinthian attitude of γνῶσις. Hence this problem is given first priority.[26]

a. 1 Corinthians 8:1-6

It is clear both from the abruptness of the break after the mention of εἰδωλόθυτα in 8:1 and the resumptive force of the οὖν in 8:4 that these two verses (1 and 4) belong together. Furthermore, it is generally agreed (because of the repeated οἴδαμεν ὅτι . . . καὶ ὅτι and the clear contradiction of v. 1 found in v. 7) that the words "eating of the food sacrificed to idols," "we all possess knowledge," "an idol has no real existence," and "there is no God but one," are quotations from the Corinthian letter to Paul. This means that they were using these propositions to support their right to eat εἰδωλόθυτα.

Thus Paul begins in 8:1 by citing their letter; but he gets only to "we all have knowledge" and immediately feels the need for rebuttal. The problem in Corinth is not first of all that they have so misunderstood idolatry as to allow participation in the temple meals. This is indeed a problem, as 8:4 and 10:19 make clear. But their greater problem is that they have misunderstood the basis of Christian ethical behavior. It is not predicated on γνῶσις, but on love.

Then in 8:4, Paul begins to take up the *content* of their γνῶσις, which he also must sharply qualify. However, the argument that is begun here is broken off at this point in order to pursue the problem of γνῶσις begun in 8:1-3. It

---

26. It is not crucial to this paper to seek for the background of this attitude, whether in Gnosticism (Schmithals), overrealized eschatology (cf. A. C. Thiselton, "Realized Eschatology in Corinth," *NTS* 24 [1977/78]: 510-26), or the Hellenistic Jewish theology represented by Philo (Horsley, "Consciousness and Freedom").

must be noted that the matter in 8:4 is not finished; it is merely shelved for a time, to be resumed in 10:14-22. This is made clear by 10:19-20, which, we have already noted, picks up the argument from 8:4. For the present, however, even the qualification of the content of their γνῶσις is bent to serve his first concern, namely their abuse of γνῶσις. That is, the content of their γνῶσις is false in a very practical way. Although "gods" do not really exist (except as demonic powers, as 10:19-20 will make clear), Paul concedes for the moment that there are in fact many "gods" and "lords." But as 8:7 makes clear, their "existence" as "gods" is only in the minds of their devotees; which does indeed give them a kind of "subjective reality," even if not an objective one.

b. 1 Corinthians 8:7-13

This of course is the crucial passage. Paul here returns to the qualification of the *way* of "knowledge" begun in 8:1-3, but now by way of the practical qualification of the *content* of their γνῶσις given in vv. 4-6.

Despite the general statements about βρῶμα in vv. 8 and 13, the problem here is specifically spelled out in v. 10 as "reclining at table in an idol's temple." Furthermore, although Paul's answer appears simply to be laying down a "principle" (no εἰδωλόθυτα if it offends), for all practical purposes, as we noted earlier, the "principle," as well as the whole answer here, has the practical effects of prohibition. One may *not* argue from silence that if the "gnostic" were not *seen*, then his action in v. 10 is permissible.[27] Such a possible misreading of Paul is exactly what 10:14-22 seems to disallow.

The first reason Paul gives, therefore, as to why they may not go to the temples is that such activity may lead to the destruction of a brother for whom Christ died (vv. 10-12). But how does the "gnostic's" action destroy his brother?

First, because the brother has a "weak conscience." But his weak conscience has to do with idols, *not* food (v. 7). Some new converts are still among those who think of the idols as having reality. The most likely place for such failure of conscience and "defilement" to take place, however, is not by

---

27. This seems to be Conzelmann's position (*1 Corinthians*, pp. 148-49). Most commentators simply ignore the plain implications of v. 10; others have seen it only as an anticipation of 10:14-22, but not as something to be taken seriously here. W. Schmithals (*Gnosticism*, p. 227) dismisses it with a footnote: "Even in 8:10, where of course Paul chooses an extreme example, he is concerned only with the eating of εἰδωλόθυτα, not with participation in the cult as such." Thus is Paul's one explicit statement in ch. 8 ruled to mean something other than what it says in order to fit a prior scheme.

his having adopted Jewish scruples about the food itself, but by his attendance at the temple where the idols actually stood. Thus the eating of εἰδωλόθυτα in v. 7 most likely anticipates the reclining at table mentioned in v. 10, not marketplace food, which nowhere else is brought into view.

Second, the man with a weak conscience is destroyed because he *sees* the "gnostic's" action and is thereby encouraged to imitate it. Paul's ironic use of οἰκοδομηθήσεται in v. 10 suggests that the "gnostic" was perhaps urging the same action on another (as a means of emancipation from foolish notions about idolatry?). As Godet nicely put it: "He enlightens him to his loss! Fine edification!"[28] In any case, the problem, and Paul's argument, only makes sense if the "gnostic's" action is something the other person can *see* and is tempted to imitate, and thereby go against conscience.[29]

In the process of this argument Paul takes up his and their common attitude toward βρῶμα as being a matter of indifference (8:8). This text is as puzzling as it is abrupt. The puzzle is with the "worse" and "better" in 8b. This can scarcely reflect the "gnostic's" view about sacrificial food, for it is precisely the opposite of what one should have expected him to say.[30] If he were arguing with Paul over idol food, his point would have been that "we are no worse if we *do* eat, no better if we do *not*."

But is this Paul's own position on marketplace food? If so, he is speaking only to the "gnostic" (v. 9) and saying something like this: "Look, if you never eat marketplace food again, you will be none the worse for it," i.e., it surely does not put you at any disadvantage if you never again eat such food; "but neither," he says, "are you the better because you can or do eat idol food." The problem with this interpretation lies with v. 9: Βλέπετε δὲ μὴ πῶς ἡ ἐξουσία ὑμῶν, which sounds as if v. 8 is a stance *they* have taken in some way.

Probably the best solution to this verse is not to make βρῶμα = sacrificial food at all. What needs to be noted is that what Paul says of food in v. 8 is almost exactly what he says elsewhere about circumcision (1 Cor. 7:19; Gal. 5:6; 6:15). Food, as circumcision, does not present us before God; it is a matter of indifference. We are none the worse for *not* eating (or for not being cir-

---

28. F. Godet, *Commentary on the First Epistle of St. Paul to the Corinthians* (2 vols.; Edinburgh, 1886), pp. 1, 426.

29. Some have suggested that the "gnostic's" action in going to the temple merely encourages the weaker brother to eat marketplace food against conscience. See, e.g., Lenski, *Corinthians*, p. 345; cf. F. W. Grosheide, *Commentary on the First Epistle to the Corinthians* (NICNT; Grand Rapids, 1953), p. 196. But such a suggestion seems to take all the force out of the example by making it a *non sequitur*.

30. This was pointed out long ago by Lietzmann, *Korinther I/II*, p. 38; cf. P. Allo, *Saint Paul Première Épître aux Corinthiens* (EBib; Paris, 1934), p. 204.

cumcised); we are none the better for eating (or for being circumcised). I would suggest, therefore, that the Corinthians were using an argument from Paul, but applying it in a way he will disallow. Food, originally used in a context speaking about ceremonial food, is a matter of indifference to God. For Paul this would still be true. But the Corinthians were arguing that such a truth can also be applied to the food eaten at the temple, since the idol has no reality and the food is a matter of indifference. For Paul this is the wrong use of ἐξουσία (v. 9). Food as a matter of indifference is true about *what* one eats; it is not true about *where* — first of all because of what it can do to a brother.

In sum: in vv. 7-13, therefore, Paul is in fact contesting with the Corinthians about their attendance at the idol temples. But his first and greater concern is not with the attendance itself but with the attitude, or basis, on which that right was being asserted. Christian behavior, he tells them, is first of all not a matter of following the way of γνῶσις, but the way of love. Going to the temples is wrong twice: it is not acting in love and (later) it is fellowship in the demonic.

At the conclusion of the argument in this section Paul establishes a principle about food in general that clearly does move beyond the question at hand. "Why, I would forever be a vegetarian," Paul says, "if that would keep from causing a brother to fall." The very personal nature by which Paul establishes that principle probably reflects something of their accusations against him. In any case, its personal nature is no accident, for he uses it as a transition to the matter of their questioning his apostleship.

c. 1 Corinthians 9:1-27

Paul will come back to the question of their "right" (ἐξουσία) to attend the temples. But before that, he responds to their calling his own ἐξουσία and ἐλευθερία into question. This section also functions as instruction, by way of example, of the proper use of ἐξουσία. Moreover, it becomes clear at the end of this argument that Paul is defending not only his authority, but his conduct as well. Only as such can one explain the strange nature of this "defense."

"Am I not free?" he begins. "Am I not an apostle?" He first answers the second question, because it is the crucial one. His answer, in the form of rhetorical questions (9:1b), is based on his own criteria of having seen the risen Lord and having founded the Corinthian church (hence 9:2). In vv. 3-6 he moves on to argue that because he is an apostle, he has all the "rights" (ἐξουσία) of an apostle, especially to the church's financial support. This right is further argued for on the basis of the divinely given natural order (vv. 7-10), applied to their situation (vv. 11-12a), and on the basis of biblical precedent (v. 13) and the word of Jesus (v. 14). Then in 9:12b + 15-18 (vv. 13-14 interrupt for further illustration what he begins in 9:12b) Paul goes on to explain why he has given up this right: so that his "free" preaching of the gospel will illustrate the "free" nature of the gospel.

In 9:19-23 Paul returns to the first question, "Am I not free?" Here it is his conduct that he defends. For Paul "apostolic freedom" means to become everyone else's servant, for the sake of the gospel. This is how he explains his apparent "two-facedness." Marketplace food, animal flesh, or whatever you have may be freely eaten or refused, depending upon the context. But "freedom" does not mean *necessity* (cf. their use of the slogan, πάντα [μοι] ἔξεστιν: 6:12; 10:23); it means *freedom*, which includes both the eating and the non-eating of idol food. Thus when he is with Gentiles he does, when with Jews he doesn't — because it really *is* a matter of indifference. All things to all men to save some, is the apostolic "rule" of conduct.

Finally, he argues (9:24-27) that ἐξουσία and ἐλευθερία must also function in a context of discipline, a point that nicely serves as a transition back to their arguing for the right to eat at the temple meals and especially so since it is based on a false security. If Paul the "free" apostle lives under no false guarantees but must exercise discipline, then how much more the Corinthians, who also have the example from Israel?

d. 1 Corinthians 10:1-13

The content of this section, as we have already noted, leads very specifically to the prohibition of vv. 14-22. But it does so by attacking the Corinthians' false security in the sacraments. It should be noted here that the whole argument scarcely makes sense unless two things are true: (1) The Corinthians really thought they were secure because of a somewhat magical view of baptism and the Lord's Supper. Otherwise it is difficult to imagine the reason for the analogies, which, though reflections of rabbinic thinking, are remote at best. (2) From Paul's perspective the Corinthians were in real danger of "falling away." The warnings are much too strong for merely hypothetical possibilities.

Thus, as we have already noted, Paul uses the history of Israel in two ways. First, these incidents serve as examples of those who, even though they had their "spiritual sacraments," were not secured by them. Second, specific sins in the desert, which caused Israel's "fall," are now warned against in Corinth: idolatry as eating meals before the idol, sexual immorality, testing God, grumbling. Paul concludes with a warning and a word of hope. The one who thinks he stands, in this case the one who has a false security, should take heed lest he fall (10:12). But it is difficult for Paul to end his argument here on a negative note, or on a note that suggests they were to stand firm in their own strength. Thus he once more reminds them of God's gracious provision — even in the time of temptation or testing (= a strong desire or encouragement from friends to attend the temples?). So he concludes: take heed; but remember God's grace.

e. 1 Corinthians 10:14-22

With a very strong "therefore" (διόπερ), Paul brings the preceding argument to its logical conclusion. Conzelmann has suggested that "the train of thought in this section is self-contained" and that "it is hardly possible to discern a strict connection of thought with the preceding section, in spite of διόπερ."[31] To the contrary, the διόπερ is especially appropriate. In vv. 1-13 Paul has warned that Israel's εἰδωλολατρία and πορνεία caused their overthrow, despite their "sacraments." Having warned Corinth of the same possibility, he concludes the argument, "*therefore,* flee εἰδωλολατρία." And εἰδωλολατρία of course means eating at the temples.

The basis of Paul's prohibition is twofold: (1) His understanding of the sacred meal as an actual participation in and fellowship with the deity; (2) his understanding, based on the OT,[32] of idolatry as the locus of the demonic. Thus as he qualified the Corinthians' *way* of knowledge in 8:7-13 by the way of love, so now he qualifies the *content* of their knowledge by a biblical view of idolatry.

Israel had recognized that idols were dumb, yet they also knew the non-existent "gods" had power. They had learned to explain this not on the basis that the "dumb" idols really *represented* "gods" — true monotheism would never allow such henotheism — but on the basis that Satan had originated idolatry to turn people away from the worship of God. The idols, and the "gods," are therefore the dwelling places of demons.

For Paul the demonic powers are real. Even though Christ has triumphed over them (Col. 2:15; Eph. 1:20-21), they nonetheless are still at work in the present age (2 Cor. 4:4; 1 Thess. 2:18; Eph. 6:12; etc.) until they are completely defeated at the Eschaton (1 Cor. 15:24). Since they are real, to eat at the

---

31. Conzelmann, *1 Corinthians*, p. 170.

32. See the various texts listed in Str-B 3.51-52; *inter alia* Deut. 32:17; Ps. 106:37 (LXX 105:37); LXX Ps. 95:5; LXX Isa. 65:11; *1 Enoch* 19:1; 99:7; *Jub.* 22:17.

table in the idol temple is to expose oneself to, indeed to fellowship with, the demons. Such eating is not a display of ἐξουσία, it is to test the Lord (1 Cor. 10:22).

Furthermore, such eating is simply incompatible with life in Christ. For to sit at table for the Christian meal was to fellowship in Christ and his body (10:16-17). And just as in 6:12-20 one may not take what has been joined to Christ by the Spirit and join it to a πορνή, so also one may not take fellowship with Christ at His meal and with Satan at his. These are mutually exclusive options. Therefore, εἰδωλόθυτα finally is prohibited because it is totally incompatible with Christian existence as it is experienced and expressed at the Lord's Table.

f. 1 Corinthians 10:23–11:1

Paul has now basically finished his argument with them over the assertions in their letter. But there are some loose threads, which must still be tied together. Εἰδωλόθυτα are forbidden because it means to participate in the demonic. But marketplace idol food, which apparently Paul *has* been known to eat and for which he has been judged (κρίνεται, v. 29), is another matter altogether. This question comes under the rubric of ἐλευθερία alone, but not as the "right" or "freedom" to do anything one pleases. Here, as one might expect in Paul, his answer is, "Follow my example as I follow Christ" (11:1). And what was Paul's example? To eat or not to eat, according to the context (9:20-23). What rules Christian conduct is not the Law, but neither is it ἐξουσία. What rules is ἐλευθερία set in a context of "benefit" and "edification" on the one hand (vv. 23-24, 32-33), and the glory of God on the other (v. 31).

Thus one is free to eat marketplace food at home, and in a neighbor's home as well, because "the earth and its provisions are the Lord's." But one is also free *not* to eat, if such eating "offends." Nonetheless Paul does not allow the other person (ἄλλης συνειδήσεως = another conscience) to judge him on this matter, for he has said "the grace" and eats with thanksgiving. Therefore, he affirms that he may still eat with impunity, even though he may have refrained from doing so for the sake of the conscience of the one who informed him.

This is probably the best way to understand vv. 29b-30, which are a well-known crux.[33] Paul has begun his advice with the "benefit," "edification," and

---

33. For a summary of options, see C. K. Barrett, *A Commentary on the First Epistle to the Corinthians* (HNTC; New York, 1968), pp. 242-44.

"care for another" framework within which freedom is to operate (vv. 23-24). But then he insists on total freedom with regard to the eating of marketplace food, whatever its context (vv. 25-27). However, in the context of another person's home, the "framework" of vv. 23-24 is to prevail (vv. 28-29a). Nonetheless, his greater concern here is the *freedom* to eat such food, so he cannot conclude the discussion with the "proviso." Once again, despite his willingness to forego eating in a given context, he reaffirms the freedom to eat such food. The sudden shift to the first person singular, and the combined use of ἐλευθερία, κρίνεται, and βλασφημοῦμαι, which recall the defense of Paul's *conduct* in ch. 9, suggest that this is the touchy issue which calls forth this final word.[34]

Finally, he says, in such matters they are to follow his example (11:1). So many of the ideas, as well as the language, of 10:31-33 recall 9:20-23 that one can be confident that this is the example he is referring to. Thus whether one eats, or whether one refrains from eating (= εἴτε τι ποιεῖτε), everything must be done to God's glory and with a concern for others.

IV. Law and Gospel in 1 Corinthians 8–10

If what has been argued in this paper is the correct understanding of εἰδωλόθυτα in 1 Corinthians, there remain two questions that must be answered: (1) If εἰδωλόθυτα in 8:1-13 refers to temple meals, why does Paul not simply forbid it from the beginning? Why does he begin with an attack on γνῶσις that lacks love and then wait until 10:14-22 before he out-and-out condemns attendance at the temple meals? (2) If prohibition is what is ultimately to be the answer, how does one escape the charge that we have thus turned gospel into Law and thereby made Paul self-contradictory?

The latter concern has especially controlled the exegesis of both von Soden and Conzelmann, so that von Soden disallows that even in 10:14-22 Paul is absolutely forbidding meals at the temple,[35] and Conzelmann argues the same for 8:10[36] despite what Paul says in 10:14-22. Thus Conzelmann says of 8:10: "Paul declares: your conduct does not affect *you;* your inner freedom to go to these places is no problem. The problem is the demonstration you give to your brother; not purposely, but in an objective sense — in other words, the way in which he understands your conduct."

---

34. The relationship of 10:29b-30 to 9:19-23 has also been noted, and cogently argued, by Hurd, in *Origin*, pp. 130-31.

35. "Sacrament and Ethics," p. 264.

36. Conzelmann, *1 Corinthians*, pp. 148-49.

In a certain sense the answers to these two questions go together and have to do with Paul's understanding of the relationship between the indicative and imperative. An imperative that precedes the indicative (obedience in order to be justified) is anathema to Paul; but so also is an indicative with *no* imperative. For Paul the imperative is man's grateful response to God's indicative (obedience because of justification). There is plenty of imperative in Paul, but it must never be turned into Law. Obedience does not secure one before God; nonetheless obedience is expected of one whom God has secured.

For this reason Paul invariably treats the imperative in a new way. The divine order still has moral and ethical absolutes; there is conduct that is totally incompatible with life in Christ. Hatred is wrong — absolutely; sexual immorality is wrong — absolutely; idolatry is wrong — absolutely. But Paul never begins there. For the person in Christ they are first of all wrong precisely because the person is "in Christ." With Christ he had died; in Christ he has been raised to live a new existence — κατὰ πνεῦμα instead of κατὰ σάρκα. Such a participant in the new order is to realize the fruit of the Spirit; and for such a person Law has ceased to function as Law. He is no longer enslaved either to the Law or to the sin brought to life or exposed by the Law.

For this reason Paul rarely ever corrects sub-Christian or non-Christian behavior simply by prohibition. Ordinarily he seeks to correct the problem at a deeper level, namely at the level of a person's misunderstanding of the gospel. This pattern occurs several times in 1 Corinthians, most notably in 1:10–4:21; 6:12-20; 12-14 — and 8:1–11:1.

Thus in 6:12-20, for example, he must finally say, φεύγετε τὴν πορνείαν (v. 18). In no situation is πορνεία compatible with life in Christ; it is absolutely forbidden. But it is not forbidden as Law; it is forbidden because it is incompatible with Life in Christ. Why then does he not begin here with the prohibition? Because that might turn ethical response into legal obligation. Therefore, it is not Law they need to hear, but a Christian understanding of freedom (6:12) and a correct understanding of the σῶμα as belonging to the Lord (6:13-14, 19-20). Together these make πορνεία quite impossible for the one who has been joined to Christ, who is "one Spirit with him."

In chs. 1–4 Paul will eventually "forbid" their divisions over leaders with the strongest kind of judgment: "Whoever thus destroys the church, God will destroy him" (3:17); as he will also threaten them with his authority (4:14-21) despite what he has said earlier about being "nothing" or only a servant (3:5-7). But their divisions are only symptoms of far greater ills; they are thereby contradicting the very nature of the gospel itself. For Paul that is the far greater urgency, although their division itself finally comes under reproof.

127

Likewise in these chapters. Eating at the idols' table finally will be forbidden outright: φεύγετε ἀπὸ τῆς εἰδωλολατρίας (10:14). It is incompatible with life in Christ as it is experienced at His table. But their abuse of ἐξουσία in this matter, based on false γνῶσις and issuing in failure to love, is the far greater urgency. Both their attitude and their action are incompatible with the gospel; but their action has resulted from their attitude, and it is this matter to which Paul first addresses himself.

Thus we may conclude that our exegesis not only offers a good explanation of all the data in the text, but it also fits Paul's theology and his ordinary way of arguing.

CHAPTER 10

2 Corinthians 6:14–7:1 and
Food Offered to Idols
(1976)

I

The problems surrounding the integrity of 2 Cor. 6:14–7:1 are well known. In the first place, 6:11-13 and 7:2-4 flow together rather easily as a single piece of personal appeal. "My heart is opened wide toward you . . . In a like reciprocation, I speak as to children, you also open wide (your hearts toward me) . . . Make room for me." The parenesis of 6:14–7:1 abruptly breaks this flow of thought. Moreover, 6:14–7:1 is a self-contained unit, which begins with a concrete prohibition supported by five balanced rhetorical questions, which in turn is supported by a catena of Old Testament passages, and concludes with a general parenesis. Nothing within this passage seems even remotely related, either in language or concept, to the personal appeal within which it is embedded.

All of this is so apparent that most scholars have despaired of finding any relationship to the present context. Even some who argue for integrity have posited that it is an *unrelated* interruption brought on by new information, with a considerable time lapse intervening between vv. 13 and 14.[1] The more common solution, however, has been the denial of the integrity of 2 Corinthians at this point and the identification of 6:14–7:1 as a fragment of the misunderstood "previous letter" of 1 Cor. 5:9, which for some unknown reason was interpolated here by the redactor of 2 Corinthians.[2] This solution

---

1. See especially H. Lietzmann, *An die Korinther I/II* (Tübingen, 1949[4]), p. 129.
2. For a short history of the problem and proposed solutions, with full bibliography up to 1956, see E.-B. Allo, *Saint Paul, Seconde Epître aux Corinthiens* (Paris, 1956[2]), pp. 189-93.

therefore is usually related to other partitioning theories of 2 Corinthians (1:1–2:13; 7:5-16; 2:14–7:4 [minus 6:14–7:1]; 8; 9; 10–13) and often to partitioning theories of 1 Corinthians, which see some similarities in the "spirit" of this passage, if not also in content, with 1 Cor. 6:12-20; 9:24–10:22; and 11:2-34.[3]

The problem of integrity, however, is further complicated by questions of authenticity. There is, for example, an unusually high incidence of *hapax legomena* for such a short unit. ἑτεροζυγοῦντες, μετοχή, συμφώνησις, Βελιάρ, συγκατάθεσις and μολυσμοῦ are all NT hapaxes;[4] and the παντοκράτωρ that concludes the catena of OT citations is found elsewhere in the NT only in the Apocalypse.[5] Furthermore, it has been argued that many of the Pauline words are used with non-Pauline meanings (e.g., δικαιοσύνη, ἀνομία, πιστός, and the collocation of σάρξ and πνεῦμα) and that the dualism and spirit of exclusivism exhibited in the passage are foreign to Paul.

Since many of the words and ideas peculiar to this passage are common stock in the Qumran literature, a growing number of scholars[6] have argued either that it had its origins in Qumran itself and was later Christianized (by Paul[7] or otherwise[8]) or that it was written by a Christian who had imbibed Qumran ideas.[9] Of those who hold this view only J. Gnilka has taken seriously the problem as to how such a text found its way into 2 Corinthians, and even he does not take seriously the problem of its immediate context.

3. See the excellent summary in J. C. Hurd, *The Origin of 1 Corinthians* (London, 1965), pp. 43-47.

4. ἐμπεριπατήσω (6:16) and εἰσδέξομαι (6:17) are also *hapax legomena* and are sometimes listed; but these are wholly irrelevant since they occur in citations of the LXX.

5. μερίς is found elsewhere in Paul only in Col. 1:12, and is therefore considered a *hapax legomenon* by H. D. Betz, "2 Cor. 6:14–7:1: An Anti-Pauline Fragment?" *JBL* 92 (1973): 91, n. 13. However, the authorship of Colossians is a moot point; and since the epistle is Pauline, even if deutero-Pauline, the question of the relationship of its vocabulary to that of the other Pauline letters must remain open.

6. See the discussion in H. Braun, *Qumran und das Neuen Testament*, 1 (Tübingen, 1966), pp. 201-4.

7. E.g., K. G. Kuhn, "Les rouleaux de cuivre de Qumran," *RB* 61 (1954): 193-205.

8. J. A. Fitzmyer, "Qumran and the Interpolated Paragraph in 2 Cor 6:14–7:1," in *Essays on the Semitic Background of the New Testament* (London, 1971), pp. 205-17 [originally published in *CBQ* 23 (1961): 271-80].

9. E.g. J. Gnilka, "2 Kor 6,14–7,1 im Lichte der Qumranschriften und der Zwölf-Patriarchen-Testamente," in *Neutestamentliche Aufsätze* (Festschrift für J. Schmid, ed. J. Blinzler et al., Regensburg, 1963), pp. 86-99; cited here from ET in J. Murphy-O'Connor, ed., *Paul and Qumran* (Chicago, 1968), pp. 48-68. More recently, G. Klinzing (*Die Umdeutung des Kultus in der Qumrangemeinde und im Neuen Testament* [Göttingen, 1971], pp. 172-82) has argued that it came to Paul by way of a Qumran baptismal liturgy. But as with others he offers no explanation as to how Paul may have received it or why it was inserted here.

The two most recent analyses of the passage (apart from Barrett's commentary) are remarkable for their unique, but almost diametrically opposite, solutions. On the one hand, J.-F. Collange[10] has argued that Paul himself was responsible for two editions of 2:14–7:4, one of which concluded with 6:3-13, the other with 6:14–7:4, both of which were included in the final redaction of 2 Corinthians. He argues that the ἄπιστοι with whom the Corinthians should not be ἑτεροζυγοῦντες were Paul's adversaries, the false apostles of chs. 10–13.

By way of contrast, H. D. Betz[11] has carried the argument of the non-Pauline origins of the passage to its ingenious, logical end — it is an *anti*-Pauline fragment reflecting the theology of Paul's opponents in Galatia! Betz argues that ἄπιστος and ἀνομία are forensic terms in this passage, used by its Jewish-Christian author to refer to those such as Paul who were ἑτεροζυγοῦντες because they had abandoned the "yoke of the Torah" with its cultic regulations. This, then, was a piece of self-contained parenesis urging his community *not* to follow Paul. Its presence in 2 Corinthians is to be explained as due to "the redactor of the Pauline corpus [who], for reasons unknown to us, has transmitted [the] document among Paul's letters."[12]

What strikes one as he reads the vast array of literature on this passage is the general unwillingness, except for a few who believe in the letter's integrity, to deal with the contextual question. Nonetheless, the questions of integrity and authenticity must ultimately be answered at this one point: Which hypothesis can make the best sense of the letter in its present form? For after all, whether authentic or spurious, whether put there by Paul or by some redactor, there it sits, right there between 6:13 and 7:2. And *someone* put it there, unless of course one is willing to allow with Père Benoit that it is "a meteor fallen from the heaven of Qumran into Paul's epistle."[13]

The problem, it should be noted, exists for either hypothesis. The person who holds to the traditional view of integrity must show *exegetically* that the best hypothesis of all is that Paul is ultimately responsible for 2 Corinthians in its present form. The person who holds to the "collection of letters" hypothesis *must* show not only that the extant text makes little sense, but also how such a wild state of affairs came about. That is, he has solved nothing by saying that it does not fit; and to keep repeating, "for reasons unknown to us,"

10. *Enigmes de la Deuxième Epître de Paul aux Corinthiens* (SNTS Monograph Series 18; Cambridge, 1972), esp. pp. 302-17.

11. "An Anti-Pauline Fragment?" *JBL* 92 (1973): 88-108.

12. "An Anti-Pauline Fragment?" *JBL* 92 (1973): 108.

13. "Qumrân et le Nouveau Testament," *NTS* 7 (1961): 279 (ET in J. Murphy-O'Connor, ed., *Paul and Qumran* [Chicago, 1968], p. 5).

will not do. One could say that of Paul! He must therefore offer an acceptable hypothesis as to how the present letter came about.

Such hypotheses have been forthcoming at other points where the integrity of, or interpolation into, the NT documents has been questioned. For example, as long as 2 Corinthians was divided into only two parts (1–9, 10–13), it was easy to suppose that a redactor may simply have joined two letters into one, without regard for chronology or logical sequence. When it was divided into several parts, Günther Bornkamm finally recognized the problem and offered a possible solution, based on formal considerations,[14] even though to this writer it lacks conviction. But even he evaded the problem of 6:14–7:1.[15] Likewise for those places in the NT where textual variation appears to be the result of interpolation (e.g., John 5:3b-4; 7:52–8:2; Acts 8:37; 1 John 5:7-8) good reasons can be shown as to *why* a scribe interpolated the text. But here alone in the NT one has an inexplicable interpolation. The only hypothesis ever offered — that a papyrus leaf became detached and was wrongly replaced — is so implausible that few have taken it seriously.[16] Plummer's answer is still valid.

> We have to suppose that the stray leaf chanced to begin and end with a complete sentence, and that, of the leaves between which it was erroneously inserted, one chanced to end with a complete sentence and the other to begin with one. Such a combination of chances is improbable.[17]

Furthermore, if we suppose a redactor to have inserted the loose leaf in this way, then we are also implying that the original of 2 Corinthians was a codex, which though not impossible also seems highly improbable. If, on the other hand, we assume such an error to have occurred at some stage in the transmission of the text, then the traditional response as to lack of textual evidence becomes valid.[18]

The fact is that no theory of interpolation can make any sense of the passage in its present context. For if an interpolation of this kind cannot be

14. "The History of the Origin of the So-Called Second Letter to the Corinthians," *NTS* 8 (1962): 258-64.

15. Cf. his *Paul* (New York, 1971), pp. 244-46.

16. Exceptions are R. Whitelaw, "A Fragment of the Lost Epistle to the Corinthians," *Classical Review* 4 (1890): 12; G. Milligan, *The New Testament Documents* (1913), pp. 181-83; and W. F. Howard, "Second Corinthians," in *The Abingdon Bible Commentary* (New York, 1929).

17. *ICC* (Edinburgh, 1915), p. xxv.

18. It should be noted that this argument is otherwise invalid. For if the compilation of 2 Corinthians was by a redactor, then the interpolation belongs to the "original" text. The lack of textual variation therefore becomes irrelevant.

explained on the hypothesis of a redactor's having thus put together existing documents or fragments — and it cannot — then the only alternative hypothesis is that the redactor edited by copying existing letters or fragments of letters. This means that in this instance he was copying from a fragment which, without punctuation or a break in letters, read something like this:

ΤΗΝΔΕΑΥΤΗΝΑΝΤΙΜΙΣΘΙ
ΑΝΩΣΤΕΚΝΟΙΣΛΕΓΩΠΛΑΤ
ΥΝΘΗΤΥΕΚΑΙΥΜΕΙΣΧΩΡΗΣ
ΑΤΕΗΜΑΣΟΥΔΕΝΑΗΔΥΚΗΣ
ΑΜΕΝΟΥΔΕΝΑΕΦΘΕΙΡΑΜΕΝ

and without reason he arbitrarily decided to insert this piece of parenesis, which he thought to be Pauline, between the ΥΜΕΙΣ and ΧΩΡΗΣΑΤΕ.[19] No redactor in his right mind — or otherwise — would have done such a thing.

Therefore, in spite of the inherent difficulties of the passage and the several plausible options as to its meaning when taken in isolation, I find myself where William Sanday was seventy-five years ago: "I confess that this view [that 6:14–7:1 corresponds to the lost letter of 1 Cor. 5:9] would have a rather strong attraction for me, if I could get over the initial difficulty . . . of framing to myself a satisfactory hypothesis as to the way in which the interpolation came in."[20] We are left then with the option that Paul is responsible for the passage in its present setting. The purpose of this paper is to offer a possible solution within this framework, i.e., to suggest that the passage makes sense in its present context if one takes seriously its relationship to 1 Corinthians.

I propose that this parenesis has a direct relationship to the question of food offered to idols. The proposal is: (1) that 1 Cor. 8–10 is not, as has always been maintained, an answer to a question about idol food in general, but rather a prohibition against joining unbelievers at table in the idol's temple, (2) that the Corinthians (or some of them) rejected this prohibition, (3) that part of their rejection was an *argumentum ad hominem,* and (4) that Paul is in 2 Cor. 6:1ff. responding to the *ad hominem* argument, while at the same time reinforcing his arguments against participation at the temple meal.[21]

---

19. This stichometry, of course, is arbitrary. But by any other stichometry, including one where one column on the scroll concluded with ΥΜΕΙΣ and the top of the next column began with ΧΩΡΗΣΑΤΕ, the fact remains that the copyist had to insert this piece of parenesis by copying it into his basic text at a most illogical juncture.

20. "2 Corinthians vi.14–vii.1," *Classical Review* 4 (1890): 359-60.

21. I am not the first to see the connection between this passage and 1 Corinthians 8–10. After I had finished the major portion of the exegesis for this paper, I discovered that this inter-

It goes without saying, of course, that authenticity is thereby assumed. Some of the arguments against authenticity will be noted in the course of the exegesis in part IV, but the most significant argument — the unusually high incidence of *hapax legomena* — deserves special attention at the outset.

II

The question of the relationship of *hapax legomena* to authenticity is neither an easy nor an obvious one. It can seldom if ever be the sole factor in determining authorship, and it must include several contingencies such as (1) an extraordinary quantity of them, (2) whether or not the subject matter has created the quantitative factor, (3) the author's ordinary vocabulary to express similar ideas, and (4) whether or not the words are truly foreign to the author or his times. In other words, it cannot be simply a question of quantity; it must also be shown that the alleged author is most unlikely to have included these words in his ordinary vocabulary.

When such criteria are applied to the interpolation at John 5:3b-4, for example, they add such an overwhelming weight to the textual evidence that no one can seriously consider the interpolation Johannine. Likewise the high incidence of NT hapaxes in 2 Peter, plus other weighty factors, makes it difficult to believe its author was the writer of 1 Peter. But these contingencies do not seem to exist here.

The quantitative factor must be tempered by several observations. First, five of the alleged NT hapaxes occur in a burst of rhetoric (vv. 14-16a), and it is the nature of Pauline rhetoric to have a sudden influx of *hapax legomena*. For example, the outburst in 1 Cor. 4:7-13 has six NT hapaxes (ἐπιθανάτιος, γυμνιτεύω, ἀστατέω, δυσφημέω, περικάθαρμα, περίψημα) and two other words found only here in Paul (κορέννυμαι, θέατρον). Similarly, the rhetorical expression of apostolic ministry in 2 Cor. 6:3-10 has four NT hapaxes (προσκοπή, ἁγνότης, δυσφημία, εὐφημία), plus one Pauline hapax (ἀριστερός) and four others found in Paul (or the NT) only here and in the comparable passage in 11:22-29 (πληγή, φυλακή, ἀγρυπνία, νηστεία). The quantity of hapaxes in 6:14–7:1 is therefore not a particularly unusual feature.

Moreover, the alleged hapaxes of this passage serve as a perfect example of our need to use greater precision in our use of the term *hapax legomenon.*

---

pretation had been suggested by Calvin in his commentary. Since then it has received only slight notice. To my knowledge the only other commentator who took it seriously was J. J. Lias (Cambridge, 1897).

For it is highly questionable whether the noun form of a verb used elsewhere by an author with precisely, or even nearly, the same meaning is really a hapax. If ἐλπίς and ἐλπίζω, or γνῶσις and γινώσκω, or πίστις and πιστεύω belong together in discussion, then surely the same is true of μετοχή and μετέχω and μολυσμός and μολύνω, especially since the only occurrence in Paul of their verbal counterparts is in 1 Corinthians 8–10 in the discussion of food offered to idols. In fact, the rhetorical question in 2 Cor. 6:14b, "For what participation (μετοχή) have righteousness and iniquity?" is most likely raised precisely because "we all have participation (μετέχομεν) in the one bread" (1 Cor. 10:17) and therefore "cannot participate (μετέχειν) at the table of the Lord and the table of demons" (10:21). Likewise there were some in Corinth whose conscience, being weak, would be defiled (μολύνεται) if they were to eat food offered to idols because they do not have γνῶσις, i.e., they simply cannot get over past associations (1 Cor. 8:7). If our text is dealing with the same issue, as I think it is, then the exhortation for the Corinthians to cleanse themselves from every defilement (μολυσμοῦ) of flesh and spirit is thus to be understood as an extrapolation of the prohibition against sitting at table in the temple of the idol. It is therefore more than simply of passing interest that the second rhetorical question, "Or what fellowship (κοινωνία) has light with darkness?" is also linguistically related to 1 Cor. 10:14-22: "The cup of blessing which we bless, is it not a fellowship (κοινωνία) in the blood of Christ?" Therefore, although food offered to idols is nothing, and idols themselves are nothing, there are demons behind those idols and Paul does not want the Corinthian believers to be "fellows" (κοινωνούς) with demons.[22]

Again, although ἑτεροζυγοῦντες is indeed a *hapax legomenon*, its meaning is very similar to another Pauline compound with ζυγός, viz. σύζυγος, which is *also* a NT *hapax legomenon*.[23] If someone who shares in the gospel, or in Paul's sufferings, can be called a true σύζυγος, then contrariwise Christians may not participate at the table of demons because they would thereby be ἑτεροζυγοῦντες, i.e., involved in an impossible yoke (= sharing) with paganism. ἑτεροζυγέω would therefore be the precise antonym of συζυγέω.

Finally, it should be noted that although συμφώνησις and συγκατάθεσις are NT hapaxes, their verbal counterparts *are* NT words (even though Paul does not use them). He does, however, use the word σύμφωνος (1 Cor. 7:5), which is also a NT hapax, with approximately the same meaning. Further-

---

22. Cf. A. Schlatter, *Paulus der Bote Jesu, eine Deutung seiner Briefe an die Korinther* (Stuttgart, 1956), pp. 580-81, who previously noted this conjunction of μετοχή and κοινωνία, but did not go on to note its implications for the exegesis of this passage.

23. I consider the word to be an appellation, not a proper name.

more, the Pauline letters abound in σύν-compounds which are NT *hapax legomena* (eighteen others in all, not counting strictly Pauline σύν- compounds which occur more than once in his letters). The argument, therefore, may be turned on its head at this point. Instead of these two words supporting *non-Pauline* authorship because they are *hapax legomena,* they rather support *Pauline* authorship because they are of a kind with other Pauline hapaxes.

We are left, therefore, with only two words that are troublesome to Pauline authorship, Βελίαρ and παντοκράτωρ. The appearance of παντοκράτωρ, however, is of little significance to the question of authenticity because it is related to the larger questions raised by the catena itself. The possibility has been entertained that the catena is some kind of pre-Pauline *testimonium*.[24] If so, then the problem of a possible *hapax* vanishes. And even if Paul created the catena., the λέγει κύριος παντοκράτωρ is so thoroughly septuagintal that it is either the final in a series of LXX texts or else he has inserted another λέγει κύριος formula under the influence of the LXX. Because such a formula is found nowhere else in Paul, I tend to think that here he has taken over something that already existed;[25] but in either case παντοκράτωρ will have little bearing on the question of authenticity.

It is perhaps otherwise with the term Βελίαρ, for here one is brought face to face with the question of affinities with Qumran. These affinities have been analyzed in detail by J. A. Fitzmyer and J. Gnilka, both of whom are convinced that they are of such nature as to preclude Pauline authorship. Fitzmyer lists the following ties between this passage and Qumran ideas: (a) the triple dualism of uprightness and iniquity, light and darkness, Christ and Beliar (together with the underlying notion of the "lot"); (b) the opposition to idols; (c) the concept of the temple of God; (d) the separation from impurity; (e) the concatenation of Old Testament texts.[26]

No one can deny that this is a remarkable concurrence in such a brief span. However, it should be noted that the real force of the argument is quantitative, i.e., it is cumulative in effect. For in each case except (d) these are Pauline phenomena in the NT,[27] and in the case of (d), as subsequent exegesis will show, it is highly questionable whether "separation from impurity" is the intended force of that citation. And as for the concurrence of (a), (b), and (c),

24. See especially the excellent discussion in E. E. Ellis, *Paul's Use of the Old Testament* (Edinburgh, 1957), pp. 98-113.

25. Cf. *ibid.,* p. 113: "The λέγει κύριος quotations and a few other striking parallels indicate that some OT texts were already in stereotyped form when Paul used them."

26. Fitzmyer, "Qumran and the Interpolated Paragraph," p. 208.

27. The contrast, Christ and Beliar, of course, does not exist elsewhere in Paul or the NT.

it is precisely the point of this paper that these ideas, which are *inherent to 1 Corinthians,* are brought into collocation in this passage *because* the church is the temple of God (c), and therefore must not have partnership with idols (b), because those idols represent demonic forces (= Βελίαρ) which are over against Christ (a). As Fitzmyer acknowledges, the concept of Belial as the Prince of Evil did not originate in Qumran. It is a thoroughgoing trademark of the Jewish apocalyptic period.[28] Therefore, the force of the argument lies not in the appearance of the word itself, but in the coincidence of this word in a passage that also has other linguistic affinities with Qumran. In any case, as interesting and remarkable as these affinities are, the occurrence of these ideas elsewhere in Paul speaks *for* authenticity, not against it. And it is equally doubtful whether Qumran ideas are the clue to understanding this passage.

We may conclude, therefore, that the authenticity of this passage is not called into question by the *hapax legomena.* What should be noted, on the other hand, are the many genuinely Pauline characteristics found in the passage. Many of these have been noted by others.[29] I add several of my own and simply list them here without argument or comment:

1. μὴ γίνεσθε is a common form of parenesis in Paul (Rom. 12:16; 1 Cor. 7:23; 10:7; 14:20; Eph. 5:7, 17), but is seldom found elsewhere in the NT.

2. ἄπιστος(οι) occurs twelve other times in 1 and 2 Corinthians to refer to unbelievers in contrast to the church.

3. The use of rhetorical questions to make a point is a recurring feature in Paul.

4. The pair δικαιοσύνη/ἀνομία is found in Rom. 6:19; φῶς/σκότος is found in Rom. 2:19; 1 Cor. 4:5; Eph. 5:8; 1 Thess. 5:4-5.

5. The concept of the church as the temple of God is a significantly Pauline idea in the NT.

6. The phrase ζῶν θεός is found elsewhere in Paul at 2 Cor. 3:3 and 1 Thess. 1:9.

7. Paul has merged quotations of OT passages elsewhere at Rom. 3:10-18; 9:25-26, 33; 11:8, 26-27, 34-35; 1 Cor. 15:54-55.

8. Quotations with the λέγει κύριος formula are found at Rom. 12:19; 14:11; 1 Cor. 14:21.

---

28. See the discussion by R. H. Charles, *The Ascension of Isaiah* (London, 1900), pp. lv-lvii, 6-7. The term appears as a name for the devil in Jubilees (1:20), The Testaments of the Twelve Patriarchs (Reub. 4, 6; Lev. 3, 19; Dan. 5), and the Ascension of Isaiah *(passim).* Charles notes: "At the beginning of the Christian era, if not much earlier, Beliar was regarded as a Satanic spirit" (p. lvii).

29. F. H. Chase, "On 2 Cor. vi.14–vii.1," *Classical Review* 4 (1890): 317; A. Schlatter, *Paulus der Bote Jesu,* pp. 580-81.

9. The phrase ταύτας οὖν ἔχοντες is a peculiarity of 2 Corinthians in the NT (3:12; 4:1, 13; cf. 3:4).

10. The plural τὰς ἐπαγγελίας is also found in 2 Cor. 1:20.

11. The appeal of ἀγαπητοί is also found in 2 Cor. 12:19, as well as 1 Thess. 2:8; Rom. 12:19; Phil. 2:12; and 1 Cor. 10:14 (!).

12. ἐπιτελέω is a generally Pauline word in the NT, and ἁγιωσύνη is found *only* in Paul (Rom. 1:4; 1 Thess. 3:13).

13. ἐν φόβῳ θεοῦ has its counterpart in 2 Cor. 5:11, τὸν φόβον τοῦ κυρίου.

This passage is therefore almost certainly Pauline; the real question is, what does it mean and what is it doing there?

III

The clue to understanding 2 Cor. 6:14–7:1 lies in taking seriously its linguistic and conceptual affinities with 1 Cor. 10:14-22 and 3:16-17. Therefore, another look at the nature of the problem of food offered to idols and Paul's answer to it is in order.

If we regard 1 Cor. 8:1–11:1 as a unit — and there are good reasons for doing so[30] — then it is altogether likely that the real problem in this section is not idol food *per se.* As most commentators have seen, it is clear from 10:25–11:1 that for Paul idol food is ultimately a matter of indifference (cf. Rom. 14 on "eating and drinking"). Here he clearly articulates: "Eat whatever is sold in the meat market without raising any question *on the ground of conscience;* for the earth is the Lord's, and everything in it" (10:25-26). Furthermore, if one is invited to dinner at an unbeliever's home, and the Christian is disposed to go, he should eat whatever is set before him, again "without raising any question on the ground of conscience" (10:27). In both cases the conscience of the individual believer is in view, since vv. 28-29 raise the stipulation about the other person's conscience.[31] About food offered to idols in general, therefore, Paul says, "whether you eat or drink, or whatever you do [= refrain from eating or drinking?], do all to the glory of God," with the proviso that one always seeks the good of his neighbor, rather than his own (10:32-33; cf. 10:24).

30. For the latest evaluation of the attempts to divide 1 Corinthians see J. C. Hurd, *The Origin of 1 Corinthians,* pp. 43-47. Hurd and Barrett (*A Commentary on the First Epistle to the Corinthians* [London, 1968], pp. 13-17) independently present strong cases for unity.

31. Although the text is ambiguous, Paul is probably referring to a fellow believer's conscience, who was also invited to dinner, rather than that of the host or another pagan. Cf. the discussion in Barrett, *A Commentary,* p. 242. This means that this is the *only* exception specifically mentioned with regard to idol food in general.

That answer is clear enough. The problem is that it seems to stand somewhat in contradiction to 8:7-13, where Paul has already enjoined a kind of self-imposed abstinence from idol food for the sake of the weaker brother, *whose conscience might otherwise be defiled.* Several ways out of this difficulty have been offered. One has been to assume that Paul is addressing two different parties. He speaks to the "strong" in ch. 8 and urges self-imposed abstinence for the sake of the "weak"; to the weak in 10:25-28 he urges the buying of meat at the *macellum* without trying to ferret out its source.[32] Others have felt that no reconciliation between chs. 8 and 10 is possible and have posited two different letters with various stages of development in Paul's own thinking on the matter.[33] J. C. Hurd[34] has recently suggested that there were no actual "weak" and "strong" in Corinth, but that the church as a whole was responsible for the letter to Paul in which they had taken a somewhat anti-Pauline stance. The problems of "weak" and "strong" and of "eating at the temple" are therefore *hypothetical* suggestions from Paul, which he used in order to strengthen his own case against them, a case in which he essentially agreed with them but did not wish to appear to agree overmuch. Still more recently C. K. Barrett[35] has suggested that 8:1–10:22 is Paul's basic response to the Corinthian letter, while 10:23–11:1 serves "to sum up in terms of practical advice and precept." But he does not thereby take seriously the apparently contradictory nature of 8:7-13 and 10:25-30.

The solution would seem to lie with yet another option; for 8:7-13 and 10:25-30 are contradictory only if one assumes them both to be dealing with idol food in general, i.e., with food sold in the *macellum.* However, if we start with what is perfectly clear, viz. that in 10:25-30 Paul insists that such food is a matter of indifference, then the real problem raised in the Corinthian letter probably lies in the immediately preceding section, 10:14-22, which equally explicitly forbids Christians to eat at the idol temple. In fact the entire section 8:1–10:22 makes perfectly good sense when viewed in its entirety as an answer to this problem. This would mean that the question of whether to eat such food when it was sold in the market in 10:23–11:1 is something of an addendum that Paul felt to be necessary in the light of his answer to the specific problem.

---

32. E.g., Kirsopp Lake, *The Earlier Epistles of St Paul* (London, 1914²), pp. 199-200; cf. the discussion in Hurd, *The Origin of 1 Corinthians,* pp. 115ff.

33. E.g., J. Weiss, *Der erste Korintherbrief* (Göttingen, 1925²), pp. xl-xliii; cf. J. Héring, *The First Epistle of St Paul to the Corinthians* (London, 1962), pp. xii-xv, and all others who hold to a partition theory of 1 Corinthians (e.g., A. Loisy, M. Goguel, J. de Zwaan, W. Schmithals, E. Dinkler).

34. Hurd, *The Origin of 1 Corinthians,* pp. 146-49.

35. Barrett, *A Commentary,* p. 239.

The possibilities of such a problem for the church in Corinth seem considerable. As with the Athens Luke describes (Acts 17:16), Corinth seems to have been a city "wholly given to idolatry." A century after Paul, Pausanias[36] describes a city whose people had "gods many and lords many" (1 Cor. 8:5). Besides the imposing temples of Apollo and Aphrodite, he mentions at least twenty images "in the open" (ἐν ὑπαίθρῳ), six other temples of the Greek "gods," and at least five temples or precincts (τεμένη) for the "lords" of the mysteries.[37] That sacred meals were eaten at these various shrines in Greek antiquity is well known. The worship of the deity included "the offering [which] was burnt, so as to send a sweet smell to the deity above; after [which] the rest of the victim formed part of a feast shared in by both worshippers and priest."[38] There are in fact among the papyri two extant invitations to such meals, both of them "to dine at the table of the *lord* Serapis," probably at the Serapeum in Alexandria.[39] It is perhaps of more than passing interest that two of the sacred precincts in Corinth were of Serapis, who is later described by Porphyry as the chief of the malevolent demons![40]

To be sure, Hurd has argued that "there is nothing in 10:1-22 to suggest either that Paul had heard of idolatrous worship by the Corinthians, or that they specifically asked whether participation in pagan worship was permissible for Christians."[41] But there are several hints within the text of 1 Corinthians that would suggest otherwise. First of all, the problem as it is raised in ch. 8 is given specificity at only one point: "If anyone *sees* you, the one having knowledge, *reclining at table* in the idol's temple" (8:10). The problem is raised precisely because the "gnostic's" action was something the weaker brother could *see*. Otherwise, how does food offered to idols become a point of contention? Did the "gnostic" deliberately nettle the weak? Has the weak man argued for Christian *kosher* markets, which the gnostic disdains? But nothing of

---

36. *Description of Greece*, Book II, 2-5 (Loeb, pp. 253-73).

37. Pausanias does not make such distinctions, but Paul apparently does (see 1 Cor. 8:5-6); cf. W. Bousset, *Kyrios Christos* (ET, Nashville, 1970), pp. 146-47.

38. W. H. S. Jones, *Pausanias' Description of Greece* (London, 1918), Loeb, I, xxi.

39. P. Oxy. 1.110² (ii/A.D.): ἐρωτᾷ δε Χαιρήμων δειπνῆσαι εἰς κλείνην τοῦ κυρίου Σαράπιδος ἐν τῷ Σαραπείῳ αὔριον, ἥτις ἐστὶν ἰε, ἀπὸ ὥρας θ' ("Chaeremon requests your company at the table of the lord Serapis at the Serapeum tomorrow, the 15th, at 9 o'clock"); cf. P. Oxy. 3.523 (ii/A.D.): ἐρωτᾷ σε Ἀντώνιο(ς) Πτολεμ(αίου) διπνῆσ(αι) παρ' αὐτῷ εἰς κλείνην τοῦ κυρίου Σαράπιδος ἐν τοῖς Κλαυδ(ίου) Σαραπίω(νος) τῇ ἰς ἀπὸ ὥρας θ' ("Antonius, son of Ptolemy, requests your company at the table of the lord Serapis in the house of Claudius Serapion on the 16th at 9 o'clock").

40. *De phil. ex orac. haur.* See F. Cumont, *Oriental Religions in Roman Paganism* (New York, 1911; repr. 1956), p. 266, n. 37.

41. Hurd, *The Origin of 1 Corinthians*, p. 143.

this kind is suggested in the text, and 10:25-30 implies the opposite. The problem, after all, is *not* that the weak brother will be merely offended by the action of the one having knowledge. The "offense" is that he will possibly himself be tempted to emulate the action of the "gnostic" and thereby "be destroyed" because he cannot make the fine distinctions the "gnostic" can.

Furthermore, the problem in 10:1-22 seems inexplicable if it is merely hypothetical. In 10:1-13 Paul is making a strong case against a kind of false security based on the Christian sacraments. The point of this argument comes into sharp focus in a series of four OT examples, wherein the Corinthians are told "not to . . . even as some of them did." The first of these is idolatry, and of all the possible supporting texts, Paul quotes Exod. 32:6: "And the people *sat down to eat and drink*"! The third prohibition is against putting the Lord to the test. Probably the scathing conclusion of v. 22 finds *its* meaning right here. The "gnostics" are probably accepting invitations to temple meals, which Paul sees as putting the Lord to the test. "Shall we provoke the Lord to jealousy?" he asks. "Are we stronger than he?"[42]

I submit, therefore, that the problem raised by the Corinthians in their letter to Paul was probably related to two factors: (1) the conduct of Paul and (2) the "gnosis" of (some of) the Corinthians.

(i) Paul's conduct in Corinth is not at all easy to ascertain. I suggest the clue lies in 9:19-23. As to idol meat in general, which he obviously considers a matter of indifference, he has himself become all things (= both eaten and refrained from food offered to idols) to all men (= those who eat and those who refrain from such food), that by all means he might save some. But however noble the intent of such a principle, it is inherently destined for misunderstanding. In this case, those who examine him (9:3) do so because his overall conduct has not appeared to be consonant with apostolic authority. In fact, his conduct has had all the earmarks of weakness rather than authority. He has not only not "got his living by the Gospel" (9:14) — a recognized apostolic right — but neither has he exercised his authority in the matter of idol food, by either commanding abstinence or allowing free partaking. In fact, he has himself probably been known to indulge or refrain in differing contexts. Such conduct by Paul will eventuate, on the one hand, in some not accepting

---

42. It is perhaps of special significance that the second μηδέ (10:8), which immediately follows the prohibition against idolatry with its sitting down to eat and drink, is a prohibition against fornication. One is tempted to see here the problem of temple prostitution brought into close proximity with eating at the idol temple. This is almost certainly how one is to understand the combination of εἰδωλόθυτον and πορνεία elsewhere in the NT (Acts 15:29 [cf. 15:20]; Rev. 2:14, 20). This combination, plus several interesting parallels between 1 Cor. 6:12-20 and 10:1-22, strengthens the conviction that Paul is dealing with temple prostitution in the former passage.

his word as authority at all, and on the other hand in some using his ἐξουσία (which for him meant freedom to do *either* with regard to idol food in general) as grounds for their ἐξουσία to recline at table in the temple. It is arguable, therefore, that ch. 9, although an apparent digression, is directly related to the way the Corinthian "gnostics" had raised the issue in their letter.

(2) The "gnosis" of the Corinthians is basically a theological issue, one with which they can be sure that Paul will be in essential agreement. In some ways the argument seems impeccable. In the first place, in the same way that Paul has argued that neither circumcision nor uncircumcision is of any avail, they have affirmed that "food will not commend us to God" (8:8), since neither eating nor abstaining is of any avail. And since Paul in all likelihood has himself eaten food offered to idols, the eating of such food is surely not wrong. Furthermore, they have argued, since we know that there is only one God, the Father, and only one lord, Jesus Christ, then it is also true that neither Apollo nor Serapis has any real existence. Therefore, it is not only a matter of indifference as to *what* we eat, but also as to *where*. Their question, therefore, or affirmation, was that if the question of food is irrelevant and the idol has no reality, then why can we not eat such food in the idol's temple?

But what would have prompted such a question? I submit that Paul, either by former letter or by envoy, has already pronounced negatively on this issue, but that the "gnostics" have taken exception to the prohibition; and they have done so partly on the basis of Pauline conduct and partly on Pauline doctrine. Therefore, their question is not simply "may we" or "why can't we" eat food offered to idols, but "Why can't we accept the invitation to join our unbelieving friends at table in the temple of Apollo or Serapis?"

To this question Paul has given a four-part answer: (1) 8:1-13, where he examines the theological basis for their question, (2) 9:1-27, where he defends his own conduct in this matter as it relates to his apostolic rights, (3) 10:1-22, where he explicitly forbids eating at the idol-demon temple, and (4) 10:23–11:1, where he addresses the more general question of idol food and generalizes the principles. A brief examination of the first three of these further supports this analysis.

1. In 8:1-6 Paul generally agrees with their position. He is not anti-γνῶσις; indeed, one of the charismata in chs. 12–14 is the word of knowledge. But as with all charismata, and many other Christian things as well, they are worthless apart from love. Therefore, just as in 6:12, the basic qualification to Christian conduct is concern for a brother: "but love builds up."

Furthermore, he goes on to argue in 8:7, the fact is that not all have the same degree of knowledge. While it is true that the idol does not really exist, he qualifies it by saying that *for us* there is only one God. This does not mean that the idol really *is* a god, but rather that *for them* it has meaning as a god. Some Christians, who formerly attributed reality to Apollo, may now indeed accede in principle that "an idol has no real existence," but in fact the heart has not caught up with the head. Such a man simply cannot free himself from former associations.

Therefore, Paul answers in effect, although all that you say about idols is true, you cannot go — and one must take seriously that the διόπερ in 8:13 amounts to a prohibition — to the temple, first of all because of the stumbling-block principle. Such conduct endangers the Christian life of a brother who does not share your γνῶσις. Therefore, this "ἐξουσία of yours" must be subjected to love.

2. In the same way, Paul goes on to say in 9:1-23, in spite of whatever reasons for it you may suspect, I have not always made use of my ἐξουσία lest I put an obstacle (9:12, ἐγκοπήν = 8:9, πρόσκομμα) in the way of the gospel of Christ. Lest this failure to use his ἐξουσία — here in the matter of accepting provision — be interpreted as lacking that authority, he makes a spirited defense both of his apostleship and of his "rights." But for Paul ἐλευθερία *and* ἐξουσία mean freedom to do all things for the sake of the gospel (9:23). Any other use of freedom and authority, especially freedom and authority that demands being exercised, becomes self-destructive (9:24-27; cf. 6:12, where it becomes self-enslavement), as well as fails to build up or help a brother (10:23-24).

3. In 10:1-22 Paul goes on to argue that in any case Christian life is totally incompatible with participation in the feasts at the idol's temple. The reason is not that Apollo exists, or that the food eaten there is somehow contaminated (10:19). The reason lies rather in Paul's apocalyptic eschatology, with its recognition of the demonic nature of evil and the cosmic dimensions of the Christ event. Attendance at the temple is not forbidden because, as in the Didache, it represents "the worship of dead gods" (Did. 6:3), but because the idol temple is for Paul the (or a) locus of the demonic. Although this is not explicitly said elsewhere in Paul, it is in keeping with his Jewish tradition, which has already made this equation.[43] But for Paul this equation is probably sharpened by his eschatological understanding of the principalities and powers.[44]

For Paul Christ has triumphed over these powers (Col. 2:15); he is now sitting in heavenly places above them (Eph. 1:20-21; cf. Phil. 2:9-11) and has

---

43. See the various texts listed in Strack-Billerbeck, III, 51-52; *inter alia* Deut. 32:17; Ps. 96:5 (LXX 95:5), 106:37 (LXX 105:37); Isa. 66:11; 1 Enoch 19:1; 99:7; Jub. 22:17.

44. A similar logical sequence is found in Galatians 4, where "beings which by nature are not gods" (= idols?) are in turn called "weak and beggarly elemental spirits" (RSV) to which the Galatians are seen to "return" in their new enslavement.

thereby delivered humans "from this present evil age" (Gal. 1:4). Nonetheless the demonic powers, which are ultimately to be completely defeated at the τέλος (1 Cor. 15:24; cf. Rom. 16:20), still are at work in the present age. Satan is still "the prince of darkness grim" (cf. Eph. 2:2), the "god of this age" who "has blinded the minds of unbelievers" (2 Cor. 4:4; ἀπίστων! cf. 2 Cor. 6:14). To be excommunicated from the (table?) fellowship of the church is to be turned over to Satan (= put back into the sphere of Satan's power [1 Cor. 5:3-5]). And even though Satan is a defeated foe, Paul himself can yet be hindered by him (1 Thess. 2:18) or buffeted by an ἄγγελος Σατανᾶ (2 Cor. 12:7); and Christians in the world continue to contend with the satanic powers (Eph. 6:12).

It is in the light of this perspective that one is to understand 1 Cor. 10:1-22. To eat at table in the idol temple is to expose oneself to, and participate in, the demonic powers. And these powers are not to be tampered with for two reasons. (a) The powers are real, and even participation in the Christian sacraments is no special guarantee of protection. There are, Paul says, many OT examples of such failings, which "were written down for our instruction, upon whom the end of the ages has come" (1 Cor. 10:11). And if anyone thinks otherwise, he is apt to fall (10:12). Therefore, to eat in the presence of demons is not a display of "authority" or "strength"; it is foolhardy. One is thereby "testing the Lord" (10:9) and appears to be provoking him to jealousy, or at least pitting his own strength against God's (10:22).

(b) But finally such actions are simply incompatible with life in Christ. For one who ate at table in the Christian community did so not simply to take nourishment, but somehow to participate in the Lord himself. Likewise to sit at table in the temple is to participate in the demonic itself. And just as in 1 Cor. 6:12-20, where the Christian's σῶμα, which by the habitation of the Spirit is a temple of God and thereby belongs to him, cannot be joined to a harlot, so also the church, which too is a temple by the habitation of the Spirit, may not eat at the Lord's table and the table of demons. Such "mixed mating," Paul says further in 2 Cor. 6:14–7:1, is simply unthinkable. For what accord has Christ with Belial (= the prince of the demonic)? Or what agreement has the temple of God with idols?

Therefore, there is no openness in Paul on this question. It is prohibited pure and simple. But such a prohibition does not obtain apart from the temple of the idol-demon, probably because eating at home or with friends is not a cultic meal with the concomitant participation in the deity (demon). Thus one may otherwise eat or drink without restriction, given that he is always aware of the concerns of others (whether Jew, pagan, or Christian).

It should be noted that this apparently circuitous path to prohibition is quite in keeping with patterns Paul has established elsewhere. For one might well ask, Why the stumbling-block principle in ch. 8 if the answer is simply, No! The reason would seem to lie in Paul's understanding of the Christian imperative as always to be an outflow of grace. For example, following the pattern of the stumbling-block principle, the prohibition has an exact parallel in 1 Cor. 6:12-20. In v. 18 he out-and-out forbids fornication (with the temple prostitute?); yet the basic answer to fornication lies in a proper understanding of Christian freedom, which seeks to be helpful and refuses to be enslaved even to one's own concept of freedom (which in such case turns into license). Furthermore, as in 1 Corinthians 8–10, this prohibition is supported by theology. The doctrine of the resurrection tells believers that their bodies are not destined for destruction but for the Lord. Therefore, φεύγετε τὴν πορνείαν. It is perhaps noteworthy that the only other occurrence of φεύγω in Paul (apart from the Pastorals) is in the passage under comment. The first reason for avoiding the table in the temple is care for the one for whom Christ died; nonetheless there are theological reasons. Therefore, φεύγετε ἀπὸ τῆς εἰδωλολατρίας.[45]

IV

It is against this background that 2 Cor. 6:14–7:1 can be shown to make perfectly good sense, and to do so within the context of 2 Corinthians 1–7. But this requires at least a partial reconstruction of the events and relationships between Paul and Corinth between the writing of our 1 and 2 Corinthians. Such a reconstruction is admittedly difficult; however, the recent proposal by C. K. Barrett offers a reasonable base from which to proceed.[46]

Pertinent to this study are the following observations. (1) Although the flare-up that caused the strained relationships seems to have been accelerated by outside influences, an anti-Pauline sentiment, partly related to his refusal to accept their support, already existed in the church (1 Cor. 9:1-18; cf. 4:14-21). Therefore, all the problems addressed in 2 Corinthians may not be assumed to have arisen after 1 Corinthians. (2) 2 Cor. 7:12 clearly implies that the now lost intermediate letter, written by Paul "out of much affliction and anguish and tears" (2 Cor. 2:4), had to do basically with the church's relaxed attitude toward the one who had wronged Paul (presumably; cf. 2:5). That letter, according to Titus, had accomplished its purpose: the church had repented, was ready to re-

---

45. One might observe further that the prohibition in Gal. 5:16, "do not gratify the desires of the flesh," follows an understanding of grace: "faith working through love" and "through love be servants of one another."

46. *A Commentary on the Second Epistle to the Corinthians* (London, 1973), pp. 5-21.

affirm its loyalty to Paul, and had taken steps to that end by its discipline of the wrongdoer (ὁ ἀδικῶν). (3) But many of the former problems appear still to be smoldering. The matter of the collection still needed further attention. Apparently the looseness toward sexual sins was still among them (12:21, πολλοὺς τῶν προημαρτηκότων καὶ μὴ μετανοησάντων).[47] And certainly, from Paul's point of view, the continuing attitudes of some of them toward him reflected an inadequate understanding of the apostolic office and ministry.

2 Cor. 6:14–7:1 appears to have its *Sitz im Leben* within these latter concerns. Titus had informed Paul of their repentance over the specific matter of the wrongdoer — and Paul is comforted by that; but Titus had also informed him that some of the prior problems still persisted. Probably some of the "gnostics" were still "holding out" against his authority and some of his specific responses given in 1 Corinthians. One such position which they rejected, and where they also questioned his authority, was the prohibition of 1 Cor. 8:1–11:1. Still unconvinced by his argument, they had informed Titus in no uncertain terms that Paul's position had the effect of restricting them (6:12; στενοχῶρος in the classical sense), and therefore he is wronging (ἀδικέω) or misleading (φθείρω) them (7:2).

It is toward this response of theirs that Paul begins specifically to address himself at the conclusion of the "great apology of the apostolic office" (2:14–7:4).[48] Toward the end of ch. 5 the "apology" begins to assume the form of personal appeal. "Be ye reconciled to God" (5:20), he pleads. "As a fellow worker with God himself," he goes on, "I beseech you not to have received the grace of God in vain" (6:1; = sharing table with demons?); "for we put no obstacle in anyone's way" (6:3). Then after a rhetorical expansion of his understanding of the true marks of apostleship (sufferings, purity of motive, etc.), he turns and appeals directly to those who have rejected his authority and the prohibition against participation at the temple feasts. "It is not I who have restricted you. Your action has caused you to become restricted in your own affections. I appeal to you as children, reciprocate our love." In such case, then, Paul's prohibition to attend the feasts at the idol-demon temple was to be viewed as an expression of his love for them. However, right at this point he interrupts the appeal, not simply to reiterate the prohibition but to reinforce the reasons for it in a more positive way.

The rest of the argument should then be reconstructed thus:

---

47. This assumes that chs. 10–13 *follow* 1–9. Barrett has convincingly demonstrated this, even if one is not necessarily convinced that it represents a fifth letter, which followed hard on the heels of the fourth (2 Cor. 1–9).

48. So called by G. Bornkamm, *NTS* 8 (1962): 260.

A. Opening parenesis (reiterating the point of 1 Cor. 10:14-22)

Μὴ γίνεσθε ἑτεροζυγοῦντες ἀπίστοις.

B. Rhetorical expansion of the opening parenesis (again reflecting 1 Cor. 10:14-22)

τίς γὰρ μετοχὴ δικαιοσύνῃ καὶ ἀνομίᾳ; ἢ τίς κοινωνία φωτὶ πρὸς σκότος;
τίς δὲ συμφώνησις Χριστοῦ πρὸς Βελιάρ; ἢ τίς μερὶς πιστῷ μετὰ ἀπίστου;

This final question leads directly to

τίς δὲ ουγκατάθεσις ναῷ θεοῦ μετὰ εἰδώλων;

C. The basis for the parenesis (reflecting the argument of 1 Cor. 3:16-17)

ἡμεῖς γὰρ ναὸς θεοῦ ἐσμεν ζῶντος.

D. He then supports (C) with a biblical base:

καθὼς εἶπεν ὁ θεὸς ὅτι

(i) The first "promise": God will dwell in the midst of his people (= the church)

ἐνοικήσω ἐν αὐτοῖς καὶ ἐμπεριπατήσω [Lev. 26:12]
    καὶ ἔσομαι αὐτῶν θεός, [cf. Ezek. 37:27]
    καὶ αὐτοὶ ἔσονταί μου λαός.

(2) But God's people must avoid idolatry at all costs

διὸ ἐξέλθατε ἐκ μέσου αὐτῶν [cf. Isa. 52:2]
    καὶ ἀφορίσθητε, λέγει κύριος,
    καὶ ἀκαθάρτου μὴ ἅπτεσθε.

(3) The second "promise" — God will father his people

κἀγὼ εἰσδέξομαι ὑμᾶς, [cf. Ezek. 20:34]
    καὶ ἔσομαι ὑμῖν εἰς πατέρα, [cf. 2 Sam. 7:14]
    καὶ ὑμεῖς ἔσεσθέ μοι εἰς υἱοὺς καὶ θυγατέρας, λέγει κύριος παντοκράτωρ. [cf. Amos 3:13 LXX]

E. Concluding parenesis, based on the promises, but demanding avoidance of idolatry

ταύτας οὖν ἔχοντες τὰς ἐπαγγελίας, ἀγαπητοί, καθαρίσωμεν ἑαυτοὺς ἀπὸ παντὸς μολυσμοῦ σαρκὸς καὶ πνεύματος, ἐπιτελοῦντες ἁγιωσύνην ἐν φόβῳ θεοῦ.

Further detailed examination of the five parts supports this analysis.

A. The opening prohibition, "Do not bear a foreign yoke with unbelievers," has usually been seen as the key to the whole section. Historically it has been the *locus classicus* for all forms of Christian separatism, from marriage, to business partnerships, to the kind of withdrawal from "the world" that Paul expressly condemns in 1 Cor. 5:9-11. And such an interpretation continues to hold sway; for those who see the passage as a piece of christianized Essenism or as a Jewish-Christian attack on Pauline freedom (Betz) continue to take the text to be related basically to ritual, ethical, or "worldly" separation.[49]

The more traditional separatist stance usually had four basic reference points in the passage — all negative prohibitions: (1) "be not unequally yoked together with unbelievers," (2) "come out from among them and be ye separate," (3) "touch not the unclean thing," and (4) "let us cleanse ourselves from every defilement." Thus "holiness" was viewed as obedience to these negatives. Even as careful a scholar as Betz has fallen prey to this when he says that "the ἄπιστοι are those who represent ἀνομία (6:14), 'idol-worship' (6:16), 'impurity' (6:17; 7:1)."[50] But this equation of unbeliever with impurity abuses both the inner structure of the argument and the intent of the OT catena. One simply *must not start* with the OT quotations, nor should one consider the language of the LXX as determinative for finding the meaning of ἑτεροζυγοῦντες ἀπίστοις. The point of those citations is *promises* — granted they are promises contingent on separation from idolatry, but *promises* nevertheless.

It is highly questionable whether μὴ γίνεσθε ἑτεροζυγοῦντες ἀπίστοις is to be viewed at all as a separatist text in the traditional sense. In the first place, ἑτεροζυγέω is metaphor pure and simple — and not necessarily a metaphor which, as Betz insists, presupposes "two yokes," one for believers, another for unbelievers.[51] The figure almost certainly derives from Lev. 19:19, where the LXX reads ἑτερόζυγος for cross-breeding, and from Deut. 22:10, where it is forbidden to plow with an ox and ass together. It is a simple metaphor which suggests that just as it is forbidden to men of old to plow with different kinds of animals under the same yoke, so the Christian is a different "breed" from the unbeliever and is forbidden an improper relationship with him. What that relationship is, however, is *not* inherent in the prohibition itself; nor does one find help in the metaphorical use of "yoke" in the OT, where it usually refers to the burden imposed by the foreign oppressor (e.g., Isa. 9:4; 10:27; 14:25;

---

49. Thus Gnilka, "2 Kor 6,14–7,1," pp. 88-99, on the one hand, and H. D. Betz, "2 Cor. 6:14–7:1," p. 91, on the other.

50. Gnilka, "2 Kor 6,14–7,1," p. 90.

51. *Ibid.*, p. 89.

Jer. 27:8, 11, 12; cf. Gen. 27:40; 1 Kings 12:4). In any case, the clue to the passage lies not in the metaphor itself, but in the sets of contrasts in the following rhetorical questions.

The meaning of ἀπίστοις, however, can be more easily determined. In the first place it is a word used by Paul only in the Corinthian correspondence (apart from the Pastorals) and always to set the pagan in sharp contrast to those within the church. They are the ones whom the god of this world (= Satan/Belial) has blinded (kept in darkness!) so that they cannot see the light (!) of the gospel of Christ (2 Cor. 4:4); they are the unrighteous (ἄδικοι) before whom members of the community are not to redress their internal grievances (1 Cor. 6:6). But Paul does not forbid the believer to have close associations with them. If married to one who is ἄπιστος, the believer should not seek divorce (1 Cor. 7:12-15) and if invited to their homes for dinner, believers are at liberty to go (1 Cor. 10:27). Furthermore, it is possible that from time to time the ἄπιστοι found their way into the Christian assembly gathered for worship (1 Cor. 14:22-25). The problem, then, in 1 Cor. 6:14 is not in deciding who they are but, in the light of the free association allowed elsewhere, to determine what kind of association with them constitutes becoming ἑτεροζυγοῦντες.[52] That that relationship is related to the prohibition in 1 Cor. 10:14-22 is especially to be seen in the rhetorical expansion that follows.

B-C. The rhetorical questions that expand the opening parenesis are apparently given for effect, both to drive home the inviolable nature of the prohibition and to give once again the theological basis for it. They are set out in balanced pairs, of which the fifth (ναὸς θεοῦ/εἴδωλα) is the most important. "For what συγκατάθεσις has the temple of God with idols?" is *the* great question to which the others lead; and the affirmation, "for we are the temple of the living God," not only derives its meaning from the contrasts of the fifth question but also serves in turn as the premise on which the rest of the argument rests. Therefore, the content of the pairs in this question gives meaning to the other pairs as well as to the ἑτεροζυγοῦντες ἀπίστοις.

Just as in 1 Cor. 10:14, the concern here is not with idolatry in general. That is something from which Christians have turned to serve the living and true God (1 Thess. 1:9), and which therefore is automatically banned (Gal. 5:20; 1 Cor. 5:11). Nor is one to "spiritualize" the term "idol" and thereby make it equal to sin and uncleanness.[53] It is rather a specific expression of idolatry that is in view. To support the prohibition of eating at the temple of the idol-

---

52. For another view see *ibid.*, pp. 89-90.

53. As does B. Gärtner, *The Temple and the Community in Qumran and the New Testament* (SNTS Monograph Series 1; Cambridge, 1965), p. 51.

demon, Paul reaffirms the argument of 1 Cor. 3:16-17. There he had argued that the church was the temple of God in Corinth because God's Spirit dwelt among them (especially when they were assembled in the name of the Lord; cf. 1 Cor. 5:3-5). As such they were God's alternative — his only alternative — to Corinth, including Apollo, Serapis, *et al.* Therefore, to destroy God's temple by division meant to place oneself under the awful judgment of God.

It is precisely this figure, which was already implicit in the argument based on the cultic meal ("all who partake are one body," 1 Cor. 10:16-17), which now becomes the explicit grounds for the prohibition. Those who have a share (μερίς)[54] in the meal in the temple of God cannot also participate (μετοχή) or have fellowship (κοινωνία) at the table of idols, because they would thereby sacrifice to demons, and Christ has no συμφώνησις with Belial, the prince of demons.

Thus it is in this sense only that the church is not to be ἑτεροζυγοῦντες. The church is not to "come out from among" the unbelievers *per se,* but rather, as the temple of God, it cannot associate with unbelievers in the temple of the demons. The pairs in the first four rhetorical questions, therefore, are various contrasts that represent the impossibility of the association of the church with idols. To participate at the table of Belial means that the believer (πιστός) is trying to have a share in the demonic with the unbeliever (ἄπιστος),[55] that he has tried to be a partner both in righteousness and lawlessness, both in light and darkness. It is in the context of the cultic meals (and perhaps also temple prostitution, cf. 1 Cor. 6:15 and 10:7-8) that these pairs would appear in sharpest contrast as mutually exclusive options (i.e., ἑτεροζυγοῦντες ἀπίστοις).

D. It is also in this light that the supporting catena of OT texts makes the most sense. As indicated earlier, one cannot be sure whether the catena originated with Paul or whether he borrowed from some previous source. But in any case, the present meaning of the catena is *not* to be found by isolating what it may have meant at its place of origin,[56] for it now has been filled with

---

54. Fitzmyer ("Qumran and the Interpolated Paragraph," pp. 209-10) has seen μερίς as reflecting the concept of "lot" in Qumran, as in the "lot of light" or "lot of God." But the word also means precisely what is suggested here, a "share of food." Cf. Moulton-Milligan, p. 398.

55. I grant that this substantival usage of πιστός is unusual for Paul; but it is surely not impossible — nor improbable. When he says that one who is justified by faith is blessed σὺν τῷ ποστῷ Ἀβραάμ (Gal. 3:9), he uses the adjective with nearly the same meaning as he does the substantive here.

56. E.g., in Jewish Christianity as Betz, "2 Cor. 6:14–7:1," pp. 92-99 (cf. L. Cerfaux, *The Church in the Theology of St. Paul* [New York, 1959], pp. 151-52); in Qumran as Fitzmyer, "Qumran and the Interpolated Paragraph," pp. 215-16.

Pauline content. In the present context it serves a double purpose: (1) to support the claim that the church is God's temple because they are God's people, and (2), because of that, to reinforce the church's absolute dissociation from idolatry.

Part 1 of the catena is a promise, taken basically from Lev. 26:1-2 (perhaps influenced by Ezek. 37:27) and now fulfilled in the church, that they are marked off as the people (λαός) of God because God himself dwells in their midst. Thus the passage serves to join two Pauline images of the church (ναός — λαός). In its OT setting, Israel is promised to be the λαός of God within the context of keeping God's covenant, which begins with the prohibition of idolatry (cf. Exod. 19:5 and 20:2-3); and it is their idolatry that leads to the judgment, "You are not my people" (Hos. 1:10). But here the significance of the text lies primarily with the words, "and I shall dwell among them." For Paul the church is the new people of God because they are a habitation of the Spirit. They are all baptized "in the one Spirit" and all given that same Spirit to drink (1 Cor. 12:13);[57] it is the Spirit dwelling among them that makes them God's temple (1 Cor. 3:16), and the presence of the prophetic Spirit will cause even the ἄπιστοι to confess: "Surely God is among you" (1 Cor. 14:22-25).

It is this promise of God's dwelling among them that leads to the reiterated prohibition in part 2. The church is "to come out from among *them*." "Them" in this context, therefore, refers only indirectly to the ἄπιστοι in v. 14. It is not unbelievers *per se* who are in view — that *is* indeed foreign to Paul — but neither in this context is ritual uncleanness or Gentiles (a true absurdity) in view. Nor should one reverse the text to suggest that it involves the cleansing of impurity from the church.[58] It simply repeats the prohibition to join in the temple feasts. The language used, of course, is determined by its OT origins (Isa. 52:11), which indeed is primarily cultic in its intent. Even there the departure is from idolatrous Babylon. But as is often true in Paul's use of the OT, although the text is chosen because of its language, the point is no longer in the language itself but in the larger context to which the passage can be seen to pertain. Because the church through the Spirit is the new people of God, she must avoid the unclean thing, the habitation of demonic spirits.

The second promise, that God will welcome them and be their Father, probably existed in the original catena and is here merely carried over. In any

---

57. For a discussion of the options that led to the choice "in the one Spirit" as over against "by the one Spirit," see J. D. G. Dunn, *Baptism in the Holy Spirit* (SBT 15 [2nd series], London, 1970), pp. 127-31.

58. R. J. McKelvey suggests this in *The New Temple: The Church in the New Testament* (Oxford, 1969), p. 95.

case, it simply reaffirms the intent of the previous promise. And it is on the basis of these promises that Paul is ready to make a concluding parenesis.

E. As usual with Paul, the OT texts are not the final word; they need a concluding interpretation or Christian affirmation. And even here — or perhaps especially here — the temple imagery of 6:16 is again determinative. The church is God's temple in Corinth. This is affirmed by OT promises of God's dwelling presence among his people; it is now fulfilled by the presence of the Spirit in their midst. It is because the church has these promises, now fulfilled, that they are to exhibit "cleanness" and "holiness." Thus the cultic language (καθαρίσωμεν ἑαυτούς, μολυσμοῦ, ἁγιωσύνην) of this concluding word, which has been so troublesome, derives directly from the temple imagery, *not* from the OT catena. The defilement that is in view therefore is *not* to be interpreted as being either ritualistic (*à la* Qumran) or as simply ethical and moral.

The troublesome words in the passage are the collocation of "flesh" and "spirit" with defilement. It has been argued that "flesh" for Paul is basically a pejorative term, describing the sinful nature, and is therefore impossible to cleanse. "Spirit" likewise is not thought of as needing cleansing by Paul, since it refers primarily to the Spirit by whom and in whom the Christian now lives. However, Paul does not always use these terms in their full theological sense. In fact, as Barrett has pointed out, "both [terms] are used in a loose popular way in this epistle. At 7:5 Paul says, 'Our flesh found no relief,' meaning exactly what he had said at 2:13, 'I got no relief for my spirit.' In each case he means, 'I got no relief,' both *flesh* and *spirit* standing for the self."[59] What Paul therefore means here is either "inwardly" and "outwardly," much the same as he uses σῶμα and πνεῦμα in 1 Cor. 7:34, or simply the whole man, such as he does by the combination πνεῦμα/ψυχή/σῶμα in 1 Thess. 5:23 (also in the context of "holiness"). Most likely he means "outwardly" and "inwardly." The inward cleansing is that which Paul regularly has in view when he speaks of the ethical imperative of the Christian life. But the church must cleanse itself from *every* defilement, including the defilement of attendance at meals in the presence of the demons.

Having thus repeated what for him was a most important truth, namely, that as the temple of God the church could have no association with the demonic worship at the demon's temple, Paul resumes the personal appeal. "Open wide to us," he pleads, "for this prohibition is not restrictive, nor do we thereby wrong or take advantage of you. And finally, not even this appeal of mine is to be considered condemnatory."

59. *Second Corinthians*, p. 202.

It is significant to note here that the χωρήσατε ἡμᾶς is clearly resumptive, and it is a cumbersome intrusion if 6:14–7:1 is taken out. That is, the oft-repeated assertion that 6:13 and 7:2 read smoothly without 6:14–7:1 is not altogether true. What would read smoothly would be 6:13 and 7:2 beginning with οὐδένα ἠδικήσαμεν.[60]

In conclusion, and in all candor, it is admitted that the one real difficulty with this interpretation is that "food offered to idols" is not specifically mentioned either in this passage or its immediate context. However, one can scarcely deny its linguistic and conceptual affinities both with 1 Cor. 3:16-17 and 10:14-22. Furthermore, this is not the only place where 2 Corinthians presents difficulties. The problem, of course, is that there was so much that went on between Paul and Corinth which they knew, and which therefore could be assumed in the correspondence, but where we are simply on the outside looking in — and that, sometimes it seems, "through a glass, darkly."

---

60. One might compare the resumptive ζηλοῦτε δὲ τὰ πνευματικά in 1 Cor. 14:1 after the long digression on love.

CHAPTER 11

Freedom and the Life of Obedience
(Galatians 5:1–6:18)[1]
(1994)

Historically this passage has been understood to reflect a major shift in the letter, from the argument proper to a section of parenesis (exhortation). Thus these chapters are most often viewed as "ethical instruction" following "right thinking about the Christian gospel" set forth in chs. 3–4.[2] But despite the popularity of this view, these chapters are much better understood as bringing the *argument*[3] of Galatians to its proper conclusion.[4] In his transitional

1. The following commentaries are referred to by the last name of the author: D. C. Arichea and E. A. Nida (1976); H. D. Betz (Hermeneia, 1979); J. M. Boice (EBC, 1976); F. F. Bruce (NIGTC, 1982); E. D. Burton (ICC, 1921); J. Calvin (ET, 1963); R. A. Cole (TNTC, 1965); G. S. Duncan (MNTC, 1934); R. Y. K. Fung (NICNT, 1988); D. Guthrie (NCBC, 1974); W. Hendriksen (1968); M.-E. Lagrange (EB, 1925); J. B. Lightfoot (1865); R. N. Longenecker (WBC, 1991); H. A. W. Meyer (MeyerK, 1870); F. Mussner (HTKNT, 1974); H. Ridderbos (NICNT, 1953); H. Schlier (MeyerK, 1965); J. R. W. Stott (1968).

2. A view perpetuated most recently by Fung, p. 243. For an especially helpful overview of how this section has been understood within the letter, see John M. G. Barclay, *Obeying the Truth: A Study of Paul's Ethics in Galatians* (Edinburgh: T. & T. Clark, 1988), pp. 9-26.

3. On the question of the *form* of the letter, especially its "rhetoric" (as found, e.g., in the commentaries by Betz and Longenecker; cf. B. H. Brinsmead, *Galatians' Dialogical Response to Opponents*, SBLDS 65 [Chico, Calif.: Scholars Press, 1982]), see esp. C. H. Cosgrove, *The Cross and the Spirit: A Study in the Argument and Theology of Galatians* (Macon, Ga.: Mercer University Press, 1988), pp. 23-38. His observation (p. 26) that whatever else Galatians might be, it is a *letter,* is too easily forgotten by those enamored by first-century rhetoric. If rhetorical categories are useful at all, then the persuasive nature of the argument as a whole, in which Paul is trying to convince the Galatians that he is right and the agitators are wrong, demands that it is deliberative, not apologetic. The "apologetic" nature of some parts are to be explained on the grounds that Paul's opponents have tried to discredit his gospel in part by discrediting him.

4. It functions, in fact, as Paul's own response to his question in 3:3: "Having *begun* by the

"speech"[5] in 2:15-21 — ostensibly to Peter but more obviously for the sake of the Galatians — Paul sets forth the basic theological propositions of the argument that follows: (a) that righteousness is "not by works of Torah" (vv. 16, 21); (b) that righteousness is "by faith in Christ Jesus" (v. 16), who also brought an end to Torah observance (vv. 18, 21); and (c) that the indwelling Christ (by his Spirit, is implied) is the effective agent for living out true righteousness (v. 20).

Paul supports the first two of these propositions in the immediately following argument (3:1–4:7), appealing, first, to their own experience of the Spirit (3:1-5) and, second, to Scripture and the work of Christ (3:6-29), concluding in 4:1-7 by bringing the work of Christ and the Spirit together. After several paragraphs that apply this argument (4:8-11), appeal to their loyalty (4:12-20), argue from scriptural analogy (4:21-31), and make application and appeal once more (5:1-11), Paul finally, in 5:13–6:10, picks up the third concern in the "speech" — the sufficiency of the Spirit, now over against both Torah (by effecting the true righteousness that Torah called for but could not produce) and the flesh (which characterized their former life as Gentiles and had made Torah ineffective for Jews).

At issue in this letter is the inclusion of Gentiles as full and equal members of the people of God — whether, having believed in Christ, they must also accept the "identity markers" of Jewishness[6] in order to be genuine "chil-

---

Spirit, do you now *come to completion* by the flesh?" For a more complete presentation similar to what is offered here, see Barclay, *Obeying*. One should especially notice in this regard the general paucity of imperatives. For example, in vv. 13-26 there are only two second person plural imperatives ("become slaves of one another" in v. 13 and "walk by the Spirit" in v. 16). As vv. 25-26 move the argument back to application, Paul shifts to "hortatory" imperatives ("let us . . ."). The number of imperatives do increase in the practical application of 6:1-10 (three second plural imperatives; two hortatory subjunctives; and two third singular imperatives). The whole is thus framed by imperatives; and the argument is carried forward at crucial places by an imperative (e.g., 5:16, 25; 6:1, 7). But by and large the imperatives are regularly explained or elaborated by material that is consistently in the indicative. Whatever else, this is not simply a series of exhortations; it is argument by way of exhortation. Thus, both the nature and structure of this material in themselves suggest that the section functions as part of the argument of the letter.

5. The transition is between the three narratives defending his apostleship and gospel with which the letter begins (1:13-24; 2:1-10; 2:11-14) and the theological arguments and appeals that begin in 3:1.

6. Especially circumcision (3:3; 5:11-12, 23; 6:12) and the observance of the Jewish calendar (4:10-11); probably also food laws, given their significance as "identity markers" in the Diaspora and the way Paul weaves them into the argument in the crucial narrative of 2:11-14. This does not necessarily exclude the theological view of the law — Torah as a means of right standing with God. In this letter the two ways of understanding the law coalesce; but the predominant issue is not "works-righteousness" (= doing Torah to gain favor with God), but eccle-

dren of Abraham."[7] The issue raised by the (apparently Jewish Christian) "agitators"[8] is not how one *enters* life in Christ (surely they would have agreed that this was through the death and resurrection of Christ), but how such life is brought to completion (3:3) — especially for Gentiles.[9]

Crucial to the argument as a whole is the role of the Spirit in the life of the believer — both at the beginning and throughout one's entire life in Christ. The key element of Christian *conversion* is the Spirit, dynamically experienced (3:2-5; 4:6), as the fulfillment of the promise to Abraham (3:14). So too with the *whole of Christian life*. The Christian experience of the Spirit sets off the believer in Christ from all other existences, which are alternatively seen either as "under law" (5:18) or as "carrying out the desire of the flesh" (5:16). The Galatians had previously lived the latter; the agitators had turned up to place them under the former. Paul will have none of it. The Spirit alone is the antidote to the "works of the flesh"; Torah not only does not help, but rather leads to bondage. Set free from that bondage through Christ, the per-

---

siological (= doing Torah as necessary to belong to the people of God). The former flows naturally out of the latter.

7. And thereby receive the promises of God's covenant with Abraham as expressed in Gen. 12:3 and 18:18. This is what one might call the "new look" on Galatians, which may be traced back as far as K. Stendahl's "The Apostle Paul and the Introspective Conscience of the West," in *Paul among Jews and Gentiles and Other Essays* (Philadelphia: Fortress, 1976), pp. 78-96 [repr. from *HTR* 56 (1963)]; cf. *inter alia*, T. D. Gordon, "The Problem at Galatia," *Interpretation* 41 (1987): 32-43; Barclay, *Obeying*, pp. 36-74; J. D. G. Dunn, "The Theology of Galatians: The Issue of Covenantal Nomism," in *Jesus, Paul, and the Law* (Philadelphia: Westminster, 1990), pp. 242-64.

8. This is Paul's own language about his opponents, found in 1:7 and 5:10. According to 6:12, these agitators were "compelling" Paul's Gentile converts to accept circumcision (cf. 2:3; 5:23). Since they are referred to in the third person, over against the Galatians themselves, one may assume they are also outsiders.

9. For the agitators, the gift of the Spirit probably signaled the need to be "completed" by adhering to Torah. This, after all, was common Jewish expectation, derived from Jer. 31:31-34 and Ezek. 11:19-20; 36:26-27, that the gift of the eschatological Spirit would lead people to obey the law. Thus, to use the language of E. P. Sanders, but not his conclusions in this case, at stake are not *entrance* requirements, but *maintenance* requirements (for full membership into God's covenant people Gentiles must become Abraham's true children by means of circumcision). Sanders understands the issue in Galatians as "entrance requirements" (see *Paul, the Law, and the Jewish People* [Philadelphia: Fortress, 1983]). Cf. the critique in Cosgrove, *Cross*, pp. 11-13. Cosgrove himself offers a different view altogether; he considers the question Paul raises in 3:5 as the essential matter and therefore understands the agitators to be promoting Torah as the proper means for "sustaining and promoting life in the Spirit" (86); see esp. pp. 39-86. This view was anticipated in part by J. Louis Martyn, "A Law-Observant Mission to Gentiles: The Background of Galatians," *SJT* 38 (1985): 307-24.

son who walks, lives, and is led by the Spirit is not only not under law, but by the Spirit produces the very fruit the law aimed at but could not produce.

But for Paul all is not automatic. One must sow to the Spirit (6:8), and be led by the Spirit (5:18); indeed, "if we live [= have been brought to life after the crucifixion of the flesh, v. 24] by the Spirit," we must therefore also "accordingly behave by the Spirit" (v. 25). This final argument in the letter (5:13–6:10) thus becomes one of the most significant in the Pauline corpus for our understanding of Pauline ethics, as Spirit-empowered Christ-likeness lived out in Christian community as loving servanthood. At issue is *not* a Spirit-flesh struggle within the believer's heart, but *the sufficiency of the Spirit* — over against both the law and the flesh, as God's replacement of the former and antidote to the latter.

Appeal: Stay with Freedom (5:1-12)

The imperative with which this paragraph begins flows directly out of the language about the two mothers in 4:31[10] and functions as the transition between the argument to this point and the application (5:2-12) and final argument (5:13–6:10) that follow. Thus it picks up the motifs of slavery and freedom from 3:23–4:7, now by way of the analogy of Abraham's sons (4:21-31), the one born into slavery, the other freedom. "Stay with freedom," Paul urges in a two-part argument. The first (vv. 2-6) is directed toward the Galatians themselves; the second (vv. 7-12) toward them still, but now once again appealing to their loyalty while indicting the agitators (vv. 7-12).

It's Freedom or Else (5:1-6)

In the strongest words in the epistle since the curse formula in 1:6-9, Paul turns his guns full bore on his readers, who by their (near?) capitulation to circumcision are thereby in danger of losing their freedom in Christ. Indeed, they are in danger of losing Christ altogether, since this appeal spells out what has been indicated right along: that Christ and Torah observance are absolutely mutually incompatible.

10. In the original letter the first words in our v. 1 were directly connected to the final words of our v. 31 without a word or paragraph break (*eleutheras tē eleutheria*, "of the free woman for freedom . . ."). This is in part responsible for the several textual variations in v. 1, as scribes variously tried to show the connection between the two sentences.

The point of the paragraph is to force the Galatians to take seriously the *consequences* of yielding to circumcision. Paul begins (vv. 2-3) with two basic assertions about those who so yield: First, to receive circumcision renders the work of Christ as *totally without value*. Whatever else, it is a matter of either/or; one simply cannot add Torah observance to faith in Christ and keep Christ at the same time. Second, to receive circumcision as evidence of a covenantal relationship with God means to put oneself under obligation to the whole law. This minimally suggests that they cannot be selective about the law; more significantly it means that by submitting to circumcision they now bind themselves to live by Torah, which by that very fact excludes living "by faith" (cf. 3:10-12).

In v. 4 Paul spells out the theological-existential consequences of vv. 2-3:[11] to submit to righteousness by Torah observance means that they (1) have been severed from Christ (since by so doing Christ "profits them nothing" [v. 2]) and (2) have likewise fallen from grace (since by so doing they are now under obligation to live by Torah itself — all of Torah [v. 31]). While this sentence at least refers to the mutually exclusive nature of Christ and Torah, the explanatory "for" of v. 5, with its emphasis on eschatological realization, suggests further that anyone who capitulates really has abandoned Christ and thus does not have eschatological hope.[12]

Verses 5-6 offer two supporting reasons for the assertions of v. 4. The first (v. 5) brings together the three key words of the argument so far[13] — the Spirit, faith [in Christ, is implied], and righteousness — placing them now within the framework of Paul's "already but not yet" eschatological perspective. We live now by the Spirit, based on faith in Christ's justifying work, as we await our sure hope of final eschatological justification.

---

11. This is expressed with rhetorically powerful chiasmus:

You have . . .
   (You who . .
      from grace . . .

The English translations and most commentaries understand the verb in the middle clause to say, "you who are *trying* to be righteous by Torah." But in fact there is not a hint of "attempting" such, which Paul is perfectly capable of saying had he so intended (cf. 4:21). This phrase speaks directly to those who are *assuming* to be righteous before God on the basis of Torah.

12. We may not like such an implication, but to keep integrity with the text itself, we probably have to own up to it. Offense at such an implication is based on a prior theological commitment, which is difficult to derive from Pauline texts on their own.

13. It has been (correctly) noted (e.g., Arichea-Nida, Betz, and Longenecker) that this verse recapitulates much of 2:15–4:7. Nonetheless, the new elements — the eschatological and ethical thrusts — are what give significance to the present passage.

The second reason (v. 6) further elaborates: for those in Christ Jesus circumcision is a total irrelevancy. At the same time it anticipates the final argument that begins in v. 13: true faith expresses itself through love, the primary fruit of the Spirit. This is Paul's ultimate verdict on the twin issues of Torah observance and true righteousness: On the one hand, Christ has made circumcision — and by implication all Torah observance — obsolete; neither circumcision nor uncircumcision counts for anything. On the other hand, what counts is true righteousness, faith that expresses itself in love, thus fulfilling the aim of Torah in the first place (v. 14).

Here, then, is the heart of Paul's gospel: eschatological hope through faith in Christ, as lived out in the present by the power of the Spirit in a life of loving servanthood (= the law of Christ, 6:2).

Condemnation of the Agitators (5:7-12)

This paragraph continues the appeal that began in v. 1. As with the earlier appeal (4:12-20), the passage is full of emotion — leading to several exegetical difficulties — and is therefore not altogether easy to follow. It consists basically of a series of indictments against the agitators: they have cut in on the Galatians (v. 7), thus troubling and upsetting them, and they will be judged by God for it (v. 10); they are like leaven, corrupting the whole loaf (v. 9), whose point of view does not come from God (v. 8, hence by implication, from Satan), since it attempts to circumvent the scandal of the cross (v. 11); if they are going to use a knife on someone, rather than circumcise the Galatians they should castrate themselves (v. 12). At the same time, Paul sets out his own ministry in sharp contrast to that of the agitators, sure evidence, along with chs. 1–2, that they have tried to discredit him along with his gospel. All of this will be picked up again in the conclusion (6:11-16). But before that, Paul returns to the final point of the argument, picking up the language and concerns expressed in vv. 1 and 5-6.

Life in the Spirit (5:13–6:10)

Paul now returns to the theme of freedom, which soon gives way to the larger issue — life in the Spirit as the gospel alternative to life under law and in the flesh. Two matters appear to drive the whole of this section. On the one hand stands Paul's deep conviction of the failure of Torah to effect righteousness, both as right standing with God and as behavior conformed to the character of God. The argument from 2:15 to 4:31 basically dealt with the work of Christ as effecting righteousness in the first sense, evidence for which was the experienced reality of the Spirit. The present passage now picks up the second conviction, the failure of Torah to effect righteousness in terms of behavior.

On the other hand, in terms of the argument of Galatians proper, there is the reverse side of the coin, and one that was — or would be — raised by his opposition: If you eliminate Torah observance altogether — as Paul does indeed — what happens to obedience? What is to keep people from doing "whatever they wish" (5:17)?[14]

The present passage is Paul's answer to both issues. Having begun by the Spirit, one comes to completion by the Spirit (cf. 3:3). The key to ethical life, including everyday behavior in its every form, is to be found in the primary Pauline imperative: "Walk by/in the Spirit, and you will not fulfill the desire of the flesh" (v. 16). The Spirit is God's empowering presence for life that is both over against the flesh (so that one may not do as one wishes, v. 17) and in conformity to the character of God (here as the "fruit of the Spirit").

Paul's essential point in the argument, predicated on their *experience* of the Spirit, is twofold: First, precisely because of the inadequacy of Torah to empower, he argues that life in the Spirit means that one is *no longer under law* (v. 18). But it does not mean that one is thereby "lawless." To the contrary, the Spirit person evidences the fruit of the Spirit and thus "fulfills" the whole of Torah (5:14; cf. 5:3) — by "fulfilling" the "law of Christ" (6:2).

Second, in an argument that anticipates Romans 6 and 8, Paul here

14. Cf. Burton, p. 290; A. T. Lincoln, *Paradise Now and Not Yet: Studies in the Role of the Heavenly Dimension in Paul's Thought with Special Reference to His Eschatology,* SNTSMS 43 (Cambridge: Cambridge University Press, 1981), p. 26; Barclay, *Obeying,* p. 111. This seems to be the best response to the issue raised by some, "How can Paul proclaim freedom from the law in Galatians 3–4 and then go on 'to lay down the law' in Galatians 5–6?" rather than to see Paul as fighting on two fronts: with "Judaizers" in 1:6–5:12 and with "libertines" in 5:13–6:10 (Ropes and Lutgert; see the discussion in Barclay, *Obeying,* pp. 141-45). That the concern is with "libertine tendencies" within Galatia is also held by R. Jewett ("The Agitators and the Galatian Congregation," *New Testament Studies* 17 [1970/71]: 198-212) and Longenecker; Betz takes a slightly different view, that the Galatians themselves were struggling against fleshly desires. A "libertarian" point of view in Galatians is read into the situation from a text like 5:16; but in fact the only *specifics* mentioned (vv. 15, 26; 6:1-5) do not betray "libertine" tendencies but conflict within the community. To call community conflict "libertine" is to stretch the meaning of that word beyond recognizable limits. Part of the reason for this view came about because of the alleged difficulty that "those who want to be under Torah" (4:21) would not thereby also live so contrary to Torah as to need these correctives. But this misses too much, especially the fact that "works of Law" have to do with Torah *observance,* not with genuinely Christian ethics. That is, "works of Torah" have to do with being "religious"; this section has to do with being truly "righteous" once Torah is gone.

maintains that life in the Spirit also means life *over against the flesh.* The Spirit stands in absolute opposition to life in the flesh, so that one may not do whatever one wishes (v. 17) — as one could when living in the flesh and apart from Torah. Those who "walk by the Spirit," he affirms, will not carry out the "desire" of the flesh (v. 16), precisely because those who are Christ's have crucified the flesh with its "desires" (v. 24).

Thus for Paul both flesh and Torah belong to the old eon whose essential power has been crippled by Christ's death and resurrection, which marked the dawning of the new eon, the time of the Spirit. Although the flesh is still about, and stands in mortal opposition to the Spirit, Christ's death has brought about our death — both to Torah (2:19) and to the flesh (5:24). Having been brought to life by the Spirit (v. 25), believers now walk by the Spirit (i.e., with the Spirit's empowering) and are thereby subject neither to the flesh's bidding (5:16) nor to the law's enslaving (5:18).

A final very important observation needs to be made. Quite in contrast to how this material is read by the most of us and is presented in many of the commentaries[15] — the concern from beginning to end is with *Christian life in community, not with the interior life of the individual Christian.* Apart from 5:17c, which is usually completely decontextualized and thus misread (see below), there is not a hint that Paul is here dealing with a "tension" between flesh and Spirit that rages within the human breast — in which the flesh most often appears as the stronger opponent. To the contrary, the issue from the beginning (vv. 13-15) and throughout (vv. 19-21, 26; 6:1-4, 7-10) has to do with Spirit life within the believing community. The individual is not thereby brushed aside; after all, one both enters and lives within the Christian community at the individual level, which is where the individual believer fits into the argument. Within the context of the church each one is to live out his or her freedom by becoming love slaves to one another (v. 13). The imperative "walk by the Spirit" does not emphasize "the introspective conscience of the Western mind,"[16] but rather calls for a life in the Spirit that does not "eat and devour" one another (v. 15) and that does not through conceit provoke and envy others (v. 26). The "fruit of the Spirit" engenders "love, joy, and peace" *within the community,* not primarily within the believer's own heart. Such a Spirit person will be among those who restore an individual who "is over-

15. Meyer and Duncan are happy exceptions, but even Duncan does not take this seriously until v. 25.

16. Language based on Stendahl's essay by that name (n. 7 above). Stendahl has shown, convincingly to my mind, that one rather thoroughly misreads Paul, and especially this text, if one begins with the assumption that Paul is basically concerned with the problem of sin and conscience.

taken in a fault" (6:1). And the final expression of "sowing in the Spirit" is "to do good to all people, especially those of the household of faith" (v. 10).

Freedom Means Enslavement to Love (5:13-15)

This paragraph functions as a kind of thesis statement for the rest of the argument-appeal of the letter. In v. 6 Paul asserted that observance or nonobservance of religious obligation, in the form of circumcision, counts for absolutely nothing — in terms either of one's relationship with God or of one's membership in the people of God. What counts, on the contrary, is "faith that expresses itself through love." That is now spelled out by specific application to their own situation. Indeed, v. 15 suggests that the whole section (5:13–6:10) has been determined by Paul's knowledge of their local situation(s). Thus, by the very nature of the material, the section that ties up the remaining loose threads of the argument of the letter at the same time serves in a very practical way to bring truly Christian behavior back into these communities.

Several matters emerge and converge in this first paragraph: First, in v. 13 Paul deliberately sets out to bring together the two crucial items from v. 16 — "freedom" (from Torah) and "love" (as the way faith "works"). Freedom from the enslavement of Torah paradoxically means to take on a new form of "slavery" — that of loving servanthood to one another.

Second, love of this kind is the way the whole of Torah (in terms of human relationships) is "fulfilled," which is why Paul is not anxious about Christ's having brought the time of Torah to an end. The aim of Torah, although helpless to bring it off, was to create a loving community in which God's own character and purposes are fulfilled as God's people love one another the way God loves them. Since love is later expressed as a "fruit of the Spirit," one may thus see in v. 14 what will be spelled out clearly in vv. 18 and 23, namely that the Spirit has "replaced" Torah by the Spirit's bringing the aim of Torah to fulfillment.[17] Thus "love of neighbor" as the "fulfillment of Torah" fully anticipates the role of the Spirit in the argument that follows.[18]

---

17. Thus the perfect passive, "has been fulfilled," almost certainly does not mean that the love-command "sums up" the whole of the law, since there is no certain evidence for such a meaning for this word. Rather it means what the verb ordinarily denotes that the whole point of Torah is fulfilled, completed, by the practice of this one command, which, of course, as vv. 16-26 make clear, is now to be carried out by believers through the empowering of the Spirit. On this word see esp. Barclay, *Obeying*, pp. 135-42, and Stephen Westerholm, "On Fulfilling the Whole Law (Gal. 5:14)," *Svensk exegetisk Årsbok* 512 (1986/87): 229-37.

18. A point often overlooked in the commentaries (e.g., Ridderbos, Guthrie, Boice, Fung).

Third, and what seems to be the driving concern of the whole argument, "freedom [from Torah]," does not mean "lawlessness," expressed here as "providing an opportunity[19] for the flesh." Although hinted at before (3:3; 4:23, 29), "flesh" is now the new element in the argument, replacing "works of law" as the dominant negative motif. In the present paragraph, the "flesh" reveals itself in the form of community strife, in which believers "bite and devour" one another.[20] It is precisely at this point, the "life of the flesh," that Torah had demonstrated itself to be inadequate. Torah obviously "laid down the law" against such behavior; but by deflecting Torah toward "works of law" in the form of Jewish identity symbols, one could be "religious" without being "righteous." Christ brought an end to Torah observance in part for that very reason; the Spirit replaced Torah, so that God's people, Jew and Gentile alike, would have a new "identity." The indwelling Spirit of the living God would at the same time be sufficient to accomplish what Torah could not: effectively stand in opposition to the flesh.

Thus, even though the Spirit is not directly mentioned in this foundational opening exhortation, the Western text of v. 14 ("by the love of the Spirit serve one another") has it right in terms of Paul's meaning, which will be made plain in the argument that follows.

The Spirit Opposes the Flesh (5:16-18)

The (otherwise difficult) flow of thought in this paragraph is easily accounted for when viewed as Paul's response to the various matters presented in vv. 13-15. Thus, the solemn assertion with which it begins, "but I say," stands in direct contrast to v. 15 with its warning that their kind of "works of the flesh" lead eventually to their being "consumed" by one another. In v. 16 the anti-

19. Greek *aphormē*, which literally referred to the starting point or base of operations for an expedition. In its metaphorical denotations, especially in Paul, it is often used pejoratively to express a kind of "pretext" for some action (e.g., 2 Cor. 5:12; 11:12; 1 Tim. 5:14); but here, even though clearly pejorative, the literal sense seems to be the point of its metaphorical usage. Freedom is not to be turned into a kind of "base of operations" for the flesh. Otherwise Betz, p. 272.

20. There is considerable difference of opinion as to the place of v. 15 (and therefore 26 and 6:1-3) in the argument. Lightfoot (p. 209), e.g., suggests that it is "a sort of parenthetic warning"; those who see the whole as general parenesis also tend to view it this way; Betz, p. 277, sees it as belonging to a "typos" and therefore unrelated to any specific situation in Galatia (cf. Meyer, Mussner); most, however, see it as at least reflecting something going on in Galatia (e.g., Calvin, Burton, Duncan, Schlier, Hendriksen, Boice, Bruce, Fung, Cole, Longenecker). Seldom, however, do they also make what seems to be the obvious connection between vv. 13, 15, 16, and 19-21 in terms of "works of the *flesh*" (Bruce is a singular exception).

dote to the possibility that freedom from Torah might provide a "base of operations for the flesh" resides in the primary Pauline ethical imperative, "walk by the Spirit." By so doing, Paul now promises,[21] one will thereby "not carry out the desire of [= make provision for] the flesh."

Verse 17 in turn offers an *explanation* as to *how* the assertion in v. 16 is true.[22] The reason walking by the Spirit means that one will thereby not carry out the desire of the flesh is that the Spirit and the flesh are absolutely antithetical to each other; and the Spirit opposes the flesh precisely so that, even though Torah is gone, one may not do whatever one wishes. Rather, one will carry out the purposes of the Spirit that oppose those of the flesh.[23]

So also, the sudden, seemingly disjointed, mention of Torah in v. 18 is accounted for at this point as a response to v. 14. That is, the Spirit who empowers love thereby "fulfills" Torah, so that the one led by the Spirit is "not under law." Its mention at this point in the argument suggests that Paul's concern is to put forth the Spirit as God's response to *both* the flesh and Torah because the latter could *not* counteract the desire of the flesh, but the Spirit can and does.

At issue, therefore, is not some internal tension in the life of the individual believer,[24] but the sufficiency of the Spirit for life without Torah — a suffi-

---

21. Contrary to the RSV, the apodosis of this sentence must be taken as a promise, not an imperative. That is, Paul is hereby indicating the result of "walking by the Spirit," not commanding them "not to fulfill the desire of the flesh."

22. As over against the many who see v. 17 as "explaining" the implied assumption of "warfare" found in v. 16, which might be possible if in fact it fitted at all with Paul's clear point: the sufficiency of the Spirit vis-à-vis life under law and against the flesh.

23. This way of looking at the text goes back to Chrysostom, and is advocated by Duncan, pp. 166-69, and R. Jewett, *Paul's Anthropological Terms: A Study of Their Use in Conflict Settings* (Leiden: Brill, 1971), pp. 106-7. See the full defense of it in my monograph, *God's Empowering Presence: The Holy Spirit in the Letters of Paul* (Peabody, Mass.: Hendrickson, 1994); cf. Barclay, *Obeying*, pp. 112-19, whose solution is slightly different. He sees the final clause as reflecting the result of the warfare imagery itself: "As [the Galatians] walk in the Spirit, they are caught up into a warfare which determines their moral choices. The warfare imagery is invoked *not to indicate that the two sides are evenly balanced* [my emphasis] but to show the Galatians that they are already committed *to* some forms of activity (the Spirit) and *against* others (the flesh)." Cf. Fung, p. 251. This may very well be the correct nuance; in any case it comes out at the same place as the one presented here.

24. It should be pointed out here that those who take this (decidedly majority) view of vv. 16-17 to a person fail to show how it fits into the overall argument of the letter, which to this point has singularly had to do with Gentiles' not needing to come under (now passé) Torah observance. How, one wonders, does this sudden shift to Christian existence as primarily one of (basically unsuccessful) conflict fit into this argument at all? No wonder it has been so popular to see this section (5:13–6:10) as generally unconnected "practical" exhortation. Cf. Barclay,

ciency that enables them to live so as not to *revert* to their former life as pagans (i.e., in the flesh, as vv. 19-21 make clear).

The Two Ways of Life Contrasted (5:19-23)

The contrasting lists of fifteen vices and nine virtues that follow are so well known that it is difficult for the modern reader to keep them in context, to listen to them as if in a Galatian assembly and for the first time. After the slight digression in v. 18, Paul now returns to the theme of v. 17, spelling out with specifics why flesh and Spirit stand in such unrelieved opposition to each other. The one describes the world *in which they once lived,* and in which their pagan neighbors still live. These are the "evident works" of those who live according to "the desire of the flesh," and thus offer a vivid illustration of the kind of life to which those who "walk by the Spirit" shall no longer be a party. The second describes what people will look like who walk by following the leading of the Spirit. It is difficult to imagine two more utterly contradictory ways of life.

Vice and virtue lists such as these occur elsewhere in the Greco-Roman world,[25] and are found throughout the Pauline corpus;[26] many of the same vices and virtues are repeated in several of them, although no two of them are alike either in content, order, or kinds of items listed. As in other cases, both of the present lists are adapted to the situation in Galatia as that which emerges in v. 15.

The lists, therefore, are intended to be neither delimiting nor exhaustive. Rather, by his use of "such things as these" (v. 21; cf. v. 23), Paul specifically indicates that the lists are merely representative. Furthermore, even though the present lists describe unbelievers and believers as such, Paul also intends by these lists to describe the "before" and "after" of the Galatians

---

Obeying, p. 112, who makes the further observation that "the [immediate] context rules this interpretation out," because it places v. 17 in such unabashed contradiction to v. 16 and thereby "wholly undermines Paul's purpose in this passage." Not only so, but in terms of "reader response criticism," which understands the letter to be an attempt to *persuade*, one wonders what could possibly be the point of such persuasion that in effect contravenes the very thing he was trying to persuade them of in v. 16.

25. For a helpful overview see Longenecker, pp. 249-52.

26. Vice lists occur in 1 Cor. 5:11; 6:9-10; 2 Cor. 12:20; Rom. 1:29-31; 13:13; Col. 3:5, 8; Eph. 4:31–5:5; 1 Tim. 1:9-10; 2 Tim. 3:24; Titus 3:3. Elsewhere in the NT see Mark 7:21-22 (Matt. 15:19-20); 1 Pet. 4:3; Rev. 9:21; 21:8; 22:15. Virtue lists are far less common, since in the Pauline corpus the items that make this list occur in the context of Pauline parenesis; but see Col. 3:12.

themselves.[27] These "works of the flesh," and others like them, are the very things that "those who belong to Christ Jesus have crucified" (v. 24) and therefore are no longer an option for those who "walk by the Spirit" (vv. 13, 16).

The Vice List — "Works of the Flesh" (vv. 19-21)

Paul's entitling this vice list as "the *works* of the flesh" is most likely a deliberate association with the repeated "by *works* of Torah" in the earlier part of this letter (2:16 [3x]; 3:2, 5, 11). This is not to suggest that Paul saw similarity between these two kinds of "works." Rather, by means of word association, this is his way of reminding the Galatians that *both categories of "work"* (religious observance and sins of the flesh) *belong to the past* for those who are in Christ and thus walk by the Spirit. These "works" express the "desire of the flesh" against which the Spirit stands in such unrelieved opposition and God's people heartily respond.

The fifteen items fall into four clear categories:[28] illicit sex (3 — sexual immorality, impurity, licentiousness), illicit worship (2 — idolatry, sorcery), breakdown in relationships (8 — hostilities, strife, jealousy, outbursts of rage, selfish ambitions, dissensions, factions, envies), and excesses (2 — drunken orgies, revelries).[29] This, of course, is not a list of sins of the *flesh* per se, i.e., having to do with the physical body or bodily appetites. The only items that fit this category are the three sexual aberrations that appear first and the two excesses that appear at the end.[30] Moreover, for the most part the various sins

27. As vv. 24-26 make clear, and in keeping with other such listings. See esp. in this regard the vice lists in 1 Cor. 6:9-11 ("but such were some of you") and Col. 3:5-8 ("in which things you also once walked, when you lived in such things; but now . . .").

28. An observation frequently made; see, e.g., Lightfoot, p. 210; Burton, p. 304; Lagrange, p. 149; Duncan, p. 170; Hendriksen, pp. 218-19; et al. For reasons that are not at all clear, Betz (p. 283), followed by Longenecker (p. 254), thinks the opposite — that this list is "chaotic" and the next "orderly."

29. What is striking in this case are the missing items, especially covetousness or greed, which appear on most of the other lists (cf. Schlier, p. 254), and the related sins of theft and robbery, as well as sins of violence (murder, etc.) and the various sins of the tongue, which is the category with the largest number of words when all the lists are collated. This suggests that whatever else "eating and devouring one another" meant, it most likely was not primarily various forms of verbal abuse.

30. The majority of the items, in fact, can scarcely be located in the human body, indicating that the suggested alternative ("satisfy one's physical desire") offered in Bauer's lexicon for "the desire of the flesh" in v. 16 cannot possibly be Paul's own intent, but is rather a carryover into this lexicon of the view of a former day.

are not the kind associated with internal warfare within the human breast. Noticeably missing are "lust" or "covetousness," matters over which the individual often struggles in the face of temptation. Rather, this list basically describes human *behavior,* which for the most part is very visible and identifiable, "works" that people do who live in keeping with their basic fallenness and that of the world around them.

Most noticeably, the majority (8 of 15) are sins of discord — actions (or motivations) that express breakdowns in social relationships. Since such sins often make the Pauline lists, one should perhaps not make too much of their appearance here; but in light of what Paul says negatively in 5:15 and 26 and positively in 6:2 and 10, one appears justified in seeing their large number as the present adaptation of a common rhetorical device.[31]

But having said all of that, a list is still a list; and one that concludes with "such things" is to be taken seriously by believers of all generations and geography. God is against such "works." Christ has died to deliver us from their grip (v. 24); and the Spirit has come to empower us not to cave in to their "desire."

This first list concludes on an eschatological note: "those who practice such things as these will not inherit the kingdom of God." For Paul "inheriting" or "not inheriting" the final eschatological glory is predicated on whether or not one is a Spirit person, having become so through faith in Christ Jesus. The "works of the flesh," therefore, do not describe the behavior of believers, but of unbelievers.[32] It is not that believers cannot or do not indulge in such sins;[33] Paul's point is that "people who *practice* such sins" are those who have no inheritance with God's people. His concern here, as in 1 Cor. 6:9-11 and Eph. 5:5, is to warn believers that they must therefore not live as others who are destined to experience the wrath of God (Col. 3:6).

Even though Paul is here speaking negatively about the destiny of the ungodly, the positive implication of believers' inheriting the kingdom should not be missed, especially since the question of "inheritance" played such a major role in the argument of 3:6–4:7 (cf. 4:30). As earlier (4:6-7), "inheritance" belongs to those who, by the Spirit, give evidence that they are God's rightful "heirs." Because such an inheritance is here *implied* for those who live by the Spirit, Paul concludes the next list by taking it in another direction altogether, namely to come back to the issue of the Spirit and Torah observance.

31. Cf. Barclay, *Obeying,* p. 153.

32. A point too often missed in the commentaries, apparently because of the way they handle v. 17. See, e.g., Calvin, Meyer, Fung, Betz, Longenecker.

33. After all, Paul's emphasis on his having warned them before and now again makes that point plain enough!

The Virtue List — "Fruit of the Spirit" (vv. 22-23)

By describing the list of virtues as "fruit of the Spirit," Paul once more sets the Spirit in sharp contrast to the flesh: the vices are "works," the virtues "fruit." But "fruit" does not mean passivity on the part of the believer. To be sure, "works" puts emphasis on human endeavor, "fruit" on divine empowerment.[34] But the emphasis in this argument is on the Spirit's effective replacement of Torah. Not only do people who walk by the Spirit *not* walk in the ways of the flesh just described, but also the Spirit effectively produces in them the very character of God.[35] Thus, the activities and attitudes of those who are "led by the Spirit" are designated as the "product" of life in the Spirit. Paul's point in context, of course, is that when the Galatians properly use their freedom by serving one another through love, they are empowered to do so by the Spirit, who produces such "fruit" in/among them. But they themselves must walk, live, conform to the Spirit. After all, in almost every case these various "fruit" appear elsewhere in the form of imperatives![36]

As with the preceding list, this one is representative, not exhaustive. That love has pride of place reflects the Pauline perspective (cf. v. 14); the rest of the list appears to be much more random, where one word, for reasons not fully clear, calls for the next. For the most part the virtues chosen stand in marked contrast to many of the preceding "works of the flesh." Again, what is surprising are the "omissions" of items that Paul elsewhere so clearly includes in such lists or in his parenesis.[37] What results, therefore — and this

34. It should be noted, however, that when "human endeavor" is Paul's emphasis for the Spirit side of things, "works" is also the word that Paul will use, as at the end of the present argument (6:10, "let us work what is good," which becomes the "good works" of Eph. 2:10). Anyone who thinks that Paul is not keen on good works has either not read Paul carefully or has come to the subject with emotional resistance to this language, usually predicated on the theological agenda of the Reformation.

35. Several of these words are used elsewhere by Paul with reference to the character of God, often in terms of God's motivation toward, and relationship to, his people. This reality, plus the fact that this language is so deeply embedded in Paul through his lifelong association with the OT and the Jesus traditions, makes Betz's comment (p. 282) seem exceedingly strange: "The individual concepts are not in any way specifically 'Christian,' but represent the conventional morality of the time."

36. It is common to make more of the singular "fruit," in contrast to the plural "works," than the language itself will allow. Paul himself probably had no such contrast in mind, nor does he think of the "works" as many and individual but the "fruit" as one cluster with several kinds on it. The fact is that *karpos* in Greek functions as a collective singular, very much as "fruit" does in English. In both Greek and English one would refer to "the fruit in the bowl," whether "they" are all of one kind or of several.

37. Missing, for example, are thankfulness, forgiveness, humility, gracious talk, and en-

does become significant for Pauline theology — is a list of virtues which tends to cover a broad range of Christian life, both collectively and individually, and which thereby helps to broaden our own perspective as to the breadth, and all-encompassing nature, of the activity of the Spirit in Paul's understanding.

As noted above, the decided majority of these items have not to do with the internal life of the individual believer, but with the corporate life of the community. While it is true that individuals must love, work toward peace, express forbearance, kindness, and goodness, or be characterized by gentleness, nonetheless in Pauline parenesis these virtues characterize God and motivate his conduct toward his own, and therefore must do the same within the believing community. Again, lying behind much of this is the situation of the Galatian churches as we get some insight into that from 5:15 and 26.

Significantly, Paul does not conclude, as one might expect, with an eschatological word of promise.[38] His present interest lies once more with the main point of the argument of the letter, that the work of Christ and the coming of the Spirit have eliminated Torah altogether from the agenda of God's people. Hence he concludes, "against such things as these there is no law."

This is stated a bit awkwardly to our thinking: law, after all, exists because people are evil, not because they are good; it exists therefore "against" sin not "against" virtue. Nonetheless, Paul's point seems clear enough: when these virtues are evident in the life because of the presence of the Spirit, Torah is an irrelevancy.[39] There is no need of Torah to say, "you shall not kill," to people who by the Spirit are loving one another, nor to say, "don't covet," to those who are actively pursuing the good of others out of kindness. This does not mean, of course, that such *reminders* are irrelevant — Paul himself is long on such — but that the need for Torah to "hem in human conduct because of the transgressions" (3:19, 22) has come to an end with the advent of the Spirit, God's own way of fulfilling his promised new covenant. This is Torah being etched on the heart, so that God's people will obey him (Jer. 31:33; Ezek. 36:27). Here also is the clear evidence that for Paul the elimination of Torah does not mean the end of righteousness. To the contrary, the Spirit produces

---

durance. In this regard see esp. 2 Cor. 8:7; Rom. 12:9-21; Col. 3:12-17; Eph. 4:32-5:2; the only other real "list" of this kind occurs in Col. 3:12, where three of the five items in that list appear here as well.

38. Probably, as noted above, because such a promise is already inherent in the previous concluding word.

39. Calvin, p. 168, put it slightly differently: "When the Spirit reigns, the law has no longer any dominion." I'm not sure that "dominion" is the issue as much as relevancy; cf. Duncan, pp. 175-76; Betz, p. 289.

the real thing, the righteousness of God, as his children reflect his likeness in their lives together and in the world.

The Sum of the Matter (5:24-26)

With these sentences Paul brings the present argument full circle, first by drawing the work of Christ back into the picture (v. 24), now vis-à-vis the flesh rather than Torah, and then in v. 25 by restating the basic imperative from v. 16, concluding in v. 26 with the reasons for these admonitions from v. 15. These sentences, therefore, belong integrally to what has preceded, but at the same time lead directly into the specific application that follows in 6:16. The appeal in v. 25 to conform our behavior to the Spirit thus wraps up what has been said in vv. 16-24 about life in the Spirit over against the flesh — repeating with different imagery the imperative to walk by the Spirit, now in light of the description of Spirit life in vv. 22-23 and on the basis of our having received life through the Spirit. Verse 26 once again sets out the "fleshly" contrast, by noting the specific kinds of sins that led to the breakdown in relationships noted in v. 15.

The Application (6:1-10)

Paul now directly applies what has preceded to their corporate life. He begins with a series of imperatives that illustrate how Spirit people should behave in their everyday relationships. The context is clearly that of the community, in which believers are to care for one another and thus "fill to the full the law of Christ" (vv. 1-2),[40] and thereby to have a proper estimation as to their own worth (v. 3) by taking proper stock of themselves (v. 4) so as to know how to "carry their own weight" (v. 5).

Because a sequential flow to these various imperatives and their elabo-

---

40. This turn of phrase is one more gentle reminder that life free from Torah and flesh, empowered by the Spirit, does not lead to "lawlessness." Rather it leads to patterning one's life after the ultimate expression of the law, Christ himself, who through his death and resurrection "bore the burdens" of one and all. Above all, Christ is the one "who gave himself for our sins" (1:4) and "who loved us and gave himself for us" (2:20). This is "the law of Christ" which Spirit people are called to reproduce. Thus, "the law of Christ" is not an appeal to some new set of laws or even to some ethical standards that the gospel imposes on believers, but to Christ himself (on this debate see esp. R. B. Hays, "Christology and Ethics in Galatians: The Law of Christ," *Catholic Biblical Quarterly* 49 [1987]: 268-90, and Barclay, *Obeying*, pp. 126-31).

rations is not immediately evident, it is common to look upon all of 6:1-10 as a series of "gnomic sentences," somewhat randomly strung together.[41] On the other hand, if one assumes that 5:15 and 26 actually refer to specific matters within the Galatian congregations, then most of the material can be shown to have an "inner logic" to it.[42] On this view vv. 1-3 form something of a unit in response to vv. 25-26. "Let us behave in keeping with the Spirit," Paul has urged in v. 25, meaning, let us *not* be full of empty conceit and provocation. To the contrary, as Spirit people you should, for example, restore a fallen brother or sister, remembering your own susceptibility to temptation. Indeed, you ought to bear any and all of one another's burdens, and so fulfill the law of Christ; for those who think themselves to be something when in fact they are nothing (who are thus full of empty conceit and thereby provoke rather than restore and assist others) are merely deceiving themselves. On the other hand, Paul goes on in vv. 4-5, each one should put his or her own work to the test, and then alone will there be grounds for "boasting." In that sense, each person must mind his or her own affairs, carry his or her own load, and thus not envy or challenge one another. In any case, the Galatians are now about to see how love, peace, gentleness, self-denial, and goodness, for example, work out in everyday life.[43]

If this is the "flow" of thought, even if it takes the form of "stream of consciousness," the two parts to the first paragraph (vv. 1-3, 4-5) are thus a double-sided response to the "empty conceit" and "provocation/envy" of 5:26, while vv. 7-10 bring the whole section (from 5:13, but now especially in light of 6:1-5) to its proper conclusion, by means of the metaphor of sowing and reaping. Since what one sows one also reaps, the Galatians are urged not to "sow to the flesh" (as described above), but to "sow to the Spirit," in the form of "doing good" to one another (vv. 9-10), so that they might also "reap" the eternal life that living in the Spirit promises (v. 8). Thus, the final word is like the first one: no occasion for flesh, but loving one another by doing good to one and all, and the Spirit as the essential — and sufficient (!) — constituent for it to happen.

41. For an articulation of this view, see Betz, pp. 291-92 (cf. Schlier, p. 269); for an overview and critique see Barclay, *Obeying,* pp. 147-55; cf. Longenecker, pp. 269-71.

42. Betz, pp. 291-92, allows as much, himself using the language "inner logic" (which he never elaborates). In any case, one must take seriously that the connectives in vv. 3-5 *(gar, de, gar)* are those of "argument," not randomly strung-together sayings.

43. Cf. Barclay, *Obeying,* p. 146 (note his chapter title for this material, "The Practical Value of the Spirit").

The Wrap-up in Big Letters with His Own Hand (6:11-18)

At the end of this letter, written with vigor and at times with great agitation, Paul takes the pen from his amanuensis and brings it to conclusion with his own hand (v. 11). What we get is a genuine conclusion, in which he basically reiterates the significant matters of the letter. He begins with a final, especially strong, indictment of the agitators, who from his point of view are "compelling" the Galatians to be circumcised for two ignoble reasons: to avoid being persecuted because of the cross; and to "glory" in the "flesh" of the Galatians (vv. 12-13). As in 5:7-12, Paul sets this indictment in contrast to his own ministry: he will "glory" only in the cross they disdain (by their compelling circumcision); through that same cross he has died to the former way of life (the world, v. 14). The outcome (in repetition of 5:6b): neither circumcision nor uncircumcision means a thing; the only thing that counts is the new creation that arises out of death. God's benediction, he concludes in v. 16, rests upon all who live by this rule (spelled out in v. 15); such people are God's true Israel. The net result is that the agitators should trouble him no further — either in Galatia or elsewhere — since he bears in his body the "marks of Christ," which thereby authenticate his ministry.

Here, then, in conclusion are the great themes of the letter: (1) the genuineness of Paul's apostolic ministry, based strictly on the cross and Paul's continuation of the ministry of the cross in his own sufferings (cf. 1:10–2:14; 4:12-20; 5:10-11); (2) the cross has brought an end to Torah observance; any form of return to righteousness by law is to run roughshod over the cross and thus to glory in the flesh (cf. 2:15-21; 3:1, 10-29; 4:4-5; 5:2-6, 24); and (3) the cross which does away with circumcision does not thereby exalt the uncircumcised status of the Gentiles; rather both former states are irrelevant because of the work of Christ and the coming of the Spirit (5:5-6, 13-26). God's peace and mercy rest upon all who so believe and so live.

CHAPTER 12

Philippians 2:5-11:
Hymn or Exalted Pauline Prose?
(1992)

This remarkable passage is at once one of the most exalted, one of the most beloved, and one of the most discussed and debated passages in the Pauline corpus. Because of its sheer grandeur, it has assumed a role both in the church and in private devotional life quite apart from its original context, as a piece of early christology. Scholarship, on the other hand, because of the passage's exalted description of Christ in the midst of a piece of parenesis, has long debated its meaning and role in its present context. Indeed, so much is this so that one can easily be intimidated by the sheer bulk of the literature, which is enough to daunt even the hardiest of souls.[1] The debate covers a broad range of concerns: form, origins, background of ideas, its overall meaning and place in context, and the meaning of several key words and phrases (ἁρπαγμός, μορφή, τὸ εἶναι ἴσα θεῷ, κενόω). But the one place where there has been a general consensus is that it was originally a hymn; in fact the language "Christ-hymn" has become a semi-technical term in our discipline to refer to this passage in particular.

The present paper finds its starting point in two recent studies on this passage. First, in N. T. Wright's especially helpful overview both of the ἁρπαγμός debate and the overall meaning of the passage in its context, he concludes by challenging: "But if someone were to take it upon themselves to argue, on the basis of my conclusions, that the 'hymn' was originally written

---

1. Martin's *Carmen Christi* is 319 pages long and includes a bibliography of over 500 items, to which one may now add at least 50 more items. See R. P. Martin, *Carmen Christi: Philippians ii:5-11 in Recent Interpretation and in the Setting of Early Christian Worship* (2nd edn.; Grand Rapids: Eerdmans, 1983).

by Paul himself . . . I should find it hard to produce convincing counterarguments."[2] Second, in Moisés Silva's recent and very helpful commentary,[3] he argues for its being a hymn,[4] very much as it is displayed in NA[26], yet in the subsequent commentary, he frankly admits that "the structure of vv. 9-11 is not characterized by the large number of parallel and contrasting items that have been recognized in vv. 6-8" and then proceeds to describe the sentence in thoroughly non-strophic, non-hymnic terms.[5]

My concern in this brief paper is a modest one: primarily I want to call into question the whole matter of the passage as a hymn, which, despite most scholarship to the contrary, it almost certainly is not; and second I hope to show that one can best understand its role in the context by a structural analysis of the kind one would do with any piece of Pauline prose. The net result is an argument in favor of its Pauline origins in this context and for a meaning very much like that offered by Wright and Silva.

My own exegetical concerns, therefore, remain constant: to discover the meaning of this passage in terms of its place in its own context.[6] But in this case several issues must be noted, since they affect one's view of so much: (1) its form; (2) two closely related concerns — (a) authorship and (b) background; and (3) its place in context. The larger issues of the meaning of some key words and phrases will be noted only in passing as they affect these other concerns.

I. The Question of Form

The almost universal judgment of scholarship is that in Phil. 2:6-11 we are dealing with an early hymn about Christ.[7] The reasons for this judgment are

2. N. T. Wright, "ἁρπαγμός and the Meaning of Philippians 2:5-11," *JTS* n.s. 37 (1986): 321-52.

3. Moisés Silva, *The Wycliffe Exegetical Commentary: Philippians* (Chicago: Moody Press, 1988).

4. Indeed, he specifically rejects the language "elevated prose" as not doing "justice to the rhythm, parallelisms, lexical links, and other features that characterize these verses" (p. 105).

5. Silva, p. 127.

6. I should note here that this paper was completed before the monograph by Stephen E. Fowl was available (*The Story of Christ in the Ethics of Paul: An Analysis of the Function of the Hymnic Material in the Pauline Corpus* [JSNTSS 36; Sheffield: JSOT Press, 1990]). Fowl's concerns are quite similar to those of this paper. He clearly calls into question whether Phil. 2:6-11 is a hymn in any meaningful sense of that term ("these passages are hymns in the very general sense of poetic accounts of the nature and/or activity of a divine figure"), yet finally treats the passage as a "hymn" in his totally watered down sense. His conclusion as to its role in the present context and in the letter as a whole is very similar to what I argue for here.

7. Thus the title of Martin's monograph.

basically four: (1) The ὅς with which it begins is paralleled in other passages in the NT also understood to be christological hymns (Col. 1:15, 18; 1 Tim. 3:16); (2) the exalted language and rhythmic quality of the whole; (3) the conviction that the whole can be displayed to show structured parallelism, of a kind with other pieces of Semitic poetry; (4) the language and structure seem to give these verses an internal coherence that separates them from the discourse of the epistle itself at this point.[8]

But despite the nearly universal acceptance of this point of view, there are good reasons to pause:

First, one must note that if it was originally a hymn of some kind, it contains nothing at all of the nature of Greek hymnody or poetry. Therefore, it must be Semitic in origin. But as will be pointed out, the alleged Semitic parallelism of this piece is quite unlike any known example of Hebrew psalmody. The word "hymn" properly refers to a *song* in praise of deity; in its present form — and even in its several reconstructed forms — this passage lacks the rhythm and parallelism that one might expect of material that is to be sung. And in any case, it fits very poorly with the clearly hymnic material in the Psalter — or in Luke 1:46-55, 68-79, or in 1 Tim. 3:16b, to name but a few clear NT examples of hymns.

Second, one must insist that exalted *prose* does not necessarily mean that one is dealing with a hymn. The same objections that I have raised as to the hymnic character of 1 Corinthians 13 must also be raised here.[9] Paul is capable of especially exalted prose whenever he thinks on the work of Christ.

Third, the ὅς in this case is not precisely like its alleged parallels in Col. 1:15 (18b) and 1 Tim. 3:16. In the former case, even though its antecedent is the υἱοῦ of the preceding clause, the resultant connection of the "hymn" with its antecedent is not at all smooth.[10] In the latter case, the connection of the ὅς to the rest of the sentence is ungrammatical, thus suggesting that it belonged to an original hymn (and should be translated with a "soft" antecedent, "he who"). But in the present case the ὅς does not belong to an original hymn, but

---

8. On the matter of criteria for distinguishing hymns and confessional materials in the NT, see esp. W. Hulitt Gloer, "Homologies and Hymns in the New Testament: Form, Content and Criteria for Identification," *PRS* 11 (1984): 115-32. Although this passage reflects several of Gloer's criteria, the fact that vv. 9-11 fit them all so poorly should give us all reason to pause.

9. See G. D. Fee, *The First Epistle to the Corinthians* (Grand Rapids: Eerdmans, 1987), p. 626.

10. Indeed, there is nothing else quite like this in Paul, where one has the order ἐν ᾧ - ὅς ("in whom" — "who"), rather than the expected ὅς — ἐν ᾧ. The subsequent ὅτι in v. 16b, which looks like a *berakoth* formula from the Psalter, plus the second ὅς in 18b, also makes one think that we are here dealing with a hymn fragment of some kind.

to a perfectly normal Pauline sentence in which it immediately follows its antecedent, Ἰησοῦ Χριστοῦ.

Fourth, and for me this is the clinching matter, in Paul's Greek, as exalted as it is, the sentences follow one another in perfectly orderly prose — all quite in Pauline style. It begins (a) with a relative clause, in which two ideas are set off with a typically Pauline οὐκ/ἀλλά contrast, followed (b) by another clause begun with καί, all of which (c) is followed by a final sentence begun with an inferential διὸ καί, and concluding with a ἵνα (probably result) clause in two parts, plus a ὅτι clause. What needs to be noted is, first, that this is as typically Pauline argumentation as one can find anywhere in his letters; and, second, that there are scores of places in Paul where there are more balanced structures than this, but where, because of the subject matter, no one suspects Paul of citing poetry or writing hymnody.[11] His own rhetorical style is simply replete with examples of balanced structures, parallelism, chiasmus, etc.

Fifth and finally, one must note how irregular so many of the alleged lines are, if they are supposed to function as lines of Semitic poetry. For example, in the most commonly accepted structural arrangement, as it is displayed in the NA[26],[12] there are no verbs at all in six of the "lines":[13]

> 6c τὸ εἶναι ἴσα θεῷ
> 8d θανάτου δὲ σταυροῦ
> 9c τὸ ὑπὲρ πᾶν ὄνομα
> 10a ἵνα ἐν ὀνόματι Ἰησοῦ
> 10c ἐπουρανίων καὶ ἐπιγείων καὶ καταχθονίων
> 11c εἰς δόξαν θεοῦ πατρός

Moreover, the placement of the verbs that do appear are anything but in a balanced poetic pattern; the verb appears last in lines 6a, b, 7a, b, c, 9a, and first in 8b, c.

This is simply not the "stuff" of poetry. Indeed, any alleged "lines" of

---

11. E.g., several passages in 1 Corinthians come immediately to mind: 1:22-25; 1:26-28; 6:12-13; 7:2-4; 9:19-22, etc.

12. For convenience I have put this display in Appendix I, with each of the lines numbered. This in fact is basically the proposal of E. Lohmeyer, who omitted line 8d (θανάτου δὲ σταυροῦ) as a "Pauline interpolation." It has also been adopted *inter alia* by Beare, Benoit, Bernard, Cullmann, and Héring (see Martin, *Carmen Christi*, p. 30, n. 1, for other bibliography).

13. There is also no verb expressed in line 11b, κύριος Ἰησοῦς Χριστός, but this is a nominal sentence in which an ἐστιν is presupposed. It is not surprising that four of these verbless "lines" are in vv. 9-11, which has nothing at all of the quality of poetry to it.

poetry like those listed above are not natural to the text, but are simply the creation of the scholars who have here found a "hymn."

It should be noted, of course, that not all scholars adopt this scheme; indeed, there are at least five other basic proposals, with modifications in several of them: (1) L. Cerfaux[14] and J. Jeremias[15] adopted a scheme of three stanzas each (Cerfaux's strophes have four, five, and six lines each; Jeremias's strophes have four lines each, excising lines 8d, 10c, 11c). The stanzas in this case correspond to the three states of Jesus' existence: pre-existence, earthly life, and exaltation. As over against Lohmeyer's proposal, these, of course, catch the point of Paul's argument, but they are less successful as "lines." (2) Ralph Martin[16] offered a modification of Lohmeyer, in which there are six stanzas of two lines each. This proposal has the advantage of trying to establish lines of generally equal length (although not totally successfully), each of which has a verb form; but to do so he omits lines 8d, 10c, and 11c, and performs rather radical surgery on the sense, especially his stanzas C and D:

(α) ἐν ὁμοιώματι ἀνθρώπων γενόμενος
(β) καὶ σχήματι εὑρεθεὶς ὡς ἄνθρωπος

(α) ἐταπείνωσεν ἑαυτόν
(β) γενόμενος ὑπήκοος μέχρι θανάτου

(3) Collange,[17] followed by Talbert,[18] offers four stanzas of four lines each. The advantage of this scheme is that it does not resort to omissions to make it work; on the other hand, it leaves one with lines of unequal length, some of which are without verb forms, and must (quite unsuccessfully) divide vv. 9-11 into two stanzas. (4) M. Dibelius[19] suggested an arrangement of five stanzas of varying length, and varying lines, which also included several modifications of the text. But such a proposal almost eliminates any feature of what

14. "L'hymne au Christ — Serviteur de Dieu (*Phil.,* II, 6-11 = *Is.* LII,13–LIII,12)," in *Miscellanea historica in honorem Alberti de Meyer* (Louvain: Bibliothèque de l'université, 1946), I, 117-30.

15. "Zur Gedankenführung in den paulinischen Briefen," in *Studia Paulina in honorem J. de Zwaan,* ed. J. W. Sevenster and W. C. van Unnik (Haarlem, 1953), pp. 152-54; cf. "Zu Phil ii 7: Ἑαυτὸν Ἐκένωσεν," *NovT* 6 (1963): 182-88.

16. In *Carmen Christi,* pp. 36-38.

17. *L'Epître de Saint Paul aux Philippiens* (Neuchâtel, 1973).

18. C. H. Talbert, "The Problem of Pre-existence in Philippians 2:6-11," *JBL* 86 (1967): 141-53.

19. *An die Thessalonicher, an die Philipper* (HNT; Tübingen: Mohr [Siebeck], ³1937), pp. 72-74.

one might consider poetry. (5) G. Strecker[20] offered the most radical surgery of all. Excising all of v. 8 as Pauline, he then adduced two strophes with six lines divided into couplets of two.

It is difficult to know how to assess all of this. When one reads Martin or Talbert, for example, the discussion is carried on with the presupposition that everyone recognizes the passage as a hymn; they only differ as to its original form. On the other hand, such reading also makes one feel like the little boy in the fairy tale, who exclaimed that the emperor had no clothes. From this perspective the very lack of agreement should call into question the whole procedure. And if one respond that there is agreement at least on the fact that it is a hymn, the rebuttal still remains: if so, then one should expect that its parts would be more plainly visible to all. Such is certainly the case with Col. 1:15-18 and 1 Tim. 3:16, but here all the arrangements are flawed in some way or another. Either one must (1) excise lines, (2) dismiss the obvious inner logic of the whole, or (3) create lines that are either without parallelism or verbless.

It should be noted further in this regard that any excision of words or lines is an exercise in exegetical futility. It implies, and this is sometimes vigorously defended,[21] that the real concern of exegesis is the meaning of the "hymn" on its own, apart from its present context. But this is exegetically indefensible, since (1) our only access to the "hymn" is in its present form and present position, and (2) we must begin any legitimate exegesis by assuming that all the present words are included because they contribute in some way to Paul's own concerns. To assume otherwise is a form of exegetical nihilism, in which on non-demonstrable prior grounds, one determines that an author did not mean anything by the words he uses.

All of this leads me to pick up on the suggestion made above (reason 4) that, in the final analysis, the passage can best be understood in terms of its three clear sentences (vv. 6-7; v. 8; vv. 9-11), which, of course, is a modification of Jeremias's analysis without the need to resort to a hymn or excision of its parts. In this scheme the first two sentences emphasize the two concerns of vv. 3-4 — humility and selflessness — but pick them up in reverse order, while the third emphasizes the divine vindication of such. This is not to deny that some of it may have had prior existence — perhaps as something creedal? But it is to argue that all of this has become subservient to Paul's present interests, which is to urge harmony in the Philippian community, by pressing for those Christ-like qualities most necessary for it, selflessness and humility.

---

20. "Redaktion und Tradition im Christushymnus, Phil. 2:6-11," *ZNW* 55 (1964): 63-78.
21. E.g., by Käsemann, Martin, and O'Connor.

II. The Question of Background/Authorship

The questions of background and authorship are closely related, in that once the passage was isolated as a "hymn," then certain features were "discovered" to be "un-Pauline" (with alleged Pauline features "missing"), which in turn led many to argue that the whole was both pre-Pauline and therefore non-Pauline.[22] Once that was established, then it was necessary to find its original *Sitz im Leben*. It should not surprise us, given the assumptions of the methodology, that scholars found what they were looking for. Nor should it surprise one that, as with form, every imaginable background has been argued for:

a. Heterodox Judaism (Lohmeyer)
b. Iranian myth of the Heavenly Redeemer (Beare)
c. Hellenistic, pre-Christian Gnosticism (Käsemann)
d. Jewish Gnosticism (J. A. Sanders)
e. OT Servant passages (Coppens, Moule, Strimple)
f. Genesis account of Adam (Murphy-O'Connor, Dunn)
g. Hellenistic Jewish Wisdom speculation (Georgi)

The very diversity of these proposals suggests something of the futility (dare one say irrelevance?) of this exercise. After all, one comes by this by guessing at what are alleged to be "Pauline adaptations and interpolations," which means that one is fairly free to create as one wills.

Furthermore, all of this becomes especially pernicious when one argues, as does J. Murphy-O'Connor,[23] that since Paul did *not* compose it, then one may not use other Pauline words — or even the present context! — to interpret it. That is, not only *can* it be isolated from its context, it is argued, but since Paul did not write it, it *must* be so isolated and must be understood on its own, without reference either to Paul or to its present Pauline context. That is an exegetical tour de force of almost unparalleled boldness.

Furthermore, I would argue, such a view shows very little sensitivity either to Paul or to the nature of composition in antiquity. On the one hand, Paul is quite capable of citing[24] when that suits him. Sometimes he adapts;

---

22. By "un-Pauline" I mean "that which is uncharacteristic of Paul"; "non-Pauline" means that it is judged as quite foreign to Paul.

23. J. Murphy-O'Connor, "Christological Anthropology in Phil. II:6-11," *RB* 83 (1976): 25-50.

24. By "citing" I refer to that kind of quotation from the OT or elsewhere, where some kind of introductory formula is used, or as in the case of 1 Cor. 10:26, a γάρ is used with a quote that the Apostle can assume will be well known to his readers.

sometimes he cites rather closely. But in all cases, the citation is both clearly identifiable and capable of making at least fairly good sense in its context. That is, Paul apparently chooses to cite because he wants to support or elaborate a point. On the other hand, there are all kinds of evidence that in other cases ancient authors — and Paul should most likely be included here — also took over other material rather wholesale and adapted it to fit their own compositions (the Gospels being a clear case in point). In these latter cases, even when they may have carried over some of the language from their source(s), they clearly intend for the present material not to be identifiable as to its source precisely because for them it is now their own material. So in the present case. Here Paul dictates, and the amanuensis transcribes, letter by letter (or syllable by syllable), without any sense that a source needs to be noted. One must always keep in mind that in the original letter what we call vv. 5 and 6 would have been "run on," something like this:

. . . ΕΝΧΡΙΣΤΩΙΗΣΟΥΟΣΕΝΜΟΡΦΗΘΕΟΥΥΠΑΡΧΩΝΟΥΧΑΡΠΑΓΜΟΝ . . .

What must be noted is that in this kind of process, one can only speak of "writing in" or "composition"; the language "interpolation" or "insertion" simply will not do, since they mislead as to the actual historical process. Therefore, to take out some of this "written in" material, as if it were an extraneous citation, when there is not a hint of citation anywhere, and then to urge that it can only be understood apart from its original context, is to argue for exegetical anarchy.[25]

Others, especially Käsemann[26] and Martin, seem to make the same exegetical error, though a little more subtly. In their case the meaning of the "hymn" is discovered first of all in isolation from its present context, then *that* meaning is contended for as the one *Paul himself intends* in context. There is an obvious circularity to this kind of reasoning; thus it does not surprise one that almost all who go this route have the common denominator of opposition to the so-called ethical interpretation of the passage.

But as before, it needs to be stressed (1) that Paul is the *author* in terms of its inclusion, including *all* the present words, and (2) that although Paul often quotes, this does *not* come by way of quotation; the alleged "hymn" is a grammatical piece within the present context. Whereas one might legiti-

25. Cf. the critique by Robert B. Strimple, "Philippians 2:5-11 in Recent Studies: Some Exegetical Conclusions," *WTJ* 41 (1979): 247-68, esp. 250-51.

26. E. Käsemann, "Kritische Analyse von Phil. 2,5-11," *ZThK* 47 (1950): 313-60; Eng. trans., "A Critical Analysis of Philippians 2:5-11," in *God and Christ: Existence and Province* (*Journal for Theology and Church* 5, ed. R. W. Funk [New York: Harper, 1968], pp. 45-88).

mately look separately at a piece of quoted material, speculate as to its original meaning, and then wonder whether an author has correctly understood that original meaning, neither the grammar, the content, nor the context allows such a procedure here. As Morna Hooker put it: "For even if the material is non-Pauline, we may expect Paul himself to have interpreted it and used it in a Pauline manner."[27] Indeed, of this whole enterprise Hooker says (correctly):

> If the passage is pre-Pauline, then we have no guidelines to help us in understanding its meaning. Commentators may speculate about the background — but we know very little about pre-Pauline Christianity, and nothing at all about the context in which the passage originated. It may therefore be more profitable to look first at the function of these verses in the present context and to enquire about possible parallels within Paul's own writings.[28]

"Of course," one wishes to respond to such an eminently reasonable proposal; otherwise why did Paul write it into this context as something that in v. 12 he will argue from?[29]

III. The Question of Its Place in Context

Käsemann notes that the so-called ethical interpretation had held sway universally up to the 1920s. As Strimple notes,[30] one can well understand *why*, since this is such an obvious reading of the passage in its present context (*pace* Martin, who continually refers to "the thin thread"). However, as Hurtado has decisively demonstrated,[31] Käsemann objects not primarily on exegetical, but theological, grounds. Here one can see, and sympathize with, his fierce antipathy to the Old Liberalism. His point, therefore, and in this he is fol-

---

27. See Morna D. Hooker, "Philippians 2:6-11," in *Jesus und Paulus: Festschrift für Werner Georg Kümmel zum 70. Geburtstag*, ed. E. Earle Ellis and Erich Grässer (Göttingen: Vandenhoeck & Ruprecht, 1975), pp. 151-64 (from p. 152).

28. Hooker, "Philippians 2:6-11," pp. 151-64.

29. Most of those who write on this passage simply fail to come to terms with the ὥστε that begins v. 12. Not only is this a thoroughly Pauline form of argumentation, but it is so in such a way that what precedes it forms the theological basis for the concluding parenesis.

30. Strimple, "Conclusions," p. 252.

31. Larry W. Hurtado, "Jesus as Lordly Example in Philippians 2:5-11," in *From Jesus to Paul: Studies in Honour of Francis Wright Beare,* ed. P. Richardson and J. C. Hurd (Waterloo, Ont.: Wilfrid Laurier University Press, 1984), pp. 113-26.

lowed by Martin, is that Paul's reason for including it is *not* example, but to provide the *ground* (basis) for Christian behavior. Hence an understanding of the ἐν Χριστῷ in v. 5 as locative of sphere (i.e., the common sphere of Christian existence) is absolutely crucial to this enterprise. The emphasis is thus placed *not* on Christ's humiliation in vv. 6-8, which functions merely to set up the real point, but on Christ's victory in vv. 9-11. Christians are being urged to live in the realm where Christ has triumphed for us over the demonic powers.

Although one might object to that theologically — as Marshall points out,[32] the reason for Christ's death is no longer sin but subjection to the "powers" — the ultimate problem is still contextual *per se*. First, the use of the verb φρονεῖτε in v. 5 demands that Paul is still concerned with the issue of vv. 1-4; otherwise, the use of language becomes nearly meaningless. Furthermore, the points made about Christ in vv. 6-8 are precisely those of vv. 3-4 — selflessness and humility. Indeed, the key sentence (v. 8) includes the two key words found on either side in the context: ταπεινόω (v. 3) and ὑπήκοος (v. 12). What the Philippian believers are being called to, humility toward one another and obedience in this matter, is what Christ did as man. Again, it must be urged that it is a cardinal rule in exegesis to assume a logical thread to an argument, unless there are especially convincing reasons for thinking otherwise. In this case, 1:27; 2:1-4, 5-8; and 2:12-13 hold together very nicely. Harmony is the issue: humility and selflessness are the way to it. The final exhortation to obedience in vv. 12-13 therefore also has to do with unity/harmony. Since the first half of the "hymn" makes precisely that point, why go elsewhere for understanding?

Martin, following Käsemann, raises two objections: (1) One cannot really follow Christ's example, which, according to Martin, is not his self-sacrifice on earth, but "the incarnation of a heavenly being"; and (2) in any case, the main point of the passage is vv. 9-11, Christ's *present* lordly triumph, which we cannot follow.

But in response, as has often been pointed out: (1) The issue is not "imitating" Christ in the sense of *repeating* what he did — that is seldom the sense of "imitation" in the NT[33] — but in being *like* him "in mind." For Paul "imitatio" does not ordinarily mean, "Do as I did," but "Be as I am." In Jesus' self-emptying and self-sacrifice, which are significant precisely because they

32. See I. Howard Marshall, "The Christ-Hymn in Philippians 2:5-11: A Review Article," *TynBul* 19 (1968): 104-27.

33. The closest thing to it might be 1 Thess. 1:6, but even here it was in the Thessalonians' own reception of the gospel with joy and suffering, an experience that in one way is uniquely theirs but in other ways is like that of Jesus and Paul, that they became "imitators of us and of the Lord."

secured redemption for us, he also exemplified for us proper selflessness and humility. Here we have the truest expression of the character of God himself, which through Christ and the Spirit he is trying to recreate in his people. In this regard one should note the use of the example of Christ in Rom. 15:1-7, 2 Cor. 8:9, and 1 Cor. 10:31–11:1 (see also 1 Pet. 2:21!). Such an appeal *assumes* the life and death of Christ as the ground of our being — that, after all, is precisely what makes the example such a powerful one — but that is not the point Paul himself makes here.

(2) The role of vv. 9-11 is divine *eschatological* vindication, not unlike the argument of 3:17-21 (perhaps 3:2-11 as well). However we are finally to understand the complex argument of ch. 3, one can scarcely deny Paul's concern to emphasize that "knowing Christ" in the *present* includes both the power of his resurrection and the fellowship of his sufferings, and that for those who so know Christ there is a certain future, which they have not yet attained. The present fellowship of his sufferings awaits final vindication at Jesus' coming, when this body of ταπείνωσις is transformed into the likeness of his present glory. So with the present argument, which seems in this regard to anticipate the argument of ch. 3. At the same time, as Wright has suggested,[34] this final inferential sentence serves as the divine approval of the way Jesus demonstrated what it meant to be τὸ εἶναι ἴσα θεῷ.

IV. How Then Shall We View the Whole? A Proposal

In what follows I do not contend that I have discovered anything new as to the meaning of the passage in its context. Rather, what is offered in the rest of this paper is a modest proposal for viewing the *whole* of the passage. What is proposed is that instead of looking for strophes, lines, parallels, etc., all of which are the result of faulty presuppositions in approaching the text, one should begin with the actual structures of Paul's Greek sentences and see how he himself is arguing (for what follows see the structural analysis in Appendix II).

First, let us begin with the obvious, that on which almost everyone agrees, namely that the whole is in two parts, the transition being signaled by the διὸ καί of v. 9: vv. 6-8 express humiliation; vv. 9-11, exaltation.

Part I has two sentences, controlled by the two main verbs accompanied by the reflexive pronoun:

---

34. Wright, "ἁρπαγμός," pp. 350-52.

v. 7 — ἑαυτόν ἐκένωσεν
v. 8 — ἐταπείνωσεν ἑαυτόν

The two parts pick up respectively how Christ thought/behaved in both expressions of his existence:

(1) ἐν μορφῇ θεοῦ — as the pre-existent one
(2) μορφὴν δούλου — during his incarnation[35]

Thus Part I¹ is syntactically balanced, though not perfectly:

Participial phrase
    Contrasting clause   (οὐκ)
    Main clause   (ἀλλά)
Participial phrase
Participial phrase   (γενόμενος).[36]

In Part I¹ᵃ, with a participle preceding, Paul begins by stating how Christ did *not* think (οὐχ ἡγήσατο) in his pre-existence as God.[37] On the one hand, the present participle asserts that he *had* prior existence as God (ὑπάρχων = *being* ἐν μορφῇ θεοῦ); on the other hand, the οὐχ ἡγήσατο tells us how he did *not* treat his deity,[38] with an eye, of course, to his incarnation that follows.

35. The choice of μορφή almost certainly has nothing to do with the long debates over its fine nuances, but rather was chosen precisely because Paul needed a word that would fit both modes of Jesus' existence.

36. Gloer, "Homologies," p. 132, lists the use of participles as one of the criteria for hymnic material. But these same participles appear in the apparently homological material found in Gal. 4:4-6. As here, this passage may reflect Paul's dipping into the church's pool of creedal/homological material. But the sentences in their present form are Paul's; and the double γενόμενος, followed by the double ἵνα clauses, reflect Paul's own skillful prose.

37. One has great difficulty taking seriously the arguments of O'Connor, Talbert, Dunn (*Christology in the Making: An Inquiry into the Origins of the Doctrine of the Incarnation* [Philadelphia: Westminster, 1980]), et al., who propose that this text does not speak to pre-existence, but to a kind of Adam-christology in which the Second Adam did *not* as Adam seek/hold onto divine privileges. Not only are the language and grammar against it, but such a view seems to miss the thrust of the passage by a long way.

38. On the whole question of the meaning of the two key terms, ἁρπαγμός and ἐκένωσεν, see Wright, "ἁρπαγμός" (who follows R. W. Hoover on the meaning of this difficult word ["The Harpagmos Enigma: A Philological Solution," *HTR* 56 (1971): 95-119]). With Wright I am convinced that these words have not to do with grasping anything, but with the basic character of God, who is not a "grasping" being, but a "giving" one, best seen in Christ's pouring himself out. Thus, he did not "empty himself" *of anything*. The verb and its reflexive (which functions as the direct object, after all) simply describe his action.

Part I[1b] then starts with the main clause, thus keeping the οὐ/ἀλλά contrast together, and asserts what he *did* do instead (become incarnate), followed by two *explanatory* participial phrases.[39] Three notes need to be made about structure and interpretation: (1) The ἀλλὰ ἐκένωσεν must be held in contrast to οὐχ ἡγήσατο as its opposite in some way. This is a typically Pauline way of setting up an argument, especially when he wants to emphasize the point of the ἀλλά-clause. (2) The first participial phrase in Part I[1b] indicates *how* ἑαυτὸν ἐκένωσεν; the λαβών is thus circumstantial/ modal (= "by" or "in"; "by/in having taken the form of a servant").[40] (3) The second participial phrase then elaborates/clarifies the first; the emphasis is on servanthood, which finds its expression in his taking on humanity.[41]

Part I[2] then picks up the reality of the Incarnation and spells out how Christ behaved (what he did) while μορφῇ δούλου. The basic structure is similar to that of Part I[1]: after a paratactic καί which joins the two clauses,[42] it also begins with a participial phrase, now stressing his humanity, followed by the main verb, which in turn is followed by a circumstantial/modal γενόμενος participial phrase. But there are also three notable differences: (1) This sentence lacks an οὐ/ἀλλά contrast; (2) the word order of the participles in their respective phrases is irregular; and (3) in place of the second (final) qualifying *participle,* there is a simple, but powerful, appositional coda. Thus:

39. Cf. the very similar structure to the comparable "creedal" material in Gal. 4:4-5.

40. Cf. Paul D. Feinberg, "The Kenosis and Christology: An Exegetical-Theological Analysis of Phil 2:6-11," *TrinJ* n.s. 1 (1980): 21-46 (p. 42).

41. These two aorist participles, it should be pointed out, which stand in contrast to ὑπάρχων (note their final position in each case, which does not occur in the next section), seem to spell death to all attempts to see I[1a] as an Adam-analogy, at least in the human/human sense (see n. 37).

42. One of the weaknesses of many of the alleged strophic reconstructions of this passage is the choice on the part of some to disregard the clear force of this καί as parataxis, which joins the first two sentences together, and to make it a conjunction joining the two lines ἐν ὁμοιώματι ἀνθρώπων γενόμενος and σχήματι εὑρεθεὶς ὡς ἄνθρωπος. Such a reconstruction has every possible thing against it. (1) There is a sparing use of conjunctions in the passage; those that do occur join clauses, not phrases; (2) in a series of sentences that are full of Semitic coloring, the καί is normal parataxis; (3) one can make almost no sense at all of εὑρεθείς as modifying ἐκένωσεν (To say "He poured himself out, by having taken the form of a servant, by having come to be in the likeness of men and by having been found in appearance as a man," and then to start the next sentence, "He humbled himself by having become obedient unto death," is to talk syntactical nonsense). Finally, since Paul himself *did not write in strophes,* one should first understand Paul's sentences in their normal syntactical arrangements.

καί   (joining the two sentences [parts] of Part I)
Participial phrase
   Main clause
Participial phrase   (γενόμενος)
        (with coda)

Several notes need to be made here about structure and interpretation:
(1) The opening participial phrase noticeably flows directly out of the last
phrase of I¹ᵇ, picking up the key word ἄνθρωπος, but now emphasizing not
just his having come in the ὁμοιώματι of ἄνθρωπος, but in fact his having
been found σχήματι as ἄνθρωπος. (2) At the same time this phrase intentionally corresponds to the opening phrase of Part I, the operative words being
θεός and ἄνθρωπος. This structural phenomenon, it seems to me, is the clear
evidence that any attempt to make the two ἄνθρωπος phrases into a single
stanza of an alleged hymn is thoroughly misguided. (3) The main clause similarly corresponds to the main clause of Part I. Thus as God, he emptied himself (poured himself out); as man, he humbled himself. These two clauses
thus express the main concern of the passage as a whole. (4) The γενόμενος
participial phrase, also as in Part I, is circumstantial/modal, indicating *how*
ἐταπείνωσεν ἑαυτόν, by his having become obedient to the point of death.
(5) Finally, and again as in Part I, only now with an appositional phrase rather
than a participle, the final phrase elaborates the preceding participle by indicating the *kind of death* (which is full of theological grist, of a kind that one
can be sure the Philippians knew well; cf. esp. 3:10).

Thus all of this is not so much "hymnic" as it is full of the kinds of balanced structures found everywhere in Paul. That it should be expressed in
such exalted language, and in language that tends to be somewhat unique to
this passage, probably is an indicator of how much of Paul we do *not* know
from his preserved literary remains. What needs to be noted is that such
"unique language" occurs in every instance of this kind in Paul, where he
seems to dip into his own, and the church's, creedal/liturgical pool to express
himself soteriologically or christologically — and no two are alike![43]

Finally, it must be insisted that Part II has *nothing* of the quality of a

43. These moments occur in all the preserved letters except Philemon. Cf., e.g., 1 Thess.
1:9-10; 5:9-10; 2 Thess. 2:13-14; 1 Cor. 5:7; 6:11; 6:20; 15:3-5; 2 Cor. 5:18-21; 8:9; Gal. 1:4; 4:4-6; Rom.
3:23-25; 4:24-25; Col. 1:15-20; 1:21-22; 2:11-15; Eph. 1:3-14; Phil. 3:8-11; 3:20-21; 1 Tim. 1:15; 2:4-5; 3:16;
Titus 2:11-14; 2 Tim. 1:9-10; 3:5-7. One could easily show the "non-Pauline" character of all of these
passages, since each of them has unique language and no two of them are alike. It is the very richness of these passages, and their obviously having been adapted to their contexts, that makes so
much of the argumentation about the non-Pauline character of the present passage so tenuous.

hymn to it, nor much in the way of the balanced structures of Part I. In fact it is a single complex sentence with a main clause, a compound ἵνα-clause, the latter of which concludes with a noun clause. The structure is easily displayed; a few additional words are in order about structure and meaning:

(1) It begins with διό, an inferential conjunction, which when joined with καί denotes "that the inference is self-evident" (BAGD). This a thoroughly Pauline expression, and belongs to argumentation, not poetry.

(2) In contrast to Part I, where Ἰησοῦς, by way of the relative ὅς, is the subject of every verb form, here Jesus is the object (direct or indirect) of the verbs, and ὁ θεός is the subject of the sentence (the main clause), as the one who bestows "the name" on Jesus. The cosmic response (heavenly/earthly) to Jesus — every knee and every tongue — is the grammatical subject of the purpose/result clause, with Jesus as the "object" of worship.

(3) Thus God the Father's action (v. 11) is twofold, both probably referring to the same basic reality: (a) God highly exalted Jesus; and (b) he did so by bestowing on him an exalted name.

(4) The ἵνα-clause expresses purpose or result with regard to his exalted name and is also twofold (i.e., two ways of speaking of essentially the same reality): (a) Every knee shall bow (= expression of homage); (b) at the *name* of Jesus every tongue shall confess: κύριος is Ἰησοῦς Χριστός.

(5) All of this is for (telic εἰς) God's ultimate glory.

There remain, then, two final structural notes about Part II, with regard to poetry. First, there is nothing like vv. 9-11 in any known Greek poetry; nor is there anything like it in the Hebrew Psalter. (a) διό appears once (Ps. 115[116]:1), but not in this kind of structural way (at the beginning of a new clause/sentence); (b) ἵνα (without μή) appears only twice (Ps. 38[39]:4, 13), and in both cases in prayer, not in descriptions of God.

Second, although this combination (διό . . . ἵνα) as such does not occur in Paul, the form itself does (an inferential conjunction followed by a purpose/result clause = "therefore/so then . . . in order that . . .").[44] This combination is the language of argumentation, not of singing.

All of this is, then, to argue that the passage is not only Pauline, but is meaningful — and precise — in its present context. If it had prior form of some kind, and this can be neither proved nor disproved (although I would tend to lean in the latter direction), in its present form it has been so thoroughly taken over by Paul as to render discussions of its prior existence as to its form, authorship, and background needless or meaningless.

---

44. See, e.g., Rom. 4:16 (διὰ τοῦτο . . . ἵνα); Rom. 7:4 (ὥστε . . . εἰς τό); Gal. 3:24 (ὥστε . . . ἵνα).

V. A Theological Postscript

Let me conclude with a theological postscript, once again picking up the concern of Käsemann and Martin. To argue that this marvelous passage is written as a theological reinforcement for harmony or unity in an early Christian community does not make the passage unworthy of Paul or a betrayal of his gospel. What it does in fact is to reinforce a significant aspect of Paul's gospel, namely that there is no genuine *life in Christ* that is not at the same time, by the power of the Holy Spirit, being regularly transformed into the *likeness of Christ*. A gospel of grace that omits obedience is not Pauline in any sense. To be sure, the indicative must *precede* the imperative or all is lost; but it does not eliminate the imperative, or all is likewise lost.

The behavioral concern of this passage is precisely in keeping with the Pauline parenesis found everywhere. Paul's gospel has inherent in it that those who are in Christ will also walk worthy of Christ (1:27). Thus, in Pauline ethics, the principle is love, the pattern is Christ, and the power is the Spirit, all of which have been provided for in the death and resurrection of Christ. The appeal in the present passage, which I take to begin at 1:27, is to a unity in Christ that for Paul was a *sine qua non* of the evidential reality of his gospel at work in his communities. The bases of the appeal — Christ, love, and the Spirit — were set forth in v. 1. The Christian graces absolutely necessary for such behavior are selflessness and humility, in which one looks not only to one's own interests but also — especially — to those of others (vv. 3-4). Here is where the example of Christ comes in. Those who are "in Christ" (v. 1) must also "think" like him (vv. 5-11), which is exactly as Paul has argued elsewhere (2 Cor. 8:9; Rom. 15:1-6).

However, to insist that in context the basic thrust of this passage is "Christ as paradigm" does not mean that there are no other agenda. Both the length and pattern of the passage suggest that Paul is laying a much broader theological foundation, probably for the whole letter. In the first place, the mention of Christ's death on the cross, even though the emphasis lies on his "humbling himself" to that extent, surely at the same time reminds them of the basis of their faith in the first place. It is that death, after all, that lies at the heart of everything. To put that in another way, the appeal to Christ's *example* in his suffering and death makes its point precisely because it presupposes that they will simultaneously recall the saving significance of that death. In 1 Pet. 2:21-25 that is explicitly stated. Paul does it differently; he does not add, "by whose stripes you were healed," but such an intent almost certainly lies behind his mention of the cross.

Second, there is also an emphasis in this letter on *imitatio* with regard to suffering (1:29-30; 3:10, 21). Those who are privileged to believe in Christ are also privileged to suffer for him; indeed, to share in those sufferings is part of knowing him. Hence, this passage, with Christ's humbling himself to the point of death on the cross, will also serve as the theological ground for that concern. Indeed, that seems to make the best sense of the otherwise unusual emphasis in 3:10 that knowing Christ includes the "fellowship (κοινωνία) of his sufferings, συμμορφιζόμενος τῷ θανάτῳ αὐτοῦ." That certainly sounds as if Christ's death is once again serving as paradigm. Both "participation" and "following" are implied here.

Third, the note of eschatological reward or vindication in vv. 9-11 is also struck more than once in this letter (1:6; 1:10-11; 1:21-23; 3:11-14; 3:20-21). For this, too, Christ serves both as exalted Lord and as example or forerunner. His vindication, which followed his humiliation, is found in his present and future lordship, to which both the Philippians and their opponents will ultimately bow. But that vindication also becomes paradigm. Those who now suffer for Christ, and walk worthy of Christ, shall also at his coming be transformed so as to be conformed to "the body of his (present) glory."

Thus the centrality of Christ in Pauline theology. His death secured redemption for his people; but at the same time it serves as the pattern for their present life in the Spirit, while finally we shall share in the eschatological glory and likeness that are presently his. And all of this is, as our present passage concludes, "to the glory of God the Father."

In the final analysis, therefore, this passage stands at the heart of Paul's understanding of God himself. Christ serves as the pattern, to be sure; but he does so as the one who most truly expresses God's nature. As God, Christ poured himself out, not seeking his own advantage. As man, in his incarnation, he humbled himself unto death on the cross. That this is what God is like is the underlying Pauline point; and since God is in process of re-creating us in his image, this becomes the heart of the present appeal. The Philippians — and we ourselves — are not called upon simply to "imitate God" by what we do, but to have this very mind, the mind of Christ, developed in us, so that we too bear God's image in our attitudes and relationships within the Christian community — and beyond.

Appendix 1
The NA[26] Structural Display of Philippians 2:6-11

6 (a) ὃς ἐν μορφῇ θεοῦ ὑπάρχων

   (b) οὐχ ἁρπαγμὸν ἡγήσατο

   (c) τὸ εἶναι ἴσα θεῷ,

7 (a) ἀλλὰ ἑαυτὸν ἐκένωσεν

   (b) μορφὴν δούλου λαβών,

   (c) ἐν ὁμοιώματι ἀνθρώπων γενόμενος·

   (d) καὶ σχήματι εὑρεθεὶς ὡς ἄνθρωπος

8 (a) ἐταπείνωσεν ἑαυτὸν

   (b) γενόμενος ὑπήκοος μέχρι θανάτου

   (c) θανάτου δὲ σταυροῦ.

9 (a) διὸ καὶ ὁ θεὸς αὐτὸν ὑπερύψωσεν

   (b) καὶ ἐχαρίσατο αὐτῷ τὸ ὄνομα

   (c) τὸ ὑπὲρ πᾶν ὄνομα,

10 (a) ἵνα ἐν τῷ ὀνόματι Ἰησοῦ

   (b) πᾶν γόνυ κάμψῃ

   (c) ἐπουρανίων καὶ ἐπιγείων καὶ καταχθονίων

11 (a) καὶ πᾶσα γλῶσσα ἐξομολογήσεται ὅτι

   (b) κύριος Ἰησοῦ Χριστὸς

   (c) εἰς δόξαν θεοῦ πατρός.

Appendix 2
Structural Analysis of Phil. 2:5-11

5 τοῦτο   φρονεῖτε
                 ἐν ὑμῖν
        <u>ὃ καὶ</u>
                 ἐν Χριστῷ Ἰησοῦ
6 [Part I]
        I¹ᵃ   <u>ὃς</u>   ἐν μορφῇ θεοῦ ὑπάρχων,
                 οὐχ   ἁρπαγμὸν ἡγήσατο   τὸ εἶναι ἴσα θεῷ
7   I¹ᵇ   ἀλλά   ἑαυτὸν   ἐκένωσεν
                 μορφὴν δούλου λαβών,
                 ἐν ὁμοιώματι ἀνθρώπων γενόμενος.

        I²   <u>καί</u>
                 σχήματι εὑρεθεὶς ὡς ἄνθρωπος,
8   ἐταπείνωσεν ἑαυτὸν,
                 γενόμενος ὑπήκοος μέχρι θανάτου
                 θανάτου δὲ σταυροῦ

_____

        [Part II]
9   <u>διὸ καὶ</u>
        ὁ θεὸς αὐτὸν   ὑπερύψωσεν
                 καὶ
        ἐχαρίσατο αὐτῷ   τὸ ὄνομα
                         τὸ ὑπὲρ πᾶν ὄνομα
10   <u>ἵνα</u>
                         ἐν τῷ ὀνόματι Ἰησοῦ
        πᾶν   γόνυ   κάμψῃ
                 ἐπουρανίων
                 καὶ
                 ἐπιγείων
                 καὶ
                 καταχθονίων
11   <u>καὶ</u>
        πᾶσα γλῶσσα ἐξομολογήσεται
                         ὅτι
                 κύριος Ἰησοῦς Χριστός
                 εἰς δόξαν θεοῦ πατρός

THEOLOGICAL STUDIES

CHAPTER 13

Toward a Theology of 1 Corinthians[1]
(1989)

It seems neither possible nor desirable to analyze the theology of a letter like this without some degree of "mirror reading" of the historical situation presupposed by the text.[2] Thus my own views on this matter, which at times will color my understanding: (I) This is the third in a *series* of letters between Paul

---

1. The tentative nature of my title is related to the fact that of all the literature on 1 Corinthians (some 2500 journal articles alone), there is not a single piece known to me that attempts this particular task: to deal with the theology of the letter as a whole. The reasons for which are obvious. Our interests in this letter tend to reflect Paul's in writing it — the behavioral aberrations that he addresses.

There are, of course, scores of items that deal with various aspects of its theology; and several of the commentaries (Barrett, Fee, etc.) offer a section in their Introductions on "Theological Contributions," but these tend to highlight the unique contributions of this letter to Paul's overall theology.

2. A few words are also in order about basic assumptions: (a) In keeping with the ground rules [of the seminar], I have tried to write this paper as if 1 Corinthians were Paul's only extant letter. This is an especially difficult exercise, since one is regularly tempted to point out what Paul does *not* say here in light of other letters (e.g., the relatively sparse use of *dikai-* words). And how does one make sense of 15:56 ("the power of sin is the law") without outside help?

(b) My task is primarily descriptive; at times, however, such description must consider Paul's assumed symbolic universe — both his own and that shared with his readers. Otherwise, one is bound to create distortions.

(c) In keeping with these assumptions, I have approached the task inductively, trying to look at the theology of 1 Corinthians on its own grounds. I have therefore, and without apology, purposely avoided much interaction with the work of others.

(d) In much of what follows I assume the exegesis of my recent commentary *The First Epistle to the Corinthians* (NICNT; Eerdmans, 1987). In the interest of space, I do not here repeat arguments that appear there; hence the embarrassingly high incidence of footnotes to that work.

and this church; (II) the letter basically reflects *conflict between Paul and the church* on most of the issues addressed; (III) the basic theological point of tension between them is over what it means to be *pneumatikos* (a Spirit person); (IV) their view of being *pneumatikos* involved a "spiritualized eschatology,"[3] wherein because of their experience of glossolalia they considered themselves to be "as the angels" and needed finally only to slough off the body; (V) their false "theology" was informed by popular philosophy tainted with Hellenistic dualism; (VI) the net result was a "spirituality" and "higher wisdom" that was generally divorced from ethical behavior, at least as Paul perceived it.

I. The Central Issue

Because Paul primarily, and in seriatim fashion,[4] addresses *behavioral* issues, it is easy to miss the intensely theological nature of 1 Corinthians. Here Paul's understanding of the gospel and its ethical demands — his theology if you will[5] — is getting its full workout.

What is at stake is Paul's singular urgency, the gospel itself,[6] which from this letter may be defined as "God's eschatological salvation, effected through the death and resurrection of Christ, and resulting in an eschatological community who by the power of the Spirit live out the life of the future in the present age as they await the consummation."[7] The *way* the gospel is at stake is in their non-Christian *behavior*, which completely misses its redemptive, transformational nature. More simply, then, the central issue in 1 Corinthians is "salvation in Christ as that manifests itself in the behavior of those 'who are being saved.'" This is what their misguided spirituality is effectively destroying.

3. Cf. H. Koester's "radicalized spiritualistic eschatology" as his description of alleged pneumatics in Philippi ("The Purpose of the Polemic of a Pauline Fragment [Philippians iii]," *NTS* 8 [1961/62]: 330).

4. At least apparently so. I have argued that a "crisis of authority and gospel" holds all of chs. 1–6 together; and "worship" is what holds chs. 8–14 together.

5. With regard to the discussion generated by Sampley's paper at the 1986 meeting, I am still prepared to understand Paul as speaking out of his *theological* convictions; but in this case, as in most cases, what is being explicated is his understanding of the gospel.

6. See esp. ch. 9, where in defense of his own behavior (apparently regarding the eating of marketplace food), Paul emphasizes that he does all things *for the sake of the gospel* (vv. 12, 16-18, 23).

7. One will recognize that in its own way, although I will not hereafter make a point of it as such, this view of things further supports Richard Hays's model of the narrative framework that shapes Paul's theological reflection (see "Crucified with Christ: A Synthesis of 1 and 2 Thessalonians, Philemon, Philippians, and Galatians," *SBL 1988 Seminar Papers*, 324-33).

Thus three phenomena must be reckoned with in attempting a theology of this letter: (1) Behavioral issues (= ethical concerns) predominate. Paul is urging, cajoling, remonstrating, using every kind of rhetorical device, to get this community both to see things his way and to conform their behavior accordingly, i.e., in keeping with the gospel.

(2) Even though Paul is clearly after behavioral *change*, his greater concern is with the theological distortions that have allowed, or perhaps even promoted, their behavior. This alone accounts for the unusual nature of so much of the argumentation. For example, the simple and clear response to "division over leaders" (1:10–4:21) is to prohibit it in the name of Christian unity. But Paul scarcely touches on such; his primary concern is with their radical misunderstanding of the gospel (1:18–2:16), and of the church (3:5-17) and apostleship (4:1-13), which their sloganeering in the name of wisdom represents.[8]

(3) In every case but two,[9] Paul's basic theological appeal for right behavior is the work of Christ in their behalf. Such appeal begins in the thanksgiving,[10] and is thoroughgoing thereafter. Note, e.g., how crucial to Paul's response the following texts are to their respective issues:

a) 1:18-25, 26, 30; 2:1-2; 3:11; and 4:15 ("Christ crucified" as God's "wisdom" which effected their salvation) — to strife, both internal and over against Paul, carried out in the name of wisdom.

b) 5:7 ("Christ our passover has been sacrificed") — to the church's complacent attitude toward a brother's incest.

c) 6:11 ("Such were some of you; but you were washed, sanctified, justified, through Christ and the Spirit") — to the church's failure to arbitrate between two brothers.

d) 6:20 ("You were bought at a price") — to some men going to the prostitutes (and apparently arguing for the right to do so on grounds that the body is destined for destruction).

e) 7:23 ("You were bought at a price") — to their considering change of status a matter of religious value.

f) 8:11 (". . . destroy a brother for whom Christ died") and 10:16 (our

---

8. So also with sexual immorality in 6:12-20 and with their insisting on the right to attend temple feasts in 8:1–11:1. See below on "The Ethical Response." Even in chs. 12–14 a theology of church (the need for diversity in unity) and of love precedes the specific correctives in ch. 14.

9. 11:2-16 and 12-14, both of which involve community worship, and thus take on a different form of theological argumentation.

10. One can scarcely miss the christological emphasis that pervades both the salutation and thanksgiving. The past, present, and future of salvation dominate the paragraph — salvation that God his initiated and Christ has brought about.

"fellowship in the blood of Christ" that makes temple attendance totally incongruous) — to the Corinthians' insisting on the right to continue to eat meals in the pagan temples; and 9:12-23 (Paul's defense of his actions as totally for the sake of the gospel) — to their questioning his authority to prohibit temple attendance.

g) 11:23-25, 26 (the bread and wine of the Table as proclaiming Christ's death until he comes) — to σχίσμα between rich and poor at the Table.

h) 15:1-5, 11 (Christ's death "for our sins" and his resurrection) — to their denial of a future bodily resurrection of believers.

These texts in particular illustrate that the gospel is the central issue. My concern in this paper is to reflect on the various strands of Paul's understanding of the gospel as saving event, including both its theological basis and its necessary ethical response, which alone brings the experience of the gospel to proper fruition.

II. God and Salvation

The gospel ultimately has to do with God, who alone stands at the beginning and end of all things. Salvation is wholly the result of God's own initiative and activity; God foreordained it and effected it — through Christ. Both the fact and the way he did so reflect his character. Moreover, God's own glory is the ultimate foundation of Pauline ethics (10:31). Since salvation finally has to do with being known by and knowing God (13:12), what makes the Corinthians' persisting in sin so culpable is that it keeps others from the knowledge of God (15:34).

At the same time, however, Paul's own experience of God's saving activity through Christ (as Savior and risen Lord) and through the Spirit (who appropriated it to his life) meant for him, as for the early church before him, an expanded understanding of the one God as Father, Son, and Spirit.[11]

---

11. Several texts suggest or imply that salvation is the joint work of the Father, Son, and Spirit. In 2:1-5, Paul's preaching of Christ crucified came with the Spirit's power, so that their faith might rest only in God's power (as defined in 1:18-25). In 6:11 the divine passives point to God as the initiator, while the saving activity is effected "in/by the name of our Lord Jesus Christ and in/by the Spirit of our God." In 6:19-20 the body participates in redemption as the temple of the Spirit, whom God has given them, having been purchased by Christ. And in 12:4-6 the diversity of God, as Spirit, Lord, and God (= the Father), is the theological foundation for the necessity of diversity in the Spirit's manifestations in their midst.

a. God the Father[12]

In keeping with Paul's Jewish roots, the one and only God is the primary reality, who stands at the beginning of all things as Creator[13] and at the consummation of all things as their goal (8:6).[14] Even though there is little reflection on God's character as such,[15] the God of grace and mercy is always the cause and goal of the saving event. Thus, e.g., in the argument of 1:18–2:16, God the Father is the subject of all the saving activity. Having foreordained (2:7) and purposed salvation (1:21), God thus thwarted human wisdom (1:19-20) by setting forth a crucified Messiah as his wisdom and power at work in the world (1:18-25). God also chose for salvation those of humble origins and status, whose only "boast," therefore, must be God alone (1:26-31). And since God's purposes stand in such bold contrast — indeed, as absolute contradiction — to merely human wisdom, human access to those purposes is only through revelation, which God himself made possible through his Spirit (2:7-13).

Likewise, God's *call* is what initiates the believer's experience of salvation (1:9; 7:17-24). The "divine passives" in 1:4-8 and 6:11 assume God as the one who "washes, sanctifies, justifies, enriches, and confirms" those who are being saved. The resultant church thus belongs to God (1:2; 3:9), who made it grow (3:6-7); and because the church is *his* temple, God will destroy anyone

---

12. Although Paul does not often so designate God — he most often uses the simple designation "God" when referring to the Father — the fact that Christ is God's Son (1:9; 15:28) means that when the two are spoken of conjointly, either one or the other is often called "Father" or "Son" (1:3, 9; 8:6; 15:28).

13. Although creation language as such is used only once, in an incidental way in 11:9, creation is the point of 8:6 (ἐξ οὗ τὰ πάντα [against Murphy-O'Connor; see Fee, *Corinthians*, pp. 374-75]) and is assumed in the analogies of the body in 12:18 and 12:24 ("God has arranged/composed the body as he willed") and of the seed in 15:38 ("God gives it a body as he willed"). Note especially the aorist ἐθέλησεν in both cases, although Paul's interest in the latter instance is in the continuation of the creative activity.

14. See esp. 15:23-28, where after all things (esp. the final enemy, Death) are subjected to Christ, then Christ himself is subject to God (= "hands over the Rule to God the Father," v. 24), "so that God might be all in all." So also the second half of 8:6, "and we for [εἰς = purpose/goal] him."

15. The reason for this is simple: this is the symbolic universe that the Corinthian believers, even though Gentiles, share with Paul through both the gospel and the Scriptures that had become a fixed part of their religious life. Cf. 15:3, 4 ("according to the Scriptures") and the frequent appeals to the OT as the final court of appeal for a point Paul wants to make (1:19, 31; 2:9; 3:19, 20; and passim).

The little that is said in this letter that reflects on God's character (that God is faithful [1:9; 10:13], a "God of *shalom*" [14:33], who is the source of grace and peace [1:3], etc.) is especially in keeping with the OT revelation.

who destroys it (3:16-17). Moreover, it is God's faithfulness that provides escape from too severe testing (10:13); and even the manifestations of the Spirit in their midst are the activity of God, who works all things in all of them (12:6-7). Prayer and thanksgiving are thus always directed toward God the Father.[16] Finally, it is God who will judge (5:13) or praise (4:5) at the Eschaton.

That the true source of the Corinthians' illicit behavior is bad theology — ultimately a misunderstanding of God and his ways — is evident from the beginning, especially with Paul's use of crucifixion language in 1:10–2:16. This language, which occurs only here, stands in deliberate contrast to their fascination with σοφία ("wisdom") and λόγος ("word").[17] God's choice of the cross as his way of salvation, and the subsequent bypassing of the world's beautiful people for the nobodies, was the deliberate expression of his own wisdom to nullify every human machination and idolatry. To those seeking signs — demanding that God perform powerfully in their behalf — the cross is an egregious scandal; to those seeking wisdom — demanding that God be at least as smart as our better selves — the cross is unmitigated folly. But for Paul a crucified Messiah was God's way of turning the tables on these two most common of human idolatries.

The cross, therefore, turns out to be the ultimate expression of God's power *and* wisdom, because it alone could achieve what the gods of human expectations could never do — redeem and sanctify sinners from all ranks of humanity, who by believing (placing their trust in God's folly and weakness) thus lose their own grounds for boasting before God. Here God "outsmarted" the wise, and "overpowered" the strong, with lavish grace and forgiveness, and thereby divested them of their strength (1:25). Thus in his crucifixion Christ not only effected salvation for the "called," but ultimately revealed the essential character of God, which is revealed further in the servant character of Paul's apostleship (3:5; 4:1-2, 9-13), and which stands over against every human pretension and boasting. This is what is at issue in 1:10–4:21, their understanding of God and his ways, not mere sloganeering, with its ἔρις and σχίσμα. These latter but reflect human fallenness that has lost its vision of the eternal God.

At issue, it should be noted further, is not mere belief in the reality of

16. For prayer see 14:2, 28; for thanksgiving, 1:4, 14; 14:18; 15:57.

17. That these two terms together form one dimension of the problem is to be seen not only by the contrasts in 2:1-5, but especially in the subtle but significant way the whole argument begins in vv. 17-18. Christ sent Paul to preach the gospel "not with σοφία λόγου (= wisdom characterized by λόγος [reason? rhetoric?])," since that would empty the cross of Christ of its significance. "For," he goes on in v. 18, "there is another λόγος, that of the cross, which is God's power for salvation."

the one God. Paul's argument is made possible, both here and elsewhere, precisely because these former idolaters (6:9, 11; 12:2) now share this conviction with Paul. Indeed, in their letter to him they play back the twin themes of "one God" and "no reality to an idol" as grounds for their continuing to attend meals in the idol temples (8:4).[18] At issue is their misapprehension of the *nature* of the one God and the nature of idolatry. Paul's response is twofold, and allows us to see how the coherence-contingency model works out in his thinking.

On the one hand, coherence demands that he agree with the fundamental premise that there is only one God. That is the only *objective* reality. Contingency is found in people's *subjective experience* of a variety of "gods" and "lords" as divine beings; and this, too, is a reality that must be reckoned with — especially in the lives of some converts for whom that "reality" has been a powerful conviction (8:7, 10-12). Thus the gods and lords are "so-called," but there is also reality to them, even though not reality as "gods." Rather, Paul argues, on the basis of the OT, that idols are the locus of demons (10:19-22). Thus what (for former pagans) was subjective reality as a god is in fact also (for Paul) objective reality as demonic. In that way he not only works within their now shared — and for him unwavering — monotheism, but provides the ultimate reason for the incompatibility of participation in both Christian and pagan meals.

On the other hand, Paul's experience of Christ as Savior and risen Lord has meant for him an expanded understanding of the one God as Father and Son. Thus, picking up the language of the so-called gods and lords (8:5), Paul affirms that "for us" (in contrast to them and their obvious polytheism) there is only *one God,* namely the Father, the source and goal of all things, including us, and *one Lord,* namely Jesus Christ, the divine agent of all things, including our redemption (v. 6).

Paul does this in such a way as to affirm two realities simultaneously: first, he speaks of the Father and the Son together in the language of deity (one God, one Lord), and second, he does so in a context where he is at the same time affirming the strictest kind of monotheism. Which leads us directly to Paul's christology.

---

18. Their point seems to have been that "since there is only one God, and thus no reality to the idol, and since food itself is a matter of indifference to God (8:8), then why can't we continue to join our friends at these feasts? We can scarcely be honoring a god, since the god doesn't exist." See Fee, *Corinthians,* pp. 361-63.

b. Christ the Son, Savior, and Lord

This is one of the more complex theological issues in this letter. First, as noted, there is every kind of evidence that Paul's thinking about God has been expanded to include the reality of Christ as Son and Lord. Yet, second, there are texts that also seem to suggest a kind of subordination between Christ and God (3:23; 11:3; 15:27-28). Third, and most problematic, is to determine the relationship between christology and soteriology, which is not immediately discernible. Paul does not himself resolve these tensions, first, because either their resolution or simply their affirmation belongs to his and their shared symbolic universe, and second, because his interest in Christ in this letter is almost entirely soteriological. Christ both saves and sets the pattern for the ethical life of those who are being saved (11:1).

One can scarcely doubt that Paul sees Christ in terms of deity. The basic appellation is the primary Christian confession of "Lord," whose deep roots in the LXX as the appellation for God,[19] however, allows (causes?) Paul to attribute every kind of divine activity to Christ. Thus, believers pray to Christ;[20] to know the mind of the Lord (from Isa. 14:13) is now to have the mind of Christ (2:16). The OT "day of the Lord" has become the "day of our Lord Jesus Christ" (1:8). The Lord whom Israel "provoked to jealousy" in the Song of Moses (Deut. 32:21) is now the Lord Christ, whom the Corinthians are provoking by attending idolatrous feasts (10:22). The divine will is both God's (1:1) and the Lord's (4:19; cf. 16:7); and judgment is now the prerogative of the Lord (4:4-5; 11:31). With fine irony Paul designates the one whom the rulers of this age killed as the "Lord of glory" (2:8), picking up the language "for our glory" in the preceding verse, and thus designating the Crucified One as Lord of all the ages and inheritor — as Lord — of the final glory that is both his and his people's.

Moreover, one must take seriously that grace and peace come from both God our Father and the Lord Jesus Christ (1:3), since one preposition controls both nouns. Thus the Father and Son (and Spirit) cooperate in the saving event. The Father calls, the Lord assigns (7:17); God washes, sanctifies, and justifies by the authority of Christ and by the Spirit (6:11); everything God does is "in/by Christ Jesus."[21]

---

19. There have been occasional objections to this (see P. Kahle, *The Cairo Geniza* [Oxford: Basil Blackwell, 1959], p. 222; G. Howard, "The Tetragram and the NT," *JBL* 96 [1977]: 65), but the evidence from the independent use of the LXX in Paul, Luke, Hebrews, and Matthew seems overwhelmingly in favor of the commonly held understanding.

20. By "calling upon the name of the Lord," 1:2; cf. the early Aramaic prayer to Jesus recalled in 16:22 (Μαρανα θα, "Come, Lord").

21. This formula occurs some 22 times in the letter; its precise nuance is especially diffi-

All of this is unthinkable language for a strict monotheist such as Paul, and can only be explained in light of his own encounter with the risen Christ. He had "seen Jesus our Lord" (9:1), which serves as the basis for his christology.[22] The resurrection and the designation "Son of God" probably lead to Paul's conviction of Christ's pre-existence, which is implied by the affirmation that "all things are through him" (8:6).[23] In any case, such is almost certainly their shared conviction.

What, then, does one do with, "and Christ is God's" (3:23) and "even the Son will be subjected to him . . . so that God might be all in all" (15:28)? The answer seems to lie in Paul's primary interest in soteriology. Whenever he uses Father and Son language (1:9; 8:6; 15:28), his interest is in salvation, which lies ultimately in the one God. Hence, the language of subordination is primarily functional, i.e., referring to Christ's function as savior, not to his being as God. In any case, these two realities hold together for Paul: God the Father is the source and goal of all that is; Christ the Lord functions as Savior, who effects the saving work of God in human history.

Although Paul does not *explicitly* make this point, Christ the Lord's role as Savior further establishes the connection between theology, gospel, and ethics. This is surely the way we are to understand the "hardship catalogue" of 4:11-13. Here is Paul's theology of the cross being applied to Christian life: the whole point of the next paragraph (vv. 14-17) is to urge them to "follow his way of life *in Christ Jesus.*" So also with his "not seeking his own good but the good of the many" as his way of "imitating Christ," which they again are commanded to follow. The life of the Son of God on earth, exemplified ultimately in his crucifixion, serves as the basis and goal of Christian ethics; this is to do all things for God's glory (10:31–11:1).

---

cult to pin down. Sometimes it seems to be clearly locative (Christ is the sphere of their new existence); but in other cases it seems just as certainly instrumental (God has acted "in" Christ Jesus). In both cases the high christology is unmistakable.

22. As well as for much else, I would argue, esp. his understanding of grace and apostleship.

23. So also with "and the Rock *was* Christ," which probably intends to designate Christ not simply typologically as the rock at Horeb that "followed them," but also as the Lord, their Rock, whom Israel rejected in the wilderness (cf. Deut. 32:4, 15, etc.). On the other hand, 15:47, which is often seen this way, almost certainly refers to his present resurrection existence as "of heaven (= heavenly)" rather than "from heaven" in terms of his origins (see Fee, *Corinthians,* 792).

c. The Role of the Spirit

More than anywhere else this crucial issue is where the Corinthians and Paul are at odds. For them "Spirit" has been their entrée to life in the realm of σοφία and γνῶσις, with their consequent rejection of the material order, both now (7:1-7) and for the future (15:12), as well as their rejection of Christian life as modeled by Paul's imitation of Christ (4:15-21). Their experience of tongues as the language(s) of angels had allowed them to assume heavenly existence now (4:8), thought of primarily in terms of non-material existence rather than of ethical-moral life in the present. Thus Paul tries to disabuse them of their singular and overly enthusiastic emphasis on tongues (the point of chs. 12–14); but in so doing, he tries to retool their understanding of the Spirit to bring it into line with the gospel. There are therefore three emphases as to the role of the Spirit.

First, despite an emphasis on sanctification, Paul only twice uses the full designation, *Holy* Spirit (6:19; 12:3). Most often he refers to the Spirit *of God* (2:11, 14, 16; 6:11; 7:40; 12:3) or the Spirit who is *from God* (2:12; 6:19). Thus the Spirit's activities are first of all the activities of God. With especially pointed irony Paul argues in 2:6-16 that since the Corinthians are πνευματικοί (Spirit people), they should have understood the cross as God's wisdom; for the Spirit alone knows the mind of God and has thus revealed what was formerly hidden. Since "like is known by like," the Spirit, who alone knows the thoughts of God and whom they have received, becomes the link on the human side for their knowing the thoughts of God. Moreover, by "the Spirit of our God" they have been washed, sanctified, and justified (6:11); only by the Spirit of God is the basic confession made as to the Lordship of Christ (12:3); and through one and the same Spirit God gives to the church the variety of manifestations for their common good (12:7-8). Thus Paul does not think of the Spirit as some energy or influence, but as God's own presence at work in their midst.

Second, and related to the first, the Spirit effectively appropriates the work of Christ to the life of the individual believer and the community. Paul's preaching in weakness a message of "divine weakness" brought about their conversion — through the power of the Spirit (2:4-5; cf. 4:20). It is the prophetic Spirit who reveals the secrets of the heart that lead to conversion (14:24-25). Hence it was by the Spirit they themselves were converted (6:11); and by the Spirit they confess Jesus as Lord (12:3). On the analogy of the one-flesh relationship in sexual intercourse, the believer has been so joined to the Lord as to become one S/spirit with him.[24] Furthermore, the Corinthians to-

24. On the translation of this term see Fee, *Corinthians*, pp. 204-5.

gether became the one body of Christ by their common, lavish experience of Spirit (12:13);[25] and the Spirit's presence in/among them forms them into God's temple in Corinth (3:16).[26] Thus the Spirit belongs to the gospel, not to σοφία or γνῶσις[27] or non-material existence.

Third, the Spirit is also the key to ethical and community life. It is especially because they have received the Spirit of God, who is *in you,* that makes the body a temple of the Spirit and thus disallows sin against the body in the form of sexual immorality. This becomes the more pronounced in chs. 12–14, where the key to true Spirit manifestations among them is to be found in the language of οἰκοδομή ("building up"). After the description of love in ch. 13, which is first of all a description of the character of God and Christ (see how it begins with "love [= God] suffereth long and is kind"),[28] he urges that they pursue love, and in that context eagerly desire the things of the Spirit, especially intelligible utterances, because they *build up.*

Thus "salvation in Christ" is the great concern in this letter, because such salvation is at once God's activity in their behalf and the revelation of his character. Therefore, salvation calls them to conform their own behavior to God's, as it is reflected and modeled by Christ and made effective by the Spirit.

III. Salvation and Ethics

The gospel that effects eschatological salvation also brings about a radical change in the way people live. That is the burden of this letter, and the theological presupposition behind every imperative. Therefore, although apocalyptic-cosmological language is also found, salvation is expressed primarily in ethical-moral language.

---

25. As noted in the commentary (Fee, *Corinthians,* pp. 603-6), the basic issue in this text is not how people become believers, but how the many of them (Jew, Greek, slave, free) became the one body of Christ.

26. Thus the two basic images of the church in this letter (body, temple) are tied directly to the activity of the Spirit.

27. Surely Paul's heading the list of Spirit manifestations in 12:8 with the λόγος σοφίας ("word/message of wisdom") and λόγος γνώσεως ("word/message of knowledge") is another moment of irony. These "gifts" that are their special province are thus reshaped in terms consonant with the gospel (= message of wisdom, etc.).

28. Here is one of the places where the "rules" of the seminar are especially constricting, since in Rom. 2:4 Paul specifically refers to God's character in terms of these two words; but I am not supposed to know that, so this matter cannot be pursued here.

a. The Human Predicament

In a former day Paul had divided the world into two basic groups: Jew and Gentile. When he became a Christian the world was still divided into two groups: "us who are being saved" and "those who are perishing" (1:18), the latter now including both the former groups, seen in light of their basic idolatries (power and wisdom) and in terms of their response to the cross as God's saving event (1:20-24). For Paul the preaching of the gospel is intended to save people *from* the one existence and *for* the other. "Such were some of you," he says to them, following a major sin list (6:11); "when you were pagans," he says in 12:2 of their former life in idolatry.

Given the eschatological framework of Paul's thinking (see below), one is not surprised to find him at times referring to human fallenness in apocalyptic-cosmological terms. Idolatry is fellowship with demons (10:20-21); Satan tempts those who lack self-control (7:5); death is the final enemy, obviously one of the ἀρχαί, ἐξουσίαι, and δυνάμεις ("principalities, authorities, and powers") that Christ will destroy at his parousia (15:24-26). Likewise the five items mentioned in 3:22 (world, life, death, present, future) are best understood as the tyrannies to which people are in lifelong bondage as slaves, and over which Christ has already taken jurisdiction.

The human predicament is also expressed in terms of people's living in the present age, apart from, and over against, God. Three terms describe this existence. The ψυχικοί ("natural persons") because they do not have the Spirit of God, cannot know what God is about in Christ (2:14). They are also σάρκινοι/σαρκικοί ("made of flesh/of the flesh")[29] — still in the physical body, and as such giving way to the flesh (= sinful nature). The ultimate censure of such people is that they are living κατὰ ἄνθρωπον[30] (as "mere human beings," 3:3-4).

In each case this depiction of the fallen condition stands in contrast to those who are Spirit people, who have thus entered the realm of eschatological existence that stands in contradiction to what is merely human. What is "merely human" belongs to "this world/age" that is passing away (2:6-8); the "disputer of this age" and the "wisdom of this world" do not know God (1:20-21), just as the "rulers of this age" did not understand God's wisdom revealed

29. I have argued that Paul uses these terms with precision in 3:1-3, to refer to physical existence (3:1, σάρκινος) and to the "sinful nature" (σαρκικός, 3:3), as a twin blow against their false spirituality (see Fee, *Corinthians*, pp. 121-24).

30. I would also include here the usage of σάρξ ("flesh") in 5:5. On this much debated text and reasons for seeing it as referring to the incestuous man's sinful nature, see Fee, *Corinthians*, pp. 208-12.

in Christ crucified (2:8). Because they lack the Spirit, such people have eyes that cannot see, ears that cannot hear, nor can their (merely) human minds conceive what God has done in Christ (2:9).

Despite such ways of expressing the human predicament, however, and because the letter deals mostly with behavioral aberrations, salvation is most often seen in terms of moral failure. People are sinners, and what God has provided in Christ is salvation from sin. Sin is the deadly poison that leads to death (15:56). Christ died "for our sins" (15:3); and to deny a future resurrection means to deny Christ's resurrection, thus leaving the living still in their sins and the dead without hope (vv. 17-18). Although ἁμαρτ- ("sin") language does not abound,[31] this is the burden throughout. The ultimate exhortation is to "sober up as you ought and stop sinning," precisely because others do not know God (15:34). Those who are perishing are thus described as ἄδικοι ("wicked") (6:1, 9) or ἄπιστοι ("unbelieving").[32] If the latter term is most often descriptive, for Paul it is never merely descriptive. People are "wicked," not simply overtly so, but also because they do not believe.

The specific forms of wickedness that lead to the world's being condemned (11:32) are many and varied. Often they reflect Paul's Jewish view of the pagan environment of Corinth: idolatry (5:10-11; 6:10; 8:10; 10:7, 14); various forms of πορνεία ("sexual immorality") (5:1-2, 10-11; 6:10 [several words]; 6:18; 10:8); greed (5:10-11; 6:1-6, 10); robbery (5:10-11; 6:10); drunkenness (5:11; 6:10); and delighting in wickedness (13:6). But just as often it includes particularly self-centered sins: pride (4:6, 18-19; 5:2, 6; 8:1; 13:4); seeking one's own interests (10:33; 13:5); shaming those who have nothing (11:22); keeping records of the evil done by others (13:5); and various sins of discord (σχίσμα, "division" [1:10; 11:18], ἔρις, "strife" [1:11; 3:3], ζῆλος, "envy" [3:3; 13:5], λοιδορία, "abuse" [5:11; 6:10], ἀποστερεῖν, "to defraud" [6:8; 7:5], γογγύζειν, "to murmur" [10:10]).

People are wicked and sinful; they do not know God. But Christ died "for our sins," not only to forgive, but also to free people from their sins. Hence Paul's extreme agitation at the Corinthians' sinfulness, because they are thereby persisting in the very sins from which God in Christ has saved them. This, after all, is what most of the letter is all about.

---

31. ἁμαρτία ("sin") 15:3, 17, 56 [2x]; ἁμάρτημα ("sinful deed") 6:18; ἁμαρτάνω ("to sin") 6:18; 7:28 [2x], 36; 8:12 [2x]; 15:34.

32. 6:6; 7:12, 13, 14 [2x], 15; 10:27; 14:22 [2x], 23, 24.

b. The Saving Event

The focus of Paul's gospel is on the saving event effected by Christ's death (8:11; 11:26; 15:3), and especially on his *crucifixion* (1:13, 17, 18, 23; 2:2, 8; cf. 5:7), which is variously asserted to be "for you" (ὑπὲρ ὑμῶν; 1:13; 11:24) or "for (ὑπέρ) our sins" (15:3). In the words of institution the wine represents "the new covenant in my blood" (11:25), and those who partake of the table are thus said to "fellowship in the blood of Christ" (10:16).

Despite the frequency of these references, it is not easy to determine how Paul understood Christ's death as "for us." The combination of 5:7 (Christ as the sacrificed paschal lamb), 11:24-25 (my body "for you"; the new covenant in my blood), and 15:3 (Christ died for our sins) suggests a much richer understanding than is actually spelled out. Most likely, this language reflects Isaiah 53 (LXX), where God's suffering servant bears the sins of the many. In any case, this is the language of atonement, in which a combination of motifs from both the Exodus and the sacrificial system combine into a rich tapestry. It presupposes alienation between God and humans because of human sinfulness, for which the just penalty is death. The death of Christ "for our sins" means that one died on behalf of others to satisfy the penalty and to overcome the alienation. For Paul this almost certainly includes not only forgiveness of past sins, but in a very real sense deliverance from the bondage of one's sinfulness as well. That, at least, is what the primary metaphors for salvation in this letter suggest, especially so in light of the overall concern of the letter.

It is not surprising, therefore, that the predominant metaphors for salvation all touch on the ethical sphere. At issue is human sinfulness; not only in its boasting over against God, but in its various forms of behavior that reflect that boasting. Salvation involves both deliverance *from* sin and *for* righteousness. This is especially true of the two sets of three metaphors in 1:30 (as nouns: righteousness, sanctification, redemption) and 6:11 (as verbs: washed, sanctified, justified [made righteous?]). Thus:[33]

Δικαιοσύνη (1:30; cf. ἐδικαιώθητε, "you were made righteous/justified," 6:11) most likely places emphasis on "righteousness," both as gift and requirement, rather than on right standing before the Law. Nothing else in the letter

---

33. Since the emphasis throughout is on God's initiative and Christ's redemptive work, there is very little emphasis on the believer's own response. Most often Paul refers simply to their "believing" (1:21; 3:5; 15:2, 11; cf. πίστις, 2:5; 15:14, 17); but the near equation of "your faith" in 15:14 and 17 with "having put our hope in Christ" in v. 19 suggests that "faith" means to respond to Christ's saving activity with full trust, including a total confidence that he has secured the believer's future.

suggests a forensic metaphor, whereas, especially in the context of 6:1-11, the verb seems to be used in a kind of wordplay over against the ἄδικοι (the unbelieving "wicked," vv. 1, 9) and the one who by "wronging (ἀδικεῖσθε, vv. 7-8) his brother is acting just like the ἄδικοι. "Such were some of you," Paul says, "but you ἐδικαιώθητε (have been made right[eous])."

Sanctification is also a metaphor for conversion in this letter (1:30; 6:11; cf. 1:2). In calling people to himself, and in effecting their salvation through Christ's death, God has determined to set them apart for himself as his "holy people," which in this letter regularly entails observable behavior.

Redemption, which occurs as a noun in 1:30, also occurs as a full metaphor in 6:20 and 7:23 ("You were bought at a price"). The noun most likely reflects Exodus imagery, thus the deliverance of slaves held in bondage to sin. But the usage in 6:20 (and partly so in 7:23) seems to put emphasis on being purchased *for God,* so that one is now his "slave," to walk in his ways.

Washing (6:11), although very likely also referring to Christian baptism, in the context of 6:1-11 refers primarily to being "washed" from the sins just mentioned in vv. 9-10.

Thus God's aim in salvation is not merely to create a people for his name who will inherit his kingdom, but to create a people for his name who will be "sanctified," i.e., who will be like Christ himself and thus live and behave in the present in ways that will glorify God's name.

c. The Ethical Consequence[34]

1 Corinthians emphasizes that the gospel issues in transformed lives, that salvation in Christ is not complete without God/Christ-like attitudes and behavior. This is assumed at every point; it is also frequently stated. In the context of demanding that the community exclude the incestuous man,

---

34. I am especially indebted to Professor William A. Beardslee, in his formal response at the seminar, both for his insightful critique of this section of the paper and for the fact that he took this matter seriously as the control issue of Pauline theology in the letter. Some of his observations and suggestions have been incorporated into the present paper. In particular Professor Beardslee expressed concern over (1) the paradigm of "indicative/imperative" that I had set forth (too neatly, I would agree, even if unintentionally), which seemed to make ethics too consequential and not sufficiently transformational as gift and Spirit activity, and (2) the eschatological paradigm of "already/not yet," which I use to "resolve" this tension. Since I tend to agree with much of his critique, though not all (I think the tension "resolves" itself in Paul more than Professor Beardslee appears to), I have adjusted the wording at several places, so as to reflect this more "transformative" view of the ethical imperative in this letter.

Paul asserts that they are a "new lump" because "Christ our Passover has been sacrificed" (5:7). That is, the sacrifice of Christ for sin is the basis of their transfer from the old to the new. "So then," he concludes, still playing on Passover imagery, "let us keep the feast without the old leaven of κακίας καὶ πονηρίας ("malice and evil," two synonyms that gather under their umbrella every form of iniquity), but with the new leaven of sincerity and truth (fully authentic behavior, without sham or deceit, that can stand the light of day)."

Likewise, in 6:11, after a severe warning, which includes a considerable sin catalogue describing the ἄδικοι ("wicked") who will *not* inherit the eschatological kingdom, Paul reasserts with equal vigor: "And these things are what some of you *were;* but you were washed, etc." Paul simply cannot let warning be the final word; but neither will he allow the warning to be taken lightly.[35] It is precisely this tension that needs theological resolution. What seems to miss Paul's theology are resolutions that either turn the imperatives into "Christian rules," on the one hand, or effectively emasculate them, on the other. That is, whatever else, the "imperative" in this letter is never simply imperative — either as "Christian Torah" or "calculated response" to God's gift of salvation; but neither is there anything close to genuine salvation that does not take the Spirit-filled, Spirit-led life seriously as simultaneously expressing both gift and demand.

The classic expression of Paul's understanding of the relationship between gospel and ethics (indicative and imperative) is to be found in 5:7. With reference to the incestuous man, he commands the church, "cleanse out the old leaven, in order that you might become a new batch of dough." But that comes perilously close to sounding as if the imperative preceded the indicative, so he immediately qualifies, "even as you really are." Thus "become what you are" is a basic form of Pauline parenesis.

But to say the imperative now follows the indicative is not quite adequate, since there are different kinds of imperative, both before and after the indicative. What Christ has done is forever to abolish the old imperatives, the Jewish boundary-markers of circumcision (7:18-19) and food laws (9:19-22; 10:23–11:1), which gave privilege. These may *not* be placed after the indicative as imperatives, either in their Jewish form or in any new Christian form. Neither circumcision nor uncircumcision counts for anything (7:19); and food will not commend us to God (8:8). Since in Christ neither kosher nor nonkosher has significance, Paul does or does not depending on context (9:19-

---

35. Cf. esp. the combination in ch. 10 of warning (vv. 6-12), affirmation (v. 13), and imperative (v. 14).

22). Likewise Jewish Christians may continue to eat as Jews. What they may not do is to superimpose these regulations on the one who is free in Christ.[36]

On the other hand, because Paul dismisses all such boundary-markers as totally outside questions of Christian conscience (10:25), one may not infer that for Paul there are no absolutes with regard to conduct. Paul warns that those who persist in the sins of 6:9-10 will not inherit the kingdom; they are commanded to stop sinning in 15:34. While it is true that neither circumcision nor uncircumcision counts for anything, something does count, namely "keeping the commandments of God"! (7:19). If Paul eats as one who is ἄνομος ("outside the Jewish law") with those outside the Law, this does not mean he is truly ἄνομος (= "lawless"). To the contrary, he is ἔννομος Χριστοῦ ("under Christ's law" 9:21). Both of these phrases ("keeping the commandments of God" and "under Christ's law") must be understood as requiring obedience to the Christian imperatives, in the form of Pauline parenesis.[37]

Thus, idolatry in the form of attendance at idol meals is incompatible with life in Christ — absolutely (10:14-22); sexual immorality is wrong — absolutely (6:18-20). And so also are strife and slander and greed, and all those other sins mentioned in this letter. Ethical life is not optional; it is the only viable fruition of the work of the gospel.

But even here, Paul never begins with the imperative. For him it must be living out the gospel as grace and gift of the Spirit, or it is nothing at all. That is why so much of the content of this letter, in all of the behavioral sections, takes the form of theological argumentation. The divine order still has moral and ethical absolutes; there is conduct that is totally incompatible with "being in Christ." But Paul never begins here. Going to the prostitutes (6:12-20) is wrong first of all because their own case is based on a faulty view of ἐξουσία ("authority, rights") and of the body, and exhibits an invalid understanding of the nature of the sexual relationship. But it is finally prohibited

36. Which, of course, is what makes the whole argument of 11:2-16 so surprising, the best solution to which is not Paul's basic cultural conservatism, but their apparent disregard for sexual distinctions in the present age. They are not yet as the angels!

37. Which, in response to Professor Beardslee, is precisely where the theological tensions lie. The person "in Christ" is expected to act like/reflect Christ's own character/activity; thus Paul can speak of "Christ's law" and "keeping the commandments of God." But these are not now encoded in some form of "rules for believers to live by." Salvation as gift and the transformed life as Spirit indwelt are always the predicates for such behavior. Ideally, perhaps, the latter should eliminate the imperative altogether (as Professor Beardslee would seem to urge). But that is precisely what awaits the final consummation. For the present the imperative, which reflects the character of God, thus "describes" the life of the future that is to be lived out in the present. The reason for its being imperative (or so it would seem) is precisely as a reflection of the tension of the "already/not yet."

because the body, which is destined for resurrection, has been thus redeemed by Christ and invaded by the Holy Spirit. Going to the temples is prohibited because their case is based on a false view of idolatry and an incorrect basis for conduct (γνῶσις, "knowledge"), but it is finally prohibited because fellowship with demons is incompatible with fellowship with Christ at his table, where one reaffirms the benefits of the new covenant (8:1-13; 10:1-22).

But all has not been said. Ethics for Paul is ultimately a *theological* issue pure and simple. Everything has to do with God, and what God is about in Christ and the Spirit. Thus (1) the *purpose* (or basis) of Christian ethics is the glory of God (10:31); (2) the *pattern* for such ethics is Christ (11:1); (3) the *principle* is love, precisely because it alone reflects God's character (8:2-3; 13:1-8); (4) and the *power* is the Spirit (6:11, 19). Since we have already made note of items 1, 2, and 4, a further word is needed about love.

Although Paul clearly understands that the gospel sets one free and thus gives one ἐξουσία ("authority, rights," 6:12; 9:1-2, 19; 10:23), this is not for him the basis of ethical conduct — because as in the case of the Corinthians it can be abused (6:12-20; 8:9). So also with γνῶσις ("knowledge") — Paul is not against it,[38] it simply fails as the predicate for behavior in the "new age." In both cases it leads to abuse of others (8:7, 9); indeed, ethics predicated on γνῶσις invariably "puffs up," gives one too high a view of oneself and a correspondingly too low a view of others.[39]

Love, on the other hand, is the ultimate expression of the character of God. Therefore, it "builds up" (8:2); indeed the one who loves is the truly "knowing [or known] one."[40] The basis of Christian conduct is what is beneficial, what builds up; therefore, it does not seek its own good but that of the other (10:23-24, 33; 13:5). And this of course is what God himself is all about in the gospel.

d. The Church, the Sphere of Salvation

Finally, 1 Corinthians is about the church, the local community of believers, who live out the gospel in relationship to one another and over against the world. If the gospel is at stake in the Corinthian theology and behavior, so also is its visible expression in the local community of redeemed people. This

38. See esp. 12:8; 13:2; 14:6.

39. See esp. the biting rhetoric of 4:7, "What have you that you have not received?" expressed in the context of condemning their pride. Such people fail to see everything as gift; hence they also fail to live out of gratitude.

40. See my argument for this as the original text of 8:2-3 (Fee, *Corinthians*, pp. 367-68).

is made clear both by Paul's basic images for the church (temple of God, body of Christ) and by the nature of the argument in several sections, especially 5:1-13 and 6:1-12.

Two great images predominate. First, the local church is God's temple in Corinth (3:16-17). With this imagery Paul makes several points: (a) As temples of God they are expected to live as his alternative both to the pagan temples and to the way of life that surround them. Indeed, this is precisely the concern throughout so much of the letter, that there are too many gray areas so that they are hardly distinguishable from the Corinth in which they live (cf. 5:1; 6:7; 10:32; 14:23). (b) What makes them God's temple is the presence of the Holy Spirit in their midst. Thus, in contrast to the mute idols around them, they are themselves the sanctuary of the living God by his Spirit. And when God's Spirit is manifested among them by prophetic utterance, pagans will have their hearts searched and judged and they will come to recognize that God is among his people (14:24-25). (c) So sacred (ἅγιος) to God is his temple that those who would destroy it — as they are doing by their quarrels and worldly wisdom — will themselves be destroyed by God (3:17). This understanding of their existence as a people among whom God is powerfully present by his Spirit makes possible our understanding of 5:1-13, where the church is purified by removing the incestuous man, yet he himself will experience salvation from such an action. Apparently being removed from such a community will lead to his repentance.

Second, the church is the body of Christ (10:17; 11:29; 12:12-26). With this image Paul makes essentially two points: (a) Underlying the imagery is the necessity of unity. As with the preceding image, the key to this unity is their common, lavish experience of the Spirit (12:13). Whether Jew or Greek, slave or free, they are one in Christ through the Spirit. Precisely because they are *one* body in Christ, the rich must cease abusing the poor at the Lord's table (11:22, 29); and those who are more visible may not say to the less visible, "we have no need of you" (12:21-26). God has so arranged the body that all the members are essential to one another. (b) But his greater concern with this image is the concomitant necessity of diversity. Rather than the uniformity that the Corinthians value, Paul urges that they recognize the need for all the various manifestations of the one Spirit. Otherwise there is no body, only a monstrosity (12:15-20).

Therefore, neither the gospel nor its ethical response is individualistic. God is not gathering individuals into his kingdom; he is saving a *people* for his name. Above all, it is as a people that they must live out the gospel. Thus, every argument is aimed at their becoming this people. This is especially spelled out in the most highly unusual arguments of 5:1-13 and 6:1-11, where in both cases the sins of individuals, grievous as they are, and as strongly as Paul condemns them, play a secondary role to his consternation with the church.

In 5:1-13 the argument is addressed almost entirely to the church and its arrogance. What is at issue is not simply a low view of sin; rather, it is the church itself: Will it follow Paul's gospel with its ethical implications? or will it continue its present "spirituality," one that tolerates (or condones) such sin and thereby destroys God's temple in Corinth?

In 6:1-11 the two great urgencies, besides his concern over the two men themselves (taken up in vv. 7-11),[41] are the church's self-understanding as God's eschatological people (vv. 2-4) and its witness before the world (vv. 5-6). Their existence as an eschatological people, who are to judge both the world and angels, trivializes all matters that belong merely to this present age. But what concerns him in this is their "defeat" before the world, their shooting down the gospel and its "new-age" behavior "in front of unbelievers" (v. 6; cf. 15:34).

And so it goes throughout. God's eschatological salvation is creating a new people, who collectively must live the life of the future in the present age, as they await its consummation. This leads to the final matter — the eschatological goal of salvation.

IV. The Eschatological Goal of Salvation

It is now time to return to the longer definition of the gospel suggested earlier: "God's *eschatological* salvation, effected through the death and resurrection of Christ, and resulting in an *eschatological community* who live out *the life of the future in the present age* by the power of the Spirit, as they *await the consummation*." Salvation is not simply a matter of changed behavior in the present. The absolutely essential framework of all of Paul's theological thinking, as well as the goal of God's saving event, is eschatological. This note is struck at the beginning in the thanksgiving (1:7-8, they "await the revelation of our Lord Jesus Christ" at which time God "will confirm them blameless on the day of our Lord Jesus Christ"), and it is the final note before the concluding grace-benediction (16:22, Μαρανα θα; "Come, O Lord"). So, too, it is the assumption of the theologoumenon in 8:6 ("one God, the Father, from whom are all things and we *for* him"). Since salvation is essentially eschatological, al-

---

41. See Fee, *Corinthians*, pp. 240-42, for the argument that these verses speak in turn to the one who was wronged and the one who perpetrated the wrong in the first place.

ways pointing toward its final consummation at the parousia, the future is therefore understood to condition everything in the present. Which is why ethical life is not optional; life in Christ in the present age is but the life of the future already begun.

a. The Framework Itself

Paul's eschatological thinking has its focus in the event of Christ, his death and resurrection, and the subsequent gift of the Spirit. Christ's resurrection marks the turning of the ages (15:20-23; cf. 10:11); the subsequent gift of the eschatological Spirit is the certain evidence that the end has begun (cf. 1:7; 13:8-13). But the facts that believers still live in bodies subject to decay (15:49-53), that the χαρίσματα ("gracious endowments") are *only* for the present (13:8-13), and that there is yet a future parousia of the Lord (11:26; 15:23) with a subsequent resurrection (15:20-28), also offer clear evidence that what has begun has not yet been fully brought to consummation. Thus, salvation is both "already" and "not yet."

This framework is thoroughgoing: God's Rule, begun by Christ who *now* reigns until his Parousia (15:24-25), is both present (4:20) and future (6:9-10; 15:50). At the Lord's table they proclaim his death until he comes (11:26). Judgment belongs essentially to the future (4:4-5; 5:13), but the death of some is God's "judgment" at work now so that they will escape final condemnation (11:30-32).

b. The Future as "Already"

This perspective can be seen especially in Paul's ethics. The believer's present existence is entirely determined by the future that has already been set in motion ("the time has been foreshortened"; 7:29-31). God's people live "as if not"; they are not, as others, conditioned by the present order that is passing away.[42] Such a point of view controls Paul's ethical imperatives at every step. Believers may not take one another to pagan courts because their lives are

---

42. Paul uses the terms "this age" and "this world" somewhat interchangeably (cf. 1:20 and 3:18-19). The use of the demonstrative "*this* age/world" (1:20; 2:6 [2x]; 2:8; 3:18/3:19; 5:10; 7:31) tends to emphasize its present character in contrast to that to come, while the use of the verb καταργεῖν ("abolish, do away with") especially emphasizes that this present age and that which belongs to it have been judged and rendered ineffective through the cross and resurrection (see 1:28; 2:6; 6:13; 13:8 [2x], 10, 11; 15:24, 26; cf. παράγει ["is passing away"] in 7:31).

conditioned by eschatological realities that render the redressing of one's grievances a mere triviality (6:1-6); believers may not attend pagan feasts because the judgments against idolatry of a former time have been written down to warn those upon whom the end of the ages has come (10:11). All merely human values and behavior have already been judged by God in Christ; already the present age is passing away (1:26-28; 7:31). Thus believers must exercise internal judgments in the present (5:12-13); the church must cleanse out the old leaven so that it might be a new loaf (5:7-8).

c. The Future as "Not Yet"

Yet the future that has begun and absolutely conditions present existence still awaits its final consummation. In contrast to the Corinthians' overly spiritualized present realization of future realities,[43] Paul frequently reminds them that they still await the revelation of the Lord (1:7), that they themselves must yet face the day of the Lord (1:8; 3:13-15), that they are to withhold judgment until the appointed time when the Lord comes and will expose hearts (4:5), that even though Christ reigns now (15:25) and death is already theirs (3:22), only at the still future parousia will all the powers finally be destroyed (15:23-26).

Such a future is as certain as life itself. Being Christ's means that both life and death, both the present and the future belong to those who are his (3:22-23). Again, this certainty has been guaranteed by the resurrection. Just as God raised up the Lord, so he will raise up believers (6:14; 15:1-28). Christ is the firstfruits, God's own surety of the full harvest (15:20). When Christ comes again, not only will he raise the dead and transform the living, but by these events he will also have finally destroyed the last enemy, death itself (15:24-28, 54-57). So certain is Paul that Christ's resurrection guarantees the future of believers that he finally taunts death in the language of Hos. 13:14 (15:55). When death is thus rendered helpless by resurrection, then salvation will have reached its conclusion; and the present reigning Lord, having destroyed all other dominions, will hand over the rule to God the Father, so that the God who initiated salvation will thus be "all in all."

But even here the final word is one of exhortation (15:58). Despite the

---

43. Despite some demurrers, both the nature of the rhetoric and the combination of "already" and "ruling" in 4:8 seem to reflect Paul's own view of their present perspective. Whether this is a carefully thought-through position and whether it is an overrealized eschatology in a linear sense of time are more debatable. Most likely their experience of the Spirit has simply put them "above" the present age, having already assumed angelic existence.

magnificent crescendo with which Paul brings the argument of ch. 15 to its climax, the last word is not the sure word of future hope and triumph of vv. 50-57; rather, in light of such realities, the last word is an exhortation to Christian living (v. 58). Thus, eschatological salvation, the great concern of the epistle, includes proper behavior or it simply is not the gospel Paul preaches.

CHAPTER 14

Christology and Pneumatology
in Romans 8:9-11 — and Elsewhere:
Some Reflections on Paul as a Trinitarian
(1994)

Most discussions of christology in Paul, as elsewhere in the NT, are primarily concerned with the twin issues of how Paul perceived Christ's deity and how he perceived Christ's relationship with the Father. The concern of this essay is to come at the other side of the christological/trinitarian issue in Paul, namely how he perceived the relationship of Christ to the Spirit, an issue on which much in fact has been written,[1] but at times with what appears to be far more confidence than the data or methodology seems to allow. The contention of this essay is that the idea, common in some quarters, that Paul blurred the relationship of the Risen Lord with the Spirit with a kind of

---

1. In addition to the studies cited below in section I, see G. W. Bromiley, "The Spirit of Christ," in *Essays in Christology for Karl Barth*, ed. T. H. L. Parker (London: Lutterworth, 1956), pp. 135-52; and F. F. Bruce, "Christ and Spirit in Paul," *BJRL* 59 (1976-77): 259-85 (= *A Mind for What Matters: Collected Essays of F. F. Bruce* [Grand Rapids: Eerdmans, 1990], pp. 114-32). There are many other works on this subject that deal primarily with the historical Jesus and the Spirit, as the avenue to a Spirit christology, which are not included here since my concern in this essay is with Pauline theology. See, e.g., among many others, G. W. H. Lampe, "The Holy Spirit and the Person of Christ," in *Christ, Faith and History: Cambridge Studies in Christology*, ed. S. W. Sykes and J. P. Clayton (Cambridge: Cambridge University Press, 1972), pp. 111-30. Among many other studies whose interests are primarily from the standpoint of systematic theology, see N. Hook, "Spirit Christology," *Theology* 75 (1972): 226-32; P. Rosato, "Spirit Christology: Ambiguity and Promise," *TS* 38 (1977): 423-40; and O. Hansen, "Spirit Christology: A Way Out of Our Dilemma?" in *The Holy Spirit in the Life of the Church*, ed. P. Opsahl (Minneapolis: Augsburg, 1978), pp. 171-98.

"Spirit christology" is in fact the invention of scholarship, and that Paul himself knew nothing about such.[2]

After a brief survey, therefore, I propose (I) to critique both the exegesis and methodology of much of this discussion,[3] (II) to offer an exposition of the one text that is always mentioned in this discussion — Rom. 8:9-11 — but which is never carefully analyzed in light of it, and (III) to contend for a methodological alternative that is much more in keeping with the instincts of the early church that led finally to Chalcedon.[4]

I

That Paul perceived the closest kind of ties between the exalted Christ and the Holy Spirit can scarcely be gainsaid. Just as the coming of Christ forever marked Paul's understanding of God,[5] so also the coming of Christ forever marked his understanding of the Spirit. The Spirit of God is now also de-

2. Any more than he would have understood one's speaking of God in terms of a "Christ theology" or a "Spirit theology," because he sometimes interchanges the functions of Christ or the Spirit with those of God the Father.

3. I am grateful to the editors for graciously calling my attention to an article by M. Turner that deals with some of these same issues, and comes to many of the same conclusions ("out of the mouth of two witnesses"?) — although the basic concern of that paper is quite different from mine. See "The Significance of Spirit Endowment for Paul," *VE* 9 (1975): 56-69. My attention has also been called to K. Stalder, *Das Werk des Geistes in der Heiligung bei Paulus* (Zürich: Evz-Verlag, 1962), esp. pp. 26-69, who also makes many of the points made in this essay. Cf. also H. D. Hunter, *Spirit-Baptism: A Pentecostal Perspective* (Lanham, Md.: University Press of America, 1983), pp. 212-30, in an excursus on "Spirit Christology," which, although it overviews the biblical data, comes at the question from the urgencies of systematic theology.

4. I am delighted to offer these musings in honor of my friend Howard Marshall, whose work has been both a model and inspiration to me ever since his "The Synoptic Son of Man Sayings in Recent Discussion," *NTS* 12 (1965-66): 327-51. A presuppositional word about references and the Pauline corpus: (1) Although no argument will hinge on such, I will regularly include references to the entire Pauline corpus, on the grounds that Colossians, Ephesians, 2 Thessalonians, and the Pastorals are first of all Pauline, whatever else. In every case, the inclusion of references from these letters will only serve to demonstrate that the same theology is at work in these matters (the one great exception being Titus 3:6, where, alone in the Pauline corpus, the Spirit is understood to be poured out through the agency of Christ). (2) All references will appear in their chronological order, as I perceive that to be (1-2 Thessalonians, 1-2 Corinthians, Galatians, Romans, Colossians, Philemon, Ephesians, Philippians, 1 Timothy, Titus, 2 Timothy).

5. So that the transcendent God of the universe is henceforth known as "the Father of our Lord Jesus Christ" (2 Cor. 1:3; Eph. 1:3) who "sent his Son" into the world to redeem (Gal. 4:4-5).

noted as the Spirit of Christ (Gal. 4:6; Rom. 8:9; Phil. 1:19),[6] who carries on the work of Christ following his resurrection and subsequent assumption of the place of authority at God's right hand. To have received the Spirit of God (1 Cor. 2:12) is to have the mind of Christ (v. 16). For Paul, therefore, Christ also gives new definition to the Spirit: Spirit people are God's children, who by the Spirit address God in the language of the Son ("Abba") and are thus his fellow heirs (Rom. 8:14-17), for whom the Spirit also serves as the ἀρραβών, σφραγίς, or ἀπαρχή ("down payment, seal, firstfruits") of their final inheritance. At the same time Christ is the absolute criterion for what is truly Spirit activity (e.g., 1 Cor. 12:3). Thus it is fair to say that Paul's doctrine of the Spirit moves toward christocentricity,[7] in the sense that Christ and *his* work often give definition and focus to the Spirit and his work in the Christian life.

So much is this so that it became popular in NT scholarship — and still is in some quarters — to speak of this relationship in a way that tends to blur the distinctions between Christ and the Spirit. This tendency is due primarily to a (mis)understanding of a few Pauline texts (especially 2 Cor. 3:17 and 1 Cor. 14:45; sometimes 1 Cor. 6:17; Rom. 1:4; and Rom. 8:9-11); but it is also partly due, one suspects, to a predilection to not take the *person* of the Spirit very seriously in Pauline thought and experience and therefore to resolve both of these matters — the texts and personhood — by suggesting that Paul thought of some kind of loose identification between the Risen Lord and the Holy Spirit — that the Holy Spirit received "personality" by his identification with the Risen Lord.[8]

One can trace this tendency at least as far back as H. Gunkel's seminal work on the Spirit.[9] It was carried forward with special vigor in the influential

---

6. Some would add 2 Cor. 3:17, "the Spirit of the Lord." But despite arguments for this based on v. 14 — "because in Christ [the veil] is abolished" — the contextual evidence would seem to support a reference to Yahweh: Paul is citing the LXX in v. 16, where "the Lord" refers to Yahweh; the passage is not christological at all, but pneumatological, and Paul far more often refers to the "Spirit of God" than to "the Spirit of Christ"; the use of τὸ πνεῦμα κυρίου, with its articular πνεῦμα and anarthrous κυρίου, is unique to the Pauline corpus, and is best explained as Paul's picking up the reference to Yahweh in v. 16; and finally — and decisively for me — the "glory" of the Lord in v. 18 almost certainly refers to Christ, as 4:6 makes certain, so that the Lord of whom Christ is the "glory" is Yahweh of the Exodus passage.

7. But not absolutely so, as is often asserted; see section II below.

8. Cf. J. D. G. Dunn, *Jesus and the Spirit* (Philadelphia: Westminster, 1975), pp. 324-25.

9. By which he "felled the giant" of nineteenth-century liberalism, wherein the Spirit had been identified with consciousness. See *Die Wirkungen des heiligen Geistes nach der populären Anschauung der apostolischen Zeit und der Lehre des Apostels Paulus* (Göttingen: Vandenhoeck & Ruprecht, 1888); ET: *The Influence of the Holy Spirit: The Popular View of the Apostolic Age and the Teaching of the Apostle Paul* (Philadelphia: Fortress, 1979). The giant-killing analogy is from

work of A. Deissmann[10] and W. Bousset,[11] so much so that by 1923 E. F. Scott could say that "in many presentations of Paulinism it has become customary to assume, almost as self-evident, that in Paul the Spirit and Christ are one and the same."[12] The post–World War II impetus to this theological perspective came especially from N. Q. Hamilton,[13] I. Hermann,[14] and, more recently, J. D. G. Dunn.[15]

The common thread in all of these studies, from Gunkel to Dunn — and in many whom they have influenced[16] — is to start by noting the Pauline texts, usually beginning with 2 Cor. 3:17, and then to use such language as "identification,"[17] "equation" (Gunkel, Dunn), or "merge" (Bousset) to speak

---

the introduction to the ET by R. A. Harrisvflle (x). Gunkel's discussion can be found on pp. 112-15; his supporting texts, in his order, are 1 Cor. 15:45; 6:7; and 2 Cor. 3:17.

10. See esp. *Die neutestamentliche Formel "in Christo Jesu"* (Marburg: N. G. Elwert, 1892). For English readers a succinct overview of his position can be found in *St. Paul: A Study in Social and Religious History* (London: Hodder and Stoughton, 1912 [Ger. original 1911]), pp. 123-35.

11. In *Kyrios Christos* (Göttingen: Vandenhoeck & Ruprecht, 1913); ET: *Kyrios Christos* (Nashville: Abingdon, 1970), pp. 154-55, 160-64.

12. *The Spirit in the New Testament* (London: Hodder and Stoughton, 1923), p. 178. In keeping with the nature of the book this is stated without documentation.

13. In his published Basel dissertation (under O. Cullmann), *The Holy Spirit and Eschatology in Paul*, SJT Occasional Papers 6 (Edinburgh: Oliver and Boyd, 1957). In his first chapter (3-16), Hamilton offers a (much too brief to be convincing) analysis of the key texts (2 Cor. 3:17; 1 Cor. 12:3; Rom. 8:9; Gal. 4:6; Phil. 1:19; Rom. 1:3-4; 1 Cor. 14:45) so as to demonstrate that "Christology [is] the key to pneumatology." One can trace the influence of this study in almost all the subsequent literature.

14. *Kyrios und Pneuma: Studien zur Christologie der paulinischen Hauptbriefe* (München: Kösel, 1961). This study has also had considerable influence, but only among those who really do think that 2 Cor. 3:17 is saying something christological, since in effect Hermann's whole case is based on a demonstrable misunderstanding of this passage.

15. First in articles on two of the key texts ("Jesus — Flesh and Spirit: An Exposition of Romans i.3-4," *JTS* 24 [1973]: 40-68; and "I Corinthians 15.45 — Last Adam, Life-giving Spirit," in *Christ and Spirit in the New Testament: Studies in Honour of C. F. D. Moule*, ed. B. Lindars and S. S. Smalley [Cambridge: Cambridge University Press, 1973], pp. 127-41); later in summary form in *Jesus and the Spirit*, pp. 318-26; and *Christology in the Making* (Philadelphia: Westminster, 1980), pp. 141-49. On the other hand, Dunn also wrote specifically against finding support for this view in 2 Cor. 3:17 ("II Corinthians 3.17 — 'The Lord Is the Spirit,'" *JTS* 21 [1970]: 309-20). For those who write on this issue, and have been influenced by these various scholars, one can trace a parting of the ways between those who follow Hermann and Dunn as the result of this latter article.

16. See, among others, H. Berkhof, *The Doctrine of the Holy Spirit* (London: Epworth, 1964), pp. 21-28; D. Hill, *Greek Words and Hebrew Meanings*, SNTSMS 5 (Cambridge: Cambridge University Press, 1967), pp. 275-83 — although Hill, to be sure, does so with considerable qualification.

17. This is the obviously operative word; see, e.g., Gunkel, Scott (hesitantly), Hamilton,

about this relationship.[18] To be sure, in most cases all of this is said with the proper demurrers, that Paul does indeed also recognize the distinctions,[19] that the identity is "dynamic" rather than "ontological,"[20] or that the identity is not so complete that the one is wholly dissolved in the other.[21] But there can be little question that "identification" is the stronger motif, especially at the level of Christian experience of the Risen Christ and the Spirit, which is asserted for all practical purposes to be one and the same thing.[22]

That the emphasis clearly lies with "identification" rather than "distinction" is evidenced by another thread that runs through these studies as well, namely the rather strong denial that Paul's experience and understanding of God can be properly termed "trinitarian." This is pressed vigorously by Hermann, who goes so far as to argue that the identification of Christ with

---

Hermann, Berkhof, Hill ("virtual identification"); cf. Walter Kasper: "That is why Paul can actually identify the two (2 Cor. 3.17)" (in *Jesus the Christ* [New York: Paulist, 1976], p. 256).

18. Another thread common to many of these studies is the assertion that Paul's "in Christ" and "in the Spirit" formulas amount to one and the same thing, a view that in particular may be traced back to Deissmann *(Formel)*, whose thesis in part depends on this interchange; cf. Bousset (p. 160): "The two formulas coincide so completely that they can be interchanged at will." Cf. Hill, *Greek Words*, p. 276. But this seems to be a considerable overstatement, since in fact there are some significant differences: Paul always uses the preposition (ἐν) with "Christ"; he alternates between πνεύματι and ἐν πνεύματι with "Spirit"; this reflects the fact that the predominant usage of πνεύματι/ἐν πνεύματι is instrumental, whereas the predominant usage of "in Christ" is locative. The differences are demonstrated in Rom. 9:1, the one sentence where both formulas appear together. In his asseverations as to his own truthfulness, Paul "speaks the truth [as one who, with them] is in Christ Jesus"; moreover, his own conscience, "by the [inner witness of] the Holy Spirit," bears witness to the same. Thus the two formulas are scarcely interchangeable, except for those places where the soteriological activity of Christ and the Spirit overlap, such as "sanctified in/by Christ Jesus" in 1 Cor. 1:2, where the emphasis lies on Christ's redemptive activity, and "sanctified by the Holy Spirit" in Rom. 15:16, where the emphasis is on the appropriation by the Spirit of the prior work of Christ. Cf. the more detailed critique of Deissmann in F. Büchsel, "'In Christus' bei Paulus," *ZNW* 42 (1949): 141-58; F. Neugebauer, "Das paulinische 'in Christ,'" *NTS* 4 (1957-58): 124-38; and M. Bouttier, *En Christ: Etude d'exégèse et de théologie pauliniennes* (Paris: Presses Universitaires, 1962).

19. Scott, *Spirit*, p. 183, in fact stands apart from the others mentioned above in that he thinks the "identification" was not deliberate on Paul's part, that it was "forced upon him in spite of himself."

20. Hamilton, *Holy Spirit*, pp. 6, 10.

21. This is the demurral language of H. Ridderbos, *Paul: An Outline of His Theology* (Grand Rapids: Eerdmans, 1975), p. 88, who takes a position similar to the one argued for in this essay, except that he is willing to allow that some of these texts point toward "a certain relationship of identity with each other" (p. 87).

22. Cf. Dunn, "*If Christ is now experienced as Spirit, Spirit is now experienced as Christ* [emphasis his]" (*Jesus and the Spirit*, p. 323).

Spirit is so complete that one can no longer press for a personal identity to the Spirit, separate and distinct from Christ, hence distinct in traditional trinitarian terms.[23] The demurrers of Hamilton and (especially) Dunn are not far from this, so much so that in effect to speak of trinitarianism in Paul is probably to use inappropriate language altogether.[24]

But one may properly question whether all of this is a genuine reflection of Paul's own christology and pneumatology. Three matters give reason to pause: the data from the Pauline Spirit texts taken as a whole; an analysis of the key texts used to support a Spirit christology; and the methodological issue of finding a proper starting point in talking about Paul's understanding of God, including his understanding of Christ and the Spirit. To each of these we turn in brief.

II

We noted above that the coming of Christ forever marked Paul's understanding of the Spirit.[25] But what does *not* seem to cohere with the data is the oft-repeated suggestion that "we have to think of the Spirit in *strictly* christocentric terms."[26] The data themselves indicate that this is something of an overstatement.

---

23. *Kyrios und Pneuma,* pp. 132-36.

24. Thus Hamilton (*Holy Spirit,* p. 3): "An attempt to deal with the Spirit in the traditional way as an aspect of the doctrine of the Trinity would be inappropriate to Paul. This is not to deny that the Spirit is for Paul a distinct entity over against the Father and the Son. The problem of the Trinity, which is the occasion of the doctrine of the Trinity, was for Paul no problem." Thus "to deal with the Spirit in the tradition of the New Testament is to avoid all speculation about the nature of the being of the Spirit." (One of course could say the same about Paul's assertions about Christ, which means therefore that one in effect should cease christological discussion altogether!) Dunn ("1 Corinthians 15.45," p. 139): "*Immanent christology is for Paul pneumatology* [emphasis mine]; in the believer's experience there is *no* [Dunn's emphasis] distinction between Christ and the Spirit. This does not mean of course that Paul makes no distinction between Christ and Spirit. But it does mean that later Trinitarian dogma cannot readily look to Paul for support at this point." If by "immanent christology" Dunn denotes the traditional sense of "Christ as he is in himself," then this statement seems far removed from Pauline realities.

25. One must put it that way, of course, because even though the *experience* of the Spirit for earliest believers follows their experience with Christ, Incarnate and Risen, their *understanding* of the Spirit begins with the OT, and it is that understanding which is being transformed by Christ, just as was their understanding of what it meant for Jesus to be the Messiah, not to mention their understanding of God himself.

26. This is the language of Berkhof, *Doctrine,* p. 24 (emphasis mine). Cf. M. E. Isaacs, *The*

The use of πνεῦμα and πνευματικός language, referring specifically to the Holy Spirit, occurs over 140 times in the Pauline corpus,[27] the vast majority of which occur in the so-called *Hauptbriefe*. The full name, Holy Spirit, occurs in 17 instances. Depending on how one understands "the Spirit of the Lord" in 2 Cor. 3:17, Paul refers to "the Spirit of God"/"His Spirit" 16 (or 15) times, and to "the Spirit of Christ," or its equivalent, but 3 (or 4) times. Some observations about these statistics:

(1) Paul refers to the Holy Spirit as a full name in the same way as, and at about the same ratio that, he refers to Christ by the full name, our Lord Jesus Christ. This use of the full name in itself suggests "distinction from," not "identity with," as the *Pauline presupposition*.

(2) Despite suggestions to the contrary, Paul thinks of the Spirit *primarily* in terms of the Spirit's relationship to God (the Father, although he never uses this imagery of this relationship). Not only does he more often speak of the "Spirit of God" than of the "Spirit of Christ," but God is invariably the subject of the verb when Paul speaks of human reception of the Spirit. Thus God "sent forth the Spirit of his Son into our hearts" (Gal. 4:6), or "gives" us his Spirit (1 Thess. 4:8; 2 Cor. 1:22; 5:5; Gal. 3:5; Rom. 5:5; Eph. 1:17), an understanding that in Paul's case is almost certainly determined by his OT roots, where God "fills with" (Exod. 31:3) or "pours out" his Spirit (Joel 2:28), and the "Spirit of God" comes on people for all sorts of extraordinary ("charismatic") activities (e.g., Num. 24:2; Judg. 3:10).

Two passages in particular give insight into Paul's understanding of this primary, presuppositional relationship. In 1 Cor. 2:10-12 he uses the analogy of human interior consciousness (only one's "spirit" knows one's mind) to insist that the Spirit alone knows the mind of God. Paul's own concern in this analogy is with the Spirit as the source of *our* understanding the cross as God's wisdom; nonetheless the analogy itself draws the closest kind of relationship between God and his Spirit. The Spirit alone "searches all things," even "the depths of God";[28] and because of this singular relationship with God, the Spirit alone knows and reveals God's otherwise hidden wisdom (1 Cor. 2:7).

In Rom. 8:26-27 this same idea is expressed obversely. Among other

---

Concept of Spirit: A Study of Pneuma in Hellenistic Judaism and Its Bearing on the New Testament, HeyM 1 (London: Heythrop College, 1976), p. 124: "For all N.T. writers the power and presence of God, signified by πνεῦμα, is grounded exclusively in Jesus, the Christ."

27. For a full discussion of these data on usage in Paul, see ch. 2 in my monograph, *God's Empowering Presence: The Holy Spirit in the Letters of Paul* (Peabody, Mass.: Hendrickson, 1994).

28. An idea that reflects Paul's background in the OT and Jewish apocalyptic (cf. Dan. 2:22-23).

matters, Paul is here concerned to show how the Spirit, in the presence of our own weaknesses and inability to speak for ourselves, is able to intercede adequately on our behalf. The effectiveness of the Spirit's intercession lies precisely in the fact that God, who searches our hearts, likewise "knows the mind of the Spirit," who is making intercession for us.

(3) Given these data, the cause for wonder is that Paul should *also* refer to the Spirit as "the Spirit of Christ." That he does so at all says something far more significant about his christology than about his pneumatology — although the latter is significant as well. Here is evidence for Paul's "high christology," that a person steeped in the OT understanding of the Spirit of God as Paul was, should so easily, on the basis of his Christian experience, speak of him as the Spirit of Christ as well.[29]

(4) A careful analysis of all the texts in which Paul identifies the Spirit either as "the Spirit of God" or "the Spirit of Christ" suggests that he chose to use the genitive qualifier when he wanted to emphasize the activity of either God or Christ that is being conveyed to the believer by the Spirit. Thus the church is God's temple because God's Spirit dwells in their midst (1 Cor. 3:16),[30] or God gives his Holy Spirit to those he calls to be holy (1 Thess. 4:8), and so on. So also in the three texts in which the Spirit is called the Spirit of Christ, the emphasis lies on the work of Christ in some way. We will note below how this is so in Rom. 8:9. In Gal. 4:6 the emphasis is on the believers' "sonship," evidenced by their having received "the Spirit of God's Son," through whom they use the Son's language to address God; and in Phil. 1:19 Paul desires a fresh supply of the Spirit of Christ Jesus so that when on trial Christ will be magnified, whether by life or by death.

(5) Finally, in Rom. 8:9-11 Paul clearly and absolutely identifies "the Spirit of God" with "the Spirit of Christ"; on the other hand, as will be noted momentarily, nowhere does he make such an identification of the Risen Christ with the Spirit, including the handful of texts that might appear to suggest otherwise. To these we now turn.

---

29. It is of some interest that this point is so seldom made in the literature.

30. This is an especially important *theological,* vis-à-vis christological, understanding of the experience of the Spirit, where the OT motif of God's presence (from Sinai, to the tabernacle, to the temple, and finally in the promised new covenant) is seen to have been fillfilled by the Spirit's presence in the gathered community (and also in the life of the individual believer in 1 Cor. 6:19). One wonders in light of such passages about the language of the Spirit as "exclusively christocentric" in Paul.

III

We cannot here examine the several texts at full length. My aim is simply to offer some exegetical conclusions, supported elsewhere in more detail.[31]

(1) *2 Corinthians 3:17.* This is the text that lies at the root of all Spirit christology talk. Indeed, Hermann rests his whole case on this passage. But in fact Paul's words, "Now the Lord is the Spirit," do not even remotely suggest that the Spirit is to be identified with the Risen Lord — as Dunn himself, the most vigorous advocate of Spirit christology in the English-speaking world, acknowledges.[32]

Similar to what he does in 1 Cor. 10:4 and Gal. 4:25, Paul here uses a form of midrash pesher to offer biblical support for what is said in v. 16 — by the anaphoric use of ὁ δὲ κύριος, which picks up and interprets this word from the preceding pesher citation of Exod. 34:34 (LXX). Thus he has "cited" Exodus to the effect that "whenever anyone [not Moses] turns to the Lord [so as to be converted], the veil is removed." "Now," he goes on to interpret, for the sake of his point in context, "ὁ κύριος in that passage stands for the Spirit."

Once this literary device has been observed, much of the debate over Paul's language in this text becomes irrelevant. By "the Lord," Paul does not intend either God or Christ; he intends the Spirit. That is, he is interpreting the text of Exodus in light of the present argument, which is, after all, a pneumatological passage, not a christological one. By this interpretative device he keeps alive his argument that his ministry is that of "the new covenant of the Spirit" (v. 6). "The Lord" in the Exodus narrative, he is saying, is now to be understood (not literally, but in an analogical way) as referring to the Spirit — not because this is the proper identification of the Lord in Exod. 34:34, but because in this argument it is the proper way to understand what happens at conversion. The Spirit, who applies the work of Christ to the life of the believer, is understood to be the one who removes the veil, so that God's people can enter into freedom.

This is further made clear by the clause that follows, where the Spirit is called "the Spirit of the Lord." By this further designation Paul himself seems intent on removing any misunderstandings brought about by his previous clause. That is, "in interpreting 'the Lord' in the Exodus passage as referring to the Spirit, I do not mean that the Spirit *is* the Lord; rather, the Spirit is, as always, the Spirit *of the Lord.*"

---

31. See the full exegetical discussion of all the Spirit texts in the Pauline corpus in Fee, *God's Empowering Presence.*

32. See Hermann, *Kyrios und Pneuma.*

Thus, in this crucial text, there is not a hint of "identity" between the Risen Lord and the Holy Spirit.

(2) *1 Corinthians 15:45*.[33] Here is the more difficult passage, and the one on which Dunn ultimately rests his case.[34] In a passage whose whole point is soteriological-eschatological, Paul is intent on one thing — to demonstrate from Christ's own resurrection that there must be a future, bodily resurrection of believers as well. Thus he begins by citing the LXX of Gen. 2:7, in another expression of midrash pesher:[35]

ἐγένετο   ὁ   πρῶτος ἄνθρωπος   Ἀδὰμ εἰς ψυχὴν   ζῶσαν
          ὁ   ἔσχατος   Ἀδὰμ εἰς πνεῦμα   ζῳοποιοῦν

---

33. Cf. esp. the similar critique of Dunn on this passage by Turner, "Significance," pp. 61-63, an article of which I was unfortunately unaware when I wrote my commentary, where the details of the following exegesis are worked out in more detail.

34. Even though Dunn recognizes that the crucial clause about Christ has been shaped by the former one about Adam, he insists that Paul intends something quite christological here. His points are: (1) v. 45 is not an explanation of v. 44, but advances the argument in its own right [I would say no and yes to this]; (2) that the ἐγένετο from the first clause must be read in the second as well [yes, but not with Dunn's intent]; (3) that therefore Paul understands a fundamental change to have taken place at Christ's resurrection, in which he is now to be identified with the Spirit whom the Corinthians have experienced, but in some aberrational ways [an especially questionable point, in that it has Paul inserting a red herring into an otherwise consistent and self-contained argument]; (4) that this identification is made certain by the qualifier "life-giving" with πνεῦμα, which is elsewhere attributed to the Holy Spirit (2 Cor. 3:6); and that Paul's intent here is similar to that in 12:3, where by identifying the Spirit whom they have received with the Risen Christ, he gives christocentric content to their experience of the Spirit. Rather than refute this point by point, I will let the interpretation offered here (and given in more detail in my *The First Epistle to the Corinthians,* NICNT [Grand Rapids: Eerdmans, 1987], pp. 787-90; and *God's Empowering Presence*) stand as that refutation. But it does need to be noted that Dunn's primary assertion on the basis of Paul's use of "life-giving πνεῦμα" — namely, that the "believer's *experience of the life-giving Spirit* is for Paul proof that the risen Jesus is σῶμα πνευματικόν" (p. 131; emphasis mine; Dunn emphasizes the whole sentence) — is just that, an assertion pure and simple; it is difficult to imagine anything further removed from Paul's intent than this, which in fact turns Paul's point quite on its head, namely that Christ's now assuming a "supernatural body" is the certain evidence that the Corinthian believers, too, will eventually "bear such a body."

35. Cf. E. E. Ellis, *Paul's Use of the Old Testament* (Edinburgh: Oliver and Boyd, 1957), pp. 141-43; it is doubtful, however, whether Paul is here citing a midrash that had already taken hold in Christian circles (pp. 95-97). Paul himself is perfectly capable of such pesher. Dunn ("1 Corinthians 15.45," p. 130) argues that the whole sentence "stands under the οὕτως γέγραπται — including verse 45b, as the absence of δέ indicates." Yes and no. This is true of the pesher as such, but Paul hardly intends the second clause to be understood as Scripture — even in a targumic way — in the same sense that the first line is.

Several observations about this citation-turned-interpretation are needed: (1) Paul's *modifications* of the LXX in the first line — the additions of the adjective "first" and of the name "Adam" — seem specifically designed to lead to the second line, where his real concern lies. (2) The two words that describe Adam and Christ respectively are the cognate nouns for the adjectives ψυχικόν and πνευματικόν in v. 44. This in fact is *the only reason both for the citation and for the language used to describe Christ.* This clear linguistic connection implies that the *original bearers* of the two kinds of bodies mentioned in v. 44 are Adam and Christ.[36] That is, the two "Adams" serve as evidence that even as there is a ψυχικός body (as the first Adam demonstrates [Gen. 2:7]), so also Christ, the second Adam, by his resurrection is evidence that there must be a πνευματικός body.[37] (3) Not only so, but Paul's *reason* for saying that Christ became "a life-giving πνεῦμα" is that the LXX had said of Adam that he became "a living ψυχή." That is, the *language of the citation* called for the *parallel language about Christ.* (4) Even though the content of the second line is neither present nor inferred in the Genesis text, it nonetheless reflects the language of the prior clause in the LXX, "and he *breathed* into his face the *breath of life* (πνοὴν ζωῆς)"; now in speaking about Christ, Paul makes a play on this language. The one who will "breathe" new life into these mortal bodies — with life-giving πνεῦμα (as in Ezek. 37:14) and thus make them immortal — is none other than the Risen Christ himself. (5) The language "life-giving" thus repeats the verb used of Christ in the previous Adam-Christ analogy in v. 22, indicating decisively, it would seem, that the interest here, as before, is in Christ's resurrection as the ground of ours ("in Christ all will be made alive"). Thus the argument as a whole, as well as the immediate context, suggests that even though Christ has now assumed his exalted position in a σῶμα πνευματικόν and is thus a "life-giving πνεῦμα," *his function in this particular role will take place at the resurrection of believers,* when he "makes alive" their mortal bodies so that they too assume a σῶμα πνευματικόν like his.

The concern of line 2, therefore, is not christological, as though Christ and the Spirit were somehow now interchangeable terms for Paul. Indeed, despite the combination of "life-giving" and πνεῦμα, he almost certainly does not intend to say that Christ became *the* life-giving Spirit, but a life-giving spirit.[38] Christ is not *the* Spirit; rather, in a play on the Genesis text, Paul says

36. As Dunn also notes ("1 Corinthians 15.45," p. 130).

37. This is the point that Turner, "Significance," p. 62, makes especially strongly.

38. Grammar must still have its day in court. Paul tends to be very precise, and generally unambiguous, with his use or non-use of the definite article with "Spirit." In the nominative, both as subject or as predicate noun (as here), when Paul intends the Holy Spirit he always uses the article. For a full analysis of Pauline usage see ch. 2 in *God's Empowering Presence.*

that Christ through his resurrection assumed his new existence in the spiritual realm, the realm of course that for believers is the ultimate sphere of the Spirit, in which they will have "spiritual" bodies, adapted to the final life of the Spirit.

(3) It seems evident, therefore, that in the two basic texts where Paul is alleged to identify the Risen Christ with the Spirit, he does not in fact do so at all. His language in both cases is dictated by his "interpretation" of OT passages, in light of the urgencies of the present contexts. And without these texts, the whole idea lies in shambles, because the rest of the texts are seen merely to support one or both of the other two. Thus, for example, *1 Cor. 6:17* is often drawn in as support, "The one who joins himself to the Lord is one S/spirit[39] [with him]." Here again the language has been dictated by the argument and the immediately preceding sentence, "The one who joins himself to a prostitute is one body [with her]." Whereas the latter sentence makes perfectly good sense and is based on the clear intent of Gen. 2:24, the former sentence standing on its own is near nonsense and becomes meaningful precisely because of Paul's penchant to do this very thing — let a prior sentence or clause dictate how he expresses a contrasting clause. Paul's point seems perfectly clear, even if the language with which that point is made is less so, namely that the Spirit has forged a "uniting" relationship between the believer and the Lord of such a kind that absolutely prohibits an illicit "uniting" of the believer's body with that of a prostitute.

So also with *Rom. 1:4*, and the phrase κατὰ πνεῦμα ἁγιωσύνης, every word of which, as Cranfield points out,[40] is full of difficulty. This is Dunn's second text by which he supports a Spirit christology; but he does so by circuitous and convoluted exegesis, which proceeds as if v. 2 did not exist and as though a concern to establish "to the Jew first" were not a part of the letter. On this matter, the argument by E. Schweizer, that vv. 3 and 4 reflect the two expressions of Christ's (the Messiah's) existence as earthly and heavenly and in that succession, is to be preferred at almost every point to that of Dunn.[41]

39. For this translation see Fee, *First Corinthians*, pp. 259-60.

40. See *The Epistle to the Romans*, ICC (Edinburgh: T. & T. Clark, 1975), vol. 1, pp. 62-63.

41. See "Röm. 1:3f und der Gegensatz von Fleisch und Geist vor und bei Paulus," *EvT* 15 (1955): 563-71. The position Dunn took in his 1973 article is only slightly moderated in his commentary (*Romans 1–8*, WBC 38A [Dallas: Word, 1988], p. 13). If reader criticism counts for anything, and it must in this case since the Romans for the most part had not heard Paul in person, then it is hard to imagine the circumstances in which they could have understood Paul as Dunn presents him to be arguing. In an otherwise useful overview of the use of σάρξ in Paul, Dunn concludes that the σάρξ/πνεῦμα contrast in vv. 3-4 is primarily to be understood in Paul's more characteristically theological way, rather than as indicating two successive spheres of existence — so much so that to speak of Christ as "descended from the seed of David κατὰ σάρκα" is ultimately pejorative. He was thus "bound and determined by the weakness and inadequacy of the

And in any case, it is difficult to imagine how this phrase can be turned into: "The personality and the role of Jesus expand and swallow up the less well-defined personality and more restricted role of the Spirit. *Jesus becomes the Spirit* (1 Cor. 15:45); . . . the Spirit becomes the executive power of the exalted Christ."[42] That would indeed seem to be a bit more weight than κατὰ πνεῦμα ἁγιωσύνης can be made to handle.

(4) The final text is *Rom. 8:9-11*, which we need to look at in slightly more detail, since in fact it not only does *not* support an identification of Christ with the Spirit, but also offers some keys to getting at this relationship in Paul.

IV

On the surface, and especially in English translation, the set of clauses in Rom. 8:9-11 can seem very confused — and confusing. But a couple of observations about Pauline style and present urgencies may help us to unpack both the argument and its Spirit talk. First, a Pauline stylistic observation. As in the passages just noted, where an OT text about which he is going to make a Christian application sets up both the language and pattern of his second sentence or clause, so too Paul tends at times to let his own rhetoric dictate *the way some things are said,* which *on their own* would almost certainly have been said with much less ambiguity.[43] The present set of sentences is particularly noteworthy in this regard.

---

human condition, *allowed worldly considerations to determine his conduct* [emphasis mine], he was merely Son of David and no more — Messiah indeed, but a disappointing, ineffective, irrelevant Messiah" (57). And this in a Pauline sentence that begins: "The gospel of God which he promised beforehand, through his prophets in Sacred Scripture"! How could the Romans have so understood κατὰ σάρκα? Or that κατὰ πνεῦμα ἁγιωσύνης has also (especially) to do with Jesus' earthly life ("In Paul's view the sonship of the earthly life was constituted by the Holy Spirit" [57])? Although this latter is clearly the view of Luke, and therefore maybe assumed to be Paul's point of view, nowhere does Paul make such a point, and it can scarcely be asserted to be true by the circuitous means by which Dunn arrives at it in this article.

42. "Jesus — Flesh and Spirit," p. 59 (emphasis mine).

43. Note, e.g., the notoriously un-Pauline sentiment expressed in the final clause in 1 Cor. 6:13, that "the Lord is for the body." This has been set up by the double rhetoric of vv. 12 and 13, the latter expressing the Corinthian position (with which Paul probably agrees): "Food for the stomach and the stomach for food." But this is not true of the body itself; he goes on: "The body is [not for sexual immorality but] for the Lord, and the Lord for the body." Seen as rhetoric, and as his own construct to balance the former clause, the sentence makes perfectly good sense. It is not that the Risen Lord exists for the sake of our bodies, in the same way that the stomach exists for food, but that the resurrection of Christ has singularly marked our human bodies as not irrelevant but as belonging to him and destined for resurrection (as v. 14 goes on to explain).

Second, as to the argument itself, several observations are pertinent: (1) Both the argument as a whole (from 7:6, picked up at 8:1-2) and the paragraph itself make it clear that Paul's primary interest is in the role the Spirit plays in "the righteousness of God" that comes "apart from Torah through faith in Christ Jesus" (3:21-22); and in this instance the clear emphasis is on the role/function of the *indwelling* Spirit.[44] In v. 2 Paul had said (in a kind of thesis statement for 8:1-11) that "the 'law' of the Spirit of life has . . . freed you from the 'law' of . . . death." This paragraph elaborates that point.[45]

(2) At the same time the linguistic ties to 6:4-14 are so unmistakable[46] that it is hard to escape the conclusion that Paul is here intentionally tying together what was said there about Christ with what is said here about the Spirit. The singular difference between this passage and that one is that the "death/resurrection" motif in the former has primarily to do with sin and righteousness in terms of behavior, while this one has to do with present and future eschatology in terms of future bodily resurrection. Thus, just as he does in vv. 1-4, Paul seems intent to tie together what has been said earlier in the argument about the work of Christ with what he now says about the life of the Spirit.

(3) The present passage is thus another excellent example of the eschatological tension in Paul between the "already" (the indwelling Spirit of God/Christ means life *now*, predicated on the righteousness Christ has provided) and the "not yet" (even though sin means death for the present mortal bodies [cf. 5:12, 21], the indwelling Spirit means life both now and forever, through resurrection). Thus it is because of the Spirit's presence now, not through the Spirit's power later, that our future resurrection is guaranteed.[47]

---

44. Evidenced by the thrice-repeated, "the Spirit dwells in you," plus the language "have the Spirit of Christ" and thus "Christ in you."

45. Just as vv. 3-8 elaborate the first point, "freedom from the 'law' of sin."

46. This takes place esp. in the apodoses of vv. 10-11. (1) "The body is dead because of sin" echoes "the body of sin" and "sin reigning in our mortal bodies" in 6:6, 12; (2) "the Spirit is life because of righteousness" echoes 6:13, where we are to present ourselves as "alive" from the dead (because of Christ's death and resurrection in which by faith we participate) and our members as instruments "of righteousness" for God; (3) "He who raised Christ from the dead shall also give life to our mortal bodies" echoes "Christ was raised from the dead through the glory of the Father" in 6:4 and "if we died with Christ . . . we shall live with him" in 6:8.

47. Thus the logic of the argument itself, as well as the weight of both external and internal evidence favors the reading τὸ ἐνοικοῦν αὐτοῦ πνεῦμα ("will live *because of* his Spirit who dwells in you"; read by B D F G K Ψ 33 181 1241 1739 1881 lat MajT Origen); the alternative, τοῦ ἐνοικοῦντος αὐτοῦ πνεύματος ("*through* the Spirit who dwells in you"), is read by ℵ A C 81 88 104 326 436 2495 pc and NA²⁶/UBS³. The UBS committee made its choice first of all by negating the witness of B ("in the Pauline corpus the weight of B when associated with D G . . . is quite considerably lessened") and then favoring the genitive "on the basis of the combination of text-

With this passage, therefore, Paul seems intent to tie together the work of the Spirit with that of Christ, as well as the ethical life of righteousness effected by Christ and the Spirit with the final eschatological inheritance gained through the resurrection of the "mortal" body. The Spirit obviously plays the leading role, both in appropriating the work of Christ previously argued for and as evidence and guarantee of the future — despite present weaknesses and suffering (a matter to be taken up in detail in vv. 18-27).

Thus one can trace the flow — and concerns — of the argument through an (abbreviated) display of its basic structure:

⁹But (as for you) you are not in the flesh
                      but in the Spirit,

[A]   since indeed   the Spirit of God   dwells in you.

  [B]   Now if anyone does not have   the Spirit of Christ,
               this person is not of him   [Christ].

  [B′]   ¹⁰But if Christ is in you,

     [C]   that means: μέν   the *body* is *dead*   because of sin,

     [D]   δέ   the *Spirit* is *life*   because of righteousness.

[A′] ¹¹Now if the Spirit of him [God]   who raised Jesus . . . dwells in you,
        then   he   (who raised Christ Jesus from the dead)

  [(C)/D′]   will also give *life* to your *mortal bodies*,
                       because of his *Spirit* who dwells in you.

---

types, including the Alexandrian (א A D 81), Palestinian (syr^{pal} Cyril-Jerusalem), and Western (it^{61} Hippolytus)" (B. M. Metzger, *A Textual Commentary on the Greek New Testament* [London: United Bible Societies, 1971], p. 517). But that will scarcely do in this case. The same combination of text-types exists even more strongly for the alternative reading (B 1739, which in combination more often represent the "Alexandrian" text than otherwise; the preponderance of Western witnesses, early and widespread; and several "Palestinian" Fathers [Methodius, Origen, Theodoret]). The issue therefore must be decided on the grounds of transcriptional probability, since the variation can only have been deliberate, not accidental. Here the evidence weighs altogether in favor of the accusative, since that is not what one expects when διά modifies a verb (cf. 6:4; 1 Cor. 6:14) — all the more so when agency would make such perfectly good sense. Despite Cranfield, *Romans*, 1:392, to the contrary (who suggests that it might have been changed to the accusative on the basis of the accusatives in v. 10), one cannot in fact imagine the circumstances in which the very natural genitive would have been changed so early and often to the much less common accusative — especially so in light of 6:4, where the διὰ τῆς δόξης τοῦ πάτρος not only reflects Paul's ordinary habits but also, by its very difficulty, begs to be changed to the accusative (which would seem to make so much more sense) — yet no one ever did so. Intrinsic probability — the argument as here presented — only adds to the weight of this conclusion.

It should perhaps be pointed out in passing that this textual decision also does away with the one place in the Pauline corpus which suggested that the Spirit was involved in the resurrection of Christ. All other passages (e.g., 1 Cor. 1:14; Eph. 1:1-21), which are sometimes brought into this purview, are dependent on reading the genitive in this passage. Paul's emphasis in v. 11 is not on the Spirit's agency, but on the indwelling Spirit as eschatological guarantor.

The *point* of the paragraph seems obviously aimed at the two "D" clauses in vv. 10 and 11, which express the net result of the reality of the indwelling Spirit. First (v. 10), since the Spirit is none other than the Spirit of Christ, that means "life" for us as the direct result of the "righteousness" effected by the Christ whose Spirit now indwells the believer — despite the fact that the "body is dead" because of sin. Second (v. 11), since the indwelling Spirit is none other than the Spirit of the God who raised Christ from the dead, the Spirit therefore is also God's own surety in our lives that, just as Christ was raised, so too our "mortal" bodies are going to live again through resurrection.

The middle portion [B/B′], on the other hand, seems aimed at tying what is about to be said in A′ with what he has already said about Christ in 6:1-14. The awkwardness of the μέν/δέ contrasts, especially following the protasis, "but if Christ is in you," is the result of *these* contrasts. That is, Paul intends, "If Christ is in you, the Spirit means life for you, because of the righteousness effected by Christ." But since the concern here is with "life" also (especially) in terms of the future resurrection, he inserts — awkwardly for us — that "the body is dead because of sin." This obviously cannot mean that Christ's indwelling by his Spirit brings about the mortality of the body; sin alone has done that. Rather, he intends something like this (paraphrased to keep Paul's arrangement, but to get at his meaning): "But if Christ by his Spirit is in you, that means that *even though* the body is destined for death because of sin, the presence of Christ by his Spirit also means that the body is destined for life (because of Christ's own resurrection and the presence of the Spirit)."

Thus the A clause, a kind of "afterthought" protasis to v. 9a, simply states the reality of the indwelling Spirit — designated the Spirit of God both because this is Paul's primary understanding of the Spirit and because of the emphasis he intends to make in v. 11. In Pauline theology, God is the initiating subject of the saving action of Christ, mediated to believers through the Spirit. The second clause [B] functions in three ways: (1) It serves to reinforce the point of the preceding clause; (2) in typical fashion it sets up a "not/but" contrast so as to make the point of the "but" clause all the stronger; and (3) by changing the designation "Spirit of God" to "Spirit of Christ" Paul not only makes a considerably important point about his new understanding of the Spirit, but also makes the closest possible ties between the clearly distinct, but inseparably joined, activities of the three divine persons in bringing about our salvation — thought of in this case in terms of its eschatological culmination, the resurrection of believers from the dead.

That leads, then, to a final word about the apparently confusing switch from "having the Spirit of Christ" to "Christ in you." Both the structure of the argument as displayed above and the flow of thought between vv. 9 and 10 make it certain that Paul did not in fact perceive the Risen Christ to be one and the same as the Spirit, or that he thought of both as indwelling "side by side," as it were. The expression "Christ in you" is to be understood as short-hand for "having the Spirit of Christ" from the preceding clause. The reason for the shorthand is that the emphasis in the argument has momentarily shifted to the work of Christ; since "Christ dwells in you by his Spirit, that means life is at work in you based on his gift of righteousness." That he comes back to the language "Spirit of God" in the final clause is clear evidence that Paul saw the Spirit and his role as distinct from that of Christ and his role, even though in terms of "indwelling" Paul seems also clearly to understand that since the Spirit is both "of God" and "of Christ," this is how God and Christ both indwell the believer in the present eon — by the Spirit.

Thus, just as in Eph. 2:21-22, where the church is a "habitation for God, by his Spirit," so here — and elsewhere where Paul speaks about "Christ in me/us/you"[48] — he means "Christ by his Spirit dwells in me/us/you." All told, therefore, not only does this passage not support a Spirit christology, but it serves as one more link in a long chain that suggests quite the opposite. To this longer chain we now turn by way of conclusion.

V

In light of these data, a final word is needed, a methodological word. Another common denominator of those who claim for Paul a "Spirit christology" is that they all begin with this handful of texts, mostly obscure texts full of noto-rious exegetical difficulties, which can be demonstrated not to carry any of the weight they wish to give them. What is important here is that these texts, which serve as the starting point, also serve not simply as the primary basis but as the only basis for Paul's alleged "Spirit christology," as though it were clear to all who would read Paul. In turn, the clear and certain trinitarian texts are then either negated by disclaimers or in some cases not even considered at all. Thus they begin with what they assume Paul to be saying in a few obscure texts and either avoid or treat with diffidence what he unambiguously says elsewhere, and in all kinds of unmistakable ways.[49]

48. Which he does not in fact do very often: only here; 2 Cor. 13:5 (probably); Gal. 2:20; and Eph. 3:16. The passage in Col. 1:29 ("Christ in you the hope of glory") probably means, "Christ in you Gentiles."

49. Dunn, therefore, seems to work at cross-purposes with a methodology he has himself spoken against (*Baptism in the Holy Spirit*, SBT 15 [London: SCM, 1970], pp. 103-4). Cf. his simi-

Paul, on the other hand, began at a different point. Here is a thoroughgoing monotheist, whose encounter with Christ on the Damascus Road, and subsequent encounter with the Holy Spirit, forever radically altered his understanding of God and of his (now Christian) existence. At the heart of Pauline theology is his gospel, and his gospel is primarily *soteriology* — God's saving a people for his name through the redemptive work of Christ and the appropriating work of the Spirit. It is his encounter with God soteriologically — as Father, Son, and Holy Spirit — that accounts for the transformation of Paul's theological language and finally of his understanding of God — although this is simply never worked out at the level of immanent, or doxological, trinitarianism. In light of this reality and the preponderance of texts that support it — and do so with trinitarian language — one would think that these texts should serve as the methodological starting point, and that the more obscure ones should be interpreted in light of these, not the other way about.

That Paul's understanding of God had become functionally trinitarian and that the distinctions between Father, Son, and Spirit were presuppositional for him[50] may be demonstrated in three ways: the trinitarian texts themselves (2 Cor. 13:13; 1 Cor. 12:4-6; Eph. 4:4-6); the many soteriological texts that are expressed in trinitarian terms; and the passages in which in close proximity the *functions* of Christ and the Spirit are expressed in ways that presuppose clear distinctions.

(1) The grace-benediction with which Paul singularly concludes 2 Corinthians is so well known that it is easy to miss its several remarkable features: first, that Paul elaborates his concluding grace at all — which he does not do anywhere else, either in his earlier or later letters; second, that he does so with this trinitarian formulation, which appears here in such a presuppositional way — not as something Paul argues for, but as the assumed experienced reality of Christian life. That it is an *ad hoc* elaboration, and not part of the church's existing liturgical tradition, seems certain from its third remarkable feature: the order — Christ, God, and Spirit — which can only be explained because Paul began his standard benediction, and then felt compelled in this letter[51] to add words about the Father and the Spirit. That the three ex-

---

lar critique of Hermann in "II Corinthians iii.17," p. 309; yet he seems to turn about and do this very thing on the basis of his own exegesis of 1 Cor. 15:45 and Rom. 1:3-4.

50. On this whole question, and especially on Paul as a trinitarian, see the section entitled "What about the Trinity?" by D. Ford, in F. Young and D. Ford, *Meaning and Truth in 2 Corinthians* (Grand Rapids: Eerdmans, 1987), pp. 255-60.

51. This "compulsion" may be related to what Paul says in 11:4. By their insistence on Jewishness, those who were troubling the Corinthians had in effect offered them "another Jesus,"

pressions are precisely the Pauline understanding of the soteriological functions of the Trinity seems to clinch the matter.

The second feature in particular, its presuppositional nature — not to mention that this is said as a form of prayer — suggests that this is *the proper place to begin all discussions about Paul's understanding of God*. For here is a text that by its very off-handed, presuppositional expression reveals Paul's theology — both his theology proper and his soteriology, which is foundational for the former.

First, it serves to encapsulate what lies at the very heart of Paul's singular passion — the gospel, with its focus on salvation in Christ, equally available by faith to Gentile and Jew alike. That the *love of God* is the foundation of Paul's soteriology is expressly stated, with passion and clarity, in such passages as Rom. 5:1-11; 8:31-39; and Eph. 1:3-14. The *grace of our Lord Jesus Christ* is what gave concrete expression to that love; through Christ's suffering and death on behalf of his loved ones, God effected salvation for them at one point in our human history. The *participation in the Holy Spirit* expresses the ongoing appropriation of that love and grace in the life of the believer and the believing community. The κοινωνία τοῦ ἁγίου πνεύματος (note the full name!) is how the living God not only brings people into an intimate and abiding relationship with himself, as the God of all grace, but also causes them to participate in all the benefits of that grace and salvation, indwelling them in the present by his own presence, guaranteeing their final eschatological glory.

Second, this text also serves as our entrée into Paul's theology proper, that is, into his understanding of God himself, which had been so radically effected for him by the twin realities of the death and resurrection of Christ and the gift of the eschatological Spirit. Granted that Paul did not wrestle with the ontological questions that such statements beg to have addressed. Nor does he here *assert* the deity of Christ and the Spirit. But what he does is to *equate the activity of the three divine persons* (to use the language of a later time) *in concert and in one prayer,* with the clause about God the Father standing in second place. This would seem to suggest that Paul was truly trinitarian in any meaningful sense of that term — that the one God is Father, Son, and Spirit, and that in dealing with Christ and the Spirit one is dealing with God every bit as much as one is with God the Father.

Thus this benediction, with its affirmation of the distinctions of God, Christ, and Spirit, also expresses in shorthand form what is found everywhere

---

which in turn meant the reception of "another Spirit," both of which thereby denied Paul's preaching of the gospel. (See ch. 15, which follows.)

elsewhere in Paul, that "salvation in Christ" is in fact the cooperative work of God, Christ, and the Spirit. Such affirmations would seem to shut down all possibilities that Paul could ever identify the Risen Christ with the Spirit so that in Paul "immanent christology is pneumatology."[52]

(2) That this "soteriological trinitarianism" is foundational to Paul's understanding of the gospel is further evidenced by the large number of soteriological texts in which salvation is expressed in similar trinitarian formulation. This is especially true of the larger, explicit passages such as Rom. 5:1-8; 2 Cor. 3:1–4:6; Gal. 4:4-6; or Eph. 1:3-14 (cf. Titus 3:5-7). But it is also true of many other texts, primarily soteriological, in which salvation is either explicitly or implicitly predicated on the threefold work of the triune God, as encapsulated in 2 Cor. 13:13. Thus:

> *1 Thess. 1:4-5*, where the love of God has brought about the realization of election through the gospel (the message about Christ) empowered by the Holy Spirit.
>
> *2 Thess. 2:13*, where God's people are "beloved by the Lord [through his death]," because God elected them for salvation through the sanctifying work of the Spirit.
>
> *1 Cor. 1:4-7*, where God's grace has been given in Christ Jesus, who in turn has enriched the church with every kind of Spirit gifting.
>
> *1 Cor. 2:4-5*, where Paul's preaching of Christ crucified (v. 2) is accompanied by the Spirit's power so that their faith might rest in God.
>
> *1 Cor. 2:12*, where "we have received the Spirit that comes from God," so that we might know the things given to us ("in the cross" is implied in context) by God.
>
> *1 Cor. 6:11*, where God is the conceptual subject of the "divine passives" (you were washed, justified, sanctified), effected in the name of Christ and by the Spirit.

---

52. Cf. the two other most clearly trinitarian passages in the corpus: 1 Cor. 12:4-6 and Eph. 4:4-6. In the former, at the beginning of a long argument (12:4-30) urging the need for diversity (over against their apparently singular interest in glossolalia), Paul insists that such diversity reflects the character of God himself and is therefore the true evidence of the work of the one God in their midst. The trinitarian implications of these three sentences seem undeniable. In Eph. 4:4-6, another creedal formulation is expressed in terms of the distinguishable activities of the Triune God. The basis for Christian unity is God himself. The one body is the work of the one Spirit (cf. 1 Cor. 12:13); we live our present eschatological existence in one hope, effected for us by the one Lord, in whom all believe (= "one faith") and to which faith all have given witness through their "one baptism." The source of all these realities is the one God himself, "who is over all and through all and in all."

1 Cor. 6:19-20, where the believer has been purchased (by Christ; cf. 7:22-23) so as to become a temple for God's presence by the Spirit.

2 Cor. 1:21-22, where God is the one who has "confirmed" believers in a salvation effected by Christ, God's "Yes" (vv. 19-20), evidenced by his giving the Spirit as "down payment."

Gal. 3:1-5, where Christ crucified (v. 1, picking up on 2:16-21) is conveyed to believers by the Spirit, whom God "supplies" even yet among them (v. 5).

Rom. 8:3-4, where God sent his Son to do what the law could not in terms of securing salvation, and the Spirit does what the law could not in terms of effecting righteousness in behavior ("walking" = living the ways of God).

Rom. 8:15-17, where the God-given Spirit serves as evidence of "adoption" as children, and thus "joint-heirs" with Christ, who made it all possible.

Col. 3:16, where in worship it is all played in reverse — as the message of Christ "dwells richly among them," they worship the God from whom salvation has come, by means of a Spirit-inspired hymnody.

Eph. 1:17, where the God of our Lord Jesus Christ gives the Spirit of wisdom and revelation so that they may understand the full measure of the work of Christ in their behalf.

Eph. 2:18, where "through [the death of] Christ" (vv. 14-16) Jew and Gentile together have access to God by the one Spirit, whom both alike have received.

Eph. 2:20-22, where Christ is the "cornerstone" for the new temple, the place of God's dwelling by his Spirit.

Phil. 3:3, where believers serve (God is implied) by the Spirit of God and thus boast in the effective work of Christ Jesus.

(3) As final evidence that Paul is presuppositionally trinitarian and that he could never therefore have confused or "identified" the Risen Christ with the Spirit are several other kinds of (non-soteriological) texts, where the activities of the Risen Christ and the Spirit are clearly kept separate in the apostle's understanding. We have already noted this kind of distinction in Rom. 9:1, where the formula "in Christ" and "by the Spirit" functions quite differently — but characteristically — in one sentence. Similarly, in Rom. 15:30 ("through our Lord Jesus Christ and through the love of the Spirit") the repeated διά indicates that Paul's appeal has a twofold basis. First, it is "through our Lord Jesus Christ," meaning "on the basis of what Christ has done for us all as outlined in the argument of this letter"; second, it is "through the love

of the Spirit," meaning "on the basis of the love for all the saints, including myself, that the Spirit engenders."

Perhaps the most significant text in this regard, thinking only of passages where Christ and the Spirit appear in close approximation, is the combination of Rom. 8:26-27 (the Spirit intercedes for us) and 8:34 (Christ intercedes for us). On the surface one could argue for "identification" in function; but what one gets rather is the clearest expression not only of "distinction" but of the fact that the Risen Christ is *not* now understood by Paul to be identified with the Spirit. The role of the Spirit is on earth, indwelling believers so as to help them in the weakness of their present "already/not yet" existence and thereby to intercede in their behalf. The Risen Christ is "located" in heaven, "at the right hand of God, making intercession for us."[53] The latter text in particular, where Paul is not arguing for something but asserting it on the basis of presuppositional reality, would seem to negate altogether the idea that the Spirit in Paul's mind could possibly be identified with the Risen Christ, either ontologically or functionally, which means, of course, that there seems to be no warrant of any kind that Paul had a "Spirit christology."

VI

The net result of this study, therefore, is that Paul would not so much as recognize the language nor the theological assertions made by those who consider him to have had a Spirit christology. His presuppositions lay elsewhere, with the one God, now bringing salvation through the cooperative work of the three divine persons: God, Christ, and Spirit. At points where the work of any or all overlaps, so could Paul's language tend to be flexible — precisely because salvation for him was the activity of the one God. If his trinitarian presuppositions and formulations, which form the basis of the later formulations, never move toward calling the Spirit God and never wrestle with the ontological implications of his own presuppositions and formulations, there is no real evidence of any kind that he lacked clarity as to the distinctions between, and the specific roles of, the three divine persons who effected so great salvation for us all.

---

53. Cf. A. W. Wainwright, *The Trinity in the New Testament* (London: SPCK, 1962), p. 260.

CHAPTER 15

"Another Gospel Which You Did Not Embrace": 2 Corinthians 11:4 and the Theology of 1 and 2 Corinthians (1994)

It is fitting that a *Festschrift* in honor of my friend and sometime colleague,[1] Richard Longenecker, should focus on his lifelong allegiance, which is also that of the apostle Paul, to what Paul variously calls "the gospel of God"[2] (= from God), "the gospel of Christ"[3] (= about Christ), or "my gospel"[4] (= which I preach). Indeed, it does not take much reading of Paul's letters to recognize that the gospel is the singular passion of his life. That passion, I have suggested elsewhere,[5] holds the key to coherence in Pauline theology, despite the many contingencies that find expression in his letters. And that passion in particular is the glue that holds 1 and 2 Corinthians together. All other matters that

---

1. I have the distinct pleasure of working with Dick on the Committee for Biblical Translation (the NIV revision committee).

2. Six times in all (1 Thess. 2:2, 8, 9; 2 Cor. 11:7; Rom. 1:1; 15:16) (Note: Scripture citations in this paper will appear in their perceived chronological order; I include the disputed letters in these references, because to do otherwise is to prejudge what, for me at least, is still open for discussion).

3. Eleven times (1 Thess. 3:2; 2 Thess. 1:8; 1 Cor. 9:12; 2 Cor. 2:12; [4:4, where I understand "Christ" to be God's "glory"]; 9:13; 10:14; Gal. 1:7; Rom 1:9; 15:19; Phil. 1:27).

4. Five times (1 Thess. 1:5 ["our"]; 2 Thess. 2:24 ["our"]; 2 Cor. 4:3 ["our"]; Rom. 2:16; 16:25). Cf. "the gospel which I preach(ed)" (1 Cor. 15:1; 2 Cor. 11:7; Gal. 1:11; 2:2; cf. Eph. 3:6 ["the gospel of which I am a servant"]; and 1 Cor. 4:15 ["through the gospel I gave you birth"]).

5. See "Toward a Theology of 1 Corinthians," in *Pauline Theology,* II: *1 and 2 Corinthians,* ed. D. M. Hay (Minneapolis: Fortress Press, 1993), pp. 37-58 [see ch. 13 above]; cf. *God's Empowering Presence: The Holy Spirit in the Letters of Paul* (Peabody, Mass.: Hendrickson Publishers, 1994), pp. 11-13.

emerge as central to these letters — concern over distinctively Christian behavior, the reality and character of Paul's apostleship, the collection — find their significance in the gospel, or at least I will so argue in this paper.

In keeping with the invitation by the *Festschrift* editors, my essay focuses on "the theological aspects of 'gospel' in the Corinthian correspondence."[6] To get at that "theology," I propose: (I) to provide a preliminary sketch of Pauline usage to demonstrate that the gospel has consistent and definable *theological* content; (II) to suggest that 2 Cor. 11:4 holds the key to the basic issues raised in the second (canonical) letter; (III) to overview several key passages in the two letters as a way of demonstrating both the validity of my understanding of 2 Cor. 11:4 and the basic coherence of the theology of the gospel in both letters; and (IV) to suggest that this coherent content offers the key to understanding the contingent matters that find focus in 2 Corinthians.

I. Gospel in Paul

That the gospel lies at the heart of things for Paul needs no demonstration. That his gospel has definable (and consistent) content is illustrated by at least three factors:

1. In the most polemical letter in the corpus (Galatians), Paul on two occasions (2:5 and 2:14), in the context of controversy, refers to "the gospel I preach" (2:2) in terms of "the *truth* of the gospel." As the argument in context attests, this language does not mean "my preaching has integrity" — although it surely includes such — but that "the *content* of the gospel I preach contains the truth from God himself." In light of the argument of Galatians 3–6, it is unthinkable that Paul is not contending for a certain *understanding* of the gospel — theology, if you will — in using this language.

2. On two occasions, dictated in each case by the situation addressed, Paul offers minimal *content* to "the gospel I preached." First, in 1 Cor. 15:3-5, in an attempt to demonstrate the folly of the Corinthians' denial of a future bodily resurrection, he reminds them of the content of his gospel: that it included the *death* of Christ *for our sins* and his subsequent bodily resurrection. This is a minimal statement, to be sure, made so by the context, but it coheres with what we find everywhere else.

---

6. One should raise a proper caution at the outset that there is something inherently wrong in "theologizing" on Paul's gospel — even though he often does it himself in opposition to distortions of it. But for Paul the "gospel" had first of all to do with evangelism, with preaching Christ so that others believed on him, thus receiving the Spirit, and thereby becoming members of the newly constituted people of God.

Second, in Rom. 1:16-17, at the outset of an extended "argument" to congregations he does not know personally, Paul offers another minimal definition of his gospel: It has to do with God's power effecting *salvation,* offering righteousness, for all who trust in Christ Jesus. He surely intends the ensuing argument — to 15:13 — to flesh out this minimal definition. Whatever else, therefore, Paul's gospel is all about *salvation,* salvation in Christ.

3. When we add to these the considerable number of semi-creedal soteriological statements that surface throughout the corpus,[7] we can affirm further both that Paul's gospel had clearly defined content and that that content was consistent at its core. Especially significant here are (a) that no one of them is identical to the others,[8] (b) that most of them find expression not usually for their own (theological) sake, but to support another concern, and (c) that there is almost always an experiential dimension to what is affirmed theologically (the *experience* of salvation obviously transcends mere theologizing about it). Yet for all their variety, they express a consistent theological point of view, suggesting how deeply woven into Paul's consciousness is the basic *content* of his gospel.

There are several matters involved in Pauline soteriology, including, for example, (a) his "already/not yet" eschatological framework, (b) that God's salvation has "a people for God's name" as its goal, and (c) that God, through Christ and the Spirit, has established a new covenant with his people in which they "fulfill Torah" by walking in the Spirit. For Paul each of these is essential to his understanding of "salvation in Christ"; and each can be shown to pervade these two letters. But my concern in this essay is to focus on Paul's understanding of salvation per se — as wrought by God: Father, Son, and Holy Spirit. Here is what holds his gospel together in all of its particulars.

Paul's gospel is "God's gospel," first of all because Paul's theological roots are firmly secured in the OT; for him, therefore, the one God is ever and always the One "from whom are all things and we for him" (1 Cor. 8:6). God is

---

7. See esp. 1 Thess. 1:9-10; 5:9-10; 2 Thess. 2:13-14; 1 Cor. 6:11; 2 Cor. 1:21-22; 13:13; Gal. 4:4-7; Rom. 5:1-5; 8:3-4; 8:15-17; Eph. 1:13-14; 4:4-6; Titus 3:5-7. But see also many other such texts, soteriological or otherwise: 1 Cor. 1:4-7; 2:4-5; 6:19-20; 12:4-6; 2 Cor. 3:16-18; Gal. 3:1-5; Rom. 8:9-11; 15:16; 15:18-19; 15:30; Col. 3:16; Eph. 1:3; 1:17-20; 2:17-18; 2:19-22; 3:16-19; 5:18-19; Phil. 1:19-20; 3:3.

8. This is a feature that is often overlooked, but which is full of significance. That no two of them are alike and that they are consistent at their theological heart suggest that those who argue for "pre-formed" traditions as the "pool" from which Paul is drawing should perhaps rethink the ramifications of these arguments. One can scarcely doubt that such creedal affirmations may well have abounded in the early church; but their very variety in Paul makes more sense if Paul, however he may have been drawing on a common stock of traditional understanding, is himself finally responsible for the most of these in their present form.

thus the *initiator* of "salvation in Christ" and is almost always in Paul's sentences the subject of the "saving verbs." The *content* of "God's gospel" is Christ, crucified and risen; hence Paul's gospel is also "the gospel of Christ," the gospel that has Christ's saving death and life-giving resurrection at its heart. God put forth Christ as a "propitiation" and thus "justified the ungodly" (Rom. 3:25; 4:5). But since the event of Christ is primarily a historical reality that effected an objective, positional reality for people before the living God, enter the Spirit, whom "God [also] sent forth" (Gal. 4:6) so that those who become God's children through Christ's redemption may realize that redemption in their personal and corporate lives. Without the Spirit, there is no salvation in Christ, anymore than there would be without the work of Christ, precisely because it is through the Spirit that Christ's saving work becomes *experienced reality.*[9]

All of this is spelled out in laconic detail in Gal. 4:4-6, to isolate just one of the many soteriological texts noted above. At the propitious moment God first "sent forth his Son" into one distinct expression of our common human life (first-century Judaism; hence "born of woman, born under the law"), whose purpose was to "redeem" by affording "adoption as 'sons.'"[10] But that historical reality becomes experienced reality because God also "sent forth the Spirit of his Son into *our*[11] hearts, crying out *Abba,*" *the language of the* Son, thus offering certain evidence that we are also God's "sons," destined for divine inheritance (v. 7).

The emphases may change and the language alter from letter to letter; but the theology is ever the same: that God has executed a new covenant with

---

9. We should note, by way of reminder as to Paul's central focus on Christ, that every soteriological statement in Paul includes a mention of Christ. In some rare instances, because of emphasis in context, he can mention Christ alone (e.g., 1 Cor. 15:3-5). Sometimes he refers to salvation in terms of God and Christ without mentioning the Spirit (e.g., 1 Thess. 1:9-10; 5:9-10; 2 Cor. 5:21). But most often, especially when the focus is on the believers' *experience* of salvation, the passage is inherently or explicitly trinitarian. What Paul cannot bring himself to do is to speak of the work of the Spirit without also mentioning the work of Christ. Thus, even in passages like Rom. 8:1-4 or 9-11, or 2 Cor. 1:21-22 and 3:1–4:6 discussed below, where the focus of the argument is on the work of the Spirit, Paul cannot describe this role without also bringing the work of Christ into the argument. The Spirit is obviously not peripheral for Paul, but neither is he the center. The Spirit takes his place near the center next to Christ, but never in the center itself.

10. It is very difficult to translate v. 5 without using the language "sons" here, since the whole passage plays on the fact that God's new children ("sons") are evidenced to be so because the Spirit uses the language of *the* Son *(Abba)* in prayer.

11. The subtle shift from second or third person to first plural is a regular feature of these soteriological moments in Paul. Theology and confession go hand in hand for him.

his people, effected historically through the death and resurrection of Christ, and realized in the life of his people by the reception of the Spirit. We now turn to a demonstration of this in 1 and 2 Corinthians.

II. 1 and 2 Corinthians

One of the ongoing puzzles of Pauline studies is the relationship of Paul's two canonical letters to the church in Corinth. The problem, of course, is that when turning to 2 Corinthians from 1 Corinthians, one has the sense of entering a new world. Except for the collection,[12] none of the issues raised in the earlier letter visibly surfaces here. But this sense of newness turns out to be a surface reading of the two letters. What holds them together are not the specific issues addressed in each, but an overriding tension over Paul's apostleship, and thus over his authority and that of his gospel.[13]

Part of this problem relates to a factor that scarcely emerges in 1 Corinthians, if at all. The problems between Paul and this church that had surfaced at the writing of 1 Corinthians seem largely to have been at the instigation of a few within the community itself.[14] The letter, therefore, is addressed to the community as a whole, always in the second person plural,[15] and with scarcely a hint that there are outsiders who might make up part of the problem.[16]

But in both letters that form our 2 Corinthians[17] (chs. 1–9, 10–13) all of this has changed. Outsiders first surface in 2:14–4:6, where Paul refers to some "peddlers of the word" (2:17) who "need letters of commendation" (3:1), in

---

12. See 2 Corinthians 8–9; cf. 1 Cor. 16:1-11.

13. For a very helpful discussion in this regard, see F. Young and D. F. Ford, *Meaning and Truth in 2 Corinthians* (Grand Rapids: Eerdmans, 1987), pp. 44-52.

14. Note, e.g., "each of you says" (1:11); "some [of you] are puffed up as though I were not coming to you" (4:18); "how can some among you say" (15:12).

15. Except for a few instances where he reverts to the second person singular, so as to make his point even more telling.

16. The closest thing to it is found in 9:12, "if others share in your material benefits, should not we do so the more?" In the context of 1 Corinthians, especially since there is no other hint of outsiders being currently present among them, the "others" in this text most likely refers to Apollos and Cephas, when they were among them (cf. 9:4-6). Cf. the discussion in G. D. Fee, *The First Epistle to the Corinthians* (NICNT; Grand Rapids: Eerdmans, 1987), pp. 7-8, 409-10.

17. Although I am among the many who think this way about our canonical 2 Corinthians, I am also of a mind that the two letters were written in close proximity to each other, and that the second carries on the conversation found in the first in a more vigorous way. Hence the two letters easily form one in overall design, even if not in actual time of writing. Thus 2 Corinthians will be treated as a unit in this study.

contrast to whom Paul "does not use deception or distort the word of God" (4:2). The primary urgency of this contrast is found in 3:3-11 and 16-18: Paul's ministry and its effectiveness in Corinth is of the Spirit, theirs is of "letter" (= Torah observance).[18] This conflict emerges full blown in chs. 10–13, where Paul accuses these outsiders of preaching "another Jesus" and the Corinthians of receiving "another Spirit" and "accepting another gospel" (11:4). The purveyors of this "different gospel" are "Satan's servants, masquerading as servants of righteousness" (v. 14; cf. 3:9; 5:21).

a. 2 Corinthians 11:4

This passage is beset with difficulties, related in part to three other — not easily reconciled — phenomena in this letter: (1) that the opponents are Jewish Christians,[19] who apparently are pressing for some form of "Jewishness," in the form of Torah observance, as part of their understanding of the gospel;[20] (2) that there are nonetheless no direct attacks against the *content* of their teaching;[21] (3) that the clear majority of the content of 2 Corinthians has to do with Paul's understanding of *apostleship* over against theirs, where the contrast is between triumphalism, including revelatory experiences,[22]

18. See my full discussion of this passage in *Presence,* pp. 286-311; see also, on this meaning of "letter," S. Westerholm, "'Letter' and 'Spirit': The Foundation of Pauline Ethics," *NTS* 30 (1984): 229-48.

19. This is made certain by the rhetoric of 11:22-23a ("Are they Hebrews? So am I. Are they Israelites? So am I. Are they descendants of Abraham? So am I"). That they are Jewish *Christians* — despite Paul's rhetoric — is attested by the last question ("Are they servants of Christ? I am a better one").

20. This is verified both by the argument of 3:1-18 (where the key contrast is between the "new covenant of Spirit" and the former covenant of "letter" only, which failed to lead to righteousness, and thus dealt in death not life) and 11:14 (that the insurgents' aim to be "servants of righteousness," even though from Paul's perspective this is mere "masquerade"). To describe what they were presenting as an expression of "Jewishness" is not intended to be pejorative, but simply to find a word that covers this side of the difficulty, a difficulty exacerbated by the fact that the word νόμος does not appear in this letter — although the contrast between the old and new covenants does.

21. Although several theological moments in this letter are best understood as over against the opponents, one cannot be sure by such "mirror reading" whether, or how much of, what Paul says is in direct theological response to them.

22. This is made certain by the combination of 5:12 ("they boast in externals"; cf. 10:7) and 12:1-10, where with biting irony he affirms that he has indeed had "visions and revelations," while at the same time making clear that such experiences have no validity as authenticating apostolic ministry.

and Paul's "weaknesses," through which "Christ's power" is revealed (12:9-10).[23]

How then, in light of all this, are we to understand 11:4, which is generally agreed to be a key sentence? In a clear attempt to shame the Corinthians into seeing things his way, Paul expostulates: "For indeed if the one who comes preaches another Jesus whom we did not preach, or you receive a different Spirit whom you did not receive, or a different gospel which you did not embrace, you put up with it well enough." Three matters are debated: (a) how we are to interpret the three phrases of this passage in relationship to each other, and thus (b) whether the emphasis falls on the first, middle, or final item;[24] and (c) what, therefore, Paul intends by "another Jesus."[25]

Regarding the related matters: several converging pieces of evidence from the letter point to a simple solution regarding their simultaneous "Jewishness" and triumphalism. First, the primary "content" of their false gospel most likely has to do not with christology per se but, as elsewhere, with soteriology; but, secondly, where the insurgents have found common cause with the Corinthians is by striking the chord of triumphalism, not in terms of christology but of authentication of ministry. After all, the Corinthians them-

23. The emphasis throughout 2 Corinthians obviously lies here, both in the *apologia* and polemics of this letter. In light of the corresponding argumentation in 1 Cor. 1:18–4:21, this view of apostleship must be understood in terms of the "weakness" of "Christ crucified"; nonetheless, Paul makes very little of that in this letter until the end (13:3-4).

24. Most scholars (see next note) take it to fall on "another Jesus"; E. Käsemann on the middle item (see "Die Legitimität des Apostels: Eine Untersuchung zu 2 Korinther 10–13," *ZNW* 41 [1942]: 33-71); I will argue for the final item.

25. The bibliography here is large. See esp. the discussion in J. L. Sumney, *Identifying Paul's Opponents: The Question of Method in 2 Corinthians* (JSNTSup 40; Sheffield: JSOT Press, 1990), pp. 15-67, who discusses the proponents of the various views under the rubrics of Judaizers (F. C. Baur, D. Oostendorp, C. K. Barrett, J. Gunther, G. Lüdemann), Gnostics (W. Schmithals), Divine men (D. Georgi, G. Friedrich), and Pneumatics (E. Käsemann). More recently, see J. Murphy-O'Connor, "Another Jesus (2 Cor 11.4)," *RB* 97 (1990): 238-51, who understands the opponents to have created "another Jesus" in order to get around the crucified Jesus preached by Paul. This would seem to move in the right direction, but still makes too much of one's ability to identify the *content* of the false teaching by Paul's language here. Both Georgi and Murphy-O'Connor rest their case on Paul's use of "Jesus," as though by using this designation he "means" something that he might not have meant had he said "Christ" or "Christ Jesus." But this becomes problematic if one considers the alternatives. Had Paul said "another Christ" some would tie it to 1 Cor. 1:12 and have a heyday with that as well; and any compound form of the name (Jesus Christ, Christ Jesus) would be thoroughly un-Pauline with this verb. I would agree that the use of "Jesus" here reflects the usage in 4:10, and thus probably emphasizes the earthly Jesus who died. But it is difficult to sustain that this means anything different from his use of "preaching Christ" in 1 Cor. 15:12 or Phil. 1:15-18, in which instances he clearly means "preach the gospel which has Christ's death and resurrection as its primary content."

selves had already tried to do an end run around the cross and its implications for discipleship; they scarcely needed outsiders to teach them to do this. What the outsiders find in the triumphalistic view of ministry already present in Corinth is a beachhead from which to pursue their understanding of Christ that includes Gentile adherence to Torah as an integral component.

Moreover, despite the rhetoric of 11:21–12:18, at issue for Paul is not his apostleship alone, and especially it is not a matter of rival claimants to Corinthian affections. At issue, as always, is the gospel, and the gospel has to do with "*salvation* in Christ," which for Paul presupposes christology (that "God sent forth his Son") but focuses primarily on soteriology.[26] This seems to be verified by the argument of 11:1-15, including v. 4. Paul's jealousy is God's own (v. 2) — to present the Corinthians as a "pure virgin" to her betrothed (= the church to Christ at his Parousia). But as Eve was deceived, so too they are being led astray; their virginity is being sullied. Our verse appears at this point, not to point to the content of the false teaching but to specify what has happened to the Corinthians in following these outsiders. In coming onto Paul's turf and currying the favor of the Corinthians (10:7-8), the insurgents are ultimately leading them astray from the gospel of Christ to something that from his perspective is no gospel at all.[27] Several matters support this interpretation.

1. The problem with starting one's interpretation with "another Jesus" is that there is no hint either in this text or in the ensuing argument that a false christology is at issue. What must be stressed is that Paul does not follow up on this phrase, either here or later. Indeed, the only hint in what follows as to content appears in the accusation that the insurgents masquerade as "servants of righteousness" (v. 15); and this is how Paul has already described the essential character of his own ministry of the new covenant (3:5-11), as "life-giving" through the work of the Spirit, a ministry that has "brought righteousness" (3:9 NIV) precisely because "God made [Christ] . . . to be sin for us, so that in him we might become the righteousness of God" (5:21).

---

26. *Pace* Georgi, Murphy-O'Connor, and Schmithals; cf. R. P. Martin (*2 Corinthians,* [WBC: Waco, Tex., 1986], p. 336), "the issue is basically a christological one." That is bold indeed, considering that christology is neither pursued in this argument, nor does it emerge as such throughout 2 Corinthians. There is a sense, of course, in which one cannot have soteriology without christology. Who Christ is, for Paul, makes his salvation work at all. But in terms of focus and argument, this element is missing from both of these letters.

27. Cf. the language of Gal. 1:6-9, where the "agitators" are also accused of preaching a "different gospel." For a similar assessment as to what can be gleaned about the content of these opponents' preaching, see V. Furnish, *II Corinthians* (AB 32A; Garden City, N.Y.: Doubleday, 1984), p. 500.

2. The key to this passage, therefore, lies not in interpreting the second and third item in light of the first,[28] but the other way about, in seeing the third as the key to the whole, and the second as the clear evidence that all three together have to do with the *fact* of their capitulation to a false gospel, not with its *content*. Two points need emphasis.

First, the awkwardness of the syntax indicates that the primary concern in the text is less on what the insurgents are teaching and more on *what is now happening to the Corinthians* as a result of this teaching, and this in light of their first *experience* of the gospel, which plays the lie to their present fascination with this false gospel. Flowing directly out of vv. 2-3, the sentence begins with a contrast between the opponents' preaching and Paul's own. But since the concern is over what is happening to the Corinthians, he shifts from "if *the one who comes* preaches," to "or *you receive* another Spirit whom you did not receive; or *you embrace* another gospel which you did not embrace." Not only so, but the three contrasting verbs ("we preached," "you received," "you accepted") are all aorists and clearly point to their *experience of conversion*.[29] Just as in 1 Cor. 2:1-5, through what "we preached" ("Christ crucified") the Corinthians "received the Spirit," which for Paul equals their having "accepted" his gospel. Thus, what is going on among them now is in obvious contrast to their first encounter with Christ and the Spirit through Paul's preaching of the gospel.

Second, all kinds of evidence demonstrate that what we encounter in this passage are the essential matters for Paul with regard to the gospel — Christ and the Spirit.[30] For Paul, authentic Christian life is the combined result of Jesus, who is "preached," and the Spirit, who is "received." This combination alone makes up the genuine embracing of the gospel. Thus, as elsewhere in Paul, preaching "Jesus" refers to the proclamation of the saving event itself, and all that Christ provided for us through his death.[31] The

28. Contra Murphy-O'Connor, "Another Jesus," p. 240.

29. A point also made by Murphy-O'Connor ("Another Jesus," p. 239), although he moves in a slightly different direction with it.

30. Cf. R. P. C. Hanson, *2 Corinthians* (TBC; London: SCM Press, 1967), p. 79: "Notice St Paul's three-word summary of Christianity — Jesus, Spirit, Gospel."

31. D. Georgi (*The Opponents of Paul in Second Corinthians* [Philadelphia: Fortress Press, 1986], pp. 271-77) and Murphy-O'Connor ("Another Jesus," pp. 241-48) argue that Paul uses "Jesus" only when referring to his earthly life. But this distinction simply does not work out in Paul, except by otherwise strained exegesis (as, e.g., in 1 Cor. 5:4-5). *Pace* Murphy-O'Connor, the "death of Jesus" and "the life of Jesus" in 2 Cor. 4:10 refer to Christ's saving death and resurrection respectively (so Furnish, Barrett, Martin, and most commentaries). It is difficult to make this mean anything different from "Christ died for us," except that the former may well focus on his death as a human. But its atoning significance is clearly in view in this passage even so.

"Spirit" refers to the actual appropriation, the actualization of the saving event. This reality is what best explains the apparently unusual order, in which the gospel is mentioned last — so as to clarify the first two items as the essential matters with regard to the gospel.

Therefore, it is not that the opponents were actually preaching a different Jesus as such; rather, by their introducing the old covenant (as we may assume from 3:1-18), the net result is "another Jesus" from the one Paul preached, in this case a preaching of Jesus that included Torah observance, which is tantamount to the Corinthians' "receiving *another* Spirit," not because there is in fact another one, but precisely because the Spirit whom they received through Paul's preaching of Christ had freed them from any possible commitments to the now obsolete older covenant (3:17-18).

3. Thus the significance of the middle member. The mention of the Spirit as "received" (= experienced) by the Corinthians is what makes the use of the term "another Jesus" as a component of the false teaching a dubious exercise at best. To be sure, some have suggested otherwise, that πνεῦμα here refers to something attitudinal or to some aspect of Christian lifestyle;[32] but that will hardly do in this argument. Against it is (a) that the mention of Spirit comes between Jesus and gospel; in such a context it is difficult to imagine that it will bear some meaning unrelated to the other two; and (b) that the verb "received," which Paul uses elsewhere for the reception of the Holy Spirit,[33] hardly goes well with any other understanding of the word πνεῦμα. How does one "receive" some aspect of Christian lifestyle or attitude, one wonders? Paul, therefore, does not think of them as actually receiving another "spirit,"[34] that is, a demonic spirit, or the "spirit of the world," or a "bad attitude." After all, just as there is not actually another Jesus than the one Lord Jesus Christ, so there is only one Spirit, the Holy Spirit. Moreover, in the context of this letter and of this church, the Spirit is absolutely crucial to the argument. Whatever else, the Corinthians were into Spirit. What jars Paul is

32. See, e.g., the commentaries by Plummer (p. 297), Hughes (p. 378), Carson (pp. 87-88), Martin (p. 336). Both Martin's reason for going this way (otherwise it assumes that "we would have to suppose that they had a heterodox . . . Trinitarian teaching") and his attempt to make sense of "spirit" (as "the effects of Christian living seen in outward deportment") point out the difficulties with this position — and the basic error in presupposing that content is what is involved.

33. See Rom. 8:15; 1 Cor. 2:12; Gal. 3:2.

34. In this regard cf. the discussion in Fee, *Presence* (pp. 26-28) on "a spirit of . . ." in Paul, especially in the three texts that are set up by the negative contrasts, "not a spirit of, but the Spirit," in which he certainly does not intend in the first part to suggest that there is "another spirit" that people receive (1 Cor. 2:12; Rom. 8:13; 2 Tim. 1:7). Rather, he intends, "in receiving the Spirit of God, you did not receive this negative characteristic."

that Spirit people have now let themselves be turned aside to that which has nothing at all to do with the Spirit.[35]

Finally, although Paul makes no point of it, it is significant for our present purposes to note the trinitarian substructure that Paul here presupposes. We have already noted the role of Christ and the Spirit; that God the Father lies behind all of this is to be found in the language "the Spirit you received," which in Paul always presupposes God's "sending the Spirit," plus the fact that in v. 7 he explicitly refers to the gospel he preached as "God's gospel."

In light of this understanding of this passage, and it seems to make the best sense of the argument in context, our next task is to show that precisely these concerns also lie at the heart of most of the significant, more purely theological moments, in these two letters. We begin with 1 Corinthians.[36]

b. 1 Corinthians 1:17–2:16[37]

Most scholars (rightly) recognize this as the key theological passage to the whole of the Corinthian correspondence, arguably to the whole of the Pauline corpus. My aim here is not to examine the passage in detail, but to focus on three particulars: (1) that this is a soteriological, not christological, argument; (2) that its trinitarian substructure is essential to the argument; and (3) that the focus on Christ, which is first of all soteriological, functions also as paradigm, which is the dimension of the gospel that in particular gives unity to the "contingent theology" of these two letters.

1. As this central argument reveals, at issue in 1 Corinthians 1–4 is not simply "division in the name of leaders," but quarreling carried on in the name of *sophia*. In contrast to their new-found "wisdom," which was both "heady" and (apparently) πνεῦμα-oriented, Paul and his gospel came in a distant second. Thus, at the outset Paul sets forth three realities from their Christian origins which stand in utter contradiction to their present fascination with *sophia*: the *content* of the message by which they came to faith, the gospel of a "crucified Messiah" (1:18-25); the *people* who make up the redeemed community in Corinth — the Corinthian believers themselves, the "not many wise, influential, and well-born" (1:26-31); the *preaching* that brought them to faith, namely, Paul's, which was confessedly done in weak-

---

35. This, of course, is precisely the argument of 3:1-18 and Gal. 3:1-5.

36. In this brief space we cannot look at all of these, but those discussed will be easily recognized as among the more important theological moments in these two letters.

37. For the exegetical judgments supporting the observations made here and in the next passage see Fee, *1 Corinthians*.

ness and had nothing to do with rhetoric and "wisdom" but everything to do with the Spirit's power (2:1-5).

Throughout this argument the focus is on God's saving event — through the Crucified One. Though some would see a "wisdom christology" at work in 1:24, that is not even remotely so, at least not as christology per se. God's "wisdom" lies in the utterly contradictory nature of his choice of saving event, which stands over against human wisdom and power in every way. Thus "Christ *crucified*" — not just Christ in himself — is God's power and God's wisdom. That no one has come forward with a "*dynamis* christology," which after all is the first designation of Christ in v. 24, is sure evidence that neither does Paul here intend a "wisdom christology."[38] Moreover, in v. 30 Paul deliberately historicizes *sophia* by placing righteousness (δικαιοσύνη), holiness (ἁγιασμός), and redemption (ἀπολύτρωσις) in apposition to wisdom (σοφία). This is how God put Christ forth as "wisdom for us," by making him to be our righteousness, sanctification, and redemption.[39] Nothing could more clearly demonstrate that the issue is not christology, but soteriology.

Finally, of course, this is quite the point of the often abused passage in 2:6-16, where Paul turns the tables on the Corinthians by appealing to their experience of the Spirit. Instead of bringing them into some kind of heady *sophia*, the Spirit instead has revealed what merely human wisdom could not know — that God chose to redeem us by means of the cross. This is what the Spirit has plainly revealed, Paul argues, and if they were truly "Spirit people," as they claim and rightly are, they should have recognized the folly of their present stance and the "wisdom" of Paul's gospel.

2. The trinitarian substructure to this argumentation also needs pointing out. First, the passage is thoroughly theocentric, from beginning to end. The message of the cross is God's wisdom and God's power for "us[40] who are being saved." God chose such "weakness" and "foolishness" precisely so that he could circumvent, and thereby overturn, the wisdom of this world. Those who believe are those whom "God has called," and in doing so he chose the world's nobodies — the Corinthians themselves — as Exhibit A that his salvation is not in keeping with the *sophia* of the present age. And their experience of God's salvation came through the Spirit's power, not through wisdom

---

38. And in any case, *sophia* is a Corinthian word, which Paul is merely picking up and re-applying so as to destroy their understanding of "wisdom" altogether. (See now ch. 21 below.)

39. These three words function not to illustrate a kind of *ordo salutis* in Paul but as metaphors, which together exhibit (in some measure) the richness of God's saving work in Christ. Cf. the discussion of 6:11 below.

40. Note again the shift to the first plural as theology approaches confession (cf. n. 11, above).

(σοφία), and word (λόγος), so that their faith might rest finally in God's power — as exhibited through the cross.

Second, God's gospel is all about Christ, who through crucifixion obtained eternal redemption for those who believe in him. Thus the passage is as thoroughly christocentric as it is theocentric. A crucified Messiah, God's ultimate oxymoron, is God's wisdom and power. Christ is God's own brand of *sophia,* who became for us God's means of salvation (i.e., righteousness, sanctification, and redemption). Thus the one who now boasts in the Lord (Jer. 9:23) boasts in Christ Jesus.

As 2:4-5 make plain, all of this, thirdly, became an experienced reality for them through the Spirit, God's power at work through Paul's own weaknesses, causing them to believe in Christ and transforming them into God's people in Corinth. Thus, whatever else, the Spirit does not lead to triumphalism; rather the Spirit reveals the wisdom in God's foolishness, so that "we might know the things graciously given to us (in Christ) by God" (2:12). The Spirit alone marks off God's people from the rest of humankind, so that our "wisdom" is of a radically different kind from theirs. And this leads to the third matter.

3. It is equally important both to this argument and to the whole of this letter — and 2 Corinthians as well — that the crucifixion is not only God's means of salvation, but the paradigm of all truly Christian life as well. Since the cross is the ultimate expression of God's wisdom in the world, one should not think that it had its time only in the historic event. On the contrary, the cross forever marks the people of God, who live by the gospel that has the cross as its central reality. This finds expression in a variety of ways in the present argument — and throughout.

This is what Paul is already setting them up for in 2:1-5 — his coming in weakness and preaching "Christ crucified" together bear witness to God's "wisdom." This is revealed by the Spirit, so that the truly πνευματικοί (= Spirit people) might understand God and his ways — that the cross is the only paradigm of God's activity in the world. This is further the role of Paul's glorying in his hardships in his apostolic defense in ch. 4. They became believers through the one who is like "the rubbish of the world, the dregs of all things" (4:13 NRSV); and they are to "imitate [Paul]," who is sending Timothy precisely so as to remind them of "my ways *in the Lord.*"

This motif, of course, becomes so thoroughgoing in 2 Corinthians that it serves as the predominant expression of "contingent theology" in this letter. But one reads 2 Corinthians poorly, and this motif in the letter in particular, who does not do so in light of 1 Cor. 1:17–2:16.

c. 1 Corinthians 6:11

I include this text as the primary illustration in this letter of the brief soteriological passages noted above. My concern is to point out (1) its trinitarian substructure, (2) its rich diversity of metaphors (as in 1:30) to describe the saving event, and (3) the predominant role of the experience of salvation in such a text.

The trinitarian presuppositions of Pauline soteriology are most easily seen by a structural display of this passage, which will also help in our further discussion (the "translation" is my own and is intentionally "literal"):

> And
> these things [vv. 9-10] some of you were;
>   but   you were washed
>   but   you were sanctified
>   but   you were made righteous[41]
>   by the name of our Lord Jesus Christ
>   and
>   by the Spirit of our God

God the Father is the assumed subject of the saving verbs, which in this case appear in the "divine passive." Because the emphasis lies with their *experience* of salvation, "you" is the grammatical subject of the clauses; but the conceptual subject is God. Thus: but God washed you, but God sanctified you, but God made you righteous. This passage is not theocentric as others are (see 2 Cor. 1:21-22 below), but God, as always, is the presuppositional initiator and protagonist of their salvation.

Of greater theological moment in this passage is the dual role played by Christ and the Spirit. As displayed above, the two prepositional phrases are to be understood as together modifying the three clauses, which means that the ἐν in both cases is primarily instrumental.[42] This means further that "you were washed" is not a metaphor for baptism in this instance;[43] rather, they were "washed" (from the sins previously mentioned), "sanctified" (set apart

---

41. This translation of ἐδικαιώθητε is not so much an attempt to resolve the long-standing debate over this term as to make sure by translation that one recognizes the clear recall of the same metaphor (as a noun) in 1:30.

42. I say "primarily" because I am among those who think watertight distinctions between "instrumental" and "locative of sphere" can seldom be maintained. While the emphasis is almost always on one or the other, the companion idea usually lurks very close by.

43. That is, Paul is not saying that they had been "baptized" in the name of Jesus.

for God's purposes so as no longer to pursue these sins), and "made righteous" (given right standing with God and thus set on the path of righteousness) by the work of Christ,[44] and realized by the Spirit.

Thus, as in 1:30, Paul appropriates a triad of metaphors to express how rich and expansive is God's work on their behalf through Christ. He repeats two of the three metaphors from 1:30, but substitutes "washing" for "redemption" in this instance for obviously ad hoc reasons. The result is yet another soteriological moment, whose clear focus in this case is on the Corinthians' *experience* of this multifaceted and — because of the Spirit — effectual work of God through Christ.

This is what the gospel is all about for Paul — here and everywhere: God himself effecting salvation through Christ and making it an experienced reality through the Spirit.

III. Theological Issues in 2 Corinthians

When we turn to 2 Corinthians, we find more of the same. At issue throughout is soteriology. Even Paul's apostleship — *especially* his apostleship, both its reality and its cruciform quality — are ultimately subservient to the gospel; and the gospel is all about God's saving activity, effected through Christ and appropriated through the Spirit. We briefly note two texts (1:18-22; 13:13), which in effect frame the letter in its present form, plus the crucial theological passage in 3:1–4:6. Together these passages embrace the concerns of this letter; and together, along with the rest of the whole letter, support our understanding of 11:4 as summarizing Paul's gospel, which the insurgents are bidding fair to bring to nothing in Corinth. Christology is not at issue; rather, as always, it is "salvation in Christ."

a. 2 Corinthians 1:18-22

This remarkable passage sets the tone for the entire epistle. At stake is Paul's integrity, first over his recent (second) change of itinerary, but more significantly regarding his apostolic ministry altogether. His change of announced plans to return to Corinth after traveling to Macedonia, returning to Ephesus

44. "Name" here signifies "authority," meaning that by the authority of what Christ had done for them on the cross, they have experienced these saving realities as these were brought to bear in their lives by God's own empowering presence, the Holy Spirit.

instead, has apparently fueled the fires of his Corinthian detractors, now supported by some outside opposition. Paul can be no apostle of the truth that is in Christ, since he so obviously says both "yes" and "no" out of the same side of his mouth.

Therefore, precisely because his apostleship is at stake, Paul feels compelled not simply to explain himself, but also to establish his integrity — ultimately on theological grounds. Thus the strange and, to us, apparently convoluted nature of the present argument. He begins by giving the reason for the first change of plans (vv. 15-16), insisting that that plan had not in fact been made with levity nor did changing it mean duplicity on his part (v. 17).

With that he launches into a singular theological vindication of his integrity in which he is intent to tie his "words" (about itineraries, etc.) to his "word" (his preaching of the gospel), and thus to God's own faithfulness, as that has been revealed in Christ his Son and in the gift of the Spirit. This is bold stuff indeed. Its various pieces tell the theological story:

1. The opening declaration (v. 18a, "God is faithful") is the boldest of all. Paul's integrity (and apostleship) is predicated first of all on God's trustworthiness.

2. God's faithfulness is what guarantees Paul's "word" to them (v. 18b). A wordplay is in progress here: in its first sense this guaranteed "word" is that of vv. 15-17; but that is only first blush. The real "word" that validates all other "words" is his preaching of Christ, which is the true "word" that is "to them" (v. 18) and was preached "among them" (v. 19).

3. The clear evidence that Paul's "word" is trustworthy is to be found in the faithful God's Son, whom Paul (and his companions) preached so effectively in Corinth. The "for" with which v. 19 begins is explanatory, or evidential. Thus, "for the Son of God, Jesus Christ, whom we preached, is himself God's yes," not only to his own promises, but by implication also to Paul's "word."

4. Indeed, he will explain further (v. 20a), in apparent anticipation of ch. 3 (and 11?), all the promises God made to Israel have found their divine "yes" in Christ. There is nothing more to be had. This, it must be pointed out, altogether presupposes soteriology.

5. Not only so, he adds (v. 20b), but in our corporate worship it is "through Christ" that we (both Paul and the Corinthians) affirm God's trustworthy word, found in Christ and preached by us, by saying the "Amen" to God, unto his eternal glory.

6. Finally, he concludes (vv. 21-22), the same trustworthy God, whose Son is his "yes" to his promises, is the one who confirms me; and not only

me, but you as well. This present confirmation is the outflow of his having already "anointed" us, that is, his having "sealed" us by giving us the Holy Spirit as his down payment on our sure future.

Here is one of the most God-centered, God-focused paragraphs in the Pauline corpus. As such it is a clear reflection of Paul's essential theology, the more telling because it is such an "off-the-cuff," non-reflective moment. Paul's integrity — and their own existence in Christ that is so integrally tied up with that integrity[45] — ultimately rests in the *character* of God (his trustworthiness, all of whose promises have been realized in Christ) and in the *saving activity* of God, which is but an outflow of his character. Thus, as always in Paul, God's own character stands as both the ground and initiative of his saving activity, which was effected historically by his Son and appropriated in the lives of believers by his Spirit, who is also the present guarantor of the final eschatological glory.

Thus, Paul *theologically* confirms his integrity, and with that his apostleship, in a remarkable soteriological moment, fully trinitarian in its presuppositions as well as in its composition. Again he appeals to their own experience of God's salvation, as the combined work of Christ and the Spirit, as the sure evidence. This is the beginning of his response to their being seduced by those who offer "another Jesus" and "another Spirit," other than the Jesus and Spirit they already know and have experienced through Paul's own proclamation of the gospel.

b. 2 Corinthians 2:14–4:6

In many ways this passage, Paul's first defense of his apostleship vis-à-vis his opponents, is the theological crux of this letter. As with 1 Cor. 1:17–2:16 the passage is much too long for detailed analysis. What is crucial for us here is: (1) that it has clearly been composed vis-à-vis the "peddlers" mentioned in 2:17; (2) that even though the focus is on Paul's ministry in contrast to theirs, in terms both of its origins and effectiveness, the crucial moments are theological, not apologetic; and (3) that the passage is ultimately soteriological, not christological, as the central role played by the Spirit in the argument makes plain.[46]

45. A point that is often made in the two extant letters to this congregation. See e.g., 1 Cor. 4:14-17; 9:1-2; and in our present letter especially 3:1-3 and 13:1-10.

46. It is of some interest to note how (apparently) studiously Georgi avoids this passage in making his case for a *theios anēr* christology on the part of Paul's opponents. The argumenta-

To be sure, there is very little direct reflection on the saving event itself — although it is presupposed at the beginning by the imagery of Paul's being a captive in Christ's "triumphal procession," a passage that deliberately echoes 1 Cor. 4:9 and thereby pushes back to the crucified Messiah in 1:18-25. It is further presupposed by the various images from the "triumph" in 2:14-16: he everywhere spreads the fragrance of the knowledge of Christ (v. 14), which the imagery in v. 15 confirms to be soteriological (Paul is the aroma of Christ for salvation/judgment). The same presupposition undergirds the language of 4:1-6, where the unusual language has been set up by the imagery of 3:17-18, but the repeated emphasis on the gospel itself makes clear that we are not dealing with christology as such, but with soteriology.

What is most significant about this passage is the central role played by the Spirit, especially so in light of the Corinthians' apparently triumphalistic view of Spirit life. In contrast both to their triumphalism and the opponents' appeal (apparently) to Moses, and thereby to a continuation of Torah during the time of the new covenant, Paul's response is twofold: First, the Spirit — whom they "received" (11:4) through Paul's own preaching (1 Cor. 2:4-5; 2 Cor. 3:3) — has freed them from the "veil," which in this argument moves from Moses' face in the Exodus passage to the hearts of those who still persist in following Torah. Instead of having "veiled" hearts and thus being "veiled" from God's presence, "when anyone [now] turns to the Lord the veil has been removed [by the Spirit]" (vv. 16-17), so that by the same Spirit they have been ushered into God's very presence, there both to behold his glory (in the face of his Son, 4:4-6) and to be transformed into his likeness. While the passage is full of significance for Pauline pneumatology, at issue is soteriology. The Spirit means freedom — from the "veil" of Torah observance and from the "veil" that keeps people from beholding God's face (now in Christ).

Second, and this is the crucial point for Paul, as the Spirit transforms God's new covenant people into Christ's likeness, he does so in the way spelled out in the ensuing argument of 4:7-15. Here, in Paul's own ministry, is spelled out afresh the paradigm of the cross. Life in the Spirit, glorious as it is in terms of its saving effects (beholding God's glory in the face of Christ and being transformed into his likeness is no small thing, after all), is finally evidenced, however, not in triumphalism but in a life that is marked by "the death of Jesus."

We note again, finally, (1) the trinitarian substructure that pervades the whole argument, and (2) the experienced nature of the theological appeal.

---

tion of this passage, with its focus on the Spirit as the way the Exodus passage is now to be understood, is scarcely the "stuff" with which to oppose such a christology!

c. 2 Corinthians 13:13

The remarkable grace-benediction that concludes this letter, the only one of its kind in the extant corpus, is in many ways the most significant theological moment of all — and verifies our overall understanding of the gospel in these letters and of 11:4 in particular. Paul concludes all of his letters with a grace-benediction, usually with the simple "the grace of our Lord Jesus Christ be with you," as in the first part of the present one. But this one has two remarkable features: first, that it is elaborated at all; and second, the trinitarian form in which the elaboration is expressed.

Even though Paul may be reflecting a liturgical formulation already used in his churches, these words most likely have their origin at this point and were expressed in light of what is going on in Corinth and what has been said in this letter — especially so since nothing like this appears anywhere else in his letters, particularly in letters after this one. *Ad hoc* elaboration alone accounts for the unusual order of Lord (Christ), God, and Spirit. Paul apparently began with his ordinary benediction, and then elaborated in the now "logical" order of God and Spirit. After all, the three expressions are precisely the *Pauline* understanding of the soteriological functions of the Trinity.[47] Here, then, in capsule is Paul's basic soteriology, expressed explicitly in other passages (e.g., Gal. 4:4-6; Rom. 5:1-11). Here also is our entrée into Paul's theology proper, into his understanding of God himself, which has been so radically affected by the twin realities of the death and resurrection of Christ and the gift of the eschatological Spirit. As Barth put it with extraordinary insight, "Trinity is the Christian name for God." Here we begin to penetrate a bit into Paul's understanding of that reality, namely that to be Christian one must finally understand God in a trinitarian way. Paul's understanding begins with the OT (in part by way of the LXX), which is always presuppositional for him. God's relationship with his people is primarily predicated on his love for them (Deut. 7:7-8); what characterizes that love pre-eminently is his חֶסֶד (*hesed;* covenant love), usually translated ἔλεος in the LXX. What Paul has come to see is that God's love, which has expressed itself in compassion for his people, especially in his covenant loyalty with them, has found its singularly concrete historical expression in the death and resurrection of Christ. It is equally clear — if not always articulated with clarity — that Paul recognized that in Christ *God himself* had come present "to reconcile the world unto himself" (5:20).

---

47. In the case of Christ and God at least, these are the most characteristic words in Paul's vocabulary to express the essence of their being and activity; the Spirit is associated with *koinōnia* in Phil. 2:1.

But that is not all. Through the gift of his Holy Spirit, the Spirit of the living God, God has now come present in the new creation as an abiding, empowering presence — so that what characterizes the Holy Spirit is κοινωνία, which primarily means "participation in."[48] This is how the living God not only brings us into an intimate and abiding relationship with himself, as the God of all grace, but also causes us to participate in all the benefits of that grace and salvation, indwelling us in the present by his own presence, guaranteeing our final eschatological glory.

Granted that Paul did not wrestle with the ontological questions that such statements beg to have addressed. Nor does he here *assert* the deity of Christ and the Spirit. But what he does is to *equate the activity of the three divine persons* (to use the language of a later time) *in concert and in one prayer,* with the clause about God the Father standing in second place. This would seem to suggest that Paul was truly trinitarian in any meaningful sense of that term — that the one God is Father, Son, and Spirit, and that in dealing with Christ and the Spirit one is dealing with God every bit as much as one is with God the Father.

It is thus not difficult to see why such a profound moment of theology — in the form of *prayer* for the Corinthians — should be the single most appropriate way to conclude this letter. What Paul prays for them is all of this, and nothing less. He has brought them this gospel of God's love and Christ's grace; in turning to God they have received the Holy Spirit, who has removed the veil from their hearts (regarding the old covenant of stone and letter) and from their faces (so that they might be in fellowship with God himself, beholding his glory in the face of Christ and being transformed into that glory). For them to abandon Paul and his apostolic ministry, Paul recognizes in a most penetrating way, is to abandon Christ and the Spirit, and thus the very love of God himself. For them to continue in their sinful ways (meals in the idol temples and sexual immorality; 6:14–7:1; 12:19-21) and for them to take up

---

48. There has been some debate as to whether "of the Spirit" is an objective or subjective genitive. That is, are we in fellowship with the Spirit, or does he create the fellowship of the saints, as it were? Since the two prior clauses reflect something both of God's character and of his activity on behalf of his people in light of that character, it would seem most likely that something similar is in view here. Since the word primarily means "participation in," the view presented here seems to capture the essence both of the "direction" of the Spirit's activity and of the meaning of the word itself. This view goes back at least as far as H. A. W. Meyer, *Critical and Exegetical Handbook to the Epistles to the Corinthians* (Edinburgh: T. & T. Clark, 1879), II, p. 514. It received its recent impetus from H. Seesemann, *Der Begriff KOINONIA im Neuen Testament* (BZNW 14; Geissen: Töpelmann, 1933); cf. the commentaries by Windisch (p. 428); Lietzmann (p. 162); Bultmann (p. 251); Barrett (p. 344); Furnish (p. 584); Martin (p. 505); see also J. D. G. Dunn, *Jesus and the Spirit* (Philadelphia: Westminster, 1975), p. 261.

with their "super apostles" and be brought under "externals" (whether in the form of Jewish scruples/requirements or of the validation of spirituality by ecstasy) is to turn from true righteousness to condemnation, from life to death. It means to go after "another Jesus," who is no Lord Jesus Christ at all; and it means to "receive another spirit," who is not the Spirit whom they have received, who has brought them into this participation/fellowship (11:4).

IV. Conclusion

I need now to note briefly by way of conclusion that this understanding of 11:4 and of the "theology of gospel" in the two canonical Corinthian letters together is further verified by the two primary "contingencies" in 2 Corinthians — Paul's apostleship, both its reality and character; and the collection for the poor saints in Jerusalem. Indeed, we could have proceeded (perhaps more properly) from these and worked outward and would have achieved the same result; for in his defense of the one (apostleship) and urging of the other (the collection) we again run full face into Paul's gospel.

As we have noted above, the defense of his apostleship has been carried out right along in terms of its exemplifying the gospel he preached to them and by which they were saved. The problem lies not with him or his gospel but with them and their readiness to move beyond the gospel of the Crucified One into something much more triumphalistic. This is what makes them such ready candidates for the perverted expression of the gospel ("another Jesus, a different Spirit") brought to them by the peddlers of the word of God.

Thus Paul bases his appeal not only on their original experience of the saving grace of the gospel as he preached it — despite his personal weaknesses — but he argues throughout that his is the only valid apostleship, precisely because it stays aligned with the central truth of the gospel as he preached it and they received it: Christ and him crucified. By this alone can one make sense both of Paul's "exposition" of his understanding of apostleship in 2 Cor. 2:14–7:4 and of his "defense" of its character in 2 Corinthians 10–12.

Similarly, in appealing for their help with the collection (2 Corinthians 8–9), the ultimate theological appeal is to the gospel itself, in which "though Christ was rich, yet for your sakes he became poor, that you through his 'poverty' might become rich" (2 Cor. 8:9). This is an unabashed appeal to Christ's coming and to his death for their sakes — and to their experience of it — as the ultimate ground for their giving out of their present "riches" so that others might also become "rich" — or at least that they might have a share in the wealth of others of God's people.

Thus these letters are all about the gospel, at every turn and in every way. And the gospel has a coherence to it that is to be found ultimately in the Triune God, through whom "salvation in Christ" has been made available to all who will trust him. This is Paul's passion; for him little else matters.

CHAPTER 16

Some Exegetical and Theological Reflections on Ephesians 4:30 and Pauline Pneumatology[1] (1994)

Paul's prohibition in Eph. 4:30 is well known: "And do not[2] grieve the Holy Spirit of God by whom you were sealed for the day of redemption." As often happens in a well-known text, however, its familiarity causes us to overlook some of its significant features. In this essay I wish to offer some exegetical and theological reflections on this passage, which in its own way touches on most of the key issues in Pauline pneumatology. I offer these musings in honor of, and with gratitude to, Rodman Williams for his service and contributions on behalf of the present-day renewal of the Spirit in the churches.

Some Exegetical Observations[3]

This passage is the second of two such solemn interruptions in the series of parenetic materials that begin in v. 25. The first, "and neither give a place to

1. The substance of the exegetical observations for this paper appear in my study of the Spirit in Paul, *God's Empowering Presence: The Holy Spirit in the Letters of Paul* (Peabody, Mass.: Hendrickson, 1994). All translations are my own unless otherwise indicated.

2. This μή is omitted in P[46], thus turning the prohibition into an indicative: "And you are grieving the Holy Spirit of God." Although this is the "more difficult" reading, it is so suspect contextually that it must be judged a solecism by the scribe of P[46].

3. The following commentaries on Ephesians were consulted for this study and are cited in the footnotes by the author's last name: T. K. Abbott (Edinburgh: T. & T. Clark, 1897); M. Barth (Garden City, N.Y.: Doubleday, 1974); F. F. Bruce (Grand Rapids: Eerdmans, 1984); G. B. Caird (Oxford: Oxford University Press, 1976); R. W. Dale (London: Hodder & Stoughton, 1987); J. Eadie (Edinburgh: T. & T. Clark, 3rd edn., 1883); G. G. Findlay (London: Hodder & Stoughton, 1892); J. Gnilka (Freiburg: Herder, 1971); W. Hendriksen (Grand Rapids: Baker,

the devil" (v. 27), follows two exhortations on speaking truthfully (v. 25) and not sinning in one's anger (v. 26). These are then followed by two further contrasts between the "old person" and the "new": working with one's own hands to provide for the needy vis-à-vis stealing (v. 28), and speaking to build others up and benefit those in need vis-à-vis "unwholesome[4] talk" (v. 29). Our text appears at this point,[5] followed in turn by five vices that are to be done away with ("bitterness, rage, anger, shouting, slander"), along with all other evils (v. 31). In contrast, believers are to be kind and forgiving towards one another in the same way that God has forgiven them through Christ (v. 32). This structure is best seen by displaying it in bare outline:

> Do not lie,
>> but speak truthfully;
>
> Do not sin in your anger;
>>> *Neither give room to the devil.*
>
> Do not steal,
>> but work, and give to the needy;
>
> Do not speak garbage,
>> but speak what builds up the needy;
>>> *And do not grieve the Holy Spirit of God.*
>
> Get rid of all evils:
>> bitterness, rage, anger, shouting, slander;
>
> Be kind and forgiving,
>>> *just as God has forgiven you in Christ.*

It does not take much imagination to recognize that all of this is directed specifically towards Paul's concerns in 4:1-16, that his readers "maintain the unity of the Spirit" (v. 3) because they are the one body of Christ by the one Spirit. The sins described here destroy relationships within the community of faith;

1967); J. L Houlden (Harmondsworth: Penguin, 1970); A. T. Lincoln (Waco, Tex.: Word, 1990); J. A. Mackay (New York: Macmillan, 1953); H. A. W. Meyer (Göttingen: Vandenhoeck & Ruprecht, 1880); C. L. Mitton (Grand Rapids: Eerdmans, 1973); A. G. Patzia (Peabody, Mass.: Hendrickson, 1990); J. A. Robinson (London: Macmillan, 2nd edn. 1904); S. D. F. Salmond (Grand Rapids: Eerdmans, repr. 1961 [1903]); H. Schlier (Düsseldorf: Patmos, 1957); R. Schnackenburg (Edinburgh: T. & T. Clark, 1991 [German orig. 1982]); E. F. Scott (London: Hodder & Stoughton, 1930); J. R. W. Stott (Downers Grove, Ill.: IVP, 1979); B. F. Westcott (London: Macmillan, 1906); A. S. Wood (Grand Rapids: Zondervan, 1978).

4. Greek σαπρός, which literally means "decayed, rotten" (referring to perishables) or "unsound, crumbling" (referring to nonperishables, including buildings).

5. The close connection between the Spirit and speech has been noted by Robinson, p. 113, and re-emphasized by Lincoln, pp. 307-8; cf. 4:11 and especially 5:18-19.

likewise, the righteousness here described presupposes life in the believing community. Life in Christ means to live the life of God in the context of "one another" (v. 32).

At the same time these exhortations flow directly from vv. 17-24, where the parenesis began by setting out the two ways of "walking," and concluded with the imagery of putting off the "old person," and of "being renewed in their minds [by the Spirit]" and thereby putting on the "new." The present exhortations not only offer specific examples of the two ways of walking, but also indicate their respective sources. The sins that divide and thereby destroy the unity of the body come directly from Satan. To continue in any of them is to grieve the Spirit, who has "sealed them for the day of redemption" (v. 30) and is responsible for the behavior that maintains their unity. And, of course, the pattern for all of this is none other than the living God himself, whose Holy Spirit is grieved when his people fail to walk in his ways.

As to the prohibition itself, especially as a significant Pauline Spirit text, several items call for further attention.

1. One of the interpretive keys to this passage lies with a phenomenon literary critics call "intertextuality,"[6] the conscious embedding of fragments of an earlier text into a later one. Since Paul's spiritual life and theology are thoroughly imbued with Old Testament realities,[7] we should not be surprised to find him not only quoting the Old Testament to support an argument, as in most cases, but also at times borrowing or "echoing" the language and setting of a specific Old Testament passage or motif and refitting it into his own setting. That seems to be precisely what he has done in this sentence, which echoes the language of Isa. 63:10[8] and at the same time reflects interests similar to that passage (vv. 1-19).

6. On this question see R. B. Hays, *Echoes of Scripture in the Letters of Paul* (New Haven: Yale University Press, 1989). For another example of such intertextuality in Pauline Spirit texts, see especially Phil. 1:19, where Paul "echoes" Job 13:16 (LXX) with its literary milieu and thus apparently transfers some of that setting to his own situation. At the same time he does so with some obvious contrasts between himself and Job. Cf. the echoes of Ezek. 36:26-27 in 2 Cor. 3:3-6, and of Deut. 30:1-6 in Rom. 2:29.

7. The evidence for this is writ large in the corpus. Both Paul's theological presuppositions and therefore his thought-world are thoroughly conditioned by the Old Testament.

8. This is often noted in the commentaries but then rather summarily dismissed. Paul's Greek reads καὶ μὴ λυπεῖτε τὸ πνεῦμα τὸ ἅγιον τοῦ θεοῦ; the LXX of Isa. 63:10 reads καὶ παρώξυναν τὸ πνεῦμα τὸ ἅγιον αὐτοῦ. That Paul is here "citing" the LXX best explains both the unusual "fullness" to the name and the word order. In the only other place where he uses the full name (1 Thess. 4:8, "who gives τὸ πνεῦμα αὐτοῦ τὸ ἅγιον into you"), the αὐτοῦ in that case comes between "the Spirit" and "the holy." The two linguistic differences between Ephesians and the LXX of Isaiah are easily explained. Paul substitutes τοῦ θεοῦ for αὐτοῦ because in Paul's

First, then, a word about Isaiah 63. After picturing the messianic judgment of him who treads the winepress alone (vv. 1-6), the prophet applies that oracle to Israel's present situation, but in light of its past. Verse 10 comes at the end of the section that describes God's gracious redemption of Israel in the Exodus (vv. 7-9) and speaks of Israel's rebellion in terms of "grieving his Holy Spirit." The prophet uses this language because this is his understanding of "the divine presence" in the tabernacle in the wilderness: "It was no messenger or angel but *his presence* that saved them"[9] (v. 9) — a direct recall of Exod. 33:12-14. This in turn is followed by a call for Yahweh to return to his people's present distress, in which the prophet once more recalls the glories of the Exodus. Again in light of Exod. 33:12-14 he equates God's presence with his Holy Spirit, which is made certain in this case because "the Spirit of the Lord gave them rest" (v. 14).[10]

The rest of my observations on this text do not require that Paul, by "citing" Isa. 63:10 in a big way, is here reflecting on the whole Isaiah passage. But it would add considerably to our understanding if such were the case. Here, after all, is the one certain place in the Old Testament, whose language Paul seems clearly to be echoing, where the motif of *God's presence* is specifically equated with the Spirit of God. Such an equation is certain in Paul by his use of the temple metaphor (= the place of God's presence), now understood in terms of the Spirit's dwelling within and among his people.[11] It is very likely, therefore, that we should be prepared to hear this text in the light of Eph. 2:22, where God's dwelling in his temple, the church, is specifically

---

sentence the pronoun would have no antecedent (but in making the substitution he keeps the word order of the LXX). He substitutes λυπεῖτε for a form of παροξύνω because the latter means "irritate" or "vex," understanding the Hebrew ועצב to mean "grieve" (correctly so; this is the only instance in the LXX where עצב is rendered with παροξύνω).

9. This reflects the text of the LXX (cf. NRSV, NAB, NJB, REB), which in turn reflects one way of punctuating and reading the Hebrew text. The difficulty lies with the combination בכל־צרתם לא צר. The LXX translator understood בכל־צרתם to go with the preceding line ("became their savior in all their distress") and either had צר ("envoy") in his Hebrew text or read צי for צר ("distress"). Paul almost certainly knew the LXX in this case, although his (proper) substitution of λυπεῖτε for παροξύνω indicates that he knew the Hebrew text as well. In any case, the Greek text more accurately reflects the text of Exod. 33, to which the prophet is clearly alluding, than does the more common English translation of the Hebrew "the angel of his presence saved them" (RSV; cf. NIV, NASB).

10. Which is a direct recall of Exod. 33:14, "My presence will go with you, and I will give you rest."

11. See the four places where Paul refers either to the church or the believer as the temple of (the living) God: 1 Cor. 3:16-17; 6:19; 2 Cor. 6:16; and Eph. 2:21-22. In each case (except 2 Cor. 6:16, where it is implied), Paul specifically attributes the reality of the temple with the presence of the Spirit.

equated with the presence of the Spirit. In any case, the Spirit as God's own personal and empowering presence is the key to our hearing Paul's own concerns in this prohibition.

2. It should be noted that, in so echoing Isa. 63:10, this becomes the only place in the corpus where Paul uses the full ascription, "the *Holy* Spirit *of God.*"[12] In this context this usage is almost certainly intentional, as a deliberate recall of Isa. 63:10, and for effect.[13] Elsewhere, when Paul wants to emphasize the relationship of the Spirit to God, he refers simply to "the Spirit of God"[14]; and (sometimes) when he wants to emphasize the aspect of holiness, he uses the full name, "the Holy Spirit."[15] Here the full ascription is not just a form of solemn speech, calling special attention to the role of the Spirit in ethical life, but also an emphatic declaration that the *Holy* Spirit is none other than the Spirit *of God.* Thus the ascription itself focuses on the concluding words of the introductory paragraph (4:23-24): that they are to be renewed in their minds (by the Spirit) and thereby to put on the new person, *created to be like God* in the *righteousness and holiness* that come from the truth (the gospel). Both of these aspects — the Spirit as the presence of God and his relationship to ethical life — need closer examination.

3. One of the more noteworthy features of the long section of parenesis extending from 4:17 to 6:9 is that Paul's primary focus throughout is God himself, his character and his deeds that reflect his character. Thus Gentiles are aliens to "the life of God" (4:18), whereas those who have "learned Christ" have put on a "new person," created κατὰ θεόν (v. 24; "according to God"; "to be like God" [NIV]). Those who forgive and walk in love are "imitators of God" (4:32–5:2). For Paul the goal of the "new creation" is none other than our being recreated in the image of God, which was rolled in the dust in the Garden. Thus the "glory of God" is the ultimate purpose of all that God has done for his people and their salvation. But such glory is not simply that which comes to God as the result of his grace in redemption, which is the first and most obvious point of reference for such language.[16] It is also for the

---

12. Although see 1 Thess. 4:8, noted above (n. 8), where the companion ascription occurs: "God . . . who gives his *Holy* Spirit (τὸ πνεῦμα αὐτοῦ τὸ ἅγιον)."

13. So many interpreters (Meyer, Eadie, Salmond, Bruce); cf. Lincoln, p. 307: "that Spirit who is characterized by holiness and who is God himself at work in believers."

14. E.g., Rom. 8:9, 14; 1 Cor. 2:14; 3:16; 6:11; 7:40; 12:3; 2 Cor. 3:3. The same is true of the three instances where he designates the Spirit as "of Christ" (Rom. 8:9; Gal. 4:6; Phil. 1:19) and where he emphasizes the relationship of the Spirit to Christ.

15. E.g., 1 Cor. 6:19 and 1 Thess. 4:8.

16. See especially the repeated refrain, "the praise of his glory," in the opening *berakah* (1:3-14), which first of all has to do with redemption per se, but finally with the fact that God has

"glory of God" that we are to bear the fruit of righteousness (Phil. 1:11). That is quite the point of the prayer in Eph. 3:14-21: that being empowered by the Spirit, Christ might live in us in such a way that we come to know his love and thus *be filled unto the fullness of God.* Paul's point with this language in part is that, when God's people do *not* live "like God," they thereby grieve the Holy Spirit *of God.*

My present point, however, is not simply the ethical one, which I will note in a moment, but the personal one. This text joins many others in making it quite clear that Paul understood the Spirit in fully personal terms. Using the terminology of Isa. 63:10 and reflecting its conceptual context, Paul appeals to his readers not to *grieve* God's Holy Spirit.[17] One can only grieve a person, and our misdeeds grieve God himself, who has come to indwell us individually and corporately by his Spirit.

One of the inadequacies of the word "spirit," and concomitantly of our impersonal images of the Spirit (wind, fire, water, oil), lies right here. Since "spirit" does not tend to call forth personal images, and since our view of God is often laced with a kind of transcendence that keeps him especially distant from our everyday lives, it is easy for us to pass off our sins in a much too casual way. Here, then, is the text that forever reminds us that such sins bring grief to God himself. Presuppositional to this exhortation is the prayer in 3:16, that we are indwelt by God's own empowering presence in the person of his Holy Spirit. Therefore our misdeeds, which reflect the character of Satan, bring grief not just to ourselves and the ones whom we have injured, but to the God who in mercy has chosen to indwell us. Hence the weightiness of this solemn word to God's people, urged to walk worthy of their calling by maintaining the unity of the Spirit: And do not grieve *the Holy Spirit of God.* Do not, as Israel, reject God's very presence, his Holy Spirit, whose dwelling within and among us is the evidence of "salvation" and his giving us "rest."

4. This leads to further discussion about the role of the Spirit in ethical life from the Pauline perspective. It is clear from such passages as Gal. 5:16–6:10 and Rom. 8:4, 13-14 that Paul understood the Spirit to be the empowering presence of God, enabling the ethical life that has God's glory as its ultimate goal. That note has already been struck in Eph. 3:16, and is the presupposition

---

created a new humanity out of Jew and Gentile alike. Such a refrain recurs throughout the corpus (Rom. 15:7; 2 Cor. 4:4, 6, 15; Phil. 2:11; 1 Tim. 1:11). But so does the refrain that, by living in conformity with his character, we too reflect or reveal that glory (1 Cor. 10:31; 2 Cor. 3:17-18; Phil. 1:11).

17. Schlier, p. 227, notes that this language stands in sharp contrast to joy, one of the most distinctive evidences of the Spirit's presence.

behind 4:3-4 (and v. 23, if it refers to the Spirit). Although the present exhortation is expressed negatively, the presupposition behind these words is that the Spirit is grieved precisely because he is present to empower us for better things: truthful and edifying speech, giving to the needy, kindness, and forgiveness. But more still is involved. As with the emphasis on the full name, the Holy Spirit of God, so also the imagery of the Spirit as God's seal speaks to the ethical dimension of life in the Spirit.

This is now the third occurrence of the "seal" imagery in the corpus.[18] The imagery itself derives from a wide variety of transactions in the Greco-Roman world, most often in the form of a stamped imprint in wax bearing the seal of the owner or sender. It was used primarily to denote ownership and authenticity, but also thereby to guarantee the protection of the owner.[19] Paul uses it metaphorically seven times in all, with several different nuances.[20] The primary referent in 2 Cor. 1:21-22 and in Eph. 1:13-14 is "ownership." By the *seal of the Spirit* God has placed his own divine imprint on our lives indicating that we are his — for now and forever.[21] But inherent in this imagery is also the notion of "authentication," which seems to be the primary referent in the present usage. Granted, the final emphasis is on our eschatological future. But in this context Paul is probably urging that, by "sealing" us with his Holy Spirit so as to walk in ways that are "like God," God has thereby authenticated us as those who are truly his own. To put it another way, as we live the life of God empowered by his Holy Spirit, we demonstrate ourselves to be the authentic people of God. As always in Paul, the Spirit is the singular identification mark of believers,[22] an identification that for Paul is demonstrated pre-

18. See 2 Cor. 1:21-22; cf. 1:13-14 in the present letter.

19. See "σφραγίζω" 2b, BAGD, p. 796; MM, pp. 617-19; and the discussions by G. Fitzer, *TDNT*, VII, pp. 939-43 and R. Schippers, *NIDNTT*, III, p. 499.

20. The verb occurs here and in Rom. 15:28; 2 Cor. 1:22; Eph. 1:13; the noun in Rom. 4:11; 1 Cor. 9:2; and 2 Tim. 2:19. The usage in Rom. 15:28 is unique and apparently refers to the sealing of a bag of produce to guarantee that it was ready for market. Thus the gift for the church in Jerusalem is "handed over under seal as it were" (G. Fitzer, *TDNT*, VII, p. 948). In Rom. 4:11 circumcision functions as God's seal, ratifying Abraham's righteousness by faith before he was circumcised. In 1 Cor. 9:2 the emphasis is primarily on authentication; the Corinthians themselves are God's seal, authenticating Paul's apostleship.

21. My contemporizing language should not obscure an important Pauline point, hinted at by Robinson, p. 194, that in 1:13 this imagery functioned to certify to his Gentile readers that they had got in on God's promises to Israel. By living like (pagan) Gentiles (4:17), they grieve the Holy Spirit who has thus sealed them for the day of redemption.

22. The frequent suggestion that "sealing" refers to baptism ought forever to be laid to rest, since it has no linguistic or exegetical basis whatsoever. This linkage has a considerable history, usually on the basis of its appearance in 2 Cor. 1:21-22. It has been argued vigorously by

cisely at the point where the Spirit replaces Torah in our lives, as the one who fulfills the new covenant by indwelling us and thus causing us to walk in the ways of the Lord.

5. We need to note the eschatological dimension of this text as well. As throughout the corpus, this is the primary theological reality for Paul regarding the Spirit, that he is "the Holy Spirit of promise" (1:13), himself the fulfillment of Jewish eschatological hopes and by his presence in our lives the guarantee of our certain future. Thus Paul urges them not to grieve the Holy Spirit of God, "by whom you have been sealed *for the day of redemption*." This language is reminiscent of Rom. 8:23, where the Spirit is imaged as the firstfruits of the final redemption, the consummation of our having been "adopted as God's children." One cannot be certain why Paul has added this final touch in this instance. It may simply have been the natural continuation of his choosing to refer them back to 1:13-14 with the imagery of the Spirit as God's seal. But it may also be a way of emphasizing that, even though the future is certain and guaranteed by the presence of the Spirit, *that future is be lived out in the present* until "the day of redemption." Thus the Spirit is the sign of ownership and authentication as well as the empowering presence of God for living to the glory of God now until we finally arrive at the promised glory, which is our own inheritance (Rom. 8:17).[23]

6. Finally, it is surely not incidental that this word occurs as a somewhat balanced response to the first set of exhortations that conclude, "neither give room to the devil" (v. 27). In this letter, written in part to reassure its recipients of Christ's victory over the powers, the Spirit plays a leading role in that

---

E. Dinkler, "Die Taufterterminologie in 2 Kor. i.21f," in W. C. van Unik, ed., *Neotestamentica et Patristica* (Festschrift Oscar Cullmann; NovTSup, 6; Leiden: Brill, 1962), pp. 173-91; and G. R. Beasley-Murray, *Baptism in the New Testament* (Grand Rapids: Eerdmans, 1962), pp. 171-77. It is adopted, *inter alia,* by W. Grundmann in "χρίω," *TDNT,* IX, pp. 555-56 (vis-à-vis Fitzer, "σφράγις," *TDNT,* VII, pp. 949-50), and Schippers in "seal," *NIDNTT,* VII, p. 499; cf. the commentaries on 2 Corinthians by Barnard, Plummer, Strachan, Lietzmann, Bultmann, and Furnish (hesitantly). In fact, not one of the several metaphors found in 2 Cor. 1:21-22 is ever used in the New Testament, either individually or together, to refer to or allude to Christian baptism. Moreover, in that passage and this one Paul himself clearly designates the Spirit, not baptism, as God's seal of ownership. The linkage itself is circuitous: one begins with mid- to late-second-century evidence for the imagery of "seal" as referring directly to baptism, then presupposes the (questionable) assumption that Paul himself understood believers to receive the Spirit at baptism, then finally assumes the metaphor itself to have baptism inherently in it. Pauline understanding must be made of sterner stuff!

23. Some (e.g., Findlay, p. 316; Barth, p. 550) have seen here an underlying threat, that by so grieving the Spirit they may forfeit the future. But that is hard to discern both in the imagery and language of this sentence, which accents the reality of the future, not its possible forfeiture.

motif as well. Thus it is fitting in this first series of pareneses, which follows hard on the heels of the descriptions of the two ways of walking in vv. 17-24, that Paul should set the Spirit over against "the devil." Satan himself, the prince of the power of the air (2:2), is the "spirit" who leads people in the ways of "the Gentiles," described here in terms of speaking falsehood, giving way to anger, stealing, using unwholesome speech, slander, and all such evils. It is the "Holy Spirit of God" who leads people in the ways of God that reflect his own likeness. Thus lying close at hand in this text is also the contrast of the Spirit of God with the "false spirit," the enemy of God's people.

Some Theological Reflections

How many of these observations would have been caught by the original readers is debatable. But I am ready to contend that they reflect Paul's own understanding of the Spirit which emerges elsewhere in his letters, and that Paul's experience and understanding of the Spirit lie much closer to the center of things than New Testament scholarship tends to allow. On the basis of the various aspects of Pauline pneumatology as they emerge in this text, I would like to make a few final theological observations as to, first, the role of the Spirit in Pauline theology and, second, some crucial matters about Paul's understanding of the Spirit.

There has been a long debate in scholarship as to what constitutes the "heart" of Pauline theology.[24] The traditional view, fostered by the reformers and perpetuated by generations of Protestants, is that "justification by faith" is the key to Paul's theology. This view puts the emphasis on Christ's historical act of redemption and its appropriation by the believer through faith. The inadequacy of such a view should be apparent after any thorough reading of Paul's letters. Not only does it focus on one metaphor of salvation to the exclusion of others, but such a focus fails to throw the net broadly enough so as to capture all of Paul's theological concerns.

In response to this, others have sought this center in Paul's "mystical experience of being *in Christ*."[25] This view shifts the focus from Christ's historical work and its appropriation by the believer to the believer's (especially

24. For a very helpful overview of this debate, especially in its more recent expressions, see J. Plevnik, "The Center of Pauline Theology," *CBQ* 61 (1989): 461-79.

25. See especially A. Deissmann, *Die neutestamentliche Formel "in Christo Jesu"* (Marburg: N. G. Elwert, 1892). For English readers, see *St Paul: A Study in Social and Religious History* (London: Hodder & Stoughton, 1912 [1911]); and A. Schweitzer, *The Mysticism of Paul the Apostle* (London: Black, 1931).

Paul's) ongoing experience of Christ. While in some ways this serves as a corrective to the traditional view, most contemporary Pauline scholars have recognized the inadequacy of both of these somewhat limiting approaches.

It is my conviction that the reason the center is so "elusive" is that Paul's theology covers too much ground for one to simplify it into a single phrase. It would seem far better for us to isolate the elements that are essential to his theology, that lie at the very heart of things for Paul, and around which all other matters cluster.[26] In such a view at least four items must be included:

1. The *church* as an eschatological community formed as the new covenant people of God.
2. The *eschatological framework* of their existence and thinking.
3. Their having been constituted by God's eschatological *salvation* effected through the *death and resurrection of Christ*.
4. Their focus centered on *Jesus* as Messiah, Lord, and Son of God.

On the one hand, it seems impossible to understand Paul without beginning with eschatology as the essential framework of all his theological reflection; on the other hand, "salvation in Christ" is the essential concern within that framework. Salvation is "eschatological" in the sense that final salvation, which still awaits the believer, is already a present reality through Christ and the Spirit. It is "in Christ" in the sense that what originated in God was effected historically by the death and resurrection of Christ, and is appropriated experientially by God's people through the work of the Holy Spirit — who is also the key to Christian life "between the times," until the final consummation at Christ's parousia.

What needs to be noted is the central role the Spirit plays in each of these aspects of the Pauline "center." The eschatological framework within which Paul does all of his theologizing (the promised future as "already" but "not yet") is the direct result of his own (not to mention the rest of the early church's) direct experience with the two most significant eschatological realities within his own Jewish heritage: resurrection (in this case, his having seen the risen Christ) and the gift of the eschatological Spirit. Indeed, I am prepared to argue that any attempt to understand Paul's theology that does not take this framework as its fundamental starting point and the Spirit as the absolute key to the framework is sure to fail. Paul can scarcely speak of the Spirit without, as in the present text, reminding his readers that their own experience of the Spirit is both the *evidence* that the future has already been set in-

26. Cf. Plevnik, "Center," pp. 477-79, but without mention of the Spirit!

exorably in motion and the absolute *guarantee* of its final consummation.[27] By having been given "the Holy Spirit of God," they — and we — have been sealed ("already") for the day of redemption ("not yet").

So it is too with the central feature of Pauline theology: salvation in Christ, which in his understanding includes both "getting in" and "staying in." That is, there simply is no salvation in Paul that does not incorporate the saved person into the people of God; and there are no genuinely redeemed people of God who do not live "according to God." The latter is not a means of grace but the transforming expression of grace received. To put this another way, Paul knows nothing about a salvation that does not include the righteousness of God, both received as the gift of right standing with God and as behavior that reflects that relationship. Even the most casual reading of Paul should cause one to recognize the crucial role the Spirit plays in both of these aspects of salvation in Christ. The same Father who sent his Son to redeem (Gal. 4:4-5) likewise sent "the Spirit of his Son into our hearts," thereby appropriating that salvation for his people (v. 6). Such a trinitarian view of salvation in Christ completely dominates Paul's way of referring to God's saving activity on our behalf, especially when he intends to include our actual experience of it.[28] That the Spirit is the *sine qua non* of righteousness in terms of godly behavior is so fundamental to Paul's view of things that some think this is all Paul knows about the Spirit (see especially Gal. 5:13–6:10).

In our present text both of these realities are also present. On the one hand, the saving work of Christ (assumed in this case), appropriated by the Spirit, is to be found in the language, "by whom you were sealed." On the other hand, the Spirit as the one who effects God's righteousness in our everyday lives is quite the point of the prohibition, as I pointed out in the exegesis.

The same is true of the Spirit as the key to Paul's ecclesiology, which we should probably rename "laiology," since he cares very little for "church" in terms of structures, but everything for believers as being "the people of God." Indeed, this is one place where Paul is absolutely one with his heritage; God is not simply saving a group of individuals to be related to him one to one. Rather, God is creating a people for his name, and Paul's concerns lie here almost totally. Even the long-time passion of his life — the Gentile mission —

27. E.g., Rom. 5:1-5; 8:11, 23, 26-27; 15:13; 1 Cor. 13:8-13; 2 Cor. 1:21-22; 3:3, 6, 16-18; 5:5; Gal. 3:3, 14; 5:5-6, 21-23; 6:7-10; Eph. 1:13-14, 17-20; 4:4, 30; 2 Thess. 2:13; 1 Tim. 4:1.

28. See especially the semi-creedal soteriological passages such as Rom. 5:1-5; 8:3-4, 15-17; 1 Cor. 6:11; 2 Cor. 1:21-22; 13:13; Gal. 4:4-7; Eph. 1:13-14; 4:4-6; 2 Thess. 2:13-14; Titus 3:5-7. But see also many other such texts, soteriological or otherwise: Rom. 8:9-11; 15:16, 18-19, 30; 1 Cor. 1:4-7; 2:4-5; 6:19-20; 12:4-6; 2 Cor. 3:16-18; Gal. 3:1-5; Eph. 1:3, 17-20; 2:17-18, 19-22; 3:16-19; 5:18- 19; Phil. 1:19-20; 3:3; Col. 3:16.

reflects his "laiology," since his passion is not simply in seeing Gentiles "get saved," but in Jew and Gentile as one people glorifying the God and Father of our Lord Jesus Christ (Rom. 15:6).

This is one of the passions that lies behind Ephesians. Along with the work of Christ, which makes all of this possible, it is the Spirit who brings it off (cf. 1:13-14, "you [Gentiles] also" are heirs by the Spirit; 2:18, both together have access to the Father in the one Spirit; 4:3, "maintain the unity of the Spirit," since [v. 4] there is "one body" because there is "one Spirit"). As I pointed out in the exegesis, such a concern lies at the heart of the whole of this parenesis, that these former Gentiles will live no longer as Gentiles, but will live in and maintain the unity that the Spirit has created.

That leads us, finally, to christology,[29] which does not in fact occur in our present text. But what does occur is related to the first aspect of Paul's christology, its presuppositional trinitarianism, which in turn lies at the heart of Pauline theology proper. Here is a thoroughgoing monotheist, whose encounter with Christ on the Damascus Road, and subsequent experience of the Holy Spirit, forever radically altered his understanding of God and of his (now Christian) existence. The gospel is everything for Paul. As we have just noted, his gospel is primarily *soteriology* — God saving a people for his name through the redemptive work of Christ and the appropriating work of the Spirit. It is his encounter with God soteriologically — as Father, Son, and Holy Spirit — that accounts for the transformation of Paul's theological language and finally of his understanding of God, although this is simply never worked out at the level of immanent, or doxological, trinitarianism. That Paul's understanding of God was functionally trinitarian and that the distinctions between Father, Son, and Spirit were presuppositional for him[30] may be demonstrated from Paul's trinitarian texts themselves (1 Cor. 12:4-6; 2 Cor. 13:14; Eph. 4:4-6) as well as from the many soteriological texts noted above that are expressed in trinitarian terms.

Such an understanding of God and of the Holy Spirit as the empowering presence of God lies at the heart of the present text. This particular text should cause us to be more cautious in using impersonal images to describe the work of the Spirit, because for many in the church the Spirit is nothing

29. On the question of whether Paul knew anything at all — he did not — about the alleged "Spirit christology" so often attributed to him, see my contribution in J. Green and M. Turner, eds., *Jesus of Nazareth: Lord and Christ* (I. H. Marshall Festschrift; Grand Rapids: Eerdmans, 1993), pp. 312-31.

30. On this whole question, and especially on Paul as a trinitarian, see the section entitled "What about the Trinity?" by D. Ford, in F. Young and D. Ford, *Meaning and Truth in 2 Corinthians* (Grand Rapids: Eerdmans, 1987), pp. 255-60.

more than "a gray, oblong blur," as one former student described him. One cannot grieve wind or fire; but one can grieve the eternal God — in this case the God who has himself come present within and among us by the Holy Spirit.

Lying behind such a view is a crucial aspect of Pauline pneumatology that is often overlooked or that has received mere lip service, namely, in the coming of the Holy Spirit the promise of the return of God's presence among his people has been fulfilled. Near the core of Paul's theology of the Spirit is the idea that the Spirit is the fulfillment of the promises found in Jeremiah and Ezekiel: that God himself would breathe on us and we would live; that he would write his law in our hearts; and especially that he would give his Spirit "unto us," so that we are indwelt by him (Jer. 31:33; Ezek. 36:26-27; 37:14). What is crucial for Paul is that we are thus indwelt by the eternal God. The gathered church and the individual believer are the new locus of God's own presence with his people, and the Spirit is the way God is now present.

One of the key images, therefore, that Paul associates with the indwelling Spirit is that of "temple." Its significance in part is that it functions for Paul both for the corporate, gathered community and for the individual believer. With this imagery in particular Paul picks up the Old Testament motif of God's "presence" with the people of God. This theme is one of the keys to the structure of the book of Exodus. There Israel comes to the holy mount, the place of God's "dwelling," where they are forbidden to go on the threat of death. Only Moses is allowed into God's presence. But God plans to "move" from the mount and dwell among his people by means of a "tabernacle." So after the giving of the Book of the Covenant (chs. 20–24), Moses is given precise instructions for the construction of the tabernacle (chs. 25–31). But this is followed by the debacle in the desert (ch. 32), culminated by God's announcement that "my presence will *not* go with you"; an angel will go instead (ch. 33). Moses recognizes the inadequacy of this solution and intercedes:

> If your Presence does not go with us, do not send us up from here. How will anyone know that you are pleased with me and with your people unless you go with us? What else will distinguish me and your people from all the other people on the face of the earth? (33:15-16 NIV)

God's Presence with Israel is what distinguishes them, not the Law or other "identity markers." This in turn is followed by the further revelation of God's character (34:4-7) and the actual construction of the tabernacle, concluding with the descent of God's glory, which "filled the tabernacle" (40:35). With that they journey to the place which "the Lord your God will choose as a dwelling for his Name" (Deut. 12:11 and *passim*). Herein lies the significance of the Isaiah passage echoed by Paul in our present text, because the prophet has made a clear identification of the "presence" motif with "the Holy Spirit of Yahweh."

In a canonical reading of the Old Testament the Deuteronomy promise is finally fulfilled in the construction of Solomon's temple, where the same glory as in Exodus 40 descended and "filled his temple" (1 Kings 8:11). But Israel's failure caused them to forfeit God's presence. This is the tragedy: the temple in Jerusalem — the place where God had chosen to dwell — was finally destroyed. The people are not only carried away captive, but both the exiles and the survivors are no longer a people distinguished by the presence of the living God in their midst, although it is promised again in Ezekiel's grand vision (chs. 40–48). The second temple itself evinces mixed feelings among the people. In the light of both Solomon's temple and the promised future temple of Ezekiel, Haggai complains, "Who of you is left who saw this house in its former glory! How does it look to you now? Does it not seem to you like nothing?" (2:3).

It is this complex of ideas and images that Paul picks up in 1 Cor. 3:16-17 and 6:19. His introductory "do you not know that . . . ," followed by "you are *the* temple of God [in Corinth]," strongly suggests that this is the rich history Paul here has in mind. The church, corporately and individually, is the place of God's own personal presence by the Spirit. This is what marks God's new people off from "all the other people on the face of the earth." Hence Paul has consternation over the Corinthians' present behavior, which has the effect of banishing the Spirit, the living presence of God that makes them his temple. And it is the same motif that Paul echoes in our present text by urging his readers, in the language of Isa. 63:10, where God's presence in Israel has been equated with his Holy Spirit: "Do not grieve the Holy Spirit of God," meaning, "Do not let your conduct be such that you grieve God himself who has chosen to come present among us by his Holy Spirit."

To be sure, not all of this is to be found in Eph. 4:30. My point is a simple one: Pauline theology simply cannot be adequately done without taking seriously the central role of the Spirit. And one does not grasp Paul's understanding of the Spirit without comprehending that we are here dealing with God's empowering presence. The present text is but a part of the building blocks for his theological reflection. In both explicit and presuppositional ways this prohibition reflects the heartbeat of Pauline pneumatology.

CHAPTER 17

To What End Exegesis? Reflections on Exegesis and Spirituality in Philippians 4:10-20
(1996)

The purpose of this lecture, which begins by tracing the author's pilgrimage as an evangelical NT scholar, is to urge that the ultimate aim of exegesis is the Spiritual one — to produce in our lives and the lives of others true Spirituality, in which God's people live in faithful fellowship both with one another and with the living God, and thus in keeping with God's purposes in the world. It is further argued, therefore, that the exegesis of the biblical texts belongs primarily in the context of the believing community who are the true heirs of these texts. These concerns are then illustrated by an exegesis of Phil. 4:10-20, where it is argued that the predicates of friendship and orality not only make sense of this passage in its present placement in Philippians, but are intended likewise to lead the community into the climactic theology and doxology of 4:19-20 as the letter is read in their midst.

Key Words: Phil. 4:10-20, exegesis, spirituality, doxology

In part this lecture[1] is something of a confessional narrative of my own pilgrimage as an evangelical NT scholar. It is certainly not intended to serve as a paradigm. But as those who know me well would tell you, it is hard for Gordon to do anything that is not at least a bit hortatory.

---

1. This essay was given as the Annual Lecture for the Institute for Biblical Research at the annual meeting in New Orleans on November 23, 1996. When the editor of this journal asked me to submit it for publication, I toyed for a long while over whether to tone down some of the rhetorical features of oral speech and to give it a more academic appearance with greater interaction with scholarship in footnotes. In the end I decided to let it stand pretty much as delivered, with a few minor changes here and there, and to keep only those notes that were already in the paper when it was delivered.

I. The Pilgrimage

The crisis event that led to this lecture occurred three years ago, when I was asked to team up with my colleague Eugene Peterson for Regent's annual Pastor's Conference. The topic had been set by those responsible for the conference: Exegesis and Spirituality. In preparing for those lectures, I realized that over the years I had developed a kind of schizophrenia regarding these two topics — schizophrenia in the derivative sense of that word: of a truly "divided mind-set."

Even though I am easily the least intentional NT scholar in the history of the discipline, I had nonetheless become one, whether intentional or not. In so doing I had also entered into a concern to restore a viable evangelical voice in the academy, where scholarship in the generation preceding mine seemed pretty well committed to the agenda of modernity — to control the data by means of a historical-critical methodology, within a non-supernatural framework, which very often included a strongly anti-supernatural bias.

When my generation came on the scene, not only had such a bias rather totally taken over the playground, but it had also established some new rules for the game. These rules developed especially in Germany, where the church had long been subservient to the academy. The history of evangelical faith in such an environment is not a happy one, although there were notable exceptions in scholars like Adolf Schlatter and Joachim Jeremias. When Scripture could only reach the people of God by way of what the academy allowed it to say, the effect was particularly deadening. When these rules were transported to North America they had a still further deadening effect — especially in the United States, where the doctrine of the separation of church and state was so fundamental to our psyche that no one growing up in my generation could have imagined a world that thought, or that should think, differently. This psyche dictated that the academy must be "neutral" with regard to religion and especially must do so when looking at religious texts.

The net result was that the game had to be played on a field and by a set of rules that were *fundamentally foreign to the texts themselves.* And here is where I entered the game that brought about my schizophrenia: I had pursued a Ph.D. in NT studies so that I might teach the NT with integrity in the setting of the church. In the process I had fallen into scholarship. And to do my scholarly work well, I had learned to play the game by the current rules. This meant to yield to the premise that what we called Scripture, God's eternal word given in love to his people for their knowing and following him, had to be treated first of all (and in the academy, *exclusively*) as historical documents not unlike any other such religious documents. Since history had always been my second love, and since I too believe that the first task of exegesis is the historical one (to be as good historians as possible when dealing with anything that comes to us from an earlier time and culture), I had no trouble at all playing the game by the rules. To be sure, my bias was basically conservative toward all historical data — innocent until proven guilty — and my own experience of God also biased me historically in the direction that God had intervened in history, the *understanding* of which intervention I also took to be part of the *historical* task.

My schizophrenia came about because I never for a moment believed that these texts were nothing more than simply objects of historical research. These texts were my singular passion, because herein I had been encountered by the living God, who in Christ and by the Spirit called me to himself to be a passionate lover of God. This, and this alone, was my *only* reason for ever becoming an exegete: to become a better reader of the texts, so that I might both live out the life they called me to (that is, to enter into their own Spirituality[2]) and share this passion with others. Indeed, this is the only way I have ever taught in over thirty years in the classroom.

But it was precisely this dimension (my *only* reason ever for doing this work in the first place) that was never allowed expression in the academy. Here we had to take the first task of exegesis not only as the first or even primary one, but as the *only* one. Anything that even smacked of caring about the Spirituality of the text — be it its own theology or its doxology or its call to discipleship — on the part of the scholar was disallowed by the present rules of the game. Thus I found myself trying to play baseball but was allowed to play only by the rules of soccer, without the use of hands and arms.

As many of you will recognize, with the publication of my 1 Corinthians commentary ten years ago, I ventured to start playing by the earlier set of rules when the texts were studied primarily by scholars within the community of faith. Since I had brought much of this exegesis to bear in every kind of church setting and since in these settings I could not imagine not asking and offering some pointers toward solutions of the "so what?" questions, I regularly included these in the commentary itself. Why do the history if the Spirituality inherent in the text itself did not matter a whit? This is what I always did in the classroom, and I knew students who had taken the course in 1 Corinthians from me would sense that I had lost my integrity if I did not do the same in the commentary. I also admit that I did so with a considerable

2. For my reasons for capitalizing this word, see the discussion in the next section, "On the Meaning of Spirituality."

amount of fear and trembling: on the one hand, because I knew I was breaking the rules and therefore the commentary might have a much more limited
usefulness than I would have hoped; on the other hand, because I grew up in
a context where "Spirituality" was the only thing most people did with the
texts, and this "Spirituality" was very often based on little or no exegesis (we
children used to parody a popular gospel song: "wonderful things in the Bible
I see, some put there by you and some put there by me").

Thus back to my preparations for the Pastor's Conference. Here I was
faced with the need to articulate what I believed to be the relationship between exegesis and Spirituality, and now I was being forced to come to terms
with my schizophrenia. To be sure, those first attempts turned out to be
much too mild: I was willing to see exegesis and Spirituality as being related,
as I always had in the classroom, but still to see Spirituality as a kind of practical *addendum* to the exegetical task. However, a year and a half later, I was
to give the Ongman lectures at the Baptist seminary in Örebro, Sweden, under the invited topic, "The Word and the Spirit." Here, again, I was specifically asked to address the question of the interface between exegesis and
Spirituality.

It was while preparing the first of these lectures that the light dawned,
for between the two sets of lectures I had written the Philippians commentary, which had become for me a constant round of Spiritual engagements
with the biblical text. It finally became clear to me that during all these years I
had not been truly abiding by my own understanding of exegesis as I had articulated it in a variety of places and settings. I have long argued that the first
task of exegesis is to try to understand the intent of the author of a text, as
much as this is historically possible, with all of the tools available to us as historians. And I still believe this to be so, even in this postmodern age, where
scholars, full of inner contradictions, intentionally write books and articles to
tell me that an author's intent may be irrelevant to a good reading of a book.
The light that finally dawned, of course, was the plain reality, writ large in almost every text in our canon, that the real intent of these texts was the Spiritual one: obedience to God, be it in the form of behavior, instruction, worship, doxology, or whatever it might be, including a carefully articulated
biblical theology.[3]

---

3. See the critique of "critical" exegesis by Wayne Hankey ("The Bible in a Post-Critical
Age," in *After the Deluge: Essays toward the Desecularization of the Church,* ed. William Oddie
[London: SPCK, 1987], pp. 41-92), who urges a return to the Fathers, who "teach that the essence
of revelation is the raising of the mind of the biblical writers and of the hearers to grasp the intellectual content, the spiritual truth about God, his manner of working in us and his will for us,
which it is the proper aim of Scripture to communicate" (p. 83). While I agree with the spirit of

Thus rather than seeing exegesis and Spirituality as opposed to one another, or as one preceding or following or having precedence over the other, I came to realize — and herewith propose for our mutual consideration: (1) that faithful biblical exegesis must, by the very nature of the documents themselves, *always* take into account the Spiritual purposes for which they were written, and (2) that this exegesis belongs within the framework of the believing community, with those who follow (whether exactly or not, at least intentionally) in the train of the original believing communities for whom and to whom these documents were written.

Thus let us say with uncharacteristic passion: the ultimate aim of exegesis (as I perceive it) is to produce in our lives and the lives of others true Spirituality, in which God's people live in faithful fellowship both with one another and with the eternal and living God and thus in keeping with God's own purposes in the world. In order to do this effectively, I would further argue (but will not take the time to do so here), true "Spirituality" must *precede* exegesis as well as be the final result of it. We must begin as we would conclude, standing under the text, not over it with all of our scholarly arrogance intact. And we must end that way as well, or all is vanity, chasing after the wind.

I would therefore make bold to insist that proper exegesis should be done in the context of prayer, so that in our exegesis we hear the text with the sensitivity of the Spirit. Only as we ourselves do our exegesis in the proper posture of humility — on our knees, as it were, listening to God — can we truly expect to speak the Word of God with clarity and boldness so as to comfort, inspire, or speak prophetically to God's people, the people for whom these texts were written in the first place.

So with this confession and proposal before us as the context of this lecture, what I hope to do in the space that remains is to illustrate what some of this might look like by looking at a specific passage, Phil. 4:10-20, and assessing its role in Paul's letter to the Philippians.

I begin with a few words about the term *Spirituality*.

---

this comment, Hankey also reflects a far too sanguine attitude toward the Fathers. Indeed, this book is a bit of a mixed bag, since the next essay by Roger Beckwith ("Not in the Wisdom of Men") ironically argues on the basis of a highly questionable "critical" exegesis of 1 Corinthians 2 for a pre-critical understanding of the biblical text.

II. On the Meaning of *Spirituality*[4]

As the result of my work on the πνεῦμα word group in the letters of Paul,[5] I have found myself becoming more and more distressed by our translating of the adjective πνευματικός with a lowercase letter, "spiritual." Indeed, the word *spiritual* is what I call an *accordion* word: its meaning pretty much has to do with how much air you pump in or out of it. The point that needs to be made is that the word πνευματικός, a distinctively Pauline word in the NT, has the Holy Spirit as its primary referent. As an adjective Paul never uses it anthropologically to refer to the human spirit; and whatever else, it is *not* an adjective that sets some unseen reality in contrast, for example, to something material, secular, ritual, or tangible.[6]

In the NT, therefore, Spirituality is defined altogether in terms of the Spirit of God. One is Spiritual to the degree that one lives in and walks by the Spirit; in Scripture the word has no other meaning, and no other measurement. Thus, when Paul says that "the Law is spiritual," he means that the Law belongs to the sphere of the Spirit (inspired of the Spirit as it is), not to the sphere of flesh. And when he says to the Corinthians (14:27), "if any of you thinks he or she is spiritual," he means, "if any of you think of yourselves as a Spirit person, a person living the life of the Spirit." Likewise, when he says to the Galatians (6:1) that "those who are spiritual should restore one who has been overtaken in a transgression," he is not referring to some special or elitist group in the church, but to the rest of the believing community, who both began their life in the Spirit and come to completion by the same Spirit who produces his own fruit in their lives.

Christian existence in the NT is thus trinitarian at its very roots. At the beginning and end of all things is the eternal God, to whom both Jews and Christians refer over and again as the Living God. God's purpose in creating creatures like ourselves, fashioned in his image, was for relationship: that we

4. Some of this material has already appeared in my "Exegesis and Spirituality: Reflections on Completing the Exegetical Circle," *Crux* 31 (1995): 29-35, which was the published version of the first of the Ongman Lectures noted above. These lectures were given again in somewhat altered form as the Huber Drumwright Lectures at the Southwestern Baptist Theological Seminary in October 1995.

5. See my *God's Empowering Presence: The Holy Spirit in the Letters of Paul* (Peabody, Mass.: Hendrickson, 1994), especially the analysis of the word group in ch. 2.

6. What this means, of course, is that much that has come under this rubric both in the secular world and in Christian history is much more Greek in its basic orientation than it is biblical. For a recent brief overview of a position similar to mine, see Inagrace Dietterich, "What Is Spirituality?" *The Gospel and Our Culture* 8/3 (September 1996): 1-3, 8 [repr. from *The Center Letter,* published by The Center for Parish Development, Chicago].

might live in fellowship with and thus to the glory of the Living God, both as those who bear God's likeness and as those who carry out God's purposes on earth. Even before the fall, we are told, God's purpose was to redeem the fallen so as to reshape their misshapen vision of God and thus to restore them into the fellowship from which they fell in their rebellion. God has brought this about, we are told, by himself coming among us in the person of his Son, who at one point in our human history effected our redemption and reconciliation with the Living God, through a humiliating death and glorious resurrection. But God has not left us on our own to make a go of it; he has purposed to come to our aid — and this is the reason for God's coming to us and among us by the Holy Spirit.

Thus God's aim in our lives is "Spiritual" in this sense: that we, redeemed by the death of Christ, might be empowered by his Spirit both "to will and to do for the sake of his own pleasure." True Spirituality, therefore, is nothing more or less than life by the Spirit. "Having been brought to life by the Spirit," Paul tells the Galatians, "let us behave in ways that are in keeping with the Spirit."

Hence the aim of exegesis: to produce in our lives and the lives of others true Spirituality, in which God's people live in fellowship with the eternal and living God and thus in keeping with God's own purposes in the world. Thus it is simply wrong-headed for us ever to think that we have done exegesis at all if we have not cared about the intended Spirituality of the text — whether it be theological, doxological, relational, or behavioral.

Now on to such an exegesis of Phil. 4:10-20.

III. Philippians 4:10-20[7]

Let me begin with the scholarly agenda, which in this case I find very often to be in the way of both understanding and Spirituality. Scholarship has tended to have two difficulties with Phil. 4:10-20, and these difficulties by and large dominate the exegetical discussion of this passage: (1) Its placement at the end of the letter. "It is inconceivable," we are told, "that Paul should wait all that time to express his thanks for the gifts."[8] (2) The twin realities (a) that

7. For more detailed argumentation of many of these points, see my commentary on Philippians (NICNT; Grand Rapids: Eerdmans, 1995). In fact, some of the exegesis in the latter part of this section is lifted almost *en toto* out of the commentary, in part to illustrate the very points being argued in this essay.

8. F. W. Beare, *A Commentary on the Epistle to the Philippians* (London: Black, 1959), p. 150.

Paul never actually thanks the Philippians for the gift (in the sense of using the verb εὐχαριστεῖν) and (b) that he uses an array of commercial language to express his acknowledgment.

For those who are troubled by these things, a variety of solutions have been offered. The most common solution to the question of placement is to divide the present letter into three, making our 4:10-20 the earliest of the three, dashed off soon after Epaphroditus had arrived, and placed somewhat thoughtlessly at the end by a redactor.[9] The solution to the *linguistic matters* has basically been to describe the passage as "thankless thanks," and then to "mirror read" some form of *tension* between Paul and the Philippians as lying behind his inability genuinely to thank them.

But such resolutions are completely unnecessary in this case, because the problem is of our own making, resulting from reading our own sociology and cultural norms back into Paul's letter. Both matters find their resolution at two points: first, in the phenomenon of Greco-Roman friendship, taking seriously the fact that our Philippians is in part a letter of friendship (as well as in part a letter of moral exhortation).[10] Understood in light of the "rules" of friendship — their sociology, if you will, not ours — both its placement and language make perfectly good sense. Second, its placement in particular is best understood against the backdrop of orality and Pauline rhetoric.

I do not have time to go into the phenomenon of friendship in Greco-Roman culture, except to outline briefly what is significant for our passage (the details can be found in my commentary):

1. Greco-Roman culture took friendship far more seriously than most Western cultures — so much so that many of the philosophers, beginning with Aristotle, have considerable treatises on the nature and obligations of friendship.
2. Friendship was of several kinds; but between equals, the highest level (to cite Aristotle) was between virtuous people, whose relationship was based on goodwill and loyalty (including trust).

9. This has always struck me as an unusual "solution," since it solves nothing, and only puts the problem back one remove from Paul. As I suggest in the commentary, this seems more like a vain attempt to exonerate Paul, since we cannot really imagine that Paul would have written differently from our "better selves." That is, since we would have written it one way, therefore Paul also must write that way. But somehow it is perfectly all right to attribute what we deem "improper" on the part of Paul to "mindlessness" on the part of a redactor, who might rather have been the one whom we should suspect of more thoughtfulness.

10. On this question see the introduction to my Philippians commentary (pp. 2-7) and the further bibliography found in n. 16 (p. 4).

3. A considerable "core of ideals" was understood to be inherent in such friendship, most of which appear in some way or another in Philippians. Absolutely basic to everyone's understanding of friendship and crucial to the passage in hand was the matter of social reciprocity, in which, using the language of commerce metaphorically, they spoke of mutually "giving and receiving benefits." This matter of "benefits" called for some of the lengthiest philosophical discussions, because friendship could not be understood apart from "benefits." By their very nature, however, benefits could also be abused so as to undermine mutuality and trust.

It is this language, the language of "contractual friendship," that both dominates Phil. 4:10-20 and helps to explain why Paul does not use "thank you" language in a direct way. We know from the literary evidence that although gratitude for benefits received was an expected part of friendship, nonetheless, because of both the mutuality and goodwill inherent in friendship and its expected reciprocity with regard to benefits, the use of "thank you" language was apparently not expected among friends.[11]

If the social phenomenon of friendship explains the *language* of our passage, its *placement* at the end of the letter is most likely due to the combined influence of orality and Pauline rhetoric. We begin with the matter of orality, noting that the first century CE was primarily an oral (and thus aural) culture. This would have been especially true for the majority to whom this letter was addressed. All of Paul's letters, and Philippians in particular, were first of all oral — *dictated* to be *read aloud* in the community. Much of Paul's rhetoric comes into play precisely at this point. His use of assonance and wordplays, for example, are "designed" to be memorable precisely because oral cultures had a very high level of retention. In literary cultures we are bombarded by so many words in print that very few, if any, are kept in memory in a precise way.

Rhetoric and orality together especially explain why Paul left his acknowledgment of their gift for the very end. For most of us, such delay borders on rudeness, if not impropriety, and for scholars it has been the source of considerable speculation. But Paul had a different agenda. Having to this point dealt with his, and especially their, circumstances[12] (basic to letters of

11. See esp. Gerald W. Peterman, "'Thankless Thanks': The Epistolary Social Convention in Philippians 4:10-20," *TynB* (1991): 261-70.

12. Here especially one needs to note the repeated phrase τὰ περὶ (κατὰ) ὑμῶν (ἐμέ) (1:12, 27; 2:19, 23), which is precisely the stuff of letters of friendship. See the discussion in my Philippians commentary, p. 3 and n. 17 on 1:12.

friendship) and knowing full well what he was doing, Paul concluded the letter on the same note with which it began (1:3-7), their mutual partnership in the gospel, thus placing this matter in the emphatic, climactic position at the end. When read aloud in the gathered community, these would be the final words that were left ringing in their ears: their gift to him has been a sweet-smelling sacrifice, pleasing to God; God in turn, through Christ Jesus and in keeping with the "riches" that are his alone in the "glory" in which he dwells, will "fill them to the full" regarding all their needs; and that all of this redounds to God's eternal glory.

At the same time, of course, they would scarcely be able to overlook the exhortations and appeals that *preceded,* given the predominance of these concerns in the large middle section of the letter. This is rhetoric at its best. The theory (predicated on our own sociology) that sees a later, rather mindless, redactor "pasting" things together in this way turns out in the end to make the redactor more clever than Paul.

In this final section, therefore, three concerns intertwine: First is Paul's genuine gratitude for their recent gift, expressed three times in three variations (vv. 10a, 14, 18). Second, this is set within the framework of Greco-Roman "friendship," evidenced by the language of "giving and receiving," a relationship of friendship that goes back to the beginning of their relationship together in Christ. Third, and most significantly (and typically!), this *sociological* reality is totally subsumed under the greater reality of the *gospel;* thus the whole climaxes in doxology.

All of this section is fashioned with consummate artistry, so that their "giving," his "receiving," and their long-term friendship (expressed as a "partnership in the gospel"), which their gift reaffirms, climax in vv. 18-20 with gratitude (from Paul), accolade and promise (from God to them), and doxology (from both him and them to God). In order to get at my concern about the intended Spirituality of the passage, I want to focus on this climactic moment in the letter.

In v. 18 Paul at last mentions their gifts directly. He speaks expansively, piling up verbs at the beginning by which he indicates how richly his own needs have been met by their lavish generosity and concluding with a change of metaphors expressing God's pleasure over their gift. The first clause, "I have received (payment) in full," reflects his final use of the commercial/friendship metaphor, indicating that his "receipt" of what they have "given" puts the "obligation" of friendship back on his side.

As further indication that this passage is not "thankless," Paul starts all over again. "I am filled to the full," he says, and then mentions their gift directly. But in doing so, he describes their gift by means of a rich metaphor from the OT sacrifices ("a fragrant offering, an acceptable sacrifice"), so as also to indicate *divine* approval for what they have done. What was for them an expression of friendship and for Paul was both evidence of their partnership in the gospel and the cause of his present "abounding" while in prison is finally described as a sacrificial offering to God, in which God himself took full pleasure.

The mention of God at the end of v. 18 leads directly to the great masterstroke, v. 19. The reciprocity of friendship is now back in Paul's court. But Paul is in prison and cannot reciprocate directly. So he does an even better thing: since their gift had the effect of being a sweet-smelling sacrifice, pleasing *to God,* Paul assures them that God, whom he deliberately designates "*my* God," will assume responsibility for reciprocity. Thus, picking up the language "my need" from v. 16 and "fill to the full" from v. 18, he promises them that "my God will fill up every need of yours."

From his point of view they obviously have the better of it! First, he promises that God's reciprocation will cover "*every* need" of theirs, especially their material needs, as the context demands, and also every other kind of need, as the language demands. One cannot imagine a more fitting way for this letter to conclude, in terms of Paul's final word to them personally. In the midst of their "poverty" (2 Cor. 8:2), God will richly supply their material needs. In their present suffering in the face of opposition (1:27-30), God will richly supply what is needed (steadfastness, joy, and encouragement). In their "need" to advance in the faith with one mind-set (1:25; 2:1-4; 4:2-3), God will richly supply the grace and humility necessary. In the place of both "grumbling" (2:14) and "anxiety" (4:6), God will be present with them as the "God of peace" (4:7, 9). "*My* God," Paul says, will act for me in your behalf by "filling to the full all your needs."

And God will do so, Paul says, "in keeping with his riches in glory in Christ Jesus." The Philippians' generosity toward Paul, expressed lavishly in the beginning of v. 18, is exceeded beyond all imagination by the lavish "wealth" of the eternal God, who dwells "in glory" full of "riches" made available to his own "in Christ Jesus." God's "riches" are those inherent to his being God, Creator and Lord of all; nothing lies outside his rightful ownership and domain. They are his "in glory" in the sense that his "riches" exist in the sphere of God's glory, where God "dwells" in infinite splendor and majesty, the "glory" that is his as God alone. It is "in keeping with" all of *this* — not "out of" his riches, but *in accordance with this norm,* the infinite "riches" of grace that belong to God's own glory — that God's full supply will come their way to meet their every need. The language is deliberately expansive; after all, Paul is trying to say something concrete about the eternal God and God's relationship to his people. This is why the final word is not the heavenly one, "in glory," but the combined earthly and heavenly one, "in Christ Jesus." Because Paul has beheld the "glory of God in the face of Christ Jesus" (2 Cor. 4:6), expressed in this letter in the majestic Christ narrative in 2:6-11, Paul sees clearly that Christ Jesus is the way God has made his love known and available to his human creatures. This is what the letter has ultimately been all about. It began "in Christ Jesus"; it now concludes "in Christ Jesus." For Paul, "to live is Christ, and to die is gain." Thus the final word in the body of the letter proper is this one: "every need of yours in keeping with the wealth that is God's in glory made available to you in Christ Jesus."

This says it all; nothing more can be added, so Paul simply bursts into doxology. The indicative yields to the imperative of worship. When one thinks on the "riches of God" lavished on us in Christ Jesus, what else is there to do but to praise and worship? Christ is indeed the focus of everything that God has and is doing in this world and the next, but God the Father is always the first and last word in Paul's theology. "*My* God" is now "*our* God *and Father*"; and the living God, the everlasting one, who belongs to the "ages of ages" and who dwells "in glory," is now ascribed the "glory" that is due his name. All of this because the Philippians have sent Paul material assistance to help him through his imprisonment! True theology is expressed in doxology, and doxology is always the proper response to God, even — especially? — in response to God's prompting friends to minister to friends.

IV. Final Reflections on Spirituality

What, then, is the Spirituality that Paul intends the Philippians to enter into by these words? The answer, I would suggest, lies with the doxology. Surely we have not read the text aright until we recognize that Paul intended the Philippians — and therefore us as heirs of their text — to join him in this praise of God. Besides the implied imperative in the doxology itself, two things lead me to argue so.

First, as noted above, these words of doxology conclude a letter that is intended to be read aloud *in the gathered community* in Philippi. For most of us this is simply a text that is read silently and understood descriptively as bringing conclusion to the letter proper. For many of us praise also tends to be perfunctory. It was otherwise with Paul. He belonged to a tradition that regularly blessed God in its worship, which in its Christian expression was rooted in the salvation that God had brought about in Christ and made effectual through the Spirit. Since "rejoicing in the Lord" was enjoined on them in the hymnbook of the ancient people of God, how much more was it enjoined on them as their proper response to Christ's lavish grace. Rejoicing is precisely what Paul repeatedly urges throughout the letter. "Rejoice in the Lord," he exhorts, "and again I will say it, Rejoice." Thus the concluding doxology is intended in part to lead them to rejoicing.

Second, besides being a letter of friendship, Philippians shares all of the significant features of the so-called "letter of moral exhortation," a primary feature of which was the use of exemplary paradigms to reinforce the exhortation. Anyone reading Philippians carefully will note that the appeals in this letter are fortified by these exemplary paradigms. First, in 2:5-11 Paul points to Christ's attitude both as God and as human to reinforce his appeal to their doing nothing from selfish ambition and vain conceit but in humility considering the needs of others to come before their own. Then, in 3:4-14, Paul offers his own narrative as one who follows Christ's example. After all, the heart of his story is his counting everything else as street filth "for the surpassing worth of knowing Christ Jesus my Lord" — which means, he adds, to know simultaneously both the power of his resurrection and participation in his sufferings, thus being made like him in his death. Those who are mature, he concludes, will adopt his view of things; those who walk otherwise are censured as "enemies of the cross." Finally, the very last imperative, before the final expression of gratitude for their gift, calls them to "practice whatever they have received or heard from him or seen in him" (4:9). Thus, it seems hardly imaginable that Paul intended them only to hear his own praise of God in this doxology and not to enter into it themselves — especially so in light of the shift from "my God" in v. 19 to "our God and Father" in the doxology.

But doxology is seldom ever for its own sake. The implied imperative of doxology is rooted in the indicative of v. 19, which, I would offer, reflects the theological basis for everything else said in the letter. It is because Paul has caught a glimpse of "God's riches in glory, made available in Christ Jesus" that everything else in this letter (and in other letters) falls into place. This theological reality explains his transformation of language from Stoicism in vv. 11-13, for example; in the light of such "wealth," lavishly given in Christ, ordinary "want" and "plenty" mean nothing at all. This is also the reason for his counting all things but loss for the surpassing value of knowing Christ Jesus his Lord in 3:8-10 and for his straining with all his might in order to secure the eschatological prize, "the upward call of God in Christ Jesus" (3:13-14). Paul has caught a glimpse of God's "riches in glory," put on full display "in Christ Jesus." This is why for him to live is Christ; to die is gain. This is the Christ whom, in the humiliation of his incarnation and death on a cross, God has exalted by bestowing on him the name above all names, the name of the Lord himself; this is the Christ in whom *all of God's riches in glory* have been lavishly made available to us. For Paul this fact determines everything. This is the glory that he longs for his Philippian friends to see and experience. Thus the whole letter finds its theological focus in this final word.

Our exegesis should in this case, therefore, lead us also to enter into Paul's Spirituality. We too need to pause and reflect, to sense the wonder and awe of such a moment. For Paul these are not mere words; these are the heart of things for him. The Spiritual reality of this text helps us to make sense of his own passions, both for Christ and for Christ's people. Here is one who is in constant communion with God in prayer, who knows the eternal God as dwelling in unfathomable riches of grace, and who knows that God lavishes the riches that are his in glory upon the people through Christ Jesus.

We bring our exegesis to fruition when we ourselves sit with unspeakable wonder in the presence of God, contemplate his riches, pray that they might be poured out on our own friends and family; and stay there in contemplation long enough that our only response is doxology: "to our God and Father be glory for ever, Amen." Until we have done this, I would venture, we have done our exegesis only tentatively. We have been mere historians. To be true exegetes we must hear the words with our hearts, we must bask in God's own glory, we must be moved to a sense of overwhelming awe at God's riches in glory, we must think again on the incredible wonder that these riches are ours in Christ Jesus, and we must then worship the living God by singing praises to his glory. Then we will in some measure have entered into Paul's intent for the Philippians themselves, which, I would argue, is what our exegesis should be all about.

CHAPTER 18

Pneuma and Eschatology in 2 Thessalonians 2:1-2: A Proposal about "Testing the Prophets" and the Purpose of 2 Thessalonians[1]
(1994)

For whatever reason, Spirit movements are frequently characterized by an unusually heightened eschatological awareness or fervor.[2] Recently Robert Jewett has suggested such a *Sitz im Leben* as the most likely historical context for the Thessalonian letters.[3] While I am less persuaded than Jewett as to the presence of a pervasive millenarianism in this church, it seems highly likely that the existence of such an element, and its relationship to the activity of the Spirit in their midst, may best explain one of the more intriguing texts in the Pauline corpus, namely 2 Thess. 2:2, with its collocation of "through Spirit" and a distressing pronouncement of "realized eschatology" (probably as a

---

1. The following commentaries are referred to in this paper by author's name only: E. Best (HNTC, 1972); F. F. Bruce (WBC, 1982); E. von Dobschütz (7th edn., 1909); C. J. Ellicott (1861); G. G. Findlay (CGTC, 1925); J. E. Frame (ICC, 1912); W. Hendriksen (1955); D. E. Hiebert (1971); J. B. Lightfoot (1895 = *Notes on the Epistles of St Paul*); I. H. Marshall (NCB, 1983); G. Milligan (1908); J. Moffatt (EGT, 1910); A. L. Moore (NCB, 1969); L. Morris (NICNT, 1959); A. Plummer (1918); B. Rigaux (EBib, 1956); C. A. Wanamaker (NIGTC, 1990); D. E. H. Whiteley (NClarB, 1969). Three other significant works are referred to by short titles: Giblin, *Threat* (= C. H. Giblin, *The Threat to Faith: An Exegetical and Theological Re-Examination of 2 Thessalonians 2* [AnB, 31; Rome: Pontifical Biblical Institute, 1967]); Hughes, *Rhetoric* (= F. W. Hughes, *Early Christian Rhetoric and 2 Thessalonians* [JSNTSup, 30; Sheffield: JSOT Press, 1989]); Jewett, *Correspondence* (= R. Jewett, *The Thessalonian Correspondence: Pauline Rhetoric and Millenarian Piety* [Philadelphia: Fortress, 1986]).

2. Perhaps part of the reason for this is the close connection between the prophetic Spirit and prophecy (understood as having to do with future events).

3. See *Correspondence*, especially pp. 161-92.

"Spirit" utterance). The purpose of this present paper[4] is twofold: (1) to look more closely at 2 Thess. 2:2, and especially at the difficult phrase, ὡς δι' ἡμῶν, since I am convinced that many of our difficulties both with 2 Thessalonians as a whole and with this passage in particular are the result of a misreading of this phrase; and (2) to suggest that what Paul says later in 2:15 offers us both a key for unlocking 2:2 and the earliest clue regarding his own perspective on the "testing" of prophetic utterances, as he had encouraged in 1 Thess. 5:21, and insists on later in 1 Cor. 14:29-32.

I am happy to offer this modest proposal in honor of Robert Gundry, with appreciation both for his own work in New Testament studies and for his and Lois's hospitality on more than one occasion.

I

At the beginning of the body[5] of his second[6] letter to the Thessalonians, Paul[7] says:

---

4. The substance of much of this paper appears in quite different form in *God's Empowering Presence: The Holy Spirit in the Letters of Paul* (Peabody, Mass.: Hendrickson, 1994). Thanks are due my colleague, Sven Soderlund, whose careful reading of an earlier draft saved me from several infelicities and errors and whose disagreement on the phrase "as though through us" prodded me to think through the argument more carefully at several points.

5. This is the more traditional way of referring to the argument of the letter, which I am convinced is still the better way. For the view that this is the "petitio" of ancient rhetoric, see Hughes, *Rhetoric,* pp. 19-74; for a helpful overview of this whole question and one that takes a position similar to that of Hughes, see Jewett, *Correspondence,* pp. 61-87, 222-25.

6. I remain convinced that one can make best sense of this letter as the second of the two. For the opposite view see, most recently, Wanamaker, pp. 37-45. For a helpful overview of the issues, which concludes in favor of the traditional sequence, see Jewett, *Correspondence,* pp. 19-30.

7. One of the incongruities of New Testament scholarship is the rejection of this epistle as genuinely Pauline. The rejection in this case is based, not as elsewhere on the differences between this letter and the other Paulines, but rather on its high level of similarity to 1 Thessalonians. Paul here is too much like himself to be genuine(!) — although not very far below the surface in every case of rejection is some dissatisfaction with its content, especially the themes of judgment frequently expressed in a more apocalyptic mode of language. But the reasons for inclusion far outweigh any considerations against it. The similarities are precisely what one might expect of a letter written very shortly after the first one, and dealing for the most part with several of the same issues. Moreover, it is nearly impossible to find a reason for pseudepigraphy in this case, especially since so little seems to be gained by it. Furthermore, the exegesis of 2:1-2 and 15 offered here presents a simple and historically viable reason for the letter within the framework of the context of Paul and Thessalonica that emerges in the first letter. On this whole question, again see Jewett, *Correspondence,* pp. 3-18.

1 Now, brothers and sisters, we beg you concerning the coming of our[8] Lord Jesus Christ and our gathering unto him

2 that you not be too easily[9] shaken in mind or disturbed, whether through Spirit or through word or through letter, as though through us, to the effect that the Day of the Lord[10] has come. (2 Thess. 1:1-2, my translation)

These opening words are at once the most crucial and most problematic in this letter. They are the most crucial because Paul now articulates for his and their sakes his understanding of what has been recently reported to him about the situation in Thessalonica; thus they serve to communicate the primary occasion of the letter. Indeed, as will be noted momentarily, the other concerns — their unjust suffering (ch. 1) and the continuing difficulty with the "unruly idle"[11] (ch. 3) — are best understood as related to this one.[12]

At the same time, however, this passage is also the most problematic, because, being as crucial as it is for the interpretation of the letter, what it finally means is far from certain. The difficulty is twofold: (1) What has been communicated among them? That is, what does it mean to say, "the Day of the Lord

---

8. B, Ψ and a few others (including sy[h] and some MSS of the Vulgate) omit the ἡμῶν. Were this more widely attested, most textual critics, including this one, would think that the other witnesses had added the pronoun, since this is Paul's more usual form. But more likely here we have omission for stylistic reasons, in light of the ἡμῶν that follows a few words later and/or in conformity to the immediately preceding clause (1:12).

9. For this sense of ταχέως, see BAGD, who also offer Gal. 1:6 and 1 Tim. 5:22 as further examples. The emphasis is only partly on "haste." Rather it lies more on "quickly" in the sense of "too easily" taken in by new things.

10. Against all earlier evidence in all forms (Greek, versions, fathers), the Majority text has substituted Χριστοῦ for κυρίου. This seems to be a later attempt to make sure that "Lord" equals "Christ" in this passage, which in fact it undoubtedly does.

11. This translation of ἄτακτοι indicates agreement with the lexical evidence suggested by C. Spicq ("Les Thessaloniciens 'inquiets' étaient-ils des paresseux?," ST 10 [1956]: 1-13) that the word implies active behavior, not mere passivity (as in "laziness"), on their part. This is confirmed especially by the wordplay in 3:11 between ἐργαζομένους and περιεργαζομένους, the latter meaning something close to "busybodies."

12. One of the weaknesses in Jewett's radical (= Spirit "enthusiasm") millenarian reconstruction of the historical situation is that he sees such a realized eschatological point of view as already present when 1 Thessalonians was written, so that he can speak of this passage in terms of their "readiness to accept the message reported in 2 Thess 2:2." But that seems to downplay too much of what is said in this passage, particularly that they have been "shaken and disturbed in their minds" about this matter, and that the responsibility of the declaration has been laid at the feet of Paul, despite what he knows has been clearly communicated to them. The implication is strong that this is a "new twist" and that they are quite distressed by it.

has come"? (2) How has this "deceit" (v. 3) been communicated to them (Spirit, word, letter, or some combination of the three?), and how is that question related to Paul (i.e., how has this error been palmed off on them as Pauline)? So problematic is this passage that it is probably fair to suggest that the questions of authenticity and the sequence of the two letters[13] stem in part from its exegetical difficulties, and both of these in regard to how the problems in 2 Thessalonians relate to what Paul has written in 1 Thess. 4:13-18 and 5:1-11.

Much of the problem in interpreting this text lies with the little phrase ὡς δι' ἡμῶν ("as though through us"), mostly because it follows hard on the heels of the preceding triplet of διά clauses, "whether through Spirit, whether through word, whether through letter." Despite the fact that it so poorly represents Pauline usage, the common interpretation understands ὡς δι' ἡμῶν as qualifying one or more of these preceding phrases, suggesting that Paul's uncertainty expressed by this phrase refers to the *means* by which the miscommunication took place. That is, he does not know whether someone has prophesied in his name/behalf, communicated orally as though from him, or forged a letter in his name. In terms of Pauline usage and the literary context, however, this phrase is better understood as anticipating what follows, referring to the *content* of the miscommunication, rather than to its form. Paul is thus offering an unqualified denial that what they are presently believing about the Day of the Lord can be attributed to him at all, even though he is not quite sure, but had a pretty good idea (from my point of view) how such a thing happened. This slight shift of perspective regarding the intent of this phrase, it will be argued, not only resolves many of the difficulties in interpreting v. 2, but also clears the way for a better understanding of the letter as a whole.

II

The first matter — as to *what* had been communicated to them — will not detain us, since to discover what they had come to believe is not essential to our immediate concern. Nonetheless, since it is crucial to the whole letter and in part to how the first part of v. 2 is to be understood, a summary of conclusions is in order.

---

13. See nn. 6 and 7 above. Evidence for such a judgment may be found in Jewett's historical sketch of the question of authenticity (*Correspondence*, pp. 3-18), where, without his trying to make this point, the discussion about authorship invariably involves a prior understanding of our passage.

First, it seems most highly probable that the error referred to in v. 2 is related to some kind of misunderstanding or, more likely, misrepresentation of 1 Thess. 5:1-11, with its repeated mention of "the Day of the Lord" (vv. 2, 4) and subsequent play on the themes of "day" and "night." After all, it is not as though a letter addressing this subject had *not* come from him; one had indeed. What is at issue in our letter is that some are promoting a *different* view from what Paul had communicated earlier.

Second, very likely the content of the misrepresentation has to do with someone's teaching that the Day of the Lord is already present, or, perhaps more likely in light of the emphases in ch. 1, that it had at least already begun in some way. This alone seems to make sense of the argument that follows, in which Paul insists that, just as *he had in fact previously taught them,* both orally (vv. 5, 15) and by letter (v. 15), certain observable events must transpire *before* that Day comes. The Day not only will be preceded by certain events (vv. 3-7), but also the events surrounding the Day will simply be too visible for any of them to miss it when it does come (vv. 8-10a). Hence, he argues, it is quite impossible to derive from anything he himself ever said (whether through word or through letter) that the Day of the Lord has already made its appearance in the present age.

Third, such erroneous teaching about the "present-ness" of the Day of the Lord also helps to explain the emphases in chs. 1 and 3. In light of what Paul had said in the earlier letter, the increase — and unjust nature — of their sufferings gives them considerable reason for anxiety, if the Day has already made its appearance. This is the reason for Paul's assurance in ch. 1 both of their own (future) vindication and of the just judgment of their adversaries. The same error could also buttress the reasoning of the "unruly idle." Since the Day of the Lord has arrived, and since they probably already took a dim view of work quite apart from the eschatological ferment,[14] why should they return to their former occupations?

It is precisely the deleterious effects of such teaching that causes Paul to insist so strongly, first, that he is in no way responsible for it (the present passage), and, second, that what he had previously communicated to them by oral instruction (2:5, 15) and letter (2:15) is the singular truth about the Day of the Lord to which they should hold fast.

---

14. On this matter see esp. R. Russell, "The Idle in 2 Thess 3:6-12: An Eschatological or a Social Problem?," *NTS* 34 (1988): 105-19; and D. E. Aune, "Trouble in Thessalonica: An Exegetical Study of 1 Thess 4.9-12, 5.12-14 and II Thess 3.6-15 in Light of First-Century Social Conditions" (unpublished Th.M. thesis, Regent College, 1989).

III

The question for us, then, is *How* has this thoroughly misguided understanding arisen among them? and How is it related to anything Paul may have said or written? The problem is both *linguistic* (What does "Spirit" mean here, especially as the first member of an apparently equivalent triad that includes "word" and "letter"?) and *grammatical* (How is the phrase "as though through [διά] us" related to the preceding triad of διά phrases?). At issue is what Paul is *denying* by the little phrase ὡς δι' ἡμῶν: (a) that he had written a letter in which this had been stated; (b) that he was responsible for any one of three unknown possible sources for the error; or (c) that he is not responsible for the false pronouncement itself, however it may have been communicated to them. I will argue here that the last of these is the most likely.

1. Let us begin by noting three matters from 2 Thessalonians, two of which are explicit, and the third suggested by Paul's use of language.

a. Paul really does not know the means through which this eschatological falsehood has been communicated to them. In its barest form, Paul's sentence can be displayed thus:

> I urge you
> > concerning the Parousia
> > not to be shaken in mind
> > > that the day of the Lord has come.

His *uncertainty* has to do with the form by which this content has been communicated, as the repeated μήτε διά makes clear. Furthermore, although these three phrases (μήτε διὰ πνεύματος, μήτε διὰ λόγου, μήτε δι' ἐπιστολῆς) together modify the compound infinitives in the purpose clause, the thrice-repeated διά is probably best understood as carrying its ordinary sense of secondary agency. Thus Paul's grammar indicates that his interest is not in the *source* and *form* of the misinformation — that it came *from* the Spirit, for example, or *from* a letter — but in the *content*, by whatever *means* it may have been communicated. This may be displayed thus:

> I urge you
> > concerning the Parousia
> > not to be shaken in mind
> > > whether through the Spirit
> > > whether through a spoken word
> > > whether through a letter
> > > > that the day of the Lord has come.

Putting ὡς δι' ἡμῶν aside for the moment, one can therefore make perfectly good sense of all this. That someone has communicated to them the content of the final clause is certain; that Paul does not know how this has been communicated is equally certain, but his best guess is that it came by means of either a prophecy, another form of spoken word, or a letter.

b. What Paul takes issue with in the argument that follows is likewise not the form of the communication, but its content. Indeed, the form of communication is quite irrelevant after v. 2. One of our exegetical questions, therefore, is why this triad of phrases exists at all. At first blush, it appears to have very little bearing on what follows.

What Paul does remind them in what follows is that he himself has spoken clearly to the issue at hand, on two occasions, and that he has said quite the opposite of what is now being promulgated among them. In v. 5 he appeals, "Don't you remember that when I was with you I used to tell you these things?" (NIV). In v. 15 he again refers to his former teaching when with them, this time by picking up the expression εἴτε διὰ λόγου from v. 2;[15] at the same time he also refers to his former letter, our 1 Thessalonians, and speaks of these two earlier communications as "the *traditions* which you were *taught*." Thus, from Paul's point of view, two things matter: he has formerly taught them the precise opposite of what they are now being told; as far as he is concerned he was also quite clear in what he had taught, and they should hold fast to these "traditions."

Thus, in sum, we are faced with a situation in which Paul (1) knows that his own teaching has been either ignored, misunderstood, or misrepresented (probably the latter), and (2) that even though he is not quite sure how this came about, he himself is being promoted as responsible for *what* is currently being taught.

c. Now to the more suggestive observation. It is striking that the two realities to which Paul refers in v. 15 as "the traditions you were taught"[16] are expressed in precisely the same language as the final two members of the triad of διά phrases in v. 2. To be sure, in v. 2 he wrote μήτε διὰ λόγου, μήτε δι' ἐπιστολῆς, while in v. 15 he writes εἴτε διὰ λόγου εἴτε δι' ἐπιστολῆς; but these differences merely reflect the grammar of the two sentences. This repetition may, of course, be quite accidental, with the former referring to *later* possible communications that have recently been spoken or written among them. But

15. In this instance διὰ λόγου cannot mean "report," as the NIV translates it in v. 2, but refers to his (and his companions') own oral instruction when they were present during the founding visit. Thus the NIV here translates "word of mouth."

16. Meaning, of course, "formerly taught personally by me and my companions."

there are good reasons to think otherwise, that in both cases the phrases refer to the *same* realities, namely his own previous eschatological communications with them. And this is where the demurrer, "as though through us," most likely fits in.

2. In light of these various observations about what Paul actually says, the question then is, what is Paul primarily *denying* by the qualifying phrase, ὡς δι' ἡμῶν?[17] To be sure, both the repetition of the διά and the fact that the phrase immediately follows "whether through letter" make it appear as though Paul is denying that he has written (yet another) letter to them in which he had taken a position quite the opposite of that taken in his first letter. The qualifier is thus sometimes understood as referring only to the final διά phrase, so that the two should be read together thus: "whether through an epistle as though it came from us."[18] This understanding is seen to be supported further by the signature in 3:17; Paul "signs" off our present letter in his own hand, we are told, so that they will not mistake it for some forgery. But there are several matters that make this view highly suspect, despite its surface appearance of naturalness.

a. This reading of the sentence puts the emphasis in Paul's denial at the wrong place. As noted above, Paul's concern throughout is to deny that he can be held responsible for eschatological teaching that so thoroughly contradicts what he has clearly taught them previously, so much so that he spends the next several sentences reiterating that teaching by way of reminder. This view, on the other hand, puts the emphasis on Paul's denying that he has written a further letter to them (hence if there is such a letter, it is a forgery).

b. While it is possible, of course, that Paul could be denying both things at the same time, namely, that he could be held accountable for the false teaching since he is not responsible for any such letter, this view nonetheless has considerable difficulty with the role of the first two διά phrases. By limiting the denial to the letter only (as the NIV: "or letter supposed to have come from us"), the first two items are cast adrift as possible sources for attributing this "new teaching" to Paul. What Paul is thus uncertain

17. On this whole question, see the helpful discussion in Jewett, *Correspondence*, pp. 18-86, who categorizes three approaches to this phrase: (1) to view the phrase as the work of a forger (which Jewett rightly sees breaks down in trying to interpret 2:15); (2) to deny that the phrase has any implications of forgery; (3) to view 1 Thessalonians as the letter, but to understand it as being misrepresented in some way (the view argued for in this study).

18. See, e.g., the commentaries by Moffatt, Moore, and Bruce; this view is also assumed by those who argue for inauthenticity, as the discussion in Jewett (*Correspondence*, pp. 3-18) makes clear. Indeed, it is usually a crucial plank in the argument of the latter.

about is whether the error springs from a prophecy or an oral communication neither of which is attributed to Paul or a letter that did purport to come from him (thus a forgery). But if so, that makes the reference to λόγος especially puzzling. Why mention it at all, one wonders, if this also is not attributable to Paul? And "prophecy" also stands quite on its own, as something that sprang from within the community, but not in relation to Paul's own teaching.

The net result is that by understanding ὡς δι' ἡμῶν as denying only a forgery, the attribution to Paul of the present eschatological teaching is no longer an issue unless, of course, its source was the alleged forgery. But such a view makes very little sense either of the mention of the first two members of the triplet or of the argument that follows, where Paul sets about to overturn the attribution of this nonsense to himself.

c. These difficulties have led most scholars, therefore, to view the demurring phrase as qualifying all three of the phrases in the preceding triad.[19] Although this "solution" has more going for it grammatically, it too founders on point (a) above, but even more so on the problem of understanding how "the Spirit" might have been understood as mediated "through us," since Paul has not recently been on the scene.[20] Indeed, that Paul should ever have landed on an *alleged prophecy* as having *come from him* in some way as a possible source of this present error seems most remarkable! Someone could easily have misrepresented his earlier — or later — teaching, to be sure, not to mention the ability to forge a letter in his name. But how could a prophecy have been alleged to have come from Paul, which is what this view must necessarily require?

d. All of which leads finally to the primary objection to both of these views, the grammatical one. It seems nearly impossible that Paul could have intended this phrase to mean, "as though it [the letter] *came from* us." If reference to a forgery were Paul's present intent, then one would expect ὡς ἀπ' ἡμῶν or παρ' ἡμῶν ("as though *from* us"), not δι' ἡμῶν, which rarely if ever denotes the "originating source" of anything in Pauline usage. Overlooking or

---

19. This is by far the more common option in the English commentaries; cf. the discussion in Rigaux, pp. 650-51.

20. That this is obviously the difficulty for those who take this position can be seen by the way they struggle to make sense of it. See, e.g., Best (pp. 278-79), who waffles at best (cf. Wanamaker and others who follow Best). On the basis of 2:15, he wants the phrase to refer only to the latter two items; but he recognizes how difficult that is to maintain grammatically, so he reluctantly includes all three. Of the first he is then left to comment, "Paul was probably known to exercise ecstatic gifts . . . any oral prophecy or statement made elsewhere by Paul or one of his associates could have been wrongly reported in Thessalonica."

ignoring this point of grammar, as so often happens in the commentaries and translations,[21] will not do, since Paul elsewhere shows considerable precision in the use of these prepositions. When he refers to the originating source of something he uses παρά or ἀπό;[22] when he refers to a secondary agent, that through which something has been mediated, he uses διά.[23] In this regard one need look no further than the well-known demurrer in Gal. 1:1, that his apostleship is neither ἀπ' ἀνθρώπων nor δι' ἀνθρώπου (it neither has its source in humans nor has it been mediated through any human). We must accept it simply as wrong to translate this phrase, "either *by* spirit or *by* word or *by* letter, as though *from* us" (NRSV; cf. NIV).

3. That leads us, then, to an alternative way of understanding ὡς δι' ἡμῶν, one that takes the grammar more seriously while at the same time fitting better with the various observations made at the beginning of this section.

As noted above, the use of διά in the preceding three phrases does not emphasize the originating source of the error; rather, by means of the διά Paul is already pointing ahead to the content of the error described in the final clause of the sentence. Thus he is not suggesting that either a prophecy or an oral report or a letter may have *originated* with him, but that by any one of these unknown means the *content of the false teaching* has been *attributed* to him. For example, had Paul not gone on to mention λόγος and ἐπιστολή, we would all (correctly) understand him to be urging that the Thessalonian believers not be easily shaken "through some prophetic utterance" to the effect that "the Day of the Lord has come." The same is true with "through oral instruction" and "through letter." In each case the διά refers to a possible source by which this content has been mediated, not that the source itself came *from Paul.*

That further suggests, therefore, that when Paul inserts the qualifying phrase, ὡς δι' ἡμῶν, he is not so much concerned with the form in which the error came to them, but with the fact that the content of the error itself has been attributed to him in some way.[24] In this sense, our phrase does indeed

21. Exceptions are Dobschütz, p. 266, and Giblin, *Threat,* p. 149, n. 3.

22. See, e.g., 1 Thess. 3:6: "now that Timothy has come to us from you."

23. It should be noted in this regard that on four other occasions Paul uses διά with ἐπιστολή (2 Thess. 3:14[!]; 1 Cor. 16:3; 2 Cor. 10:9, 11) and in each case he clearly refers in some fashion to the *content* of the letter(s), not to its origins. One should note further·that the δι' ἐπιστολῆς in 2:15 does *not* refer to Paul as the source of the letter as such, but to the letter as the means whereby the "traditions" have been given to them.

24. This view has been suggested, *inter alios,* by Frame, p. 247 ("he disclaims simply all responsibility for the statement: 'the day of the Lord is present'"); cf. Dobschütz, pp. 266-67;

grammatically go with the three preceding phrases, but it is not suggesting any of the three items as being *from Paul;* rather, it refers to them as the possible means whereby he has been accredited with the content of the false teaching about the Day of the Lord. Thus Paul almost certainly does not mean, "*through* a letter, as though *from* us"; he means, "whether through [any of these means], as though through us the present teaching came to you."

4. If such is the case, and both grammar and the rest of the argument in context seem to point this way, then several matters combine to suggest (1) that the second and third phrases in the διά triad do not refer to a recent report or letter purported to come from him, but rather to his own teaching when first with them and in his previous letter to them, teachings that are now being misrepresented in some way so that they support the new "teaching"; and (2) that the first member of the triad, which does not fit easily with the second and third under any circumstances, and is noticeably missing in 2:15, may be the key to much.[25] Let us begin with the latter.

a. Much of our difficulty with v. 2 has always lain with the first of the three διά phrases. On the one hand, it is *grammatically* coordinate with the next two, but unlikely so otherwise. That is, even though the three phrases are joined grammatically in Paul's sentence, it is unlikely that they can be coordinate either as to the nature of the communication or in terms of who is doing the communicating. It is generally agreed that διὰ πνεύματος refers to a prophetic utterance of some kind.[26] Although we may be rightly puzzled as to why he may have used πνεῦμα rather than προφητεία, it is not unlike Paul to express himself in this way. This is surely the way we are to understand the use of the plural πνεύματα in 1 Cor. 14:32 (where "spirits" of the prophets are subject to the prophets; cf. 12:10 and 14:12). The reason for the plural in the 1 Corinthians passage is not that Paul believed in a plurality of "spirits," but that

---

Dibelius, p. 44; Findlay, p. 165 ("'*supposing that* it is through us,' viz. that the announcement of the arrival of 'the day' comes from the Lord through His Apostles and has their authority"). For a different solution, see Giblin, *Threat,* pp. 149-50, 243, who sees the issue not to be one of the content of the utterance itself so much as an issue over Paul's authority.

25. Cf. J. T. Ubbink, "ὡς δι' ἡμῶν (2 Thess 2,2) een exegetish-isagogische puzzle," *NedTTs* 7 (1952-53): 269-95, who, however, still takes the phrase as referring to what precedes, not to what follows.

26. So most commentaries (Best, Bruce, Dobschütz, Ellicott, Frame ["clearly"], Hendriksen, Hiebert, Marshall, Milligan ["ecstatic utterance"], Moore, Morris, Plummer [who allows tongues as well], Rigaux, Wanamaker); cf. the NIV, which actually translates, "by some prophecy." Whiteley (p. 97) suggests simply "ecstatic experience."

he understood the one Holy Spirit to be speaking through the several human spirits.[27]

It seems altogether likely, therefore, especially in light of 1 Thess. 5:19-22, that this meaning should prevail in our sentence. If so, then it also seems likely that this alleged means through which the error might have found expression took place *within the believing community at worship.* Furthermore, given that Paul includes such an option at all, one should probably take seriously both that this is a very real possibility from his point of view and that the final clause actually gives the basic content of the oracle itself.[28]

b. Such a possibility would further explain (1) why Paul repeats the final two διά phrases in v. 15, but with the "Spirit" phrase noticeably missing, and (2) how it is that he knows his own teaching is now being contradicted — even though he is not quite sure how this came about — while at the same time he is being promoted as responsible for what is currently being taught. The reasons for both phenomena lie with a recent prophetic utterance within the community, which has given expression to the present teaching, whose content at the same time has been attributed to Paul.

c. On this view, one can then also make sense of the repetition — and omission — in 2:15, by viewing the twin phrases in vv. 2 and 15 as *referring to the same reality,* namely what he had communicated both when he was himself present with them and in his former letter — our 1 Thessalonians. A prophetic utterance that either contradicts that former teaching, or reinterprets it, could at the same time also attribute to Paul what is being prophesied — if one but have the Spirit's help in "properly interpreting" what Paul had previously taught! This would explain both the inclusion of prophecy in the triad in v. 2 and also how such a clear contradiction to his former teaching could have been laid at his feet. This also means that "through letter" has nothing at all to do with yet another letter, as though someone forged such a letter in his name.[29]

27. I have suggested the cumbersome "S/spirit" as a way of translating this idea, which is also the best explanation for the (for us) awkward-sounding, "my S/spirit prays" or "sings" in 1 Cor. 14:14-15. On these various matters see the discussion of these texts in G. D. Fee, *The First Epistle to the Corinthians* (NICNT; Grand Rapids: Eerdmans, 1987).

28. As many have suggested; see, e.g., Jewett, *Correspondence,* p. 178; Giblin, *Threat,* p. 243.

29. This also suggests that the whole issue of forgery, which has caught the imagination of so many scholars, is something of a red herring. These two passages together (2:2 and 15) do not suggest as much; and the reason for 3:17 is precisely the same as in Gal. 6:11, as a way of emphasizing that, whatever else, he is indeed responsible for the (apostolic) content of what has been written in *this* letter.

Rather, Paul's (now awkward) sentence gives expression to his own frustration that his own teaching is no longer adhered to while he himself is being given credit for a clear contradiction to it. His solution is found in v. 15, where διὰ πνεύματος is noticeably missing[30] as he now urges them to "hold fast to the traditions you were taught, whether by direct speech or by letter."[31] He knows that his former teaching was not ambiguous; they must therefore hold fast to what has been "handed down" to them directly from him.

5. Putting all of this together, the "logic" of the sentence thus goes something like this. Given Paul's twofold difficulty — that he is aware that the *misinformation* has ultimately been attributed to him, while he is not quite sure *how* it was communicated — he therefore begins with the latter item, the uncertain form of miscommunication, the first member of which is most likely the key to the whole. By means of the "Spirit" someone could easily have represented himself/herself as speaking in Paul's behalf (e.g., "the same Spirit who spoke to us previously through Paul now speaks again in Paul's behalf, saying that . . ."). But for Paul it would be equally possible — more likely, perhaps, in light of the next two phrases — that such a "prophecy" had been given in the form of an authoritative interpretation of what he had previously taught or written (e.g., "the Spirit says that what Paul really meant was . . ."!). In either case, having mentioned the uncertain *form* of mediation of this error by the repeated "whether through . . . ," he begins to move toward the misrepresented *content*.[32] Using the same suppositional language, "as though through us," he now with this demurral anticipates the final clause in the sentence.

---

30. Cf. Giblin, *Threat*, p. 45, who also sees 2:15 as "factoring out" a "heavy reliance on charismatic utterances," but as a "modification," rather than a "follow up," of 1 Thess. 5:19-22 (as I will argue below).

31. It is the clear statement of 2:15 that Paul has in fact written to them *before* the writing of our 2 Thessalonians, which makes the reversal of the order of these two letters so problematic. Wanamaker's "solution" of this difficulty is highly questionable. He suggests that the "letter" mentioned in 2:15 is hypothetical on Paul's part. But that will not work at all, not only because Paul also mentions "through word," which harks back to v. 5 and therefore cannot be hypothetical, but also because "through letter" is modified by ἡμῶν, which can scarcely mean "as though from us." Paul is clearly referring to a previous letter, "our letter," which picks up the plurals from 1 Thessalonians which are carried through this letter as well. That "our letter" refers to 1 Thessalonians is made the more certain because the content of that letter, as Paul well knows and is now reminding them, stands in utter contradiction to what they are now believing.

32. Thus at issue is not simply a misunderstanding of Paul, as Jewett (*Correspondence*, pp. 185-91) would have it. "Misrepresented" or "misconstrued" makes far more sense of the twin facts that Paul knows he has been quite clear on this matter, yet that he is now being put forward as responsible for the current contradiction.

Thus, "Do not be too easily shaken or disturbed," he urges them, "whether it comes through the Spirit, or through what I have previously taught or written, as though the teaching came through us to the effect that the Day of the Lord has already come."

Finally, this also helps to make sense of the ὡς ὅτι that introduces the final clause. What Paul intends is clear enough; here finally is the content of what has been said in their midst that is currently troubling them. But the sentence has gotten away from him a bit. The ὅτι ("that") grammatically follows the various possible sources by which this content has been mediated, and thus by direct discourse introduces the content of the oracle itself; the ὡς picks up the same sense of misrepresentation as in the preceding phrase, and thus ties the two together. He does not doubt that the version of the content he is about to offer is basically correct; but he may not have it precisely correct, so he qualifies, "to the effect that." The point being made is that under no circumstances may teaching of this sort, or a prophetic oracle with this content, be laid at his feet, as though it had come to them with his imprimatur.

IV

The view suggested here, it should finally be noted, makes good sense of several matters in·these letters, and beyond.

1. Let us begin by reiterating the conclusions from above: The answer to the question, How in light of 1 Thess. 5:1-11 (δι' ἐπιστολῆς) and 2 Thess. 2:3-12 (διὰ λόγου) could anyone have attributed to Paul the realized eschatology expressed in 2:2 probably lies with the pneumatism that was apparently alive and active in this congregation. Someone speaking "by the Spirit" has declared that "the Day of the Lord has already come." By "the Spirit" this eschatological declaration has also been laid at Paul's feet. But he will have none of it. He will neither disown the Spirit nor despise prophesyings (cf. 1 Thess. 5:19-20); but neither will he allow such prophetic words to go "untested." What they are to hold onto, he declares in 2 Thess. 2:15, are "the *traditions* you were taught previously, whether orally or by our letter." This does not "factor out" the Spirit; but it does offer a guideline whereby such Spirit utterances were to be tested.

2. That leads us, in turn, back to the Spirit material in the earlier letter (1 Thess. 5:19-22), to ask how that might be related to what is said here. One of the problems with the 1 Thessalonians passage is its relationship to the larger

context of the letter and in particular to the parenesis that begins in 5:12.[33]
The problem is, how do these imperatives relate to the *formal* (structural) aspects of the letter, and how much do they *reflect the known situation* in Thessalonica (as reported to him by Timothy)?

Most likely the answer to both parts of the problem lies in a *via media*. On the one hand, they are part of a "formal" series of "staccato" imperatives such as one can find in many of the Pauline letters; on the other hand, and especially since imperatives like those in vv. 19-23 are noticeably missing in all other Pauline letters, this set probably reflects the "tailoring" of the concluding imperatives to fit the local situation in Thessalonica.

If so, then the question is, what situation? First, some structural observations: As with vv. 16-18 which immediately precede, the five imperatives in vv. 19-22 are intended to be read together. They are given in two sets (vv. 19-20; 21-22); the first is a form of parallelism in which the second member specifies the first (they are not to quench the Spirit by despising prophesying); the second set, which is in contrast to the first, specifies what they are to do instead, this time in a set of three, the first giving the general rule, which the final two spell out more specifically. Thus:

> The Spirit do not quench;
> Prophecies do not despise; *but*[34]
>> Test all things:
>>> Hold fast to the good;
>>> Avoid every evil form.

33. On the one hand, hortatory remarks such as these appear regularly as a part of the concluding materials in the Pauline letters (e.g., 1 Cor. 16:13-18; 2 Cor. 13:11; Rom. 16:17-19; cf. Fee, *1 Corinthians,* pp. 825-26), most often, as here, in the form of "staccato imperatives." Sometimes these imperatives pick up specific matters in the congregations; at other times they are simply general exhortations. On the other hand, in some of Paul's letters a section of parenesis follows the so-called doctrinal section, as a conclusion of the larger argument of the epistle, as, e.g., in Rom. 12–15, Gal. 6:1-10, Col. 3–4. In each case these can be shown to be integral to the argument of the letter, not simply "ethical instruction" following "right thinking on the Christian gospel."

34. The omission of this δέ in the TR (supported by א* A 33 81 104 614 629 630 945 pm), along with the fact that each of these imperatives was assigned a verse number, has tended to destroy altogether the meaning of this series of imperatives and to cause untold harm in separatist churches. The δέ in this case was in all likelihood omitted by scribes (in conformity to the whole series, all of which lack conjunctions), rather than added early and often by such a wide range of early witnesses (incl. B D G K P J 181 326 436 1241 1739 pm it vg cop goth eth). B. M. Metzger (*A Textual Commentary on the Greek New Testament* [London: United Bible Societies, 1971], p. 633, following Lightfoot, p. 84) suggests that the omission may have resulted from its being "absorbed by the following syllable," but it is hard to see how that could have happened in this case (since it is followed by the δοκ-, not the -τε, of δοκιμάζετε).

The basic exegetical issue is to ascertain *where the emphasis lies:* Is it on the first two imperatives (are some within the community less than delighted with such phenomena in the assembly?), or on the final three (Do the first two set up the final three so that in correcting abuses they will not over-correct?)?[35]

It is common to argue that the problem in Thessalonica results from some disenchantment with, or conflict over, these phenomena,[36] in the form either of too much "ecstasy" (usually glossolalia, as in Corinth) or of misguided "ecstasy" (either by the "unruly idle," who are using prophecy to justify their behavior or by some whose mistaken predictions about the Day of the Lord have brought prophecy into disrepute). This is arguably supported by the grammar of the prohibitions themselves.[37]

But it is just as possible, more likely in my view, that Paul is offering something preventative, perhaps related to their former experience with "ecstasy" of a more uncontrolled sort. In light of the evidence from 2 Thess. 2:1-2, it may well be that Timothy had already informed Paul of some tendencies in worship that needed "adjustment" — but not elimination. Thus, some months later (2 Thess. 2:2), even though Paul does not know the precise source of the misrepresentation of his teaching, he does know that a prophetic utterance is one of the possibilities. Thus, the evidence from 2 Thess. 2:2 and 15 leads one to think that Paul in 1 Thess. 5:19-22 already had reason to caution this community to be a bit more perceptive about "Spirit" utterances.[38]

35. It is altogether possible, of course, that Paul is simply trying to offer some guidelines for perfectly valid — and normal — Spirit activity within their own gatherings for worship, since many of his Gentile converts would already have been well acquainted with "ecstasy" from their pagan past. Wanamaker (p. 201) suggests that "Paul wished to encourage pneumatic activity as a sign of the eschatological times in which the Thessalonians found themselves." This passage, however, and others like it, implies that the phenomena are more integral to early Christian initiation and experience than Wanamaker allows. Paul hardly needs to "encourage" what would have been *presuppositional* in the Pauline churches.

36. See esp. Jewett, *Correspondence,* pp. 100-102, whose discussion notes others who share this perspective (e.g., W. Schmithals, Marshall, D. E. Aune).

37. μή with the present imperative often has the force of "stop doing something," implying the forbidden action as already taking place. This is argued, e.g., by Hiebert, p. 243, and Moore, p. 83; but see Bruce, p. 125, who correctly notes that "like the positive imperatives in vv. 16-18 and 21-22, [these negative imperatives] indicate what they must habitually do (or refrain from doing)."

38. For a different view on the relationship between 1 Thess. 5:19-22 and 2 Thess. 2:2; 2:15, see Hughes, *Rhetoric,* pp. 56-57, who interprets the author of 2 Thessalonians as denying the validity of "spirit," which is contrary to the genuine Paul in 1 Thess. 5:19-20 ("a particularly jarring contrast" to the exhortation not to quench the Spirit, as though Paul had not written vv. 21-22 as well!).

The difficulty with this passage, of course, is that in urging that they "test all things," and in so doing to "hold fast to the good and be done with every evil expression," he gives no criteria for such testing. How does one distinguish the good from the evil, in terms of prophetic utterances? Here again is where the combined evidence of 2 Thess. 2:2, 5, and 15 may help. On the one hand, the abuse of "prophetic utterances" is not in itself directly condemned in the second letter, probably in this case because Paul is not in fact certain that this is the actual cause. On the other hand, if our understanding of 2:2 moves in the right direction, then in 2:15 he is also offering a clear criterion for "testing the spirits": "the *traditions* you were taught, whether orally or by our letter."

3. It is of some interest, in light of these suggestions, to note that in the better known passage in 1 Corinthians 12–14 Paul also calls for "testing all things" when it comes to prophetic utterances. First, in 1 Cor. 12:8-10, in his list of primarily extraordinary Spirit manifestations within the gathered community, he lists "the discerning of spirits" immediately following "prophecy." That this most likely refers to "discerning prophecies" is substantiated by the use of this same language in 14:29-32, where he insists that after two or three utterances, the others "discern" what is said, and that they can take their turn in prophesying because the "spirits" of the prophets are subject to the prophets.[39] But, again, as in 1 Thess. 5:19-22 Paul neither indicates the process nor gives criteria as to how one goes about the "discerning." Earlier, however, in 14:3 he specifically says that the one who prophesies speaks edification, encouragement (or exhortation), and comfort. Even if not intended as criteria for "discerning," such a direct statement as to the goal of prophecy within the community has the effect of establishing a kind of criterion — the encouragement and building up of the community. This, of course, is precisely *not* what has resulted from a "Spirit" utterance in Thessalonica about the Day of the Lord, which has led instead to many of them being "shaken in mind and disturbed."

V

If all of this approximates both the situation being addressed in 2 Thessalonians and the meaning of these various texts, then a few brief conclusions may be drawn about the purpose of 2 Thessalonians, as well as about "testing the prophets" in the Pauline corpus.

39. For full arguments in this regard see Fee, *1 Corinthians*, pp. 596-97, 693-96.

Whether or not the Thessalonians' present distress was *actually* the direct result of a prophetic utterance that had also laid claim to Paul's authority, Paul himself at least *believed* that such could well have been the case. If so, then the purpose of 2 Thessalonians and the need to "test all things" with regard to prophecy may well coalesce in 2 Thess. 2:15.

At stake are two issues: the need expressed earlier in 1 Thess. 5:19-22 to "test" prophetic utterances, and the need to calm this community's distress over false eschatological "prophecies." The key to both of these matters is for Paul to remind them of "the *traditions* you were taught, whether orally or by previous letter." Since this latest eschatological unrest has apparently caused further distress in their suffering, as well as having furthered the cause of the "unruly idle," he reminds them of his former teaching on these matters as well. This accounts for all the data in this letter.

What this also means is that here, along with 1 Cor. 14:3, we have a primary criterion for the testing of prophetic utterances. In 2 Thess. 2:15 the basis of the "test" is *theological or doctrinal content* (= "the traditions you were taught"); in 1 Cor. 14:3 Paul offers the test of *effect,* as well as content, having to do with its helpfulness to the believing community.[40] Both of these "criteria" were being abused in Thessalonica, and that is what called for in our letter.

A final, contemporary word is perhaps in order, especially in the light of the renewal of Spirit phenomena in so many sectors of the church in our day. First, it should be noted that the earliest mention of prophecy in the New Testament (1 Thess. 5:19-22) includes the imperative that all such prophecies (and by implication all other such "Spirit utterances" in the community) are to be tested. The awe with which many contemporary charismatics hold prophecy and "prophets," which in effect causes them almost never to be "tested," stands in basic contradiction to this Pauline injunction; rather, it reflects the Thessalonian attitude toward prophetic utterances, one that needed correcting and harnessing.

Second, it is arguable that in 2 Thess. 2:15 and 1 Cor. 14:3 Paul has set the pattern for the church at a later time. On the one hand, all Spirit utterances

---

40. Among the "criteria" passages, one might add 1 Cor. 12:3, but as I have noted in my commentary (*1 Corinthians,* p. 581), "Paul's point in context is not to establish a means of 'testing the spirits,' but to remind them that 'inspired utterance' as such is not evidence of being 'led of the Spirit.'" Some might want to add Rom. 12:6 ("according to the analogy of the faith"). While this view has several things to commend it, more likely this phrase refers to the actual gifting of the prophet, that he or she is to prophesy in keeping with the faith to do so, which in turn is in keeping with the differing "portion of faith" that each has received (v. 3). For a full examination of this matter, see Fee, *Presence, ad loc.*

should be tested in light of the "traditions," which for us, of course, are now in the form of inspired sacred Scripture. On the other hand, since even "truth" can be used in an abusive way, all such Spirit utterances should also lead to the encouragement and edification of the local community of believers.

CHAPTER 19

Toward a Theology of 2 Timothy —
from a Pauline Perspective
(1997)

The task of this paper is to present the theology of 2 Timothy, both explicit and implied, on the assumption that the letter was written by Paul.[1] In order to do that, some preliminary methodological matters first need to be set forth, including an overview of the assumed rhetorical situation of the letter and how that in turn may be assumed to affect its theological emphases.

I. Some Methodological Concerns

It may be taken as a common starting point, no matter what view of authorship one holds, that 2 Timothy is not intentionally theological, in the sense that theology as such is not its primary reason for being. Nonetheless, the presupposed rhetorical situation of the letter shows deep concern for continuing loyalty to the apostle and his gospel. One may, therefore, legitimately examine the clues throughout the letter that both explicitly and more incidentally reveal the theological content of the gospel to which Timothy and the church are being urged to be loyal.[2]

1. For this reason, whatever one means in this case by "authorship," I intend to use the name "Paul" as subject of my sentences throughout, rather than a more neutral (but clumsier) circumlocution, such as "the writer" or "the Paul of this letter." By this usage I mean nothing more than that in this paper the presupposed rhetorical situation of the letter is assumed to reflect an actual historical situation of the apostle during his lifetime. While I hold this to be historically more probable than otherwise, there is no attempt to demonstrate that here. At best, I hope to show that one can make a good deal of sense of the letter as a document from early Christian history under this assumption.

2. I should point out that the paper reflects my own working through the text of 2 Timo-

Significantly, these clues emerge precisely at those places where Paul either (1) urges Timothy — and thus the church through Timothy — to "hang in there" as his faithful companion in the gospel by "joining with me in suffering" (1:8; 2:3),[3] or (2) urges faithfulness vis-à-vis some "opponents"[4] who are not loyal to Paul and his gospel, who themselves have "deviated[5] concerning the truth," and who bid fair to "overturn[6] the faith of some." Therefore, it is of some importance for us to try to establish the rhetorical situation in which these various clues emerge, if we are going to read its theology in light of its assumed contingencies.

I should also offer a definition of "theology," since in this seminar and its predecessor "theology" has become an "accordion" word, depending on how much air one pumps into or out of it. I take our task not to be a sociological or rhetorical one, but a *theological* one in the sense that biblical theology by its very nature presupposes a narrative in which *God* is the protagonist, *people* the agonists, and *redemption* the goal of plot resolution. All other theological concerns, as I perceive them, find their meaning in light of these narrative realities. My concern within this framework is to determine and analyze the *coherent nature* of Paul's (as assumed "author" of 2 Timothy) theological explication of the narrative of salvation, as that finds expression in the *contingencies* of this letter.

Finally, since my task is to read the theology of this letter in the light of Pauline theology as reflected elsewhere in the corpus, I should at least indi-

---

thy again, with almost no consultation with the secondary literature (including my own commentary!) in the first go around, which is essentially reproduced here. There are two reasons for this procedure: first, it gave me the opportunity to have a fresh encounter with the letter on its own terms; second, all of the literature to a piece that speaks to this question (the theology of 2 Timothy) does so *only* in the context of "the theology of the Pastoral Epistles"; and in this case that proves disastrous. Even in such a helpful (and corrective) study as Frances Young's *The Theology of the Pastoral Epistles* (Cambridge, 1994), much of what is there presented is almost unrecognizable as the theology of 2 Timothy. For example, no one who had read her initial theological chapter (on "theology and ethics") and then read 2 Timothy could imagine that her study were based on a careful reading of our letter, since what is presented, in reality the ethics of 1 Timothy and Titus, could not possibly have been derived from 2 Timothy on its own. Likewise with her section "God as Saviour," which would look quite different had she started with 2 Timothy, rather than amalgamating its theology into that of 1 Timothy.

3. Thus I take the συγκακοπάθησον to mean "join with me" rather than "join with Christ" or "with Christ and me" — despite the συν compounds in 2:11-12, which almost certainly intend the latter.

4. See 2:25, τοὺς ἀντιδιατιθεμένους (NT hapax), and 3:8; 4:15, where a form of ἀνθίστημι occurs (a Pauline word, but unique to 2 Timothy in the PE).

5. See 2:18, ἠστόχησαν (a PE word; see 1 Tim. 1:6; 6:21); cf. 1:15; 4:4, where ἀποστρέφω appears with reference to those within the church who have followed the "opponents of the truth."

6. See 2:18, ἀνατρέπουσιν (cf. Titus 1:11).

cate what I perceive to be the essentials of that theology. And since it is arguably impossible to understand Paul without recognizing *eschatology* as the essential framework of all his theological thinking, while *salvation in Christ* is the essential concern within that framework, at issue is the nature of the "constants" in Paul's understanding of "salvation in Christ" — even if they do not each find expression in every soteriological moment in his letters. Therefore, I have chosen to outline my understanding of those constants in Part 4 of this paper, and then to use them as a convenient framework for analyzing the theology of this letter.[7]

II. The Assumed Rhetorical Situation

Read on its own terms, 2 Timothy was written from prison[8] with the primary purpose of urging Timothy to join Paul posthaste (4:9, 21), presumably in Rome,[9] and to bring Mark and some personal items along with him (4:11, 13) when he comes.[10] Timothy is to be replaced by Tychicus, the presumed bearer of the letter (4:12). The reason for haste is the onset of winter (4:21) and the fact that the preliminary hearing has already taken place (4:16).

But the letter body is very little about this matter, and very much an appeal to Timothy to remain loyal to Paul and his gospel, and to do so by embracing suffering and hardship, in light of (1) the defection of so many (1:15), (2) the present opposition, which even though its leadership had been previ-

---

7. By adopting this methodology, of course, I lay myself wide open to the charge of reading the theology of 2 Timothy through a grid that may be foreign to the letter itself. But what happened to me in fact was quite the opposite. It was after I had finished writing parts 2 and 3 of the paper, especially part 3, that I saw the Pauline "constants" were precisely those that had to be addressed in any proper theological analysis of the gospel in 2 Timothy. That one has to analyze the gospel in order to do its theology properly is what emerged out of writing parts 2 and 3. That all of this happened during the writing of the paper will be evident to any who might chance to read both the abstract and the paper. In the strange, but necessary, workings of the SBL, abstracts are required to be in hand three months before the paper; and I therefore submitted an abstract of what I *expected* to do, which changed some in the course of things.

8. See 1:8; 4:16; and esp. 2:9, where the reference to his suffering "even to the point of being chained like a common criminal" (κακοῦργος, used elsewhere to refer to those who commit especially serious crimes; cf. Luke 23:32ff.) seems especially repugnant to him.

9. Assuming that the πρώτη ἀπολογία of 4:16 was a *prima actio*, a preliminary hearing before the emperor or another magistrate, roughly comparable in purpose to a grand jury hearing, and that the "lion's mouth" in v. 17 (echoing Ps. 22:13) is Nero, even if he was not personally present.

10. That Timothy is to pick up these items in Troas implies a journey from Ephesus by way of Troas, the Egnatian Way, across the Adriatic and on to Rome.

ously excommunicated, continues to spread its teachings like gangrene in the church (2:18; cf. 1 Tim. 1:19-20),[11] and (3) Paul's own urgencies in light of his expected execution (4:6-8).

At the same time, however, although in a more indirect way, this appeal to loyalty to Paul and his gospel is also intended for the church. This is evidenced first of all by the double "grace" at the end (4:22: "the Lord be with your spirit [singular]; grace be with you all [plural]"), and further by: (a) the instruction in 2:2 that what has been entrusted to him Timothy is to entrust to others who are reliable and qualified to continue the teaching, and (b) the plaintive note in 2:18 that the "faith of some is being overturned" by the false teachers, matched (c) by the stronger note in 4:3-4 that many within the church are quite pleased to have it this way. As with all the other Pauline letters, including Philemon, this letter was expected to be read publicly in the church(es), in this case apparently as a simultaneous final affirmation of Timothy (and therefore also of Tychicus) and an appeal to their loyalty to his gospel.

Everything in the letter presupposes this situation, starting with the thanksgiving (1:3-5), with its reminder that both Paul and Timothy have been loyal to their own pasts and that true[12] "faith" (= faith-fulness) really does reside in Timothy,[13] and concluding with the final charge (4:1-5), for which Paul himself serves as paradigm (vv. 6-8); and, of course, it continues on into the personal matters and instructions of 4:10-18.[14] But it is especially pro-

11. A word about the perceived relationship between 1 and 2 Timothy. The rhetorical situation of 1 Timothy assumes Paul to be free, having recently left Timothy in Ephesus with the specific charge to stop false teaching (apparently led by some elders in the church[es]) while he himself went on to Macedonia. Before he left he had excommunicated Hymenaeus and Alexander. That the excommunication failed to "take" in the case of Hymenaeus is assumed in the new rhetorical situation of 2 Timothy. Alexander appears to have gone on to Troas, where he is most likely in part responsible for Paul's arrest in that city (4:14-15, hence the warning for Timothy to watch out for him as he goes through Troas), while Hymenaeus is now teamed up with a Philetus. One may assume these two at least to be included in the descriptions of those who make their way into the homes of "sin-laden women" in 3:5-9, who are thus the imposters of 3:13 who deceive even as they are themselves deceived.

12. Gk ἀνυποκρίτου, a word that is often pointed out as betraying the ultimately "un-Pauline" character of "faith" in the PE. But is not this objection the clear evidence of finding what one is looking for? How is it "un-Pauline" to speak of "genuine faith" when the so-called "real Paul" speaks exactly this way of "love" (Rom. 12:9)? Given that the "faith of some" is being overturned, could it not be argued to be typically Pauline that in the thanksgiving he should remind Timothy of the "genuineness" of his own "faith-fulness" toward Christ Jesus?

13. It might be noted in passing how Pauline it is to thank God in his thanksgiving periods for the very matter(s) that are also at stake in the letter.

14. In very much the same way as Philippians, 2 Timothy may be described as a combination of a letter of friendship and of moral exhortation. Among other things, "friends" have "en-

nounced in the several appeals to loyalty that make up the body of the letter. The first of these, with which the letter begins (1:6-14), sets the stage for the whole. It is resumed in 2:1-13,[15] after a preliminary setting forth of a positive paradigm (Onesiphorus, 1:16-18) in light of negative ones (1:15). The second appeal (2:14–3:9), while made to Timothy, is specifically directed toward the church and set in the context of the opposition to Paul's gospel (2:14–3:9), while the final one (3:10-17) returns to the paradigmatic nature of Paul's ministry in light of these opponents, before giving Timothy his final charge (4:15).

Of these three (or four)[16] appeals to loyalty, the two parts of the first one (1:6-14 and 2:1-13) are the more important theologically, not only because they come first and set the course for the whole, but in both cases they are bolstered by specific references to the content of Paul's gospel. Indeed, both the positioning and the (apparently) careful structuring of 1:6-14 make it especially important for our purposes. The paragraph as a whole is framed chiastically, first by the appeal to Timothy's experience of the Spirit (vv. 6-7 and 14), and then by Paul's own loyalty in the midst of his present hardship and suffering (vv. 8 and 11-13), so that the confessional theologoumenon of vv. 9-10 serves as the centerpiece. The theological grist behind the resumed appeal appears at the end in 2:8-10 and 11-13.

What is expressed explicitly in these two passages, therefore, serves as the primary source for our inquiry. But we are also served by a score of incidental moments throughout the rest of the letter, since for Paul participation in the Story (the gospel) through the experience of grace also involves one in getting the story right, not to mention living out the story in keeping with God's own gracious character. And 2 Timothy fully fits these concerns.

We should note finally that there is an inherent uniqueness to this rhetorical situation that will predetermine its special theological emphases. That is, even though Paul has previously written a letter while "in chains" (see Phil. 1:7, 13-18; cf. 2 Tim. 2:9), in that case he clearly expected to be released (Phil. 2:24, "I am confident in the Lord that I myself will come soon"). But here he just as clearly expects to be executed (4:6-8). It should not surprise one, there-

---

emies" in common, and in letters share about each other's personal affairs, while letters of moral exhortation appeal to exemplary paradigms (cf. Phil. 3:4-14, 15-16, 17; 4:9 with 2 Tim. 1:11-12; 3:10-12; 4:6-8 [esp. v. 8!]). On these matters, see Fee, *Philippians* (pp. 1-14).

15. The basic reasons for seeing 2:1-13 as the resumption of the appeal begun in 1:6 are that (a) both begin with the imperative συγκακοπάθησον (1:8; 2:3), (b) both appeal to Timothy's own loyalty and endurance (in 2:14 the direction clearly changes toward the church), and (c) both focus on the gospel itself.

16. Three, if one assumes, as I do, that 2:1-13 belongs with 1:6-14 as its resumption. Otherwise, there are four (1:6-14; 2:1-13; 2:14–3:9; 3:10-17), plus the final charge in 4:1-5.

fore, that on the one hand the letter breathes Paul's characteristic christo-centricity, while on the other hand it focuses on the eschatological "not yet" (but without losing the eschatological "already").

III. Paul's Gospel (the Narrative)

The word "gospel" occurs three times in 2 Timothy (1:8, 10; 2:8),[17] in the first two instances as the framing words for the confessional moment that spells out its content, and in the second in the identifying prepositional phrase, "according to my gospel." Elsewhere in the letter the gospel is designated by the companion (also Pauline) words, "truth" and "word,"[18] the former always, as elsewhere in Paul, in the context of controversy.

For the sake of convenience, the two primary texts are given here:[19]

> God, . . . saved us and called us unto a holy calling,[20] not in keeping with our works but in keeping with his own purpose and grace, which was given to us by/in Christ Jesus, before the ages began, but was manifested in the present time with the appearing of our Savior, Jesus Christ, who broke death's back and brought to light life and immortality through the gospel.

> Remember Jesus Christ, raised from the dead, of the seed of David, according to my gospel; . . . but the message from God is not bound;

17. A little more frequently in ratio than in Romans, where it occurs nine times.

18. See 2:15, 18, 25; 3:7, 8; 4:4 for ἀλήθεια; see 2:9, 15; 4:2 for λόγος as referring to the message of the gospel (the combined phrase ὁ λόγος τῆς ἀληθείας occurs in 2:15); cf. 2:17 for ὁ λόγον αὐτῶν as the "message" of the false teaching. For Pauline usage see, inter alia, esp. Gal. 2:5 and 14 ("the truth of the gospel") and Phil. 1:14 and 2:14 ("the word [of life]" = the message of the gospel).

19. It should be noted that these kinds of semi-creedal soteriological sentences occur on a regular basis throughout the corpus. In *God's Empowering Presence* (p. 48, n. 39) I have isolated about 25 of these kinds of sentences in Paul, some of which are more "creedal" in appearance than others, and the most of which are "trinitarian" in composition. What is perhaps most remarkable about these various passages is that, apart from Gal. 4:4-6 and its companion in Rom. 8:15-18, none of them is even remotely similar to the others. Which in turn has been part of the reason for assuming that many of them existed in a pre-Pauline form that Paul has taken over and adapted. One would hardly deny this as a valid historical option, but it also seems to presuppose an unusually "static" Paul, who as one of the early church's premier theologians is not capable of such creedal expressions himself!

20. I take the dative κλήσει ἀγίᾳ to be a dative of interest (so REB, NIV) rather than manner (NRSV). In either case, the concern surely is with the people who are called, in terms of what they are called unto, rather than the nature of God's call as such.

> therefore, I endure all things for the sake of the elect, in order that they might obtain the salvation which is by/in Christ Jesus [and] accompanied with eternal glory.

> Faithful is the saying:

>> For if we have died with him, we shall also live with him;
>> if we endure, we shall also reign with him.
>> If we deny him, he will deny us;
>> if we are faithless, he remains faithful;
>> for he cannot deny himself.

Here are all the primary theological components of Paul's gospel: (1) eschatological salvation,[21] that is (2) brought about by the divine protagonist (God) through the death and resurrection of Christ, (3) the goal of which is a people for God's name (the "elect") who live in keeping with his own (holy) character, and which (4) is a present reality destined for a final glorious consummation. Indeed, the only missing element in the sentences themselves is the work of the Spirit, and that is presupposed in both 1:6-7 and 8. In vv. 6-7 Timothy is urged to "fan into flame the gift of the Spirit," whom God gave "us" to effect "power, love, and a wise head," and in v. 8 to "join in the suffering according to the [prior mentioned] power of God." The rest of this paper will attempt to unpack this theology as it emerges both in these sentences and throughout the letter.

IV. Salvation in Christ

One of the more significant aspects of Pauline theology is the rich variety of metaphors and images he uses to express the heart of his gospel, "salvation in Christ." There are indeed "constants" within his understanding of the gospel:

(a) salvation is a divine activity, initiated and carried out by God the Father,[22]

---

21. On the matter of eschatological salvation lying at the heart of the theology of the PE, see esp. Phil Towner, *The Goal of Our Instruction* (JSNTS 34; Sheffield Academic Press, 1989), pp. 75-119.

22. In light of the thoroughgoing nature of this reality in Paul, I was not just a little taken aback by Young's statement (*Theology*, pp. 50-51) that "the use of 'Saviour' to characterise God and his activity is one of the distinctive features of these short texts — it is not particularly Pauline." I assume by this that she is referring to the title "Savior" as applied to God, since in fact,

(b) effected through the death of Christ, who is Son and Lord, and

(c) made effectual by the gift of the Spirit,

(d) as an act of pure grace,

(e) and thus entered and sustained by trusting Christ; moreover, it is

(f) an eschatological reality that is both "already" and "not yet";

(g) its primary goal is a people for God's name,

(h) which involves "turning away from wickedness and doing good."

But these constants are expressed in so many different ways as to defy all attempts to narrow the elusive "center" down to one metaphor or way of speaking.[23] What should be clear to all is that the "form" and "imagery" his various soteriological statements take are predicated almost altogether on either (1) the aspect of the *human predicament* from which God is saving his people, or (2) the *nature of the error* that he perceives his gospel as standing in opposition to.

Thus the metaphor of "justification by faith" over against "works of law" appears only in the three letters (Galatians, Romans, Philippians) where some form of Judaizing (that is, imposing Jewish boundary-markers on Gentile believers) is at issue; the metaphor of "adoption" in those places (Romans and Galatians) where at issue is "who are the true 'children' of Abraham, hence of God," who are thus no longer "enslaved" to the Torah; the reality of "turning from idols to the living and true God, whose Son Jesus rescues us from the coming wrath" (1 Thess. 1:9-10) is played back to some early Gentile converts soon after their conversion and in the context of increasing opposition and suffering.

---

apart from a rare instance such as in Gal. 1:4, God is regularly the express or implied (as in the divine passives) subject of all of Paul's "saving verbs." Thus, as 1 Cor. 8:6 makes clear, the proper prepositions for God's activity are ἐκ and εἰς, whereas διά (or ἐν) is invariably used for Christ. This reality should have made us wonder not that *God* is called "Savior" in the PE, but that *Christ* is called "Savior" by Paul in Phil. 3:20, which, of course, as in 2 Tim. 1:10, seems to be set directly over against the emperor cult.

23. It is this fluidity of form, usage, and imagery that should cause us to distinguish more carefully between the terms "un-Pauline" and "non-Pauline." I use the former to refer to something that is uncharacteristic of the Paul we tend to think we know thoroughly from the rather scanty evidence of a few letters; "non-Pauline" refers to that which seems to lie outside Paul's linguistic and conceptual framework altogether.

Moreover, in reconstructing Pauline theology one must be especially cautious about "silence" and/or "frequency of mention." Who around our table, I wonder, would believe that they celebrated the Lord's Supper in the Pauline churches, had the Corinthians not been messing it up? And the "un-Pauline" ("non-Pauline"?) sentiments expressed in Phil. 4:8 should embarrass any self-respecting Paulinist, and would surely damn any suspect letter like this one had they occurred here.

And so it goes throughout the corpus. The theological constants are always in place, although often emerging only in implicit ways. But the lack of explicit emphasis on any one, or several, of them does not make a letter therewith less Pauline.[24] And so it is with the soteriological priorities in 2 Timothy, which are christological in emphasis, eschatological in focus, and ethical in concern. These emphases are the direct result of the concern for loyalty to Paul's gospel — and therefore endurance — in the face of error, combined with his own expectation that the end of the "already" is near at hand for him, and is expected before the final eschatological denouement. Yet most of the other "constants" characteristically find expression throughout the letter in some form or another. Thus we turn to these "constants" as they emerge in our letter.

(a) *Salvation as God's activity.* Above all else, the eternal God stands at the beginning and end of everything; God is the initiator of salvation, as well as its sustainer and final goal. Thus God is the one who "saved us" by "calling us" to himself (1:9), and did so in the present time (νῦν) on the basis of the "grace [God has] given[25] in Christ Jesus." Such salvation also expresses God's own purpose (πρόθεσις) that is rooted in God "before the ages began."[26] Furthermore, it has found prior expression in the "God-breathed Scriptures" of Israel, knowledge of which is able to make one wise with regard to "the salvation that comes through faith in Christ Jesus" (3:15-16). And even when those who have wandered away come to repentance, that too has been given by God (2:25).

God is thus the ultimate reality of all human life, especially Christian life, so that even though Timothy is "the Lord's [= Christ's] servant" (2:24), ultimately he must present himself before God (2:15; cf. 1:3) — just as those being warned regarding error must consider themselves as being called into account by God himself (2:14). For this reason the final doxology is probably

24. So, e.g., the absence of mention of God's grace in 1 Thessalonians and Philippians (appearing primarily only in the salutation and final blessing) does not make them un-Pauline. Indeed, the combination of "grace" (in the form of the verb χαρίζομαι; the only occurrence of χάρις is in 1:7, where it is not at all clear that it refers to God's act of "saving grace") and "believing [as a verb] in Christ" emerges only once in Philippians — in 1:29, in a rather off-handed way that is certain evidence for its presuppositional nature. But one could hardly consider it an "emphasis" in this letter.

25. Assuming as always that the passive δοθεῖσαν is a "divine passive" (cf. ἐγηγερμένον in 2:8).

26. I thus take the combination πρόθεσιν καὶ χάριν τὴν δοθεῖσαν ἡμῖν ἐν Χριστῷ Ἰησοῦ πρὸ χρόνων αἰωνίων to be chiastic: the grace (b) given us in Christ Jesus (b′) is also in keeping with God's purpose (a) inherent in God before the ages began (a′). Such a view, of course, is thoroughly Pauline, who understands the present "revelation" of Christ to be something "hidden in God" from πρὸ τῶν αἰώνων (1 Cor. 2:6-7; cf. Col. 1:26).

also directed toward God, as the one worthy of "glory unto the ages of ages" (4:18), even though its immediate antecedent, "the Lord," refers to Christ.[27] In this letter, therefore, the gospel is God's story, whatever else. God is its divine protagonist, who, full of grace, purposed life for the people he has called to participate in the story.

(b) Effected by Christ. If God stands at the beginning and end of things, the key player in the divine drama is Christ, whom God has "given" to effect eschatological salvation. Everything that God has done — or does — is through Christ Jesus. Our letter is thus thoroughly christocentric, in a thoroughly Pauline way, demonstrated not only by the high frequency of the name "Christ Jesus" (13 times) and of the title "Lord" (16 times, all but one of which refers to Christ), but also by the (again Pauline) idiom ἡ ἐν Χριστῷ Ἰησοῦ ("which is by/in Christ Jesus"). Every significant aspect of Christian life is made available ἐν Χριστῷ Ἰησοῦ (salvation [2:10]; the promise of life [1:1]; grace [2:1; cf. 1:9]; faith [1:13; 2:15]; love [1:13]).[28]

Furthermore, the combination that one finds elsewhere of "high christology," in terms of who Christ is, and "functional subordination," in terms of his saving work, is likewise present here, in the same kind of explicit/implicit ways.

(1) The high christology is found in the standard "subtle" ways, such as in the salutation, where one preposition serves to designate "God the Father" and "our Lord Jesus Christ" as the coordinate source of "grace, mercy, and peace."[29] It is also found especially in this letter by the (very Pauline) use of κύριος language, which is deeply rooted in the LXX, and which thus transfers to Christ[30] what originally referred to God (κύριος = Adonai = Yahweh). This

27. Indeed, the only exception to the "rule" that God is the subject of all the saving verbs and activities in this letter is the σώσει εἰς τὴν βασιλείαν αὐτοῦ τὴν ἐπουράνιον of 4:18, where Christ, who "will rescue" Paul from "every evil deed" (= from any real power of evil to destroy me), will also thus "save" him "for his heavenly kingdom." And here the structure of the sentence calls forth this exception.

28. The idiom also occurs twice in 1 Timothy (1:14; 3:13); for its occurrence elsewhere in Paul see Rom. 3:24 ("redemption"); 8:39 ("love"); Gal. 3:21 ("faith"). The idiom has been criticized as reflecting a "non-Pauline" element in the PE (see, e.g., Easton, *Pastoral Epistles*, p. 12). The methodological question that seems never to be raised by those who make these kinds of assertions is "How many times must something occur in the Pauline letters before it is considered Pauline?"

29. See also the similar phenomenon in 4:1, where the emphasis is even more christological: "I charge you ἐνώπιον τοῦ θεοῦ καὶ Χριστοῦ Ἰησοῦ," which is then elaborated altogether in terms of Christ: "who is going to judge the living and the dead, and [in the light of] his appearing and his kingdom."

30. But see Young (*Theology*, pp. 59-61) to the contrary, who notes that the first two oc-

occurs in three ways: (a) in the septuagintal echoes in such phrases as "servant of the Lord" (2:24);[31] "call upon the name of the Lord" (2:22);[32] "the Lord rescued me" (3:11; cf. 4:17-18);[33] and "the Lord . . . the righteous judge" (4:8);[34] (b) in the explicit citations of the LXX in 2:19 ("the Lord knows those who are his" [Num. 16:5]; let every one who names the Lord's name" [cf. Isa. 26:13] depart from evil);[35] and (c) in the intertextual use of Psalm 22 (21, LXX) in 4:17-18, where "the Lord" who stood with Paul and strengthened him during his first hearing and also "rescued" him "from the mouth of the lion" is the same Lord who will "save" him unto *his heavenly kingdom.*[36]

Furthermore, both the language and the implication of Christ's "sovereignty" over Caesar in this latter passage give one good reason to believe that the combination of the titles κύριος and σωτήρ with ἐπιφανεία in 1:10 also functions in direct antithesis to the cult of the emperor.[37] There is only one divine κύριος, Jesus Christ; and he will rescue his servant from the world's κύριος, Nero Caesar.

(2) Yet for all that, the emphasis in this letter is not on Christ's person or status, but on his role as Savior (as one finds also primarily in Paul). God's grace has been given to us ἐν Χριστοῦ Ἰησοῦ (1:9), having been revealed in the

---

currences (1:1 and 8) clearly refer to Christ, but then sees more ambivalence throughout the rest of the letter. But this does not seem to take seriously enough what good narratology should teach us about how an author expects his/her readers to pick up clues of meaning from first occurrences, as determining how keywords will be used throughout a document.

31. See inter alia 2 Kgs. 18:12 (Moses); Josh. 24:30 (Joshua); Jonah 1:9; Ezek. 34:23 (David).

32. This phrase, or variations thereof, occurs over 50 times in the LXX; in the Pauline corpus, cf. 1 Cor. 1:2; Rom. 10:13-14.

33. The combination of a form of ῥύεσθαι with με occurs at least 25 times in the Psalter, not counting the many instances of "rescue my soul." As noted below, that this is a septuagintalism is made certain by 4:17-18, which is full of intertextual echoes of Ps. 21 LXX (esp. vv. 1, 4-5, 21).

34. Besides all the passages that refer to God's judging righteously, see esp. Ps. 7:12 (LXX) for this very language (ὁ θεὸς κριτὴς δίκαιος; cf. 49:6; 74:8); that Paul intends Christ in this passage is made certain both by the clear assertion in 4:1 and thus by the substitution of κύριος for θεός in this septuagintal echo.

35. That κύριος in these citations refers to Christ seems certain, not only from the fact that in its first occurrences in the letter (1:2, 8) κύριος unambiguously refers to Christ, but also because in the Numbers citation the word κύριος has been substituted for the LXX's θεός.

36. That this can only refer to Christ is made certain by the prior usage in 2:12 (and 4:1).

37. On this matter, see further Young, *Theology*, pp. 64-65. The only other place in Paul where σωτήρ is used to refer to Christ, and again in conjunction with κύριος in the context of Christ's coming, is Phil. 3:20-21 — again almost certainly as direct confrontation with the emperor cult. Which is also what makes sense of the intertextual use of Isa. 45:23 in Phil. 2:9-11; even the emperor himself will someday bow before Christ and confess him alone as κύριος.

present with the "appearing of our Savior Christ Jesus," who broke the power of death and thus brought us to life (1:10); salvation is thus to be had ἐν Χριστοῦ Ἰησοῦ (2:10; 3:15). While the ultimate nuance of these ἐν's is a matter of debate, in either case, whether locative or instrumental, the effect is theologically the same. God has effected his eschatological salvation "through" Christ Jesus or "in Christ Jesus," who is the divine agent of such salvation.

The emphasis in this letter is on the eschatological results of Christ's saving activity, hence there is no explicit mention of his death as "for us." But Christ's own death as the locus of his victory over death for us, thus making him the bringer of life, is clearly presupposed. This is made certain by the "faithful saying" in 2:11-13. Here believers' present sufferings (line 2, "if we endure") and future glory ("we shall reign with him") are integrally bound up with their relationship to Christ's death and resurrection, in a manner that recalls Romans 6 (cf. 1 Thess. 5:9-10). Thus (line 1), "if we have been joined with Christ in death [i.e., if our present life, including its suffering, is bound up in Christ's redemptive suffering], then we shall also live with him [i.e., our present life in Christ shall be consummated by eternal life with him, in which we also reign with him]."[38] Therefore, even though "atonement" is not an issue in this letter, Christ's death as "for us" is the certain suppositional base for all of its soteriological statements.

But in light of Paul's own impending death and the need for Timothy and the church to remain loyal to Christ, the emphasis in this letter is on the eschatological dimensions of salvation in Christ: Christ has brought to pass the "promise of life" (1:1, 10), and has done so by breaking the power of death[39] (1:10). This same presupposition lies behind the striking imperative in 2:8: "Remember Jesus Christ raised from the dead, of the seed of David," a combination that occurs in a similar semi-creedal moment in Rom. 1:3-4. The emphasis clearly lies on the resurrection, but that presupposes the crucifixion; and whatever else is true of the Risen One, he is first of all God's kingly Messiah, who is both "from" David's seed and David's true Seed (2 Sam. 7:12-14); and his kingly messiahship has been entered through death and resurrection.

(c) *Made effectual by the Spirit.* The Spirit also plays a very typical role in this letter. To be sure, the Spirit is not mentioned in conjunction with Christ's

---

38. The first line in this saying, of course, is precisely in keeping with Rom. 6:8, and one would be bold indeed to argue that it should mean something different here from what it does there, since the present context demands such a meaning.

39. καταργήσαντος, an especially Pauline word (25 of 27 occurrences), used primarily in eschatological contexts to reflect the reality that the work of Christ has rendered the powers of the present age ineffective, so that they are currently "on their way out," and thus finally to be abolished. See further section (f) below.

saving activity in the two primary passages that speak about the gospel. But that is almost certainly due to the nature of these two passages, since neither is speaking directly about the believer's appropriation of salvation. That is, in passages such as 1 Thess. 1:4-6; 2 Thess. 2:13; 1 Cor. 6:11; 2 Cor. 1:21-22; Gal. 3:2-5; 4:4-7; Rom. 8:2-3; 8:15-17, the emphasis is on the believers' *experience* of the salvation that God has effected in Christ; hence the mention of the Spirit, who certifies that salvation by making it an experienced reality. But in passages like Rom. 1:16-17 and 3:21-26, as in our two passages, the emphasis is on the larger reality of the work of Christ as such; hence there is no mention of the Spirit's appropriating role.[40]

But the Spirit's presence in the believer's life is fully assumed by what Paul says about himself and Timothy in 1:7 and 14, and is certainly implied in the κατὰ δύναμιν θεοῦ of v. 8. Here δύναμις is something of a periphrasis for the Spirit, since in v. 7 the Spirit is declared to have been given to "us" for this very purpose. Hence Paul can say, "join together with me in suffering in keeping with the power [of the Spirit] of God." In the same way, at the end of this first appeal to loyalty to the gospel, Paul reminds Timothy that "the Spirit who dwells in us"[41] will enable him to "guard what has been entrusted to him." There is nothing either static or "defensive"[42] in this imagery; the imagery itself would not work with any other language. How Timothy is "to guard" his trust is spelled out in a whole variety of ways throughout the letter (e.g., 2:15-26; 4:1-5), none of which means merely "to sit on it." And the Spirit is the obvious presupposition for how Timothy is to "do" the gospel.

Thus the Spirit is explicitly referred to in this letter in one of the three primary ways he is mentioned throughout the corpus — as the one who enables the believer effectively to "do" and "live" the gospel in the world.[43]

(d) By grace alone. Precisely because salvation is God's act, initiated and effected by God, Christ, and the Spirit, it is also therefore an act of sheer mercy and grace, which has already been emphasized in the salutation by the

40. One can see these two aspects of salvation merge in a passage like Gal. 4:4-7, where the effective work of Christ is mentioned as a reality unto itself in vv. 4-5. But in order for Christ's redemptive work of adoption to become effectual for the "adopted children," God thus "sent the Spirit of his Son into our hearts, crying out *Abba*," the very language of the Son.

41. Gk ἐνοικέω, found elsewhere in the NT only in Rom. 8:11; cf. the non-compounded οἰκέω in Rom. 8:9 and 11, and 1 Cor. 3:16. Thus the imagery of the "indwelling Holy Spirit" is a uniquely Pauline usage in the NT.

42. That is, this is not a kind of "hold the fort" imagery. In the culture presupposed by this usage, the imagery serves as an especially powerful appeal to one's loyalty and trust.

43. On this matter see section (h) below. The other two ways, of course, are (1) for initiation into life in Christ and (2) for enabling worship and the building up of the people of God as they do so.

addition of "mercy" to the standard "grace and peace." Since there seems to be no special reason for this emphasis in the letter, this would seem to be a genuinely Pauline touch. Salvation, which is rooted in God's eternal purposes, is thus also rooted in God's own grace, which found expression as "revelation" through the saving work of Christ. But grace has to do not only with "getting saved," but with "being saved" as well. Hence Paul urges Timothy to "be strong" by means of the grace that is always to be found in Christ Jesus (2:1).

Because all is of grace, it therefore cannot be "according to our works" (1:9).[44] Even though this phrase does not reflect Paul's best-known usage ("not by works of law"), it is Pauline at its heart, as the argumentation in Rom. 9:12 and Phil. 3:3 makes certain.[45] Indeed, the tendency toward an "either/or" (between a socio-ethnic and religious-theological understanding) of "works of law" and "faith in Christ Jesus"[46] seems to miss the mark by a wide margin. In all of the contexts where the phrase "works of law" occurs, it is a contingent way of addressing a *theological* issue[47] that has admittedly deeply socio-ethnic implications that finally impact Paul's theology at its two crucial points: (1) that the people of God newly constituted by Christ and the Spirit *must* include both Jew and Gentile together for the eschatological fulfillment of the Abrahamic covenant; and (2) that the only way that can happen is by way of grace, faith, and the gift of the Spirit. Hence what is expressed in socio-ethnic terms is ultimately and profoundly theological. The only question we should therefore ask of this phrase is what shape Paul's theological concern might take in this matter once it is no longer tied to its original contingencies. And "not according to our works" but "according to God's own grace given us

44. One should perhaps not make too much of this little phrase, since nothing quite like it appears elsewhere in the letter. On the other hand, it does occur right here, precisely at a point where Paul is reminding Timothy of the gospel for which he must be ready to suffer through the power of the Spirit. Its appearance only here may simply indicate how little we know about the contingent situation of this letter, and in this case may be a faint reflection of the fact that the false teachers elsewhere in the PE think of themselves as "teachers of the law" (1 Tim. 1:7; cf. Titus 3:9). But if our letter is ultimately from Paul himself, this could just as easily simply be Paul's being Paul.

45. Cf. also the way "through law" and "nullifying the grace of God" in Gal. 2:21 (see also 3:10-14) clearly presuppose the traditional theological understanding of this contrast.

46. This, of course, assumes a traditional understanding of πίστις Χριστοῦ Ἰησοῦ; but it is based on the larger reality that when πίστις becomes a verb in all of the contexts where this phrase occurs — and it always does — the verb clearly intends the so-called traditional view.

47. After all, "works of law" are emphatically underscored by Paul to be a "means of boasting" before God (Phil. 3:3-4; Rom. 3:27). In Philippians, where this issue is raised without use of the phrase "works of law," Paul describes the contrast to "faith in Christ Jesus" in terms of "a righteousness of my own based on law."

in Christ Jesus" would seem like the most plausible way. In any case, this is surely how we are to understand the theological implications of the phrase, which is thus fully Pauline at its very core.[48]

(e) Through faith. As always in Paul, "faith" is the human response to God's saving work in Christ. This central point finds expression in our letter in an almost incidental fashion in 3:15: Salvation is through[49] faith in Christ Jesus. But we also need to be reminded that the rhetorical situation of our letter does not beg for this to be said, since at issue is not how Timothy (or the others) came to be saved, but his/their enduring "faithful" trust in Christ in the midst of a present crisis. Thus, the predominant use of πίστις in this letter is in the very Pauline way of referring to one's whole relationship to God as an expression of "faith" (1:5, 13; 2:22; 3:10), meaning one's lifelong faithful trust in Christ that also began that way.[50] In one instance "faith" does seem to come closer to being a synonym for "the content of the gospel" (4:8: "I have kept the faith").[51] Even here, however, it probably contains the same kind of ambiguity one finds in the similar usage in Phil. 1:27, where "the faith of the gospel" most likely refers to the content of the gospel, but in context also speaks to the "faith-fulness" that is essential to the gospel. In any case, the understanding of "faith" in 2 Timothy is profoundly Pauline theologically.

(f) An eschatological reality. As throughout the corpus, salvation is first of all to be understood as an eschatological reality. That is, it has to do with the promised eschatological salvation of the OT, which is believed to have come present through Christ's death and resurrection and the gift of the eschatological Spirit. Hence it is a reality that is "already" present through Christ (and the Spirit), which will eventually be consummated with the (now second) coming of Christ. One can scarcely understand "salvation in Christ" in 2 Timothy apart from this eschatological tension.

First, because of the predominantly future orientation of the letter, based on Paul's own situation, salvation has ultimately to do with "life" and "death." Through both his death and resurrection Christ has freed people from the tyranny of death and given them life, both for now and forever. Participation in Christ's death and resurrection (2:11) is what leads to the "promise of life" now made available in Christ Jesus (1:1). Hence Timothy, in the context of being urged to "join with me in suffering" (2:2; 1:8), is also urged to

48. On this phrase in our passage see especially Towner, *Goal*, pp. 96-97.

49. διά, implying secondary agency to God's prior grace, which is the primary agent.

50. This is surely its meaning as a "fruit of the Spirit" in Gal. 5:22, and is thus the preferred way of understanding πίστις in many other passages as well: Rom. 1:8, 12; 1 Cor. 16:13; Phil. 1:25; 2:17, all 8 occurrences in 1 Thessalonians, and the majority in 2 Thessalonians.

51. Which is also a Pauline way of using this word, as Gal. 1:23; Phil. 1:27, et al. make clear.

"remember Jesus Christ raised from the dead" (2:8), precisely because what God's saving grace ultimately wrought through Christ's first "appearing"[52] was to "render death ineffective" by bringing to light ζωὴν καὶ ἀφθαρσίαν ("life and incorruptibility").

This does not mean that one will not die; on the contrary, Paul is about to be "poured out," the time of his "departure" is at hand, because he has come to the end of his race (4:6-7). What has been rendered ineffective through Christ's death and resurrection is the final triumph of death (cf. 1 Cor. 15:54-55); its back has been broken. And this is the significance of the addition of the (especially Pauline) word "incorruptibility" to "life." No Pauline (and NT) word carries the *ambiguity* of the already/not yet so completely as "life," since by its very nature "life" is both for now and forever. By adding "incorruptibility," Paul is clearly pointing to his and Timothy's (and other believers') future bodily resurrection, since ἀφθαρσία is Paul's primary way of speaking about this reality in the one passage where he tackles the issue head-on (1 Cor. 15:35-58). Very likely this emphasis in 1:9-10 is directly related to the one piece of content we are given regarding the gangrenous teaching of the opponents, namely that the resurrection ("of believers" is intended) has already happened (2:18).

Furthermore, because in Christ's first ἐπιφανεία he effectively dealt with death, this guarantees that he will equally effectively deal with justice at his second ἐπιφανεία (4:1, 8), when he "the righteous judge" (4:8) will judge both the living (meaning those alive at his coming) and the dead. Those who are his, who "love his appearing" (probably meaning "who long for it to come") will receive a victor's "crown of righteousness"[53] (4:8). Therefore, the one who believes in Christ is confident that God will have guarded that one's trust until the final eschatological day (1:13). Likewise, those who have spurned grace and persist in wickedness by their resistance to Paul's gospel will also be "repaid"[54] by Christ in keeping with their deeds (4:14).

52. In an unfortunately tendentious presentation of the evidence, P.-G. Müller's discussion of ἐπιφανεία in *EDNT* (2.44-45) asserts that all five of the occurrences of this word in the PE "refer to the anticipated second appearance of the resurrected and exalted Christ." But that is to run roughshod over the plain meaning of this clause, where both the cognate verb and noun emphatically point to already present realities based on the "first" ἐπιφανεία of Christ.

53. This ambiguous phrase could mean either "the prize awarded a righteous life" (so Bernard, Barrett, Kelly), or "one which consists of the gift of righteousness, which only the Judge, as he who alone is *dikaios*, can give" (Pfitzner, *Paul and the Agon Motif*, NovTSup 16 [Leiden: Brill, 1967], p. 184). While I tend to lean toward the latter, in either case it does not mean that "righteousness" is achieved, but that it represents the appropriate crown for those who have received grace and have thus "pursued" righteousness as a way of life (2:22). See the discussion of ethics in section (h) below.

54. ἀποδώσει, the same word that first appeared in 4:8 above.

Christ's second ἐπιφάνεία will also bring about his "heavenly kingdom" (4:1, 18). Thus the use of βασιλεία in this letter refers altogether to the final reign of Christ, just as it does most often elsewhere in Paul. Very likely the comparatively heavy concentration of this language in 2 Timothy is the result of Paul's Roman custody, as a means of emphasizing eschatological certainty in light of Nero's present reign.

Nonetheless, the tension of living in the "already" as one awaits the "not yet" is also thoroughgoing in this letter, being most evident in the (again typically Pauline) theology of suffering, on the one hand, and in the context of the "last day" messianic woes, on the other. Suffering, in the form of persecution, is to be expected by all who wish to live in a godly way in Christ Jesus (3:12), for which Paul serves as paradigm (vv. 10-11; cf. 1:8/12; 2:9). Such a life, which is related to one's being joined to Christ in his death, thus calls for "endurance" (2:10, 12; 3:10) and "long-suffering" in the present.

Moreover, such suffering may be expected to intensify as the final eschatological event draws nearer (3:1-5),[55] which is the way one is to understand the present opposition to the gospel (3:5-6); indeed, such "imposters" (3:13), who are understood to be entrapped by the devil (2:26) and thus "deceived and deceiving" (3:13), will only go from bad to worse (3:9, 13). At the end they will receive their due (4:14). But so will those who endure faithfully (2:10, 12; 4:8).

(g) The goal — a people for God's name. As everywhere in Paul, even though salvation is for the individual (1:12), and is received individually and lived out at the individual level (3:14-17; cf. 1:5),[56] the goal of God's saving activity in Christ is a people who "name the name of Christ" (2:19). That this is the thoroughly presuppositional stance of 2 Timothy is made certain by the fact that such a thing is said at all in a letter directed primarily to an individual, appealing to his loyalty. But Timothy's loyalty will hopefully be manifested in the people of God as well.

---

55. For a recent and helpful survey of this motif in Paul, see J. Plevnik, *Paul and the Parousia* (Peabody, Mass.: Hendrickson, 1997), pp. 244-64.

56. In clear reaction to the unfortunate individualism in much of Protestantism, it is common in some circles in NT studies to stress the "corporateness" of the cultural-anthropological setting of first-century Christianity. That this indeed is Paul's primary focus seems clear, and in this he is simply in continuity with his OT heritage. But discontinuity with the past is equally significant for Paul, in that people become members of the believing community one by one on the basis of faith in Christ Jesus (as over against birth and the rite of circumcision). Anyone who has read the Psalter and the epistles of Paul will recognize that the significance of the individual is not an idea that began with the Reformation or Enlightenment. But to say this is a far cry from espousing the intense, and unbiblical, individualism that marks so much of contemporary Western culture. See further, Fee, *Paul, the Spirit, and the People of God* (Peabody, Mass.: Hendrickson, 1996), pp. 63-73.

At two points in the letter Paul refers to God's people in a way that makes it clear he understands them as in continuity with the former covenant people of God, even though they are obviously reconstituted by Christ and the Spirit (1:9-10, 6-7). First, they are God's "elect" (2:10), language that recalls Old Testament realities, where Israel was "chosen" by God to be his people in the world. Not only does this term evoke for the people a sense of their "secure" place in God, but it also evokes the purposeful nature of their being God's people. That comes out even more in the language καλέσαντος κλήσει ἁγίᾳ (probably, "called unto a holy calling") in 1:9.

Second, and similarly, the imagery of the people as God's temple, or at least so it would seem,[57] in 2:19 also carries this twofold thrust. The foundation of God's temple is firmly fixed, having been sealed with God's own stamp of ownership. And although this imagery is pregnant with possibilities of meaning, Paul makes his twofold point by citing or echoing OT passages: Christ "knows" those who are his (citing Num. 16:15, where those who are truly God's people will be distinguished from the false!); and those who name his name (= are thus known by his name) should therefore separate themselves from what is evil.

In these two clauses one finds the heart of Pauline ecclesiology. On the one hand, the people belong to Christ (or God). Their security and eschatological vindication rests there. And it is always so for Paul. Not that he is adverse to speaking about believers' knowing Christ (as, e.g., in Phil. 3:8, 10), but their existence as a people is predicated on the fact that God knows them (Gal. 4:9; 1 Cor. 8:3).

On the other hand, those who are so known by God and thus "name Christ's name" must themselves walk in ways that conform to God's/Christ's own character. Which is where ethical instruction comes in for Paul. Salvation is the result of God's grace, not "in accordance with our works" (1:9); nonetheless, Paul could not have understood salvation that did not include an ethical imperative. After all, the goal of salvation is not to people heaven, but to create a people who reflect God's own glory.

Thus, even though newly constituted through Christ, this now newly constituted people are not only in continuity with the former covenant people of God, but are in the true succession of that people.

What is most striking about the ecclesiology of this letter is the total

---

57. The imagery of 2:19 seems hardly applicable to a "household," the other possible imagery (and adopted by some on the basis of vv. 20-21). But the "foundation" stone affixed with the owner's seal seems to imply a more public structure. And in any case, as a Pauline document it picks up the temple imagery from 1 Cor. 3:10-17.

lack of concern for order, structures, and leadership. Indeed, if 2 Timothy were the only one of the Pastoral Epistles to have survived, no one would ever have imagined that this epistle should be read as some kind of manual for church order. The one text (2:2) that might possibly be read that way has nothing to do with order, and everything to do with loyalty to Paul's gospel by faithfully transmitting it to those who will faithfully continue the process. But there is no "appointment," no titles, nothing that hints of "order" per se. Even in the places where Timothy's role as a leader might be in view (2:3-7; 2:15-17; 2:22-26; 3:14-17), at issue is not "church order" but ethical conduct. What makes Timothy a "man of God" in this letter is not an "office" but that he serves as a model for "every good work" (3:17).

And that, too, reflects Pauline theology. It is not that order or structures did not exist; it is simply that we know very little about them except that they are plural and included ἐπίσκοποι and διάκονοι (Phil. 1:1). In his earlier letters Paul's concerns for the church lie not with its leaders getting their act together, but with the church and its leaders together living out the life of the future in the present age. That same theological concern emerges in 2 Timothy as well.

(h) From sin and for holiness. Finally, we need to note that although salvation is primarily an eschatological reality, it also has a purely "religious" dimension as well. Those who are rescued from "death" for "life" are also called "to a holy calling," which means to a life that is set apart for God and his purposes. This means both a rejection of "wickedness" (2:19) and the pursuit of "righteousness, faith-fulness, love, and peace" (2:22).[58]

Therefore, eschatological salvation, the gift of life both for now and forever, also includes being "saved from sin(s)." The women who welcome the false teachers into their homes are described as "laden down with sins," as they pursue "all kinds of lusts"; and the sins of the false teachers are given in a stereotypical vice list[59] that is undoubtedly intended to portray the pagan culture from which these men were to have been saved. Such people lack

---

58. The structure of the large middle section of the letter (2:14–3:17) is especially significant in this regard. After (a) the opening warning that the people are not to do battle with words (2:14), (b) the appeal to Timothy to obtain divine approbation (v. 15), and (c) the description of those who do not do so and who are thus leading others astray (vv. 16-18), Paul affirms the church as belonging to Christ, yet they too must "turn away from wickedness." That is followed by what some perceive as the enigmatic imagery of vv. 20-21, but which surely functions to call Timothy to modeling behavior that must be embraced (vv. 22-26), while in 3:1-5 and 6-9 the false teachers model the "wickedness" that must be rejected.

59. Which, of course, in itself is another typically Pauline feature, including the fact that no one of Paul's vice lists bear very much resemblance to any of the others.

love for God, being lovers of themselves — and of money! — and are therefore full of arrogance, ingratitude, divisive quarreling, and all other kinds of aberrant behavior.

Those who are known by Christ are obviously intended to live differently. With Timothy as their paradigm, they are to "cleanse themselves" from wickedness and thus to be "ready for every good work" (2:21). This means actively to pursue what Paul elsewhere calls "fruit of the Spirit": righteousness, faith-fulness, love, peace (2:22), and gentleness (2:25). As elsewhere in Paul, not only "power," but especially "love" (1:7, 13; 2:22; 3:10) and also "sober-mindedness"[60] are the direct result of the presence of the indwelling Spirit, given by God.

Since God is full of goodness that exhibits itself in his "doing good" to those he loves,[61] his people are to exemplify the same. They are "equipped" through the God-breathed Scriptures for doing every kind of good work (3:17), just as they are "prepared" for doing every kind of good work (2:21) by turning away from wickedness (2:19).

That this is a thoroughly Pauline view of things can be found on every page of Paul's extant letters. Indeed, "doing good" might well be argued as lying at the heart of Pauline ethics — especially since this thoroughly OT way of speaking[62] is how the argument of Galatians concludes (6:9-10: "Let us not flag in doing what is good; . . . let us do good to all, especially those of the household of the faith") and finds expression again at the end of Romans (16:19: "I want you to be wise unto what is good and guileless unto what is evil").

We may thus conclude this reading of 2 Timothy as a Pauline letter by noting again how thoroughly Pauline it is. Indeed, if one excludes arguments from silence (and they must be excluded, since every letter in the corpus can be damned for not mentioning some "important" Pauline matter), and likewise if one reads the letter on its own, apart from 1 Timothy and Titus, it has a decidedly Pauline ring at every turn. At times what we hear are old words or

60. σωφρονισμός; cf. the use of σωφρονεῖν and its compounds in the context of making sober assessments about one's own place in the body of Christ in Rom. 12:3.

61. This, of course, is not said in 2 Timothy, but one may assume it to be so on the basis of 3:16-17, where the "man of God" is "equipped" by means of the "God-breathed" Scriptures for "every good work." Whatever else those Scriptures tell us about God, they continually remind us that God is good and does what is good for his people.

62. Note, e.g., how often in the Psalter, set up on the basis of Psalm 1, the righteous and the wicked are contrasted in terms of their respectively "doing good" or "doing evil" (e.g., Ps. 14:1, 3; 34:14; 36:3; 37:3).

phrases newly configured or juxtaposed; at other times the language itself is new. But in all of it the theology is both essentially Pauline and full of what is essential to Paul.

Perhaps I may be allowed to return to the question of methodology at the end. What is striking in the literature on the theology of these letters, and the otherwise very helpful study by Frances Young is a case in point, is that it is common (1) to lump the three letters together, and thus to read their theology *en bloc,* but even so (2) to begin such a study with 1 Timothy and Titus (for understandable reasons), and then (3) to read into 2 Timothy the now presupposed theology that one has found in 1 Timothy and Titus. One wonders in passing what would happen if we were to do this in reverse. What if one were to begin with 2 Timothy and its very Pauline theology, and then read the other two letters in light of this one? Surely they would sound much more Pauline than is often asserted to the contrary, since they address contingent situations that simply have not arisen elsewhere — where current *leadership within the church* is responsible for leading whole house churches astray. In any case, this letter lives and breathes Paul's own understanding of the gospel narrative as God's gracious saving activity in Christ.

CHAPTER 20

Paul and the Trinity: The Experience of Christ and the Spirit for Paul's Understanding of God

(1999)

It has been rightly said that "the New Testament contains no doctrine of the Trinity."[1] Fully developed doctrine, no, but experienced reality, yes. At issue for the study of the Trinity in Paul (and the rest of the New Testament) is not doctrinal exposition of the One and the Three. Rather, it is the explication of his — and his churches' — experience[2] of Christ and the Spirit as the experience of the only and living God, expressed in a variety of descriptive and theological affirmations that attribute deity to both.

The reluctance on the part of New Testament scholarship to use trinitarian language when referring to these affirmations is understandable;[3] but

---

1. Donald H. Juel, "The Trinity and the New Testament," *Theology Today* 54 (1997): 313.

2. Although some may object to, or be anxious about, the language of "experience" (it raises specters of Schleiermacher or contemporary patterns of "truth based on feeling"), it has Pauline precedent (Gal. 3:4) and seems to be the best English word to express the experienced nature of the reception of the Spirit that Paul appeals to on several occasions (e.g., 1 Thess. 1:5-6; 1 Cor. 2:4-5; Gal. 3:2-5; Rom. 15:18-19); and in any case, it is not "inner feeling" or religious experience per se that I refer to, but always an experienced encounter with the living God (Father, Son, and Spirit) of a kind that the Scriptures are full of.

3. This reluctance is writ large throughout the academy in a variety of ways. It can be seen most recently in reviews of two of my recent books. In his review of *God's Empowering Presence* James Dunn takes issue with what he calls "Fee's rather glib assumption that Paul's theology can be properly described as trinitarian. It is not that he fails to attempt to justify the use

---

I wish here to extend my thanks to my Regent College colleagues, who vigorously interacted with an earlier version of this paper at a recent faculty retreat. That discussion helped me to sharpen up my concerns at several points, so much so that I rather thoroughly reconfigured the whole.

that reluctance is often expressed in ways that cause one to wonder what the real issue is. Is it the word Trinity itself, because it implies speculative onto-logical questions of a later time? Or does it have to do with what the Pauline affirmations are actually saying about Christ and the Spirit? Here is where the pigeon comes home to roost, for the denial of trinitarian language seems very often to preface denials about the *deity* of Christ and/or the Spirit as well, not to mention denials of the *personal nature* of the Spirit.

Thus, the primary issues in Paul's "economic trinitarianism" are chris-tological and pneumatological. About Christ it is ultimately a question of In-carnation and pre-existence; about the Spirit it is a question of his being "per-son," plus his relationship to both God the Father and Jesus Christ the Son expressed in later theology in terms of "equal to" but "distinct from."

The pneumatological issue has been further exacerbated by the practi-cal binitarianism of so many orthodox Christians. On the one hand, in light of the full biblical data — from Matthew's "God with us" to John's worship "of the One who sits on the throne and of the Lamb," not to mention John's Gospel and Paul's letters along the way — and despite offshoot groups like the Ebionites, one can scarcely imagine the Christian faith not having ex-pressed itself finally in terms of God as Binity. That is, the biblical texts were (correctly) understood by the orthodox majority as overwhelmingly support-ing Christ's full deity, but in the context of rigorous monotheism. Once that was resolved, then at issue, besides the christological question per se,[4] was what to do with the Spirit — how to express a trinitarian faith that included the Spirit fully in the Godhead, and not as a kind of divine stepchild.

---

of the term. . . . It is rather that to make use of a later technical term, without addressing or clari-fying the issues involved in that term . . . is to erect an orthodox flag without an adequate flag-pole" (*Theology* [1996]: 152). Likewise David Kaylor's review of *Paul's Letter to the Philippians* remonstrates: "Those who resist the tendency to let theological assumptions determine exegetical outcomes will find difficulties precisely at this point. Is there really 'an intentional Trinitarian substructure' here (see pp. 179, 302), or is Fee reading later theological constructs into Paul?" (*Int* [July 1997]: 303) — as though his view of Paul were without theological assump-tions! In both cases the objection is to the use of this word, since neither scholar would deny that Paul's understanding of salvation included God's loving initiative, Christ's effectual work on the cross, and the Spirit's making it an experienced reality. What language, one wonders, should we use for such a view of God? Is not a "rose by any other name . . ."? Paul's understand-ing of salvation was triadic, and the triad was divine. So why not Trinity, especially since the Fa-ther and Son are personal, as is the Spirit, or so it is argued here? I am not here contending for the language as such, but for a way to express Paul's insistence on the Oneness of God, while at the same time using the language of deity for Christ and the Spirit.

4. That is, how Son of God and son of man co-exist as one being, fully God and fully man — another reality supported by the biblical data but never addressed as such.

It seems to me that historically most orthodox Christians have gone the latter route (treated the Spirit as a divine stepchild);[5] the primary reason for which is probably related to the later church's understanding of the ongoing role of the Spirit in the life of the church.[6] But abetting such a view is the very real problem of human beings' relating to the concept of "spirit." Father and Son are easily recognizable metaphors for God and potentially easy to relate to. But for many the Spirit is, in the words of a former student, "a gray oblong blur"; and relating to the Spirit is especially difficult since all of our images are *im*personal. How does one relate to water, wind, oil, fire, or dove in the same way one does to a father or son?[7]

The purpose of this paper is to examine the Pauline christological and pneumatological data once again, with a view towards seeing Paul as a latent trinitarian. My thesis is that the key to Paul's new and expanded ways of talking about God as Savior — while at the same time rigorously maintaining his monotheism — is to be found in the *experience of the Spirit,* as the one who enables believers to confess the risen Christ as exalted Lord, and as the way God and Christ are personally present in the believer and the believing community.

To make this point I propose first to examine Paul's triadic statements themselves as to their latent trinitarianism, since these statements are invariably both soteriological and experiential. Then, in the light of these statements I propose to examine (a) the issue of pre-existence and (b) the implications of calling Christ *kyrios.* Finally, with regard to the Spirit, I wish to explore (a) the issue of "personhood," (b) what it means for the Spirit of God also to be the Spirit of Christ, and (c) the implications of the experience of

5. See esp. the discussion by Elizabeth Johnson, *She Who Is* (New York: Crossroad, 1992), pp. 128-31, who says, picking up the language of many whom she has just quoted, "Faceless, shadowy, anonymous, half-known, homeless, watered down, the poor relation, Cinderella, marginalized by being modeled on women — such is our heritage of language about the Spirit" (p. 131). She goes on to cite Kilian McDonnell: "Anyone writing on pneumatology . . . is hardly burdened by the past."

6. For what is involved here, see the helpful overview by George S. Hendry, *The Holy Spirit in Christian Theology,* 2nd edn. (London: SCM, 1965), pp. 53-71; cf. Johnson, *She Who Is,* who notes that in her own Roman Catholic tradition Mary has assumed the biblical role of the Spirit, citing among several examples Pope Leo XIII: "Every grace granted to human beings has three degrees in order; for by God it is communicated to Christ, from Christ it passes to the Virgin, and from the Virgin it descends to us" (p. 129).

7. Cf. a story from Dorothy Sayers (as related by Madeleine L'Engle, *A Circle of Quiet* [San Francisco: Harper, 1972], p. 50) about the Japanese gentleman who, in discussing the mysterious concept of the Trinity in Christianity, said, "Honorable Father, very good. Honorable Son, very good. Honorable Bird I do not understand at all."

the Spirit as the experience of the renewed Presence of God, understood also as the presence of the risen Christ.

At the end I raise some theological implications from these data, as to both the essentially experienced nature of the Spirit as our way of knowing God in a truly relational way, and the need for our theology to keep in step with the Pauline way of talking about the Trinity by way of narrative, which was maintained especially by the early creeds.

I. The Triadic Experience of God as Savior[8]

At the heart of Paul's theology is his gospel, and his gospel is essentially about *salvation* — God's saving a people for his name through the redeeming work of Christ and the appropriating work of the Spirit. Paul's encounter with God in salvation, as Father, Son, and Holy Spirit,[9] alone accounts for the expansion and transformation of his theological language of God and of God's saving work. In light of this reality and the great number of texts that support it — with trinitarian language — these passages rightly serve as the starting point for any study of the Trinity in Paul.

The evidence here is found in two sets of texts: several explicitly triadic texts (2 Cor. 13:14; 1 Cor. 12:4-6; Eph. 4:4-6) and the many passages where Paul succinctly encapsulates "salvation in Christ" in triadic terms, sometimes in semi-creedal fashion, but always in non-reflective, presuppositional ways.

1. The remarkable grace-benediction of 2 Cor. 13:14 offers us all kinds of theological keys to Paul's understanding of salvation, and of God himself.[10] The fact that the benediction is composed and intended for the occasion,[11] rather than as a broadly applicable formula, only increases its importance in hearing Paul. Thus what he says here in prayer appears in a *thoroughly pre-*

---

8. Much of what is said in this section has appeared earlier in very much the same form in *Paul, the Spirit, and the People of God* (Peabody, Mass.: Hendrickson, 1996), pp. 39-46.

9. Although I will fall into traditional usage (Father/Son/Spirit) from time to time, I consciously try most often to stay with Paul's most frequent usage (God/Christ/Spirit) — although Paul himself contributes to the traditional language in such passages as Gal. 4:6 ("God sent forth the Spirit of His Son into our hearts, crying *Abba*, i.e., Father").

10. For a more thorough analysis of this text, see *God's Empowering Presence: The Holy Spirit in the Letters of Paul* (Peabody, Mass.: Hendrickson, 1994), pp. 362-65.

11. That it is both ad hoc and Pauline is clearly demonstrated by the twofold reality that it functions precisely as do all of his other grace-benedictions, which all *begin* exactly this way, with "the grace of our Lord Jesus Christ," and that this beginning point thus determines the unusual order of Christ, God, and Spirit.

suppositional way — not as something Paul argues for, but as the *assumed, experienced reality* of Christian life.

First, it summarizes the core elements of Paul's unique passion: the gospel, with its focus on salvation in Christ, equally available by faith to Gentile and Jew. That the *love of God* is the foundation of Paul's view of salvation is stated with passion and clarity in passages such as Rom. 5:1-11; 8:31-39; and Eph. 1:3-14. The *grace of our Lord Jesus Christ* is what gave concrete expression to that love; through Christ's suffering and death on behalf of his loved ones, God accomplished salvation for them at one moment in human history.

The *participation in the Holy Spirit* continually actualizes that love and grace in the life of the believer and the believing community. The *koinōnia* ("fellowship/participation in") *of the Holy Spirit* is how the living God not only brings people into an intimate and abiding relationship with himself, as the God of all grace, but also causes them to participate in all the benefits of that grace and salvation — that is, by indwelling them in the present with his own presence, and guaranteeing their final eschatological glory.

Second, this text also serves as our entrée into Paul's understanding of God himself, which had been so radically affected by the twin realities of the death and resurrection of Christ and the gift of the Spirit. Granted, Paul does not here *assert* the deity of Christ and the Spirit. What he does is to *equate the activity of the three divine persons* (to use the language of a later time) in *concert and in prayer,* with the clause about God the Father standing in second place(!). This suggests that Paul was in fact trinitarian in any meaningful sense of that term — that the believer knows and experiences the one God as Father, Son, and Spirit, and that when dealing with Christ and the Spirit one is dealing with God every bit as much as when one is dealing with the Father.

Thus this benediction, while making a fundamental distinction between God, Christ, and Spirit, also expresses in shorthand form what is found everywhere throughout his letters, namely, that "salvation in Christ" is the cooperative work of God, Christ, and the Spirit.[12]

The same trinitarian implications also appear in 1 Cor. 12:4-6 and Eph. 4:4-6. In the former passage Paul is urging the Corinthians to broaden their perspective and to recognize the rich diversity of the Spirit's manifestations in their midst (over against their apparently singular interest in speaking in

12. It should also be pointed out that affirmations like this also shut down all possibilities that Paul ever identified the risen Christ with the Spirit. For a critique of this mistaken bypath taken by several recent NT scholars, see my "Christology and Pneumatology in Romans 8:9-11 — and Elsewhere: Some Reflections on Paul as a Trinitarian," in I. H. Marshall *Festschrift,* J. B. Green and M. Turner, eds., *Jesus of Nazareth: Lord and Christ: Essays on the Historical Jesus and New Testament Christology* (Grand Rapids: Eerdmans, 1994), pp. 312-31.

tongues). He begins in vv. 4-6 by noting that diversity reflects the nature of God and is therefore the true evidence of the work of the one God in their midst. Thus, the Trinity is presuppositional to the entire argument, and these opening foundational words are the more telling precisely because they are so unstudied, so freely and unselfconsciously expressed. Just as there is only One God, from whom and for whom are all things, and One Lord, through whom are all things (1 Cor. 8:6), so there is only One Spirit (1 Cor. 12:9), through whose agency the One God manifests himself in a whole variety of ways in the believing community.

In Eph. 4:4-6 one finds the same combination as in 2 Cor. 13:14 — a creedal formulation expressed in terms of the distinguishable activities of the Triune God. The basis for Christian unity is the one God. The *one body* is the work of the *one Spirit* (cf. 1 Cor. 12:13), by whom also we live our present eschatological existence in *one hope,* since the Spirit is the "down payment on our inheritance" (Eph. 1:13-14). All of this has been made possible for us by our *one Lord,* in whom all have *one faith* and to which faith all have given witness through their *one baptism.* The source of all these realities is the *one God* himself, "who is over all and through all and in all." Again, because at issue is the work of the Spirit ("the unity the Spirit creates," v. 3), the order is the same as in 1 Cor. 12:4-6 — Spirit, Lord, God — which works from present, experienced reality to the foundational reality of the one God.

If the last phrase in this passage re-emphasizes the unity of the one God, who is ultimately responsible for all things — past, present, and future — and subsumes the work of the Spirit and the Son under that of God, the entire passage at the same time puts into creedal form the affirmation that God is *experienced* as a triune reality. Precisely on the basis of such experience and language the later church maintained its biblical integrity by expressing all of this in explicitly trinitarian language. And Paul's formulations, which include the work of both Christ and the Spirit, form a part of that basis.

2. That the work of the Trinity in salvation is foundational to Paul's understanding of the gospel is further evidenced by the large number of texts in which salvation is formulated in less explicit, but clearly triadic terms, which are full of trinitarian implications. This is especially true of larger passages such as Rom. 5:1-8; 2 Cor. 3:1-4, 6; Gal. 4:4-6; Eph. 1:3-14; and Titus 3:4-7.

Let us take Gal. 4:4-6 as an example. This passage serves to sum up the argument that began in 3:1. In showing the folly of the Galatian believers' readiness to come under the provisions of the Jewish law, Paul has appealed first of all to their common, and obviously lavish, experience of the Spirit (vv. 3-5) and then second to the work of Christ, especially its bringing the time of Torah to an end. At the end of this argument, and in a context that emphasizes the temporal role of the Law, Paul concludes that "in the fullness of time God sent forth his Son," whose task was to redeem those who were under bondage to Law and do so by giving them adoption as God's own children.[13] The experiential evidence of this work of Christ in believers' lives comes about because God also "sent forth the Spirit of his Son into our hearts," who cries out from within us the *Abba*-cry of the Son to the Father, thus indicating that we, too, are "sons" of the Father. It is a passage like this that caused H. B. Swete to remark so perceptively, "Without the mission of the Spirit the mission of the Son would have been fruitless; without the mission of the Son the Spirit could not have been sent."[14]

Such texts reveal an unmistakably trinitarian experience of God on the part of the Apostle. God sends the Son who redeems; God sends *the Spirit of his Son* into *our hearts,* so that we may realize God's "so great salvation" — and the experienced evidence of all this is the Spirit of the Son prompting us to use the language of the Son in our own relationship with God.

But besides these grand and thus well-known moments in Paul, this "trinitarian" understanding of salvation is also true of many other texts in which salvation is portrayed in the same triadic way as is encapsulated in 2 Cor. 13:14. (Among these passages, listed in my view of their chronological order, see especially the semi-creedal soteriological passages, such as 1 Thess. 1:4-6; 2 Thess. 2:13-14; 1 Cor. 6:11; 2 Cor. 1:21-12; Rom. 8:3-4; and 8:15-17. But see also many other such texts, soteriological or otherwise: 1 Cor. 1:4-7; 2:4-5; 2:12; 6:19-20; 2 Cor. 3:16-18; Gal. 3:1-5; Rom. 8:9-11; 15:16; 15:18-19; 15:30; Col. 3:16; Eph. 1:3, 17-20; 2:17-18, 19-22; 3:16-19; 5:18-19; Phil. 1:19-20; 3:3.)

All of these in some form or another reflect the threefold activity of Father, Christ, and Spirit in effecting salvation. Take, for example, 2 Thess. 2:13, where God's people are "beloved by the Lord [through his death]," because God elected them for salvation through the sanctifying work of the Spirit; or 1 Cor. 6:11, where God is the implied subject of the "divine passives" (you were washed, justified, sanctified), accomplished in the name of Christ and by the Spirit. And so with each of these texts; only those with eyes deliberately closed could fail to see how thoroughgoing this three-dimensional understanding of God as Savior is in Paul.

One of the more remarkable features of these passages is the frequency and consistency with which the Spirit is mentioned in purely soteriological

13. While "children" is certainly the correct sense of the Greek, it has the misfortune of losing Paul's play on the word υἱός, where Christ as "Son" brings about adoption as "sons" evidenced by the Spirit of the Son being sent into our hearts to cry the *Abba*-prayer of the Son to the Father.

14. *The Holy Spirit in the New Testament* (London: Macmillan, 1910), p. 206.

texts. Equally remarkable is the paucity of such texts (e.g., 1 Thess. 1:9-10; 5:9-10), where the Spirit is not mentioned. What makes this so noteworthy is that most often when Paul refers to God's saving work as it was effected in history, he (understandably) focuses altogether on the work of Christ; but when that work is effectively applied to the life of the individual, that is, when he refers to the experienced reality of salvation, the narrative almost always includes the agency of the Spirit.

The point of all of this, of course, is that salvation in Christ is not simply a theological truth, predicated on God's prior action and the historical work of Christ. Salvation is an experienced reality, made so by the person of the Spirit coming into our lives. One simply cannot be a Christian in any Pauline sense without the effective work of God as Father, Son, and Holy Spirit.

But these statements serve only as the beginning point in our investigation of Paul as a "trinitarian." Equally important is a careful look at what he says about who Christ and the Spirit are, whether what is implied theologically in the benediction in 2 Cor. 13:14 noted above can be found elsewhere. We begin with christology.

II. Christ: Pre-existent and Exalted Lord

All trinitarian conversation must begin with the Incarnation; here the reality of God as Trinity stands or falls in terms of divine self-disclosure.[15] And the presupposition of the Incarnation is our Savior's pre-existence. Thus, those scholars who wish to contest whether Paul understood Christ in terms of deity have especially contested pre-existence as a Pauline category. The five texts[16] that have traditionally been so understood are thus given alternative interpretations, so as to cast doubt on whether Paul should be understood in a Johannine way.

My concern here is not to offer a full rebuttal of these views, but simply to note the exegetical weaknesses of the alternative exegesis[17] — vis-à-vis the

---

15. On this matter, see esp. Catherine Mowry LaCugna, *God for Us: The Trinity and Christian Life* (San Francisco: HarperSanFrancisco, 1993), pp. 209-41.

16. Rom. 8:3; 2 Cor. 8:9; Gal. 4:4; Phil. 2:6; Col. 1:16-17, to which one should probably add such texts as 1 Cor. 8:6.

17. See, *inter alia*, Norman K. Bakken, "The New Humanity: Christ and the Modern Age: A Study Centering in the Christ-Hymn: Philippians 2:6-11," *Int* 22 (1968): 71-82; J. D. G. Dunn, *Christology in the Making* (London: SCM, 1980), pp. 114-21; John Harvey, "A New Look at the Christ Hymn in Philippians 2:11," *ExpTim* 76 (1964-65): 337-39; George Howard, "Phil 2:6-11 and the Human Christ," *CBQ* 40 (1978): 368-87; Jerome Murphy-O'Connor, "Christological Anthro-

strengths of the traditional understanding — of the most significant of these texts, Phil. 2:6-11, which I have had recent occasion to examine in some detail.[18]

The alternative understanding begins with two important presuppositions: that Paul is citing a prior text, with whose particulars he may not necessarily be in full agreement; and that vv. 6-8 are a reflection of Paul's Adam-Christ christology, in which Paul sees Christ here merely in his humanity, who was (as Adam) in God's "image," but vis-à-vis Adam did not try to seize God-likeness.

Whether the passage had prior existence or not is a debatable point, but the suggestion that the text may not reflect Paul's own christology should be forever laid to rest. The obvious fact is that, now embedded as it is in a thoroughly Pauline sentence which *the Apostle dictated as his own,* one may assume that what Paul "cites" as a model to be emulated he thoroughly agrees with.

On the second point, several observations: (1) Whether there is an Adam-Christ analogy at work here is a highly debated point. If so, it is purely "conceptual," not linguistic.[19] On the other hand, if so, it must also be urged that Paul's perspective in the opening sentence (vv. 6-7c) has little to do with Christ in his humanity; that is, if the analogy is intended, it has nothing to do with the two Adams' being in God's image *in their humanity,* and everything to do with how each Adam *handled* being in that "image." To press the analogy to suggest "mere humanity without pre-existence" is to stretch Paul's own grammar and language nearly beyond recognition.[20] (2) The metaphor inherent in

---

pology in Phil. II, 6-11," *RB* 83 (1976): 25-50; Charles H. Talbert, "The Problem of Pre-existence in Philippians 2:6-11," *JBL* 86 (1967): 141-53.

18. For a fuller exposition of what is given in outline form here, see *Paul's Letter to the Philippians* (Grand Rapids: Eerdmans, 1995), pp. 191-229.

19. The one tie that is often suggested, that there is a semantic overlap between Paul's μορφή and the LXX's εἰκών, is both an assertion that has not been demonstrated and a thoroughly illegitimate use of linguistic data. That the two words are fully interchangeable and would have automatically been understood so by the readers is scholarly mythology based on untenable semantics. This is to imply that because in certain instances they share a degree of semantic overlap, therefore an author could — or would — use either one or the other at will. Since Paul is quite ready to speak of Christ as "in the image (εἰκών) of God," and since that is the word used in Genesis, how is it possible, one wonders, that Paul was *intending* this analogy and then wrote μορφή?

For an objection to the need for a linguistic tie in order for the Philippians to have perceived a conceptual tie, see J. D. G. Dunn, *The Theology of Paul the Apostle* (Grand Rapids: Eerdmans, 1997), pp. 274-75. While his point, that one does not necessarily need linguistic ties for there to be an allusion, is conceded, the question still remains as to how in this instance the Philippians would have had a clue without such a tie.

20. In fact, one of the major weaknesses of the view is methodological, in that it requires a considerable accumulation of merely possible, but highly improbable, meanings, *all of which*

the main verb of the first sentence, ἐκένωσεν ("he emptied himself), seems strikingly inappropriate to refer to one who is already (and merely) human. Paul's point is that it was while "being in God's nature" and thus "equal with God"[21] that Christ disdained acting out of "selfish ambition or vain conceit" (v. 3), but rather showed God-likeness precisely in his "pouring himself out by taking on the form of a slave." (3) The one described in the opening participle (v. 6) as "being in the form of God" and thus "equal with God" is described at the end of the sentence as being "made/born in human likeness"; which is then picked up as the first item in the second sentence in terms of his being "found in human appearance." This, too, is an especially strange thing to say of one who was merely human from the start. (4) This view ultimately divests the narrative of its essential power, which rests in the pointed contrast between the opening participle ("being in the form of God") and the final coda ("death on the cross").[22] (5) Finally, the structure itself supports the traditional view, in which the participle that begins the second clause ("and being found in appearance as a human being") stands in clear contrast to that which begins the first clause ("who being in the 'form' of God"), so that the first sentence narrates how Christ acted as God and the second how he acted in his humanity.

Paul's nicely balanced sentences are in fact written precisely to counter the two negative attitudes expressed in v. 3 ("selfish ambition" and "vain glory"), so that Christ as God "emptied himself by taking the form of a slave" and as man "humbled himself by becoming obedient to the point of death on the cross." All of this makes perfectly good sense in terms of Paul's understanding of Christ as pre-existent and "equal with God," but very little sense

---

are necessary to make it work. Conclusions based on such a procedure are always suspect. For refutations, see Paul D. Feinberg, "The Kenosis and Christology: An Exegetical-Theological Analysis of Phil 2:6-11," *TrinJ* 1 (1980): 21-46; L. D. Hurst, "Re-enter the Pre-existent Christ in Philippians 2:5-11?," *NTS* 32 (1986): 449-57; Peter O'Brien, *Commentary on Philippians*, NIGTC (Grand Rapids, 1991), 263-68; C. A. Wanamaker, "Philippians 2.6-11: Son of God or Adamic Christology," *NTS* 33 (1987): 179-93; T. Y.-C. Wong, "The Problem of Pre-existence in Philippians 2, 6-11," *ETL* 62 (1986): 167-82. For a helpful overview and sane conclusions on this matter, see L. W. Hurtado, *DPL* 743-46.

21. Too many NT scholars have passed over the plain sense of Paul's grammar in these opening clauses, where the anaphoric τό before εἶναι ἴσα θεῷ points back to Christ's "being in μορφή θεοῦ"; thus the clause grammatically reads: "being in the form of God, he did not consider (the afore-mentioned being) equal with God to be ἁρπαγμόν." See further my *Philippians*, pp. 207-8.

22. Indeed, in order to make this view work, one must resort to the dreadful redundancy of making *both* participles that refer to Christ's humanity begin the final sentence ("Coming to be in the likeness of human beings and being found in appearance as a human being, he humbled himself . . ."). For a refutation, see my *Philippians*, p. 214, n. 3.

in this context as emphasizing his role in contrast to Adam, which assumes a view of Christ that begins from below.

When we turn to vv. 9-11, we come to the other point I wish to make regarding Paul's presuppositional christology, namely the appellation of κύριος given him at his exaltation by God the Father. As long as the heavy hand of Wilhelm Bousset, with his rich learning but *religionsgeschichtlich* presuppositions, was laid upon our discipline,[23] many NT scholars found it convenient to back away from the christological implications of the earliest Christian confession that "Jesus is Lord." But it is clear from a large variety of data that the early believers came by this title through the Septuagint, not from pagan or imperial influences; and Paul serves as both our earliest and most definitive witness to this.

In the first place the very subtlety of many of the Pauline usages must catch our attention. Without hesitation Paul takes a series of κύριος phrases and sentences from the OT that refer to Yahweh and applies them to Christ: e.g., "the day of the Lord" is for him "the day of our Lord Jesus Christ" (1 Cor. 1:8 *et al.*), and the "Spirit of the Lord" is now also "the Spirit of Christ" (see esp. Rom. 8:9). In contrast to the "gods many and lords many" of the pagan cults, "for us [believers in Christ]," Paul says, "there is one God, the Father, from whom are all things and we for him, and one Lord, Jesus Christ, *through whom are all things* and we through him." Thus, the one God of Israel, Yahweh, who is designated *kyrios* in the LXX, is now, on the basis of Jesus' own use of *Abba* that he passed on to his followers (Gal. 4:6; Rom. 8:15), designated "Father," while the appellation *kyrios* comes to be used almost exclusively of Christ.[24]

But none of these is perhaps as telling as is the way Paul uses Isa. 45:23 in Phil. 2:10-11. First, "at the name of Jesus," who in his exaltation has been given The Name (i.e., κύριος/the Lord), "every knee shall bow." The whole created order shall give him obeisance. The "bowing of the knee" is a common idiom for doing homage, sometimes in prayer, but always in recognition of the authority of the god or person to whom one is offering such obeisance.[25] The

---

23. See *Kyrios Christos* (first German edition, 1913); translated by J. E. Steely from the fifth German edition with a foreword by Rudolf Bultmann (Nashville: Abingdon, 1970). For an assessment and critique, see L. W. Hurtado, "New Testament Christology: A Critique of Bousset's Influence," *TS* 40 (1979): 306-17.

24. Among scores of such passages, see the interesting usage in Rom. 14:1-12, where "the Lord" before whom one does or does not eat is Christ, who assumed the role of Lord of both the living and the dead through his own death and resurrection.

25. See, e.g., Ps. 95:6; Mark 15:19; Luke 5:8; 22:41; Acts 7:60; 9:40; Eph. 3:14; cf. the discussions in *NIDNTT*, 2.859-60 (Schönweiss), and *EDNT*, 1.257-58 (Nützel).

significance of Paul's using the language of Isaiah in this way lies with his substituting "at the name of Jesus" for the "to me" of Isa. 45:23, which refers to Yahweh, the God of Israel. In this stirring oracle (Isa. 45:18-24a), Yahweh is declared to be God alone, over all that he has created and thus over all other gods and nations. And he is Israel's savior, whom they can fully trust. In vv. 22-24a Yahweh, while offering salvation to all but receiving obeisance in any case, declares that "*to me* every knee shall bow." Paul now asserts that through Christ's resurrection and at his ascension God has transferred this right of obeisance to the Son; he is the Lord to whom every knee shall eventually bow.

Also in keeping with the Isaianic oracle, but now interrupting the language of the citation itself, Paul declares the full scope of the homage that Christ will one day receive: every knee "of those in the heavens and of those on earth and of those under the earth" shall bow to the authority inherent in his name. In keeping with the oracle, especially that "the Lord" is the creator of the heavens and the earth (45:18), Paul is purposely throwing the net of Christ's sovereignty over the whole of created beings.[26]

Second, not only shall every creature bend the knee and offer the worship that is due Christ's name, but "every tongue" shall express that homage in the language of the confessing — but currently suffering — church: Jesus Christ is Lord. In its Pauline occurrences this confession always takes the form, "the Lord is Jesus," to which he here adds "Christ." For Paul this confession is the line of demarcation between believer and non-believer (Rom. 10:9). In Rom. 10:9, this confession is linked with conviction about the resurrection of Jesus; that same combination is undoubtedly in view here.

Such a passage thus affirms the deity of Christ in unmistakable terms: equal with God, he became incarnate; in his humanity he became obedient to the point of death on the cross, all the while never ceasing to be God; raised and exalted, he is given The Name, so that the Lord is none other than Jesus Christ, at whose name every created being shall eventually do obeisance. Such language seems to force upon us at least a binitarian view of God on the part of Paul.

But for all the well-known christocentricity of Paul's theology, he was not in fact a binitarian, but a thoroughgoing trinitarian in his experience of God and his articulation of that experience. Crucial to all of this is the reality that for Paul the confession of Jesus as Lord is possible solely through the experience of the Spirit (1 Cor. 12:3). Thus, Paul's "high christology" does not

26. Those "of heaven" refer to all heavenly beings, angels and demons (so most interpreters); those of earth refer to all those who are living on earth at his Parousia, including those who are currently causing suffering in Philippi; and those "under the earth" probably refer to "the dead," who also shall be raised to acknowledge his lordship over all.

begin with doctrinal reflection but with experienced conviction. Those who have received the Spirit of God have been enabled to see the crucifixion in new, divine light. Those who walk "according to the Spirit" can no longer look on Christ from their old "according to the flesh" point of view (2 Cor. 5:15-16). They now know him to be the exalted Lord, ever present at the Father's right hand making intercession for them (Rom. 8:34).

It is in this light that we now turn to Paul's understanding of the Spirit, since his thoroughly trinitarian experience of God was ultimately determined by his and his churches' experience of the Spirit — as the fulfillment of God's promise, including especially the promise of the renewal of the divine Presence with God's people.

III. The Spirit: The Personal Presence of God and Christ

Since the difficulty most people face when dealing with the Holy Spirit is with "personal-ness," that is the rightful place for this discussion to begin. Unfortunately, this very understandable difficulty has been abetted by the reticence of NT scholarship on this matter, which has taken two forms. On the one hand, it is argued that Paul is largely dependent on the OT for his understanding of the Spirit, and that there the Spirit appears most often as not much more than some kind of extension or emanation of God, or of power coming from God. And since in the OT — and in Paul — the primary function of the Spirit of God is some form of agency, there is nothing inherent in Paul's understanding that would require us to think of the Spirit in personal terms.

On the other hand, some have argued that Paul's understanding of the Spirit is best viewed in terms of identification with the risen Christ, that is, that the risen, exalted Christ and the Spirit are essentially the same reality. If by this one means that the Spirit is how the risen Christ is continually present with his people, there are no objections to be raised. After all, this is exactly how we understand God the Father to be with us as well. But the language in the literature suggests far more than that, moving very close to full identification, so that "distinct from" is almost totally lost in the rhetoric of identification.

Since I have addressed this latter issue at some length in an earlier paper,[27] here I wish only to revisit some Pauline texts that seem to demand (a) that Paul understood the Spirit in very personal terms, and not simply as an extension of God, personifying his power as it were, (b) that he understood the Spirit as the "Spirit of Christ" as well as the "Spirit of God (the Fa-

27. See n. 12 above.

342

ther)," and clearly as "distinct from" Christ, and (c) that one key to Paul's enlarged understanding of the one God in trinitarian terms lies with his understanding the Spirit to be the renewed Presence of God and thus also the presence of the risen Christ.

1. While it is true that Paul does not speak directly to the question of the Spirit's *personal nature,* nonetheless, two passages in particular make it clear that he understood the Spirit in personal terms, intimately associated with God, yet distinct from him.

(a) In 1 Cor. 2:10-12 Paul uses the analogy of human interior consciousness (only one's "spirit" knows one's mind) to insist that the Spirit alone knows the mind of God. At issue in this passage is the Corinthians' radical misunderstanding of the Spirit, which in turn has led to a radical revaluation of the cross (actually devaluation). Having argued vigorously for the centrality of the cross (1:18 to 2:5), Paul now sets out to demonstrate that the Spirit — whom the Corinthian believers have indeed received as the source of their supernatural giftings (chs. 12–14; cf. 1:5-7) — must first of all be understood as the one who has revealed God's heretofore hidden mystery: that the "foolishness and weakness" of the crucifixion is in fact the ultimate expression of God's wisdom and power.

Paul's concern with the analogy in vv. 10-11, therefore, is not ontological (that God is like us in his being, in that he has a "spirit"), but epistemological (how we can know the mystery of the cross that has lain hidden in the "depths of God"). His point is that only through self-revelation one can penetrate into another's consciousness. Indeed, the analogy breaks down precisely at the point of ontology; but with regard to ours, not God's. Whatever else is clear in Paul's pneumatology, the present *locus* of God's Spirit is not interior to God as a way of expressing self-consciousness, but "external" to God, in the sense that the Spirit presently dwells in and among God's people.[28] Thus, Paul's concern in using the analogy has to do with revelation, pure and simple. The Spirit whom they have come to understand in a triumphalistic way is rather to be understood as the source both of their getting it right with regard to the cross (as God's wisdom) and also of their living life in the present in a cruciform way, as their maligned apostle does (which is quite the point of 1 Cor. 4).

28. The passages here are numerous, most of them reflecting Paul's use of the language of the LXX from Ezek. 36:26 (πνεῦμα καινὸν δώσω ἐν ὑμῖν; "I will give a new Spirit in you," followed by the analogy of a heart of "flesh" replacing the heart of stone) and 37:14 (καὶ δώσω τὸ πνεῦμα μου εἰς ὑμᾶς καὶ ζήσεσθε; "and I will give my Spirit into you, and you shall live"). Among many texts in Paul, see 1 Thess. 4:8 (for the precise language of Ezekiel); Rom. 8:11, and 1 Cor. 3:16 (for the concept of "indwelling"); Gal. 4:6 (for the location as "in our hearts"); and 1 Cor. 6:19 (for the abbreviated "in you").

Nonetheless, by use of this analogy Paul does in fact draw the closest kind of relationship between God and the Spirit. The Spirit alone "searches all things," even "the depths of God"; and because of this unique relationship with God, the Spirit alone knows and reveals God's otherwise hidden wisdom (1 Cor. 2:7). What is significant for our present purposes is that such language assumes personhood in a most straightforward way. The Spirit "searches, knows, reveals, and teaches" the "mind of God," so that having received the Spirit ourselves, "we have the mind of Christ," Paul concludes (2:16).

Some mystery is involved here, of course, because finally we are dealing with divine mysteries. But there can be little question that Paul sees the Spirit as distinct from God; yet at the same time the Spirit is both the interior expression of the unseen God's personality and the visible manifestation of God's activity in the world. The Spirit is truly God in action; yet he is neither simply an outworking of God's personality nor all there is to say about God.

(b) Even more significantly, in Rom. 8:26-27 this same reality is expressed in reverse; now it is God who *knows the mind* of the Spirit. This passage comes at the end of a sudden and extraordinary influx of σύν- compounds that express our relationship with the Spirit and Christ (and includes the now-subjected creation as joining with us in "sighing" in our present "already/not yet" eschatological existence). In v. 16 Paul has stated that the Spirit "bears witness together [συμμαρτυρεῖ] with our spirits that we are God's children"; now, following the brief, but theologically significant, interlude describing our present existence in weakness (vv. 18-25), he concludes with this final word about our present life as life in the Spirit: "Likewise [just as the Spirit bears witness with our spirits], the Spirit also joins together with us to aid us (συναντιλαμβάνεται) in our weakness, by interceding from within us with inarticulate groanings." Paul's ultimate concern here is to show the absolute sufficiency and adequacy of such praying in the Spirit, the effectiveness of whose intercession lies precisely in the fact that God, who searches *our* hearts, likewise "knows the mind of the Spirit," that he is interceding for us κατὰ θεόν (according to God!).

Thus, not only does the Spirit himself (αὐτὸ τὸ πνεῦμα) intercede on behalf of the saints (a very personal activity, it must be pointed out), but the saints can have complete confidence in such prayer, even if they do not understand the words, because *God knows the mind of the Spirit, that the Spirit intercedes according to God.* One can scarcely miss the significance of such a sentence for Paul's understanding of the Spirit, as both personal (the Spirit intercedes; God knows the Spirit's mind) and "distinct from" God the Father.

2. It is of further importance with regard to this latter text to note that some few sentences later (v. 34) Paul mentions the present intercessory activity

of Christ in our behalf. Whereas the Spirit intercedes from "within us" (see 8:9, 15), Christ in his exaltation intercedes for us "at the right hand of God." This collocation of intercessory texts, one by the Spirit (from within the human breast) and the other by Christ (at the right hand of the Father) should put to rest any idea that Paul identified the risen Christ with the gift of the Spirit.

On the other hand, and here is the crucial matter, on three occasions, when at issue is the risen Christ's presence with him, Paul freely and readily denominates the Spirit of God to be "the Spirit of Christ (Jesus)" (Rom. 8:9; Gal. 4:6; Phil. 1:19). Although such usage admittedly says something more christological than pneumatological, what it does say of the Spirit is especially significant, since herein most likely lies an important key to Paul's trinitarian understanding of God. As he insists elsewhere, there is only one Spirit (1 Cor. 12:4, 9; Eph. 4:4); but as his usage in various contexts makes plain, the one Spirit is the Spirit of both the Father and the Son.

Crucial here is that the reception of the Spirit is thus the way Paul experiences — and therefore relates to — both the Father and Christ. It would be hard to minimize the significance of this reality for our understanding of Paul's latent trinitarianism. To some Gentile believers who are sorely tempted to relate to God by means of (impersonal) Torah observance, Paul asserts that the Son of God who loved me and gave himself for me (past tense) also "lives in me" (present tense), so that I am dead with reference to Torah and alive to God (Gal. 2:19-20). And it is equally clear from Rom. 8:9-10 that "Christ lives in me" is Pauline shorthand for "the risen Christ lives in me by his Spirit [i.e., by the Spirit of God who is also the Spirit of Christ]."

Thus, just as Paul knows God to be personally present with him through his experience of the Spirit, so also when Paul speaks of Christ as living in me/you/your hearts (as he does on five occasions[29]) this is realized by the Spirit as well. This, surely, is of no small consequence for our coming to terms with Paul's own enlarged understanding of God as Savior.

What this says in terms of our understanding the Spirit is equally important, of course, since this combination of realities (that the Spirit of God is equally the Spirit of Christ) means that just as Christ put a human face on God, as it were, so also has he put a human face on the Spirit. No longer can one think of the Spirit as some "it," some emanation from God; the Spirit of God is also to be henceforth known as the Spirit of Christ. He is thus the very personal presence of Christ with and within us during our present between-the-times existence.

3. That leads us at last to a final set of texts, which make clear what we

---

29. Rom. 8:10; 2 Cor. 13:5; Gal. 2:20; Eph. 3:17; Col. 1:23.

have been noting right along — that Paul views the Spirit as the eschatological renewal of God's presence with his people. While this motif stems in part from the language of "indwelling" found in the new covenant promises of Jeremiah and Ezekiel, it emerges especially in Paul's use of temple imagery, part of the significance of which is that the metaphor functions both for the corporate, gathered community as well as for the individual believer.

The theme of God's presence with his people is one of the keys to the structure of the book of Exodus. When Israel comes at last to the holy mount, the place of God's "dwelling," it is also a place where they are forbidden to go on the threat of death. Only Moses is allowed into God's presence. But God plans to "move" from the mount and dwell among his people by means of a "tabernacle." So after the giving of the Book of the Covenant (chs. 20–24), Moses receives the precise instructions for constructing the tabernacle (chs. 25–31). But this is followed by the debacle in the desert (ch. 32), followed by God's announcing that "my presence will *not* go with you"; an angel will go instead (ch. 33). Moses recognizes the inadequacy of this solution and intercedes: "If your Presence does not go with us, do not send us up from here. How will anyone know that you are pleased with me and with your people unless you go with us? What else will distinguish me and your people from all the other people on the face of the earth?" (33:15-16 NIV). God's Presence with Israel is what distinguishes them, not the Law or other "identity markers." This in turn is followed by the further revelation of God's character (34:4-7) and the actual construction of the tabernacle, all of which concludes with the descent of God's *glory* (his Presence), which "filled the tabernacle" (40:35). With that, they set out for the place that "the Lord your God will choose as a dwelling for his name" (Deut. 12:11 and *passim*). At a later point in time the motif of the divine presence, as outlined here, was specifically equated with "the Holy Spirit of the Lord" (Isa. 63:9-14; cf. Ps. 106:33), which language and theme Paul himself deliberately echoes in Eph. 4:30.[30]

The deuteronomic promise is finally fulfilled in the construction of Sol-

---

30. This is often noted in the commentaries, but then rather summarily dismissed. Paul's Greek reads καὶ μὴ λυπεῖτε τὸ πνεῦμα τὸ ἅγιον τοῦ θεοῦ; the LXX of Isa. 63:10 reads παρώξυναν τὸ πνεῦμα τὸ ἅγιον αὐτοῦ. That Paul is here "citing" the LXX best explains both the unusual "fullness" to the name ("the Spirit, the Holy, of God") and the word order. The two linguistic differences between Paul and LXX Isaiah are easily explained. Paul substitutes τοῦ θεοῦ for αὐτοῦ because in Paul's sentence the pronoun would otherwise have no antecedent (but in making the substitution he keeps the word order of the LXX). He substitutes λυπεῖτε for a form of παρωξύνω most likely because the latter means "irritate" or "vex," and Paul understands the Piel of עצב to mean "grieve" (correctly so; this is the only instance in the LXX where עצב is rendered with παρωξύνω).

omon's temple, where the same "glory" as in Exodus 40 descended and "filled his temple" (1 Kgs. 8:11). But Israel's failure caused them to forfeit God's presence. This is the tragedy. The temple in Jerusalem, the place where God has chosen to dwell, is finally destroyed; and the people are not only carried away captive, but both the captives and those who remained were no longer a people distinguished by the presence of the living God in their midst — although it is promised again in Ezekiel's grand vision (40–48). The second temple itself evinces mixed feelings among the people. In light of Solomon's temple and the promised future temple of Ezekiel, Haggai complains, "Who of you is left who saw this house in its former *glory?* How does it look to you now? Does it not seem to you like nothing?" (2:3). In many circles, therefore, the hope of a grand, rebuilt temple with the renewal of God's presence — his glory — still awaited the people of God.

It is this complex of ideas and images that Paul picks up in 1 Cor. 3:16-17 and elsewhere (cf. 6:19; 2 Cor. 6:16; Eph. 2:21-22), as his introductory, "do you not know that, . . . followed by "you are *the* temple of God [in Corinth]," strongly suggests. And what makes them God's temple in Corinth, his alternative to all the pagan deities to which they were formerly enslaved (1 Cor. 12:2), is the Spirit. The church, corporately and individually (1 Cor. 6:19), is now the place of God's own personal presence, by the Spirit. This is what marks God's new people off from "all the other people on the face of the earth." Hence Paul's consternation with the Corinthians' present behavior that has the effect of banishing the Spirit, the living presence of God that makes them his temple, the place of God's present dwelling.

Thus, this imagery, which understands God's presence with Israel in terms of the Spirit, is what is exploited by Paul. Their corporate experience of the Spirit's gifting, rather than being turned into demonic self-focused spirituality, must be for their corporate building up. All things the Spirit does among them is for their common good and for the edification of the body. And this, precisely because the evident manifestations of the Spirit among them are evidence of God's own presence among them.

All together these series of texts indicate in the strongest kind of way that Paul understood the Spirit in personal terms. It is in light of what seems reasonably clear in these texts that then causes one to see the same reality in all of the other texts where the Spirit's agency is personal — in the same way as Christ's is[31] — and where the Spirit is the subject of verbs that presuppose personhood.[32]

31. For this discussion, see esp. my *Paul, the Spirit, and the People of God*, pp. 26-27.
32. Besides the texts noted above, the Spirit also *teaches* the content of the gospel to be-

Not only so, but these texts also give certain evidence that for Paul this new eschatological experience of God's presence is also the experience of the presence of the risen Christ "living in me." The net result is that the experience of the Spirit finally provides the key to Paul's trinitarianism. The Spirit whom God "sent into our hearts" is thus "distinct from" God himself, just as is the Son whom God sent to redeem. At the same time the Spirit is the Spirit of Christ and is thus "distinct from" Christ, who now lives in us by means of "the Spirit of Christ."

To be sure, Paul's experience and understanding of the Spirit as God's personal presence inevitably leads us into some deep waters. At issue *for us* is *how* God exists in his essential being as triune. How can God be known as Father, Son, and Spirit, one being, yet each "person" distinct from the other? And we tend to think that a person is not a true trinitarian unless he or she has a working formulation in response to this question.

To put the question this way, however, is to get ahead of Paul, not to mention to define trinitarianism by later standards. What makes this an issue for us at all is the fact that Paul, the strictest of monotheists, who never doubted that "the Lord thy God is one," wrote letters to his churches that are full of presuppositions and assertions which reveal that he *experienced* God, and then *expressed* that experience, in a fundamentally trinitarian way. Thus Paul affirms, asserts, and presupposes the Trinity in every kind of way, but especially soteriologically — the very heart of Pauline theology. And those affirmations — that the one God known and experienced as Father, Son, and Holy Spirit, each distinct from the other, is yet only one God — are precisely the reason the later church took up the question of "how."

IV. Conclusions and Implications

In sum: Paul's various triadic expressions of God's saving activity, as the combined activity of Father, Christ, and Spirit, stem not only from his prior understanding of God as Savior and his encounter with the risen Christ on the Damascus Road, but especially from his experience of the Spirit, who made that work effectual in his and others' lives. Furthermore, the risen Christ is

---

lievers (1 Cor. 2:13), *dwells* among or within believers (1 Cor. 3:16; Rom. 8:11; 2 Tim. 1:14), *accomplishes* all things (1 Cor. 12:11), *gives life* to those who believe (2 Cor. 3:6), *cries out* from within our hearts (Gal. 4:6), *leads* us in the ways of God (Gal. 5:18; Rom. 8:14), *bears witness* with our own spirits (Rom. 8:16), *has desires* that are in opposition to the flesh (Gal. 5:17), *works* all things *together* for our ultimate good (Rom. 8:28), *strengthens* believers (Eph. 3:16). Furthermore, the fruit of the Spirit's indwelling are the personal attributes of God (Gal. 5:22-23).

now the exalted "Lord," the OT language for God, about whom Paul spoke as the pre-existent Son of God and to whom he attributed every imaginable activity that Paul's Judaism reserved for God alone. That the issue is Trinity, however, and not Binity, comes directly out of the church's personal experience with God through the Spirit, who is at once the renewed Presence of God and the way the risen Christ lives in him/them. The question is, Did Paul in fact have a trinitarian faith, even if he did not use the language of a later time to describe God? Our analysis of the Pauline data suggests that indeed he did.[33]

One may grant that Paul's trinitarian assumptions and descriptions, which form the basis of the later formulas, never move towards calling the Spirit "God" and never wrestle with the philosophical and theological implications of those assumptions and descriptions. But neither is there evidence that he lacked clarity as to the distinctions between, and the specific roles of, the three divine "persons" who accomplished so great salvation for us all.

I would thus urge my colleagues in the NT academy that in our desire to be good historians we not dismiss too easily the fact that the "historical Paul" had plenty of theological muscle. If his concern is less with "God in his being" and more with "God our Savior," there is plenty of good reason to see Paul as presuppositionally an ontological trinitarian as well. The fact that the Spirit alone knows the mind of God, "the deep things of God," as Paul puts it, and that God knows the mind of the Spirit indicates not only functional trinitarianism, but something moving very close to "ontological" trinitarianism. So also with the clear evidence of the Spirit's "unity" with Christ — in receiving a fresh supply of the Spirit, it is the Spirit of Jesus Christ whom Paul receives (Phil. 1:19) — yet the clear distinction between Christ and the Spirit remains.

We may wish for more, but then on what theological point might we not always be wishing for more? Such is the way of ad hoc documents whose concern is primarily, as in the Judaism to which Paul is heir, with the way God's people live in the world, so that even when he addresses their thinking it is to change the way they are living. May our own trinitarian discussions never lose sight of this end as well.

Which leads me to note that perhaps even more important than how Paul contributes to later ontological articulation, is what he may contribute to our own experience of and relationship with God. Fundamental to Paul's Judaism is that God's people are expected to "know God," which of course has

---

33. On this whole question, and especially on Paul as a trinitarian, see further the section entitled "What about the Trinity?" by David Ford, in Frances Young and David Ford, *Meaning and Truth in 2 Corinthians* (Grand Rapids: Eerdmans, 1987), pp. 255-60.

little to do with doctrinal articulation and everything to do with knowing God relationally, in terms of his character and nature. Paul carries this fundamental understanding with him, but insists on putting it into perspective: our knowing is preceded by God's "knowing us" (Gal. 4:9; cf. 1 Cor. 13:12).

As a follower of Christ, Paul rephrases "knowing" in terms of "knowing Christ," for the surpassing value of which he has "suffered the loss of all things" (Phil. 3:8). "*Being found* in him," he goes on, has as its final goal "to know him, both the power of his resurrection and participation in his sufferings, so as to be made like him in his death" (v. 10). It is clear from any number of passages that for Paul "knowing God" comes by way of "knowing Christ" (cf. 2 Cor. 4:6); and "knowing Christ" comes by way of "the Spirit's wisdom and revelation" (Eph. 1:17). At the heart of all of this is Paul's conviction that Christian life means to "live by, walk in, be led by" the Spirit. Living the life of the Spirit means for the Spirit to bear his fruit in our individual and corporate lives; and that fruit is nothing other than God's character, as lived out by Christ, being reproduced in his people.

Hence to be a trinitarian of the Pauline kind means to be a person of the Spirit; for it is through the Spirit's indwelling that we know God and Christ relationally, and through the same Spirit's indwelling that we are being transformed into God's own likeness "from glory to glory" (2 Cor. 3:18).

Finally, whatever else we learn from Paul's kind of trinitarianism, we need to recognize that if Rahner is right, that the economic and immanent Trinity are one, then our trinitarianism is terribly defective if we spend our labors on the ontological questions in such a way as to lose the essential narrative about God and salvation that raised those questions in the first place. The instincts of the earlier creeds were right on at this point, by insisting that we confess our faith in God by way of this narrative (God as Creator, Christ as Redeemer); where their instincts failed was in excluding the Holy Spirit from the narrative as such — although one could argue that "the holy catholic church" is the Spirit's role in the narrative.

In any case, rather than simply use Paul as the quarry for later theological reflection, something might be said for keeping Paul's form of trinitarian expression as part of the final equation.[34]

---

34. Which, it should be noted, is also part of Catherine LaCugna's agenda in *God for Us* (see esp. ch. 7).

CHAPTER 21

Wisdom Christology in Paul:
A Dissenting View
(2000)

When I did my doctoral studies in the 1960s, the phrase "wisdom christology" was rarely heard. Although the roots of the idea go back much earlier[1] — such language was tentatively used as early as 1947 by C. H. Dodd[2] — the term

---

1. Especially in Hans Windisch, "Die göttliche Weisheit der Jüden und die paulinische Christologie," in *Neutestamentliche Studien für Georg Heinrici*, ed. H. Windisch (Leipzig: J. D. Hinrichs, 1914), pp. 220-34. For a convenient overview of this history see E. J. Schnabel, *Law and Wisdom from Ben Sira to Paul: A Tradition History Enquiry into the Relation of Law, Wisdom, and Ethics* (WUNT 2/16; Tübingen: J. C. B. Mohr [Siebeck], 1985), pp. 236-63. For a brief, helpful overview see E. Elizabeth Johnson, "Wisdom and Apocalyptic in Paul," in *In Search of Wisdom: Essays in Memory of John C. Gammie*, ed. L. G. Perdue et al. (Louisville: Westminster John Knox, 1993), pp. 263-83.

2. See C. H. Dodd, "The History and Doctrine of the Apostolic Age," in *A Companion to the Bible*, ed. T. W. Manson (Edinburgh: T. & T. Clark, 1947), pp. 390-417. Dodd broaches the subject with due caution: "It seems probable also, though the proof is not complete, that some teachers, independently of Paul, had associated [Christ's] authority as the revealer of God with the OT idea of the divine Wisdom" (p. 409). But then he cites 1 Cor. 1:24 quite out of context to the effect that Paul considered Christ to be the Wisdom of God. He finally asserts, without giv-

---

I am pleased to offer these musings in honor of my dear friend and colleague, Bruce Waltke, with whom I have team-taught both biblical exegesis and biblical theology for the past decade. Bruce is a man of great integrity and personal piety, whom students and colleagues alike have learned to treasure. My wife Maudine and I have especially enjoyed the friendship of Bruce and his wife Elaine over these years, one of the highlights of which has been regular evenings out for dinner and a concert by the Vancouver Symphony. Without his knowing what I was about, I was able to discuss the basic concerns of this essay with Bruce and found him to have the same reservations about personified Wisdom that I have carried for many years; so it is appropriate that I should offer this study in his honor.

has picked up momentum since the 1970s, so that it has now become coin of the realm in the New Testament guild. This is evidenced especially by the prominent billing it is given in J. D. G. Dunn's recent comprehensive study of Pauline theology.[3] But the catalog of those who speak thus of Paul's christology is large and includes, in addition to Dunn, many scholars of considerable reputation. It is therefore with some apprehension that I offer a dissenting voice; nonetheless, I will do so in this essay, in part because I am convinced that the evidence brought forward in support of it is tenuous at best and in part because the logic of the argument in its favor seems flawed in both its major and minor premises.

What I offer here is another reading of the texts involved (the Wisdom literature and Paul's letters) with the suggestion that such a reading of these texts — independently of each other and on their own terms — does not support the many assertions being made about the influence of Jewish Wisdom on Paul's christology. I will begin with a brief overview of the issues, the texts, and the methodology.

I. Overview

A. *The Issues*

It is interesting that even though the phrase "wisdom christology"[4] is now so commonplace, it emerges at only one point in the discussions of Paul's theology: on the issue of pre-existence,[5] and especially in the interest of tracing out

---

ing the evidence, that "in Col. 1:15-19, without mentioning the word 'wisdom,' he [Paul] uses language which can be traced *in every point* (except the one word 'fullness') to Jewish Wisdom theology" (italics mine). Nonetheless, when starting his next paragraph, Dodd is content to put the term in quotes ("This 'Wisdom-Christology' made it possible for Paul to give a more adequate account of what was meant by calling Christ the Son of God"). I have not found an earlier use, but further research is needed.

3. J. D. G. Dunn, *The Theology of Paul the Apostle* (Grand Rapids: Eerdmans, 1998), pp. 266-81. Cf. his earlier *Christology in the Making* (Philadelphia: Westminster, 1980), pp. 176-96.

4. How to capitalize *wisdom* in this study is problematic. I have capitalized it when referring to the Jewish sapiential tradition and, following the lead of the NJB, when I intend its personification; it is lowercase when it refers simply to an attribute of God or when it is used synonymously with understanding or knowledge. I refer to the deuterocanonical Wisdom of Solomon as Ps-Solomon except when the reference is followed by chapter and verse numbers (e.g., Wis. 1:6), for the sake of clearer distinctions between the book and the concept.

5. It is of some interest at this point to note that Dunn uses Wisdom Christology in order to diminish the concept of *personal* pre-existence in Paul. See, e.g., on 1 Cor. 8:6: "Is there then a

the origins of this idea. That is, even though a great deal is said about Wisdom in the Jewish texts, and even though Paul has much to say about Christ in his letters, the only place these two literary traditions intersect is on the matter of Christ's pre-existence. Furthermore, this issue is most often brought forward at only one point in discussions of pre-existence, namely, Wisdom's role in creation, where assertions are made over and again to the effect that "the ultimate source of this doctrine [Christ as Wisdom] is Prov. 8 where Wisdom is conceived as pre-existent and as God's agent in creation."[6]

B. The Texts

Although God is said to have created "all things in wisdom" (Ps. 104:24; LXX 103:24: πάντα ἐν σοφίᾳ ἐποίησας; cf. Prov. 3:19), the crucial texts from the Jewish Wisdom tradition are those where Wisdom is personified and pictured as present with God when he created. These texts are basically three:[7] Prov. 8:22-

---

thought of pre-existence in 1 Cor. 8.6 . . . ? Of course there is. But it is the pre-existence of divine Wisdom. That is, the pre-existence of God. . . . Whether the subtlety of the theology is best expressed as 'the pre-existence of Christ' *simpliciter* is another question" (*Theology*, pp. 274-75).

On the other side — and the list is long here — are those who find in Wisdom Christology support for a more traditional understanding of pre-existence in Paul; see *inter alios* M. Hengel, "Jesus as Messianic Teacher of Wisdom and the Beginnings of Christology," in *Studies in Early Christology* (Edinburgh: T. & T. Clark, 1995), pp. 95-117; Hengel, *The Son of God* (Philadelphia: Fortress, 1976), pp. 48-51; S. Kim, *The Origin of Paul's Gospel* (WUNT 2/4; Tübingen: J. C. B. Mohr [Paul Siebeck], 1981), pp. 114-23; Ben Witherington III, *Jesus the Sage: The Pilgrimage of Wisdom* (Minneapolis: Fortress, 1994), pp. 295-333; E. J. Schnabel, "Wisdom," in *DPL*, pp. 967-71.

It has also become an especially crucial construct in the Roman Catholic feminist theology of Elizabeth A. Johnson (see "Jesus, the Wisdom of God: A Biblical Basis for Non-Androcentric Christology," *ETL* 61 [1985]: 261-94 [esp. pp. 276-89]).

6. The citation is from A. M. Hunter, *The Gospel According to St. Paul* (Philadelphia: Westminster, 1966), p. 68, and is used here because of its brevity and clarity. But whether in brief or at length, this encapsulates the position held by a large number of scholars who have either written on the subject or who are (as is Hunter here) dependent on those who have.

7. They are also discussed in an essay by Karen Jobes, who was kind enough to let me read her paper when I was at the beginning of my research for an examination of the concept of incarnation and pre-existence in Paul presented at the Incarnation Summit, Dumwoodie, N.Y., at Easter 2000, and to be published with the other papers under an Oxford University Press title. While working on that paper, I experienced dis-ease over the matter at hand and included my reservations as part of that presentation. Although these studies have quite different concerns, in both cases I go over much of the same exegetical ground, so that there is some repetition (and reproduction) in the two exegetical sections of the two papers — after all, I have scarcely changed my mind on these matters over the six-month period between working on the two essays!

31 (in light of 3:19); Sir. 24:3-22; and Wis. 6:1–10:21 (esp. 7:12, 22; 8:4-5; 9:1-9). On the Pauline side the crucial texts are 1 Cor. 8:6 (in light of 1:24, 30) and Col. 1:15-17 (in light of 2:3).

C. The Methodology

My concerns here go in two directions: First, as will be pointed out, there is no *significant* linguistic correspondence — indeed, if any *linguistic* correspondence at all — between Paul and these texts. The question, then, is how one determines *conceptual* influence in such cases. After all, we have abundant evidence that Paul both cites and "echoes" the Hebrew Bible in a variety of ways. But what is missing in the case of pre-existent Wisdom as the agent of creation is not only verbal correspondence between Paul and the Wisdom tradition at this point, but also clearly identifiable echoes from these texts.

Second, the method used to establish the links between Paul and the Wisdom tradition on these matters takes a form of logic that goes like this:[8]

> *Major premise:* In the Jewish Wisdom tradition, personified Wisdom is pictured as the divine agent of creation.
> *Minor premise:* The Jewish Paul specifically calls Christ the Wisdom of God (1 Cor. 1:24) and sees him as the agent of creation (8:6).
> *Conclusion:* Therefore, when Paul speaks of Christ as the agent of creation, he is both relying on this tradition and putting Christ in the role of Wisdom.

As with many such syllogisms, however, when there are questions about how one reaches a given conclusion, the problem often lies with one or both of the premises. And so it is in this case. The minor premise is especially suspect, as exegesis of these passages on their own terms seems to make certain. But there are flaws in the major premise as well, especially as to what one means by "agent of creation." Together these flaws make the whole argument

---

8. By imposing a logical syllogism on the discussion, I do not mean to caricature those with whom I differ. In fact, I have gone over the arguments several times with painstaking care to make sure that this proposed syllogism fairly represents the actual "steps" in the argumentation. See Dunn, e.g., who begins his argument (*Theology*, pp. 267-69) with a brief look at the two key Pauline texts (1 Cor. 8:6; Col. 1:15-20); he then turns to examine personified Wisdom in the Jewish Wisdom texts (ibid., pp. 269-72), stating unequivocally, "Clearly, then, Paul was attributing to *Christ* the role previously attributed to divine Wisdom" (p. 270). I doubt whether this is clear at all (see sec. II.B).

tenuous — or at least so it seems to me. Here is another case where "it is very doubtful whether a set of weak arguments adds up to one powerful one."[9]

II. Another Look at the Pauline Texts

Instead of beginning with the major premise — as is normally done in the conventions of scholarship — I wish to begin the discussion with the minor premise, looking closely at the primary texts in 1 Corinthians and Colossians. The problem with starting with the role of Wisdom lies with the inherent danger (and, from my perspective, the fundamental error) of reading too much into Paul and, as is often the case, of not paying close enough attention to his own argumentation in context.[10] We begin, therefore, with the key text, 1 Cor. 8:6, and its alleged support in 1:24, 30.

A. 1 Corinthians 8:6

At issue in this section of 1 Corinthians is an ongoing argument between Paul and the Corinthians over their insistence on the right to attend festive meals in pagan temples.[11] Apparently Paul has already forbidden such practice (5:9), but in their return letter, they have argued vigorously for their right (ἐξουσία) to continue attending (8:9). Their argument can be reconstructed with a measure of confidence from Paul's citations from their letter: "We all have knowledge" (8:1)[12] that "an idol has no reality" since "there is only one

---

9. See I. H. Marshall, *1 and 2 Thessalonians* (NCB; Grand Rapids: Eerdmans, 1983), p. 35, about Trilling's arguments for the inauthenticity of 2 Thessalonians.

10. See also N. T. Wright, "Poetry and Theology in Colossians 1.15-20," *NTS* 36 (1990): 445-58 [452]. Although his concern is slightly different, he questions whether starting with Wisdom is the best procedure.

11. For the full argumentation in support of this perspective see Gordon D. Fee, "Εἰδωλόθυτα Once Again: An Interpretation of 1 Corinthians 8–10," *Bib* 61 (1980): 172-97; cf. Fee, *The First Epistle to the Corinthians* (NICNT; Grand Rapids: Eerdmans, 1987), pp. 357-63. The objection to this point of view presented by Bruce Fisk ("Eating Meat Offered to Idols: Corinthian Behavior and Pauline Response in 1 Corinthians 8–10," *TJ* 10 [1989]: 49-70) is flawed at several key points in both his lexical analysis and his theological presuppositions about Corinth and Paul, which will be pointed out in a forthcoming publication.

12. There is every good reason to believe that the Corinthians came to this view of *knowledge,* as they did of *wisdom* in 1:10–4:21, by way of their experience of the Spirit, since these two are the first items Paul picks up in his listing of Spirit manifestations in 12:8. In fact, chs. 1–4, 8–10, and 12–14 constitute the three largest blocks of argumentation in this letter, and in each case

God" (v. 4); therefore since food is a matter of indifference to God (v. 8), it matters neither what we eat nor where we eat it (v. 10).

Paul's response to this specious reasoning is especially noteworthy. For even though he will eventually condemn their *theology* — as a radical misunderstanding of the demonic nature of idolatry (10:14-22) — he begins by appealing to the nature of Christian *love*, which should forbid their casual destruction of the faith of others (8:2-3, 9-13). But even at this early stage in the argument he offers a preliminary correction to their theology per se (vv. 5-6, in response to their basically correct assertions in v. 4). In doing so, he acknowledges the "subjective reality"[13] of idolatry in the form of the "gods many and lords many" of the Greco-Roman pantheon and the mystery cults (v. 5). But before spelling out in v. 7 the consequences for "weaker" believers, for whom the subjective reality of idolatry still outweighs the objective reality being denied by those "in the know," Paul does an even more remarkable thing: he insists that their understanding of the "one God" needs to be broadened to include Christ as well (v. 6); and he does so because, at the end of the day, the attitudes and actions of the "knowing ones" who assert their "rights" serve potentially to destroy the work of Christ in others (vv. 10-13).

Our interest lies in v. 6, where in nicely balanced clauses Paul affirms,[14]

(1) ἀλλ' ἡμῶν	εἷς θεὸς	ὁ πατήρ,					
	ἐξ	οὗ	τὰ τάντα	καὶ	ἡμεῖς · εἰς		αὐτόν,
(2) καὶ	εἷς κύριος	Ἰησοῦς Χριστός,					
	δι'	οὗ	τὰ τάντα	καὶ	ἡμεῖς δι'		αὐτοῦ,
(1) But for us	one God	the Father,					
	from	whom	all things	and	we	*for*	him,
(2) and	one Lord	Jesus Christ,					
	through	whom	all things	and	we	*through*	him.

a part of Paul's argument with the Corinthians takes the form, "If anyone thinks that he/she . . ." ("is wise" — 3:18; "has knowledge" — 8:2; "is spiritual" — 14:37). See Fee, *Corinthians*, pp. 10-15.

13. This is my own term for the nature of Paul's argumentation. In 10:14-22 he asserts, in effect, that despite "idols being nothing," they nonetheless have an objective reality as the habitation of demons. In the present argument (ch. 8), besides v. 5 where he affirms that for pagans there are "gods many and lords many," he acknowledges in v. 7 that some with weak consciences do not have the "knowledge" of the others. This surely does not mean that they did not understand the truth that God is one and therefore that idols have no reality as gods; rather, because they had long attributed reality to the idols, when the "weak" became believers they were unable to shake themselves free from these former associations with pagan worship — which is why it would be so deadly for them to return to the temples for festive meals that honored a "god" (vv. 11-12).

14. Translations throughout are my own, unless otherwise noted.

This is clearly a Christian restatement of the Shema (Deut. 6:4: "Hear, O Israel: The Lord our God, the Lord is one"), with *God* now referring to the Father and *Lord* referring to the Son.[15] Because Paul's interests here are pastoral, he identifies the "one Lord" as none other than the historical Jesus Christ, the one who died for all, especially those with a weak conscience (v. 11). Thus, over against the "gods many" of paganism, the Shema rightly asserts — as the Corinthians themselves have caught on — that there is only one God; and typical of Paul's Jewish monotheism, the one God stands over against all pagan deities at one crucial point: creation. Thus God the Father is ἐκ/εἰς (from/for) in relation to everything that exists; he is its source and goal (or purpose) of being, although the final phrase ("we for him"), noticeably Pauline, moves easily from creation to redemption, where God is the goal of his people in particular.[16]

The surprising moment comes in line 2. Over against the "lords many" of paganism, there is only *one* Lord, Jesus Christ, whose relation to creation is that of mediator. Thus the Father has created all things through the agency of the Son, who is also — and now Paul's second point is being established — the agent of their redemption ("and we through him"). The whole, therefore, typically for Paul, encloses the work of the Son within that of the Father; that is, the two διά phrases regarding the one Lord's role as agent of creation and redemption are (logically) framed by the ἐκ and εἰς phrases regarding the Father as the ultimate source and goal of all things — both creation and redemption.

15. To be sure, Paul does not here use "son" language in referring to Christ. But since he has just referred to God as Father, this is one of those certain places where Paul's presuppositions allow us to identify Christ as Son, just as he assumes God as Father when he speaks only of the Son. The evidence for this is writ large in his letters; in the present letter, see 1:3, 9, where in v. 3 "God" is "our Father," while in v. 9 the God who has already been so designated has called believers "into fellowship with his Son, Jesus Christ." Only sophistry of the worst kind would deny the same relationship being in view in 8:6 simply because Paul does not use "son" language. Of the large literature on this matter, see esp. Larry W. Hurtado, "Son of God," in *DPL*, pp. 900-906; cf. Hurtado, "Jesus' Divine Sonship in Paul's Epistle to the Romans," in *Romans and the People of God*, ed. Sven K. Soderlund and N. T. Wright (Grand Rapids: Eerdmans, 1999), pp. 217-33.

16. Because of this, and because he is enamored with the text as a pre-Pauline creed, K.-J. Kuschel, in his *Born before All Time? The Dispute over Christ's Origin*, trans. J. Bowden (London: SCM Press, 1992), pp. 285-91, argues that this passage has to do only with soteriology (as did J. Murphy-O'Connor before him; see "I Cor. VIII, 6: Cosmology or Soteriology?" *RB* 85 [1978]: 253-67). But that is to misread the passage in context; the analogy for Pauline usage here is Rom. 11:36, not 2 Cor. 5:18, as argued by Kuschel. What seems to make this creational reading of 8:6 certain is the identical use of τὰ πάντα δι᾽ αὐτοῦ in Col. 1:16, which Kuschel gets around by denying Pauline authorship of Colossians (a circular argument that assumes what is questionable; see n. 33 below). Compare the critique in Dunn, *Theology*, p. 268 n. 5.

For our present purposes, three additional things must be noted about this passage. First, although the *conceptual* frame for this construction can be found elsewhere in the NT,[17] there is nothing quite like this use of prepositional phrases apart from Paul himself. Indeed, the only other known use of this specific scheme of prepositions in all of ancient literature is in Rom. 11:36, where the full phrase ἐξ αὐτοῦ καὶ δι' αὐτοῦ καὶ εἰς αὐτὸν τὰ πάντα ("from him and through him and for him [are] all things") appears in a doxology without this christological modification.[18] It is of significant theological interest that in the Romans doxology *God* is the one "through whom" are all things, while in Col. 1:16 *Christ* is the one "for whom" are all things. As Richard Bauckham has recently argued in a slightly different way, this interchange of prepositions indicates full identity of Christ with God.[19] My point here is simply to note that this formulation is a uniquely Pauline construct in the NT and in Paul's Jewish heritage; furthermore, as we will note later, there is nothing even remotely like it in the Jewish Wisdom tradition.

Second, this assertion is striking because at one level it is unnecessary to the present argument, since nothing *christological* is at stake. That is, Paul is not trying to demonstrate Christ's creative agency here; he simply assumes it by assertion. Nonetheless, at a deeper level this is precisely the assertion that will make both the theological and ethical dimensions of the argument work. By naming Christ as the "one Lord" through whom both creation and redemption were effected, Paul not only broadens the Corinthians' narrow perspective on the Shema but at the same time anticipates the role Christ is to

17. Most notably Heb. 1:1-2, where God has "appointed the Son" as "heir of all things, *through* whom also he made the universe."

18. In Dunn's commentary on Romans (*Romans 9–16* [WBC 38B; Dallas: Word, 1988], p. 701), he notes that "the use of prepositions like [these three] when speaking of God and the cosmos . . . was widespread in the ancient world and typically Stoic." But apart from the three Pauline texts (Rom. 11:36; 1 Cor. 8:6; Col. 1:16-17) he lists only six others, none of which contains another instance of all three prepositions occurring together. In his *Theology* (p. 269) Dunn has further suggested that one of the texts (Philo, *Cher.* 125-27) serves as an illustration of one who has made "a similar division in the 'by, from, and through' formulation, between the originating role of God . . . and the instrumental role of the Logos." While this is partly true, Philo's context and concerns are quite different from Paul's; and he does not come close to Paul's formulation as such. In fact, he would be mortified to think that Paul would use διά to refer to the "one Lord," since such a usage about Cain ("I have gotten a man through God") is to Philo an abomination ("even in these last two words he erred") and is the cause of the discussion that leads to the distinction between "by" (not "from") and "through."

19. Richard Bauckham, *God Crucified: Monotheism and Christology in the New Testament* (Grand Rapids: Eerdmans, 1999), pp. 37-40.

play in the argument that follows (esp. 8:11-12; 10:4, 9, 16-22),[20] where every-thing hinges on their ongoing relationship to Christ himself. What is impor-tant for our present purposes is (1) Paul's deliberate use of κύριος for Christ, language that in the Septuagint was substituted for the divine name of the one God; and (2) the *presuppositional* nature in these passages of the *historical person*, Jesus Christ, as pre-existent and as the personal agent of creation it-self. There is simply nothing like this to be found in Jewish Wisdom or any-where else in Paul's heritage.

Third, there is nothing inherent in this passage nor in its surrounding context that would suggest that Jewish Wisdom lies behind Paul's formula-tion. At issue in the present context is behavior predicated on *gnōsis,* not *sophia.* An insistence that Wisdom nonetheless lies behind Paul's formulation will have to remain in the category of scholarly discovery, not Pauline disclo-sure. And one should not expect a reader of Paul's text, including the Corin-thians themselves, to catch such subtlety. This leads us directly to the texts that are understood to be presupposed in Paul's present formulation.

B. 1 Corinthians 1:24, 30

Those who read 8:6 as a Pauline construct based on personified Wisdom's role as "agent of creation" invariably turn to these two passages in the argu-ment of 1 Cor. 1:10–4:21, usually in terms like "at this point we need to recall that Paul in fact already explicitly identified Christ as God's Wisdom — in 1 Cor. 1.24 and 30."[21] But such an understanding of 1:24 is highly question-

---

20. It should be noted here that Dunn would have us see an allusion to Wis. 11:4 (where Wisdom is associated with "the water [that] was given them out of the flinty rock") in the refer-ence to Christ as the "spiritual rock" that "followed" Israel in the desert in 10:4. While one need not doubt the association with Wisdom in Ps-Solomon (see Wis. 11:1), it is in fact at this point in the poetry that the author begins to address God (as the "you" makes plain; see esp. in context Wis. 10:20 and 11:26). This author is simply too Jewish at the core for him to address Wisdom and say, "When they were ⴕthirsty, they called upon you [Wisdom], and water was given them. . . ." All such addresses in this book are toward God alone. Thus the role of Wisdom is left a bit ambiguous here, although it is likely that Wisdom is to be understood as the divine instru-ment behind the various favors from God in the desert. But this is a far cry from Paul's bald as-sertion that "the rock that followed them *was* Christ," where he is picking up a rabbinic tradi-tion that had the rock accompanying Israel in the desert, since Moses struck it twice: once at the beginning of the wilderness experience (Exod. 17:6) and once toward the end (Num. 20:11). For details see Fee, *Corinthians,* pp. 447-49.

21. Dunn, *Theology,* p. 274. This is an invariable in all such discussions, because without it no one could possibly have seen "Wisdom" as lying behind 8:6. In fairness to Dunn, as over

able, especially if one reads the passage on its own terms, without a prior agenda.

It must be noted at the outset that it is especially doubtful whether *wisdom* is a truly Pauline word at all and whether, therefore, Paul ever thinks of Christ in terms of Jewish Wisdom.[22] The linguistic data tell much of the story: The noun σοφία and its cognate adjective σόφος occur 44 times in the Pauline corpus — 28 in 1 Corinthians, 26 of these in chs. 1–3,[23] and most of them pejorative! Of the remaining 17, one occurs in a similarly pejorative way in 2 Cor. 1:12, while ten occur in Colossians and Ephesians, where the "heady" nature of the false teaching being addressed again calls forth this language. This means that in the rest of the corpus this word group appears only five times, only one of which is the noun (Rom. 11:33), where it echoes OT usage referring to God's attribute of wisdom. These statistics, therefore, not to mention the argument itself, indicate that wisdom is actually a Corinthian thing and that Paul is trying to counter it by appealing to God's foolishness[24] as evidence that the gospel that saved them is not to be confused with σοφία in any form![25]

Indeed, Paul's assertion of Christ as "God's power" and "God's wisdom" in 1:24 (note Paul's order) is not a christological pronouncement at all,[26] as

---

against many others, he at least recognizes that Paul turns divine wisdom into the proclamation of Christ crucified; but even so, he treats v. 24 altogether as a christological, rather than soteriological, statement.

22. Contra Witherington, e.g., who (typical of many) is bold here: "[Paul] saw Christ as Wisdom come in the flesh (cf. 1 Cor. 1:24)." Ben Witherington III, "Christology," in *DPL*, p. 103.

23. And the remaining two (6:5; 12:8) seem clearly to hark back to the issue raised here. In 6:5, the question "Can it be that there is no one wise enough to adjudicate between brothers?" is straight irony, predicated on the Corinthians' own position as it has emerged in chs. 1–3. In 12:8, in Paul's listing of Spirit manifestations in the community, he begins with the two that played high court in Corinth (λόγος σοφίας; λόγος γνώσεως) so as to recapture them for the vital life of the Spirit within the community ("for the common good," 12:7).

24. His foolishness is seen, first, in his saving through a crucified Messiah (1:18-25); second, in his choosing the Corinthian "nobodies" to be among his new eschatological people (1:26-31); and third, in his calling them through Paul's preaching in personal weakness (2:1-5). For details see Fee, *Corinthians*, ad stet.

25. In fact Paul asserts categorically that "in the wisdom of God" (as attribute) the world through wisdom (διὰ τῆς σοφίας) did not know God; it seems altogether unlikely that he would then turn about and say that Christ is Wisdom and, by implication, suggest that one can know God through Wisdom after all.

26. That is, a pronouncement about Christ's *person* as over against his *work* (soteriology). I grant that in the final analysis one can scarcely do justice to Paul's theology if person and work are separated. But in the present case, the question is whether these statements are saying something fundamental about who Christ is or about what he accomplished on the cross. That is, in

though Paul were reflecting either a *dynamis* or *sophia* christology.[27] Rather, he is taking the *Corinthians'* word, however they understood it, and demythologizing it by anchoring it firmly in history — in a crucified Messiah, God's "foolishness" and "weakness," whereby that same Messiah turned the tables on all human schemes and wisdom that try to "find out God." After all, the presenting statement in v. 18 makes clear that the issue is *salvation* through the *message of the cross,* which divides all humankind into those perishing and those being saved. For the former, the cross is "folly and weakness." Paul now asserts that for "those who believe" the message of a crucified Messiah is the precise opposite: not "folly and weakness" but "power and wisdom." "Christ the power of God and the wisdom of God," therefore, is shorthand for "God's true power and wisdom, that belong to him alone, are to be found in the weakness and sheer folly of redeeming humankind by means of the cross," which by God's own design is intended to nullify the wisdom of the wise (hence the citation of Isa. 29:14 in v. 19). If Jewish Wisdom were to lie behind this at all, the use of δύναμις and σοφία here would seem most likely to echo a passage like Job 12:13,[28] having to do with God's attributes of "power and wisdom." These divine attributes, Paul argues with the Corinthians, have been put on full display in the ultimate oxymoron of a "crucified Messiah."

This understanding is further confirmed by v. 30. Having reaffirmed that God has made Christ to be "wisdom for us," Paul immediately qualifies it in such a way that the Corinthians could not have imagined that he had a personified Wisdom in mind. "Wisdom for us" is again clarified in terms of Christ's saving work — righteousness/justification, sanctification, and re-

---

saying Christ is the "power of God," is this a christological referent about Christ's embodying God's power in his person, or is it a shorthand way of referring to the effectiveness of the cross as God's power for salvation to those who believe (v. 18)? The answer lies with the obvious point of the passage, which is to eliminate Corinthian boasting in wisdom altogether by pointing to Christ's humiliating *death* (not to Christ as embodying pre-existent Wisdom) on a Roman gibbet as the ultimate expression of divine wisdom; and only the Spirit can reveal it as such.

27. In fact (*pace* J. A. Davis, *Wisdom and Spirit: An Investigation of 1 Corinthians 1.18–3.20 against the Background of Jewish Sapiential Traditions in the Greco-Roman Period* [Lanham, Md.: University Press of America, 1984]), nothing in the argument suggests that those in Corinth enamored with "wisdom" had any interest at all in the Jewish Wisdom tradition, since the contrast "wisdom/folly" belongs on the Greek side of the equation, with "power/weakness" on the Jewish side, as vv. 20, 22-24 make plain.

28. LXX παρ' αὐτῷ σοφία καὶ δύναμις, αὐτῷ βουλὴ καὶ σύνεσις ("with him are wisdom and strength; he has counsel and understanding," NRSV). The significance of this text is not so much that Paul would be echoing it as that these two words occur together in an expression of Jewish Wisdom in which wisdom is not personified — very much the same way it is found in Prov. 3:19-20 ("The Lord in wisdom laid the earth's foundations").

demption,[29] three nouns that appear later as "saving verbs" (6:11) or as metaphor (6:20).

Finally, in 2:7 Paul argues again that wisdom can indeed be found in the gospel he preached; but it is a (formerly) "hidden wisdom" that is so contradictory to mere human wisdom it can only be known by the revelation of the Spirit (v. 10), which the whole context and v. 12 in particular (by use of χαρίζομαι) indicate is to be found in the cross. Again, if there is Jewish background to this idea at all, it is to be found in Jewish apocalyptic, not Jewish Wisdom.[30]

This means that when Paul refers to Christ in 8:6 as our "one Lord, Jesus Christ, through whom are all things and we through him," it is altogether unlikely that he now is thinking christologically of something that he historicized in 1:18-31. To argue so would require significant *linguistic and conceptual* evidence, which is exactly what is lacking in this passage. Conceptually,[31] God created all things not through Christ as Wisdom but through the one Lord whom the Corinthians know historically as Jesus the Christ. This seems to be made certain by the fact that the designation employed for the "one God" is *Father*, which implies not Wisdom Christology but the "Son of God" christology that explicitly dominates the text to which we turn next. And linguistically, as we will note momentarily, there is not a single tie of any kind between Paul and the Jewish Wisdom texts.

C. Colossians 1:15-17

When we turn from 1 Corinthians to Colossians, we find very much the same thing. Here Paul refers to the pre-existent *Son*[32] as the divine agent of creation

---

29. Witherington (*Sage*, pp. 310-11) tries to circumvent this by (1) making the ἐν Χριστῷ Ἰησοῦ instrumental (a possible but unusual sense for this phrase), (2) making the relative clause, toward which the whole sentence is pointing, parenthetical, and (3) thus turning the three nouns, which sit in apposition with σοφία, into predicate nouns with "you are." Thus, "But from God *you* are through Christ (who was made Wisdom for us by God), righteousness and sanctification and redemption" (both italics and comma in the original). Rather than the "natural sense of the grammar" as he asserts, this looks like a "translation" intended to get around the plain implications of the text.

30. On this matter see Gordon D. Fee, *God's Empowering Presence: The Holy Spirit in the Letters of Paul* (Peabody, Mass.: Hendrickson, 1994), pp. 97-101, and especially the discussion of the relationship of Paul to the Wisdom of Solomon in the final chapter, "The Pauline Antecedents," pp. 911-13.

31. For the missing linguistic evidence, see the argument in section II.C.2 below.

32. The contextual point that must be made here, and one that is seldom noted in the lit-

in a deliberately programmatic way at the beginning of a letter[33] to a church where some false teaching has emerged with the damaging effect of diminishing both the person and work of Christ.[34] Thus a sentence that began as thanksgiving to God the Father for redemption in "his beloved Son" (vv. 12-14) now proceeds — in what appears to be a two-stanza hymn[35] (vv. 15-20) — to exalt the Son by picking up the two sides of his agency in creation and redemption expressed in creed-like fashion in 1 Cor. 8:6. Our interest lies in the first strophe (vv. 15-17), which is a considerable elaboration on the δι' οὗ τὰ πάντα of line 2 in 1 Cor. 8:6.[36]

(a)	ὅς ἐστιν εἰκὼν	τοῦ θεοῦ	τοῦ ἀοράτου,	
(a′)		πρωτότοκος	πάσης κτίσεως,	
(b)	ὅτι	ἐν αὐτῷ	ἐκτίσθη τὰ πάντα	
(b¹)				ἐν τοῖς οὐρανοῖς καὶ ἐπὶ τῆς γῆς
(b²)				τὰ ὁρατὰ καὶ τὰ ἀόρατα,
(b³)				εἴτε θρόνοι εἴτε κυριότητες
(b⁴)				εἴτε ἀρχαὶ εἴτε ἐξουσίαι,
(b′)	τὰ πάντα	δι' αὐτοῦ καὶ εἰς αὐτὸν	ἔκτισται	
(c)	καὶ αὐτός ἐστιν πρὸ πάντων			
(c′)	καὶ τὰ πάντα ἐν αὐτῷ συνέστηκεν			

The strophe is expressed in three pairs of parallels, with a considerable expansion of the first line of the second pair. Together these lines emphasize

---

erature because of our fascination with the hymn as allegedly pre-Pauline, is that the *grammatical* — and therefore contextual — *antecedent* of all the pronouns, beginning with the relative pronoun in v. 14, is "God's beloved Son" at the end of v. 13. A new sentence does not begin until the final clause in v. 16; and even here all the pronouns that follow have "the beloved Son" as their antecedent. In fact, the term *Christ* does not occur in the entire passage (vv. 9-23) and does not emerge until v. 24, where Paul picks up on his own role as messenger of the gospel.

33. I will not belabor here the historical difficulties I have with the rejection of the Pauline authorship of Colossians. One wonders how a pseudepigrapher would have had access only to the semiprivate letter to Philemon among the letters of Paul and used only its incidental data as the basis for a letter like this written in Paul's name. To accept Philemon as written by Paul and yet reject Colossians seems historically illogical. See further Fee, *God's Empowering Presence*, p. 636, n. 4.

34. For a convincing presentation that the "false teaching" was a syncretism of the gospel with folk religion (including magic and belief in intermediate beings), see C. E. Arnold, *The Colossian Syncretism: The Interface between Christianity and Folk Belief at Colossae* (Grand Rapids: Baker, 1996).

35. But see Wright, "Poetry and Theology," who prefers to see it simply as a poem.

36. While not all may agree with my structural arrangement, my concern here is simply to have a convenient display of the whole passage so as to comment briefly on its relevant parts.

the Son's supremacy over the whole created order, especially over the powers. The first doublet affirms the two essential matters: the Son as the εἰκών (image) of the otherwise invisible God, thus using *Pauline* language to emphasize that the Father is revealed in the Son (cf. 2 Cor. 4:4-6); and the Son as the πρωτότοκος of every created thing, which points to his holding the privileged position of "firstborn" — both heir and sovereign with regard to creation.

The ὅτι that begins the *b* lines, typical of many psalms, gives reasons for exulting in the one who is the "image" of God and holds primacy over creation. The two lines are synonymous and together emphasize that "all things" were created "in him," which is elaborated in the second line in terms of both "through him" and "for him." Line *b'* begins as a direct echo of 1 Cor. 8:6; its second half, however, now asserts that God's "firstborn" Son is also the *goal* of creation, the one for whom all creation exists and toward whom it points. Thus two (διά, εἰς) of the three all-encompassing prepositions in Rom. 11:36 are found here and attributed to the Son. The ἐκ, which belongs to the Father alone, is conceptually present in the divine passive (ἐκτίσθη, were created), but even that is moderated (remarkably so) by the assertion that all things were created *in him* (i.e., in the Son).

Finally, line *c* reemphasizes what was implied in lines *a'*, *b*, and *b'*: that the Son *is* — not was — *before* all things, where the Greek preposition bears the same ambiguity (temporal and spatial) found in the English word *before*, thus emphasizing both his existence prior to the created order and his having the position of primacy over it because he is the agent of its existence. In the final line *(c')* his role as the pre-existent creator of all things is furthered by emphasizing that they are currently "held together" in and through him.

The linguistic ties between this passage and 1 Cor. 8:6, not to mention 2 Cor. 4:4, suggest that the same christological point of view lies behind both of them, especially so since the next stanza (vv. 18-20) spells out in similar detail the καὶ ἡμεῖς δι' αὐτοῦ (and we through him) of the earlier passage. The Colossians passage simply spells out in greater detail what is already presupposed in 1 Corinthians.

But here in particular, Dunn has argued for "a sequence of correlation [between Paul and personified Wisdom that] can hardly be a matter of coincidence." Indeed, he asserts that Paul's language in this passage (and in 1 Cor. 8:6) offers "classic expressions of Wisdom Christology."[37] But despite this as-

---

37. Dunn, *Theology,* p. 269; the whole of his presentation here rebutted appears in pp. 268-70, concluding with "Clearly, then, Paul was attributing to *Christ* the role previously attributed to divine Wisdom." "Clear," it would seem, as with beauty, is surely in the eye of the beholder!

sertion, there is an almost complete lack of both linguistic and conceptual ties to this tradition. Dunn's "sequence of correlation" consists of basically five points (including Christ's role in creation, the controversial point that will be picked up in the next section). Let me first address the other four:

1. Dunn points out that the same term "image [εἰκών]" is used of both personified Wisdom (Wis. 7:26)[38] and of Christ (Col. 1:15). Indeed, C. K. Barrett makes bold to say that "*image* is a word that belongs to the Wisdom literature"; he then cites Wis. 7:26 as evidence.[39] But this is a plain overstatement of the case, since this use in Ps-Solomon is in fact the *only* occurrence of the word with this sense in the literature.[40] Furthermore, Paul and Ps-Solomon scarcely reflect truly parallel uses of language; for personified Wisdom is not "the εἰκών of *God*," but is merely "an image of his *goodness*" (εἰκὼν τῆς ἀγαθότητος αὐτοῦ), one of the clear concerns of this author. Paul, on the other hand, is intending something very much like what he says in 2 Cor. 4:4-6: that God is now to be known not through personified Wisdom but in his beloved Son (Col. 1:13), who alone bears the true image of the Father to whom Paul has been giving thanks (v. 12).

2. Wisdom is further alleged to be called "God's 'firstborn' in creation." But this is quite misleading, since Paul's word (πρωτότοκος) does not occur at all in the Wisdom tradition — at least not in Paul's sense.[41] Not only do the

---

38. In this and in the following cases, Dunn also draws on several references from Philo, assuming Philo to be representative of a Wisdom tradition similar to Ps-Solomon. But as noted below (n. 49), what appears to be the best reading of the evidence puts Ps-Solomon and Philo in Alexandria basically as contemporaries. Their relationship, therefore, is unlikely to be literary; it is rather the reflection of a common milieu. What cannot be demonstrated in any way is Pauline dependence on Philo. Nonetheless I shall also examine the Philo materials here, since the issue could be argued not in terms of direct dependency but of a point of view that is "in the air," as it were.

39. C. K. Barrett, *Paul: An Introduction to His Thought* (Louisville: Westminster John Knox, 1994), pp. 146-47.

40. It is elsewhere found in Sir. 17:3 and Wis. 2:23 with direct reference to Gen. 1:27, and in Ps-Solomon in several instances referring to idols (Wis. 13:13, 16; 14:15, 17; 15:5) and once in a metaphorical way (17:21) referring to darkness.

41. In fact the only other occurrences are in a textual variation of Sir. 36:17 and as a plural in Wis. 18:13 referring to the slaughter of Israel's firstborn. Dunn also gives two references to Philo as supporting this "parallel" (*Ebr.* 30–31; *QG* 4.97); but these are especially dubious. In the first instance Philo speaks of God's having union with knowledge, who "bore the only beloved son who is apprehended by the senses, the world which we see" (LCL 3.335); "knowledge" is then equated with wisdom, at which point Philo "cites" Prov. 8:22 in his own way: "God obtained me first (πρωτίστην) of all his works." But that is not remotely related to Paul's use of πρωτότοκος, which has to do not with the Son's being created first, but with his having the role of firstborn, heir, and sovereign over all creation. The other passage exists only in an Armenian translation,

texts brought forward (Prov. 8:22, 25) have totally different words in the LXX, but also their point (the fact that Wisdom is the first of God's "creations" so that she might be present to frolic as he creates all else) is something radically different from Paul's use of πρωτότοκος here, where Christ *as Son* holds the rights of primogeniture with regard to every created thing, since they were all created *through* him and *for* him.

3. It is further argued that when Sir. 1:4 speaks of Wisdom as "before all things," this correlates with what Paul says here of the Son. But this is particularly dubious, since Sirach's phrase has an altogether different word and he means something almost the opposite of Paul. Sirach says that "Wisdom was *created* before all things [προτέρα πάντων]," which Skehan and Di Lella (correctly) translate "before all things else."[42] Paul, on the other hand, says that the Son ἐστιν πρὸ πάντων (*is* before all things), by which he means that the Son through whom all things were created *is* "before them" both by virtue of his pre-existence temporally and by his primacy of rank. Therefore this is not a correspondence of any kind.

4. Finally, Paul's assertion that "in him [the Son] all things hold together [συνέστηκεν]" is alleged to correspond to Wis. 1:6-7, where the author refers to "*that which* holds all things together [τὸ συνέχον]," referring in this case specifically to the Spirit of the Lord. This one is a bit tricky, since it is related to a very complex issue regarding the translation of v. 6: When Ps-Solomon says that "wisdom is a kindly spirit," does the author mean to equate a personified Wisdom with the Spirit of the Lord, or (which seems far more likely) does he refer to the "spiritual" quality of wisdom? In any case, he does not in fact say that "Wisdom holds all things together";[43] rather, he says it is the Spirit who does.

These various strands of a questionable use of parallels, therefore, hardly constitute the kind of "sequence of correlation" asserted by Dunn. Indeed, there are no certain linguistic ties in the Colossians passage with the

which has been rendered in English as "And who is to be considered the daughter of God but Wisdom, who is the first-born mother of all things." It would be of great interest to see what Philo's Greek actually looked like in this instance. But in any case this helps very little, since the Wisdom literature itself does not use this language, and to argue for dependence of Paul on Philo is more than most would wish to do. What it does point out is that such a view existed in Alexandria at the turn of the Christian era; but what is of interest is that it fails to make its way into Ps-Solomon.

42. See Patrick W. Skehan and Alexander A. Di Lella, *The Wisdom of Ben Sira* (AB 39; Garden City, N.Y.: Doubleday, 1987), p. 136.

43. Dunn also appeals to several instances in Philo where he says the same thing of Logos; but that is to assume what must be proven, not simply asserted: namely that Logos and Sophia are interchangeable ideas for the author of Wisdom of Solomon (on the basis of 9:1-2; but see the interpretation of this text offered below).

Wisdom literature at all, certainly not of a kind to allow the use of such a term as "Wisdom Christology."[44] What Paul's sentences point to instead is a Son of God christology, which may have some distant echoes conceptually to things said about Wisdom in the earlier literature, but even this is doubtful. A case of clear *literary* or *conceptual* dependence of Paul on this literature needs to be demonstrated for us to entertain the idea of a Wisdom Christology in Paul. So we turn next to these texts themselves to see whether they actually posit personified Wisdom as the agent of creation, which is the sticking point.

III. Is Wisdom the Agent of Creation?

When one turns from Paul to examine the Wisdom tradition itself more closely (the major premise), one is surprised to find how much mileage is made on what appears to be far more vapor than petrol. At issue first is whether, by the various personifications of Wisdom found in Prov. 8:22-31, Sir. 24:3-12, and Wis. 6:1–10:21, their authors have a divine hypostasis in view — that is, an actual divine (or quasi-divine) being who exists alongside (or in relationship with) God in some unique way.[45] Or are these merely literary moments in which the feminine nouns *(ḥokmâ, sophia)* are made powerfully present through means of the literary device of personification? The significance of this is, as Dunn's own work demonstrates, that one may draw quite different conclusions if Wisdom is more a literary device than a divine hypostasis.

Although there has been considerable debate on this matter, the consensus of those who have worked closely with these texts — without our agenda in view — is that in Proverbs and Ben Sirach we are dealing with a literary device, pure and simple.[46] On the other hand, the personification of

44. It should be noted that Col. 2:3 ("in whom [Christ] are hidden all the treasures of wisdom and knowledge") is sometimes brought forward as supporting the view that this passage reflects an alleged Wisdom Christology (in somewhat the same way 1 Cor. 1:24 is said to support such a view of 1 Cor. 8:6). But that will hardly do in this case, since Paul does not refer to Christ as "wisdom," but, vis-à-vis all lesser "powers," as God's (now revealed) "mystery," in whom the divine attributes of "wisdom and knowledge" are found as treasures. This is several leagues short of referring to Christ as personified Wisdom, present as agent at creation. Indeed, it is most unlikely that anyone would have found a reference here to Wisdom Christology who was not looking for it in the first place.

45. A point made by Dunn (*Christology*, pp. 168-76; cf. *Theology*, pp. 270-72) that has seemed to fall on deaf ears. My disagreement with Dunn is in his finding a Wisdom motif at all in the Pauline texts, when there does not appear to be one.

46. For Proverbs, see the commentary by R. B. Y. Scott, *Proverbs and Ecclesiastes* (AB 18; Garden City, N.Y.: Doubleday, 1965), pp. 69-72, to which one might now add the forthcoming

Wisdom in Ps-Solomon seems to move much more toward some kind of hypostasis, so that the consensus here is to be found in the following oft-quoted definition: "a quasi-personification of certain attributes proper to God, occupying an intermediate position between personalities and abstract beings."[47] The nature of this "intermediate position," however, is taken by scholars each in their own way, depending on the degree to which they perceive the author to regard Wisdom as both personified and separate from her originator.[48] The point to make here is that if Paul were in fact dependent on this tradition, which seems doubtful at best, it is not at all clear that he would have understood Wisdom in terms of *personal pre-existence in the same way that he so considered Christ.*[49]

At issue finally in this discussion is the relationship of Wisdom to creation. And it is crucial here to note again that, despite some attempts at find-

---

commentary by the honoree of this *Festschrift;* for Sirach, see the commentary by Skehan and Di Lella, *Ben Sira,* p. 332. This is also affirmed by David Winston (*The Wisdom of Solomon* [AB 43; Garden City, N.Y.: Doubleday, 1979], p. 34), who sees Philo and Ps-Solomon in contrast to Proverbs and Sirach at this very point.

47. W. O. E. Oesterley and G. H. Box, *The Religion and Worship of the Synagogue* (London: Pitman, 1911), p. 169, and cited, e.g., by Winston, both in his commentary (see n. 46, above) and in his contribution to the Gammie Memorial volume ("Wisdom in the Wisdom of Solomon," in *In Search of Wisdom: Essays in Memory of John C. Gammie,* ed. L. G. Perdue et al. [Louisville: Westminster John Knox, 1993], p. 150); cf. R. Marcus, "On Biblical Hypostases of Wisdom," *HUCA* 23 (1950-1951): 159, who in turn is cited by Witherington, *Sage,* p. 109. But see also the cautions raised by Dunn, *Theology,* p. 272.

48. This ambivalence can be found especially in Winston, who in his commentary cites the Oesterley-Box definition but in the footnote goes on to aver, "In Philo and Wisd . . . where Sophia is considered to be an eternal emanation of the deity, we undoubtedly have a conception of her as a divine hypostasis, coeternal with him" (p. 34). This would seem to go beyond Oesterley-Box by some margin. Winston's commitment both to a much more hypostatic understanding, as well as to this pre-existent hypostasis as being God's agent of creation, can be found in the introduction (p. 59), where he asserts, "The central figure in Wisd is Sophia, described as an 'effluence' or 'effulgence' of God's glory, and his agent in creation (7:25-6; 8:4; 9:1-2)." The reference in 7:25-26 is to Sophia: "while remaining in herself she renews all things *(ta panta kainizei)*." But in the commentary on this passage he does not so much as mention creation — for good reason, one might add, since it simply is not in the text. The same ambivalence is to be found in the attempt to distinguish between wisdom as God's attribute and Wisdom in the NJB, especially in its handling of the three occurrences of σοφία in Wis. 1:4-6, as well as in 3:11. The consistent use in that translation of the capitalized Wisdom in 6:9–10:21 can only be described as prejudicial.

49. After all, the author of the Wisdom of Solomon, who may well have been an older contemporary of Paul himself (Winston, e.g., dates the work within the reign of Caligula [37-41 C.E.]), is most likely merely heightening the effect of the personification, rather than thinking of an actual being distinguishable from God. As will be pointed out below, the latter seems to be an unfortunate misreading of our author's text, not to mention his theology.

ing other echoes of Wisdom in Paul, this is the one point at which the whole enterprise seems to have found its origins and continues to find support in the literature. Thus it is to these texts in particular that we now turn.

I begin by noting that, in contrast to repeated assertions to the contrary, it is doubtful whether anywhere in the tradition it is explicitly stated that personified Wisdom was the *mediating agent* of creation. In none of the passages brought forward to defend such a view does one find language similar to that found in Paul; that is, these authors do not come close to saying that God created τὰ πάντα διὰ σοφίας (all things through Wisdom).[50] Rather, Wisdom is personified as present in another sense, namely as the attribute of God that is manifest through the masterful design exhibited in creation.

A. Psalm 104:24

This way of speaking about creation finds its first expression in the exalted poetry of Ps. 104:24 (LXX 103:24). After reflecting on the heavens, the earth, the living creatures on the earth, the sun, and the moon, the author bursts forth, "How many are your works, O Lord! In wisdom you made them all." Wisdom here is "neither instrument nor agent but the attribute displayed by Yahweh in creating."[51] My contention in what follows is that all of our subsequent authors are guided by this same theology, so that even when they express in a heightened personified way Wisdom's presence with Yahweh at creation, she as such is never the *agent* but instead the attribute made manifest in God's own creative work. Nor is it likely that Paul would himself have understood such language in terms of personal agency, so it would never have occurred to him to identify the historical, now exalted *kyrios,* Jesus Christ, with a mere literary personification.

B. Proverbs 8:22-31

This literary interpretation of wisdom is most evident in Prov. 8, the passage from which all others take their lead. For example, Prov. 3:19 affirms that "in

---

50. The closest thing to it in the LXX is Ps. 103:24 (EVV 104:24), πάντα ἐν σοφίᾳ ἐποίησας, which is not only in a non-wisdom passage but also reflects what the Wisdom tradition does indeed affirm: that "God in his own wisdom created" things so that they reflect his wisdom of design and purpose — which scarcely amounts to mediation.

51. Quoting Scott, *Proverbs,* p. 70, who applies these words to the companion passage in Prov. 3:19.

wisdom the Lord laid the earth's foundations"; that this does not mean Wisdom personified is made plain by the rest of the quatrain: "by understanding he set the heavens in place; by his knowledge the deeps were divided, and the clouds let drop the dew." When Wisdom is later personified in a literary way in the marvelous poetry of 8:22-31,[52] she is pictured as *present* at creation, precisely because of what is said in 3:19, but not as its mediator: "I was there when [God] set the heavens in place, when he marked out the horizon on the face of the deep" (8:27). Thus Prov. 8:22-26 asserts in a variety of ways that Wisdom was the first of God's creations, emphasizing her priority in time, so that her being *present* with God when he alone created the universe would thus reflect — as it actually does — God's wise blueprint. This, then, is the point picked up in vv. 27-31, which further depict Wisdom as present at creation, again in the sense of 3:19.

Those who think otherwise find their hope in the ambiguous Hebrew term *'āmōn* in v. 30, which is assumed to lie behind the Greek τεχνῖτις/τεχνίτης (fashioner, designer) in Wis. 7:21 (7:22 NRSV); 8:6; 14:2, which meaning is then read back into the Hebrew of Proverbs. In another context the author's poetry might be stretched to mean "that [he] sees Wisdom as pre-existing and probably as having an active role in the work of creation."[53] But this assumes a more hypostatic view of Wisdom than can be demonstrated in Proverbs, not to mention that it fails to take the point of the poetry seriously in the context of Prov. 8 itself. To be sure, Wisdom is the "master worker" at God's side, but she is not the *mediator* through whom creation came into being. Rather, to our author the whole created order is so full of evidences of design and glory that God's wisdom, now personified in a literary way, can be the only possible explanation for it. It needs only to be pointed out that this falls considerably short of Paul's understanding of Christ's role in creation.

C. Sirach 24:1-22

The next appearance of these ideas is in "The Praise of Wisdom" in Sir. 24:1-22. While creating his own (equally magnificent) poem, Sirach at the same time remains absolutely faithful to the understanding of his predecessor in Proverbs, on whom he is obviously dependent. For Sirach, who delights in the literary personification of Wisdom, God alone is nonetheless the sole Creator

---

52. See ibid., pp. 70-71; Scott argues convincingly that this poem is written by the same author as 3:19.

53. Witherington, *Sage*, p. 44.

of all things, including Wisdom herself ("Before the ages, from the beginning, he created me," 24:9 [ἀπ᾽ ἀρχῆς ἔκτισέν με]; cf. v. 8, "my Creator").

Those who find pre-existent, personified Wisdom as having a role in creation appeal to v. 3 ("I came forth from the mouth of the Most High, and covered the earth like a mist," NRSV).[54] But that is surely to come to the text with an agenda in hand, not to read it on its own terms.[55] This passage reflects Sirach's view that Wisdom is there "before the ages," since "from the first, he created [Wisdom]" (24:9), and it is Sirach's own interpretation of "the Spirit of God . . . hovering over the waters" in Gen. 1:2. His referent is not to her creative agency but to her having "sought a resting place" (v. 5), which took place historically *not* in creation but in her presence with Israel in the exodus!

D. Wisdom of Solomon 6:1–9:18

That brings us, then, to the Wisdom of Solomon, which by everyone's reckoning has the crucial texts (found in the adulation of and prayer for wisdom in 6:1–9:18).[56] But here especially one needs to read what the author says in the context of the entire poetic narrative. Ps-Solomon's concern seems ultimately to be semi-apologetic (toward the Greeks as well as for the Jewish community's encouragement), since the opening section (1:1–6:11), allegedly written by one who is himself a king, is framed by appeals to "the rulers of the earth," variously called "kings" or "despots." This opening appeal also sets forth his basic agenda: that "living well" (doing justly and living righteously) is rewarded by immortality, whereas death awaits those who are evil. The way one lives well in this sense is to emulate Solomon and his own request for wisdom, a theme that is taken up in the crucial central section of the narrative (6:1–9:18: "If you delight in thrones and scepters, O monarchs over the peoples,

54. Compare ibid., p. 95; Witherington appeals to H. Ringgren, *Word and Wisdom: Studies in the Hypostatization of Divine Qualities and Functions in the Ancient Near East* (Lund: Ohlssons, 1947), pp. 108-9.

55. Compare Skehan and Di Lella, *Ben Sira*, pp. 332-33, who do not so much as mention a view that reads this passage as Wisdom's having a role in creation itself.

56. One of the problematic features of "dependency" on the part of Paul with regard to Ps-Solomon is, of course, its date. If Winston is correct that it should be dated during the reign of Caligula (see n. 49), then there seems almost no chance that Paul, who had become a follower of Christ by this time, would have known about this work — or given it the time of day, had he known of it. But since this dating (which I think is to be preferred for the reasons Winston sets forth) is much debated, I have chosen to enter this discussion on the playing field and under the assumed rules by which the game has been played by others.

honor wisdom, so that you may reign forever," 6:21 NRSV),[57] where "Solomon" sets out "to tell you [the monarchs] what wisdom is and how she came to be" (6:22 NRSV).

One can easily trace the author's progression of thought in this central section. He begins with Solomon's adulation of (now personified) Wisdom (6:12-21), which he proposes to describe (vv. 22-25). But before doing so the author reminds his readers of Solomon's ordinary humanity (7:1-6) and also of the great things that happened to him when he received wisdom (vv. 7-21), the secret to which he now hopes to "pass on liberally" (v. 13 NJB). That leads to his "eulogy of Wisdom" (7:22–8:1), which the NJB note describes as "the peak of OT writings on Wisdom." Because of Wisdom's undoubted greatness — both for understanding and uprightness, which alone leads to immortality — the author returns to Solomon's own love for Wisdom (8:2-18), who knows that he could never have it unless it be given by God (vv. 19-21). Thus this author's own version of "In Praise of Wisdom" concludes with Solomon's prayer for Wisdom (9:1-18).

The rest of the narrative is an intriguing mixture of reflection on God's goodness to Israel in its history — especially in the exodus, with several antitheses between this goodness received and its opposites that befell Israel's opponents. What is fascinating structurally is that this narrative begins with Wisdom playing the leading role (10:1–11:3), from Adam (10:1-2) to the exodus (10:15–11:3). But after the first antithesis — a contrast between Israel's gift of water from the rock and the water that punished their enemies (11:4-14) — the rest of the poetry takes the form of personal address to God, while Wisdom fades altogether from view (except for a cameo appearance as the "artisan" of boats in 14:2, 5).[58] It is in this last section in particular, all of it addressed to God and quite apart from reference to wisdom of any kind, that the author's "theology" in true Jewish fashion emerges over and again: namely, that it is their God who is the sole Creator and Ruler of all that is (11:17, 24-25; 13:3-5; 16:24).

My reason for rehearsing this narrative and its structure is that it must

---

57. Unless otherwise noted, this and other translations will be from the NRSV from this point on, in part because in keeping with its translation style it tends to be close to the Greek text and in part because it consistently translates σοφία in the lowercase (just as in Proverbs and Sirach), thus not prejudicing the reader toward any view of personification.

58. While some would see this text as supporting a view of Wisdom as agent of creation, that is to make too much of almost nothing. Verse 5 offers the author's perspective on the personification of v. 2, and it has nothing to do with the creation of the world as such: "It is your will that works of your wisdom [in this case, ships!] should not be without effect." Here the usage is simply in keeping with the whole sapiential tradition.

affect the way one reads the eulogy of Wisdom in the brief central section. Our author's concern with wisdom is not theological per se but practical and ethical. Only by having wisdom will rulers rule well, and only by having wisdom will people live well. This concern leads to his expansive praise of Wisdom and her "works." At issue is whether agency in the original creation of the world is seen by the author as part of these works. As indicated, and quite in keeping with the traditions to which he is indebted and despite his enthusiasm for Wisdom's greatness, he sees Wisdom as only *present* at creation, not as its divine agent.

This comes out especially in the crucial texts in 9:1-2, 9, at the beginning of Solomon's prayer. Precisely because he is now praying for Wisdom — not describing her — and thus addressing God in the second person, he says of God, "you who have made all things by your word [τὰ πάντα ἐν λόγῳ σου]," thus reflecting the Genesis narrative by way of the loaded Greek term *logos*, while adding in the parallel, "and by your wisdom [τῇ σοφίᾳ σου] have formed humankind to have dominion over the creatures you have made." This is so obviously not a personification, either of a divine *logos* or divine *sophia*, that even the NJB with its bias toward personified Wisdom translates these in the lowercase. The only way one can find hypostatic Wisdom as the agent of creation in this passage is by bringing to the text a prior disposition to do so and by misreading the parallelism so as to make *logos* and *sophia* interchangeable. Our author's obvious concern is not with Wisdom's role in creation as such but with her role in God's "equipping or constructing" (κατασκευάζας) human beings for their life in the world that God created by his word. And because the world is so wondrously arrayed by the God who created it, he goes on to add in v. 9 (NRSV), "With you is wisdom, she who knows your works and was present when you made the world." This is a straightforward reflection of Prov. 8:27-31.

This is precisely the role Wisdom plays in the other texts brought forward to support her agency in creation, where the author says of her, for example, that she is "the fashioner [τεχνῖτις] of all things" (7:21; 7:22 NRSV), which in context has nothing to do with creating as such but with the design of the world as it exists (including the elements, the cycles of nature, and the natures of animals and of human beings). So also in 7:24, where Wisdom is said to "pervade and penetrate all things," Ps-Solomon is not at all interested in her *creative* role but in her obvious place in the world as he knows it — a world created by the God whose attribute is wisdom. This is also the case, finally, in 8:4-7, where Solomon expresses his desire for Wisdom. Why? Because evidence of her "work is everywhere," be it in wealth (v. 5), intellect (v. 6), or uprightness (v. 7). That she is described in the present tense in v. 6 as "the fashioner of what exists" is not a theological statement about original creation; it is a typical personification of her role in making the present world work well.

E. Conclusion

Where, then, does this overview of the texts from the Wisdom literature leave us? Hardly with the kind of statements on which Paul could have built his theology of Christ's pre-existence. It is never quite certain even in Ps-Solomon that the author thought of Wisdom as a hypostasis with existence and being apart from God; nor do the texts themselves ever explicitly spell out a *mediating* role for her in creation. And what is most lacking in all of this material is a verbal or conceptual linkage between Wisdom and creation of the kind explicitly found in Paul with reference to Christ. On the contrary, Wisdom is regularly referred to as "created" before all other things (Prov. 8:22; Sir. 24:9), a motif never applied to Christ. Instead, in keeping with the Genesis narrative — and its later echoes in the OT[59] — God created by *speaking* "all things" into existence (or by fashioning everything with "his hands"). Wisdom is present only because creation so obviously proclaims God's wisdom in design and sustenance.

When we return to 1 Cor. 8:6 from this material, what we see is not similarity but contrast. Paul asserts that along with the one θεός, "the Father," there is an (uncreated) one κύριος, who is distinguished in *strictly personal terms based on his incarnation in human history* as "Jesus the Christ." Thus Paul does not understand Christ as agent of creation in some nebulous way akin to Wisdom's presence with God at creation; rather, it is Jesus Christ, the Son of God himself, who is not simply present at creation but the actual agent of creation. "All things" came to be "through him." This understanding is made certain by the fact that in the final phrase about the "one Lord" (καὶ ἡμεῖς δι' αὐτοῦ), Paul uses the same preposition to refer to Christ's historical work of redemption.[60] Nothing like this is even hinted at in the Wisdom literature.

I realize that some might see this exercise as undercutting the concept of pre-existence in Paul's view of Christ.[61] But not so; my point is first of all a

59. Thus in Ps. 33:6, "By the word of the Lord were the heavens made, their starry host by the breath of his mouth."

60. Some (e.g., E. J. Schnabel, "Wisdom," *DPL*, p. 970) see here a second "transfer" to Christ of personified Wisdom's role in the Wisdom tradition, namely a soteriological one. But this rests on an even shakier understanding of the relevant texts.

61. This is because for them the predicate for the "origins" of the idea of pre-existence is so integrally tied to an alleged pre-existent Wisdom.

purely academic one, to call into question personified Wisdom as the *source* of Paul's understanding and thus to challenge the use of terms like *transferring, adopting,* and *adapting* as being applied to Wisdom when referring to Paul's christology because of the highly suspect nature of the data themselves. Second, I want to point out that the use of Wisdom to diminish the aspect of pre-existence in Paul's theology (cf. Dunn) is equally suspect. Wisdom is of virtually no — or very little — help in understanding Paul's view of the pre-existent Christ; and if hypostatic Wisdom must be barred from the front door, it does no good to bring a diminished view of pre-existent Wisdom in through the back door, as Dunn and others try to do.[62]

IV. Some Concluding Observations about Method

If my reading of these texts is close to what both Paul and the Wisdom writers intended, then the question remains, Why have so many read these texts in a different way? The possibility remains, of course, that my reading is simply a poor one. But another very real possibility is that scholarship at this point was driven by a need to discover the *origins* of Paul's high christology. The way forward seemed to be the "discovery" that personified Wisdom played a similar role to Christ's in Paul's own Jewish heritage, so the transfer of ideas from Wisdom to Christ was an easy, natural one.

But that raises for me several questions about method. My first concern arises out of the fact that one cannot find elsewhere in Paul a single trace of influence from Wisdom, neither in his theology in general[63] nor in his christology in particular. That is, how at the end of the day does the term "wisdom christology" fit Paul at all, if this very questionable "correspondence" is the only significant christological relationship between Paul and the Wisdom tradition? It is true, of course, that Paul is quite ready to use texts from this tradition where they support his own theology, especially those passages that dis-

---

62. A further way that personified Wisdom has been "found" in Paul stems from Eduard Schweizer's influential study, in which he argued for a double "sending" formula in Wis. 9:10-17 as "background" for Paul's words in Gal. 4:4, 6, about the Father's having sent the Son and the Spirit ("Zum religionsgeschichtlichen Hintergrund der 'Sendungsformel' Gal 4,4f., Rm 8,3f., Joh 3,16f., 1 Joh 4,9," *ZNW* 57 [1966]: 199-210). I have had previous occasion to call much of this study into question, regarding both the "formula" itself as well as the way Schweizer (and others following him) uses the Spirit material (see Fee, *God's Empowering Presence,* pp. 911-13).

63. I am well aware of the long history of trying to find Ps-Solomon behind Paul's pneumatology, but as I pointed out in *God's Empowering Presence* (pp. 911-13), that is a demonstrably wrong use of sources.

play the folly of human beings trying to "match wits" with God. This is how he cites Job, for example, in the two certain citations of this book — in 1 Cor. 3:19 (of Job 5:13) and Rom. 11:35 (of Job 41:3) — whereas his only citation of Proverbs (22:8 in 2 Cor. 9:7) is precisely as one might expect: to reinforce a very practical expression of Christ's love.

But at issue here is the use of the term "wisdom christology," when in fact these texts say any number of things about Wisdom not found in Paul's language or patterns of thought. Paul, on the other hand, says a great deal more about Christ, both his person and work, that has no connection — or at least no perceptible one — with anything that is said of Wisdom. I would think that this fact alone would cause the New Testament guild to back away from such language and use more modest terms.

The greater methodological issue, of course, has to do with what Samuel Sandmel some years ago caricatured as "parallelomania," which (in my terms) is a tendency to turn every *linguistic* correspondence between a Jewish or Hellenistic document and Paul's writings into a *conceptual* parallel and every alleged "parallel" into an "influence" or "borrowing." In this case the issue is slightly different, since *linguistic* parallels of any useful kind are lacking. The methodological concern, therefore, has to do with how one goes about establishing *conceptual* parallels in such a case.

Here in particular is where Paul's use of the OT should perhaps play a role in one's method, since Paul uses these documents in at least three ways: (a) by direct citation, (b) by clear allusion, and (c) by intertextual echo. Direct citation is easy enough; and it must be noted here again that Paul does not cite either Sirach or the Wisdom of Solomon, and when he cites Proverbs, it is for purposes other than christological ones. Clear allusion is also easy to see, such as in the argument of 1 Cor. 10:1-13, where what happened to "our fathers" serves as a warning to the Corinthians not to test Christ by idolatrous practices as some of them did, who then fell in the desert.

On the other hand, the identification of "intertextual echo" is much less certain. Richard Hays and I, for example, find Paul's use in Phil. 1:19 of the exact language from the LXX of Job 16:13 and the similar kinds of historical settings of Philippians and Job to be compelling reasons for interpreting Paul in light of Job.[64] Others, however, are less sure here. I find the same kind of phenomena to be present in Phil. 2:15-16, which has a series of linguistic echoes from the Pentateuch with reference to the story of Israel. Similarly, the debate

---

64. See Richard B. Hays, *Echoes of Scripture in the Letters of Paul* (New Haven: Yale University Press, 1989), pp. 21-24; cf. Gordon D. Fee, *Paul's Letter to the Philippians* (NICNT; Grand Rapids: Eerdmans, 1995), pp. 130-32.

over whether "all his holy ones" who accompany Christ's Parousia in 1 Thess. 3:13 refers to angels or the Christian dead seems to me to be settled conclusively by the specific echo of the language of Zech. 14:5 (LXX) in a similar apocalyptic context.

But what about echoes or allusions where there is no linguistic correspondence at all, as is the case in the present matter? This is not to say that conceptual allusions may not exist in Paul's use of the OT. Take, for example, the possibility that there is a conceptual allusion to Adam in the description of Christ in Phil. 2:6. I am less enamored with this option than many others are; but I am open to the possibility precisely because one can imagine that those who know the biblical story well — as Paul's readers in this case would — might hear such an echo even if Paul did not intend such himself.[65] But that kind of possible allusion to a well-known biblical narrative is the very thing lacking in this case.[66] That is, the biblical narrative of creation itself does not make reference to wisdom at all, and when later writers bring that concept in, they do so in a way that is not central to their concerns. This is where the issue of "what one is looking for" comes into the methodological discussion. Those who find Wisdom behind 1 Cor. 8:6 in particular, and somewhat less so in Col. 1:15-17, are not reading Paul on his own terms, it would seem; instead, they are especially interested in the question of where this idea came from. When one starts with that kind of question, one is far more apt to find what one is looking for than otherwise.

All of this is to say, finally, that the most fruitful way to approach the question of origins almost certainly does not lie with such nebulous findings based on a questionable methodology. More likely it lies with Paul's *kyrios* christology, which is not only firmly established in Paul himself, but also provides the key to much of his christology. Pre-existence in Paul is an easy step back in time, if you will, from Christ's having been exalted to God's right hand, thus fulfilling Ps. 110:1 (see esp. Rom. 8:34),[67] as well as Christ's assuming Yahweh's role in all kinds of OT texts and phrases through the title "Lord."

65. My hesitation in this case is due both to the lack of any linguistic parallels at all (*pace* Dunn's and others' wanting to make μορφή equal to εἰκών) and to the fact that the case of Christ in this passage and the case of Adam in the Genesis narrative are simply not parallel. See the discussion in Fee, *Philippians*, pp. 209-10, esp. n. 73; Dunn's (now more moderated) view can be found in *Theology*, pp. 282-88.

66. Here I have the same difficulty with Dunn's (and others') allusions to Wisdom in 1 Cor. 8:6 — where both linguistic and certain conceptual echoes are missing — as he does with various attempts to find it (and other motifs) in Phil. 2:6-11; see Dunn, *Theology*, p. 282, n. 68.

67. So I have argued in a preliminary way in my contribution to the Incarnation Summit (see n. 7 above); see now esp. Bauckham, *God Crucified*, pp. 29-31.

Here, at least, one is on *terra firma* with regard to Paul's own use of texts and allusions.

But that is for another essay. For now I trust that my friend and colleague, Bruce Waltke, will find these ruminations worthy of further reflection.